D1564121

INTERESTING TIMES

INTERESTING TIMES

Uganda Diaries 1955–1986

Sir Peter Allen

The Book Guild Ltd
Sussex, England

The Book Guild Ltd
25 High Street,
Lewes, Sussex

First published 2000
© Sir Peter Allen, 2000

The right of Sir Peter Allen to be identified as the Author
of the Work has been asserted by him in accordance
with the Copyright, Designs and Patents Act 1988.

Set in Times
Typesetting by Keyboard Services, Luton, Bedfordshire

Printed in Great Britain by
Antony Rowe Ltd, Chippenham, Wilts

A catalogue record for this book is
available from the British Library

ISBN 1 85776 468 4

For my mother
Edith Jane Allen
1895–1995

CONTENTS

LIST OF ILLUSTRATIONS

Uganda Police H.Q. Security staff and drivers with Staff Officer (P.A.) and police dog Blister

On top of Mt Kilimanjaro (19,565 feet) with Outward Bound Course 1959

Uganda Police identification parade, Kampala 1959

P.A. on a cattle seizure operation, Karamoja, N. Uganda, 1960

Investiture at Government House, Entebbe 1957, P.A. standing left

Karamojong (Pian) Warrior at Nabilatuk, Karamoja, North Uganda 1960

Sir Frederick Crawford, The Governor of Uganda at the Mayor of Kampala's garden party (visiting the police bandstand) P.A. on right, 1957

Queen Elizabeth National Park, Western Uganda

Magistrates course graduation, Uganda Law School May 1967. Left to right: Vice-president Babiiha, Chief Justice Udo Udoma, Attorney General Binaisa, P.A.

Amin with three newly appointed judges at State House. The Solicitor General is on the left and Chief Justice Wambuzi on Amin's right. P.A. is on the extreme right

Entebbe Airport raid: the bullet-riddled building which held the Israeli hostages seen after the raid and rescue

INTRODUCTION

Some years ago I read that 'May you live in interesting times' was supposed to be an ancient Chinese curse. I can't think why it should have been so regarded. How very boring to live in dull, uninteresting times and so miss out on possible chances of adventure, fame, fortune and surprising events. At any rate, I think that I have been fortunate enough to live through some very interesting times, the best of which was the period of over 30 years which I spent living and working in the East African country of Uganda.

When I was a schoolboy during the Second World War I was listening to the wireless one day after lunch and heard a talk by a former district officer in Africa. I was fascinated by it and can remember thinking at the time: What a wonderful life. That's for me. I shall go to Africa. However, I was only 14, so instead of packing my bags, I wrote to the Colonial Office, told them of my career interest and, in return, was sent a booklet setting out the various types of work and divisions in the British Colonial Service. The two branches that most interested me were the Administrative Service and the Police Service, for both of which preference was given to those who had first served in the armed forces. That suited me as I intended to go into the Army first anyway.

After nearly eight years in the Royal Artillery, during which I had twice served in Hong Kong but had been unsuccessful in obtaining a posting to Africa, sudden defence cuts in 1954 required that I should transfer to another branch where there were vacancies, or leave the Army. Fortunately, while reading *The Times*, I came across an advertisement asking for officers about to relinquish their commissions to join the Colonial Police Service. So I applied and was called to the Colonial Office for an interview.

In a dim and gloomy room in Great Smith Street one of the three elderly interviewers suggested that I should go to the Far East as I was 'in the picture' and 'knew the ground'. But I made it clear that for me it was Africa that I really wanted. Fortunately there were then plenty of vacancies in various parts of Africa so there was no problem.

I put in my papers to the War Office and was due to complete my final leave and army active service in January 1955 when I would transfer to the reserve. Meanwhile I received a letter from the Colonial Office stating that the writer had been directed by Mr Secretary Lennox-Boyd to inform me that I had been selected for probationary appointment to Her Majesty's Overseas Civil Service as an Assistant Superintendent of Police (Cadet) in the Uganda Protectorate in East Africa. The appointment was to take effect from the date of leaving the UK and I would be on half pay until arrival in the Protectorate, whereupon the Governor would provide me with a letter of appointment. The pay was attractive since it was almost twice what I'd been receiving in the Army. Having been a keen collector of British Empire stamps as a schoolboy, I knew that Uganda was on the equator next to Lake Victoria and inland from the Crown Colony of Kenya. In those days colonial officers were sent on first posting with kit and trunks by sea and I was informed that my sailing date was 22 February 1955.

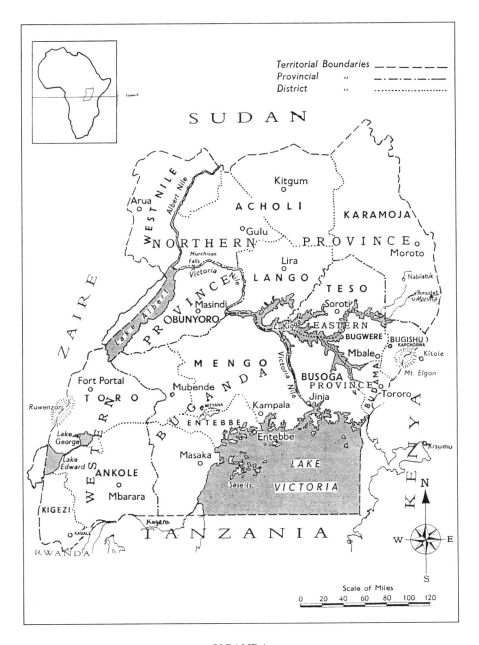

UGANDA

1

The Uganda Police: February 1955–April 1962

Monday 14 February

In order to get my jabs – inoculations and vaccinations, for yellow fever, smallpox and so on, required by the Colonial Office for service in East Africa – I went by train to Oxford yesterday to a tropical disease research place hidden away behind one of the colleges.

My passport arrived this morning. It describes my occupation as 'overseas civil servant'. For all sorts of reasons one does not describe oneself as police officer in a passport.

This afternoon I decided to go to the cinema for the last time before departure, particularly as the film was about Kenya. It was called *Simba* (Swahili for lion) and was a rather gory tale about a chap (Dirk Bogarde) who goes out to Kenya after hearing that his settler brother has been murdered there by Mau Mau. Food for thought.

I'm required to learn and qualify in Swahili, or Kiswahili as I gather it is more correctly called, and I've managed to get a book of grammar, vocabulary and simple exercises which I shall start swotting up during the trip out.

According to my letter of appointment tours in East Africa are for three years followed by six months home leave, with some local leave each year.

Saturday 19 February

By train to Liverpool with my luggage. There was a heavy fall of snow last night. A taxi to the docks where the driver eventually located the rather unimpressive Ellerman Lines ship *The City of Agra*. Nobody was in sight and the driver and I unloaded my kit and stacked it at the foot of the gangway. After hunting around on board for a while I found a character who showed me to a cabin. This is a cargo ship that carries only two passengers in the one cabin available. Hardly worth their while I would have thought.

1

The other occupant had not yet arrived so I had first choice of bunk and quickly settled in, pleased to find slightly more space than I'd had on troopships. My cabin companion turned up about an hour later. He said he's been a district officer in the Sudan but, as the Sudan is to become independent at the end of this year, he has secured a transfer to Kenya. He's been in the administration since the end of the war, which he finished as a captain in the Army. He was then given the honorary rank of major and prefers to be addressed as such. Apart from this small piece of vanity he seems to be quite a pleasant chap.

There is one steward to tidy the cabin and deal with the laundry and we are to take our meals with the ship's officers. The captain, a friendly middle-aged type, says we can go on to the bridge whenever we like but, apart from one visit, I think I'll stay out of the way. There's very little deck space as it's all cluttered up with derricks, winches and deck cargo, all under a thick coating of snow at the moment. What a relief to know that, during the three weeks of the voyage, there will be no deck games, fancy dress balls and suchlike passenger ship jollifications.

We sailed with this evening's tide passing a familiar-looking empty troopship parked alongside one of the docks. It was the *MV Empire Pride* in which my regiment had sailed to Hong Kong in June 1952. No bands or waving crowds for us this time, though, as Liverpool faded away in the darkness. It was too cold to remain on deck so I came below to the cabin.

Saturday 26 February

Having long since lost our snow covering, and after a thankfully not too rough passage through the Bay of Biscay, we entered slightly warmer climes and passed Gibraltar with a very superior-looking cruiser of the Royal Navy swooshing disdainfully past us in the opposite direction. A fighter aircraft then swooped down, decided we were of no consequence, and flew on towards the Rock while we plodded on into the Med.

The steward has produced two deck chairs, passengers, for the use of, and there is just enough space on deck for them. Not much chance of anyone playing deck quoits here – might just find room for a game of ludo. I've started work on *Teach Yourself Swahili*. It doesn't appear to be a very difficult language since it hasn't any awful irregularities and complicated grammatical constructions that one finds elsewhere. It seems to be based mainly on a mixture of Arabic, Hindustani and Africanised English words developed on the east coast of Africa. My big problem, as with other languages I've tackled, is remembering the vocabulary. So I sit muttering words as if learning a part in a play. So far no really useful phrases have cropped up like: 'My grandmother's carriage has been struck by lightning.'

Friday 4 March

Yesterday we were at anchor in the harbour at Port Said, but with no arrangements for going ashore; so I watched some cargo being offloaded on to a lighter. Having seen the sights of the place on four previous occasions I had no wish to revisit the Simon Artz Store or be entertained by the conjuring of a *Gully Gully* man, an Egyptian street magician. Even the bumboats left us alone. We are definitely downmarket.

Early this morning we up-anchored and joined the queue of vessels going through the Suez Canal, chugging slowly between the lines of sand dunes. It seemed odd not being in a troopship with British troops in khaki drill on the canal shore shouting: 'Get yer knees brown, mate!' Instead all was silent with just an occasional Arab pottering about on the bank.

Wednesday 9 March

I ought to know about the hazards of the burning sun in the Red Sea by now. The day before yesterday I was so deep into my Swahili exercises in the afternoon that I sat out too long exposed to the sun and my forearms are burned red and sore. Now we are parked offshore at Aden and again nobody's going ashore. It's cooler on board anyway and there's not much cargo being unloaded on to the lighters here.

Thursday 17 March

We have been ploughing steadily southwards through the Indian Ocean in very bright sunlight with flying fish and even occasional dolphins cavorting around our bows; glorious sunsets painted across the whole horizon. At dawn today we crept slowly into Mombasa harbour with dhows dodging about and everywhere the intriguing and exciting smell of tropical lands with palm trees and sandy beaches in view.

The ship anchored offshore and once more prepared to unload on to lighters. Before that commenced a launch came out and collected the major and myself with our luggage and took us ashore. The major was carried off by khaki-clad Kenyan officials and the local district officer deputed to look after me took me through customs and immigration and then by car to an old-style colonial hotel in town. Tomorrow morning I start my two days journey by East African

Railways to Kampala, the capital of Uganda, 884 miles away west-wards across the whole width of Kenya.

Before he left me the DO remarked that today is St Patrick's Day and there is an Irish regiment stationed in Mombasa, so it's likely to be a lively night. I had the whole day to spend walking around Mombasa, which is not large but has an interesting old harbour and fort. A soldier's first requirement in new territory is a good map of the area, so I located the government offices and from the Lands and Survey Department purchased an excellent Ordnance Survey map of East Africa which will be useful on the train journey – and later, of course. After dinner in the hotel I went for a stroll outside and a breath of fresh air, though in fact it was humid and didn't feel much cooler. There seemed to be drunken Paddies everywhere and I suspect the Redcaps will be busy later on. Leaving the night to them I came up to my room, where the bed has been made up with a roomy mosquito net over a frame; so I know I'm back in the tropics.

Friday 18 March

The DO collected me at the hotel this morning and took me to Mombasa railway station. We wandered along the platform until we found the first-class carriage with a 'reserved' card in a slot outside a two-bunk cabin showing my name and that of a doctor. By departure time the doctor had not shown up so I have the compartment to myself. There are very smart aluminium fittings with a small foldaway wash-basin and comfortable seats and bunk beds. The next carriage down is a restaurant car, where I enjoyed an efficiently served lunch.

Starting at sea level, we've been climbing steadily all day, with occasional flat stretches and stops at local stations where Africans carrying bundles on their heads get on or off. Others, mostly small boys, walk along the platform offering varied fruits, cakes, cooked yams, roasted corn cobs and cold drinks for sale. The railway staff, some Asians but mostly Africans, wear neat khaki uniforms and are very polite.

We've passed small stations or halts with names like Voi, Tsavo, Simba and Athi River (a game reserve at 5,000 feet). There seems to be plenty of game about, mostly buck of various sorts and sizes, also giraffe, zebra, monkeys and lots of highly coloured birds. Mount Kilimanjaro could be seen in the distance to the south with snow on its summit of almost 20,000 feet.

Saturday 19 March

It was still dark when we stopped at Nairobi station (5,500 feet) and we've continued in daylight through Kikuyu – which is also the name of the main tribe in this area. After Longonot there was a long stop at Gilgil, where some passengers got off to go on a branch line to Thomson's Falls.

The sun was setting as we passed through the Aberdare mountains, which is the area where Mau Mau activity has been mainly centred though there seemed to be no visible signs of the emergency. At Nakuru the main line divides into two routes; one goes west to Kisumu and Lake Victoria, the other, via Eldoret, crosses the border into Uganda at Tororo and then on to Kampala.

At the trading centre called Equator – which is actually where it's at – we were at the highest point of the railway at 9,000 feet. It was a long slow climb with two engines pulling and stops to pick up fuel and water. Altogether it's quite a journey but very interesting and the meals are fine. In the restaurant car I met a chap who's a superintendent on transfer to the Uganda Police from Tanganyika. Odd sort of chap – but then he's a policeman, what can you expect? No doubt I'll be seeing more of him later.

Sunday 20 March

Early this morning we crossed into Uganda at a small halt called Malaba and, after a brief stop, moved on to a larger station at Tororo in Uganda's Eastern Province. There was a good view of Mount Elgon, which rises to over 14,000 feet, to the north. We chugged on to the Busoga district headquarters of Jinja, which is where the Ripon Falls are – or were until last year when the Queen opened the new Owen Falls dam and hydroelectric scheme on the site.

The train rattled across the bridge here and work is still in progress on a part of the power station. From Jinja it's about 55 miles to Kampala, passing through the dense forests and lush greenery of Busoga at an altitude of about 4,000 feet. I was told that the arrival of the Uganda mail train at Kampala on Sunday mornings before lunch is treated as a social occasion and there's always a crowd of people on the platform either meeting people or just gossiping and inspecting new arrivals. Indeed that is how it was and porters swarmed around energetically pulling suitcases out and dumping them on to the platform.

A huge, obvious rugger type loomed over me and introduced himself as Mac in a broad Scots accent. He had my trunks loaded into a police truck and then I was in his car with a suitcase. We drove to his married quarters on Kololo hill, where I am to spend the night. Tomorrow I gather I'm to move into the Kitante government hostel, which is at the bottom of this hill next to the golf course and accommodates single European officers.

From what I could see driving from the station, Kampala appears to be a pleasant-looking town with lots of greenery and buildings perched on a number of surrounding hills. I met Mac's very pregnant Scots wife, infant daughter and excitable small dog and enjoyed a pleasant lunch. A couple of other police chaps called in to inspect the newcomer. One of them, also clearly a rugger type, asked what games I play. When I replied: 'None at all, if I can help it,' he looked shocked and disappointed.

'However did you get into the police then?' he cried with disgust as he was leaving.

'I bribed the Colonial Secretary,' I said.

Tomorrow's going to be a busy day, I'm told. Mac says I've been posted to the Police Training School (PTS), where he is the second in command and chief instructor. What on earth can I teach them? Sounds a bit like the blind leading the blind.

Monday 21 March

A full day. First to Police Headquarters, which is on another hill in the centre of town. Here I met the Commissioner of Police, a short, stocky, quietly spoken mild type called Joe Deegan, who welcomed me with the rather ominous words that someone in London had bungled. Apparently I was supposed to have attended a UK police college course for colonial officers before coming out here. I had known nothing of this, of course, and for an awful moment thought I was about to sent back to the UK as an export reject. However, the Commissioner didn't seem to be too worried about it and said: 'Well, too late for that now, you'll have to pick it up as you go along just like we had to do in the old days.'

What a sensible chap, I thought. I next met the Deputy Commissioner, a very keen-eyed and competent-looking type named Cleland, and then the Senior Assistant Commissioner in charge of administration, a rather grim-looking, prune-faced chap, who gave me the impression of being a humourless numbers man.

Next a brief meeting with the Chief Accountant, then along to a small room where the police photographer took mugshots for my warrant card, driving permit and their file. Then to Barclays Bank to confirm that my UK bank had opened an account for me and to collect a cheque book and some local cash. After that Mac took me to the shop in Kampala Road of the only local British tailor, W. E. Green, known, of course, as Wee Green. A self-important little man whose old-fashioned ideas on tropical uniforms were clearly in need of updating. I ordered the minimum from him; too expensive. Having some experience with this sort of thing and wishing to acquire several spares, I asked Mac to take me to a good Indian tailor, so we went to a shop called 'Men's Wear' further along Kampala Road. Here, just as I suspected, they make not only perfectly good uniforms but are much quicker and cheaper and more inclined to pay attention to the customer's requirements.

Off again up another hill, called Nakasero, to an old-time stone fort which is now used as the police quartermaster's stores. The QM is a standard gloomy ex-Army quartermaster type who still uses his military rank of captain. The QM's a very necessary and important chap in a unit who can be quite helpful and affect one's comfort and convenience in many ways if so minded. A spot of respect and friendliness costs nothing and can produce all sorts of useful items and occasional assistance. For now I collected the standard issue of a cap, badges, buttons, black Sam Browne belt, sword (for ceremonial duties, I was told), long khaki stockings, blue puttees, black boots and shoes, a swagger cane, helmet and riot baton, a .38 revolver, a police whistle and blue lanyard, a lightweight raincoat and a thick blanket.

After lunch I was taken to Kitante Hostel and introduced to Mr and Mrs Broome, the co-managers, who showed me first the communal dining room and then a small flatlet in a two-storey block consisting of a sitting room and a small, partially partitioned-off bedroom. The bathrooms are at the end of the corridor and available to all inmates. My trunks had already been delivered. Not very exciting accommodation, but Broome explained that I should be able to move into one of the separate thatched cottages eventually. He said that as people go on transfer up-country or on leave or get married, so others can move into better accommodation. There are a lot of people here so it looks as if I'll be stuck in this one for about a year unless there's a very selective massacre or upheaval organised. However, it's not too bad. There's standard PWD furniture and, with my own bedding, pictures, books, radio and record player unpacked, I'm reasonably comfortable. I gather that Kampala is now mosquito-free so it's no longer necessary to sleep under a net – but it is needed up-country.

Tuesday 22 March

This morning I was taken to the High Court, an impressive old colonial building in the middle of town, to the chambers of the Chief Justice, a friendly old buffer called John Griffin, who said a few welcoming words then swore me in as a Justice of the Peace. Apparently this is necessary so that, wherever I happen to be stationed in Uganda, I can take and record oaths of service of summonses from constables who are process servers. Then, if the accused or a witness fails to attend court, service on him is proved by production of the sworn summons endorsed at the back by a JP. An arrest warrant can then be issued by a magistrate, and Bob's your uncle.

Afterwards Mac took me to one of the local car dealers and agents, Twentsche Overseas Motor Trading Company (TOM) on Kampala Road, the main street through the town. TOM have sold a number of Standard Vanguards to police officers because they are reasonably priced and have strong engines and sturdy bodies. Mac has one in which he has been driving me around. A fat car, not elegant or attractive but good for these roads. Government car loans are available for all colonial officials as one has to be able to get about on duty and the police have very few vehicles of their own. Monthly deductions are made from one's salary to repay the loan.

In the showroom my eyes lighted upon a very smart red MG sports car and I said: 'That's for me.' Mac tut-tutted, shook his head and said I had no hope as Finance would never agree to a loan for that. Apparently a suitable car in the eyes of police officialdom is one in which dead bodies can be carried up-country as well as live constables. Well, I didn't know that. So a Vanguard it will have to be and I'll clear it with Finance tomorrow and obtain a chit from them to take to TOM so that I can collect a car.

On arrival at the hostel for lunch I found a line of six young African men each clutching small books waiting outside my flat. Word had gone forth that I was available to be selected as an employer of a houseboy. Each produced his *kitabu*, the small book issued by the government containing his photograph, thumb print, names, age, tribe, record of previous employment and reason for discharge. Most of them were from Kenya and all spoke Swahili.

One of them was a rather shifty-looking type with a wall-eye. He had clearly made an impression on his last employer who had written in his *kitabu*: 'If Yozefu has talents he has so far kept them well hidden. On the day he started work for us he simultaneously reached his level of incompetence. I can safely recommend him for any minor post requiring no productivity, capability or responsibility.'

Clearly Yozefu is a politician in the making. I handed his *kitabu* back to him with a 'best of British luck to you, chum'. Instead I chose a smart-looking young chap called Ephraim Timothy from Northern Rhodesia.* He has very little English so I'll have to get a move on

*Now called Zambia.

with my Swahili studies. All he has to do at the moment is make my bed, do the *dhobi* (laundry) and clean my shoes for the princely sum of 20 shillings a month. Servants quarters are provided at the other end of the hostel compound so he can be on hand when needed. A fairly idle life I would imagine.

This afternoon I've had a chance to look around the PTS at last. The Officer-in-Charge (usually referred to as the OC) is a senior superintendent called John Thomson (another Scot). He's quiet spoken with a sense of humour and a friendly approach, apparently at one time a drill instructor in the Scots Guards. He doesn't seem worried that I know nothing of police work. 'Aye, it's no bother,' he said, 'ye'll pick it up as ye go along.'

The PTS is on the side of Kibuli, yet another of Kampala's hills. On the top of the hill is the attractive Kibuli Mosque, a white rectangular building with a tower at each corner and a large onion dome over the centre part. The PTS grounds extend down the hill to a level part where there is a grass parade ground and sports field with a drill shed at one side. Apart from classrooms there are dormitories for the recruits, a cookhouse, an administration block and quarters for staff NCOs. The recruits are aged about 18 and come from all tribes, although those from the north and east predominate. They spend a year here training. Most are taught in Swahili but there are a few more recently recruited youngsters who speak English and recruiting is now concentrating on getting more of them into the force. The entry standards are being steadily raised so that eventually all recruits will be English-speakers. At the PTS they wear khaki pillbox hats, white *merduff* (thick cotton) shirts with no collars, khaki shorts and go barefooted. After their basic training they wear full police uniform for guard duty and ceremonial parades. When addressing an officer or NCO they use the term *afendi* which is the Swahili version of the Turkish *effendi*.

I've been given two jobs here at the school. One is as first-aid instructor (OC Bandages). Recruits are given a full course in first aid and are then examined by the St John Ambulance Brigade superintendent, a British woman who speaks to the recruits in a garbled mix of Swahili and Luganda. Those who pass are allowed to wear the silver circular badge of the Brigade on their sleeves. I was a first-aider as a boy scout so I see no problems there; just a matter of brushing up on bandaging, splints and pressure points.

The second hat I'm to wear is the new post of Assistant Editor of the Force monthly magazine called *Habari* (news). The OC of the PTS is automatically the editor but he usually just writes the editorial. The work of putting the magazine together so far has been in the hands of the sub-editor, an old coast Arab called Zubeir Aboubakar, who is also the chief Swahili instructor. He has been sub-editor since *Habari* was started in 1931. Most of the issues have been written in Swahili with a few English articles, generally copied from Force Orders, showing who has gone on leave or been promoted or transferred. The Swahili articles tend to be old Arab and African stories or parables about animals that talk, rather like Aesop's fables and, in my view, not suitable for a police magazine. I've had a look through several back issues and pretty dull and boring and uninspired they are. The whole thing needs pulling together and bringing up to date and made relevant to the Force.

Obviously I'll have to go carefully about this as the old man has no doubt worked hard to keep the magazine going for years, though the sales are right down, and I don't want to upset him if it can be avoided. Having been involved with magazines both at school and in the army, I have some idea of what to do. We need to drop the childish talking animal stories and replace them with articles of interest about general police work, interesting cases, various laws that need explaining; things going on in the Force itself – parades, sporting events, special functions and so on – some simple competitions, photographs, cartoons and other humour. We need reports from stations all over the country for 'District Notes' and I'll start writing a series of 'Improve Your English' articles to help those who are trying to do just that.

It's sold for 50 cents at the moment, which nowhere near covers the printing costs – especially as so many are unsold. It has to be subsidised by Headquarters plus whatever advertising can be obtained – another area that needs some attention. I've been to see the printers, Patel Press in Kampala Road, to discuss a brighter cover and layout inside. This all has interesting possibilities and is worth doing because it can be a good morale booster and provide interest and entertainment and a chance for any member of the Force to send in contributions and get his name in print. Involvement is what it's all about.

Friday 25 March

The recruits do PT before breakfast while it's still relatively cool, then at eight o'clock everyone attends morning parade. The inspection is followed by drill under squad sergeants. For those squads nearing the end of their training there is passing-out parade practice. Officers on the staff watch over different squads.

On Fridays the OC requires his officers to take part in revolver-shooting on the small range near the obstacle course. He is an expert pistol shot and captains the Force pistol team, which usually wins the

East and West Africa cup, so he expects a high standard. The recruits have to qualify on the rifle ranges with the old British Lee-Enfield .303 army rifles before they pass out and usually there are one or two marksmen produced. These wear a crossed rifles badge on their sleeve cuffs, as in the army. We work on Saturday mornings from nine o'clock to noon then break off for the weekend. I gather that Saturday noon is when the local *Wazungu* (Europeans) descend upon the club at each station, the serious drinkers for a session, others for a drink or two and a natter before heading for lunch.

Sunday 27 March

A few days ago I purchased a street plan of Kampala, and Chas, a Scot who works in CID headquarters, with whom I share a table in the hostel dining room, took me on a leisurely tour around Kampala in his car this morning. It was very quiet in town, hardly any traffic. There are two large, fine-looking cathedrals, each on a separate hill, of course. The Anglican is at Namirembe and the Catholic at Rubaga. In addition to the mosque on Kibuli there are other mosques and Hindu temples scattered around the town. Many of the Asians live on Old Kampala hill, where there are the remains of Lugard's Fort, a different fort from that on Nakasero hill, where the QM presides. There are several Indian schools in Old Kampala and others elsewhere in Kampala. The government education system here provides separate schools for Africans and Asians. There is an Aga Khan school and a European junior school. For higher education European children are sent to the excellent schools in Kenya or to the UK.

Across the road from the PTS is the large Nsambya police barracks with lines of quarters for the NCOs and constables who provide staff for Central Police Station, Police Headquarters and supporting staff belonging to the radio section, drivers, vehicle inspection and repair section and so on. On the outskirts of town there are stations at Katwe, Old Kampala, Jinja Road and Kira Road, each with its own lines. Eastwards, outside town on the road to Jinja, is Naguru Police College, where courses are held for promotion to various ranks and for the CID.

The road to Katwe is called Queensway, with a tower at the town end containing a clock, known as the Queen's Clock, declared open last year when the Queen visited to inaugurate the Owen Falls electric power scheme. From Katwe there are three roads: one to Entebbe 20 miles to the south on the shore of Lake Victoria; the eastern road climbs yet another hill to Makindye, at the top of which is the Governor's Lodge, used when the Governor is in Kampala for any length of time. Around and below this are the residences of various

11

wealthy business people. The road to the west does not lead to such a desirable residential area but to the very crowded and, in parts, slum-like Katwe-Kisenyi which is the haunt of low-life bars, thieves, receivers and some politicians. Constables going into that area go in pairs, unlike in the rest of Kampala, where they patrol their beats singly on foot. I gather that it's one of the areas where you can buy cheap replacements of parts or tools stolen from your vehicle; often you buy the original parts back.

North-west of the town, on yet another hill, is Makerere University College, which is affiliated to London University. It has a high reputation academically and there's a lot of competition for places from all over Africa.

Wednesday 30 March

I've started oral Swahili lessons after work in the early evenings. Mr Kamoga, who is a Swahili teacher at the PTS and a Luganda teacher outside, comes to my flat twice a week. He asked if another of his students, who works in some other government department, could join us and I agreed. His name is Pollock, though I'm told he's known as 'The Pillock' – a tall, skinny civilian who has been out here for some years but has not so far mastered this very simple language. We do 'conversation', which consists mostly of questions and answers to prepare us for the oral part of the exam.

The Pillock has a family and collects guns, which he would much rather talk about – also how important his work is – than Swahili. However, like all government officials, he has to qualify in it for substantive appointment and promotion. Kamoga's a good methodical teacher, cheerful and painstaking. His favourite expression for describing any situation or problem is that 'it's a piece of cake'. Probably picked it up from some ex-Riff-RAF type.

For confirmation of appointment at the end of the two years probationary period we are also required to pass the Police Law examination, consisting of five papers covering the Law of Evidence, the Penal Code, Criminal Procedure Code, Local and Special Laws and a paper on Police Standing Orders (police duties). Some find it difficult to pass the language and law exams in the two years because of other outside interests, general idleness, procrastination or just lack of brains. I don't like exams or studying for them and my solution is to dispose of them as soon as possible. So I've decided to sit for the law exam at the end of this July and the Swahili exam in August.

Nobody I've spoken to thinks I have a hope of passing the two exams together like this so soon after my arrival, and they may be right, but I'm going to give it a try. I've prepared for exams before and worked out some exam techniques that will give me a chance. I've plenty of time in the evenings to do the necessary swotting as I'm not interested in bars, clubs and such.

Having missed the UK police course, I've not a clue about the legal subjects, except for a slight knowledge of military law, but Chas has kindly offered to coach me for an hour or so on a couple of evenings a week, so my tutoring in both law and Swahili is organised. The rest is up to me. Looking at some of the senior characters around here, especially the ex-Palestine Police types, I can only conclude that if they managed to qualify then so can I. Well, we shall see.

Monday 4 April

Finance haven't yet processed my car loan so I still get lifts to the PTS from the hostel and back from other police types resident here. It's not always convenient and sometimes I hitch a lift home in the PTS tender (as police trucks are called). If it drops me in town on its way somewhere else then I walk the mile and a half to the hostel. I also like to walk about in the early evening so as to learn my way around. But I'm pointedly told that it's not on for Europeans to walk here as we are expected to move around in cars. So, naturally, I go on walking and 'letting the side down'. Sometimes helpful African drivers stop and offer me a lift and when I say I like walking they look astonished and reply: 'But, sir, Europeans don't walk here.'

At last I've been able to collect my first batch of khaki uniforms, which Ephraim has washed and starched; so now I can go on parade properly dressed instead of appearing in tinker's *mufti*.

Thursday 7 April

There's a residents common room above the hostel dining room, where tea is served in the afternoons. I rarely go up there as I'm not usually back at that time or busy being tutored. But it's Good Friday tomorrow and we finished early today so I popped up for tea and cakes. Several police types were there scoffing away and exchanging gossip. Paddy, who is a most un-serious and charming person, was as usual causing hilarity.

He prosecutes in the Resident Magistrate's criminal court. It seems that proceedings this morning were very dull and boring and everyone was getting sleepy, even the defence advocate who was doing the talking. So Paddy picked up some African's disreputable old felt hat that was an exhibit in a case, put it on, with the brim down all round, turned round to face the Africans in the public spectators seats and pulled a gormless, Worzel Gummidge-type face. They all collapsed with loud laughter and the RM was obliged to stop the proceedings, call for order and ask Paddy, whom he knows well, to behave himself.

Friday 15 April

I was invited to dinner with the Commissioner of Police this evening. I got a lift up yet another hill to his residence at 1 Baker Road – which seems almost an apt address. The CP then drove me in his car to the Uganda Club, which must have been a journey of almost 150 yards. His wife is away and nobody else had been invited so we dined *à deux*. A good meal with some excellent wine and he was a pleasant, friendly and interesting host. Afterwards, when he was backing his car in the club car park, a wall collided with us. I didn't know whether to take his name and address or just ignore it.

Saturday 23 April

Fred, a hostel inmate who works in the Labour Department, offered to drive me to Jinja this afternoon to look at the dam and the town. He has an old Morris on the point of disintegration and we reached Jinja rattling and backfiring and emitting clouds of exhaust fumes after following behind buses and lorries, many of which were in a similar state. We passed through large forests in Busoga with tall *Mvule* trees, from which furniture of a beautiful grain and colour is made, and many smaller different-coloured flowering trees. The dam and power station are where the Ripon Falls used to be, and there is an inscribed stone proclaiming that it is where Speke discovered the source of the Nile on 28 July 1862. After the remarkable and presentient Winston Churchill stood there back in 1908 he wrote: 'It would be perfectly easy to harness the whole river and let the Nile begin its long and beneficent journey to the sea by leaping through a turbine.' Forty-six years later, in April last year, the Queen opened the Owen Falls hydro-electric scheme, built just as he predicted.

There were several Africans standing in the water and on the rocks below the dam with home-made fishing rods and, further down, I saw the upper parts of two hippos in the water doing absolutely nothing. Lake Victoria is huge, the second largest in the world and about the size of the whole of Ireland. Fred showed me where some parts of the Bogart/Hepburn *African Queen* were filmed four years ago. Jinja is not a large town and today the main street was quiet. It was lined with Asian-owned *dukas* and, at the other end, is the *boma*, where the various government offices are located. At the roadside we stood under a tree with fragrant purplish flowers and small pale green leaves on weeping branchlets. It was like a slow, fine shower-bath. Fred calls it the wee-wee tree. We had tea and cakes at the Ripon Falls Hotel not far from the lakeside, then back to Kampala, once he could get the reluctant car to start. On the way we had a slow puncture and, of course, he had no spare wheel. So we kept stopping while I hopped out and used an ancient foot pump to put some air back in while Fred kept the engine running in case it wouldn't restart. Over 50 miles of such energetic fun was rather exhausting and I was quite relieved when Fred's ramshackle conveyance finally reached the hostel.

Sunday 24 April

After lunch Chas took me in his car the 20-odd miles to Entebbe, where there is a long sandy beach on the lake shore. At the roadside where the rough track starts to the beach there's an ambiguous sign saying CROCODILES IT IS DANGEROUS TO BATHE. Since this is where people come to swim, perhaps the message is intended for the crocodiles. It's a very pleasant, quiet place with only a few people around. Across the road the airport runway commences but nothing was using it while we were there. I gather there's one flight out on Sundays. After a swim and a walk along the beach, with no sign of any crocodiles, we drove around Entebbe, which is mainly government offices collectively called the Secretariat, Government House and a well-spread residential area with a few shops in the main street and a very pleasant botanical gardens down by the lakeside, which one can either walk or drive through. It has a large collection of exotic plants, shrubs and trees, some of which are not native to this country. There are also masses of brightly coloured birds flitting about making bird noises. We called at the airport in time to see the four-engined BOAC Argonaut taking passengers aboard and having its elastic band wound before taking off for London. Since our working tours out here are for three years, it's going to be some time before I make use of that flight.

Finally tea on the large verandah of the Lake Victoria Hotel, Entebbe's only hotel, an attractive old building, before returning to Kampala at dusk, which, as we are on the equator, lasts for only a few minutes before darkness suddenly descends.

Tuesday 26 April

This afternoon I was able at last to collect my new car; my first car, in fact. Actually it's a Standard Vanguard panel van – being the cheapest – with the panels cut out and replaced with glass to make it look almost like a car, but with no back seats. That is all the loan rate at my miserable salary would stand. Still, it's not too bad and the colour I chose was British racing green with a white roof for coolness. I learned to drive in army jeeps and haven't driven a right-hand drive civilian car before, so I took it out after work and drove around Kampala feeling rather grand. I was advised that, as it was designed to carry a load, the vehicle would be more stable on the road if I put ballast in the empty back space. For this I've obtained some gunny bags (sacks) which will be filled with sand the first time I drive it down to Entebbe beach.

Wednesday 27 April

For the last week or so at the PTS we were rehearsing for a guard of honour for yesterday's opening of this session of the Legislative Council (LegCo). The two senior squads of recruits and some staff were formed into one company with Mac commanding and myself as number two. This is my first public ceremonial parade here. The Police Band also took part and they're very good. We all wore full dress – khaki tunics over a white shirt and black tie, shorts and long blue put-tees and boots with Sam Browne and sword for us. The men wore a tasselled blue fez (or tarboosh) with khaki high-collared tunic and shorts and a wide blue cummerbund under a black leather belt, with rifle and bayonet.

We were inspected by the acting Governor, who is the Chief Secretary, Colin Thornley, as Sir Andrew Cohen is on leave. The Chief Justice and the Buganda Regents were present all in robes and there was quite a crowd of spectators, many no doubt attracted by the sound of the band. It went off very well; a piece of cake, as Kamoga would say. There was quite a good photo of us in today's *Uganda Argus*.

Sunday 8 May

In the course of studying the long list of local and special laws I read the Game Ordinance today. According to most books and films Kenya is the place for white hunters and expensive hunting safaris. In fact, they also take place here with hunting licences issued by the Game Department.

For instance, a visitor's full licence allowing him to shoot through the list of animals costs the equivalent of £50, while the same for a resident costs only £5. A licence to shoot one elephant costs £5, one black rhinoceros is £10, one bull giraffe is £15 and a bird licence is 10 shillings. Nobody is allowed to shoot a gorilla or a white rhinoceros. The annual fee for a firearm is only 5 shillings. Personally, I've no use for any of them.

Thursday 19 May

Officers on the PTS staff have to take their turn as night duty officer at the Central Police Station on Kampala Road, going out at irregular intervals in the old and rickety Ford Pilot patrol cars and checking through the list of buildings and compounds requiring security visits around Kampala. These ancient vehicles wouldn't be much use for chasing after another car – except, perhaps, a reversing lorry.

I was on this duty all last night, sitting next to the driver with a radio used for communications with the duty officer at the CPS. In the back of the car were two constables, who spent most of the time asleep. Keystone cops. In the doorways of all the Indian-owned shops along Kampala Road and in Old Kampala could be seen African night-watchmen wearing ex-army khaki greatcoats and maintaining a high and efficient standard of security for the shops and offices of their employers by remaining in a deep sleep. They refused to be disturbed even when I had to seize hold of an occasional greatcoat collar to haul one or other of them aside in order to check the door locks.

No calls for help came over the air from the CPS and, after I'd been out for about an hour, at around midnight Sandy, the duty officer, called up asking if anything was happening out there. I replied: 'Not a sausage.' Perhaps the local criminal fraternity was sleeping as soundly as everyone else seemed to be, apart from the driver and myself. Probably just as well. By the time the old Ford reached the scene of a crime all concerned would have long been gone. We're hardly a fast-response unit.

Those on night duty get the following day off, presumably to catch up on sleep, but I decided instead to take a book and some sandwiches and spend the day on Entebbe beach. Being a weekday it was deserted except for half a dozen Ankole cattle with their characteristic huge curved horns grazing at the far end. A quiet, idle, pleasantly hot day. This is the life.

Sunday 29 May

After class last week my Swahili co-student, The Pillock, kindly invited me to his home on Saturday (yesterday) for dinner. So I drove over to Entebbe and eventually located his place. His wife's sole topic of conversation consisted of a string of complaints about their African domestic servants. There was also a sullen young son covered with freckles who didn't speak at all.

After a reasonable meal – nothing wrong with their cook – we sat with coffee and he went on and on about his gun collection, which I didn't ask to see, and she went on about the servants and I was so bored I fell asleep. I woke up, disturbed by a sudden silence, to find that I was being glared at very angrily by the whole family of Pillocks. Very embarrassing. I apologised and said I'd been on duty all the previous night and so without sleep. Then I stood not upon my departure. Somehow I don't think that I'll be invited there again.

Friday 10 June

The 4th Battalion of the King's African Rifles (4 KAR) is the Uganda battalion of this famous regiment. Other KAR battalions are located in Tanganyika, Kenya and Northern Rhodesia. Most of these, including ours, have been stationed in Kenya these last few years during the Mau Mau emergency there. Meanwhile the Uganda Police took over the duty of performing the annual parade for the Queen's birthday. This parade took place today after several weeks of practising and rehearsing with the band. In order to produce the necessary three companies almost all the recruits and staff at the PTS have been involved. Jock Thomson was parade commander. He is soon going on leave and his replacement is already here and took command of one of the companies. Mac had another company and I the third.

We paraded at the Kampala Sports Club ground, where there is plenty of space for the necessary complicated manoeuvres involved in this special parade. The Governor is still on leave so the acting Governor, Mr Thornley, took the salute. He was escorted by the Commissioner and Deputy Commissioner. It seemed to go well, and afterwards I was told that it had been most impressive. There was plenty of applause from spectators as we marched off.

Friday 1 July

The Protectorate Government has introduced the ministerial system as from today. So the various related departments are grouped together under a minister. For instance the Police, Prisons Service and Fire Brigade come under the Minister of Internal Affairs. The Customs and Immigration Departments ought to as well, but they are a part of the East African High Commission, which runs them, as well as such other organisations as EA Posts and Telegraphs, agricultural and veterinary research stations, EA Airlines, EA Currency Board, EA Railways and Harbours and so on, for the combined benefit of Kenya, Uganda, Tanganyika and Zanzibar.

Wednesday 6 July

A bit of a flap on last night as CPS had a clean-up operation. They roped in bods from all Kampala stations and Nsambya Barracks. Officers were also detailed from all over and our OC kindly volunteered my expert services as the PTS contribution. There was an officers briefing at the CPS at 7 p.m. when the OC/CPS told us that the raid was on the upper part of Kisenyi and the object was to bring in illegal *waragi* (locally distilled spirit from bananas), the stills used, home-made guns, wanted persons and Mau Mau in hiding from Kenya, and other assorted villains. Road-blocks were to be established at both ends of the long top road and teams led by officers would search all the buildings. The OC said: 'Right then, let's go and feel some collars.' The constables were loaded into a collection of police tenders with an officer in the front of each one and we trundled off through Katwe. Our target area was not street-lit but a moonlight night had been chosen.

Later, when I was about half-way along the road in Kisenyi and about to search some windowless store, there was a shout from several of the men as a lorry suddenly started up in the dark beside another building. The driver had either been hiding in the cab or had crept in unseen. The open back of the truck was loaded with large 40-gallon drums, possibly containing *waragi*. As the lorry headed towards me at increasing speed, the OC/CPS from further along the road shouted: 'Stop him!'

So I stood in the road with my hand up thinking: this is what policemen do. 'Stop! Halt! *Simama*!' I shouted as the vehicle careered towards me. I then realised that he was not going to be good enough to obey my order and, at the last moment, I jumped aside. Unfortunately, I timed it rather badly and the very edge of something on the side of the truck caught me quite lightly on the shoulder. It spun me round two and a half times like a ballet dancer and I struck the closed door of the store behind me. The door burst open and I disappeared inside and knocked some boxes over with a crash and then fell on to some sacks of maize flour, which burst, sending up a cloud of dust and white flour that billowed up and out through the doorway. I got to my feet and staggered outside spluttering and coughing and covered with white dust. The constables were hugely entertained and, holding their sides, fell about laughing. I sent a corporal down the road to see if the lorry had been stopped at the roadblock and he came back grinning and reported that the vehicle had disappeared. Apparently the barricade at that end had not been in place. Somebody had bungled – apart from me.

However, the other sections had been busy and, after a couple of hours, we made our way back to the CPS with all sorts of seized items, including several scruffy-looking characters carefully disguised as members of the local criminal fraternity who were wanted for one thing or another. The OC/CPS referring to my earlier escapade said: 'Ha! Must have been self-raising flour. Not to worry; can't catch 'em all you know.'

Sunday 10 July

I wonder if the reason that sound carries so well here has something to do with the very clear air at an altitude of 4,000 feet. The sound of drumming from various parts of Kampala and the outskirts can often be heard. I gather that the Baganda have drums at weddings and funerals, which perhaps explains the frequency. Nsambya police barracks is almost 2 miles away from Kitante but I can usually hear the various bugle calls quite clearly, especially the Last Post.

Once or twice a month, on Sundays, the Police Band gives an excellent afternoon concert in the King George V Memorial Park in the centre of town. There's a bandstand in the park and plenty of smooth grass on the slope for spectators of all races to sit or stand and enjoy the programme and exchange greetings.

Friday 29 July

After just over three months here I sat for the five papers in the Police Law exam this week, having been studying for it on most evenings when I wasn't doing Swahili. The papers didn't seem to be too bad – at least I could get some sort of answers down. I was previously warned by several types, some of whom had taken two, three or more years to pass the law exams, that I hadn't a hope of passing with no police experience or training and that it was a waste of time. Why hurry, anyway, they asked, since there's two years to go before confirmation of appointment? So be it. We shall see what we shall see. As far as I'm concerned I'm glad I tried.

Wednesday 10 August

The two senior PTS squads passed out this morning. I was parade commander, with an inspector and a sub-inspector as squad commanders. The Commissioner took the parade and afterwards expressed satisfaction with the drill and turnout. The best recruit receives the Commissioner's Prize, which is a truncheon with an engraved silver plate on it and a blue and silver lanyard which he will always wear when in uniform as a permanent mark of distinction.

Friday 19 August

Today I sat for the Swahili exams – translation papers both ways and an oral test by some character learned in the language. Not too bad. I think I'm reasonably confident about it. Did plenty of swotting for it anyway. Afterwards I saw Kamoga and he asked how it went. 'Piece of cake,' I said.

Monday 22 August

Three cheers. I was informed today that I've passed the Police Law exams. Two of us passed with distinction in all subjects; the first ever in the Force, so I'm told. The Jeremiahs are not looking too happy that I not only did it in less than four months out here but also passed well. Fat lot I care. All I want is to put the exams behind me, then I can get on with putting it all into actual practice, which is the important part.

Friday 26 August

Police Sports Day today. It was held at the PTS sports ground across from Nsambya barracks. Most of the Kampala officers were acting as recording officials, judges and starters. I was a track judge. Athletes took part from units all over the country and the results were turned into an inter-Provincial competition. There are some first-rate runners and jumpers. Many Africans seem to have very long legs, which helps, I suppose. I was particularly interested in the 440 yards relay and the 110 yards high hurdles, which I used to take part in. Some of these chaps, if properly coached, could make a very good showing in international athletics. Heaven knows what hidden talent there is out in the bush where children, from a very young age, run several miles to school and back every day, so I'm told.

There were some very impressive times, distances and heights recorded. There were also the usual entertaining events such as races for veterans and clerks, a tug-of-war, a bicycle race which ended in a pile-up and a police children's race that ended in a fight. Cups and other more useful prizes were presented by the Commissioner's wife and the band played and everyone seemed to enjoy the day.

Monday 29 August

Because Uganda is a British Protectorate and not a colony, there are no European settlers here as in Kenya. Land here can only be owned by Africans but they can lease it to non-Africans for commercial purposes such as cotton ginneries, sugar, tea and coffee planta-

21

tions and so on. Most of these enterprises are owned and run by Asians.

The government administration is by the Governor at the top, then the Provincial Commissioners over the Northern, Eastern and Western Provinces and the Resident, Buganda Kingdom. District Commissioners (DCs) assisted by Assistant District Commissioners (ADCs) administer the districts. The DC is the top man in the district and he chairs the African District Council – consisting of chiefs and elders of that particular tribe – and the District Team of department heads from public works, labour, agriculture, police, prisons, veterinary, and so on.

The judicial side is separate, with a Resident Magistrate (RM) either stationed at the district HQ town or visiting from time to time. The DC and the ADCs also sit as lesser magistrates of the first, second and third class depending on their seniority and having passed the Administration Law exam, which is similar to the Police Law exam.

Within Uganda there are four kingdoms and other parts of the country where the highest ranking Africans are the county chiefs. The Buganda Kingdom is a separate provincial area ruled over by the Kabaka; the other three kingdoms are located in the Western Province, where Bunyoro and Toro are each ruled over by an Omukama and Ankole, in the south-west, by an Omugabe. For administration purposes each of the western kingdoms is regarded as a district under a DC. In the Eastern Province the district of Busoga has a paramount chief called the Kyabasinga. These rulers have limited powers according to the individual treaties signed by earlier rulers with the British.

HE the Governor, Sir Andrew Cohen, is a left-wing intellectual type who, unusually for such an appointment, has never served in the Colonial Service but is a political appointee. He is very keen to make Africans politically aware and to encourage the development of democratic local governments. In 1952, his first year in office, the first political party, the Uganda National Congress, was formed under his benevolent eye. He decided that African District Councils should run themselves and their departments and that the DC should no longer be the Council chairman. The Councils from then on took over the appointment of chiefs and the collection of taxes.

As a consequence of this decision the 1933 Bunyoro Agreement has had to be amended and the ceremony of signing the new Agreement will take place at Hoima in Bunyoro, where the Omukama has his palace, on 3 September. It will be a full-dress affair with the Governor in blue uniform and cocked hat with feathers, the Omukama and his chiefs in robes and everyone else in best bib and tucker. There will be a police guard of honour for HE and the Omukama to inspect and, to add to the grandeur of the occasion, the Police Band is being sent to Hoima by bus to take part. However, the Bandmaster, Teddy Beare, apparently cannot be with them on that day and the OC/PTS told me that I am to take the band to Hoima as Band Conducting Officer (but not, alas, as conductor) to ensure that all goes well and the programme is adhered to. Teddy has asked me to drive him to Hoima tomorrow in order to recce the sites and positions for the band over the two days. The musical programme has all been worked out and rehearsed to perfection as always, of course. With any luck it should be a piece of cake.

Tuesday 30 August

Very early this morning I picked up Teddy at his quarters in Kololo and drove off to Hoima, which is 128 miles to the north-west of Kampala. It was hot and the road was hard, red *murram* (laterite), very dry and dusty. Stirling-Astaldi are working on the road in Bunyoro, upgrading it so that it becomes all-weather and most will eventually be tarmacked.

There were many large white ant (termite) hills beside the road, and some troops of baboons, without any road sense, were playing about on the road in a most careless manner. Because of the dryness and the dust the choice was to close the car windows and be baked in the heat or open the windows to let in the hot air and the dust. The answer was to compromise and drive with the windows open for as long as possible and then, when another vehicle approached, close the windows quickly to keep the dust out, with both driver and passenger frantically winding the windows up and down. One still arrives at the end of the safari covered with a film of rust-coloured dust anyway, as it gets in whatever one does. A shower and cold drink on arrival usually help to restore the soul.

Africans were plodding along beside the road, or in it, with loads on their heads and often chewing on thick sticks of green raw sugar cane with their strong white teeth. One small girl was walking along with a soda bottle balanced upright on her head without any apparent difficulty.

We arrived at Hoima Police Station before lunch. The OC Police is Inspector John Bainbridge, who is about to be gazetted as Assistant Superintendent as he's the other chap who recently passed the Police Law exam with distinction. He led us to the site of the treaty signing ceremony and indicated the places for the police guard of honour and the band. Then to the DC's residence, where the band will play first at the garden party and then beat Retreat at dusk. We sorted out various matters to do with positions and moves and then had a quick look round the small township of Hoima before adjourning for lunch. Then back to Kampala. The car went very well on its first safari up-country.

Friday 2 September

Another early start. First to Nsambya barracks to see the band and instruments off in the bus with the excellent Drum Major in charge. Then I followed behind until we were on the Hoima road when, having no wish to eat the dust from the bus, I overtook them and sped on my way. I wanted to be in Hoima first anyway to make sure that accommodation for the band was prepared and to meet them on arrival.

A dusty safari again but all went well and the bus duly arrived and the band soon settled in. Later I took the Drum Major over the two sites for the ceremonies and, when he was satisfied, took him back. I went up to the quarters of the OC Police, where I'm staying for two nights. John will be dealing with whatever crowd and traffic control is required tomorrow. It shouldn't be much of a problem.

In the course of our conversation he mentioned that an African had come into the station the other day and reported that he had been attacked by a leopard. His arm and shoulder were bleeding. The OB constable had entered it in the Occurrence Book as an assault and John was wondering who to send out and make the arrest. I couldn't resist saying: 'Of course, the leopard will have to be spotted first.' Yes, well.

Saturday 3 September

The big day. Everyone who's anyone was here. Apart from HE and the Omukama, Sir Tito Winyi III, there was the Attorney-General, Ralph Dreschfield, QC, in wig and gown; the Provincial Commissioner, Sir George Duntze, Bart., and the DC both in white uniforms and pith helmets, and many other dignitaries. Lurking in the background, but ever present, was the mysterious Band Conducting Officer keeping an eye on everyone.

At the *boma* a smart guard of honour was commanded by the OC Police Masindi, with the band playing for a Royal Salute. Then followed the actual signing ceremony with speeches and everyone getting hotter and hotter in their uniforms and robes. In the late afternoon the band played light music at the garden party held on the large lawn at the DC's residence. Later the band beat Retreat there as evening came and it cooled down. They marched and countermarched, making full use of what space there was on the lawn and playing well-known marches and tunes. The dignitaries, now in suits, sat relaxed on cane chairs and clearly enjoyed the programme. Afterwards I took the Drum Major to HE, who congratulated him on the band's performance.

Once I'd got the band back to their accommodation for the night and arranged for their early departure to Kampala tomorrow morning, I drove to John's quarters and changed out of uniform and then went with him to attend the sundowner at the Omukama's Palace, which was on a hill, of course.

Instead of standing and moving about in haphazard fashion as we like to do at parties, Africans generally seem to prefer that everyone sits down and remains static. This means that you are stuck with whomever happens to be sitting beside you, which I find a bit of a bore. The room or hall we were in was reasonably large and chairs were placed in a line along each wall, so we all sat facing inwards like a collection of wallflowers at a ball. Fortunately servants kept moving around with plenty of drinks and plates of small food. At one point the younger females of the Omukama's large family came around greeting all the visitors. They first knelt on the floor before the Omukama and then moved around from chair to chair, sitting on the lap of each male visitor for a moment or two before moving on to the next. It was like some stately party game. John was sitting next to me and he whispered: 'I hope I get the cheeky one,' and put his knees together ready. But he was disappointed as the ceremony ended before they reached us; we were probably sitting below the salt.

When HE was about to leave he saw me and came over and repeated how pleased he was with the band's performances today. I said I'd pass it on to the Commissioner of Police and the Bandmaster. Back to Kampala tomorrow morning.

Sunday 18 September

Yesterday was the Annual Police Ball, which was held in Makerere University College hall. Teddy has just trained a section of the band as a dance band. This was their first appearance and very good they are too. The hall had been well decorated by the wives of some of the senior officers with banners, flags, striped poles, flowers and so on. There was an excellent buffet and a very busy bar. It went on until 3 a.m. The Chief Justice, the Attorney-General and various other senior officials and friends were guests. All Force officers wore the newly introduced mess kit of white monkey jacket and dark blue trousers with light blue stripes.

1955

Tuesday 20 September

At Nsambya barracks there's a small club with a badminton court for gazetted officers and their wives where functions such as farewell parties, Christmas parties, etc. are sometimes held. One can also purchase weekly alcohol supplies at a reduced rate to take away. This evening we were treated to a showing of the 1953 Kenneth More film *Genevieve* in black and white. The original version was in colour but our simple projector can't cope with that. It was very enjoyable anyway.

I've designed and drawn a new cover for *Habari* to replace the old plain one. This has a large drawing of the Force badge and alongside it a full-length drawing of a constable in ceremonial dress uniform with the necessary words and figures above and below the design. The printer's proof doesn't look too bad at all.

Friday 23 September

Because I'd much rather be outdoors than in, if it isn't raining, I usually take first-aid classes in the open air under a tree in the PTS grounds. These are on the side of the hill with plenty of grass around to sit on. That's where we were this morning.

We were dealing with burns and shock and, after going through it all a few times, I asked a recruit who was not showing much interest what was the treatment for shock. He replied: 'Cover the patient with a blanket and hot tea.' In an earlier lesson dealing with delivering a baby he had declared it necessary to cut the umbrella cord. He's unlikely to achieve the status of Commissioner's prizeman. Still, he tries.

There was a commotion from about 50 yards up the hill and I looked up to see the OC/PTS standing with his hands cupped round his mouth shouting in Swahili. He stopped and seemed to wait for something. I couldn't understand a word he was saying. I turned to the squad sergeant and said: 'What's the OC saying?' The recruits were all grinning and the sergeant replied: 'He's congratulating you on passing the Swahili examination, sir.'

How very embarrassing. I waved my hand in acknowledgement and carried on. That's my other qualification for confirmation disposed of, thank heavens.

Tuesday 11 October

We have been practising the recruits in crowd control and riot drill all week in readiness for the Kabaka's return from exile on 17 October.

26

All the police in Buganda will be on duty because the whole population of the kingdom will be out to welcome him.

HH the Kabaka Mutesa II is now aged 31 and he was educated at Uganda's finest school, King's College, Budo. He was crowned at the age of 18 and then went to Magdalene College, Cambridge for a couple of years. While there he was made an honorary captain in the Grenadier Guards, became a bit of a playboy and, with his easy manner, was popular with the wealthy set. He was having marital troubles before going to London to attend the Queen's coronation in 1953. Apparently, the problem was that he preferred his wife's sister to her and didn't hide it. That same year in June the Secretary of State for the Colonies, Oliver Lyttleton, made a speech at the East African Association's annual dinner in London in which he referred to the controversial proposed Central African Federation of Nyasaland and Northern and Southern Rhodesia. He went on to speak of 'possibly still larger measures of federation of the whole East African territories'.

The East African Standard, a popular newspaper published in Kenya and read all over East Africa, carried the matter too far and unfortunately headlined a possible 'great new dominion' by the union of East and Central Africa. This considerably upset the Baganda traditionalists, who could not bear the idea of possibly being subject to Kenyan white settlers and suchlike.

Although assured by the Governor and the Colonial Office that this was not planned at all, the Kabaka and his Ministers chose to believe it was and refused any further co-operation with the Protectorate Government. Consequently the British Government withdrew recognition of the Kabaka as ruler of Buganda and he was sent in exile to London, where he resumed his high living with plenty of booze and girls. Regents were appointed to rule in his absence and the Baganda were naturally very upset about this but, after a couple of years of negotiations, conditions for the Kabaka's return were made and agreed. So he's now due to arrive here on Monday amidst what we are told to expect will be wild rejoicing. Thus, even our junior recruits will be needed to reinforce general duties men in crowd control. No trouble is expected but a lot of high spirits and people in large numbers will be trying to get as close to the Kabaka as possible.

Monday 17 October

Very early this morning police from all over Kampala assembled in various places and moved to their assigned positions. The Kabaka arrived at Entebbe airport at about 9 a.m., to be met by the Governor and a huge crowd of cheering Baganda. He then slowly drove the 20 miles to Kampala, passing under arches constructed of bamboo and barkcloth with messages on them in Luganda welcoming him back every few miles along the route.

I collected my group of recruits and took them in the PTS tender to our first position about 8 miles out from Kampala on the Entebbe road. There they were spread between two arches about half a mile apart. There were a number of people around already but they waited quietly until the Kabaka appeared with his wife Damale, the Nabagereka, sitting in the back of an open Rolls-Royce and followed by other Baganda notables in cars. There was a lot of shouting, ululating, cheering and drumming. They then disappeared down the road.

The plan was for him to be seen by as many people as possible by driving slowly all round Kampala, where there were bigger crowds gathered. This also gave us time to move to our second position, which, for my group, was on Mengo hill itself. We were to do the crowd control outside the *Twekobe*, the Kabaka's palace, a white building with a central tower. The *Lubiri*, or palace compound, is enclosed by a traditionally woven fence of crossed reeds which we had been instructed not to enter.

Outside the *Lubiri* the Baganda drums were beaten and the huge crowd was very noisy and excited. My chaps were lined on either side of the narrow road leading up to the palace gates so as to keep the entrance clear. I remained near the gate keeping an eye on things. When the Kabaka's Rolls appeared there was much cheering and ululating and people started to push forward into the roadway. The mere presence of the police was not sufficient to hold them back so I shouted to them to link arms and form a barrier. By the gates the men were not holding them back so I grabbed a couple of arms and joined the barrier, calling to them to lean back into the crowd. We made just enough space for the Rolls to pass through us. It was very hot work with a great deal of pushing and shoving going on but nothing more than that. No rough stuff.

The Kabaka was sitting back in his car waving to the crowds. When he was about 3 feet away he looked at me, grinned and said 'Hot work, isn't it?' then passed through the gateway. Nobody tried to follow him in there, of course; they wouldn't dare. The crowd broke up and we were able to relax as they moved about outside and started to celebrate with drumming and dancing. No doubt the *pombe* (locally brewed beer) would soon appear and they would get stuck into their rejoicing. I loaded my chaps into the tender and off we trundled back to the PTS.

Tuesday 18 October

I was chatting to some Special Branch (SB) chaps who were on duty at the airport yesterday for the Kabaka's arrival. It seems he brought a souvenir back from London, a blonde popsy with whom he'd been having an affair. The aircraft captain quietly informed the authorities and HE gave orders that she was not to be allowed off the aircraft, but was to remain in the cabin and be flown back to the UK. A senior SB officer went aboard as soon as it landed to ensure that this was done in spite of any protests from the Kabaka. The matter is to be kept very quiet, of course. How on earth did he think he'd get away with it with his wife and all the Baganda dignitaries plus the press and crowds at the airport? Not a peep about it on the radio or in the newspaper today, though.

Friday 21 October

The large rugger type whom I met at Mac's house on the day I arrived here also lives at the hostel and is on the PTS staff. He asked me for a lift to work this morning as he has a wonky knee, the result of playing rugger too heartily, and so he can't drive his car. We were driving down Kitante Road beside the golf course when we passed an African on a bicycle. As we came level with the cyclist my esteemed passenger stuck his head and large shoulders out of the side window and, waving his swagger cane in the air, gave a tremendous shout. The poor chap, startled out of his wits, lost control of his bike, which left the road, struck a grassy mound and fortunately pitched him on to the grass of the course, where he and his bike landed in a heap. 'What on earth did you do that for?' I asked, 'I thought we were supposed to prevent traffic accidents, not cause them.'

'Keeps them on their toes,' he replied, grinning.

'Well,' I said, 'he's hardly on his toes now, is he?'

Saturday 22 October

After work this afternoon I went to have a look at the Kampala Trade Show at Nakivubo sports stadium. A large crowd there and booths displaying all sorts of commercial enterprises – mostly Asian-owned, but some government departments such as Education. The band of 4 KAR beat Retreat at the end of the afternoon. Not yet up to the standard of our band but quite good. Their programme included one of my favourite marches, 'Imperial Echoes'. As the 4 KAR is a rifle regiment, which from its formation has invariably been officered by those seconded from Scottish regiments, the Drum Major wears a rifle green kilt and the bandsmen wear khaki kilts. They looked very smart. The first jet fighters to be stationed at RAF Nairobi in Kenya flew over on a special visit and performed aerobatics which clearly enthralled the crowd, they not having seen anything like it before.

Saturday 19 November

The size of the Force is being increased this year and yesterday two more squads were passed out by the Commissioner. I commanded the parade and all went well. But the new constables will not be leaving us until Monday as they were required to take part in a special cere- mony this morning. It's the Kabaka's birthday, the first since his return, and somebody decided that we should supply a guard of honour as a friendly gesture to start off the celebrations up at Mengo. Since these squads have just completed their training they were the obvious choice for this duty. Mac commanded the guard, I went as number two and the band accompanied us.

I had rather expected the Kabaka to appear in robes but, instead, he was disguised as a Grenadier Guards captain, in khaki service dress with riding breeches, well-shined boots and sword. Some guards drill sergeant had taught him how to salute properly and, after inspecting us, he said: 'Jolly good turnout, chaps.' He then sloped off, no doubt in the direction of liquid refreshment. Well, it is his birthday.

Wednesday 30 November

I was caught for night car duty last night, so I went out and about in a Ford Pilot which I think is the only one still roadworthy. Bars are supposed to close at midnight unless they have a night-club licence. Just after half past we were in Kisenyi, moving slowly along a badly pot-holed road, and I decided to check that a certain sleazy bar there was closed. It was not a very wise thing to do in that area as there had been no trouble reported. The constables had more sense and stayed firmly in the car while I got out and walked across some flat ground towards the ramshackle bar, which had a light on and seemed to be still open. As I approached it a bunch of drunks lurched out through the door and started shouting and throwing bottles at me – and we hadn't even been introduced. Not wishing to be involved in an unnec- essary incident I retreated to the car and radioed the CPS, where Sandy was on duty again. I reported that I had been subjected to a barrage of bottles from the bar customers and all Sandy asked was whether they were empty or full bottles and whether any hits had been scored. I replied contents unchecked and no hits. He advised a strategic with- drawal and to leave them to it. So that's what I did.

As I have today off duty I drove over to Entebbe beach for a quiet swim and a read. Unfortunately as I was swimming there was a heavy rainfall and I got wet through. Should have brought my brolly with me.

Sunday 4 December

I took a leisurely stroll across the golf course this morning in the direction of Kira Road and, when I reached the Uganda Museum, found a small group of men sitting on the ground under an acacia tree by the building wall. Four of them were playing the popular game of *mweso* and the others were spectating and making laughing comments. It's a complicated board game with, I'm told, many variations in different parts of Africa. There are normally four rows of eight or ten holes or saucer-like depressions in a wooden board and the pieces used are usually pebbles or beans. A player tries to capture all of his opponent's counters or manoeuvre them into positions from where he can't move. These Baganda didn't have a wooden board and they were using depressions made in the soft soil and small stones gathered from round about.

Monday 19 December

I've been told I'm to leave the PTS at the end of this month and start the new year at Central Police Station to do some practical police work. At the PTS we're practising a ceremonial parade for the Annual Police Review, which will be performed before the Governor and assorted VIPs. Various medals and cups are to be presented. The company I've been training for this will now have to be taken over by my replacement here.

Thursday 22 December

For my farewell effort at the PTS I organised as a Christmas entertainment a football match between the officers and the senior NCOs on the staff, which was played this afternoon. The Firemaster was referee and it was well attended by families, staff and recruits. The sergeants won, of course.

Friday 30 December

The Commissioner of Police is leaving in a day or two to become the Deputy Inspector General of Colonial Police at the Colonial Office in London, just as his predecessor here did. We gave the Deegans a farewell Sundowner party at the Nsambya police officers club with

31

speeches and presentation, of course. The new Commissioner arrives in January from Mauritius, where he was Commissioner of a smaller force. A chap called Neil Hadow, who is only 42 so he must be some sort of a high-flyer, since I gather that normally promotion in the Colonial Police is considered to be rather slow.

1956

Sunday 1 January

I've had an interesting first year in the Uganda Police and learned a lot. Mainly I'm very glad to be working in Africa at last. I enjoyed the PTS and especially working up the Police *Habari* into what I hope is now a more organised and readable magazine. The OC/PTS wrote in his December issue editorial: 'The demand for *Habari* each month has so increased that we would like to think that it is not only due to the excellent salesmanship of those officers concerned at the pay table, but also, perhaps, to the fact that it is now a magazine which people *want* to buy and not just one which they feel they ought to buy.' I shall continue to contribute articles and cartoons every month as before and assist in any way I can to improve the magazine even more.

Sunday 8 January

I reported for duty at the CPS on Monday and found that, as European officers have to be OC of something, I'm now OC Nuts. This is the dignified post held by the newest member of the staff. I have a couple of constables whom I send out into the highways and byways of the town to bring in street hawkers selling without a licence from the town council. They are usually youngsters selling groundnuts in the street from woven baskets. Most of them scoot away safely at the sight of a uniform, but sometimes the odd one is caught in a street sweep collecting beggars and other pavement inhabitants. There's not a lot to be done with them. They only make a few cents on their sales and can't pay fines and we don't want to put them in prison for such a petty offence. What to us is a street nuisance is a street service to peckish passing pedestrians.

Last week the magistrate, fed up with these time-wasting cases, ordered four of them with quite full baskets of nuts to sit outside the court under the eye of a large constable and to eat their entire stock themselves. Bulging cheeks.

'Just a skeleton staff on duty today, sir'

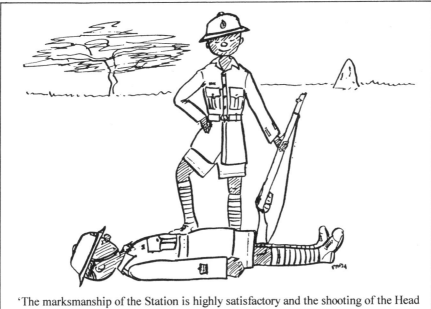

'The marksmanship of the Station is highly satisfactory and the shooting of the Head Constable was especially praiseworthy.' (from an inspection report.)

Two of P.A.'s cartoons from the Uganda Police *Habari* magazine

33

Wednesday 18 January

N. K. Mehta, an extremely wealthy Asian businessman, owns, among other things, the Uganda Sugar Company and Tea Estates at Lugazi, which is about 30 miles east of Kampala on the Jinja road and covers a large area of land. They are having an industrial dispute with the labour force of several thousands of temporary and seasonal workers, who are not well paid. Some agitators among them demanded an increase, which was refused, and so they went on strike. Unfortunately it has become violent and the Asian manager and overseers were attacked and damage done to some buildings. Lugazi police station is small and asked for assistance, so four officers – I am one – and twenty men were sent to Lugazi today. The men are squeezing into the small barracks and we four are camping in the living room of the OC's flat over the station.

Saturday 21 January

For three days we've been driving round the vast estates searching for and arresting the ringleaders of the violent part of the strike. Everything quietened down once the police reinforcements were seen moving about the area, but the ones we're after went into hiding. Each section drives around with one of the Asian managerial staff to identify particular assailants whom we've been bringing in each day. This morning we located the last of them and it is now quiet. There was a reluctant agreement to increase the pay slightly and the trouble seemed to be over, so we headed back to Kampala this afternoon.

Tuesday 24 January

I have been detailed for duty as High Court officer-in-attendance during the present criminal sessions in Kampala, which commenced this week. There are murders, manslaughters and a robbery for trial. A gazetted police officer acts as assistant to prosecuting Crown Counsel during the trials. My main job is to check that the witnesses are present and waiting outside the correct court room and that they don't stray or mix with those who have already given their evidence. In fact I have a corporal who does most of the work – that's what corporals are for – and during the trial I sit next to Crown Counsel and tell the corporal which witness to bring in next. After the verdict I fill in a CID form with the details of the accused, the offences, the result and sentence for the Criminal Records Office (CRO).

The judge wears a wig and red robes and the prosecuting and defending counsel are in black gowns and wigs since they are barristers. It's all quite interesting really, though the judge does get rather upset if a particular witness is missing when called. Sometimes, especially if witnesses are from up-country and haven't been to Kampala before, they get bored with waiting for hours outside the courtroom and they wander off to see what's going on in the big town. Then the corporal and I go spare, dashing about trying to locate them.

At the end of each day witnesses are paid a very small attendance allowance to enable them to buy food. The police usually have to find accommodation for those who don't have relatives or friends to stay with and they may end up at Nsambya barracks or on the verandah or in an empty cell at the CPS.

Friday 27 January

We started a new murder case this morning at the High Court. The defence advocate has the extremely common Indian name of Patel and seems to be very proud of his degree from Bombay University, which he keeps mentioning. At the opening of the trial there was an exchange between him and the judge which I noted down. It went like this:

Judge: How many witnesses are you calling for the defence, Mr Patel?
Patel: Ooooh, my Lord, I am having many splendid witnesses. Your Lordship will be believing them entirely, isn't it?
Judge: Well, we shall see. But how many will there be?
Patel: Oooooh, my Lord, they are truly magnificent witnesses I am calling to do the needful in this case. Prosecution is having no hopes. No hopes at all. Most excellent and learned judge like your Lordship is believing only my witnesses, isn't it? And I am winning my case without doubts.
Judge: But I need to know how many witnesses you intend to call, Mr Patel, so that I can estimate how long the trial will last. I have other cases like this one to fit in the sessions, you know.
Patel: Ooooh, my Lord, other cases are not like this one. This case will be very excellent for my client, isn't it?
Judge: (loudly and clearly) HOW MANY WITNESSES ARE YOU CALLING?
Patel: Ooooh, my Lord, I am not knowing at this wery moment.
Judge: But, Mr Patel, if you are not knowing how many witnesses then how will you know when you have finished your case?

35

Patel:	Ooooh, my God, I am not finishing yet. I am still having many first-class, wery fine witnesses to call.
Judge:	Mr Patel, please address me as 'my Lord' not 'my God.'
Patel:	Oooooh, my God, my Lord, my goodness, whatever am I saying, your Lordship? I am most humbly apologising, my Lord, isn't it?
Judge:	So how many, Mr Patel?
Patel:	How many, my Lord? Ooooh, many, many apologies.
Judge:	No, I mean witnesses, Mr Patel. How many are you calling?
Patel:	My Lord, I have many very fine, smart witnesses. Wery splendid, outstanding peoples, my Lord. They are telling remarkable truths. I personally am knowing them all well. They are absolutely first-class and most reliable, I am hoping, isn't it?
Judge:	Oh, very well. Do let's get on. Call your first reliable witness please, Mr Patel.
Patel:	Ooooh, your Lordship is having little joke. Most amusing and frolicsome, isn't it?

Friday 17 February

When the High Court criminal sessions finished a few days ago I was told that I am to transfer to Kampala Traffic Branch at the end of this month as the OC Traffic Prosecutions is going on long leave and I am to replace him. When I mentioned my ignorance of such work I was rather sarcastically told that, since I had passed my law exams so quickly, I must be a brilliant lawyer, so I'd better get on and prove it. So I'm stuck with it.

Anyway, I've been out here for a year now and I'm entitled to some local leave before I transfer. Another Peter in the police, who shares a hostel dining table with Chas and me, has also asked for local leave and he has suggested that we should go down to have a look at the Queen Elizabeth National Park in Toro in the Western Province for the purpose of inspecting and photographing the animals. So that's what we're going to do tomorrow.

Saturday 18 February

We started our safari early this morning as it's over 230 miles to the QE Park on a very dry and dusty road. We decided to take my car and share the driving. I hung a *chuggle* (canvas water bag) filled with drinking water on the outside of the car so that it would keep cool by evaporation. Parts of the *murram* road were corrugated for long distances. Somehow constant traffic over the hard *murram* surface leaves it like corrugated iron sheets and it's shattering and most uncomfortable to drive over until one can find the right speed to move smoothly over the tops of the bumps. At the same time one has to watch the speed because of other hazards, such as wild or domestic animals wandering into the road and occasional people with no developed road sense.

We travelled south-westwards from Kampala via Masaka and Mbarara, crossing the equator on the way – marked by concrete arches and a white line. Then turned northwards to the Kichwamba Hotel, where we're staying as it's smaller and cheaper than Mweya Safari Lodge inside the park. We arrived at the hotel covered with dust and hot and thirsty. There was no hot water until the evening so it meant a cold bath in the rust-coloured water, which was better than nothing. Hurricane lamps and candles were provided as the electricity generator is switched off at 10 p.m.

On our way into the park this morning we went across a Bailey bridge over the Kazinga Channel between Lake Edward and Lake George. There was an inscription on a board fixed to it which said: 'This bridge originally formed part of an emergency bridge in London over the Thames during the World War 1939–1945. Re-erected here in 1954.'

The safari lodge stands on a bluff on the Mweya peninsula with fine panoramic views of the lakes and mountains. As we drove there we could see a largish herd of elephant not far away and plenty of hippos in the water and buck and zebra all over the place in disorganised groups posing for photographs.

Monday 20 February

We visited the fishing village of Katwe, which is just outside the park boundary. This is where The Uganda Fish Marketing Corporation (TUFMAC) have a factory producing frozen lake fish for sale all over Uganda. The park tracks are dry at the moment and so not too bad for driving on. There are plenty of animals all over the place: buffalo, hippos, buck of all types and sizes, zebra and elephants. There was a well-fed lion lying in the shade of a large tree near the remains of a buffalo. I drove up close for a photograph and it could not be bothered to move. Many vultures on the ground and in the trees were waiting for the lion to move away and give them a chance at the meat. Four or five wild dogs were lurking hopefully a little further away. Everyone gets a turn but there's clearly a strict order of precedence. There are large black and white fish eagles perched on branches at the water's edge making their wailing cries as they keep an eye open for fish. Piles of elephant droppings on the tracks with very busy dung beetles rolling away balls of dung larger than themselves.

Tuesday 21 February

We took packed lunches and went up to the craters. The volcanoes are dormant and the craters full of water, which has caused all sorts of greenery to grow up the insides including some spectacular large cacti. The result is like a magnificent sort of African Lake District with curiously shaped plants and trees and, down by the water, many colourful birds such as the African darter or snake-bird, the Goliath heron and other herons and egrets, storks and ibis and the noisy fish eagle.

Wednesday 22 February

We decided to return to Kampala by the more northern route and so drove through Kasese to Fort Portal with, on our left, the tremendous mountain range of the Ruwenzoris – the Mountains of the Moon – which mark the western border of Uganda with the Belgian Congo. The mountains were mostly hidden by clouds and mist but occasionally parts of them peeped through.

Fort Portal is the district HQ of Toro District, which is also a kingdom ruled over by the Omukama of Toro, Sir George Rukidi III. It's a small, quiet town and we soon passed through it. Then eastwards to Buganda through Mubende and Mityana until we arrived at Kampala in the late afternoon, hot, tired and dusty. It was an enjoyable trip and the car went well – no punctures in spite of some quite bad roads.

Saturday 25 February

At the hostel I was told that I could at last move into a cottage that had become vacant suddenly. So today Ephraim and I shifted my goods and chattels across the 100 yards to my new home. It has a bathroom, a bedroom, living room and a small storage space by the entrance. The roof is thatched and the walls made of thick stone to keep it cool inside and it's mine, all mine. I drove down to the Industrial Area and collected a very well made *mvule* bookcase that an Indian *fundi* has made to my measurements.

Monday 27 February

I reported for duty to the OC Kampala Traffic Branch at the Traffic

Section office behind the CPS building but in the same compound. I was shown to the tiny prosecutions office at the end of the building, where I met John, the chap whose job I'm taking over. Apart from my recent spell in the High Court the only other court work I've done is as a member of several army courts martial. I acted as defending officer in three cases but I've never prosecuted. We went up to the traffic court, which is an old wooden building just outside the CPS compound up the hill a bit, so it's not far to walk. The constable who acts as court orderly came with us, carrying the files and books. First we went to the chambers of the Traffic RM, where John introduced me as his replacement and explained that I am new to prosecution work. The RM's pained expression showed how pleased he was to hear this news.

I watched while John prosecuted a careless driving case that ended with a conviction and fine. Then came a more serious case of dangerous driving defended by a European solicitor in practice in Kampala. This had just got going when a constable came into court and whispered to John, who then turned to the RM and informed him that he was required immediately across the road in the High Court as a witness in a manslaughter trial which had suddenly been brought forward. However, he added, as I was taking over from him today I would now be able to continue with this prosecution. With that he turned to me and said: 'OK, carry on from here. It's quite straight-forward. Here's the file – and the best of luck.' Then he was gone.

I hadn't read the file and so hadn't much of a clue about the case, which, of course, would have to be a defended one. However, I struggled on and did what I could. Defence counsel objected to some of my questions to witnesses but the RM merely said: 'Well, the prosecutor's new to the game so we have to make allowances.' After the evidence counsel managed to persuade the RM to reduce the offence to careless driving but, at least, it was a conviction so not a total loss and I was quite satisfied.

In the only other case down for trial the accused changed his plea to guilty so, after dealing with that, I went back to what was now my office with two convictions on my first day in court. I looked through the files for tomorrow's cases and then dealt with a pile of petty traffic offences which John had earlier told me had to be sorted into those which were to go to court and those to which could be sent a standard written warning of a likely prosecution if they were repeated. For some minor offences a traffic constable can give a verbal warning on the spot, recorded in his notebook and reported in writing on his return to the station, where it is filed. Another constable, who always keeps a ball-point pen stuck horizontally through his wiry hair, records on forms the convictions and warnings, which he then forwards to CRO for future reference.

Friday 2 March

I'm in court prosecuting each day except for Friday, which is plea day for the new cases, when my sub-inspector takes over with a huge pile of files. Many people come to court and plead guilty to traffic offences. There's also a list of minor offences for which a written plea of guilty is acceptable. This can be recorded on the back of the summons, which is rubber-stamped with an endorsement to this effect. The plea is witnessed by the constable serving it and then brought to my office. This saves a lot of time and means that those concerned need not attend court unless they fail to pay the fine after being notified of it.

Pleas are taken at high speed by the traffic RM and for anyone pleading not guilty the RM consults his diary and fixes a date for hearing the case. Back in my office, the witness summonses are then prepared. The constables who are process servers go out daily into the highways and byways seeking out and serving people required in court. For those who fail to pay fines by the due date, or who fail to appear in court when summoned, they take out and execute arrest warrants issued by the RM.

Friday 9 March

A gazetted officer usually goes to the scene of a bad traffic accident, and one has to if it is a fatal. Ted, who is number two in the Section, was on his way out to one this morning. As it's plea day I was not in court so he took me with him in the section Land Rover. Ted remarked that as it's the start of the long rains, which go on until June, the roads get very slippery so the traffic accident rate goes up.

We drove to Wandegeya roundabout, where the road branches to Hoima in the west and Bombo in the north. Near the roundabout is Makerere University College on one side and Mulago Hospital on the other. There was a scruffy-looking lorry lying on one side with gunny bags of *posho* (maize flour) and bunches of *matoke* (green cooking plantains) all over the place. It looked as if it had been grossly overloaded, as usual, and had taken the roundabout too fast, run out of road and toppled over. There were two constables at the scene keeping the traffic moving and trying to hold back a growing crowd of curious sightseers and others intent on helping themselves to the items lying around. The turnboy (or driver's mate), who, as usual, had been sitting on top of the load, had been thrown out with it and had sustained a broken arm and leg. The driver was covered with blood from head and chest injuries and didn't look too happy to be there. Usually lorry drivers, if not badly injured, run away from the scene of their accidents. Just then the tender arrived and took them both to the nearby hospital. As we were walking round the lorry I drew Ted's attention to the tailboard, on which was painted the slogan: GOD IS MY PILOT. Ted said: 'No comment.'

Friday 16 March

This morning as I was about to wash and shave at the basin in my cottage bathroom, I turned on the tap and, as the water hit the basin, there was a quick scuffle underneath and a snake fell from the U-shaped pipe on to my bare feet. With a startled yelp I performed a record-breaking standing leap. Fortunately the snake was equally surprised and made off about its business. I called in Ephraim, who ferreted and fossicked around with a broom handle for a while before giving up with a nil report.

Back at Wandegeya, this time on duty for the opening of the new police station recently built near the roundabout. This is part of the recent expansion of the Force and because there was no station conveniently covering this area. The opening ceremony was performed by the Mayor, Councillor Lewis (a local European businessman); the Commissioner of Police and the Resident of Buganda were present. The first OC of the station is also the first African gazetted officer to command a Kampala police station.

Thursday 29 March

Today I had the disagreeable task of prosecuting one of my own staff for a traffic offence. During a weekend some time back he had borrowed a friend's car and had driven it in town and collided with a lorry, and his passenger was badly injured. The OC Traffic decided that the constable was to blame and ordered his prosecution for dangerous driving. I asked the OC if we could proceed in some other way as the man was working well in my office, and it wasn't a criminal offence. The OC said it was a bad case due to the injured passenger and the fact that the driver was a policeman.

I walked with the constable to court this morning. I had given him a list of suggested questions he could ask the witnesses, which was all the help I could offer. I presented the bare facts to the RM and left it to him without emphasising any part. The constable said that it was his first offence and asked for the charge to be reduced, to which I made no objection. However, the conviction for dangerous driving was inevitable and the fine a large one, which he said he had absolutely no hope of paying. The sentence of imprisonment for non-payment then came into effect. Instead of handing him straight over to the prison warders, I took him to the barracks in my car and instructed them to arrange his automatic discharge from the Force and prepare travel warrants for his family to go home. I waited for a while outside while he explained to his wife and changed out of uniform. When he was ready, I took him back to the court and handed him over to the warder. Although clearly upset he had remained calm and sensible throughout this unpleasant ordeal ending a promising career.

Saturday 4 April

Kampala Road Safety Week has been on since last Saturday and it has been a busy time for Traffic Branch although, until today, because of my court duties I've had little to do with it. There was a motor show last Sunday with highly polished new and old cars on display. The section organised a demonstration of mock traffic accidents to show how they they are caused and how best avoided, with St John Ambulance volunteers dealing with the 'casualties'. There have been road safety pedestrian and cycling demonstrations at various schools in town and special cinema shows for children. This weekend there is a good drivers contest at Kololo airstrip and that is where I've been helping out today; testing volunteers driving on a mock-up of various road hazards.

Sunday 29 April

Last weekend was the visit of Prince Aly Khan. There are quite a number of his people, the Aga Khan's Ismaili Khojas, living in Kampala and they had organised various functions at the Jamath Khana Mosque and other places for this visit, so we had to control traffic, while the barracks supplied the crowd-control men. There was heavy rain and we all got very wet. Up-country lightning killed three people, a frequent occurrence here, it seems.

Last night I was duty traffic officer and a report came in late of a fatal cycle accident on the Bombo road. At the scene the constable, a keen church attender, was standing doing nothing. He solemnly reported to me: 'Sir, the victim has bled to death and there is no health in him, the miserable offender, Amen.' I made no reply as I couldn't think of one. The new street lights going up in Kampala have not yet reached this part so it was quite dark. Lying in the road was a decrepit old man with his legs tangled in an equally ancient bicycle. A large pool of reddish liquid had spread out from under his body, which was absolutely still. There was a very strong smell and I shone my torch down and lifted his shoulders. There was a broken gourd underneath him with some evil-smelling booze which was definitely not blood. The old man was, in fact, fast asleep in a drunken stupor and appeared to me to be unhurt. He'd simply fallen off his bike and the world had gone on without him. 'This corpse is drunk,' I declared.

The tender eventually arrived and we put him aboard, still in a deep sleep, with his old bike and took them to the CPS for him to sleep it off. This morning the station sergeant gave him a good finger-wagging and sent him on his way, a quite happy and unrepentant sinner.

Thursday 3 May

In addition to the Swahili and law qualifications that are required for confirmation, we are later expected to pass an exam in a second African language before being eligible for higher promotion. There are several years before this can come about but, as I want to clear away all necessary exams as soon as possible, I've decided to start work on a second language now. It could also be useful in everyday work. Because I'm here in Buganda I'm told that I am expected to learn Luganda, which no doubt would be useful and I might have a go at it later on. However, I'm hoping to be stationed in the north sometime. Many of our NCOs and constables are from Acholi District, which is just south of the border with the Sudan, so that is the language I've selected. I shall be able to practise the oral part on them once I have some vocabulary.

The grammar is simple and straightforward, like Swahili, but it is a Lwo language and Nilotic rather then Bantu and consequently tonal. Thus one word can have several different meanings according to how it is pronounced or stressed. For instance, the word *gwok* can mean 'dog' or 'shoulder' or introduce a negative injunction like 'take care not to...' or it can be used as *gwok nyo*, which means 'perhaps'.

Okello, the civilian clerk in my office, is an intelligent young Acholi with quite good English. Like the other clerks, he wears a white shirt and tie to indicate his status. By pressing money into his hand I've persuaded him to agree to stay behind after office hours one day each week and practise me in Acholi conversation, pronunciation and the use of colloquialisms. One of the superintendents in Buganda Provincial HQ, who was stationed up there for a number of years and is a fluent Acholi-speaker, has lent me a mission-produced grammar and dictionary so I can get on with that part by myself, with Okello occasionally checking through the written exercises when we meet for our conversation sessions.

43

One of the first things one learns with any African language is the system of greetings. These are very important and it is regarded as impolite to start talking without first exchanging the conventional greetings. In Luganda, for instance, they go on and on. People passing each other in opposite directions start the greetings as they approach each other and continue as they pass and draw apart. If they stop to talk then handshakes are also exchanged, even if one has met the other before on that day.

Saturday 5 May

I went with Chas to the Black Cat nightclub in Kampala Road this evening. It's the only one in town and very popular, with a small space for dancing, dim lights, music and lots of booze. I was not surprised to find several police types there, including Ted from Traffic. He's a very amusing chap but he has this habit, which I find uncomfortable, of standing very close to one when speaking so that we are literally face to face. I automatically move back in such a situation so that our conversations are mobile as we shuffle across the room face to face like partners in a dance. I usually end up with my back to a wall or fall over some furniture.

Wednesday 9 May

There was a bit of a flap on as for some time the CID have been after a gang of robbers, one of whom, the leader, is believed to be armed with a pistol. They claim to have received information that the gang would be doing a job on a shop in Shimoni Road last night; so extra officers were called upon to assist. We all had loaded revolvers in our pockets and met at a café in the same road at 8 p.m. and sat about drinking Pepsi-Cola or Mirinda (orangeade). Two of us were required to be in uniform, for some reason not made clear, but were supposed to hide the fact, so we left our caps in the car and wore a raincoat to hide the uniform. This, I thought, looked pretty daft as it was a very hot, dry night and there was absolutely no natural reason for us to be dressed in raincoats. Also I had a heavy pistol dragging down the coat pocket on one side, ready for a fast draw. Eventually the senior officer, Mike, said: 'Chummy should be arriving about now.' So we trooped out of the boring café and took up positions behind some parked vehicles along the dark street. Then we waited. And waited. Nothing happened at all. It looked as if the informer had got it wrong or maybe the robbers had lost their way or been unable to get transport or changed their minds. Or maybe someone had told them about a group of very suspicious-looking *wazungu* lurking around the area. Well, that's show business.

Saturday 12 May

These CID and SB types seem to spend a lot of time in bars where they claim they pick up a lot of useful information. It's a good excuse and it may even be partly true. Yesterday evening Chas told me he wanted to call at the City Bar, which is in Kampala Road and much frequented by police and other legal types, so I went along too. It's a single-storey building, as are most of them in Kampala Road, with a corrugated-iron roof and a wide verandah where one can sit and drink outside and watch the world passing by.

Among others I met there was Old Duffy, who runs a small, not too successful local newspaper, the *Uganda Herald*, and a printing business in competition with the *Uganda Argus*. It seems that years ago before the war he was an officer in the British regular army until one evening, while stationed in the UK, he came back to his quarters a day early from an exercise and found his wife in bed with his commanding officer discussing tactics. Taking out his revolver he shot them both dead and later went to prison for manslaughter. After serving his sentence he left England and came to East Africa, where he has stayed ever since. Sounds like something by Somerset Maugham.

Tuesday 15 May

The Traffic Ordinance requires a driver to stop at the scene if he is involved in an accident; but a problem arises if he knocks down and kills or seriously injures a child. No matter if the child has dashed out into the road so close in front of the vehicle that there is absolutely no chance of avoiding hitting the child, the local villagers will not only blame the driver but, if he has stopped as required and got out to try and give help, the invariable result will be that the people will beat the driver to death, whether that driver is a man or woman of any race. In practice, therefore, it's acceptable and sensible if the driver keeps going and stops and reports to the first police officer or station he comes to.

Friday 25 May

Today is the fiftieth anniversary of the founding of the Uganda Police Force. So this month there have been and will be functions of various sorts celebrating the Jubilee of the force. The Queen sent a special congratulatory message, which has appeared in Force Orders and in *Habari*.

From 1899 there had been an armed constabulary under military control acting as soldier-policemen to quell the frequent tribal wars and disturbances. The Colonial Office took over control of the Uganda Protectorate from the Foreign Office in 1905 and, on 25 May 1906, Captain (later Brigadier-General) W. F. S. Edwards DSO arrived in Uganda to take up the newly-created post of Inspector General of the Uganda Protectorate Police.

In 1908 a beat system was introduced in Entebbe and a Fingerprint Bureau established. The Kampala Police Depot barracks was opened in 1910. There were no prisons at first and punishments in those days seemed to consist mainly of strokes of the *kiboko* (hippo-hide whip), later replaced by a cane.

Saturday 26 May

There was a public display for the Jubilee at the PTS playing field this afternoon. The band was in fine form and there was a motor-cycle formation riding display by Mobile Traffic Section and static displays in the Drill Shed of radio equipment, home-made firearms recovered, fingerprinting, various police vehicles, the photographic section, the Fire Brigade and so on. The afternoon ended with the band beating Retreat. The Governor, the Chief Justice and many other people attended and it went very well. In the evening there was a Fiftieth Anniversary Dance at the Nsambya Police Officers Club.

This month we have at last got rid of the old Ford Pilot patrol cars and they've been replaced by black Humber Super Snipe saloon cars or, as one well-oiled officer described them at the club, 'Slumber Hooper Hipes'. The new motor-cycles issued to the Mobiles have radios fitted to each machine, which will solve their communication problem. The riders wore police caps for the display but, from now on, will be wearing white crash helmets. In a recent letter applying for recruitment to that section a school leaver said he wants to be a 'moving traphician'.

Saturday 2 June

I was traffic duty officer last night. Just after midnight some drunken character crashed his car into an electricity pole near Makerere College; so I drove to the scene and found a power cable down across the road. I couldn't tell whether it was live but, if so, it was in a most dangerous position. The driver, as with most drunks involved in accidents, was completely unhurt. There is a very busy patron saint of drunkards who watches over them with considerable efficiency.

I sent a message to the UEB office but nobody came out. As children would be going to school and women to market early in the morning along this road, I decided to try to clear it myself. With the aid of a length of wood, I carefully wrapped my rubberised raincoat around the cable and pulled it to the side of the road. I told the constable who was with me to stay there until the repairmen arrived and prevent any passers-by from touching it, or even trying to steal it, which was quite likely. When I checked again just before dawn a European from the UEB had just arrived and he assured me that the power was now off in that area and that they'd soon fix it.

Thursday 8 June

Kampala's inhabitants find the new street lights in town very useful for supplementing their diets. The bright lights attract swarms of *enzige* (large green grasshoppers) in their season which fly around them and are easily caught. In addition to the ubiquitous black and white crows, which are for once out after dark, groups of Africans of all ages gather around the light poles at night with boxes, baskets, gunny bags, *debes*, or any other container and grab the *enzige* by the handful from the air or on the ground and fill them. The 'hoppers are later fried or boiled and eaten with great zest, providing all sorts of nourishment, protein and the rest. Vehicle drivers at night have to keep a sharp eye open as the street light groups are a considerable traffic hazard. They are so busy chasing and catching the 'hoppers that they frequently ignore passing traffic and are occasionally knocked down as a consequence, thus adding to the accident statistics and not doing themselves a lot of good either.

Sunday 17 June

Yesterday afternoon the Governor held a garden party at Government House, Entebbe, for the Queen's birthday. Some of us drove over to supervise the traffic arrangements and, before it was time to start, we went to the airport to inspect the new four-engined Bristol Britannia turbojet aircraft which is here on its flight trials. The airport was deserted apart from mechanics working on it, so we were able to get a good close look at it.

Friday 29 June

As I'm in court all week I tend to catch these Friday evening and weekend duties quite frequently. This evening the Governor was attending some function at the Indian Women's Association clubhouse on Queen's Road. It's a slightly awkward place for traffic as it has a narrow entrance drive and exit only about 30 feet apart. I posted a constable to keep arriving cars moving one way only; in at one end to drop passengers and out the other end, to be parked at the roadside under the direction of the other two constables. As HE should be the last to arrive, I decided to leave his car in the drive outside the main entrance of the IWA. Any late arrivals would have to stay on the road outside.

All went well until we saw the Government House Austin Princess approaching. There is a street light at the entrance and the constable clearly signalled to the driver where to enter and I stood near him also pointing the way in. I saw Cohen lean forward and say something to his driver, who then drove straight past us, turned into the exit and stopped outside the IWA the wrong way round, so that HE got out on the opposite side from where those waiting to greet him were shuffling around in some confusion.

I've been told that Cohen has an anti-police attitude and dislikes seeing us on duty at functions, but this seemed to me very childish. Perhaps he thinks that the rules don't apply to him or that nobody will dare to complain. I walked quickly up to HE's driver, ignoring Cohen, and said to him loudly: 'You must obey all police signals, driver, or you'll find yourself in very serious trouble.'

Cohen looked startled and said: 'Oh, it's my fault, I'm sorry. I told him to go in that way. I thought it was the proper way in.' He then went inside with his hosts.

It was an obvious lie, with the two of us clearly directing him under a bright light. Perhaps he'd had a bad day and was taking it out on us. I had a blank written warning form in my pocket, so I filled it in, putting the offence as failing to obey the directions of a police officer, and gave it to the driver. 'Here,' I said to him, 'show this to the *Bwana Mkubwa* when you get back to Entebbe.' That should round off HE's day nicely.

Tuesday 3 July

At last Friday's plea day in the traffic court, one of the accused who failed to appear for plea after being summoned turned out to be a professor at Makerere. The sub-inspector obtained and collected several arrest warrants from the magistrate for these people and gave them to the process servers to execute. He mentioned this particular one so I took the warrant from the constable and said I'd serve it myself. I didn't think it would look too good for a British university professor to be led away in handcuffs by one of our constables. I rang up Makerere and, after a long wait, he came on the line and identified himself and asked what was up. 'You failed to attend traffic court here last Friday, professor; you received a summons didn't you?' I asked.

'Good heavens, I'm so sorry. I was lecturing and completely forgot about it. Am I in dire trouble?' he asked anxiously.

'Well, the magistrate wasn't too pleased about it and he's issued a warrant. So you can now consider yourself under arrest, but I can't get these handcuffs down the telephone line, so you'd better come to my office right now and I'll take you before the magistrate and we'll sort it out. Bring some cash with you to pay the fine.'

Afterwards he said to me: 'Do you usually arrest people by telephone?'

I replied: 'Only if I think they may be violent.'

Monday 16 July

During term-time we send traffic constables to the various Kampala schools at arrival and departure times in an effort to instil some traffic sense into the little horrors. They will persist in rushing out of school, in very noisy groups, straight into and across the road no matter how busy the traffic is. It's not a popular duty and there are sighs of relief from all our personnel when school holidays begin and groans when they end.

Saturday 21 July

Yesterday I had to call in at Katwe Police Station on a traffic matter. The OC there is Tony Constable – a very suitable name for a cop; when he was in the UK police he was Constable Constable (= PC^2).

King's College, Budo, is so called because it's built on Budo hill, which is regarded by the Baganda as a royal hill. Situated about 12 miles outside Kampala, it started as a Church Missionary Society (CMS) boys high school 50 years ago and so it's celebrating the jubilee this year. It's considered to be Uganda's best school with some first-rate British teachers and many leading Ugandans were educated there, including the Kabaka, who is its most distinguished old boy. Traffic Branch was out there in force today as the Governor and the Kabaka and all sorts of VIPs were attending the weekend celebrations. I had a good look round and admired the fine views from the hill and the pleasant classrooms and well-equipped laboratory.

49

Tuesday 24 July

Clerks in Police HQ personnel section were rather shaken the other day. When one of them opened a drawer in a filing cabinet out popped an 18-inch snake. It was the fastest evacuation of that end of PHQ for a long time, they say. The Fire Brigade was called in, since it is their job to deal with uninvited snakes and wild bees and hornets. Sometimes they even get a fire to play with. The big question was: how did the snake get into a locked metal filing cabinet? CID's best brains failed to produce an answer and, as it got clean away, it could not be interrogated. The clerk who told me about it said: 'Without a word of warning the snake dashed out and disappeared completely.' But I wonder whose file it was looking for.

Thursday 26 July

At teatime in the hostel common room Paddy was relating about an African he had prosecuted in the RM's court for being idle and disorderly – he was found drunk in the middle of Kampala Road offering to fight anyone who approached him. His name was Musa and he was employed as a houseboy by an Irishman who works in the PWD roads department. His employer was in court and paid the fine since Musa, of course, had no money. As they were leaving the court afterwards the Irishman said: 'There now, Musa, if ye hadn't spent all yer money on drink ye'd be able to pay the fine yourself, wouldn't ye?'

Friday 27 July

This afternoon I'd been up to Mengo checking on some details for a function which will involve the Traffic Branch and I was returning via Nakivubo. I drove past the stadium, where the final of some football match was being played which I knew the Governor was attending. It was not one of our functions and the police on crowd control were general duties men from the barracks. As I drove slowly past I could hear quite a lot of noise from inside the covered stadium and there were a number of people milling about outside which seemed to indicate that the match was over. One well-dressed African, seeing my uniform, ran up to my car and waved me to stop. He said: 'The police in the stadium are fighting our people! Help us! Save us, please.'

I quickly parked my car and walked into the stadium, where there was considerable pandemonium. Instead of spectators leaving through the gates they were all over the pitch in groups, fighting and struggling with a few uniformed constables who were dotted about singly. The Governor hadn't left and I could see him sitting in his box. There seemed to be no officer, inspector or NCO on duty. I walked on to the pitch and moved from group to group. In each case I seized hold of a constable and separated him from his assailants and loudly ordered the people around to leave the stadium immediately. I then ordered each constable to go over to the clear end of the pitch and wait there for me. I was quite surprised to find that everyone quite docilely did exactly as I told them and soon I had the eight constables standing at one end of the pitch and the spectators leaving through the far gates. I questioned Okot, an Acholi and the senior constable there, and he said that the Baganda, whom he naturally regarded with contempt, had thought that the wrong team had won so they came on to the field to dispute the matter. The players and the referee had fled from the pitch, leaving the battlefield to the rather disorganised spectators and the handful of constables who had tried to get them to depart, but some of the fans had become aggressive.

It had looked like a rather rumbustious riot but, in fact, nobody had been hurt. I sent a constable to bring the Governor's car to the grandstand and walked over the rapidly emptying pitch to where HE was still sitting. He looked quite pale and alarmed and asked: 'Is everything all right? Can I leave now?'

I said: 'Yes, sir, it's OK to go now. I'm bringing your car here and I've put two constables on the nearest exit.'

He looked hard at me and said: 'I've seen you somewhere before, haven't I?'

Hoping to distract him from recalling our little car parking episode last month outside the Indian Women's Association, I replied: 'Yes, sir, your car's here now.'

Fortunately he went off without another word and, after waiting until the stadium was clear of people, I buzzed off. Probably one of the very few times when he was pleased, or at least relieved, to see the police around.

Tuesday 31 July

In an accident report this morning there was a statement from a lorry driver who had knocked down a pedestrian, or possibly a cyclist. It read: 'The man was walking on his bicycle. I admit that my lorry hit him but he agreed that it was his fault because he had been knocked down before.'

One of the new constables recently posted to the branch handed in a report today complaining about a European who he said had abused him by calling him a 'block'. I sent for him and he was quite upset. He told me that he had checked the driving permit and insurance certificate of a European car driver who had turned to his companion and said: 'This block says my DP has expired.' I explained that probably he had said 'bloke', which was just a friendly word like 'chap' or 'fellow' and was not insulting or abusive at all. 'Oh,' he said, 'I didn't know that.'

Saturday 4 August

Another night duty yesterday. It was a quiet night, so, after midnight, I decided to take a walk around the town centre, up and down Kampala Road, taking the reserve constable with me and thus interrupting his sleep. He was pleased, of course. It was pleasantly cool and the road was empty. The only sign of life, if that's how it can be described, was the usual collection of deeply slumbering nightwatchmen in the shop doorways or even on the pavement, keeping their ever-alert guard over the property of their employers. Who needs insurance with such magnificent security?

When we reached the compound of the Police Inspectorate of Vehicles, where I knew there was supposed to be a GD constable on guard, I decided to take a look around to see if all was well. No sign of any constable but, from army experience, I know what sentries get up to, so I opened the cab doors of the various police vehicles parked there. In the passenger seat of one of the tenders I found a constable fast asleep. What a surprise, I said to myself. I spoke to him and shook him but, like many Africans, when he's asleep he's dead. So I reached up into the cab and pulled him by the shoulder and he toppled out and hit the ground. Still fast asleep. There was no smell of alcohol. When he eventually condescended to wake up I took his name and number and warned him for *maktab* (orderly room) for sleeping on sentry duty. 'But I wasn't sleeping,' he protested, 'I was thinking.'

Wednesday 8 August

In this climate dead bodies commence to decay and decompose very soon after death and the usual procedure is to bury them on the same day, or the next day at the latest. However, with violent or accidental deaths the bodies have to go the mortuary to await a post-mortem examination, which is quite often delayed if nobody's available to perform it. On one occasion, for instance, the doctor who carries out the PMs was himself on the slab, having taken a leading part in a fatal traffic accident the night before. At the municipal mortuary there is no refrigeration or air-conditioning in the small brick building, which is located down in the Industrial Area, and it's not a place to linger in, unless you happen to be dead.

I was there this morning concerning the body of a man we'd pulled out of a nasty traffic accident. He'd been identified and I wanted to put his name on the label tied to one of his big toes, also to enquire about another PM. The slabs and the wooden racks were all occupied by bodies from accidents, crimes and the less successful efforts of hospitals. The smell of decomposition was appalling. The superannuated police corporal who acted as mortuary attendant didn't seem to notice it, but he'd been there for years. Afterwards the constable who had accompanied me said: 'That is the smellymost place.'

Tuesday 14 August

One of the traffic officers from Jinja called in today on some business or other. He said they had had an earth tremor in Jinja yesterday evening which sounded like thunder and passed under the town without any reported damage; just a few bricks or blocks dislodged from low walls here and there. Their station diary constable had entered in the SD: 'Earthquickker passed. Takes about two minutes only.'

From time to time herdsmen drive herds of cattle through the Kampala traffic, just as they used to in the old days when few vehicles were around. It causes even more chaos than usual, of course, but they don't seem to care. Yesterday I received a file charging someone with being a careless person in charge of an animal – which is a traffic offence if committed on a public road. The reporting constable took a statement from a cyclist complainant. It read:

The vehicle was a bull, full aged, walking from one side of the road to the other in a zigzag way as if it was drunk. The cow was on its own. The man in charge was six hundred yards away. The cow gave me a signal to pass but when I tried to pass by it hit my bicycle with its back end and I fell off and died.

Wednesday 22 August

Today I sat for the Lwo (Acholi) language exam. The written papers for translation both ways were quite reasonable. The Secretary of the Languages Board, a European expert in Lwo and other languages, took me for the oral exam, with questions and conversation about the job and so on. While speaking about police work I flummoxed him with a colloquial expression that I'd picked up from Okello. He turned to his silent Acholi assistant, who, I suppose, was there for that purpose and, perhaps, to comment on pronunciation, and asked if I had used an acceptable expression. The chap replied that it was in quite common use among those Acholi who had served in the army or police some time ago; so I suppose Okello had picked it up from his father or one of his uncles, as most of the men in the tribe have service backgrounds. So my life was spared. But I wonder if the old boy will take umbrage at a mere beginner catching him out. Still, he didn't seem to mind at the time.

Tuesday 26 August

A report in the *Uganda Argus* this morning reads:

> Confused by the noise of traffic, an Ankole bull that was probably experiencing its first taste of town life got mixed up with vehicles on the Entebbe Road yesterday and was struck by a lorry. It was so badly injured that the Officer-in-Charge of Central Police Station, who was passing, ended his life with a bullet.

Friday 7 September

Last week when I was checking some summonses just issued for service, I saw one charging a European with a traffic offence. His home address was in Kitante Road near the hostel, so I decided to serve it myself on my way home. He was naturally not overjoyed to see me, but it was a petty offence for which he could and did sign a written plea of guilty on the back. His wife came into the room then with a very good-looking wire-haired fox terrier which I admired, saying we'd had one like it at home. She said that there was a litter and was I interested in acquiring one of the pups? I most certainly was, so we agreed a price and she said mine would be ready to pick up in a week's time – which was today.

So now I've got this splendid little pup which, as he's a pedigree, will be registered with the East African Kennel Club in Nairobi. A delightful little creature, and most of my hostel neighbours have dropped in to inspect and make a fuss of him. I've decided to call him Blister, as he's a little lump that matters.

Wednesday 12 September

Today I prosecuted an African RC priest for dangerous driving. Father M was driving a motor scooter, and came out of a side turning without stopping and hit and injured a pedestrian. The victim and an eyewitness testified that the priest did not stop at the junction before entering the main road and he made no signal there and apparently didn't even see the pedestrian. The priest's version was that he stopped, signalled and turned into the main road and the victim then stepped into the road directly in front of him and he couldn't avoid hitting him. The magistrate preferred to believe the testimony of the pedestrian and the independent witness, particularly as the priest rode off without stopping at the scene (the witness noted his vehicle registration number) and offered no explanation for doing so, and expressed no regret for injuring the man and failing to help him. The RM said that he regretted having to hold that the priest had deliberately lied on oath, but that was how it was. The priest was lucky there was no journalist in court to report it.

Monday 17 September

I was on night duty last Friday with a brand new cadet ASP who is learning the ropes. He looks about 15 years old and is very enthusiastic. There was a commotion outside at about 1 a.m. as an Asian-owned hardware shop on the other side of Kampala Road was on fire. I told the new chap to ring the Fire Brigade and report it. He finally got through and said: 'I say, I'm awfully sorry to bother you at this hour, but would you mind popping round to Kampala Road as there's a bit of a fire near the CPS.' I pointed out that an emergency call should be brief, brisk and to the point and not as if it were an invitation to a game of whist at the club. A fire engine eventually arrived and firemen jumped out clutching large axes with which they zealously set about smashing the shop door and windows in an orgy of unnecessary destruction. It even woke up several nightwatchmen, who thoroughly enjoyed the spectacle, applauding loudly when the main glass display window went for a burton. Water was squirted everywhere, even after the fire was out, and it flooded the area. A very anxious Indian arrived and rushed inside to gather up what was probably his second set of account books. He kept throwing his arms into the air and saying: 'Oh my goodness.' On my way to work this morning I stopped for a look. Over the weekend the owner and his family had tidied the area and boarded up the windows. There was a notice fastened to the front which said: SELLING BACKSIDES NOW.

Thursday 20 September

One of the traffic constables brought into the station a Land Rover driven by an angry European. On its radiator was fixed what must have been a record spread of buffalo horns. The constable reported him for driving his motor vehicle while in a dangerous condition, as indeed it was with those very sharp horns pointing outwards at the front. The driver complained about being arrested in Kampala. According to him, only last week he'd been out in the bush in Teso and some short-

55

sighted Yank with a hunting licence had taken a pot-shot at him, claiming later that he only saw the horns through the heavy undergrowth. Now, he said, he was in trouble again and it was too bad. I pointed out that it was dangerous and illegal to display the horns in this manner, so he'd better remove them right away before another traffic type ran him in. Surely he could stick them on the wall at home or somewhere? So he untied them and I gave him a written warning and sent him on his way muttering and grumbling. Another dissatisfied customer.

Sunday 23 September

Kampala roads are usually quiet on Sundays so the first metal Cat's-eyes were put down this morning at one of the junctions on Kampala Road as an experiment instead of the usual yellow line painted on the road at a halt sign. The heavy traffic apparently wears out the paint quickly, and constantly replacing it is expensive. I was down for the duty of seeing that all went well. The Sikh in charge of the work crew said he needed 14 Cat's-eyes to do the job but, when he opened the box, he found only 11 there, so he couldn't do a proper job. What a nonsense; I suggested that surely he could just spread them slightly further apart and who would notice? So he did. But who would want to pinch three Cat's-eyes? Three one-eyed cats, I suppose.

Monday 24 September

Paddy's latest story is about Governor Cohen. A European who knew no Swahili went to see HE at his Government House office. At the main entrance to the house he saw a uniformed messenger and asked him in English: 'Where is the Governor?'

The messenger answered in Swahili: '*Iko juu*,' (he's upstairs).

'I know he's a Jew,' said the visitor, 'but where is he? I want to see him.'

Tuesday 25 September

For some unexplained reason the traffic police motorcyclists in their white helmets are known to the African public as 'Mau Mau'. It seems they are regarded as terrorists. A case in court this morning was a prosecution for exceeding the speed limit. The evidence of a 'Mau Mau' was that the accused Indian driver was going at 80 miles an hour, which is 20 above the limit along that particular road. The owner of the car was the father of the driver and was a passenger in the car at the time. He testified for the defence that the car speed never exceeded 55 m.p.h. When I challenged him on this in cross-examination the old man replied: 'My son would never drive at such high speed. If he had done so I would have been getting out of the car immediately.'

I asked: 'Wouldn't that have been rather painful?'

Thursday 27 September

Hallelujah! I received notification today that I've passed the Acholi exam that I sat last month. So all of the necessary exams for confirmation and future promotion are completed and out of the way. What a relief.

My prosecutions office is dealing with about 1,200 traffic prosecutions every month in the Kampala area. Luckily most plead guilty or we'd never get through them. Even more written and verbal warnings are issued. The standard of driving and vehicle maintenance is not very high. In today's fan mail: 'I object to this written warning being put on my record as I have a long carrier (sic) in driving and I therefore request that it be whitewashed.'

It's noticeable that, no matter how many people witness a traffic accident, none of them sees the same things as anyone else and the version of each witness is different from the others. Describing people and vehicles produces extraordinary differences and disagreements. One can't help wondering just how reliable is the evidence of even the most truthful eyewitness who can possibly be mistaken, misunderstood or misled.

Monday 1 October

The Traffic RM is on leave so one of the Crown Counsel is acting as our magistrate. He's fairly new out from the UK and hasn't much of a clue yet. In a motor manslaughter case this morning he caused an interpretation problem. Being a lawyer and unused to this country, he persists in using long complicated words instead of the perfectly good short ones available, and the interpreter had the greatest difficulty in understanding him. The magistrate became so agitated at one stage that he banged on his table very sharply to make his point. The interpreter was sitting just below the dais and to one side of the table. When the magistrate thumped the table the vibration caused a line of heavy law books to slide over and they toppled one by one on to the head of the interpreter below, punctuated by his cries of: 'Ouch! Ow! Ooooh!' as each one bounced off his noggin. He looked up, rubbing his head, puzzled why he was being so brutally assaulted.

Later, instead of just getting on and sentencing a convicted accused, the magistrate launched into a long-winded tirade of flowery phrases and pomposity concerning the accused's 'disgraceful attitude towards the safety of other users of the highway' and used expressions like 'this heinous offence' and 'blatant malfeasance' and 'felonious disregard for the lives of others' followed by 'the paramount necessity for a custodial sentence' and 'deserved incarceration for an extended period'. The interpreter listened to this prolonged diatribe open-mouthed and with very little comprehension. When the magistrate appeared to have finished the interpreter turned to the accused and said in Swahili: *'Wewe mshenzi bure. Mahabusi kwa wewe'* (You useless savage. Prison for you).

Thursday 4 October

The short rains have started and will go on till November. In the way these things work there are bound to be lots of functions requiring traffic arrangements outside and we shall all get very wet. As a result of walking around barefooted in the cottage, I picked up a jigger in my left big toe and it was most uncomfortable. I should know better by now. These are sand fleas which burrow into the skin and hatch out eggs which cause irritation and inflammation and have to be extracted whole. Africans are usually very skilful at this so I asked Ephraim to perform the operation. He used a safety-pin because a needle is too sharp-pointed and is liable to pierce the egg sac. After sterilizing the pin in the flame of a match, he dug it carefully in and removed the egg sac whole. I washed out the cavity, put in some antiseptic cream and stuck on a piece of sticky plaster and the operation was completed without much loss of life.

Sunday 7 October

On Friday I was on night duty and, while patrolling on foot along Kampala Road with a traffic constable, we came across a couple of types who had broken into a shop and were helping themselves to the contents. So we arrested them and the Indian *duka-wallah* came down from his room above the shop and overwhelmed us with his verbal gratitude. Of course, I couldn't accept any of the gifts that he tried to press on me but, as I was leaving, he gave me the cured skin of a vervet monkey, which he insisted I must accept and put it where I could rub my feet on it daily so that it would bring me great good fortune in the future. As it was of no apparent value I took it and departed, followed by his noisy thanks. So, we shall see.

On Saturday evening Chas and I attended the charity premiere of the film of *Madame Butterfly* in glorious Technicolor. The Governor and others were present and, it being a formal occasion, the gents wore DJ and the ladies were in long gowns and family jools. I'd had no sleep the previous night and, when the lights went out and the film commenced with the first chords of the beautiful music, I immediately drifted off into a deep sleep. When I woke up refreshed everyone was standing for the Governor to leave first. It was all over, and I had gone to great expense to secure the special performance ticket, and the bother of changing into DJ, all for nothing. I asked Chas why on earth he didn't wake me, but he merely grinned and said, as I seemed so peaceful and was not snoring or disturbing anyone, he had left me to it.

Thursday 25 October

Diwali, the annual Hindu Festival of Illumination, is over once more. Fireworks going off everywhere and shops all lit up; cars crammed with Indian families driving round and round Kampala at night. Higher authority in the past decreed that African constables should not be on the streets at night during Diwali and all European officers they can dig out are sent patrolling Kampala in uniform. Chas and I were wandering slowly along Wilson Road, parallel but below Kampala Road. The streets were brightly lit and noisy with crowds on foot. Chas suddenly shouted: 'After him!' and started to chase an African who dodged into a very narrow, dark passage-way leading up to Kampala Road. I followed him, though I'd seen nothing. In the dark alley Chas fell over something and, as I ran past, he called: 'Careful, he's got a knife.' I reached Kampala Road, where many people passed both ways and I couldn't pick out our quarry. I seized a watchman's arm – all awake on this night – and asked if he'd seen a man with a knife go past, but he cried: '*Bwana*, it wasn't me. I didn't do it.' Must have had a guilty conscience.

Saturday 27 October

I've been told that I'm to transfer from Traffic to Katwe Police Station next month, so once more I'm on the move, though I shall still stay at the hostel. First, I applied for some local leave and last week I drove down to Kisumu in the southern part of Nyanza Province in western Kenya, just over our border. I took with me as a passenger a traffic constable called Abwoga, who comes from that area and had asked for a lift as he was going on leave to see his family. This is where the Jaluo tribe live. Many of them are fishermen on Lake Victoria using small dhows. It was pleasant to wander down to the lakeside in the late afternoons to watch them unloading their catch. One of the dhows had the name *Fro and To* painted on the bows. At Abwoga's invitation I visited him and his large family and inspected their *shamba*. After a meal with them they took me to a local football match. Not my favourite sport. Before the game started each side was administered to by its own personal witch doctor, who paraded about dressed in his professional outfit doing what was necessary to ensure a win for his team. I suppose that their spells must have been of equal strength since the result was a draw. I wonder if they have witch doctor transfer fees? In the afternoons I sometimes went down from the hotel to watch the hyrax (coneys) sunning themselves on the rocks near the lake. They are strange little rodent-like creatures but apparently they belong to the elephant family. I can't see any resemblance though. I also took a close look at Mount Elgon from the Kenya side. It looks just as high from this end.

Monday 29 October

Driving to Nairobi took all day. At the steep escarpment there was an excellent long winding road built by Italian prisoners of war during the war, with the prisoners' small chapel cut into the hillside part-way down opposite an abutment from which there's a magnificent view across the vast Rift Valley, which cuts Africa in two. There were long lines of Kikuyu women staggering along bent almost double under huge loads of *kuni* (firewood) usually with a man walking nonchalantly in front carrying only a walking stick. I checked in at the New Avenue Hotel just off Delamere Avenue in the centre of Nairobi. Hotel guests' cars are parked diagonally on the road outside the front of the hotel. From my room window I can see a large mosque and several buildings of four or five storeys as well as many much older single-storey shops and offices. These are mostly Asian-owned but, since Kenya, unlike Uganda, is a colony, there are a lot of white settlers with farms and other Europeans in business competing with the Asians.

Tuesday 30 October

This morning I drove to the Royal Nairobi National Park, which is only just outside and within sight of Nairobi, yet full of all the usual animals. The entrance fee was one shilling. I took photos of giraffe, ostriches, wild pig, herds of zebra and buck of all kinds. There was even a very satisfied-looking leopard lying down under a tree some distance off the track. I drove on to the rough ground to get a closer photograph and promptly collected a puncture. After taking the picture I drove slowly back to the track and, against regulations, got out of the car and changed the wheel. Meanwhile, the leopard yawned and fortunately ignored me.

Thursday 1 November

When I first obtained my car I joined the Royal East African Automobile Association (REAAA). They patrol the main roads occasionally and are useful for supplying information about road conditions and weather before one sets out on a long safari. I checked with their main Nairobi office before I started back to drive the 450 miles to Kampala. In some parts the road was good tarmac and in others it was under construction or repair or just hard dusty *murram*. At one of these latter parts I was waved down by an African patrolman of the REAAA, who told me that his patrol van had broken down. I then did my good deed for the day and gave him a lift to Kitale so that he could arrange for a breakdown truck. However, I thought that this sort of thing was supposed to be other way round. I think I should get a rebate on my annual subs.

Sunday 4 November

Just before I left for my Kenya safari I was at Nsambya barracks on some business. As I was driving through the lines I saw the constable who is my court orderly and stopped to have a word with him. He was standing near a row of quarters, which are single rooms joined together in a row. He pointed to one of them and said it was his. In its doorway stood a tall, well-built young man wearing a white shirt and khaki drill trousers. He looked like a fairly typical Nubian from the Sudan whereas my orderly is a Lugbara from West Nile, so I asked who he was and what he was doing there. The constable introduced him as his relative, Sergeant Idi* of 4 KAR and the present heavyweight boxing champion, over from Jinja army barracks for training for the Uganda Amateur Boxing Association Championships which would be held in the PTS Drill Shed on Saturday 3 November (yesterday).

There were eight police boxers entered in the championships and the finals night is regarded as an important Force occasion, so we officers wore mess kit or DJ. Four of our men reached the finals but three of them lost their fights. The last fight of the evening was the heavyweight finals between Les Peach of the Police and the newly promoted Sergeant Major Idi, who, when still a corporal two years earlier, had defeated Peach to become champion. They slugged it out

*Later Field Marshal Idi Amin, Life President of Uganda (half Nubian, half Lugbara).

for the full three rounds, each knocking the other down for partial counts. Peach then delivered a punch that put Idi through the ropes for the full count – our only win of the evening.

Monday 5 November

I reported to Chas this morning as he is the present OC Katwe Police Station. He tells me that I'm to look after the traffic section as well as doing ordinary criminal work. There's plenty of crime in the Katwe/Kisenyi and Mengo area and it's a very busy station. The room I've been allocated as an office is a former storeroom and still half full of junk. There's a plank shelf high on the wall behind my desk and I placed all my law books on it. All was well until I decided to put my first-aid box up there. Thereupon the whole construction collapsed on top of me, with heavy books and other items cascading on to my desk and the floor, making a tremendous din and a billowing cloud of dust. Chas with a sergeant and a constable came rushing in alarmed until I explained what had happened. Chas said: 'Thought you were having problems extracting a confession so we came to help.'

Friday 9 November

A cyclist going the wrong way round the roundabout outside the station was knocked off his bike by a car coming round the correct way but too fast. The station tender was out on a job and we had no means of getting him to hospital until it returned, so I carried on doing a spot of first aid on the cyclist's fractured arm and leg. Chas came to help and we splinted and bandaged him at the roadside in correct St John's fashion. The leg fracture was bad and we had to move him around a bit but he never made a sound. The tender arrived and we loaded the casualty in and sent him to Mulago Hospital. I commented on his courage – keeping so quiet, no crying out or even a groan. A constable, who has been at the station for some years and knows all the locals, said: 'Well, he's deaf and dumb.'

Saturday 10 November

Lady Baden-Powell is visiting Uganda from Kenya, where she lives, and today laid the foundation stone of the Scouts and Guides HQ building at Wandegeya, next to a line of very tall trees which house many hundreds of large fruit bats. The Governor and the Kabaka both attended. It's not in our area but I went along disguised as a spectator because I had been a King's Scout and, as a small Wolf Cub, had once paraded at a rally in Leicester before the founder, Lord Baden-Powell.

Wednesday 14 November

Chas and I have joined a small group of people taking a Luganda language course in a room at Police HQ one evening each week. It will be a useful third language for us both. Mr Kamoga, who took me for Swahili, is running the course and assures us it will be a piece of cake. He's very good and explains the complicated grammatical constructions very clearly. It's not an easy language with its prefixes, infixes and suffixes, but at least there's plenty of opportunity to practise outside since it is the local language.

Friday 16 November

There were two fatal traffic accidents here this week. On Tuesday a cyclist was knocked off his bike outside the shops in Katwe by a fast-moving lorry that didn't stop. The man was lying in a pool of blood with his head caved in and the bike smashed up. By the time it was reported and I reached the scene any witnesses had either disappeared or decided to keep quiet, so we couldn't locate the lorry involved.

This morning I was called to another one just outside Kisenyi. A pedestrian was knocked down, also by a passing lorry. Lorry and taxi drivers are the worst on the roads and that's saying something; they have a great deal of competition from other road users. This victim had been struck on his right side at about hip level by some sharp edge of the lorry or its load, and the femoral artery had been sliced through. He had lain and bled to death while the inevitable crowd had gathered and eagerly watched. Nobody tried to help him nor did anyone report it until later. The more blood at the scene of an accident or crime, the more entertainment it seems to provide. When I arrived I naturally first checked the man's pulse and examined him. A man in the crowd said jeeringly: '*Unapoteza nafasi yako. Sasa ye nyama tu*' (You are wasting your time. He's just meat now).

Tuesday 20 November

This morning I had to go to Luzira Prison, which some still call the King Georgi Hotel, just outside Kampala on the road leading to Port Bell on Lake Victoria. I wanted to interview a prisoner who was a witness, and possibly a participant, in a case I'm looking into. The prison staff seem to be quite efficient and the prisoners and surroundings looked clean and smart. I managed to obtain a fairly useful statement from the prisoner and then secured my release from prison, only to find that someone had backed or turned into my car in the prison car park and had left a long scratch and dent in the wing and then disappeared.

Thursday 22 November

Since the beginning of the month I've been putting together my Record of Noted Persons – or Noted Blokes Book – which is a record of all prominent people of every race who are of any importance or interest in our station area. There are quite a few scattered around, especially on Makindye Hill. All discoverable details and, if available, a photograph are included so that, if any of them is involved in an incident or we have to deal with them for any reason, we can locate them and know something about them in advance.

There's a large-scale map of the area with their locations marked as well as other places of importance and concern. It's been an interesting and enjoyable side job, driving and walking around, locating and interviewing people and mapping the area. Most were very helpful and even suggested other people I should contact and places to include.

Friday 30 November

I've already made use of information in my Noted Blokes Book. Today I was called to the Sabens' house at Makindye, where they had a burglary last night. He's a bigwig in insurance, motor cars and other business here. She's an Alderman and a member of Legislative Council and busy in many activities. I sat in her large, comfortable room with coffee and biscuits, taking her statement, while one of our detective constables questioned the domestic staff. Personally, I thought the butler did it. The detective called me to come to where he had been searching the compound and, just outside, there were some items of clothing lying on the ground which Mrs S identified as hers. After some further questioning of people in the vicinity the detective found the two culprits hiding in a nearby hut with the rest of the stolen property, so it was all wrapped up fairly quickly and Mrs S was very pleased.

Thursday 6 December

There's been a rabies warning issued for this area so stray dogs are being rounded up and destroyed. A government notice rather ambiguously states: 'Owners of dogs are reminded that they must be chained up.'

Wednesday 12 December

The Native Authority (NA) Police (*askaris*) are very basically trained and assist the chiefs in tax-collecting and other duties. When I checked the Occurrence Book (OB) this morning I saw a report that an NA *askari* had reported being assaulted and robbed in Makindye village. Included in his list of stolen property was 'one red face'. I asked the OB Constable why embarrassment was listed but it turned out to be one red fez, the *askari*'s headdress.

Friday 14 December

Early this morning I went with Chas to the bungalow of an old Englishman on a track leading up a small hill well off the main Entebbe road. The old man was a retired commercial type with no family or relations. He had been lying dead on the floor of his bedroom for about three days, with the windows and door closed, before anyone had noticed and reported it. The body was decomposed, crawling with maggots and flies and the smell was unpleasant. His houseboy was nowhere around and had probably fled in case he might be blamed although there were no signs of violence or robbery. The PM report was available late this afternoon and he'd apparently died of a heart attack.

Saturday 15 December

At a ceremonial parade by the Force at Nakivubo this afternoon, before the Governor departs at the end of his five-year term of office, various medals were dished out. HE then presented on behalf of the Protectorate Government a set of seven silver fanfare trumpets to mark the fiftieth anniversary of the formation of the Force. Each trumpet has a blue and silver banner bearing an embroidered Force badge. The selected bandsmen have been practising playing fanfares recently and these will no doubt be the opening part of many ceremonies from now on.

Sunday 16 December

My dog Blister is growing well and proving to be quite a character. He came dashing through my cottage this afternoon yelping with fear and pain. He had been snoozing on the floor of the bedroom until a line of *siafu* (safari ants) had reached him and marched onwards. He was covered with the fiercely biting small brown ants. They travel about in huge swarms, moving along in a narrow line, about six abreast, relentlessly passing through gardens, houses or wherever, in as straight a line as they can manage. They attack all in their path regardless of size and their bites are maddeningly painful. If one happens to stand in the way of an unnoticed approaching column they will in no time be all over one's body biting painfully, and people have been known to get undressed in public in record time in order to pull off the ants and stop the agonising biting.

Blister could do nothing to get rid of them but, fortunately, he came straight to me and I held him firmly while I quickly pulled them off and squashed them. Back in the cottage the safari line stretched through the house, across the living room and was approaching the doorway. I grabbed the DDT container and rapidly pumped the handle to spread the insecticide as I moved along the column of ants, slaughtering them by the thousand. The other tens of thousands on the way evidently got the message because the line changed course slightly and went past the cottage instead of through it.

Saturday 22 December

I was told that certain officers didn't think much of my idea last Christmas of organising a non-serious football match between the officers and the African senior NCOs of the PTS staff – although everyone seemed to enjoy it at the time. So this year someone else organised an all-officers fancy dress soccer match at the PTS ground, with a requirement that players could only walk and had to raise their headgear before kicking the ball. I went there as a spectator and saw a lot of families present. It was amusing and entertaining but I was sorry to see there were no African officers involved.

Sunday 23 December

Sir Andrew Cohen's term as Governor is up in January and he has been going round Uganda this last month on a farewell safari. Several of us were down at Entebbe today and, after visiting the beach for a while, we went to the airport and watched Cohen's departure. Various senior officials were there, of course, but only a small number of spectators. I don't think he was very popular among Europeans though the African politicians will miss his eager support. The police certainly won't miss him – he never seemed to like seeing us around the place. At two public functions where I was on duty I heard him order that the uniformed police should be removed out of sight, which didn't seem very sensible. Other officers told me that he had done this sort of thing throughout his tour. Perhaps, when he was a politically active student, as I hear he was, he had been frightened by a policeman.

Among the people leaving the airport I saw the back of a familiar figure and said to Chas: 'You must meet this chap, I knew him in the army.'

I went over and tapped him on the shoulder and, when he turned round he was a complete stranger.

I said: 'I'm sorry, I thought you were somebody else but I see you're somebody else.'

He replied: 'Of course I'm somebody else.'

As he walked away I turned to Chas: 'He was somebody else', I explained.

Chas said: 'Well, I'm glad we've got that sorted out.'

Friday 28 December

This morning when I was going through a collection of bizarre and curious items to check whether we had sufficient evidence to proceed with charges under the Witchcraft Ordinance, Chas asked me to go with a sergeant and a plain-clothes constable to a village in the bush some miles off the Entebbe road, where a young man had been reported killed. It was a thief-beating as he'd been caught stealing a handful of cassava. The owner probably made an alarm and the villagers quickly assembled and proceeded to beat the boy with sticks and kick and stamp on him, as is the long-established custom. Afterwards they dispersed, leaving the body lying on the path, and nobody is now talking since all were involved. Unless the police arrive while such a beating is taking place it's often impossible to make any useful arrests.

In a volume of old law reports I found a typical case here back in 1944 when two men set upon some herdsmen in the honest but mistaken belief that they were stealing *matoke*. One of the men died from the beating and both accused men were convicted of manslaughter by the High Court and sentenced to ten years' imprisonment. The Court of Appeal (all British judges) held that:

Theft of food by night is regarded by Africans as a very serious offence. Before British rule killing such persons was considered justifiable. While such a severe beating cannot be justified or allowed to go unpunished, we are of the opinion that, in the circumstances, the sentences were excessive and they are reduced to five years imprisonment each.

I see that in a Kenya report, back in 1932, seventy villagers were found guilty of murder as a result of beating with sticks a woman believed to be a witch, when she refused to remove a spell on the wife of one of the accused. All 70 pleaded guilty and 10 juveniles were detained, while the 60 adults were all sentenced to death which does seem rather excessive. Obviously this local custom was totally disregarded in that case but, since then, things have changed considerably. If we can find some of the culprits in the present case they will most probably be charged with manslaughter rather than murder. There seems to be no apparent sign of any slackening in following this old custom, though.

1957

Tuesday 1 January

Another year gone and I feel really at home here now. Although I'm not wildly excited about being a policeman, at least the job's proving interesting and diverse and occasionally amusing; and I do like working with Africans. Ugandans seem generally to be naturally polite, friendly and easy to get on with. The climate is excellent; plenty of sunshine and the altitude of 4,000 feet very considerably reduces the humidity factor. There's plenty of lush greenery and colourful plants and flowering trees everywhere to brighten things up. I'm looking forward to whatever this year brings.

Monday 7 January

I was summoned to Police HQ this morning to see the Commissioner. He told me that the next Governor, Sir Frederick Crawford, had written asking for a police aide-de-camp to be appointed and to report to Government House before he arrives from the UK. The Commissioner said that he had selected me for the job because it would provide little or no spare time, for which I had no need as I had already completed all my required examinations. Besides, he added, he couldn't spare an experienced officer for a job where such experience would be wasted. What a recommendation. I was definitely not pleased; I said that I was too independently-minded to be effective as anyone's dogsbody and runabout, that I had no interest in the job and that I was hoping for an up-country posting with ordinary police work to do. I also mentioned that, in the army, I had once been approached in Hong Kong about being ADC to the GOC there and had said I was not interested. The Commissioner was not overjoyed and, perhaps, had thought that I would snap up such a high-society job; but he knows that I know that it's not the sort of job that one can be forced into against one's will. So he said: 'Well, I've chosen you as the most suitable officer available for the job. Are you doubting my judgement in this matter?' Put like that, I didn't see that I had a lot of choice if I didn't want my career blighted. So I said that I was not willing to do it for a full tour but I would agree to act as a stand-in until the Governor could obtain a more permanent candidate from elsewhere to fill the post. The Commissioner agreed to this and said he would inform the Private Secretary at Government House accordingly; he added that I should also contact the PS to arrange about moving to Entebbe as soon as possible; and that in all police or administrative matters and problems, while I'm at Government House I should report to him (the Commissioner) directly without going through anyone else. The Commissioner said that, as I'm soon due to be confirmed in my appointment, I can put up my second pip right away instead of waiting until mid-February. He added that there's no need to bother about obtaining and wearing ADC's aiguillettes 'or any of that fancy stuff'. But this is sloppy civilian thinking, in my opinion. My military training tells me that I should be properly dressed for the job and so I intend to be.

When I left the Commissioner's office the prune-faced Senior Assistant Commissioner (Administration) popped out of his office, where I think he'd been waiting in ambush, and told me sternly that it was quite wrong for me to put up my confirmed rank before the correct date and he was definitely opposed to such a move. I said nothing; as I now report directly to the Commissioner and he had allowed it, so I would do it.

On arriving back at Katwe Police Station I rang up Peter Gibson, the Private Secretary at Government House, a seconded admin type of District Commissioner rank, and introduced myself. He asked me to pop over tomorrow and see him at GH to discuss arrangements. This is what comes of being a clever clogs and getting rid of my exam requirements quickly. No good deed ever goes unpunished. To quote Paddy: 'So there you are; before you know where you are, you're where you are.' However, as always when I've been given a job to do, I shall put my best efforts into it because that's what it deserves and that's the way I was brought up.

Wednesday 9 January

I drove over to Entebbe this morning and entered the well-laid-out grounds of GH. The white building itself is spacious and attractive, with a pillared portico at the imposing entrance. An Edwardian-type colonial residence built in 1908 on a hill, of course, with a swimming pool and a tennis court in the grounds. There is a guardroom at the main gates and the police sentry stands outside. The office wing is part of the main building, with the Governor's office and those of his personal secretary and the Private Secretary upstairs. On the ground floor are the offices for the ADC and the Goan accountant and the social secretary for the Governor's wife.

I am to live in the house – there are two bedroom-and-bathroom suites at the end of one corridor; one is for me and the other for the elderly woman who used to be nanny to the Crawfords' two sons, who are now well beyond that stage. Apparently Lady Crawford has retained her as a sort of general companion/dogsbody. I shall therefore live and eat *en famille*, which seems to indicate absolutely no freedom at all. I must form an escape committee and start digging a tunnel out of the prison compound as soon as possible.

I pointed out to the PS that I have a dog and am not prepared to give it up. He promptly trumped that card by saying that the Crawfords have two dogs and two cats so that one more will hardly be noticeable. I'm moving over on Monday in order to get used to the set-up before the Crawfords arrive by sea from the UK on 27 February. Meanwhile I'm to practise being ADC to the acting Governor, who is the Chief Secretary, Charles Hartwell.

Monday 14 January

This morning I had my boxes and trunks loaded on to a police tender and sent it off to Entebbe with Ephraim riding shotgun. Then into my car, filled with all sorts of loose items plus an excited Blister, and away to a completely different type of life. I overtook the tender on the way and arrived at GH in good time. I was met by the Head Houseboy, Francesco, looking very smart in the GH uniform of white drill high-collared frock coat and trousers, red cummerbund and fez. He arranged for some of the staff to unload my kit and take it up to my room. I've brought Ephraim with me as he and I both want him to stay working for me after I've finished this hopefully short spell at GH. I secured agreement that he is to be taken on as a temporary member of GH staff but working for me and not available for ordinary GH duties, in which he hasn't been trained.

The Housekeeper is Mrs W, a British widow whose son works for the Secretariat as some sort of admin type. She has the cooks, kitchen boys and the laundry under her control. The Governor's junior office staff come under the Head Office Boy, Suleimani, to whom Blister attached himself immediately. The ADC controls the GH vehicles, which are kept down in the garages. The Head Chauffeur is a very dignified old man called Alfairi who proudly wears a row of medals, being ex-KAR, headed by the Royal Victorian Medal, presented to him by the Queen after he had driven her around on her visit to Uganda in 1954.

The GH vehicles all look old and much used and would seem to be in need of replacement, though the PS says there's no money available for this. There's an ancient Daimler that, I'm told, is very unreliable and so seldom used now; a newer Austin Princess, which is giving occasional trouble and would obviously prefer smooth British roads; a Rover 90 saloon for the Lady's shopping and other activities. For safari up-country there's a Plymouth saloon, a Land Rover and a lorry to carry all the safari gear and servants. There's also a battered Standard Vanguard Estate, which the ADC uses for general running about. Apparently Governor's safaris during Cohen's and his predecessor's days were on a very grand scale with tents, furniture, tables and white tablecloths, fine cutlery, china and silverware. Well, I shan't be the one to try and change this; I'm quite prepared to rough it in comfort and luxury while I'm here.

Alison, who was Lady Cohen's social secretary, is a bossy type who was a commandant in the ATS during the war. She's staying on temporarily to do the same for Lady Crawford while they see if they can stand each other. Da Souza, the GH accountant, is one of the small army of highly efficient Goans who keep the financial side of government departments, as well as banks, well documented and organised.

Tuesday 15 January

The acting Governor, Charles Hartwell, came over from the Secretariat this morning to do some work in the Governor's office here, so I had an opportunity to meet him. I had only seen him at a distance before. He is known throughout the administrative service as *Kali* Charlie (*kali* is Swahili for fierce, sharp or cruel) and most of the civil servants are scared stiff of him. He is 6 feet 7 inches tall and looms over everyone with a very serious and fierce appearance and, apparently, will take no nonsense and has no time for fools and wafflers who waste his time and don't get quickly to the point. However, he was very pleasant and friendly and welcomed me to the job and said I shouldn't hesitate to approach him if I had any problems. Perhaps he's just a big softy who hides a kind heart under a gruff exterior; or not, as the case may be.

Friday 25 January

Timing is very important for ceremonial and official occasions and, since most of these occur over 20 miles away in or around Kampala, I've made sure that I know the distances and speeds required for whatever time we leave GH and have to arrive. I instruct Alfairi at what speed to drive and then adjust it on the way according to circumstances and traffic so that we arrive on the dot. After all, people put a lot of work and preparation into these functions, so I must see to it that HE does not upset their timetable or hold things up unnecessarily.

Kali Charlie is obviously not used to having an ADC. He should leave things to me, but he interferes. For instance, on Tuesday evening there was some exhibition on at Makerere College Main Hall and Alfairi was keeping up the steady speed I had given him for a punctual arrival when Charlie decided to intervene. With a grunt he moved his huge body forward and, instead of telling me, spoke directly to Alfairi: 'Faster, driver, go faster, you're much too slow.'

I said: 'If we increase speed, sir, we'll arrive too early.'

'No, no,' he barked, 'we're hanging about. We must go faster or we'll be late.'

So we speeded up considerably and arrived over eight minutes before the programmed time for his arrival. There was no reception committee standing at the hall entrance; in fact, nobody was in sight. I rushed into the hall and grabbed the organiser and sent him outside. Nobody else was ready for him so they had to find a small room where he could sit and wait until they had sorted themselves out and it was the proper time for him to arrive. The organiser was most upset and cursed me for bringing him in too early, for which I apologised. When I went to fetch him from the room Charlie grinned sheepishly and said: 'Sorry about that; I should leave these things to the ADC, of course.'

Last Sunday there was a special service at Namirembe Cathedral. The arrival timing was crucial because the Kabaka was also to attend and precedence is considered so important. He was supposed to arrive five minutes before the acting Governor, although he is notorious for being late, sometimes, it seems, on purpose just to cause embarrassment. We arrived exactly on time and HE took his seat at the front after we had been told that the Kabaka had not yet arrived. I had suggested that we should wait in the car or a side room but Charlie, impatient as usual, brushed that aside saying: 'We won't wait for him.' The drill was that everyone was to stand on the arrival of the Kabaka, followed by all, including the Kabaka, standing for the entrance of HE. Now we were the wrong way round. ADCs are supposed to prevent this.

The service should have begun straight away, which would have helped, but there was a delay and the Kabaka came bouncing in four minutes later and everyone started to get up. I leaned forward and whispered to Charlie: 'The Kabaka's just come in; better remain seated.' But he stood up with the others, perhaps forgetting he was not just the Chief Secretary. The Kabaka looked pleased and no doubt mentally chalked one up. If HE's car was fitted with a radio linked to the police net we could probably sort these things out better. When I had earlier suggested this I was told that there was no money to waste on 'such fripperies' and that an efficient ADC ought to be able to manage without.

Tuesday 29 January

This morning I had to pop down to the single row of shops in Entebbe township so I took the GH Vanguard and left by the back gate. The hill slopes sharply there and as I was going down to the main road a PWD lorry came from nowhere (as the witnesses in court usually say) and, although I was moving slowly and braked hard, it hit the car in the side. Fortunately only a dent and some scratches to add to old ones, but annoying nevertheless and I said words to the lorry driver. As it was an accident involving two government vehicles, neither being insured, it had to be reported. Entebbe Police Station is only a short distance from the scene, so I trundled in and wrote my report and duly had my leg pulled by the OC Police.

On Friday we're off on the acting Governor's safari in Eastern Province, which means he wants to get in some fishing. Since the new Governor will want to tour the whole country soon after arrival, this will serve as an introduction to such safaris and I can learn the form. The programme is fairly low-key, with no wives taking part. The Minister for Local Government, Lachie Boyd, a former district officer and a close chum of Charlie's, is coming along, and the Eastern Provincial Commissioner, Tom Cox, will also stay with us throughout.

Friday 1 February

We arrived at Jinja at 10 a.m., visited Namasagali and Kamuli, where the PC had laid on a picnic lunch. Then to Kaliro county and dinner and the night at Namugongo Rest Camp, to which the GH lorry had come directly so that they could unload and fix up the camp. In fact, with all the kit and seven domestic staff, including a laundry boy and the Minister's two, we had had to borrow an extra lorry from Works. And this is just a simple non-ceremonial safari. There seemed to be little for me to do. The GH staff have been on far more elaborate safaris before and they know their jobs. Later, a large campfire was lit, the smoke keeping the mosquitoes away, and when everyone had had hot baths and changed into informal safari clothes and had enjoyed drinks round the fire, dinner was served on a beautifully laid table. It's a rough life on safari; survival of the fattest.

We left Busoga District early to go up to Kumi in Teso District. There's no direct road so we had to cross the Lwere River at Terinyi, where it forms a small lake. All round is papyrus swamp and the locals cross the open bits of water in long dug-out canoes. The main vehicle ferry is a Heath Robinson contraption of wooden planks with supports for a flat corrugated-iron roof and just space for one vehicle and a few people. It's propelled by twin wooden paddle wheels driven by a small motor. The GH Plymouth was driven on board to the accompaniment of drummers and under the watchful eyes of villagers, chiefs and the District Commissioner. The PC stayed with HE and his car. I was using the PC's small car which was put on to the smaller second ferry of similar construction but without the luxury corrugated-iron roof. Everyone waved and the drummers increased their tempo and away we all chugged across the water. A long canoe full of bicycles with their owners sitting two by two passed us in the opposite direction and they and the ferrymen exchanged lengthy greetings as we drew further apart.

During the morning we visited two leprosy centres in Teso, at Kumi and Ongino, where sufferers from this dreadful disease are looked after and treated. The small staff at each centre seemed to be kind and helpful and doing their best for the unfortunate patients. I had sent the lorries and staff straight on to Odwarat Rest Camp, where we are to stay for two nights. We spent the afternoon inspecting the Teso local government prison and prison farm. There are African Local Government (ALG) prisons as well as Protectorate prisons all over Uganda. The ALG prisons receive customers from the chiefs' and elders' customary courts.

Monday 4 February

Yesterday, Sunday, we spent on a long, dusty safari in the bush in north-west Teso on the boundary with Karamoja, using very rough tracks. None of our vehicles was suitable for this so the District Police Superintendent had driven the short distance across into Kenya and borrowed a long-wheel-based Land Rover, properly fitted with padded seats, from a wealthy white settler chum of his with a farm not far from Kitale. The Superintendent drove the vehicle and Charlie, the

Minister and I were the only passengers, so we had plenty of room to stretch our legs and bounce about uncomfortably as we hit pot-holes and rough ground and raised clouds of dust. We passed through large areas of thorn bush and vast, empty Africa with game of various sorts wandering carelessly around and occasional naked Karamojong herdsmen carrying spears and tending their large herds of cattle. We stopped under some shady trees to stretch our legs and unbend our backs while we enjoyed a picnic lunch and cold drinks before wending our way back to the rest camp.

Today we visited north Bugisu with a short stop at the town of Mbale, the district HQ, then on to Sipi for a picnic lunch. Afterwards we followed a rough *murram* track around the north of Mount Elgon to Bukwa Rest Camp close to the Kenya border. The lorries had gone straight there and so all was set up for the night. Charlie and the Minister grabbed their fishing gear and toddled off to the nearby Suam River, which has been well stocked.

Tuesday 5 February

Early this morning we left the rest camp and, still using the borrowed Land Rover, drove northwards into Karamoja on the new road that is being built, eventually to reach the District HQ of Moroto. We went as far as Greek River and Karita, where there is a small police post. The Karamojong are tall, slim cattle nomads who do not live in permanent villages. They put up extended family *manyattas* consisting of groups of mud and wattle huts which they surround with a thick thorn-bush fence to keep out marauding lions and other unwanted visitors, including their enemies the Suk, who live on the border of Kenya and Uganda mostly disregarding the authorities on both sides.

Karamoja is by far the driest district in Uganda and is mostly covered with thorn-bush desert. It is a closed district, which means that, if you are not in the police or district administration, it can only be visited after obtaining an Outlying Districts Permit. Like the NFD (Northern Frontier District) in Kenya, it seems to be regarded as the badlands and so unsafe for ordinary members of the public of any race. Certainly, Africans of other tribes would not be received by the majority of the Karamojong in a friendly fashion.

There were plenty of ostriches and giraffe and some eland galumphing about in all directions, ignoring the heavy passing traffic – i.e. our Land Rover. Then back to Bukwa for more fishing and roughing it with a four-course dinner. But first the Superintendent wanted to return the borrowed Land Rover, so he asked me to follow him in his car for the return journey while he led the way to the settler's farm. On the

Kenya side, when we were on a steep slope down Mount Elgon towards Kitale, the tube carrying the brake fluid snapped or burst and I lost the brakes in his car. The vehicle hurtled downhill and I just managed to pass the startled Superintendent without hitting the Land Rover. I was going much too fast on the narrow road but luckily there was no other traffic using it then. I wrestled with the handbrake and tried not to strip the gears, steering as best I could. Three baboons playing about in the road just made it out of the way in time and, after hurtling down for about a mile, at the bottom of the hill I managed to force the car up on to a steep rocky bank beside the road and stopped without turning over. The Superintendent caught up with me and said he'd guessed what had happened and was relieved I'd made it down safely. But not as relieved as I was. We then drove on very sedately on fairly level ground to the farm and handed over the Land Rover to the owner.

Thursday 7 February

Yesterday morning we left Bukwa camp and followed the *murram* road which wends its way around Mount Elgon to Kitale. This time I was not driving and we had no brake problems. Once in Kenya, we stopped and the driver removed the Governor's flag from the car bonnet as HE is only a visitor and Kenya, of course, has its own Governor. We drove through Kitale after calling at the police station to report our presence in Kenya, and then turned on to a good tarmac road heading south-west back into Uganda. After visiting the ALG prison at Morukatipe, we spent the night at Kwapa Rest Camp, where our lorries awaited.

This morning at Tororo District HQ we met the county chief, visited the hospital and called on Bishop Greif, an Austrian missionary type, and then to the mines in the Sukulu hills, where at present the Tororo Exploration Corporation is exploring mineral deposits while mining phosphates for farming purposes. Farming is very important in Uganda so there's a big demand for their products. We also looked in at the Tororo asbestos factory, which is very busy. There was a lot of unpleasant dust around though.

This afternoon HE went to Bunyole County HQ to present some certificates won by local farmers. The county chief arrived at the camp with a crowd of men who had brought about 20 bicycles to ride along the narrow track to the HQ about half a mile away. The bicycles were distributed and Charlie looked a sight on his with his knees coming up well above the handlebars. The Minister, PC and DC grabbed bikes, followed by the chiefs, and all rode merrily off. I had waited politely till the last and found the only remaining bike was, in traffic section terms, in a dangerous mechanical condition. I had no intention of even trying to ride the dreadful old wreck.

Being in no hurry to attend the long, boring speechifying, I sauntered slowly along the track used by the mass cyclist brigade and, on arrival, stayed well at the back of the crowd. However, Charlie spotted me across from where he sat and he grinned and winked. Afterwards he said: 'I see you craftily managed to avoid most of that lengthy rigmarole. Wish I could've done so.'

Friday 8 February

The last day of the safari. After breakfast the staff packed up and loaded the trucks and set off back to Entebbe. Meanwhile, we went to look at a sleeping-sickness resettlement area at Ikulwe then on to yet another ALG prison, at Bufulubi. Charlie seems to be very interested in prisons but, of course, security comes under the Chief Secretary's portfolio. Then a sumptuous lunch with Muljibhai Madhvani at his large residence close to the Kakira sugar factory and plantation, which he owns. He is probably the wealthiest businessman in Uganda, owning cotton ginneries, oil mills and soap factories and the giant Madhvani Industries Ltd.

After lunch we looked at the sugar factory and drove round parts of the vast sugar estate, which covers 20,000 acres and employs 10,000 Africans. It even has its own small narrow-gauge railway with 65 miles of lines. Apart from providing Uganda with sugar, it produces large quantities of very popular and cheap boiled sweets. Several boxes of these were put into the boot of HE's car and I shall distribute them among the GH staff on our return. Then tea with the PC at his residence in Jinja followed by – what a surprise – a visit to the Protectorate prison just outside Jinja township. From there the Minister buzzed off in his own car and we set off back to Entebbe. At GH I found that the trucks had been unloaded and all was well. The wives and *totos* (small children) came from the servants' quarters like vultures for their prey. The *totos* danced excitedly around grabbing sweeties and played with their new friend, an equally excited Blister; the whole lot in a noisy tangled mass while I tried to distribute equal shares.

Sunday 10 February

Apart from the usual deafening dawn chorus of tropical birds around the eaves of GH, it was a quiet weekend. The safari was an interesting and useful experience and I look forward to seeing the rest of the country in such style when the Crawfords arrive.

Wednesday 13 February

Yesterday evening Charlie and Mrs Charlie, who is also very tall, decided to go to the cinema. We drove to Kampala to see the première of the film *Reach for the Sky*, the story of Douglas Bader, the legless wartime fighter pilot. It was very good; not the sort of film to fall asleep in. I got in free too. Ted and some of the traffic constables were on duty outside the cinema. As I passed him I said: 'Good work, my man', and gave him a 10 cents tip. He was speechless for once.

While routing around in a cupboard in the ADC's office this morning, I found a box of brass badges, each with a crown above the letters GH, clearly meant for the staff and never issued. So I gave each of the house staff one to wear in his red fez and to Francesco, as Head Steward, the same badge with a laurel wreath around it. It looks quite smart. I have also had Works produce pin-on metal strips with a name stamped on each so that visitors and guests will know the name of any servant they are dealing with and, I hope, so avoid that awful habit of calling adult Africans 'boy'.

Wednesday 20 February

I went to the airport to pick up the diplomatic bag which BOAC brings in on their flights from the UK. Also I met Roger, who is the permanent, but junior, ADC. He's just down from Oxford and answered Sir Frederick's request to his old college to find a graduate to come out for a couple of years as his ADC. He wants two ADCs, which is why I'm here. Roger did his national service as a sub-lieutenant in the RNVR. When he showed me his uniform at GH there were two stripes on the sleeves although he is not entitled to that rank. He said that Sir Frederick is pulling strings at the Admiralty to persuade their lordships to grant Roger the temporary rank of lieutenant while he is ADC here. I gather that they are being rather sticky about it.

On Sir Frederick's instructions Roger has brought out two sets of ADC's right shoulder aiguillettes for us; gold for him and silver for me. So much for the Commissioner's views on the subject. I shall certainly wear mine.

The Crawfords are coming by sea with all their kit on the SS *Uganda*, disembarking at Mombasa and then flying up to Entebbe by special aircraft. He was Governor of the Seychelles until recently and, before that, Deputy Governor in Kenya, dealing mainly with the Mau Mau uprising security situation. I am to go down to Mombasa by train on Saturday to meet them and fly back here with them. Tomorrow I shall go into Kampala with Roger for a rehearsal of the Governor's swearing-in ceremony outside the High Court. As 4 KAR are supplying the guard of honour with their band, we shall go through the inspection and movements and placings and generally tie up everything with those involved.

Sunday 24 February

A pleasant two days journey on the train down to Mombasa, where I was met at the railway station this morning by some friends of the Crawfords with whom they will stay for a night on arrival tomorrow. This afternoon they lent me one of their several cars and I drove to Nyali beach and enjoyed a swim in the warm water of the Indian Ocean.

Monday 25 February

We took two cars to the docks, showed our special passes and went aboard the *Uganda*, an impressive-looking liner. Met the Crawfords in their cabin. He seems to be a pleasant enough chap, with a sense of humour, thank heavens, and a faint Yorkshire accent. Lady C is slim, with a Grecian nose and rather haughty, very aware of her status. While they were talking to their friends I arranged to have their luggage taken ashore and loaded into the second vehicle. There was no bother with the Customs or Immigration, of course. We drove to the house, where, after lunch, they took a siesta. Lady C has Nanny with her. That's what they all call her, so I have to as well. She is a very quiet, unobtrusive mouse, but seems to be a nice old thing.

There are two Government Houses in Kenya – the main one in Nairobi and the secondary one here in Mombasa, used for coastal visits and holidays. This evening we are going there for dinner with the Governor of Kenya, Sir Evelyn Baring, and Lady Baring; a black tie affair. The Barings are old friends of the Crawfords from his term as Deputy Governor here, although most of Sir Frederick's colonial service was in Tanganyika.

Tuesday 26 February

The dinner at Mombasa GH was very grand. Sir Evelyn comes from a long line of imperial proconsuls and seems to be related to a number of other great families in Britain. In fact, I was the only one present without a title. They had guests staying who were peers and wives of peers, and even their two ADCs had courtesy titles as sons of peers. When I was introduced, one of them, a captain in the Guards, said: 'Good heavens, a policeman.' I was rather expecting him to add:

79

'They'll be giving the job to postmen next.' Nevertheless it was a pleasant evening and an excellent dinner.

This morning we were driven to the small local airport, where we boarded the East African Airways DC3 specially fitted out and used during the Queen's last visit. Very comfortable inside, with armchairs and a bar. We were the only passengers, with a steward to do the necessary. Apart from a quick circuit and bump in an army AOP Auster in Hong Kong, this was my first flight, having travelled abroad only by sea so far. We landed at Nakuru airstrip to pick up their pets, which had been in kennels there. They have a friendly Alsatian called Hank, a bad-tempered Sealyham terrier called Susie and two Siamese cats, one of which has a deformed hind leg. I mentioned to Lady C about my Blister and she replied that as long as he was friendly with their animals there would be no problem. Good.

We landed at Entebbe just before noon and there was a police guard of honour and a line of dignitaries to meet them, with *Kali* Charlie in charge of the proceedings and making the introductions while photographs were taken. Roger had brought two cars and the lorry for their luggage and I left him to it and went with the Crawfords to GH. The staff had all lined up at the entrance and HE greeted them in Swahili, in which he is fluent. He had sent on ahead his personal valet, Mohamed, a very superior and disdainful Somali, who wears a turban and clearly wouldn't be seen dead in a fez.

At 5 p.m. today HE was sworn in by the Chief Justice at a ceremony in the grounds of the High Court, as we rehearsed the other day. On the way into Kampala we were picked up by a police motor cycle escort with sirens going. HE turned to me and said: 'I don't want any of that. Tell them no sirens in future.' Everyone was in robes or full dress uniform; HE in dark blue tailed tunic with silver facings and cocked hat with plumes. I noticed that his London tailor had boobed when putting his three medals on a bar. The middle one was a Second World War Africa Star instead of the Africa General Service Medal with 'Kenya' clasp, for his work during the Mau Mau period, that he is entitled to and should have been wearing. I shall take the necessary steps tomorrow to sort that out before some sharp-eyed nit-picking type spots it and blames me for allowing him to parade improperly dressed.

Wednesday 27 February

Lady C has decreed that every night is to be a black tie night; whether there are guests or just the family, we must dress for dinner. Fortunately I have an excellent lightweight DJ made for me in Hong

Kong, but I'll have to buy some more white shirts. HE's very busy interviewing ministers and heads of government departments in his office, but I managed to catch him just after lunch and mentioned that the medal was being sorted out. I also referred to my hope that this would be a short appointment as I wanted to get back to normal police duties. He said that the Commissioner had already informed him of this and he was going to arrange to take on another possibility whom he had interviewed in London. However, this fellow would not be available until the middle of August and he wanted me to stay on until then so, of course, I agreed. That's fine, my escape is fixed up.

In the *Uganda Argus* this morning there's a report about a part of the Jinja road being surfaced by Stirling-Astaldi. It said: 'Roads constructed of this material are not subject to the murram dust nuisance caused to pedestrians over which motor cars run.'

Saturday 2 March

Alderman Lewis, who is the Mayor of Kampala and a director of the Uganda Company, arranged a Mayor's Garden Party for this afternoon so that HE could meet the prominent Kampala residents of all races. It took place in the King George V Jubilee Park, with the Police Band in the bandstand entertaining the guests with popular music from films and shows while everyone chatted and took tea or cold drinks with cakes. The men in natty suits and the women in hats and afternoon gowns. I stayed with HE while Roger went circulating with Lady C, each finding cronies from their Kenya days.

After tea I ushered HE up to the bandstand and presented the Director of Music, Teddy Beare, and HE had a few words in Swahili with members of the band, complimenting them on their efforts. Teddy was quite chuffed. Several of the wives sidled up to me and asked me to present them to HE. I suppose there's going to be quite a lot of that sort of thing as we go along, especially for invitations to GH.

Sunday 3 March

I'm not a church-goer but HE and Lady C seem to be quite enthusiastic as they indicated that they would attend the Entebbe Anglican church twice every Sunday, and ADCs are required to be in attendance, as always; both of us for the morning service and one for the evening service. So one of us gets a couple of hours off on alternate Sundays. Such lavish leisure time. If HE is so keen on church why does he have to borrow my Bible each time when he reads the lessons? It seems that most evenings there will be guests for dinner or functions to attend and visitors staying over the weekends who have to be looked after. This is what I most dislike about this job; there's little or no time to myself.

Tuesday 5 March

This afternoon the Kabaka came over from Mengo to meet HE for an informal discussion. He came in one of his Rolls-Royces and I met him at the portico, introduced myself and took him up to HE's office. He seems quite a pleasant chap; just hope he's not going to cause the sort of upheaval and nonsense he had with Cohen; but there are some wild men in the Lukiiko. Afterwards HE brought him down for tea on the verandah so that he could meet Lady C. He has a good line in social chit-chat and is very suave and self-assured. I don't think Lady C took to him at all, though.

Monday 11 March

Richard Nixon, who is Vice-President to the indolent President Eisenhower in the US of A, is doing an African tour American-style, which pretty well means one country a day; here he has spent all of one and a half days. Before he arrived HE held a security meeting at GH at which the advance team of US Secret Service characters tried to take over everything. They even suggested that those of us living in GH should move out for the period of the visit, so that they could fill the place with their 'guys' and control all comings and goings. HE very firmly vetoed this and said nobody moves out and nobody is to be interfered with. They clearly didn't like it but they had to accept it or cancel the visit, which might worry them but certainly wouldn't bother us as it has no particular significance to Uganda either now or in the future.

The Nixons arrived in a large American Boeing aircraft yesterday morning, accompanied by another large aircraft filled with very noisy and pushy journalists. I heard one of the SB officers on duty at the airport muttering: 'Feed them to the crocodiles, say I.'

The PTS provided a guard of honour on the tarmac with the band in attendance. When he had inspected it Nixon turned to the Commissioner of Police and said: 'That was great. Your guys sure know their stuff.' Then, just as we got them loaded into the cars, the heavens opened and we were deluged. The guard of honour and band rapidly disappeared into the airport building and we drove up to GH, followed by several million Yankee pressmen waving wet cameras and yelling before being carted off to the Lake Victoria Hotel. At GH there was an informal cold lunch on the long verandah with a fine view of the colourful garden steaming in the sun after the rain. Actually the

Nixons seem to be very pleasant, amiable and intelligent people with a good social touch.

After lunch the Nixons went with HE to Jinja in what they call a 'motorcade', a convoy of cars, to view the Owen Falls Dam. Roger caught that duty while I stayed at GH to mind the shop, and had a quiet afternoon for once. They returned from their arduous safari in time to change for the formal dinner at which the Chief Justice and the Ministers and their wives were guests.

First the Police Band beat Retreat on the back lawn, which was lit up for the purpose, while we stood on the verandah and spectated. Teddy had inserted a couple of Sousa marches into his programme and they went down very well. They concluded with the Force March, which is Teddy's arrangement of Offenbach's 'Bold Gendarmes'. One of the Vice-President's Escort Officers, a major in the dress uniform of the US Marines standing next to me said, 'Say, they're playing our toon'. I realised that he was nearly right; Teddy's march version of the 'Gendarmes', in fact, bears a close resemblance to 'The Shores of Tripoli' or whatever the US Marines call their march. I didn't bother to explain all this to the major but, next time I see Teddy, I must remember to pull his leg about it. In the course of my conversation with the major I was intrigued to hear him describe the Vice-President as 'a wunnerful hooman bean'.

After the guests had left and the Crawfords and the Nixons had retired to their rooms, I walked around the house as usual for a final check-up. When I passed the Nixons' bedroom there was a Secret Serviceman in a chair outside their door. I felt like asking if he was waiting for a bus, but he might have pulled a gun on me so I just wished him goodnight. This morning Mrs Nixon went with Lady C and Alison to Kampala for exciting visits to YWCA and community development projects while Nixon gave a press conference on the verandah. It was attended by all the visiting pressmen. Two locals, from the *Uganda Argus* and the Government Information Department, were allowed to squeeze in at the back. Secret Servicemen stood around looking exactly like Secret Servicemen. Probably from Central Casting in Hollywood.

Nixon was most impressive at handling the Yank journalists who, without much respect, heckled and badgered him with awkward questions, which he fielded expertly. No doubt he's had a lot of practice at this but he did it with considerable panache. The press then dashed off to the airport to fly in advance to Nairobi, his next port of call. Meanwhile Nixon and HE sat drinking coffee and waiting for the ladies to return from Kampala. Nixon then asked me a tricky question, did I really like doing this job? Copying his evasive style I said that it was interesting and a chance to meet all sorts of people. He grinned and said: 'You mean like the Nixons?'

Mrs Nixon arrived and we took them straight down to the airport for their noon departure. Roger and I were each handed one of the Vice-President's visiting cards signed by him, and the American invasion was over. Just as well, as HE had to go to Kampala for his first opening of the Legislative Council at 2 p.m. So a quick change into full dress uniform and off we went in the Austin Princess. Outside LegCo HE inspected the police guard of honour while the band tootled away and then we processed into the building. I led the way and entered the chamber first to announce in a loud voice 'His Excellency the Governor' and the members rose to their feet.

Wednesday 13 March

While LegCo is sitting HE goes in each afternoon to preside over the Council as a sort of chairman/speaker. Roger and I take it in turns to go with him and sit through their boring debates. Fortunately, after the opening we all wear suits. It was my turn today and we set off in the Austin Princess and, at mile 9 from Kampala, the engine gave a gasp and expired. Alfairi turned on to the *murram* at the side of the road and cruised to a halt. As HE won't have a police escort – he says I'm enough – and we have no radio we were stuck in the middle of nowhere at lunch-time when traffic is at its sparsest; there was nothing in sight and we had to be at LegCo at 2 p.m.

Time was running out and HE was getting tetchy when a scruffy-looking European in an equally scruffy small car came chugging along, with the exhaust trailing a cloud of smoke behind. I stepped into the road and waved him down and asked for a lift to Kampala. HE looked a bit doubtful about sitting in the untidy and not too clean back seat but there was nothing else in sight so he got in. I sat in front and told the driver to get us to the LegCo building as fast as he could. I had instructed Alfairi to stay with the Austin and said I would send a PWD mechanic out from Kampala to rescue him and hopefully bring him to us at LegCo. The engine of the small car sounded very rough and I wondered if we were going to have a second breakdown but we made it.

When we turned into King George VI Way and approached the LegCo building, which is also the Town Hall, we were stopped by a traffic constable. He looked disdainfully at the car, correctly assessing it as probably in a dangerous mechanical condition, and said to the driver: 'You can't enter this road; it's closed for LegCo.'

I recognised the constable and stuck my head out of the window and said: 'It's OK, Byamugisa, the Governor's in the back as we had a breakdown on the way.'

He stepped back, saluted and waved us on in one cleverly combined movement and we drew up in front of a puzzled reception official at the steps. I quickly jumped out, said, 'HE's here', and opened the back door for HE to scramble out from the dusty interior and startle all beholders with his unconventional appearance.

I thanked the unknown European for the lift and suggested that he should disappear before keen types in the traffic police took a closer look at his decrepit vehicle. Off he went in a cloud of exhaust smoke and was seen no more. HE turned to me and said: 'This sort of thing will just not do, you know.' I shrugged; I had already said several times that we needed to replace the car or at least have a radio fitted, but to no avail. Once HE was in with LegCo I slipped out and rang my contact in the PWD mechanical section and arranged for the Austin to be collected. I then rang Roger at GH and asked him to keep in touch with PWD and, if the Austin was unlikely to be ready in time, to send the Plymouth to Kampala to collect us.

In fact, they fixed up the Austin and we returned to Entebbe in it and I had a go at HE on the way back about a replacement, but I gather Finance is being awkward about it. On our arrival at GH Lady C said: 'Somebody must be told.' She says things like that.

Friday 15 March

I was disappointed to hear that HE's first safari would be in the Eastern Province and we would be covering similar ground to last month's safari, but this one will be more formal and ceremonial as it's a first visit. We drove over to Jinja this afternoon to start it. Both ADCs are needed as HE and Lady C have separate programmes. They are staying with the PC, Tom Cox, while we ADCs are at the rest house, half a mile away, but not eating there, thank goodness. I checked the refrigerator in the kitchen and it was full of cockroaches. Apart from a dinner party at the PC's residence this evening there's nothing until tomorrow, when the fun starts.

Saturday 16 March

We started off with a ceremony and *baraza* at the Busoga District Council building, with the Kyabazinga and other officials in colourful robes and all the admin officers in white uniforms, pith helmets, medals, swords, the lot. A guard of honour by the ALG Police and their band, a drum and bugle Boys Brigade type, playing their original version of the National Anthem. The interpreted speeches inside the hall were followed by a prolonged march past by millions of barefooted children looking very smart in their school uniforms, all giving an eyes right – or left, as the inclination took them – as they passed the high platform from which HE saluted them. After that visits to places and projects.

This evening there was a reception at the PC's to meet the prominent locals, for whom we supplied the booze from GH stocks brought with us, which they very rapidly depleted; grabbing free booze being the name of the game at these sprees. Tomorrow church, followed by a drive to Tororo after lunch for more of the same.

Wednesday 20 March

After Tororo we went to Mbale for the usual guards of honour, ceremonies, district council *baraza*, speeches, visits to schools, hospitals, prisons and so on. At the evening drinks parties the ADC's job seems to be to see that all attending get their share of free GH booze but do not noticeably over-indulge; which they do, of course. And then close the bar at the time laid down for guests to bid farewell to HE and Lady C. We more or less act as bouncers, a part I do not really enjoy.

Friday 22 March

At Soroti in Teso the evening party was held at the DC's residence and the chiefs and other prominent citizens who attended seemed to be the keenest so far to lace their beer with whisky or gin – a popular mixture that ensures a satisfyingly quick intoxication. When the time came for guests to bid farewell one old senior chief was so far gone on the mixture that he couldn't walk or talk. He was totally legless and euphoric. There was no way I could allow someone in such a condition to approach HE, even if he could manage it, so instead of inserting him in the line of departing guests I instructed the duty GH houseboy, Paulo, to help me pick him up by the shoulders and feet and we dropped him out of the front window of the bungalow on to the densely planted flower-bed, from where he eventually crawled off into the night. He clearly felt no pain.

Later, when everyone had left and we were relaxing in armchairs, at last able to have a drink ourselves, Lady C, whose beady eyes miss very little, said: 'I saw what you did to that poor old man, Peter. I think you ought to show more respect for senior chiefs. In future I don't expect our guests to be chucked out of the window.'

I said: 'Yes, Lady C,' and she gave me one of her looks. I must remember in future not to defenestrate well-oiled chiefs when Lady C is around.

Saturday 23 March

We left for Entebbe this morning. The Crawford's first Uganda safari has been satisfactory and they seem to have gone down well with all and sundry. Of course, they are old East Africa hands and know the ropes and HE is very good at chatting up politicians, chiefs and self-important personages. Having gone through all the administrative grades himself in Tanganyika, he knows just what to look for and how to deal with district officers. They can't pull the wool over his eyes as his deceptively mild and quiet approach hides very sharp and percep-tive questions and comments. When we arrived back at GH I found a letter awaiting me from Police HQ informing me that my appointment as an Assistant Superintendent in the Colonial Police had been con-firmed on 17 March.

Thursday 28 March

A couple of days ago we had a British MP staying here, Lord Balniel, the son of the Earl of Crawford and Balcarres. A pleasant enough chap, in spite of being a politician. He had talks with various people and then enjoyed a slow drive which I took him on through the Botanical Gardens. Today another visitor arrived with his wife. He is a short, stout, pompous and exceedingly self-important character who insists on using his full title: Commander Sir Stephen King-Hall. I remem-ber during the war he used to give regular pep talks to the nation on the wireless. He also publishes and circulates a UK newsletter and has already given me half a dozen samples of it; hoping for a subscrip-tion, perhaps.

He came in a hired car with his equally short and stout wife, who keeps fairly quiet in The Great Man's presence. I met them at the portico and introduced myself. He announced his rank, title and name in full, which I already knew, of course, and then asked me: 'What is your rank?' I replied that as I'm a police officer we merely call our-selves mister. 'Oh,' he said, 'that won't do at all. I shall call you Captain.' I felt like asking the silly little man: Navy or Army? But said nothing. Fortunately, it's Roger's turn to look after this one. They're both ex-Navy anyway.

Friday 29 March

There is a push-button alarm bell up on the main landing in GH which rings in the guardroom at the main gates to summon assistance if required. This morning I decided to test it so I pressed the button and waited. And waited. Nothing happened. What a surprise. I phoned the guardroom and asked the corporal if he had heard the bell. 'Yes, sir,' he said, 'I thought it was the telephone, but nobody answered when I picked it up.' So I went down to the guardroom to sort them out. Apparently nobody can remember when the alarm bell was last tested, if ever, so they hadn't a clue about it, although I found it mentioned at the end of the standing orders for the guard. So much for security. Somebody must be told, as Lady C would say.

Monday 1 April

I was in Kampala this morning to tie up some arrangements for a function in the near future and at the CPS I was told that, at the UABA boxing championships last Saturday, the Force won five finals matches and Les Peach once again fought Sergeant Major Idi of 4 KAR and knocked him all round the ring, winning easily on points. Everyone in the police considerably chuffed.

Tuesday 2 April

Lady C summoned me into the presence this afternoon and complained: 'Blister has treed my cats again. You must do something about it.' It's difficult really as she is well aware that fox terriers notoriously chase cats. All small moving animals are fair game to them and her cats are eminently chaseable. I called Blister and gave him a good finger-wagging about his behaviour. 'Fat lot of good that will do', sniffed Lady C. In fact both she and HE are very fond of Blister and, when HE goes down to Entebbe Golf Club for his mid-week golf, he always takes Blister with him, but not his own dogs. Helps him to concentrate, so HE claims. I never go on these expeditions so I don't know what those two get up to. The PS is the golfer and he accompanies HE. He says that Blister is very well behaved and sits snootily beside HE in the car and keeps still while HE swings his bat or racquet or whatever they play the game with.

In the evenings the five resident animals, three dogs and two cats, assemble in the kitchen yard, where their food is prepared and put out in separate bowls by Nanny assisted by Yowana, a kitchen assistant. The animals all sit quietly in the same positions each day and are well behaved in her presence, just like children would be. Everyone calls her Nanny, even the household staff address her as Memsahib Nanny and probably think it's her name. Apart from feeding the animals she looks after Lady C's clothes and generally potters about, eating in her room and keeping out of the way, hardly saying anything and never upsetting anyone. But I suspect she can be firm when she needs to be.

Wednesday 3 April

Barrington-Ward, the editor of the *Uganda Argus*, came over this morning to see HE in his office; probably about some proposed government project or legislation. Apparently his father was once editor of *The Times*. A bit of a comedown. HE has a low opinion of the *Argus*, which he reads at breakfast every morning. He calls it 'the two minutes silence'.

Friday 5 April

Since I came to GH it has bothered me that the police sentry at the main gates stands out there in the open in full dress uniform regardless of the hot sun or rain. It doesn't look right to me; there obviously should be a sentry box. Consequently I prevailed upon the Sikh *fundi*, who is in charge of small building works at Entebbe PWD, to build a proper sentry box, for which I provided the design. It was completed today, a fine-looking white-painted concrete structure with a small tiled roof and side windows. The tallest constable at Entebbe Police Station is PC Mpande, who is 6 feet 6 inches and, with his tall blue fez, reaches 7 feet. I had the sentry box made to fit him – a tailor-made sentry box, in fact – and probably the tallest sentry box in the whole British Empire.

There are two First World War grey-painted German field guns placed one on each side of the main gates facing outwards, and now, with the sentry box in place and the guardroom just inside the gates – where the visitors book is kept – it all looks tickety-boo to me. The guard commander sends a constable to the ADCs' office each morning with the visitors book to check the names of those who called in and signed it on the previous day, in case there is anyone HE should be informed about and possibly invite to a meal.

Tuesday 9 April

Yesterday we commenced the first of two planned Northern Province safaris, divided because there's a large area to cover. It's very hot up in the north at the moment so Lady C has not come, nor has Roger. Since the roads are not too good and far too much time is lost in travelling by car, it was decided to go up by air and send the Plymouth to meet us at the various district HQs. So, yesterday morning we left Entebbe in a chartered De Havilland Rapide, a twin-engined biplane belonging to Caspair Ltd, and flew to Gulu in Acholi, which is both the Provincial HQ and the District HQ. We were met by both the PC, Powell-Cotton, and the DC, Gotch, and with them was the Plymouth driven by the number two driver, Badiru. There was a smart guard of honour by the ALG Police, nearly all ex-KAR, and full dress ceremonies and a *baraza*, where HE addressed the District Council, with the necessary interpreter doubling the time these speeches take. Then visits to the hospital, prison and the pride of the north, Sir Samuel Baker Senior Secondary School, followed by a sundowner party in the evening. I even managed to try out a few of my Acholi conversation pieces.

Late this afternoon we flew to Moyo, which is in the very north of Madi District of West Nile, only just below the Sudanese border. Here we were met by the DC, Basil Duke, an old-time bush type recently transferred from the Sudan. We are spending the night in his fine old thatched bungalow.

Wednesday 10 April

After a quiet night we started the morning in ceremonial uniforms, HE and the PC in white with pith helmets and, outside, inspected a guard of honour of eight ALG barefoot police, which is all they have here. Then we walked across to the nearby District Council *baraza*, a small thatched roof building with open sides. We changed into khakis after that and went by car to visit the hospital and the RC mission school, where the children all paraded outside holding a Union Jack and the mission flag on poles with spear tops and sang the National Anthem. The mission staff wore long white robes – the brothers with khaki topis and the sisters with white hoods.

After lunch a dusty drive westwards and then south to the West Nile District HQ at Arua, stopping on the way to visit the Ladonga White Fathers RC Mission at Aringa – more white-robed Italian priests – and then to Maraca, where the local chief had gathered a crowd of people by the roadside to greet HE, including the pupils from a small primary school. So we stopped and got out of the car and HE shook a few hands and exchanged Swahili greetings and thanked them for turning out. The chief was very pleased and there was much hand-clapping as we drove off.

Many of the West Nilers wear modern-style clothes now but in the villages there are still a number of women who wear the traditional bunch of leafy twigs fore and aft, held in place with a string around the waist.

Thursday 11 April

Here at Arua we stayed last night with the DC, Roy Thompson (both he and the PC wear the ribbon of the Military Cross awarded in the last war). Another ALG guard of honour made up of ex-KAR proudly wearing their war medals. In the north they are all warrior tribes and most join the KAR or the police. After the ceremonial *baraza* at another thatched-roofed district council building, we changed and started the usual visits, including one to the Agricultural Department office, outside which there is a complete hippo skull mounted on a stone block – such enormous jaws and teeth.

After lunch with the DC we drove down to Rhino Camp on the Albert Nile and went aboard the government launch for a fishing trip to Lake Rubi where several quite large and patriotic Nile perch allowed themselves to be caught by HE. Then on to Wadelai, where we went ashore to take a look at Emin Pasha's monument, a cairn out in the now overgrown bush. The Mahdist rebellion in the Sudan in 1885 caused the German Emin to move the HQ of the huge Equatoria Province, which he governed, to Wadelai, where he built a fort to protect himself and his Sudanese *askaris* from attack by the Mahdi, who was pursuing him. He also recruited locally, where he was known as Takka Effendi; but he was completely cut off once Gordon was murdered in Khartoum in 1886. Eventually Stanley led a much publicised relief expedition, which met the indecisive Emin on his retreat from Wadelai. The ruins of the fort he built have been reclaimed by the bush and have disappeared. Incidentally, by bringing his Sudanese soldiers into Uganda he also brought the tsetse fly and sleeping sickness, for which he deserves no thanks.

There are dense masses of papyrus along the banks of the Nile and large quantities of waterbirds, egrets, grey herons, storks and goliath herons. On land we occasionally saw sausage trees with brown, hard fruits weighing from 8 to 10 pounds hanging down from the branches. Not the sort of thing that one wants falling on to the noggin. We went further south as far as Pakwach then turned the launch round and back to Rhino Camp, from where we drove to Arua.

Friday 12 April

Another night at the DC's house then to Arua airstrip this morning, where we found our biplane waiting and, leaving Badiru to drive the Plymouth back to GH, a full day's journey, we flew off to Entebbe. I would have liked to have made the trip back in the car but HE vetoed that. It seems that I'm required for duty back at GH and not joyriding around the Protectorate.

Monday 15 April

The band of the 4 KAR is off to the UK on tour, including performances at the Royal Tournament in London. As a farewell treat they came to Entebbe sports ground this afternoon and beat Retreat. We all went down to spectate and enjoyed it. They were in fine form and there was a good-sized crowd watching.

Tuesday 16 April

Three British MPs are out here on a swan under the auspices of the Commonwealth Parliamentary Association; no doubt busily stirring up local politicians, with whom they claim they had 'fruitful talks' – preaching their ideas of democracy without the slightest idea, or even concern, whether such foreign ideas are appropriate or fit in with local ways and customs.

They came to dinner this evening in their badly fitting DJs and I found myself sitting next to a Labour MP whose name I didn't catch or even try to. He told me he thought it was wrong our having all these African servants waiting on us and they should be sent back to their villages. I said: 'But then none of them would have a job.' Each time one of them brought him a plate of food or filled his wine glass he turned in his seat and said with an oily smile: 'Thank you, brother', and 'Very kind of you, my friend'. The GH staff at first looked surprised then decided to ignore this sanctimonious parade of virtue. They are a snobbish lot and they expect guests at GH to behave with decorum. I said nothing and got on with my meal. In my view politicians should be neither seen nor heard, merely hammered into the ground like tent pegs. I bet if that chap went home and found that his new neighbours were West Indian immigrants he'd go through the roof.

Friday 19 April

There was a formal dinner this evening for various local guests and some visitors. Lady C is always very strict about going into dinner exactly on time. However, the Kabaka had been invited and, as always, he was late. She was doing a certain amount of teeth-gnashing and didn't think much of my suggestion to give him another five minutes and then start without him, when there was a flurry at the door. I went into the hall and found the Kabaka coming in with Francesco, who is a Muganda, bowing almost to the floor.

I went up to him and said: 'Good evening, sir, you are late and Lady Crawford is hopping mad. Will you come straight through, please?'

He indicated the lavatory hidden behind a screen near the front door: 'I've simply got to go in there, I'm bursting,' and shot inside. I sent

Francesco to inform Lady C that the Kabaka would join them in a minute.

I hear that the Cohens used to play charades and other such games with their guests after a formal dinner, but the Crawfords don't seem to go in for that sort of thing. When the men join the ladies after coffee, brandy and cigars, everyone sits around in comfortable armchairs nattering and drinking and being reshuffled by Lady C every now and again so as to talk to somebody else. It's all very sedate and dull. Maybe the Kabaka thinks so too. He didn't stay long and buzzed off early. I don't think he's hit it off with either of the Crawfords.

Saturday 20 April

Yesterday the Buganda Lukiiko, the Kabaka's government, met and decided that their local government police force was not up to much – how right they are – and that what they need is a strong police force because Buganda is soon going to have self-government – they hope. The Katikiro (premier) said that the Buganda policemen were getting very good training with the Uganda Police special courses at the PTS. However, the Deputy Speaker challenged this claim and said: 'We want our own policemen trained by us. The kind of training they receive at Kampala is not the one we want. They are not trained to be the friends of the public, but simply to frighten us.'

The members then voted overwhelmingly in favour of this half-baked motion or resolution, totally disregarding the fact that they have neither the means nor the money to carry it out, apart from the other fact that there is absolutely no chance of Buganda getting self-government and opting out of the Uganda Protectorate, for similar reasons. Perhaps those visiting busybody MPs have been putting ideas into their heads and irresponsibly encouraging such flights of fancy. On the other hand, maybe the answer is to give the Buganda Kingdom self-government and then stand back and let them see what happens – as a lesson to them and to the other parts of the country.

Monday 22 April

This morning I went with HE to visit Namulonge Agricultural Research Station, which is a few miles north of Kampala. We arrived at 10 a.m. exactly on time and there was not a soul in sight to meet HE. I jumped out of the car and dashed into the main building, grabbed a startled passing European and said: 'Where's the Director? The Governor's waiting outside.' Panic ensued and the Director then appeared from his office and, without waiting for him to say anything, I blasted him for dereliction of duty in failing to be on hand to greet

93

the Governor. He rushed outside and came back with HE, babbling excuses (the Director was babbling, not HE). Not a good start to the day. HE was clearly not pleased; both he and I are punctuality fiends and miscreants had better beware if they want to avoid decapitation or worse.

Because of its altitude and position Uganda has a marvellous climate and the agriculture wizards are having a fine time researching and improving crops and grazing grasses. The most important crops are cotton and coffee, followed by tobacco, tea and cane sugar. The Bantu tribes inhabit the southern parts of Uganda, where the banana is the staff of life. There are many plantations of both the small, sweet eating banana and the larger green plantains called *matoke*, which are cooking bananas, a staple diet here and very easy to grow. In meals they replace European potatoes, which only grow in the cooler south-west, in Kigezi District. In the north and the east they prefer grain and grow quantities of maize, *wimbi* (finger millet) as well as *muhogo* (cassava), sweet potatoes, groundnuts, *sim sim*, beans and sorghum. Also up there cattle are extremely important, though more as a display of wealth and for paying bride price (dowry) and milk rather than as meat to eat.

Thursday 25 April

Lady C has several favourite expressions. When she's displeased with someone or with what has happened, she says; 'It just won't do' or 'Someone must be told' (to get it sorted out or to do it right). On arrival somewhere she says: 'Who's in charge?' which always sounds ominous and people tend to go into immediate hiding or take to the hills.

Lady C's grand piano finally arrived from the UK a couple of days ago. A lorry came and, accompanied by much shouting and everyone giving orders to everyone else, the staff unloaded the large crate and staggered with it into the reception room where it was to be set up. Lady C was fetched and, just as I arrived on the scene of the crime, she came into the room saying: 'Who's in charge?' Before I could slide off she spotted me and said: 'Ah, you're in charge, Peter, let's get to work,' and promptly took charge of the operation herself, issuing orders in all directions. She does that kind of thing. I call it inverted delegation.

The crate was dismembered and parts and packing removed and a very fine grand piano was revealed, but in a legless state. With everyone lifting almost together the legs were positioned and slotted into place. I tried a five-finger exercise on the keys and they sounded all right. Lady C sat down and rippled through the keys with considerable expertise and everyone cleared off and left her to it.

There was a reception here yesterday evening and, at one point, some idiot put his glass of whisky down on the piano top. I quickly whipped it away before it could make a ring on the polished surface and handed it back to him saying: 'Don't ever do that if you value your life or your job. You'd better hope that Lady C didn't see you.' But she did and later thanked me for removing it. Those beady eyes miss very little around here.

Wednesday 1 May

We usually have breakfast on the small verandah. Cereals, orange juice, milk, fruits and any other cold items are put out on a small table by the back wall and we help ourselves. The duty houseboy is around to fetch anything cooked that is ordered. I was down first this morning and noticed a large ham on the bone resting on a plate with the other cold stuff. There was no houseboy present. I took a quick look at the *Argus* before HE arrived and cornered it. When I turned to get some cereal I saw an empty plate where the ham had been. I called Francesco and said, 'Where's the ham?' He looked around and then pointed silently to the garden, where Blister could be seen sneaking off with the ham in his jaws held by the bone.

I hopped over the balustrade, calling quietly for him to stop. He was in a dilemma because the large, heavy ham was hindering his escape, so he could either drop it and make off or hold on and be caught. His strong terrier instinct never to let go decided that for him and I caught him easily, said: 'Drop it', and removed the ham and took it to Francesco. We dusted it off and turned the best-looking side up on the plate. It looked reasonably fit as Blister had held the bone and hadn't had time to bite at the meat. I carried on with my cereal and coffee as HE came on to the verandah, rubbed his hands and said: 'Ah, my favourite ham; I'll have a couple of slices please, Francesco.'

Apart from exchanging 'good mornings' with HE I said nothing and carefully avoided looking at Francesco as he sliced away. I didn't stay for Lady C's arrival but I think we got away with it. No explosions so far.

Friday 10 May

The Great Indian Mutiny began exactly 100 years ago today and, as was predicted, the British Raj failed to last for another 100 years afterwards. Well, whatever we get here at the end shouldn't be quite as bad as that was. I hope.

Saturday 11 May

Entebbe pier is a fairly large jetty really, where the lake steamers tie up on their weekly journeys round the lake from Bukoba in Tanganyika and Kisumu in Kenya. Also kept tied up there is the launch *Vigilant*, now belonging to the Entebbe Airport Air-Lake Rescue Team in case any aircraft lands or crashes in the lake. It was formerly used for taking passengers out to the flying boats at Port Bell in the days before the airport was built. It's supposed to be on standby for all aircraft arrivals and departures but HE decided he wanted to have a trip on the lake in it, so this was arranged for this afternoon. The Crawfords' younger son, aged about 16, is here on his school holidays so it was a family outing together with both ADCs, the Private Secretary and his wife. Since we were going on the water, Roger had put on his tropical white sailor suit and he had switched on his I'm-in-command, box the compass, clap 'em in irons, character. We headed southwards towards the Ssese Islands and fortunately, as far as I was concerned anyway, the lake was calm. Further out it can be very rough during storms and numerous fishermen have been lost in their canoes. Very few of them bother to learn to swim, which adds slightly to their peril.

I could see that Roger was itching to take over the helm from the African quartermaster and demonstrate his seamanship and bellow unintelligible orders at us landlubbers. The African seaman was clearly not impressed with Roger's naval uniform. Helpfully I said: 'If he won't let you take over, Captain Bligh, clap him in irons, I say. We want no mutineers here.' Very reluctantly he finally agreed to hand over the wheel. We mere passengers disported ourselves on various parts of the launch enjoying the sunshine and smooth movement. I could hear Roger singing out nautical-type words and just hoped he didn't give the order to submerge to periscope depth or to engage the enemy fleet, so I interrupted with: 'If this old tub sinks Roger, you as temporary acting unpaid Captain, will have to go down with it or I shall have to endorse your boat driver's licence.' Lady C said: 'Stop being unkind to Roger.' So I said: 'Yes, Lady C,' and stopped being unkind to Roger and, shortly after, we turned around and went home.

Wednesday 18 May

This morning, after I'd collected the diplomatic bag from the airport, I took Robin Crawford to the residence of the Chief Game Warden. He was at work, of course, but Mrs Kinlock appeared with the leopard cub that we'd come to see and photograph. It was about the size of an ordinary cat and very playful. They call it 'Aringa' because that's where it was found, in West Nile, its mother having been killed by poachers. It's a wild animal, not a pet, and they won't be able to keep it for long, but they don't seem to have decided what to do with it. There's even talk of starting a zoo in Entebbe. What an awful thought, caging wild animals. What on earth do we need a zoo for? All Africa is an open zoo anyway.

Friday 20 May

HE's formal visit to the Kabaka and the Buganda Lukiiko took place this morning at the Kibuga on Mengo Hill. Lady C accompanied him, so two ADCs were required. The New Bulange (Great Lukiiko Hall) is a fine two-storeyed building put up in Cohen's time. It has offices and law courts and is well furnished and equipped. HH the Kabaka was in robes with an elaborately embroidered pillbox hat and a Buganda Order round his neck. He looks the part of a ruler with the fine, superior cast of features sometimes seen on ancient Egyptian tombs.

After they jointly inspected a police guard of honour we all proceeded into the Lukiiko hall. This has well-carved wooden benches made of *mvule* on each side in which were sitting the senior chiefs and elders who were members of the Lukiiko appointed by the Kabaka. On a dais covered with numerous overlapping skins of leopards and lions and four steps up stood the ornate throne occupied by the Kabaka. To one side and one step down from the throne sat HE on a beautifully carved and gilded smaller throne. On the other side of the dais sat the Kabaka's family. The galleries were filled with invited guests and everyone was dressed in robes or suits.

The Kabaka made a polite speech of welcome in perfect English, slyly mentioning some of the things that they want to do, and HE replied smoothly and without promising anything but emphasising the need for full co-operation between the Protectorate and Buganda Governments. Earlier at Entebbe I suggested to HE that it would be well received if he could incorporate a sentence in Luganda at the end of his speech. He agreed, so the PS and I concocted a complimentary conclusion, translated it and then I worked out a simple phonetic pronunciation for HE to read out. Being a fluent Swahili speaker he managed well after a couple of practice readings. When he finished his speech with it there was gasp of pleasure from the audience and a tremendous burst of applause. He was a hit!

After this the Kabaka left in his Rolls to drive down *Kabaka Njagala*, the road across the same hill to the *Lubiri*, his palace grounds, and we followed on to attend a small reception for the GH party and the Buganda Ministers. Inside the *Twekobe* (palace) the Baganda present, including the *Katikiro* (premier), either knelt or prostrated themselves in the Kabaka's presence and we from GH were the only ones still standing. Personally, I'm excused prostrations; I've got a chit from the doctor.

I was handed a tumbler full of sherry – it was either that or a tumbler full of whisky. I produced the gift that HE had brought for the Kabaka from the Captain of the *SS Uganda*. It was a black plastic flip-over directory for telephone numbers and addresses with the name of the ship engraved on it. I thought it a pretty useless sort of present for someone who had others to do the telephoning or writing on his behalf. The Kabaka glanced at it and said: 'Oh, jolly good, I must get someone to plug it in.'

Friday 31 May

I went with HE to visit the Department of Information in Kampala this morning. As he wants to confer with the Resident Buganda in the latter's office this afternoon, we're having lunch at the Governor's Lodge at Makindye. Some GH staff have been sent over by the Housekeeper to open up the Lodge and prepare it for use. I also phoned the OC Police at Katwe to inform him that HE would be in his area.

HE was in an unusually bad mood in the car going to Kampala. In fact he was seething about the local politicians who have recently been more vociferous and scathing, making demands for independence by yesterday. HE had decided that the worst offenders should be prosecuted for making seditious utterances in order to make an example of them. However, the Attorney-General had strongly opposed him and advised that it would only make them worse and would do no good anyway. I put in my twopenn'orth and said that I thought that prosecutions would quite likely be successful on such a charge. HE snapped: 'Of course they would succeed. I keep saying so. What we need is a new Attorney-General.' I wonder if this AG's for the chop?

At the Information Department we were met by the Director of Information, who showed us round the offices where they produce numerous educational magazines, booklets and pamphlets, also small vernacular newspapers for distribution in each province. We moved to the broadcasting studios, where the Head of Programmes and the Chief Broadcasting Engineer demonstrated and explained their functions and those of their subordinates, who are African broadcasting assistants being trained on the job to take over technical posts eventually.

Then to Makindye for a cold lunch. The constable who had been sent by the OC Katwe popped up from behind a hedge and with a tremendous salute announced that everything was *sawasawa* (OK). I told him to stick around until the truck with the GH staff and equipment had left to return to Entebbe. We then went back into Kampala to the Resident's Office. He's the equivalent of the provincial commissioners in the other parts of the country, but, because Buganda has always been regarded by the British as well as the Baganda as being different and special, they have a Resident instead. I deposited HE there and drove down to see the OC Traffic about some future function arrangements and to find out the local gossip before collecting HE for our return to Entebbe.

Saturday 8 June

This week HE went on safari to visit Western Province. Lady C decided not to go as she has not been well, so there was no need for two ADCs. It was Roger's turn to go so I stayed behind. There were a few visitors to attend to, and several boring functions due soon required arrangements to be made, so I've been fairly busy. I gather that in Kigezi, which is very mountainous, the Plymouth left the road but fortunately stopped without rolling down the mountainside, which must have been quite a relief for the occupants. A large number of local 'volunteers' pushed and pulled it up the slope and back on to the road. It was undamaged so they continued on their way. They were lucky; there have been reports of several very bad accidents caused by vehicles, usually overloaded, leaving the road and taking a short cut down one of the mountainsides.

Sunday 9 June

We both went with HE and Lady C to Kampala this morning to the Commonwealth Youth Sunday parade in front of the High Court. All the local youth organisations took part, Boy Scouts, Girl Guides, St John Ambulance Brigade, Boys Brigade and representative groups from most of the schools in and around Kampala, all marching past, some of them in step, to the music of the Police Band. The children looked very smart in their Scout, Guide, Brigade or school uniforms and someone had rehearsed them very efficiently.

We were all in uniform for this event. HE wore his khaki service dress Commander-in-Chief's uniform and Lady C was disguised as Chief Guide. When we arrived at the imposing steps and they got out, before Lady C could say: 'Who's in charge?' a large, imposing and bossy woman, who's chairman of the Uganda Youth Council, appeared and told everyone what to do. So we did it.

Thursday 13 June

HE and Lady C attended the Queen's Birthday Parade, which was held this year at Nakivubo Stadium by the 4 KAR (The Uganda Rifles). Now that they are back in Uganda after their period in Kenya chasing Mau Mau, they have taken back this duty from the Police. However, our band provided the music, accompanied by their Corps of Drums, as their regimental band is still in the UK on tour. Roger and I attended the dress rehearsal on Monday and I introduced him to the CO, Lieutenant-Colonel John Peddie, and the Adjutant, Bill Fairhouse. Back at GH I briefed HE on his movements on the parade, which, of course, is not a new ceremony to him.

HE, Roger and I were in blue full dress uniforms and, in the stands, all the local dignitaries were also robed or in uniform or suits; the Chief Justice, the Kabaka, Chief Secretary, Bishops, Commissioner of Police and so on. On the parade the Brigadier commanding GHQ troops in Nairobi was in attendance and all four companies of the battalion took part. Roger attended HE for the inspection and I did the presentation part, which included presenting warrants to the three newly created Effendis, all warrant officers first class. This is an old-time warrant rank, senior to RSM, reintroduced to provide African platoon commanders. In my view this is a retrograde step; they should be looking for young Africans to train as commissioned officers, just as we do in the Police. One of them, Effendi Obwoya, won the Military Medal in the Mau Mau operations. The Colour was trooped in grand style and altogether it was a very well-drilled and impressive parade.

Friday 14 June

The second part of the Queen's birthday ceremonies took place at GH this morning; an investiture of 31 people who had received awards. HE stood on a red-carpet-covered dais in the main reception room with a table spread with various medals. Roger stood by it with a satin cushion on which to hand over each award to HE. On the other side stood the Chief Justice in wig and robes reading out the citation for each award. Seated beside the dais was Lady C, the Chief Secretary and Mrs Charlie, the Bishop of Uganda, and various Ministers and their wives. In the main part of the room sat relatives, friends, various civil servants and others who had been invited.

My job was to stand by the door leading to the small reception room where we had lined up the recipients in order of the seniority of their awards: CBEs, OBEs, MBEs, BEMs, and Chief's Medals and Certificates, and call out their names one by one, having checked the correct pronunciation of some of the African names. Afterwards there was a group photograph of the recipients with HE, the ADCs acting as bookends, followed by a reception with everybody congratulating everybody else and laying into the free booze.

The Commissioner of Prisons and the Deputy Commissioner of Police are about to retire and so collected their gongs today. I heard some muddled or drink-fuddled woman ask our Deputy Commissioner: 'Do tell me, Mr Cleland, is your OBE civil or criminal?'

The Head of the Uganda Civil Service and I share the same names and a woman who was introduced to me said: 'But you look too young, are you sure you are *the* Peter Allen?'

I said: 'Of course I am; the other one is an imposter.'

She looked puzzled. 'Oh,' she said, 'I didn't know that.'

In fact, Mrs Allen frequently comes to GH to 'do the flowers'. I gather she's very ambitious for her husband and likes to keep closely in touch with GH as she's hopeful that her husband, and my namesake, will eventually become a governor, which, I suppose, is possible. If there's a visitor at GH present during these flower-doing sessions and I'm in the vicinity, Lady C takes great delight in introducing us both to the visitor as 'Mr and Mrs Allen' and then adding: 'Of course, they're not married,' out of mischief and just to cause embarrassment.

Tuesday 18 June

Whenever LegCo is sitting, HE attends as Chairman/Speaker while discussions and debates go on. This means that an ADC must accompany him and sit beside the dais on which is HE's 'throne'. It's very boring and I've perfected the art of sitting upright in the chair, appearing alert and attentive but actually asleep. However, during the afternoon tea break today, *Kali* Charlie passing by me with a cup of tea and grinning, said: 'I see you had a good nap again during this afternoon's debate.' Nothing gets by him.

Wednesday 19 June

The seats of the Austin Princess are fitted with white drill covers. There are two sets so that there's always a clean, sparkling white set in use. This afternoon the Austin stood at the portico with the back door open ready for HE to step in with his golf clubs. A minute before he was due to arrive at the car there was a white blur and Blister shot past Alfairi at full pelt and landed on the back seat. He knows exactly when it's time for golf. Unfortunately, it had been raining and he'd just been playing in the garden with HE's dogs. In a moment the dazzling white seat was covered with muddy paw marks.

'Quick,' I said to Alfairi, 'get the spare covers.' I grabbed Blister

101

and handed him over to Suleimani, the Head Office Messenger, and told him to take him over to my office and shut him in until the car departed. We had just got the seat covers changed when HE arrived, with Mohamed carrying his golf clubs. 'Where's Blister?' asked HE.

'He is unseenable, *Bwana Mkubwa*,' replied Alfairi helpfully.

'I think he's playing with Hank somewhere,' was my contribution.

'Oh well, let's go,' said HE.

Thursday 27 June

The Kabaka came to see HE this morning. Or, rather, he was sent for – the second time this month. Apparently the Lukiiko has been up to its games and not co-operating with the Government as required. So HE has had to point out to the Kabaka that he was only allowed back from exile on the understanding that he co-operated and caused no trouble. The Lukiiko obeys the Kabaka and reflects his thinking, so he is responsible.

I met him at the door, we exchanged greetings and I took him up to HE's office and left him there. Up before the headmaster again. His ADC, George Male, and another aide waited outside in the Rolls, so I invited them in for coffee and we sat on the verandah and chatted, then walked around the garden. Eventually HE came down with a somewhat chastened-looking Kabaka, who jumped into his car and tootled off back to Mengo.

Saturday 29 June

I've been at GH for six months now and had no time to myself at all. Guests and visitors have to be looked after and functions attended in the evenings and weekends. There's never a proper break, which is just how I imagined it would be when I tried to avoid this appointment. One's friends are neglected and they get the idea that one is stuck-up and superior and can give them no more time. So today being Saturday and, just for once, as there are no visitors or functions, I mentioned to Lady C that I wanted to pop into Kampala and see a chum. She immediately tried to veto that, saying: 'Oh no, you're on duty here and might be required.' I pointed out that it's a quiet weekend and Roger is available anyway, so she said: 'All right, just for two hours this afternoon. But you must be back for dinner.'

Or I turn into a pumpkin, I suppose. I felt so angry and humiliated at having to beg like a child for a couple of hours break, the first in all these months, too. Nothing will make me stay in this job any longer than absolutely necessary now. I must live my own life as I've never been gregarious or particularly sociable. I dislike sundowner parties, official functions and especially entertaining other people's guests. I loathe obsequiousness; I am not servant material. A meal with a friend or just reading a book while listening to pleasant music is my idea of a good time. They can keep their high society and parties. It's odd really; here I am moaning about having to dine every night in GH when there are people out there who would give their eye-teeth for just one GH dinner invitation.

My allotted two hours was reduced by a half as it would take an hour to drive to and from Kampala, so I'd have just an hour to make my arrangements for when I leave here. For that is the good news; because HE told me yesterday that his new ADC on contract will be out from the UK early in August. So now I have an escape date when I can return to normal life. HE said that the PS would be writing on Monday to the Commissioner to inform him that I would be available for police duties in August; so I asked him to add ten days to the date to give me some local leave before returning to duty. He knows how I feel about this situation and is sympathetic, so he kindly agreed to do that. Police HQ, including Prune Face, will have to accept it if HE says that's how it will be; so I'm making my arrangements accordingly.

Monday 1 July

HE, the PS and I left this morning on the second leg of his northern safari, this time to Lango and Karamoja. This will be my last GH safari. We flew to Lira, the Lango District HQ, in the De Havilland Rapide, again having sent the Plymouth and Land Rover ahead. The vehicles met us at Lira airstrip and we drove to Agur Rest Camp, where we are staying. At the camp entrance we found a gathering of chiefs and villagers, who put on a very energetic welcoming dance with wild drumming and much stamping of feet. The DC introduced HE to the local notables and the spectators politely applauded.

After lunch we visited a place called Alito and inspected an ALG police guard of honour and HE spoke to local farmers, some of whom were proudly wearing Second World War campaign medals. Then to the Verona Fathers RC Mission School at Aboke. This is a junior secondary school for boys and girls run by Italian missionaries, although they teach in English, of course. The whole school was assembled outside the main building and they sang the National Anthem and a hymn which I could not identify.

Tuesday 3 July

This morning we were in full fig and drove into Lira for the usual ceremony and *baraza*. Afterwards, back to camp to change and have lunch, then into Lira for a round of visits to the hospital, medical training centre, prison and another school. This evening there was HE's sundowner party, where there was much chattering and swilling of free booze until chucking-out time.

Wednesday 3 July

We drove to Karamoja early this morning eastwards across Lango and into the northern part of Teso District along very dry and dusty roads. Iriri Police Post is at the boundary of Teso and Karamoja at the foot of the curiously shaped Napak Mountain. A sign here says that it's a closed district. The police post consists of aluminium rondavels called uniports, thatched to keep them slightly cooler than hot ovens. Whitewashed stones have been carefully placed around the patches of very dry, yellow grass and the Uganda Police blue and silver flag flies from the flagpole. We went into Iriri Rest Camp, where the Land Rover and some of GH staff were waiting with lunch. Afterwards HE looked around the post and spoke to the constables.

The OC Police had driven from Moroto with two armed constables to escort us the 45 miles to the District HQ. The *murram* road was very dusty and we kept the vehicles well apart so as to avoid eating the dust. On each side of the road was a huge expanse of thorn bush, dry long grass and acacia trees. On the way we stopped at Kangole, which is a small trading centre with a two-man RC mission supplied by the Verona Fathers. The shops and buildings are single-storey, made of wooden supports with corrugated iron roofs and walls. Karamojong were wandering around or just sitting on the concrete verandahs of the *dukas* thinking deep thoughts. As we neared Moroto we could see the jagged skyline of Moroto Mountain looming over the small one-street township. Tired, hot and very dusty, we sought baths and a cold drink.

Thursday 4 July

Ceremonial day. HE inspected a police guard of honour outside the District Council, which is an open-sided building. Then straight in for the *baraza*. The chiefs and elders listened as HE's speech was translated into Karamojong. They wore only black *shokas* (sheets) tied with a knot at the neck to hang on one side of the body. One or two wore ancient shirts and shorts. Their coiffures were elaborate, with matted hair in different coloured clays formed in intricate patterns and making them look as if they were wearing helmets of coloured beads drawn tightly over their heads. Some had ostrich feathers fixed to stand upright from their headpieces. Metal of various types hung from their ears and noses. Metal plugs were fitted into holes made below their lower lips. The DC, Sandy Field, has been here a long time and speaks Karamojong fluently and obviously gets on well with them. He stutters in English and is very diffident but he changes and is quite animated when chatting to his Karamojong.

After changing into everyday khakis, we visited the police station, the hospital and Moroto Primary School. Here the head (and only) master paraded the entire School, consisting of seven very small boys. The Karamojong are not yet terribly interested in education and, being semi-nomadic cattlemen, are not keen farmers either. At the prison most of the convicts are cattle-raiders, some of whom have killed herdsmen or herdsboys, and the prison uniforms are the first clothes they've ever worn. They give no trouble and produce carvings and basketware and other items, which are taken to Kampala to sell to tourists. On release they go back to their nomadic lives and cattle-raiding. Prison is merely an interlude and does not change them.

The usual getting-to-know-you sundowner party was held in the evening at the DC's residence, with the chiefs getting magnificently drunk in very quick time on beer laced with the hard stuff. We poured them out of the house at the end and sent them on their way very happy.

Friday 5 July

From Moroto we drove south on the Watershed Road, calling at the small trading centres of Loro and Amudat; one *duka* had a petrol pump worked by a hand-operated pumping lever. Both have small police posts and are very close to the Kenya border. This part of Karamoja is inhabited by the nomadic Suk, who wander between Kenya and Uganda grazing their cattle without being concerned about borders. The Suk are enemies of the Karamojong, who, in the south of the district, belong to the Pian tribe. They raid each other's *manyattas* and steal cattle, killing the herdsboys and anyone else they find nearby. Nor are they friendly towards tribesmen from other parts of Uganda, which is one reason why this is a closed area.

Amudat is overlooked by the impressive Kadam mountain range, just below which is the rest camp where we are spending the night and near which the Suk are putting on a big *ngoma* (dance). The DC presented them with a white bull for the feast. It was immediately slaughtered and cut up. HE walked around the few *dukas* in the trading centre, which today was crowded with naked Suk warriors carrying long spears or sticks. Then we called in at the cattle sale, where the Suk had brought in cattle to sell to the government buyer for transporting to Kampala for sale in the butchers' shops.

The dance commenced in the afternoon and it was still going on when we returned there after our evening meal at the rest camp. There was a great deal of prancing around in circles and of men waving sticks, spears and shields. Also much jumping up and down on the spot and chanting. HE, the PC, the DC and a junior district officer, all dressed in khaki drill and wearing pith helmets, wandered around among the dancers. Geoff from Moroto Police was also there; he's the only Australian in the Force except, as he always says, he's Tasmanian, not Australian.

Hanging down the backs of some of the senior warriors were the skins of leopards which they had speared themselves. Fantastic hairdos and lots of ostrich feathers were on display. Many of the women wore so many bead necklaces that they had difficulty in turning their heads, further weighed down by the heavy metal rings, like large curtain rings, in their ears.

Saturday 6 July

After packing up camp this morning, we drove westwards, calling at the tiny trading centre of Moruita and then Lolachat, both with police posts. We stopped at Nabilatuk, which is the trading centre for southern Karamoja, with about six shops in a dusty street. We had lunch at the rest camp after HE had walked round the area and looked in at another government cattle sale. The people here are Pian and noticeably different from the Suk.

Lunch over, we drove northwards back to Moroto, stopping on the way at Latome RC Mission and calling on the fathers and looking at the single-classroom school to which they are trying to persuade local Karamojong to send their sons, whom the Pian feel are better employed tending their cattle. At Moroto airstrip the Rapide awaited us and after bidding farewell to the assembled officials we flew back to Entebbe. A tiring but enjoyable safari. I like Karamoja, it's really Africa as I imagined it to be, and I must try to get a posting there if it's possible.

Thursday 11 July

We have a junior minister from the UK staying at GH at the moment. He is John Profumo MP, who is Parliamentary Under-Secretary of State for the Colonies. A very pleasant chap who holds an Italian barony and was a brigadier in the Second World War. With just the family and perhaps a guest or two, HE prefers to make the cocktails himself. He's very good, a mean shaker and maker or fixer and mixer, or whatever. I was aware that Profumo is married to the well-known actress Valerie Hobson and, at the cocktail hour, I mentioned that I had seen her in the musical *The King and I* at the Drury Lane Theatre when I was in the Army and had enjoyed it very much. Lady C said it was one of her favourite shows and, when she heard that I have the LP record of the show music, insisted that I should bring it down and play it on the library record player after dinner.

Tuesday 23 July

Teddy Beare, the Police Director of Music, has now left on retirement after ten years with the Force Band and his replacement is Ted Moon, who has just arrived from the Queen's Royal Lancers in Germany. He'll find things rather different here, I expect, but he's inherited a really well-trained band to play with, to coin a phrase.

Wednesday 24 July

For the last two days we've had Herbert Morrison MP, staying at GH. He was a minister in Churchill's wartime National Government and also in Attlee's post-war Labour Government. On the afternoon he arrived he decided to have a swim in the GH pool and appeared there in a 1930s-style striped swimming suit. 'Do you think I'm suitably dressed?' he asked me. 'Oh quite,' says I, somehow managing to keep a straight face as Lady C choked in her drink.

Morrison married his secretary, who has not come with him on this trip. This is a pity because he's a very disorganised and forgetful type and apparently she's the opposite and keeps him more or less put together. Wherever he goes he leaves behind him a long trail of mislaid and lost property. I seem to have spent a lot of time since he arrived organising searches for his wallet, passport, briefcase, spectacles, notes, fountain-pen, watch and so on. In exasperation I decided yesterday that it was time I lost him for a while. The local politicians invited him to meet and address a group of them, probably so that they could seek advice on strategy for obtaining instant independence, something they are very keen on these days.

The meeting was to take place in the Katwe office of one of the activist lawyer/politicians so I had to take him there in a GH car, having first made sure he had all his goods and chattels, and then hand him over into their clutches. Naturally, I had no intention of spending the day with that lot so, as they were going to give him lunch, we agreed a time for me to send a car to collect him. Apparently he had a good day, but he did report that he had mislaid his key-ring somewhere. Fortunately, Badiru later found it underneath the car seat. Thank heavens this sort of nonsense is coming to an end for me in a few days time.

Tuesday 30 July

This year there's to be held a World Boy Scout Jamboree in England to celebrate 50 years of Scouting. Uganda is sending a small contingent and the Governor, as Chief Scout of Uganda, was invited to view a replica of the bamboo and papyrus arch that will be taken and erected at the site by the Uganda Scouts. So yesterday morning HE and I drove over to Kazi, just outside Kampala, where a pre-jamboree camp is being held for the Scouts who are going, so as to rehearse what they will be doing there. There was a photo in today's *Uganda Argus* showing HE and the Organising Commissioner and other Scout officials, with me lurking in the background. As a former Scout, I was naturally interested in what was going on and it's good to see that Scouting is flourishing all over Uganda.

Saturday 3 August

During Roger's national service in the Navy, he picked up an expression that I've not heard before, certainly not in this modified form, in the Army. When someone has gone off somewhere or just disappeared he says: 'So-and-so has sugared off.' He uses this expression constantly at GH and it has obviously been noticed and picked up by some of the staff. This afternoon, at around teatime, he was nowhere to be seen and Lady C wanted him for something, possibly just to have tea; so she sent Francesco to find him. When Francesco came out alone on to the verandah after a while, she said:
    'Well, Francesco, where's *Bwana* Roger?'
    As usual looking very solemn and superior, Francesco replied: 'He has sugared off, *Memsahib Mkubwa*.'
    Lady C said: 'Well, tell him to sugar back again quickly.'

Tuesday 6 August

Roger went down to the airport a couple of days ago to collect the dip bag and to meet Alan, the new ADC and my blessed replacement. Apparently he did his national service in the RAF, flying a chair in some minor administrative capacity and so will be wearing that wingless uniform. For a few days we have a surfeit of ADCs here and I can take it easy.
    I went to Police HQ yesterday, having made an appointment to see

the Commissioner. I should complete my three years tour at the end of February but, as my brother Nick is getting married on 21 December in Germany, where he is stationed in the army, and I'm to be best man, I've asked for my leave to start in early December. This was agreed, but it doesn't leave much time for a proper posting between now and December, only a four months period, in fact. So it's been decided that I'm to take over temporarily as OC Mityana Police Station, in West Buganda, where the present OC is just about to go off to the UK on special short leave to get married there and then return to his station, which he has only recently taken over.

The Commissioner said that there was a view that I didn't have the experience necessary to run an up-country station, but he had decided that I should be given the chance as he thought I could do it, so I'd better not let him down. I bet the adverse opinion came from Prune Face. I mentioned that I'd very much like to be posted to Northern Province after my leave if there was a chance of it. He just said: 'We'll see.'

Both HE and Lady C said I must leave Blister with them while I'm away on my ten days local leave, which I'm taking in Mombasa. He'll certainly be happy here with his friends and everyone makes a fuss of him. In fact, he's going to miss GH very much more than I shall. HE and Lady C gave me signed photos of themselves, which I had asked for, and they both said that they would have liked me to stay on for the full tour. He's a very good boss and there are some good perks, but it's the job I can't stand.

Friday 23 August

I'm back refreshed from my local leave idling on the beaches at Mombasa. I drove down to the coast in two days, staying overnight in Nairobi. Some of the roads were not too good, being dry, dusty and pot-holed; others were quite fair. However, I enjoyed the break with no duties to perform, no telephone, and no wretched visitors or guests to bother about. I've obtained some excellent Wakamba carvings of animals for presents and myself.

Ephraim went home to Northern Rhodesia while I was at Mombasa and has brought back a wife, Marjorie, for whom he had saved up enough to pay the dowry. She looks about 16 and speaks no English or Swahili. Our conversation is therefore limited. He's quite sad at losing his prestigious post at GH but I told him he can keep the GH uniform and wear it on special occasions.

I put my boxes and other kit on to a PWD lorry and sent it off to Mityana with Ephraim and Marjorie and their bits and pieces. The OC

Police there has a government quarter and, as he is returning to it after the wedding, he's leaving all his stuff so I shall have his furnished house to use while I'm on the station.

Saturday 24 August

I called into GH this morning, said hello and goodbye to everyone, and Robin, who's there on school holidays, came out with Blister, who hopped into the car and we drove off to Mityana, which is on the road to Fort Portal. It's a good tarmac road so no great problems. The police station is small, with less than 30 men and, in addition, three outposts each manned by a corporal-in-charge and six constables. It's a busy area, with a number of Asian-owned cotton ginneries scattered around as it's a large cotton-growing district. There's quite a lot of crime, and homicides of one sort or another, such as murders, manslaughters and suicides, occur every week. The Mityana CID consists of one detective constable and one plain-clothes constable and they are both kept busy. I'm going to visit the three outposts with Jim, the OC, on Monday. Apart from handing over, he has to go there and hold the monthly pay parade anyway. His house is modern and well furnished, on a hill overlooking the station, and I should be comfortable here for my short stay. I've checked the admin side with him and been over the current crime files under investigation or awaiting trial in Kampala. He and his predecessor ran an efficient station so it's no problem taking over. Some of the constables were at the PTS when I was there two years ago and one was with me in Traffic Branch, so they're not all strange faces.

Tuesday 27 August

In Buganda the organisation of the administration of chiefs, starting from the most senior, is the *saza* chief over roughly a county which is divided into *gombololas*, each with a chief. Each *gombolola* is divided into *mirukas*, roughly parishes. These are subdivided into *mutongoles*, the chiefs of which are really village headmen.

Yesterday we drove round the district calling on the *saza* and *gombolola* chiefs and then visiting the three police posts at Tondola, Kasanda and Busunju. The last is actually a newly built police station on the Hoima road, but it is staffed at present as an outpost due to shortage of manpower, so they have plenty of room there. I spoke to the corporals and constables and looked at their books, files and records. After pay parade we distributed mail and vernacular newspapers obtained free from the Information Department. In the Busunju prisoners' property book there was an item shown as 'one rubber lightening'. On querying this I was told by the Station Diary constable on duty that he thought it was a mistake by the other SD constable and he probably meant 'a magnetic light'. Yes, well. The only answer was to have the item produced and it turned out to be an ordinary cigarette lighter. On the way back we came across a man on a bike with a long plywood box roped crossways on the carrier. We stopped and questioned him and he explained that he was taking his father's body for burial at his *kyalo* (village) and he produced a chit, a grubby piece of paper with the office stamp of the *gombolola* chief on it, confirming this.

Today Jim took me to visit the various cotton ginneries and at the last one the Indian manager invited us to a curry dinner. It was delicious and very hot, with all the trimmings – tasty poppadams and chapatis and plenty of ice-cold beer or water to quench the internal flames. The ginneries are quite well run and profitable because the Indian owners keep the overheads down as much as they can; and they certainly can't be accused of overpaying their African workers.

Friday 30 August

Jim left this morning with his luggage and a happy smile on his face as he headed for the UK and matrimony. So, in answer to Lady C's usual question: 'Who's in charge?' the answer is: 'I am.' I have a sub-inspector who watches over the investigations, with an excellent station sergeant and a civilian clerk. A sergeant is in charge of the barracks and discipline and runs the duty roster, with three corporals to assist wherever needed. As at all stations, the staff come from different tribes, so we can generally find someone to interpret when required. Luganda is the local language and, although the Baganda are not great ones for joining the police or army, not being warrior types, we in fact have three, the sub-inspector and two constables. Most of the staff speak Luganda anyway as they just pick up these languages with great ease in the course of their duties.

We have two drivers as our transport consists of the usual black police tender and a fairly new Land Rover; both in constant use visiting scenes of crime and picking up live and dead bodies as required. There's a largish area to be covered and crimes have a way of taking place in or near villages well off the main roads or out in the bush in the middle of nowhere; and witnesses have to be searched for and then brought into the station or post to question them and for their statements to be recorded.

Wednesday 4 September

A middle-aged African, who in fact is regarded as an old man here, was arrested after he was found leading a youth with his hands tied, on the road to Kampala. His story was that he was going to sell the boy to the Fire Brigade. For some unknown reason there was long ago established in East Africa this superstition that the Fire Brigade buys people to eat.

It's not easy to find out how this belief came about but, apparently, it is prevalent among ignorant and illiterate Africans in the bush in various parts of Uganda and Kenya. It seems to have something to do with the fact that fire engines are red. Also, with no ambulances available, firemen have been known to put injured fire victims into their vehicle and drive off with them to the hospital. Possibly some died there, or on the way, and were thus not seen locally again. Also, in the past, when police transport was even scarcer than nowadays, fire tenders were sometimes pressed into service to assist the police and pick up drunks, vagrants and beggars; so locals would see them carted off in the fearsome red vehicles equipped with axes, ropes and so on, and they jumped to the wrong conclusion.

Saturday 7 September

There's quite an interesting little tale about how this place came to be called Mityana. In the old days – or should I say, once upon a time – with no transport available people walked long distances (many still do, in fact) meeting wild animals and enemy warriors on the way. From Bunyoro in the west the Banyoro men would walk the many miles to Kampala to look for work or for other reasons. When they reached the Saza (county) of Ssingo in Buganda there was a favourite resting place for travellers where a large tree gave them good cover and shelter for a night before continuing with their safari. When there was a wind the large branches of the tree rubbed together and moved about, sighing and groaning. The Banyoro named it *Emiti-Eyana* (the tree-making-music). The local Baganda took up the name and would say in Luganda: '*Tugende emitiyana*' (we are going to the tree-making-music). When the British came and heard about it they called the place simply Mityana, and it became a trading centre. And everyone lived happily ever after. Or something.

Sunday 8 September

I obtained a couple of constable volunteers to help me do something about the station recreation room, which is just a bare roam with practically nothing in it but some wooden chairs, a table and some junk. There was also a home-made draughts board with Pepsi-Cola and Mirinda bottle tops as pieces and a *mweso* board made of *mvule* wood by a carpenter in the local prison. I had received a bundle of colourful and quite interesting posters from the Information Department, which we have put up on the walls, and I produced some magazines, books, playing cards and a ludo set of my own. I had earlier removed the welfare radio and had it repaired so the place now looked a little brighter and was slightly better equipped. I've asked Provincial HQ in Kampala for some cash to purchase other indoor games as there is a Force Welfare Fund and I don't see why we shouldn't get some benefit from it here.

Monday 23 September

About a week ago Roger phoned me from GH and said that HE was due to visit West Mengo as part of his Buganda tour and that on his way back to Entebbe he wanted to drop in and see me. It was to be a personal visit not an official one, so no ceremony. Nevertheless, I had to report to Buganda Provincial HQ that the Governor was about to visit my station, because failure to do so would have put me in deep trouble afterwards with senior officers suffering from the HQ bureaucratic tyrant syndrome.

I tried to explain to the District Superintendent, a very dour Scot, that it was just a personal visit, but senior officers cannot imagine that such an elevated personage as the Governor would call on a junior officer, so the Senior Superintendent and the Superintendent both arrived at the station after lunch today. They clearly did not approve of such a visit and I think they wanted to blame me somehow for insubordination, but it was way above their heads. However, I was ordered to produce a guard of honour, which I knew HE would definitely not want or expect; so I merely paraded the men who were available in the station without rifles or putting on full dress. This was frowned upon but there was in fact no time to do anything else.

Blister seemed to sense the impending visit of his golfing chum and he became rather overexcited and interfered somewhat with the preparations for the parade as several of the constables usually make quite a fuss of him. This upset the SSP, who said I should do something about it. As both of the cells were empty for once, I shut him in one of them to keep him out of the way (Blister, not the SSP, though I would have preferred it to be the latter).

HE duly arrived with Roger and looked rather surprised to see the senior officers and the men on parade. The Superintendents were presented to him (that was obviously why they had come) and HE had a quick look at the parade and then turned to me and said: 'But where's my little Blister?'

I replied, 'I'm afraid he's in the clink doing time as he was disturbing the peace.'

HE asked for him to be let out, so I sent a constable to release the prisoner who had been granted clemency by the Governor. Shortly after, there was a white blur as Blister came out of the station at full speed and jumped straight into HE's arms, he was so pleased and delighted to see the boss again. The two Superintendents looked shocked and aghast at this grossly insubordinate demonstration of affection and started to protest and apologise, mentally putting me down for execution, no doubt; but HE ignored them and made a great fuss of him.

We walked aside and I apologised for the unwanted ceremony and HE said not to worry and asked how I was getting on. We exchanged news and I told him the sort of cases we deal with here. Then he got into the car, waved farewell and went on his way. I had to hold on to Blister's collar very firmly or he'd have been into the car with HE in a flash. Before the Superintendents disappeared, I took advantage of their presence to ask about the welfare cash; the SSP said that if I gave him a list of what we wanted he would try to obtain them and have them delivered. I already had my list prepared and handed it over. So that's fixed.

Wednesday 25 September

Kassi, our detective constable, has put in a report about a man he went to arrest on suspicion of being in possession of stolen property. He was a spanner boy, that is, an assistant to a garage mechanic, and when Kassi entered the small garage where he worked he was busy recharging some vehicle batteries. Kassi identified himself and, without a word, the man immediately lifted up one of the batteries and hit him in the face with it and broke two of his front teeth. A clear case of assault and battery.

Tuesday 1 October

Another homicide was reported yesterday afternoon. I took the Land Rover as the site was way off the road, along a *murram* track through a village, where we picked up the *Mutongole* chief, and into the bush for several miles until we reached a forest area and a narrow track where the vehicle had to be left. Lying on a footpath inside the jungle there was the body of a man. It looked as if he had been speared several times and then an attempt made to burn the body, particularly the face. As it had taken a day and a half for the report to reach us, by a messenger on foot, decomposition was well advanced and there was an unpleasant smell in the still, hot air of the forest. I had brought my camera with me, thinking it might be useful to take a photo of the scene, but I couldn't use it as it doesn't have a flashlight fitted and the light was too dim. So I sat on a fallen tree trunk and sketched the body and surroundings and added various measurements. Meanwhile Kassi went back to the village to make enquiries. Some curious villagers had followed us to the site, so the chief gave them the unpleasant task of carrying the body to the Land Rover. This morning Kassi returned to the village and, when he returned this evening, reported that he had someone who could identify the body as a missing relative. He also had information about a suspect who had a land dispute with the deceased and had disappeared for the moment. The chief has been told to bring him in if he reappears, as he probably will in time, since he owns land there.

I drove to Kasanda post later this morning. On arrival I asked the SD constable: 'Where's the corporal?'

'Not in the post, sir.'

'I know that, so where is he?'

'Out, sir.'

'But where is he?'

'He went, sir.'

'Well, where did he went?'

'Don't know, sir.'

Friday 4 October

I drove all the way back to Entebbe today as I've been seconded there for ten days on special duty. I left the sub-inspector in charge of the station and told him to ring up the District Superintendent if there are any problems. I said: 'Don't hesitate to bother him. He's got nothing to do but push paper around anyway.'

The Secretary of State for the Colonies, Alan Lennox-Boyd, arrives by air tomorrow to hold talks with the Governors of Uganda, Kenya and Tanganyika and the Resident of Zanzibar, all of whom will be staying at GH. Special Branch are dealing with all the external security but, in view of my recent job here, I've been put in charge of internal GH security with an increased uniform police guard on both gates and patrolling the grounds. I'm staying at the Lake Victoria Hotel, but I don't expect to see much of my room there as I shall be spending each day at GH in uniform on duty. However, HE has insisted that I should rejoin the ADCs and have my meals there too.

For the talks to last so long they must be covering a lot of ground. Mainly, I suppose, they are considering the local politicians' increasingly pressing demands in each of the territories for self-government, or *uhuru* (freedom) as the political types have now taken to calling it; though many people here of all races think it's still a long way off.

Saturday 5 October

Of the visiting Governors who arrived this morning, I had previously met Sir Evelyn Baring of Kenya in Mombasa when I collected the Crawfords last February. Sir Edward Twining of Tanganyika is a large man, good-humoured and friendly, whom the others all address as 'Twinks'. Zanzibar is regarded as being too small to rate a Governor and so the ruling Sultan is provided with a British Resident, roughly equivalent to a provincial commissioner. The Colonial Secretary, who is also a large man and about as tall as *Kali* Charlie, has the permanent secretary of his ministry with him as an adviser. This evening, after I checked the guard and the perimeter and impressed on them that nobody was to be allowed into GH without my permission, I went back to the hotel to change into DJ, which I had naturally brought with me, knowing the form, then back to GH for HE's excellent cocktails and dinner.

Monday 7 October

Yesterday being Sunday, the visitors relaxed and it was decided in the afternoon that they would all go down to the Botanical Gardens and talk to the birds and trees for a change. So Roger sent for the Austin Princess and we packed all five of them in, three Governors, the Colonial Secretary and the Resident Zanzibar. It was a tight fit and there was no space left for an ADC to accompany them as Lennox-Boyd chose to sit in front with the driver where there was more leg-room. I offered to follow with Roger in my car but HE said not to bother, they'd be OK.

I'm only responsible for GH security, not outside visits, so I merely informed the only SB officer on Sunday duty where they were going and left them to it. When they returned late for tea they came into GH laughing like school kids who've been up to some mischief. Apparently, after driving into the Botanical Gardens and enjoying a pleasant afternoon there, they started back to GH for tea but, once on the main road, the Austin decided to have one of its periodical break-downs. So the local inhabitants were entertained by the edifying spectacle of a large black limousine flying a flag and being pushed by Her Majesty's Secretary of State for the Colonies and three Colonial Governors until it reached a slope and got started again. As they came in, Twinks and the others were pulling HE's leg about the state of his transport, with much laughter. They thought it was a great lark but, when Lady C heard about it, she was not amused and said: 'Somebody must be told.'

Thursday 10 October

At the cocktail hour this evening HE and *Ses Excellences*, as he refers to his colleagues, were at one end of the library, where HE was dispensing his own special concoction, while the two ADCs and I were chatting at the other end. Suddenly the huge Lennox-Boyd loomed over us asking: 'What's going on here? What are you chaps giggling at?'

So I told him about a recent political demonstration in Kampala where the participants were carrying home-made banners indicating how unpopular we are. In one case the sign was supposed to read: WE ARE FED UP WITH BRITISH RULE, This was too many words for the painter to get on to one placard, so he had divided it in two, and the two men holding the placards had been strictly instructed by the organising politician to stand next to each other all the time. However, in the general excitement and milling crowds pushing people around, they became separated. The result was that there were now two quite separate placards. One said: WE ARE FED and the other some yards away said: UP WITH BRITISH RULE.

Friday 11 October

I decided to test whether anything useful had been done about the GH security alarm bell which the gate guard had ignored when I tested it earlier in the year. So I went up to the landing inside GH and pressed the bell push. Shortly after that the corporal and two constables appeared at the main door carrying rifles and out of breath. That was OK, so I asked the corporal what else he had done. He replied that he had closed the main gates and the back gate and ordered the sentries to allow nobody through. This was correct procedure. I walked with him down to the guardroom, where we found a very angry Commissioner of Police in his staff car outside the closed gates.

Apparently he'd been sent for by HE to explain and discuss some security matters at their conference and now he was late. He was not too happy about that. I quickly had the gates opened and explained about my security alarm test and said that the sentry was just obeying standing orders. The Commissioner showed a definite lack of interest in this and sped up the slope to GH looking quite cross.

117

Sunday 13 October

The conference ended yesterday at noon and, after lunch, the Colonial Secretary and visiting Governors were taken down to the airport for their departures. We had no security upsets during the week, which was a great relief. But I've been on continuous day duty, with checks on the guard every night, since I came here, so I'll be glad to get away. Lady C asked me to a family dinner yesterday evening. As there were no visitors left and we'd all had a heavy week, she allowed us to appear in suits instead of DJs. But I still had to go back to the hotel first to change out of uniform, so it really didn't make much difference. Still, it was a pleasantly relaxed meal and I had quite enjoyed the interlude. At least I was doing my proper job here this time. I drove back to Mityana today and checked in at the station on arrival, finding all more or less in order.

Tuesday 15 October

A day for administrative matters. The elephant grass growing around my quarters on the hillside has become very long in my absence and Ephraim reports seeing snakes around; so the barracks sergeant contacted the ALG prison and had a gang of convicts marched up here with grass slashers to clear the area.

I found PC Okello in uniform pottering around the station barefooted and with no hat on. He produced a chit from the medical assistant at the local clinic excusing him from wearing boots because of a badly swollen foot, the result of a hornet sting. I told him to wear canvas shoes or flip-flops and then asked why he was not wearing his fez. Okello said that he thought that, if he couldn't wear boots with uniform, he ought not to wear a hat either. Some logic. His name ought to be O'Kelly not Okello.

On my desk I found a handwritten application for leave from PC Onyango. He wants to go home to his village, where his wife 'is almost pregnant'. I sent for him and asked how she could be only almost pregnant. He replied: 'Well, I have not been there yet.'

Thursday 17 October

I dropped in at Kasanda Police Post this morning to check up about a serious assault case – a drunken dispute that resulted in one bystander being badly cut up with a *panga*. The post was in a turmoil, both on and off duty men running around with sticks, one waving a spear that was an exhibit in a case. They were rattling around in the cupboard, under the counter and poking sticks around outside the post building, and all the time shouting excitedly. I grabbed PC Rubanga's arm as he rushed past and demanded to know what was happening. He said breathlessly: 'There is a very dangerous cobbler hiding in the post somewhere, sir.'

So there was a mad shoe repairer at large. 'What has he done? Is he armed?' I asked.

'No, sir; it's a cobbler, a bad snake.' The southern Bantu tribes have this peculiar problem with the letters *l* and *r* which, for no good reason, they switch around and interchange heedlessly and indifferently as the fancy takes them, both in their own language as well as in English. So we get 'cobbler' for cobra and 'reopards' and 'rizards', 'lerations' and 'ploblems'. Someone described as a 'royal' person is usually one who is faithful and reliable, without a title. No amount of education seems to get rid of this odd habit. I've heard a Muganda doctor speaking of a 'reper corony' and of a 'plegnant' woman being in 'rabour'. In a PM report concerning a case of strangulation the larynx was described as the 'ralynx', sounding like some rare animal. One who has flown in from abroad is likely to be asked: 'Did you have a good fright?' They can pronounce both letters with equal facility so it's not like the problem an oriental has. It's just something they do. Meanwhile, the cobra had escaped from very noisy lawful custody and sensibly disappeared.

Saturday 26 October

At the request of the station footballers, who think they're pretty good, I contacted the OC Police at Mubende, about 60 miles to the west of us, and issued a challenge to a friendly match to take place here, followed by a feast. They accepted and turned up this afternoon and utterly defeated us by five goals to two. Two of their players are really hot stuff who sometimes play in the Force team and they ran rings around our lot, after which they apparently all enjoyed the post-match booze-up. I looked in for a short while and then left them to it. Their OC had not come with them as he had had to go out on a murder enquiry.

Monday 28 October

Kassi sidled into my office this morning and reported that an *mdukizi* (informer) of his had told him where a home-made shotgun – he called it a 'short gun' – was hidden in a hut in a small village a few miles out into the bush to the north of Mityana. I took him with Corporal Omara, who was in uniform, in my car and drove first to the *Muluka* chief's hut and told him we were going to carry out a search, without mentioning what we were looking for as other people were present. The chief called his ALG askari, also in uniform, and we walked towards the other huts.

In order to protect his informer, whose identity only Kassi knew, we searched two other huts first. At the entrance of each we stopped and, according to custom, I called out: '*Hodi?*' (may I enter?) to which the occupants gave the standard reply: '*Karibu*' (come in). The chief explained that we were searching huts and then stepped aside and waited outside while we carried out our search around the meagre home-made wooden furniture covered with the usual blue cotton cloth colourfully embroidered with flowers by the wives and daughters. As usual, we made sure that anything moved was replaced and nothing was damaged and then passed on to the next hut.

When we came to the suspect's hut he greeted us effusively and tried to be very friendly and helpful – enough to make any policeman suspicious. The usual and not very original hiding place for illegal firearms is in the grass-thatched roof. Corporal Omara is well over 6 feet tall, with long arms, which was why I had brought him along, and while he checked the roof I poked around behind the furniture and inside an old suitcase looking for ammunition. With his long reach Omara rootled about in the roof thatching with a stick and, after dislodging a disgruntled rat that had been sleeping peacefully up there, he pulled out a rather primitive-looking shotgun made of a length of piping and pieces of metal probably rescued from old bicycles and cars. It was not loaded and the mechanism seemed to work reasonably well when I tried it outside.

While Kassi handcuffed the man, who loudly protested his innocence, saying that he didn't know that it was there and, in any case, he was only looking after it for his brother, the chief quickly declared his ignorance of the gun's existence, otherwise he would have reported ... etc. We continued searching for ammunition and dug up the earth floor around the hut support poles and under the beds but found nothing. While they took the accused to my car, I spoke to the chief severely and warned him to be more vigilant and watchful in future. I added that his superior chiefs at the *Saza* and *Gombolola* would not be very pleased to hear about his failure as an effective and efficient village chief responsible for its security. Meanwhile, he was to ensure that the relatives of the accused's wife and children were informed so as to look after them while the man was away for a long spell in prison. I said I'd be back next week to check that this had been done.

Thursday 31 October

The corporal in charge of Tondola Police Post is a fine marksman and a member of the Force Rifle Shooting Team. Today I tried him on orderly room on a charge of neglecting his duty. A homicide was reported at his post last week and he didn't bother to go to the scene, although he is bound by standing orders to attend the scene of any serious crime reported to him. In addition, he has to send a report to the OC station, and he did neither. When the report did reach me, brought directly by the village chief who had waited vainly for the Tondola police to appear, I went straight there with him, and called at Tondola on the way. The body was well decomposed by that time and various problems were caused by the delay, including the disappearance of the suspect.

Consequently I was not too pleased about it and, when the corporal offered no explanation for his laxity, I immediately warned him for orderly room. It was most unfortunate as, up until then, he was a competent NCO in charge of the post, but when today he still offered no explanation or excuse, I had no choice but to convict him and take away his stripes. Reduction in rank is a punishment subject to confirmation by the Commissioner, so I've sent the papers to Provincial HQ for transmission to Police HQ and requested his immediate transfer to another station, as I believe it would be embarrassing for him to remain here as a constable after being an NCO for so long. Fortunately it won't affect his membership of the rifle team, but he'll have to earn his promotion all over again, which will take some time with this black mark against his name. We all do foolish things occasionally and then we have to pay the price.

Friday 1 November

For some time now we've been searching for the *waragi* distillers around Busunju. *Waragi* is a very fierce and potent, 100 per cent proof spirit distilled from bananas, the making, possessing, selling and drinking of which is illegal. It is very popular because it's cheap to make, but it does have a tendency to kill or blind or render insane those who over-indulge. We know that it is mainly manufactured in the area around Busunju Police Station, but searching the area and questioning locals has not revealed the main hiding place where it's distilled or stocked.

However, yesterday fate stepped in and, during a very heavy and continuous rainfall, the near by Mayanja River overflowed its banks. Shortly after this a considerable number of large drums containing *waragi* were washed away from their hiding place beside the river by a strong current. They were hotly pursued along the river banks by frantic distillers. The Busunju chaps rounded them up and, with the help of men provided by the *Miruka* chief, they pulled the drums ashore as exhibits. But I wonder how much of the contents will mysteriously disappear before the case comes to court.

Monday 4 November

When I first came to Mityana I saw that there was a single bench against the wall on the public side of the station counter in the charge room. This is where the complainants, victims, witnesses and others wait until they receive some attention from whomever's on duty behind the counter. Sometimes it's a long wait. I couldn't help noticing that the men always sat on the bench and the women were left to sit on the concrete floor, even if pregnant or carrying a baby; which meant most of them. I am well aware that in Africa it's a man's world and he regards women and girls as chattels to serve him and do all the work and take second place in every aspect of life. It's something I find offensive and unacceptable.

I had seen the same at CPS Kampala and Katwe Police Station when I was there, of course, but I wasn't in charge at either of those stations. Here I am the boss, so I decided to do it my way. I therefore ordered the men off the bench and decreed it was for women only. The men could stand or sit on the floor. This didn't please anybody and the constables thought it extraordinary. The men from the public objected and protested loudly and the women were embarrassed. So I said: 'Too bad. While I'm in charge here, this is the way it will be. After that someone else can decide.' That was over two months ago. These days everybody quietly follows the new rule without any trouble or bother.

Friday 8 November

Yesterday we had a full inspection of the station by the Senior Superintendent which meant a full dress parade for everyone who was not actually on station duty and an inspection of the barracks and compound and, of course, all the records and files, the vehicles and the armoury. We were prepared for it and it went well. I left Blister at home so as to avoid any disruption of the proceedings and we had no awkward visits from snakes, straying cattle or local lunatics, which made a change. The SSP had brought with him a few items purchased for our recreation room, which I handed over to the barracks sergeant. When I saw the SSP off in his car he appeared to be reasonably well satisfied. His chief worry seemed to be that the road back is under repair and about to be resurfaced for several miles and consequently is very dusty, which might spoil his expensive new uniform cap.

He had told me that the previous OC, from whom I had taken over temporarily, is not returning to this station but has been posted elsewhere. HQ is trying an experiment and this is to be the first up-country station to have an African gazetted officer as OC. The officer selected is just completing a course at a police college in the UK and he will be arriving to take over from me on 12 December. This is fine by me as I've been informed that I'm booked to fly home on leave on 17 December.

Thursday 14 November

After a considerable amount of agitating and bothering the authorities concerned, I managed to persuade the Works people to come out and build an additional block of latrines for the barracks, as those there were inadequate for the number of people in the lines. I thought this was a useful achievement and so couldn't resist writing to the District Superintendent and inviting him to come and cut the ribbon and declare them open. Of course, I unwisely failed to take into account that he is a dour Scot with no visible sense of humour. Today I received his reply. There was practically smoke coming out of the envelope. In fact, the letter didn't reply to mine; it merely ordered me immediately on receipt of this letter to remove the copy of my letter of invitation from the station file and destroy it (should I use high explosive?) and then to report in writing, with a copy on the file, of course, that I had complied with this order. There was added an injunction that I must never again write an official letter containing such disrespectful flippancy. Och aye, the noo.

So I sent my report as follows: 'This letter is to confirm that the order contained in your letter about my previous letter has been carried out.' I suppose I shall now be posted back to CPS as OC Nuts again or as Accommodation Officer at Nsambya barracks. Still, I've been out here for almost three years and I'm leave-happy and consequently slightly doolally. Perhaps this will be taken into consideration when passing sentence.

Sunday 17 November

Each year the members of the Entebbe Club put on a Christmas show; more of a satirical review than a panto. Entebbe is the centre of government administration and it gives the club members a chance to have a go at their seniors. This year, I'm told, their scenery painter has produced an amusing backdrop. The central theme referred to the three East African Governors, Crawford of Uganda, Baring of Kenya and Twining of Tanganyika on a grocery theme. Thus, in succession from the top to bottom, the backdrop read:

TWINING'S TEA – BARING'S BISCUITS –
CRAWFORD'S CRACKERS.

Tuesday 3 December

The SD constable rang me at home late yesterday evening to tell me that Busunju post had reported that there had been a fatal traffic accident on the Hoima road. I drove down to the station and collected the traffic corporal and then on to Busunju. When I entered the post it was very dark and only a pressure lamp was burning as there's no electricity there yet. Stretched out on the top of the counter, as if lying in state, was PC Odoch, the SD constable, zizzing away happily. He was recently posted here from the PTS and is quickly learning the form. His truncheon was lying nearby so I picked it up and brought it down with a crash on to the counter, close to his head, at the same time shouting: 'FIRE!'

He shot upright, fell off the counter and ran straight out of the door into the darkness. A moment later he came back in blinking and sheepishly said: 'I can't find the fire.'

I said: 'You were asleep on duty, Odoch.'

'No, sir, I wasn't asleep; I was just thinking.' He trotted out the standard reply throughout the Force. Maybe it's taught at the PTS now.

'Well, think about this then; where exactly is the traffic accident?' Having obtained this information and collected their reserve constable, we proceeded to the scene. Policemen never go anywhere; they always proceed to and from places. So that's what we did.

Thursday 5 December

In the mail this morning there was a letter from a local school-leaver who wants to join the Force. He finished his letter with: 'In conclusion, sir, I enclose my school certificate and remains. Yours faithfully...'

Monday 16 December

After handing over the station and sending my kit and boxes by lorry to PWD storage in Kampala, I drove there for a night in a hotel before I depart by air tomorrow. After checking in at the hotel I took my car to the PWD storage, where it will be put on blocks and looked after for the eight months I shall be away. My leave is actually supposed to be for six months but, when I reported in to Police HQ, I was told that the Director of Training wanted to see me. He gave me the bad news that I am to attend a senior CID course at Wakefield Police College for four months; and that a half of the course period would come out of my leave entitlement, making it eight months that I shall be absent. Far too long, in my opinion.

What a way to spend one's leave – four months as a reluctant student. I'm definitely not looking forward to it. I saw one or two people to say cheerio to and then arranged for transport to the airport tomorrow. Ephraim and his wife came to Kampala in the lorry with my kit and they have gone off on their long safari to his home village in Northern Rhodesia until I return. I handed Blister over to the Kampala agent for Dundori Kennels in Nakuru, Kenya, where he is to board in my absence.

Thursday 19 December – At Iserlohn, West Germany

My first long-distance flight was from Entebbe in a four-engined BOAC Argonaut Speedbird. It took 22 hours, with stops to refuel in Khartoum, Benghazi and Rome. When we arrived at Heathrow I collected my luggage and then went to another terminal for European flights as I had to go straight to Germany in order to be in time for the wedding on Saturday the 21st. On arrival there I needed directions and naturally addressed a German airport official in Swahili. He seemed quite surprised. As it is a military wedding I've brought my uniform with me, which added to the bulk of my luggage. It is the middle of winter here and really cold after coming straight from the equator at the hottest time of the year. Consequently I was immediately struck down with the dreaded flu. Somehow I have to remain on my feet to do my best man stuff and then perhaps I can succumb.

Tuesday 24 December – In Wiltshire

The wedding went off well and I got through it somehow, though I was unable to remain on my feet during the service and I gave up on the speech after croaking a couple of sentences. I flew back to England yesterday with my parents, only to find that their house had been burgled in their absence. Neighbours had called the police and there is fingerprint powder everywhere plus a broken kitchen window. Nothing much is missing, I gather, but it's not the best way to celebrate Christmas.

1958

Friday 11 April – In Wakefield, Yorkshire

After a week touring the Rhine and visiting Cologne, the Möhne Dam, Luxemburg, and tasting the wonderful Rhine wines, I reported most reluctantly to the Wakefield Police College to be taught something about criminal investigation. The students on the course are from various Commonwealth police forces as well as a few, marked for promotion, from different British forces. At the opening of the course we were each asked to stand and introduce ourselves. I dislike this sort of thing and I stood up and said the first thing that came into my head, which got me off to a bad start. I said that, when I left the Army and joined the Colonial Police, I knew nothing of police work so, naturally, I was appointed to be an instructor at the Police Training School. The other students were considerably amused but there were some very sour looks from members of the College staff, who probably thought I was getting at them. He's a trouble-maker, I could imagine them thinking.

Friday 30 May

This course goes on and on. There is clearly a vast difference between police investigative practices and equipment in a British city and those in the middle of the African bush. A great deal of what they teach here is irrelevant in Africa, so I let it float past me. I'm well aware that proper policemen everywhere aim to get into CID as soon as they can manage it. However, I've no wish to get out of uniform so I shall not be volunteering for CID in Uganda. I'm happy working in an up-country police station or, even better, teaching at the PTS. I'd like to have a posting to the Police College, where they hold advanced courses; but I want to be there as an instructor not a student as I am here.

I'm told that I shall be informed of my next posting before I return to Uganda, and that one doesn't have a choice in the matter. As I've been doing since my first year in Uganda, I've continued every month to send in articles and cartoons for publication in *Habari*. It's a good little magazine now and a copy of each issue is sent to me here, or wherever I am.

Friday 13 June

I told the Chief Superintendent who runs this place that I have important business to see to in London and so have taken four days off from

126

the course, although he wasn't very happy about it. I reckon that they can carry on without me. On Wednesday I met Mike, one of our officers who recently arrived on leave, at a pub in London. He'd been delegated by the Commissioner to inform me that my next posting will be as Staff Officer to the Commissioner at HQ. It sounds ominously like another ADC-type job to me. No doubt he's sensibly taking advantage of my experience in GH but I am not overjoyed at the prospect. I prefer running my own small show to being at the beck and call of someone else. However, there it is; I'll just have to make the best of it. Mike has already done a spell in that post, which was why he'd been chosen to brief me and pass on a few hints.

Yesterday, Thursday, I attended the Queen's Birthday Parade on Horseguards. I had written for a ticket as soon as I arrived on leave. It's an impressive parade and so well done. Unfortunately, it was a rainy day and showers came and went during the parade. The Queen rode her police horse and was accompanied by the Dukes of Edinburgh and Gloucester, all three in Guards uniform. After the parade I went to a restaurant where a lunch had been arranged for past and present officers of the Uganda Police. Several officers on leave were present and I met some old-timers, blokes who had 'walked up from the coast', now long since retired. Then back to the awful Wakefield by train this evening after an enjoyable break.

Thursday 19 June – At Wakefield

I've been wearing corduroy trousers and a sports jacket while attending this wretched course and today I decided to put the corduroys in for dry-cleaning. Behind the counter of a small dry-cleaners a very snooty young woman looked at them, sniffed, and said: 'We don't take industrial clothing here.' I said that there was nothing industrial about my clothing, but she would not relent; so I withdrew and left her to her prejudice and ignorance.

Friday 11 July

The course ended and we all dispersed this morning. Last week the Chief Superintendent interviewed each student. He asked me what I would be doing when I return to Uganda and, when I told him that I'm to be Staff Officer to the Commissioner, his eyebrows rose in surprise. 'But that's an important job,' he said. So?

I went by rail down to Wiltshire for a short stay with my parents before returning to Africa and took with me one of our inspectors, Ernest Mulabi, who had been attending another course at Wakefield. I wanted him to see some other parts of England before he returns.

We took him to see Stonehenge and Salisbury Cathedral and other interesting places around Wiltshire. He showed us a photo of his wife and 11 children, his 'football team' as he calls them.

Monday 28 July

Back in Uganda at last. I arrived on Friday afternoon after a long, tiring flight and have spent the weekend in the Imperial Hotel in Kampala getting things organised. Blister arrives tomorrow by train from Kenya and I'll pick him up in the late afternoon. I reported to the Commissioner this morning. My office is opposite his in the single-storey HQ building and it's quite spacious. He knows very well that I don't care for this type of stooge job in attendance on others, but he is unrepentant and will certainly not go to heaven. Anyway, I told him that I should like to be posted up-country as soon as possible and he retaliated by making it clear that he considers that my time in GH will prove very useful in this job so I should just get on with it. So that's what I'll do. But I must try to avoid making myself indispensable in any way.

Chas is with HQ CID now and is caretaking the Deputy Commissioner's residence while he is on long leave. There are no vacant bungalows in the hostel at the moment so Chas suggested that I should move into the Deputy's house. There are plenty of rooms and it's near HQ. The Deputy's wife has left her horrible dachshund, which the Deputy had named Panya – not telling her that it is Swahili for 'rat'. Apparently he's not too fond of it either. Their houseboy feeds it and Chas takes it for walkies, under the present arrangement. I hope that Blister and Panya are able to get along without hostilities breaking out.

Wednesday 30 July

The Staff Officer looks after the Commissioner's diary with regard to official meetings and functions; the HQ staff cars for senior officers; the staff car drivers and the Commissioner's tours of inspection; and deals with files and other matters passed on by the Commissioner. All of his visitors to HQ first report to my office, no matter how senior they are, so I get some idea of what's going on. In fact, the people to ask about what's really happening are the staff car drivers and the messenger who makes the tea.

Blister arrived looking very smart, having been given a very professional clipping, and he has obviously been well looked after; and just as well, since eight months in the kennels was an expensive business. He was bursting with energy and excitement after his long train journey, so he took me for a long walk which was more of a run. He and Panya circled each other and sniffed and decided to make friends rather than make war. So that's all right.

Friday 1 August

Things have been moving while I've been away. A police dog section has been started, with four dogs and an experienced British dog handler recruited. One of the dogs is already trained; I think they obtained it from Kenya. They are to be used as tracker dogs and, of course, for chasing after and catching escaping suspects. They are not guard dogs.

Another innovation in Kampala is our first set of traffic lights. These caused a peculiar problem for African road users, who found their own inimitable solution. It seems that they saw European motorists going through the lights when they were green and noted a number of Asian drivers shooting through when the lights were yellow. From this they have deduced that green was for Europeans to go, yellow was for Asians to go; which left only red for Africans to go, so they went on red. Traffic Branch chaps report that numerous African drivers, when stopped and cautioned for driving through red lights, stated their firm belief in this three-colour go system. The word had somehow gone out. So, for a time, a traffic constable had to be stationed at the lights to stop and educate offenders.

The large new five-storey building housing Central Police Station, Kampala Traffic Branch and Provincial and District HQ, was completed and opened in May; and the old compound containing what was the comparatively small CPS and the Traffic Branch, as well as the old wooden building housing the traffic court, have all been demolished to make way for main post office extensions and other buildings.

Thursday 14 August

The news from Jinja is that the DC's house was recently broken into at night and a quantity of his clothing was stolen. The DC's residence is near the golf course (naturally) so, as soon as the report came in, the constables in the station who were about to go on night beats were taken out to search the area of the golf course, which happened to be the most likely line of retreat for the thief or thieves. A man carrying a large bundle was seen and whistles were blown, shouts were shouted and fingers were pointed. He promptly dropped the bundle and ran towards the bank of Lake Victoria, which at that point was 20 feet high. Nevertheless, he jumped into the water and made a magnificent splash.

Torches were directed at the place but he was not seen and two constables entered the water to search among the papyrus but found nothing. Then the OC Police had a brainwave and picked up a large rock, which he hurled into the water, creating a surface disturbance. At the same time he shouted: '*Mamba! Mamba!*' (crocodile). The constables on the bank took up the cry and shouted it although they could see nothing. The two constables in the water believed what they heard, panicked and rushed to the bank and were out of the lake in a shot, closely followed by the thief, who had been hiding in the papyrus close by and ran straight into the arms of the law. They didn't teach that sort of thing at Wakefield.

Wednesday 24 September

As the Deputy Commissioner is almost due back from leave, I moved out of his desirable residence last weekend and into a bungalow at Kitante Hostel, and had a telephone installed as I have to be contactable at all times, so I'm told. Last night someone broke into my car, parked outside the bungalow, and pinched the tool kit. I've reported it to Wandegeya Police Station, which covers this area, but I hold out no hope of recovering anything. Vehicle tools are easily disposed of and not so easily identifiable; so I'll just have to buy a new set.

It seems that one of the chaps living here some time ago had his car broken into on two nights and was so fed up that he deliberately left an empty briefcase on the seat as bait one night, with the car parked very close to his bungalow. He then connected a wire to the nearest car door handle and plugged it into the mains indoors. The next morning he overslept, was late for work, and rushed out to his car, seized the door handle and received a nasty electrical shock which severely rattled his teeth. No doubt it did him a power of good.

Friday 26 September

The present Commissioner, after reading history at Cambridge, served for ten years in the Ceylon Police Force; members of which, I gather, are a snobbish lot who regard themselves as the cream of the colonial police forces. He received accelerated promotions in other forces until coming here as Commissioner at an unusually early age. Obviously a high-flyer.

I was told some time ago that, if the Commissioner decides that an officer here has made it, or shown form, or been accepted, or whatever, he will be invited to join him on one of his duck shoots down in Ankole or Kigezi. I've no idea whether this is so and such things don't interest me. However, yesterday the Commissioner invited me to join his duck-shooting party this weekend. I've never been attacked or even threatened by a duck, so I explained to him that I enjoy photographing birds and animals but I won't hunt or shoot them, so it was a case of thank you, but no thank you. He merely said: 'That's all right,' and I suppose he found someone else without much difficulty. Fortunately, I don't want this job at HQ so it wouldn't worry me if I suddenly found myself transferred elsewhere. He knows this, of course, so I probably won't be. No such luck.

Tuesday 30 September

I called into Nakasero Hospital this afternoon, where Bob, one of our officers, whom I had previously served with in the Army, is in with bilharzia, caught from swimming in the lake. It's a most debilitating disease and he was not at all well. The problem is it de-energises and can be recurring and is very weakening.

Wednesday 8 October

Last year, as a result of representations and political agitation, it was decided that there must be direct elections for African representatives from all districts in the Legislative Council and an ordinance was passed by LegCo to this effect. So the elections to be held this month will be the first direct elections in Uganda. However, the chiefs and elders who make up the Buganda Lukiiko, as usual, decided to be awkward and sulk, so they have rejected direct elections in Buganda, which their own politicians had been demanding for so long. This is a part of their policy of rejecting or obstructing everything proposed by the Protectorate Government.

The Supervisor of Elections is my namesake, the Head of the Civil Service. The Commissioner told me that it would be my job to organise the movement of the massive police reinforcements from all over Buganda, where they will not now be needed, to all the other districts where elections will take place. There they will assist in policing the polling stations and generally help the locally based police to provide extra security in their areas. They will all be unarmed, of course. I have to find transport and work out a timetable of movements and select which units go to which place and how and when. So I need to produce a single, comprehensive operation order which, at the same time, is not over-complicated.

I've been given nobody to assist me in this nor have I asked for anyone. I spent a week going round town hiring buses, booking special trains and obtaining numbers and locations of all available reinforce-

131

ments and allocating suitable transport according to destinations. Next, I worked out a fairly complicated movement order and then simplified it as much as possible and put it into the operation order. This has been typed on to stencils and checked and printed, complete with movement tables and all conceivable points covered; I hope.

I took the final version to the Commissioner and asked him to sign it so as to give it his full authority. He seemed quite impressed and said that I should sign it as it was all my work. I pointed out that it gave orders and instructions to Provincial Police Commanders and other senior officers and, from their point of view, it would be better coming directly from the Commissioner. It's nonsense really since I regularly sign Force Orders for him and I haven't heard anyone complain about that. However, he did what he was told and signed it and now copies have gone out in all directions.

Thursday 16 October

I've had a busy two days as I had decided to make sure that my operation order was being carried out as written. So I've been seeing off trains and buses filled with reinforcements from various Kampala police stations and Nsambya barracks as well as from the College and PTS; making sure that they departed at their correct times in the day or night for the north, east and west. Consequently, I haven't spent much time in the office. When the Commissioner saw me pop in there today he grinned and said that I should be wearing an armband indicating that I'm a Movement Control Officer.

For additional supervision and a security overwatch generally, the Commissioner is flying north to Gulu this afternoon in an aircraft borrowed from the Kenya Police Air Wing. I've sent his staff car up there in advance to meet him on arrival. The Deputy Commissioner has driven off to Fort Portal to watch over the Western Province, and Prune Face has gone to Mbale or Jinja or somewhere in the east, and hopefully got lost. So all our senior officers and their staff cars have departed and so have two radio officers, thus leaving the place almost empty except for the duty signallers and me.

Saturday 18 October

Isn't it marvellous? In election week, when communications are most important, the Post Office has decided to bring into service the new PABX telephone system and, as Police HQ has to be connected directly to CPS and Nsambya barracks, all of our HQ telephones have had to be disconnected for this purpose. So we're out of touch with everybody. Mind you, the general feeling outside is that we are always out of touch anyway. Of course, the police radio connecting all stations is still in action, but it's extremely busy with all the additional signal traffic at this time. Anyway, it's certainly been very peaceful here with all the senior officers away and the telephones dead. I was pleased to hear over our radio that all the reinforcements arrived at their correct destinations in accordance with *Mein Fuehrer*'s orders.

Monday 20 October

The arrangement was that, as election results are published in each district, they would be telephoned by the local supervisor through the police to me at home during the weekend; and I would then pass them along by phone to my namesake, the Supervisor of Elections, at his Entebbe residence, where, no doubt, Mrs A was busily doing the flowers. So I had to stay in all weekend for this purpose. Hardly a fun-filled two days. Still, I'm pleased that it has gone more or less as planned and no unlawful incidents of any significance have been reported.

Saturday 25 October

This evening I was in the bar of the Lake Victoria Hotel at Entebbe talking to Mathias, a young Muganda who was educated in England and now works for an insurance company in Kampala. I asked him what he'd have to drink. He looked around the small bar, no doubt noticing that he was the only African present, and, smiling mischievously, said in a loud voice: 'What I'd like is a white lady. A large one, please.' There was shocked silence as the Europeans in the bar looked at us and then realised that it was a cocktail being ordered and embarrassedly got on with their drinks and conversations.

As we were leaving the bar later, one of the Europeans, whom I know slightly, said to me out of the corner of his mouth: 'I suppose you think that's funny?' I did.

Saturday 1 November

In September I decided for a lark to join the Kampala Amateur Theatrical Society (the KATS), as it is quite a few years since I last tripped the boards and they have a reputation for putting on good performances. Each year there is the Uganda Drama Festival for all local amateur dramatic societies; and there are quite a number of them, Asian, African and European. Societies that enter the competition are required to put on a one-act play or a single act selected from a longer play. It's all taken very seriously, with the Governor as Patron of the

133

Festival and the Adjudicator is a professional brought out from the UK to judge the entries. This year it's Norman Marshall, a member of the Guild of Drama Adjudicators. The performances take place over several days at the Makerere College Hall. Some of the larger societies, including the KATS, have two entries. I am in their second entry, *A Rose Without a Thorn*. This took place on the second evening and it consisted of three scenes which take place in Hampton Court and the Tower, concerning King Henry VIII and the trial of Catherine Howard for adultery on charges brought by Archbishop Cranmer in 1542.

There were two police officers in it: John, a superintendent in SB, was John Lascelles and I was the Earl of Hertford. For this amazing performance I wore a short beard and used some talcum powder to whiten the sides of my hair as I was supposed to be middle-aged; and I had quite a shock when I looked in the mirror. There was a long speech to learn for the trial scene which seemed to go all right, and the audience appeared to enjoy our play almost as much as we did.

Monday 3 November

The *Uganda Argus* has given a good write-up to the various plays in the Festival and it reported the final results. An Asian group called The Kampala Youth League (sounds more like a political party) won the cup for the best all-round performance. The Adjudicator listed seven actors, each from a different society, whom he commended for outstanding individual performances and my name was in it for the KATS. He said that I had 'portrayed a man of authority, distinction and intelligence with light and shade, variety of tone and tempo, especially with Hertford's long speech'.

What a comparison with 12 years ago when I was still in my teens. The drama society to which I then belonged entered the annual local drama festival with what was supposed to be a serious costume drama of about the same period as *Rose*. In it, at one stage, I had to pick up this fair, buxom maid and carry her, and say dramatically: 'Oh, Florence, I could hold you in my arms like this for ever.' So I picked up this girl, who was rather heavier than I, and said the words as dramatically and sincerely as I could as I sank to my knees and collapsed miserably on to the stage under my excess baggage. Instead of weeping at the wonderful sentiment, the audience fell about laughing. She was naturally furious and I was embarrassed and we were not well placed in the final marks list. Still, that's show business, as we Thespians say.

Sunday 9 November

It's Remembrance Day. The Governor and the Commissioner were among those attending the ceremony at the Kampala War Memorial. The 25-pounder field gun of the Special Constabulary fired at 11 a.m. to commence the two minutes' silence and, since they were on Gun Hill and out of sight from the War Memorial, it was essential to get the timing right. The Commissioner said: 'You were in the Artillery, so you can do it.' Thus I was at the War Memorial with a walkie-talkie in contact with the Specials chap commanding the gun detachment. I gave the order 'Fire!' at the start of the silence, hoping that they had remembered to load with blank ammunition.

Wednesday 12 November

I met Mike Kagwa in town today. He's a Muganda and the only African Crown Counsel; at present he's taking his turn as a Resident Magistrate. He was recruited while he was in England after he had been called to the Bar, so he reckons he ought to be on expatriate terms of service.

I went into Men's Wear in Kampala Road to see about some uniforms I had ordered and he came into the shop, saw me and made a pistol out of his two fingers and fired a 'shot' at me. I immediately clutched my heart and did a dramatic collapse, falling against a display stand and bringing the whole lot crashing to the floor. Mr Patel and an assistant came round the counter clucking: 'Oh dear, oh dear, oh my goodness,' and resisted my efforts to pick up the pieces. 'Can't take you anywhere,' said Mike.

Monday 17 November

The new post-election LegCo was ceremonially opened by HE this afternoon. The ceremony started with an excellent fanfare played by the police bandsmen on the silver trumpets. However, the trumpeters were lined up in position in the gallery and weren't able to see the arrival of HE, so the Commissioner volunteered my expert services to stand in a position from where I could see both the trumpeters and the entrance to the Chamber. Then, at the exact moment that HE stepped into the Chamber I signalled to the trumpeters and they let rip with the fanfare and everyone was immensely impressed. 'You see,' said the Commissioner afterwards, 'Staff Officers do have some use after all.'

1958

Thursday 20 November

One of the new and eager young politicians elected to LegCo for Lango District recently is Milton Obote*, a trade unionist who is opposed to the possible fragmentation of Uganda into various kingdoms. Referring especially to Buganda in a speech in LegCo this week he said:

> If the Government is going to develop this country on a unitary basis, how on earth can the Government develop another state within a state? Does the Government really think that, when self-government comes to this country, the state of Buganda will willingly give up the powers it has already got now, in order to join with other outlying districts or provinces? I don't think so.

I think he's right about that.

Friday 21 November

We had an Officers' Mess Guest Night last night held at the Imperial Hotel. There were 77 officers and guests, quite a few from up-country, and it went very well. This is the fourth such Mess Night, the idea being introduced by the present Commissioner, and they've become very popular. The band played during dinner and things generally livened up afterwards.

Much later on, some of us found an officer asleep on the roof of the Deputy Commissioner's car in the hotel car park. When the Deputy, very well oiled by this stage, was about to go home and he was shown his passenger, he said: 'I don't mind, y'know, but this is not a dekkle dubber bus.'

Thursday 25 November

The Commissioner is leaving the Force and going home after only three years here. His tour as Commissioner would no doubt have gone on for some time before his inevitable promotion to a larger Force in another colony. Apparently his wife is not happy here and there may be other reasons which I don't know. But it is a considerable loss for the Force and a great pity that a high-flyer like him should end his career in the Colonial Police at the age of only 45.

There are all sorts of rumours going around about who will succeed him. One of his last acts here as far as I'm concerned has been to put me up for membership of the Uganda Club, and I heard today that I'm

*Prime Minister 1962–67; President 1967–71 and 1980–85.

136

now a member. The Kampala Club is a very snooty club of the old type, known as the 'Top Club' and it's almost entirely British and difficult to join unless one is very senior. The Uganda Club was started in Cohen's time as a multiracial club, particularly for those who are members of LegCo and in other medium-to-high government positions. It has a few bedrooms so it's going to be useful when I'm stationed up-country and want to stay overnight in Kampala or if I'm going on leave or arriving from leave and need a night's accommodation before departure. There's a useful library and restaurant and members mix easily without what I regard as the objectionable and unnecessary snobbery and racial prejudice of the Kampala Club.

Thursday 27 November

A report in from West Nile tells of a driver taking a heavily-laden lorry from Kampala to Arua. He had a tyre burst on the empty road near Pakwach and the lorry overturned into the bush. The turnboy was thrown off from the top of the load and was killed. The driver decided to spend the night with his lorry and load. In the middle of the night a gang of men came armed with spears and sticks, pulled the driver out of the cab and chased him into the bush, where he ran straight into a sleeping elephant which angrily took over the chase of the poor fellow. He eventually returned to his lorry and saw the thieves ransacking it and carrying off much of the load. When they went off he started back to the lorry, only to find his way barred by a pack of hyenas which were no doubt attracted by the dead body of the turnboy. He picked up a tree branch and ran at them shouting and screaming and managed to reach the lorry cab, into which he jumped and locked himself in for the rest of the night.

Monday 1 December

A Police Air Wing has started, with a Cessna 180 high-wing monoplane, a lurid yellow colour; we haven't yet got a pilot, although one is being recruited. Meanwhile a pilot borrowed from the Kenya Police Air Wing, which has eight of these aircraft, has been taking it up for trials between Jinja and Entebbe Airport. It cost £6,000 and has slow landing speeds and high performance and is suitable for landing on roads or bush clearings. The Commissioner's making some farewell visits to up-country stations in it.

Tuesday 2 December

Rehearsals have commenced at the KATS for the Christmas musical show, which is to be *Alice in Wonderland*. It's a good script with pleasant music and we have some good singers. I've been cast as the March Hare, which doesn't seem to surprise anyone. Fortunately it's not a singing part.

I asked the Commissioner, since he's leaving, if I could now move from HQ and go up-country. But he says I must see in the new Commissioner and provide continuity. It looks as if my escape may be delayed considerably, especially as this new Commissioner is not coming here until March next year. He is currently Deputy Commissioner of the Tanganyika Police, where he has been throughout his service so far, including during the war. Meanwhile our Deputy will act as Commissioner. I should think he may well be a bit peeved at not getting the job himself; after all, he was previously Commissioner of the Bechuanaland* Police before he came here.

Thursday 11 December

I drove down to Entebbe Airport with the Commissioner and his wife and a load of luggage. He obviously intends to be properly dressed on arrival at Heathrow as he had a bowler hat and a tightly rolled umbrella with him. We said our farewells and they departed. Tomorrow I have to move into the Commissioner's residence at No. 1 Baker Road to caretake the place for three months until his replacement arrives. Mrs H gave me lengthy and strict instructions for the care of her many rose bushes, which she will never see again, but which she seems to be much concerned about; whereas I am not in the least. I think that, like most things and people, they will do better if left alone. If I'm wrong about this – too bad. I'm not a gardener and have no interest in it nor in ingratiating myself with the next occupants.

Thursday 18 December

Yesterday one of our officers, an Assistant Superintendent called Chris Webb, was killed in a traffic accident while driving back to Kampala from Jinja. He was in the Criminal Records Office and head of the police photographic department. He's only been out here about six months, having retired from the Worcestershire Constabulary after 30 years service, during which he was awarded the King's Police Medal for Gallantry for arrest of an armed burglar, when he lost an eye.

This is the hottest time of the year so I had to organise a quick funeral for this afternoon. There was a great deal of telephoning, informing people to attend and making the actual urgent funeral

*Now Botswana.

arrangements. As many officers as possible attended in dress uniform, with a firing party quickly organised by the PTS. Everyone concerned was very helpful and co-operative and we were able to give the poor chap a good send-off at the small European cemetery on Jinja Road on the outskirts of Kampala.

Friday 19 December

After I returned from leave I decided to do something more about teaching English than just writing articles in the *Habari* each month; and this month saw my thirty-ninth 'Improve Your English' article published. The Force English literacy exams, which are held twice a year, are vital qualifications for NCOs and constables seeking promotion, but the results so far are not what they should be. Some tutoring and coaching is necessary, in my view; so I put a chit up on the Nsambya barracks general notice-board to say that I'm offering free English spoken and written lessons in the evening after working hours at the barracks once a week, and anyone who is interested may attend.

I obtained some chalk and borrowed a blackboard and, for a few weeks, we stood it under a large mango tree with a pressure lamp to light it. This is necessary because, being on the equator, we have roughly 12 hours of daylight and 12 of darkness and it gets dark very quickly at around 6.30 p.m. while the class is still taking place. However, a classroom was found for us when I pointed out that the classes are being taken very seriously and many men are attending. It was quite usual to have 40 to 50 or even more (there were 80 one evening) sitting around when we had the board under the tree; and they are lively sessions with plenty of questions and discussion. Most of us there wear plain clothes, except some who come to the class straight off duty; and we don't bother about rank. I enjoy it and find it stimulating and satisfying, much more so than the job I do all day. The men obviously like it, it's free and they can come and go as they wish. Some come in late, straight off duty, and others leave part-way through to go on duty.

The important thing is that they are very keen to improve their English and their future career chances, and many are clearly doing so, as I see when I mark the written exercises which I set for them to do between weekly lessons. There's no pressure on them to attend or to work, but they know that their chances of promotion will be considerably enhanced if they do well in the next literacy exam, which will be in January. It may also help a little that they know that someone cares enough to assist them to do so.

139

The Force Education Officer, a civilian from the Education Department, heard of what I've been doing and informed his boss, the Director of Education, who has sent me a letter appointing me to be an official part-time English teacher. I've thus been able to secure a grant to purchase a sufficient number of exercise books to issue two to each student. They can now write their current exercise in one book and hand it in to me for marking, and use the second book for the following week's exercise. Which helps a lot.

Saturday 20 December

The KATS musical show *Alice in Wonderland* has gone well. We put on the first performance on Thursday evening at Makerere College Hall; another yesterday evening and two today, Saturday, a matinée and an evening performance, which was the final one. This morning's *Uganda Argus* gave us an excellent write-up, especially praising the costumes, songs, dances and scenery. The Mad Hatter's Tea Party and the Trial Scene, in both of which I was much involved as March Hare, got special mentions. Those of us taking part certainly enjoyed ourselves tremendously, which helped to put it over with considerable gusto. It was great fun.

Sunday 28 December

A quiet afternoon at Entebbe. Instead of going to the usual beach, where there were several groups of people, I went round to a deserted bay further to the south-east. I was idling along slowly through the water on my back when from the corner of my eye I noticed a movement in the water about 6 yards further out. I turned my head and saw the lumpy head of a crocodile moving smoothly along the surface in the opposite direction. I headed for the shore as quickly as I could. Fortunately the croc had other things on its mind and kept going towards its destination.

1959

Tuesday 13 January

I've recently taken to bringing Blister to the office. He is usually well behaved and, on arrival each morning, makes a tour of the other offices to check up who's in and be made a fuss of. I strongly suspect the ladies in Central Registry give him biscuits; and he spends quite a bit of time with the messenger who makes the tea – after sugar lumps.

The other day he escaped from the CID offices carrying in his mouth a small scroll of barkcloth which is an exhibit in some case due in court in a few days. By re-rolling it from the other end I think we can hide the tooth marks from the judge, provided he doesn't unroll it in court. Questions might then be asked.

The acting Commissioner trundled into my office yesterday and complained: 'Your dog, Blinker, is it? I found him asleep in my office chair when I came in this morning.'

So what was I supposed to do? 'Right, sir,' I said, 'I'll speak to him severely about it.'

He said: 'Huh!' and stumped out. He thinks I'm flippant and too casual. He has said so.

In the middle of this morning my important contemplations were interrupted by the telephone. The conversation went like this:

'Staff Officer here.'

'Ah, is that Mr Allen?' – a very superior female voice.

'Yes.'

'It's your dog again.' – RSPCA trouble; it was their Queen Bee.

'What's he done now?'

'He's holding up the traffic in Kampala Road.'

'Yes, well, he thinks he's a traffic police dog.'

'Well, it's very dangerous. I think you should do something.'

'Very well, I'll pop down and sort him out.'

So I walked down the hill from Police HQ to Kampala Road and found Blister in a supervisory capacity sitting in the middle of the main road near the Post Office, with traffic buzzing past in both directions carefully avoiding him. Naturally, I couldn't call him to me from that position so I raised my hand, in the way that policemen do, stepped into the road and asked Blister what he thought he was a-doing-of while I clipped on his lead. Then I marched him back to HQ under arrest for disrupting the traffic. Once there, he settled for a snooze on the seat of Prune Face's staff car, so I left him in the care of his friends the drivers, who said they'd keep an eye on him.

Sunday 18 January

Yesterday the Police Amateur Boxing Championships were held at the PTS Drill Shed. Officers attended in mess kit and the acting Commissioner, with me in attendance, gave out the prizes. When the championships were being planned the acting Commissioner decided that Police HQ should be represented on the Force Boxing Committee and he kindly volunteered me for the job. I am well qualified for it as I know nothing about boxing and have even less interest in it. The committee is chaired by a crusty old superintendent who is ex-Palestine Police and has long since reached his promotional ceiling and is about due for retirement. He viewed my presence at his committee meetings with grave suspicion, which I encouraged by never saying a word at any of them. This no doubt confirmed to him that I was sent by HQ to spy on them.

Wednesday 21 January

It's the Annual Police Review on Friday and I needed to extract some of the silver cups from the glass-fronted display cabinet in the corridor outside the Commissioner's office, but nobody knew where the key was. The Senior Superintendent from CID came along to see the Commissioner and, when he saw the problem, said: 'Not to worry,' took out a thief's picklock and had it open in a jiffy. There was a final dress rehearsal held at the PTS sports field this morning. I attended on behalf of the acting Commissioner to check on his positions and movements on the parade and during the presentation of medals and cups by the acting Governor. Roger was there from GH for the same purpose. HE is on leave so *Kali* Charlie is acting and will officiate.

Afterwards, when the parade had marched off and things were being put away, I chatted with some of the recruits on one of the working parties, as I always like to do with any group of constables when I come across them. As I walked towards my car afterwards I passed a group of three or four European officers and one of them turned to me and said in a sneering tone: 'I see you were talking to your friends again.'

I've heard such snide remarks before, particularly since I started the English classes at the barracks, so I said: 'What on earth's the matter with talking to Africans? We're here to work with them and help them, so why not talk and be friendly towards them?'

But it's a waste of breath, as I well know; there's a certain type of European out here, fortunately a minority, who never speaks to Africans except to complain or to give orders. They're the ones who usually take overlong to pass local language exams and they tend to be contemptuous of Africans and show no interest in them, although they came here to work. Their conversation is mostly about off-duty booze-ups and their activities on home leave and about plans for when they retire; with their wives complaining endlessly about the alleged incompetence of their servants. Their local social life is entirely expatriate and they seem to be here because it's just a way of earning money and not because it's an interesting and adventurous life or they want to help with training and development.

Friday 23 January

The Police Review went off well this afternoon. Roger and I, back in harness together, worked the medal table after the parade and *Kali* Charlie loomed over everyone and stuck medals on to people as if he were pinning butterflies on to a board. The Kabaka, the Omukama of Bunyoro, the Mayor of Kampala and other dignitaries were present, and a large crowd of spectators. The sun was shining and the band was in fine form. Cups and medals were also presented to the two Force teams, which, once again, won the East and West African Police Rifle Competition Challenge Cup and the E & WA Revolver Challenge Cup. We still have the best police shots in Africa. I was pleased to see that one member of the rifle team, the corporal whom I had been obliged to demote in Mityana in 1957, has since regained his stripes.

Wednesday 11 February

I decided to do something about the staff car drivers' uniform belts. They are the standard issue: thick black leather with silver badged buckles. For sitting in a staff car and driving long distances they are most uncomfortable. So I thought why not let them wear cloth belts with a simple flat buckle as we officers wear? Of course, I can't change uniforms or equipment at my level and I know that old Prune Face, who is in charge of Force administration, and whose Bible is Police Standing Orders, would not agree to such a change, especially as it is officers' dress. So I went over his head and put it to the acting Commissioner, who saw sense in it and agreed. The tailor on the QM's staff has produced the belts, the cost was negligible and the drivers are very pleased. How Prune Face feels I don't know.

Saturday 21 February

The Queen Mother arrived by air last Wednesday on a nine days visit to Uganda, during which she will tour the country, meet lots of people and attend various functions. The Force is naturally very busy during this period, covering all the events and visits. This afternoon there was a Royal Garden Party at GH, to which I was invited as one of the guests of all races. We were all dressed in our best, the ladies sporting Ascot-type hats in the bright sunshine. The Queen Mother was in pale blue with gracious smiles for everyone, and Special Branch types were lurking behind the bushes and shrubs. I seemed to be the only policeman there who was not on duty. The Police Band beat Retreat at the end of the afternoon and it all went very well; though the 20-mile journey back to Kampala afterwards wasn't much fun as there were long lines of cars bumper to bumper in the darkness. However, Traffic Branch as usual handled it efficiently and we kept moving.

Friday 27 February

Last Tuesday the Queen Mother went on her northern safari and spent the night at Paraa Lodge in Murchison Falls National Park after a full day of visits. At the lodge, just before dinner, the royal butler solemnly announced to HM that there was an elephant at the door. HM went to investigate and found game guards shooing away her outsize visitor. It left no message.

The Queen Mother was expected to leave Uganda by air at 8.30 a.m. today. She is travelling in a Comet IV jet aircraft of the Queen's Flight. Because of the heavy police duties all week, a call went out for more assistance and the acting Commissioner, always ready to offer my services, made me available today. It suited me as it meant I got out of the office. I was assigned to Entebbe for the departure and took station with some constables about half-way between GH and the airport. It meant a very early departure from Kampala as the royal car was due to come down to the airport at 8.10 a.m. At about that time a harried-looking senior superintendent drove from the airport, saw me at the roadside and stopped. He said he had phoned GH and been told that HE and the QM were already in the car on their way to the airport. However, the aircraft had developed some problem which the mechanics said would take an hour or two to fix. This meant informing HE of it and suggesting that they return to GH as there are no suitable facilities at the airport. He was quite clearly nervous about having to stop the royal car to tell them this and he said with some relief: 'Look, Peter, you know how to deal with these people, so you tell them, will you?' and scooted off before I could reply. Just then the Austin Princess came slowly into sight, so I stepped into the road with my hand up and walked towards it. Alfairi was driving, with Roger sitting beside him, and both knew I would have good reason to stop the car. It slowed to a halt as I reached the rear window on HE's side. He lowered his window and said: 'What's the matter, Peter?'

I aimed a salute between HE and HM and said: 'Sorry, sir, there's a slight technical hitch with the aircraft and it's not ready for take-off yet. They suggested that, as it may take at least an hour, Her Majesty might prefer to wait at Government House until it's ready, rather than at the airport.'

HE turned and spoke to HM, who nodded and then smiled at me with her head on one side. I had kept the road clear, of course, so we turned the car round on the spot and back they went to GH. When they came past again, just over an hour and a half later, I saluted as they sailed past and a white gloved arm was raised and gave a slight wave in the approved style.

Saturday 28 February

As the new Commissioner is due to arrive on 4 March I have moved out of his house today into one of the new brick-built bungalows at the hostel, which I've been lucky enough to secure, and a phone has been installed. I hope that the new occupants of No. 1 Baker Road are not too keen about roses.

Monday 2 March

The Force Education Officer rang this morning to say that the papers in the recent Force English literacy exam had now been marked. The largest number of entries always comes from Kampala units because of the numbers stationed here. He said an even greater number than before had entered from Nsambya barracks, where I've been teaching, and the pass results from there were much higher than in other years. He added that he was very pleased and hoped I would be able to continue with the classes. I told him that I was planning to hold them all through the year and not just during the run-up to exams, as my aim is for a general improvement and not just good exam results. I believe that these results will encourage others to come forward and attend the classes, which will eventually be helpful both to them and to the Force. That's what makes it worth while, apart from the fact that I really do enjoy doing it.

Wednesday 4 March

The Deputy Commissioner and I drove down to Entebbe pier to meet the new Commissioner, Michael Macoun, and his wife, who had sailed here on the Lake Steamer from Mwanza in Tanganyika with all their luggage, for which I had brought a truck. Since they are old East Africa hands all went reasonably smoothly. It will be interesting to see how my new boss turns out.

Monday 9 March

I've been collating the annual reports received from all of our stations in order to produce the Force entry in the Protectorate Annual Report, which deals with all the Government departments. There is an enormous quantity of crime statistics to put together and total up. The deterrent and preventive effect of the constable on his beat or in a patrol car cannot be calculated although it's a very important factor. The actual crime figures never work out and the totals do not cross-check. My view is that this does not matter much so long as it all looks balanced and is approximately right with no obvious anomalies. After all, who cares really? Statistics are a great waste of time in the general scheme of things. They are only read by statisticians who, like economists and anarchists, are a generally useless and unproductive bunch of thugs who do nothing to advance the steady backward march of civilisation. Nothing much is proved by them. We all know that crime is on the increase because crime is always on the increase. Personally, I blame the criminals.

Wednesday 18 March

In the *Argus* today it was reported that a doctor and his wife who live in Masaka were walking near the township with their pet spaniel when it was attacked by a large python, which coiled itself twice around the dog and then tried to swallow it. The doctor jumped on the python's head while his wife heaved at its tail. After struggling like this for a while, they managed to free the dog and the python was then dealt with by villagers who had run to the scene with spears. The dog is doing well, but the python isn't.

Friday 20 March

Since my time in the PTS I've made a point of keeping my eyes open and talent-spotting among constables for possible future senior ranks and then pushing them to get over the initial promotions, the first steps on the ladder. Previously my recommendations to attend promotion courses had to go through the chain of command and did not always meet with support. However, in this job I see the list when it comes to HQ and I can add to it without referring to anyone else or having it vetoed by anyone. Though an attempt was made to do so yesterday.

Since his recruit days at the PTS in 1955 I've kept an eye on Luke Ofungi* and I soon after put up his name for early promotion to corporal even when he was not under my command at the time. Fortunately, when I spoke of it to his then OC, he agreed with me and our combined recommendation got him on to the course, which he passed easily. I've kept in touch with him and this year he has been a training NCO on the staff of the PTS, so I've now put him up for a sergeants course; at the same time informing the OC PTS that I've done so, of course. Obviously the officers at the PTS have realised his

*Later Inspector General of Police three times under different governments.

146

value and two of them came to see me yesterday and tried hard to persuade me to withdraw my recommendation so that they can keep him in his present post, saying that he is too young and not yet ready for further promotion and too valuable on their staff to lose. My reply was that if he's that good, and we all know he is, then he's clearly ready for further promotion and none of us should stand in his way. They can always ask for him to go back to the PTS after promotion, although I hope that won't happen. He should go elsewhere and broaden his experience ready for his next move upwards. At any rate, I declined to remove his name and he will attend the course.

Tuesday 24 March

There's been a spate of housebreakings in Kampala recently, often in the daytime when the occupants are out at work. Most are carried out by what is known as fishing. The thief finds an open window, or forces one open, and puts a long pole with a hook on the end through the window bars. He then hooks and pulls out any loose items, like bed sheets, blankets, towels, clothes lying on chairs and so on.

When I reached my bungalow at lunch-time today I found that I had been the victim of a fishing thief. The bungalow is at the far side of Kitante Hostel compound and the bedroom window faces the golf course and is concealed from view by various trees. The bedroom was a mess with things lying on the floor; a blanket missing and half a sheet across the bed. For once I had not taken Blister with me to HQ and he had tried to foil the thief by seizing one end of the disappearing sheet in his strong teeth and having a tug-of-war with the thief for possession; resulting in each getting a half. He'd tried hard and, no doubt, he barked as well but nobody was around to hear. Ephraim said he'd been over at the hostel servants' quarters as usual doing some dhobi and ironing.

Last week one of our senior officers living on Kololo hill woke at about 3 a.m. and found an intruder in his house, who took off like the clappers down the road, hotly pursued by this officer clad only in pyjama trousers shouting: 'Thief! Thief!' However, the thief was much younger and fitter and soon disappeared, without any loot, and everyone in the area slept blissfully on. When the beat constable arrived from the other end of his beat, where he'd been at the time, there was nobody in sight apart from an irate but underdressed and overweight senior officer jumping up and down, shaking his fist and uttering rude words. Fitness is the key, so they say.

Thursday 9 April

The Assistant Commissioner in charge of Traffic and Communications is a pleasant, friendly chap but a great gossip and time-waster. He seems to have very little to do and lots of time to spend talking about it. He strolls into my office and sits on my desk and goes on about how he liberated a town in Belgium in 1944 or, especially, about how he was aide to Lord 'Boom' Trenchard when the latter was reorganising the Metropolitan Police before the war. All very interesting, but a bit of a bore when one has heard it all several times over, and especially when trying to get on with some work.

Saturday 11 April

I went with the Commissioner to Entebbe airport to meet Lord Perth, who is Minister of State for the Colonies. A guard of honour was provided by the PTS, with the band of the 4 KAR in attendance as our bandsmen are all on leave. There was heavy rain but the Minister insisted on inspecting the guard. They'll probably all have colds tomorrow. No umbrellas.

I stood with the Commissioner in the airport building afterwards and a crowd of that magnificent body, the UK press corps, came from the aircraft after the parade part was over and approached us. I recognised one of them as Randolph Churchill disguised as a journalist. He looked very well lubricated, red-faced and bad-tempered. As he reached me he glared irritably at me and said: 'Hey, you, where's the gents?' I think I must have given him one of my looks, which I had found effective at GH when used on people who had behaved badly, because he staggered back slightly as I pointed silently at the nearby toilet door, which was clearly marked. He said: 'Er, er...' and disappeared inside. Hardly an historical meeting.

Monday 14 April

In Buganda Province the Baganda politicians have been busy stirring up trouble again. The newly formed Uganda National Movement has started a campaign of boycotting non-African traders, which, of course, includes the majority of shops as they're owned by Asians. The activists put thugs with sticks outside the shops to intimidate Africans from entering them. The Government has quickly made it unlawful to mount pickets outside shops and to intimidate potential shoppers. Meetings of over 250 people at any one place are also prohibited. The SB boys have been busy keeping an eye on potential trouble-makers and others whom they regard with deep suspicion (i.e. everyone else).

As always, of course, the politicians have caused their own ordinary working people to suffer the most from their absurd efforts. Now the African women dare not go into the small Indian *dukas* to buy their household and family necessities and there are certainly nowhere near sufficient African-owned *dukas* to replace them. Time after time the mostly intelligent and likeable Baganda demonstrate their expertise in the well-developed trait of cutting off their noses to spite their faces.

Wednesday 16 April

I wrote an official letter to the Commissioner the other day asking him to consider promoting me, even if only to acting rank, as most of the officers I deal with are senior to me and, in any case, I feel that the Staff Officer to the Commissioner ought to hold more senior rank. It would look better and, if I'm doing the job OK, then why not? Instead of calling me in to talk about it he sent me a written reply saying that it is not possible as there are a number of officers senior in service to me who would be upset. The poor things. What a feeble excuse; as if it matters whether they're upset; they're not doing this job. Anyway, why should they be if it's only a temporary rank?

This morning he came into my office with a secret file to be returned by hand to the Central Registry, just an excuse, I believe, and said that he'd decided that the title of Staff Officer is no longer appropriate and I should henceforth be known as the Commissioner's Personal Assistant. I protested at such an obviously stooge-like, dogsbody title, but he's the boss. So I repeated my earlier request for a transfer up-country as soon as possible. He said no and I can't understand his thinking. He knows I want to escape from HQ, so why bother with this humiliating degrading of the post, especially if I'm doing the job well, as he insists I am.

He stopped on his way out of the office and added the final touch: 'Oh, as you're no longer a Staff Officer you'd better not sign Force Orders any more. The Headquarters Superintendent will do it from now on.' He has also appointed two senior officers as HQ staff officers; another slap in the eye, and I'm left with the ADC-type work. I realised that I must assemble my emergency escape kit. In despair I gave it yet another try and repeated my request for a transfer up-country. I think he could see I really meant it and he said: 'All right, you can go at the end of the year.' So another seven and a half months of this nonsense and then I'm away, with any luck.

Monday 20 April

The Commissioner has decided to make weekend visits, starting on Friday mornings, to each province in order to see as many stations and posts as can be fitted into the time. I have, therefore, produced a programme for the visits and informed those concerned. We have just returned from the first weekend safari, which was to the west, calling at Masaka, Mbarara, Bushenyi and Kasese, where we visited the Kilembe Copper Mine and were shown round by the Canadian general manager. Then to Fort Portal and back to Kampala via Mubende, with a call at my former station at Mityana.

As the Commissioner prefers to sit in the front of the car, as I do, I did most of the driving, while the driver sat comfortably in the back, occasionally waving in a regal fashion at the passing peasants. At each station or post that we visited I made notes of things observed or things to be done, so that I can produce a complete safari report after each expedition for action or whatever he indicates.

Monday 27 April

This weekend we drove to the north, calling at Hoima, Masindi and Gulu. On Saturday we went to Kitgum and then further north up to the border with the Sudan. We ate our lunch sandwiches at Lototuru Rest Camp, which is on the crest of a 3,000-feet escarpment with a wonderful panoramic view of miles and miles of Africa, all bush and distant mountains. We spent some time there with a company commander of 4 KAR discussing border security patrols because of the recent increase of incursions by southern Sudanese bandits.

On Sunday we drove down to Lira, visiting various stations and posts in Lango District, then back to Kampala. My notes are accumulating and there's no doubt that these visits are proving useful, but they are also fairly tiring with a great deal of driving on hot, dusty roads over long distances. They also ruin the weekends for quite a number of people in stations and posts, some of whom seem to think it's my fault, mainly because it's very difficult for me to forecast times of arrival as there are so many unknown factors.

Monday 4 May

Another safari weekend; to the east this time, calling at Jinja, Tororo, Mbale and Soroti plus numerous outposts. We spent a night at Bukwa Rest Camp, where we set up camp immediately on arrival. The Commissioner had with his safari kit a personally designed and rather heavy thunderbox which he said he had had made for safaris in

Tanganyika. A constable was trying to move this across to the other side of the camp where the latrine pit is sited, so I gave him a hand to carry it. When I came back the Commissioner said: 'Hey, you don't have to do that sort of thing, you know.'

I replied: 'Well, he needed a hand and there was nobody else available then.'

During the previous week the Commissioner announced that he wanted a siren fixed to his staff car. I think he's seen a film or read a book about the Flying Squad or something. We don't use such things here. Anyway, ours not to reason why, so I sent the car to the Police Vehicle Workshops with a chit telling them what was required. I was driving on a dusty, rough road in Teso, with him sitting in front obviously dying to try it out. We were stuck behind a slow-moving and heavily overloaded lorry making a lot of dust and failing to pull over to let us pass when I tooted a few times. He said: 'I'm going to do it!' and pressed the button to sound the siren, which blared out over the bush and probably gave the lorry driver the fright of his life, as he may not have heard or seen us behind his billowing cloud of dust.

He pulled over to the side of the road and I drove past and stopped in front of the lorry and signalled to him to stop. I did my traffic cop stuff and checked his vehicle and listed the various offences against traffic regulations that you can always find on such vehicles. When I warned him for prosecution, I added that the Commissioner of Police was sitting in the car and had witnessed his offences so there was not a lot of point in denying them in court. 'I enjoyed that,' said the Commissioner when I returned to the car. 'Not done that sort of thing for a long time.'

When I handed in the report at Soroti Police Station during the inspection visit, I told the OC Traffic that I'd be glad to come up and give evidence if the driver pleads not guilty. Anything to get away from HQ for a day or two. He said: 'Can I call the Commissioner as a witness too?'

Friday 8 May

A mobile traffic course, training police motor cyclists, has just ended and, so I hear, early in the course one of the student constables carrying a jug of water walked all round his *pikipiki* then approached the instructor and said: 'I can't find the radiator to put the water in.'

Yesterday the Commissioner decided to try out the new launch the Force has acquired for anti-smuggling and fish poaching patrols in Uganda's section of Lake Victoria. So we drove down to Entebbe pier and set off in the launch with an officer from the vehicle workshops as skipper. We headed well out into the lake away from land, with the engine going well until we were, by my navigational calculations, approaching the coast of communist China, when the motor gave a polite cough and stopped dead. And there we were, not up the creek, but definitely without a paddle. And no radio fixed in yet. Not even a lifeboat or a parachute. Help!

Nothing the mechanical genius could do would get it going again. I suspected that we had just run out of fuel but he didn't want to admit having failed to check before leaving port. So we drifted for almost a hour before some wealthy-looking civilian in a much larger and expensive launch or yacht, or whatever, answered our shouts for assistance and, with some rude comments, towed us back to the pier. The Commissioner was not at all impressed and expressed his displeasure cogently; the mechanical officer was extremely embarrassed and I was late for tea. It was all too, too vexing.

Sunday 17 May

The KATS musical *1066 And All That* was performed on Thursday and Friday evenings, with two shows yesterday, Saturday. It's the musical version of a book of the same title written by W. C. Sellar and R. J. Yeatman (both of whom were at Reading University with my father, who long ago introduced me to their amusing books). The performances were very well received, according to newspaper and other reports. I took four parts in it, all rulers: Julius Caesar, William the Conqueror, King Henry V and King Charles II, which I thoroughly enjoyed playing. The orchestra, made up of four assorted Europeans and seven members of the Police Band, did a first-rate job with the excellent music. One of the cast says he's planning to produce and direct some Shakespeare in the near future and, apparently unduly impressed by my extract of the Henry V Agincourt speech in the show, asked if I would be interested in taking part. As Ephraim no doubt says when he is doing the dhobi: 'Once more into the bleach.'

Sunday 24 May

From Teso comes this report: the dog belonging to an Indian trader died in January and the Indian buried it wrapped in a white sheet and poured six bottles of Pepsi-Cola into the grave to show his devotion to the animal. During the whole of March, the hot season, no rain fell in Teso and the grass and crops withered. It is contrary to custom among the Iteso to bury an animal; they are just left out in the bush to be eaten by vultures and hyenas. The villagers in the area believed that the rain had disappeared because the Indian had buried his dog.

In April they gathered together and demanded that it be dug up. The Indian indignantly refused and the villagers became threatening. Another Indian ran to Katakwi Police Post and reported the matter, and a party of police went to the scene and warned the people to disperse, but they refused. Fifteen people were arrested and a day later they were convicted by the ADC/magistrate and either fined or imprisoned. The dog was dug up in the presence of the ADC and the Usuku county chief and the corpse thrown away. Shortly afterwards there was a storm with heavy rain over the whole of that county, followed by considerable local rejoicing.

The convicted villagers believed that the DC would allow their appeals because he was known to own a rain gauge (?) but he dismissed them and shortly afterwards the dry weather returned so cotton could not be planted in that county, which was hard luck for some. So what does it all prove?

Monday 25 May

For some time now the Uganda National Movement has been causing security problems by their activities in Buganda; the politicians becoming more and more extreme and getting out of hand. The Force has had to use all of its available manpower, sometimes including PTS recruits, to police the area. On 12 May Government at last declared Buganda Province to be a disturbed area, giving the police additional powers. The UNM was proscribed as a political party but, next day, it reappeared calling itself the Uganda Freedom Movement. This too was proscribed and today it has resurfaced as the Uganda Freedom Convention. I suppose this sort of thing can go on interminably. Although the leaders of the many-named party have now renounced the use of violence and intimidation, cases are still being reported and they show no sign of decreasing.

Friday 5 June

Yesterday evening there was a bit of a flap on, with yet another illegal political assembly down in South Street taxi and bus park. When the police attempted to disperse the crowd of around a thousand people they were surrounded and heavily stoned by the mob. Riot batons and tear gas were used but they still refused to disperse and, because of the increasing violence, the police had to open fire. Nobody was killed but seven of the injured rioters were taken to hospital. In addition, an officer and eight constables were injured. Most of us in Kampala were on duty all night and Police HQ was fairly buzzing with activity as reports came in. One of the confiscated placards had

153

on it the words: BRITSH GOHOM. I think they're trying to tell us something. Things are certainly serious: the Queen's Birthday Parade is being switched this year from Kampala to Entebbe because of the unsettled situation around Kampala. Our whole world is crumbling.

Saturday 20 June

Fifty years ago, on 19 June 1909, a mixed party of KAR, Sikhs and Uganda Police was sent on foot and by steamer under the command of the DC Mbale all the way down to Lake Kigezi to set up the first British administrative post in that area. It had not yet became a part of the Uganda Protectorate and Belgian forces were also claiming it and they reacted in a hostile manner. However, what was known as the Kivu Mission was successful and Kigezi was annexed, and boundaries with the Belgian Congo were later settled.

A special jubilee celebration of the event took place yesterday at the spot where this occurred, which is marked by a small monument on a hill. The Commissioner attended with the OC Kigezi Police and local dignitaries in colourful robes, such as the Secretary-General of Kigezi (a sort of premier), the local Saza chief and the Chief Judge of Kigezi (African courts). A KAR company on duty in the area also took part and so did representatives from the Belgian Congo. Also present were two ancient Africans who, as youngsters, actually took part in the original mission.

Thursday 9 July

The Deputy Inspector General of Colonial Police, Ivo Stourton, who was once Commissioner of Police here, expressed a wish to extend his inspection visit from London to three weeks and turn it into a nostalgic trip around the stations throughout Uganda. With the difficult political situation in Buganda, the Commissioner decided that he couldn't accompany the DIG around and about, except locally, so he instructed me to draw up a programme for the three weeks tour and to accompany the DIG myself. He's put his staff car with its flag at the disposal of the DIG and I've produced a programmed tour around the Protectorate, visiting stations and staying in hotels. Copies have been sent out and I've now an excellent excuse for being away from HQ.

Meanwhile, back at the ranch, the activities of the leaders of what is now called the Uganda National Congress have become so troublesome that ten of them have been rusticated to far-flung outposts of the Protectorate, mainly as far north as they can be sent; which severely upsets them as the Baganda believe that civilisation ends at the boundary of Buganda. One of them, a lawyer named Godfrey Binaisa*, has been sent to Moroto to kick his heels in Karamoja. I've met him and he's actually a very pleasant, intelligent and amusing character and it's rather surprising that he's so involved. Another, whose strong anti-British sentiments are belied by his name, John Bull Kintu, has been sent elsewhere. Meanwhile, the trouble continues.

Sunday 12 July

An angry Commissioner on the phone disturbed my Sunday morning lie-in. The DIG is a Catholic and wished to attend early morning mass, so I had warned the duty staff car driver to pick him up at the Commissioner's residence and take him to the Church of Christ the King. But no driver or car turned up and the Commissioner was obliged to get up and take the DIG to church himself. And it was all my fault, of course. He angrily demanded to know where the driver had got to. How should I know?

For heaven's sake, what a fuss. The RC church is just down the road from his house and the DIG could have walked. It would have done him good to do so, even though Europeans don't have legs in Africa. I didn't say this, of course, not wishing to cause a disturbing explosion on Sunday morning, so I said: 'I'll go to the barracks and check up,' knowing full well that to try to phone the barracks on a Sunday was a complete waste of time as nobody would answer. I eventually found the driver, who claimed he had forgotten all about it, and sent him to the church to pick up the DIG.

Saturday 18 July

All week I've been on safari with the DIG. We visited stations in Masaka, Mbarara, Kabale, Kilembe, Fort Portal, Hoima and Masindi; then to the north, spending yesterday in Gulu and today in Lira. Again I've done a lot of the driving, as he also likes sitting in front, which suits me. On a narrow mountain road in Kigezi, with a sheer drop on one side, the DIG said suddenly: 'Oh, look at that wonderful view,' then seeing me turn my head from the road quickly added: 'No, no, don't look. Better keep your eyes on the road.' At Fort Portal the Ruwenzori (Mountains of the Moon) made one of their very rare appearances from the clouds and we had an excellent view of the range. Of course, I didn't have my camera with me to record this remarkable sight.

---

*Later Attorney-General 1962–68; President of Uganda 1979–80.

Friday 24 July

This week the DIG's safari continued across to the east, visiting Soroti, Kumi, Mbale, and Tororo; then turning westwards to Iganga and Jinja before returning to Kampala, just in time to change and go to the Police Officers Club at Nsambya for the farewell party for one of the senior superintendents who is retiring. The DIG has now finished his nationwide tour and departs on Monday. I've enjoyed it as it got me out of the office and on safari swanning merrily about the country for most of this month.

Wednesday 29 July

A short while back I was approached by Charles Potts, the civilian Force Welfare Officer, who asked me to be the Force representative at a formation meeting to establish the YMCA in Uganda. Yesterday evening, with Bishop Leslie Brown, the Anglican Bishop of Uganda, in the chair, we held a meeting of eight prominent Africans and six Europeans, from whom a formation committee was chosen. Having appointed the various members, the Bishop turned to me and made what he called his little joke: 'We must have our finances in the safe hands of the law, of course,' and appointed me to be the treasurer. I received this news with dismay as my knowledge of and interest in finance is zero. In fact I'm safe as we have no money yet. The intention is to raise funds to build a YMCA hostel in Kampala with a games room, library, swimming pool and other facilities to give youngsters of all races, including non-Christian Asians, somewhere to meet and enjoy various recreational activities together all year round and particularly during school holidays.

Friday 31 July

Prune Face is just back from an inspection tour in the Eastern Province and has complained to me that his staff car driver was absent from duty and he had to drive himself back from Jinja. He sent the man's file to me with instructions that I should try him on orderly room and then discharge him from the Force immediately. His written report stated that at Jinja the driver didn't turn up in the morning from the barracks, where he'd spent the night, at the time ordered by the SACP to leave and return here. He added that he waited for 20 minutes but the driver didn't arrive so he decided to drive himself. He opened the car boot to put in his suitcase and found that the driver had put a bunch of *matoke* in there (they all do it), which he threw out on to the roadside. He then drove to Kampala.

The driver eventually arrived half an hour late; he said his watch had stopped, and reported the loss of the SACP and his car to Jinja Police Station where he was given a bus warrant to get him back to Kampala. He's a brand-new police driver, recently out of training, but a good and experienced civilian car driver, hence this posting. Also he had been allocated this duty by the Senior Driver as none of the HQ drivers likes driving Prune Face because he is hard to please and has an unfriendly attitude.

There is no way that anyone, no matter how senior, is going to tell me to convict someone, nor what punishment to inflict. He was definitely out of line saying what he did in this respect. Unfortunately, the driver was clearly guilty and admitted this, so I had to convict him; but it was his first time and not quite a capital offence, so I awarded him a simple reprimand, the least sentence available. I didn't bother to tell Prune Face but merely sent the file back through his office. The Goan Chief Clerk told me later that the SACP was hopping mad, but he hasn't said anything to me. I don't think he will, because he must be very well aware of how improperly he acted by trying to interfere with the exercise of my joo-dicial functions in that way.

Monday 3 August

At least we've had no more riots recently, but the trade boycott campaign has continued all through July and the declaration of Buganda as a disturbed area has just been extended to 30 September. The situation in Masaka and East Mengo districts has deteriorated to such an extent that the Commissioner has had to impose a curfew there and the police stations in that area have been reinforced.

Tuesday 4 August

Mount Kilimanjaro (the Shining Mountain) is 19,340 feet high and known as the Roof of Africa because it's the highest in the continent. It's an extinct volcano, partly in Kenya and partly in Tanganyika. On the Kenya slopes at Loitokitok, above the Maasai Plains, is the East African Outward Bound School, run by Major Stroud, an ex-Royal Marine. They hold courses for young adults and schoolboys, each course a mixture of all races.

The other day the Commissioner told me that his younger son is due out here on school holidays and, for reasons which I don't know, he has decided to send him on one of these courses. This has been arranged by him through the Outward Bound representative in Kampala. At the same time he offered them my services as a volunteer instructor on the same course so that I can keep an eye on his

157

wretched son. Actually, I want to go on the course, but I would have preferred the courtesy of being asked first.

So I'm due to drive down to Kenya tomorrow for the three and a half weeks course. This afternoon the Commissioner told me that his son had decided not to go on it. I gather there was a row; maybe he also didn't trouble to consult his son before making the arrangements and there has been an understandable rebellion. Then he added: 'Anyway, you can go as arranged, but without him.' Good. Almost a month away from this place.

Thursday 6 August

A long, hot and dusty drive across Uganda and down through Kenya, but no problems until I reached the Rift Valley. Coming down a hill before Nakuru, the car brakes went completely and I had that frightening experience again of heading down a long, steep, narrow road at an uncontrolled speed. Fortunately, there were no buses or lorries coming up the hill and, after a struggle, I managed to run it into a bank beside the road at the bottom; then slowly on until I came to a small garage on the outskirts of town where they fixed my brakes, while I stretched my legs after hours of driving.

Next on to Nairobi, where I spent the night at the New Avenue Hotel. This morning I set off early south-eastwards to Voi and the Tsavo National Park, where the man-eating lions had wreaked such havoc among those building the Uganda Railway at the beginning of this century. There I turned west through the Abaseli Game park, with giraffe galloping clumsily beside the car, to Loitokitok on the lower slopes of Kilimanjaro, arriving at the Outward Bound School in the late afternoon to find the staff sitting round a table drinking tea; but no cucumber sandwiches. Major Stroud and his assistant are the permanent staff; they rely on volunteer instructors to make up the others needed. On this course there is an African schoolmaster from Kenya, a national service subaltern from 4 KAR (ex-Harrow), a Cambridge undergraduate (ex-Rugby) and an old Etonian. The 48 boys come from schools all over East Africa and are aged about 15 or 16. They are divided into four patrols, like Boy Scouts; each 12 a mixture of all races from the different territories. I have the Elgon Patrol and my accommodation is a tent, which I share with the Cambridge type, a rather priggish God-botherer. He must have been hell as a sixth-form puritan prefect.

Wednesday 19 August

The training programme here is progressive and includes daily PT, athletics, forest and mountain walking, camping, first aid, mountain rescue, rock-climbing, bivouac-building and a tough ropes exercise similar in some ways to a military obstacle course. The first of the three climbing expeditions was an acclimatisation walk up to about 12,000 feet. The second a climb up to Kibo Hut at 15,321 feet several days later, with rock-climbing and abseiling at suitable places. Everyone is much fitter now with all the training and exercise; and appetites are very keen, with a rush for second helpings at mealtimes.

When climbing we each carry 40 pounds in rucksacks with warm clothes, bedding, food, water and firewood. On the second climb the boys had to spend one night out alone on the mountain. Reaching pre-arranged areas, we patrol instructors took each boy to a separate place and left him with two matches, a *panga*, a couple of blankets and some very basic food; to make a bivouac and sleep if he could; also to make a fire and cook some food, either in the morning or before going to bed, whichever he chose. I settled into a small cave for the night. It was cold on the mountain, very dark and lonely, so a good test of the boys' initiative and ingenuity. Leaving a small white towel spread over the cave mouth so that I could find it again, I did a round of visits in the dark and one early in the morning to see how they were doing.

It's possible already to see a tremendous difference in individual boys as they have become more self-reliant and confident, more helpful to each other and have learnt to work as a team. The solo night has been the only time when they have not acted together as a patrol. Each boy also has a day when he acts as patrol captain and can demonstrate any qualities of leadership. Some of the European boys from Kenya, probably sons of white settlers, at first have found it difficult living with Africans and Asians and taking orders from them when they are patrol captains, but most have soon adapted. I've only had to rebuke one of them for using a racial slur.

Sunday 30 August

The final climb to the summit took three days to accomplish. On the first day we climbed to the level of the Second Caves and spent a cold night there. On the second day we climbed up to Kibo Hut, which is on the saddle between the summit, called Kibo, at 19,340 feet, and the second peak called Mawenzi, at 16,900 feet.

We had carried up water and firewood; some dry rations, tea, sugar and tinned milk were in the hut store. All our water was collected and poured into a large bowl and the tea, tinned milk and sugar added and mixed together. Everyone was very thirsty after a long day climbing with loads on our backs. However, when the first to receive tea tasted it, they spat it out. The Cambridge genius who shared my tent had elected to make the tea and he had put in it a large packet of salt instead of sugar, without having bothered to check the contents first before using it. The whole lot was completely undrinkable and totally wasted. All our water gone and not a drop to drink. Surely a spot of homicide is justified in such circumstances?

We were then supposed to sleep in the hut until about 1 a.m., when the hardest part of the climb would commence, that to the summit. In the hut it was very cold and draughty and we were all wearing two of everything in an attempt to get warm. We were also still very thirsty and I don't think many got much sleep. We stumbled out into the icy darkness and started up the loose ashy scree, which was almost vertical for about 3,000 feet; taking three steps up and sliding down two. It was heavy going and exhausting work. Then a pause to catch a gasping breath, with very little oxygen at that altitude, and on to the final agonising 500 feet to Gilman's Point at about 19,000 feet, where we watched dawn come up from a seat in the gods.

I was so thirsty that I removed both my mittens and gloves and broke some ice in a rocky hollow and swallowed it. Then on to the summit of Kibo, also called Kaiser Wilhelm Spitze from the days before the First World War when Tanganyika was a German colony and they claimed the mountain as theirs. Photographs were taken and the view into the huge crater and across to Mawenzi and beyond admired. It had been a tremendous effort and I believe we all felt a great sense of achievement after overcoming a terrific challenge.

When we were back down in the Outward Bound camp, we instructors sat and wrote individual reports on the boys for the record and for their sponsors. By this time it was possible to produce really comprehensive and useful reports on each boy and I should think that they will leave here rather different persons, richer in self-confidence, selflessness and self-knowledge.

The Commissioner had arranged for me to spend the following two days at the Tanganyika Police Training School at Arusha on the other side of the mountain. I was bringing back with me in the car two of the boys from Uganda and we drove round the mountain to Moshi on a very muddy road; we twice slid off the road into ditches and had to extract ourselves. At the PTS I arranged for them to sleep in a dormitory for recruits while I stayed with the second in command and was shown round the school and met various people.

We drove from Arusha northwards across the border into Kenya and up to Nairobi, where we paused for refreshments, then on through Kenya and into Uganda. Three countries in a day! It was the longest single journey I've driven and it was well into the night by the time that I reached a few miles outside Jinja, where I had to pull off the road exhausted. I couldn't keep my eyes open any longer so it wasn't safe to go on. The boys were asleep in the car when I staggered outside and sank on to the grass at the roadside and slept, completely oblivious to whatever creatures might creep or crawl over me.

Early in the morning we drove into Jinja to an hotel where they were just about to start breakfast, of which we ate heartily, two helpings of everything. When we arrived at Kampala I dropped the boys at a students hostel to await their buses, one to Mbarara and the other to Fort Portal. Then home for a bath and change before popping into HQ to see how they had managed to survive without me.

Tuesday 15 September

Some visiting British journalists came to interview the Commissioner this morning and they were sitting in my office chatting while waiting to see him. In answer to a casual question, I remarked that it would probably be nearer to ten rather than five years before Uganda was anywhere near ready for independence. 'I'll quote you on that,' said one of them. I hurriedly replied that I was merely a junior officer and giving my personal opinion not an official one, which I didn't know. The last thing I want is to be quoted in the press. Probably be drummed out of the Force. I kept my mouth closed after that.

Tuesday 3 October

Last Thursday the Commissioner made his first visit to southern Karamoja. We drove up in his staff car to Moroto, a journey which took all day. He stayed with the OC Police and I stayed in the rest house. As we walked through Moroto barracks a dust whirlwind came through the lines and took the roof off one of the uniport huts, carrying it, together with pots, pans and other household utensils, high into the air before dropping them in a clatter on to the *murram* parade ground 30 yards away. A very frightened but unhurt wife and child were found hiding under the bed in the remains of the hut.

On Friday and Saturday we used the OC's Land Rover and, with him, we visited the posts at Nakawomotheng, Loro, Achorichor, Amudat and Namalu, the accommodation being the same aluminium uniports with thatch on the roofs to reduce the heat. I was particularly interested because I have selected Karamoja for my up-country posting at the end of December and the Commissioner has agreed.

From Amudat on Saturday we drove into Kenya and spent the night at the small hotel in Kitale. Back into Uganda on Sunday with a visit to Nabilatuk, which I hope will be my next station as the present OC

161

goes on leave in January. Then back up to Moroto for a night and we returned to Kampala yesterday.

Wednesday 14 October

A great stir in Kampala as a European was murdered on Monday night. He shared a flat in the centre of town with a chap I know well as a member of KATS. Apparently the houseboy and the victim had a quarrel about pay and the houseboy stuck a knife in him and fled. The flatmate returned late at night and found the body and blood all over the place. This is such an unusual, indeed unique, event that I gather that not only did every European member of the CID visit the scene, but also all the senior officers from HQ from the Commissioner down. In fact, I seem to be the only European officer in Kampala who did not go there. The houseboy was picked up today and has confessed, so they say. Consequently, my expert investigative services will not be required. Which is probably just as well.

Friday 3 November

I went with the Commissioner to visit the Police College at Naguru this morning. He wanted to inspect some new Sterling sub-machine guns that we have acquired for Special Force, our paramilitary unit for dealing with border incursions and cattle raids and suchlike. It is based at the College. Special Force personnel were carrying out riot gas drill while we were there and a unit was going through the tear gas room one by one without gas masks. As soon as I saw that I knew what was coming, for I know this Commissioner well by now. Sure enough he turned to me and said: 'Now you go through.'

I said nothing. I've done it before in the Army in numerous internal security exercises with the Hong Kong Police and it's no big thing. I just covered my nose and mouth, squinted up my eyes, held my breath and moved through the room as quickly as possible, and out again with practically no after-effects. I think he was rather disappointed that they couldn't all have a big laugh at me staggering around coughing and weeping like some of the SF men who had been through it. Well, hard luck. I noticed he didn't go through himself. Nazi swine, putting me in the gas chamber.

Monday 6 November

Kololo airstrip was invaded by American tourists yesterday. Almost 50 huge aluminium caravans and their towing vehicles arrived. They are a group of retired business people, under the command of one

Wally Byam, who are travelling on what they call a goodwill tour of Africa from Cape Town to Cairo in their Airstream Land Yachts. Byam is a short, fast talking, energetic and enthusiastic westerner who is convinced that his caravans contribute considerably to 'innernashnal unnerstanning'. They certainly draw the crowds here, where such vehicles have not been seen before. One of the caravanners remarked: 'These sure are the friendliest injuns we've seen so far.' The traffic police motor cyclists escorting the convoy through the town were puzzled at being addressed as 'troopers' and 'youse guys'.

Tuesday 10 November

Yesterday afternoon when I was sitting quietly in my office contemplating infinity – i.e. my sojourn in Police HQ – the Commissioner stuck his head in the doorway and said: 'I can hear a disturbance outside LegCo. Go and stop it.' The Town Hall/Legislative Council building is next to HQ so I went out of the front entrance and found a huge crowd of about eight men with placards standing outside LegCo, which is in session, and chanting unintelligible words. Inside, they are debating a bill to amend the Penal Code to give the Governor power to declare a trade boycott illegal and to make it a criminal offence to support such a boycott. Nobody else was in sight, not a single spectator to this mass demonstration.

The protesters were Makerere students and I recognised their leader as one Abu Mayanja*, a Muganda lawyer, Secretary-General of the Uganda National Congress (UNC) and known to us as a trouble-maker. I spoke to him and he replied that they were protesting about the Penal Code Bill and that they were going inside LegCo to lobby the members about it. I said: 'Oh no, you're not. You're causing a disturbance outside LegCo. Do you have a permit to hold a meeting here?'

He replied: 'I am a lawyer and this is the Queen's highway and we can use it as we wish. If a crowd gathers and there's a disturbance it will be your fault. We are now going into the Legislative Assembly.' In fact, there was absolutely no sign of a crowd gathering, which must have been rather disappointing for him.

As he moved forward I put my arm out to stop him and said: 'You can't go in there.' He tried to brush aside my arm but I kept it in place and he continued to argue the toss, just like any lawyer would. Meanwhile the Commissioner had evidently phoned CPS and summoned the cavalry because a senior superintendent and same constables arrived in a police car at the same time as the Commissioner came out of HQ towards us; just as I'd decided to arrest Mayanja. When the

*Later a minister in Obote's and Idi Amin's governments.

SSP asked Mayanja if he had a permit to be there and the answer was no, Mayanja's feet didn't touch the ground. He was just swept up into the vehicle and driven away. The other student protesters were put into a police tender and followed on to the CPS.

I drove down there to write my statement for their file. When the SSP read it he said: 'I made the arrest so leave that part for me. But because of what you say about putting out your arm to stop him, I'm going to add a charge of assaulting a police officer in the execution of his duty.' I said that it was only a technical assault and it seemed to be going a bit far to charge it. The SSP said he'd decided to throw the book at him and everything would go in, adding: 'So don't argue about it.' So I left them to it.

Wednesday 18 November

The trial of Abu Mayanja and the seven others commenced yesterday before the Resident Magistrate. The *Argus* and the radio had reported the original incident, so the court was crowded. There were even brief reports about it in the airmail editions of *The Times* and *Daily Telegraph*. There were three counts against Mayanja: 1) Creating a disturbance likely to interfere with the proceedings of Legislative Council; 2) Taking part in an unlawful assembly and 3) Assaulting a police officer.

I gave my evidence about the disturbance and I explained about holding my arm out, without implying that it was an assault, saying that he had merely pushed against it. Mayanja used my presence in the witness box to rant and rave about the police and how they rode roughshod over the people's rights and arrested people without warrants and treated them roughly and even raped women, and so on. Several times the RM interrupted him and warned him to stop making scandalous remarks, but he went on doing so. I just stood there and made no reply. Then he pointed at me and declared that I was the policeman responsible for all this and that I was the one preventing them from attaining self-government in Uganda. There was a loud gasp from the spectators in court when they heard this alarming news. I didn't know that I had done all this; I really must pay more attention to what I'm doing in future. The RM turned to me and said: 'There's no need to answer this nonsense.'

In his defence Mayanja called Milton Obote, the President-General of the Uganda National Congress, who was speaking against the Penal Code Bill in LegCo at the time when the disturbance occurred. Obote said that he did not hear any chanting outside the building and that there was no interruption of the proceedings.

164

Sunday 22 November

The Annual Police Ball was held this year at the new indoor sports stadium at Lugogo on the Jinja road instead of the usual Makerere Hall. There was more room for tables here and also for dancing, with both the Police and KAR Bands playing alternately. HE attended, bringing with him the new Governor of Kenya and Lady Renison and the Resident of Zanzibar, both of whom are here for a conference. The Chief Justice, the Mayor of Kampala, *Kali* Charlie and Mrs, and various other bigwigs were present and, as most of the VIPs were at the Commissioner's large table, I found myself in attendance with a gaggle of ADCs.

Tuesday 24 November

Headlines in today's *Uganda Argus*: the RM gave his judgment in the Mayanja case yesterday. He acquitted him on two counts; that of unlawful assembly, as there was nobody else there and so no like-lihood of causing a breach of the peace; and of assaulting a police officer, as he held that the contact with my arm was like that at a foot-ball match where a man pushes against the arms of policemen form-ing a cordon and restraining a crowd. I entirely agree with that and I still think it should not have been charged, in spite of all the unkind things Mayanja accused me of in court. He was convicted on the first count of interfering with LegCo proceedings and fined 1,000 shillings (£50). The Makerere College students were also convicted on that count and all bound over to keep the peace (until the next time). The RM added that he was satisfied the police had conducted themselves with perfect propriety and correctness, and he thought it was most regrettable that a member of the English Bar should see fit to make the allegations Mayanja did in court. A pity I can't sue him.

Friday 27 November

Yesterday evening I went to a KATS audition. I don't know why since I hope and expect to be away from Kampala at the end of this year. But, of course, nothing is ever certain in life and the Uganda Police. They were reading something by Tennessee Williams, who is not a favourite of mine, called *Night of the Iguana*, I think. I started badly by irritating the very serious and earnest producer when I referred to the play as the *Day of the Lizard* by Mississippi Smith.

Apparently one of the minor characters in it is an American negro and the producer was asking for a volunteer to 'black up' and take the part. I was absolutely astonished and suggested that he couldn't be serious. Here we are, I said, in the middle of Africa. It would be absurd and deeply offensive to Africans for a European to black up, especially as there are at least two excellent African amateur theatrical societies in Kampala from which we can easily find a suitable actor. But the producer was serious and wouldn't hear of it. So I said jokingly: 'OK, I'll do it then.' He must have thought I was being serious because he refused my offer as, so he said, he wanted me for one of the male lead parts. I said: 'No thanks, I don't think I want to be involved in this piece of nonsense,' and walked out.

Wednesday, 9 December

The Commissioner usually comes to the office on time, but this morning he was late. At 8.15 a.m. I had a phone call from the Chief Secretary demanding to speak to the Commissioner immediately. He sounded in a thoroughly bad mood and no doubt all were taking cover at the Secretariat in Entebbe. I said the Commissioner hadn't come in yet. 'Where is he? I want to speak to him right away,' said *Kali* Charlie in a really bad-tempered voice. He kept ringing every five minutes, getting angrier and angrier, but the Commissioner did not appear. I could tell him nothing because I knew nothing and that simply made *Kali* C even angrier. I had phoned the Commissioner's house after the first call and been told that he had already driven away.

Eventually he arrived about an hour late. I told him about the Chief Secretary's big phone bill and he said: 'Oh, I know what that's about. Just put me through to him.' Afterwards the Commissioner came into my office and said: 'I see you still have friends in high places. The Chief Secretary asked me to tell you that he's sorry he was angry with you as he knows you were not to blame.'

I replied: 'Thank you, but I do need to know where you are in working hours otherwise I can't get in touch with you quickly.'

Thursday 17 December

Well, I've got my wish and I'm to leave here at the end of this month, take a week's local leave, then report to Moroto before taking over as OC Nabilatuk Command in southern Karamoja. I went up to see an Asian sub-inspector at Old Kampala Police Station this morning to see if any of his Indian friends has a second-hand refrigerator for sale. I shall need one in Nabilatuk as it's in the middle of the bush and very hot there. He found a chum with a second- or third-hand paraffin-burning fridge with blue glass and wicks; just what I want in a non-electric area, so we haggled over a price.

Ephraim has decided not to come up there with me and will return to his home in Northern Rhodesia. He has probably been listening to stories from other Africans here about how unfriendly the Karamojong are towards members of other tribes. I'm sorry to lose him after almost five years but I've managed to acquire Juma, a Jaluo from Kenya, who is an experienced cook/houseboy. He will travel up in the lorry with my kit and refrigerator and, of course, Blister. It's not permitted to take dogs into Murchison Falls Game Park, where I'm going for my local leave on the way up to Karamoja.

A European in the hostel who's going to the UK on retirement is selling all his kit so, today, I bought various saucepans, a frying pan and other kitchen utensils for a very reasonable price. In fact, he gave me some of the stuff. There is a general store in Moroto where I can hopefully get what else I need. Several officers have expressed surprise that I've chosen to go to Karamoja, which quite a few of them regard as a sort of punishment station because it's so far from civilisation. But that to me is the great attraction of the place.

1960

Thursday 7 January

It's been a pleasant and restful camping trip at Murchison Falls and I've seen a good selection of animals and obtained some reasonable photos. I drove up last Saturday and, once I was inside the park, where the track was quite bad, the car had two simultaneous punctures. There was a herd of elephant and another of buffalo grazing quite close, but I disobeyed park regulations and got out and put the spare wheel on. The animals looked up curiously but then carried on with the important business of eating. Slowly I drove on with one flat tyre until I reached the landing place for the open wooden ferry that carries vehicles and people across the Nile. It was on the other side when I arrived so there was a bit of a wait until it came back across and I drove the car on to the flat platform deck. Once across I drove to Paraa Lodge, where the game park vehicle mechanic kindly fixed both punctures for me. Then on to the camping ground about a mile away from the lodge, where I put up the small green tent I'd borrowed from the QM.

Later, while standing at the narrow gorge through which Murchison Falls passes, I met an Acholi game ranger and decided to practise my Acholi on him. He told me that, in January 1954, six years ago, he was on game patrol and saw a small aircraft fly into a large flock of birds and crash into the bush. He and some others went to the scene and found a big, noisy *muno* (European) with a beard called '*Ladit* Hemwi' (it was Ernest Hemingway) who had hurt his shoulder. He was with the pilot and another passenger, who was injured in the side. There were many crocodiles on the banks of the Nile at that place so they walked further upriver with them, until they met a small boat with a doctor and a woman aboard who were on a trip to Butiaba (they were Dr Ian McAdam and his wife in the old boat that was used in 1951 to make the Humphrey Bogart film of *The African Queen*) who gave a lift to the three battered Europeans from the aircraft.

He didn't know what happened to them after that but, in fact, when they reached Butiaba, Hemingway did his tough-guy act and insisted on trying to fly to Entebbe in a De Havilland Rapide – like the one I'd flown in on GH northern safaris – which took off and immediately crashed and burst into flames, giving Hemingway a cut scalp and concussion to add to his already dislocated shoulder. After that he went by road, having at last got it into his thick head that flying was for birds.

Friday 8 January

When I went outside the tent early this morning I saw that there had been visitors in the night. There were the large, clear footprints of elephant in the dewy grass. One of these was on the corner of the tent, pressing the peg and the brailing with the canvas right down into the ground. When I checked inside the tent I found it was squashed down about 10 inches from the pillow of my sleeping bag. I had wondered vaguely on waking why the tent side seemed to be much closer to my head than before. If the elephant had moved its foot even slightly I would not be writing this. The odd thing is I'm a very light sleeper yet I neither heard nor felt its fairy-like tread.

A couple of hours later, while looking for animals to photograph, I stopped the car at a place close to where buffalo and zebra were grazing and was immediately descended upon by a swarm of buffalo-flies, like huge horse-flies, with most painful bites. I departed rapidly.

Monday 11 January

I spent the whole of yesterday driving from the park to Moroto, over 320 miles, along dry and dusty roads, entering the closed district of Karamoja at Iriri. Mac, who was at the PTS with me, is now the OC Police Karamoja and I called at his house and disturbed his Sunday tea-time to report my arrival. After refreshment, I collected the mail and files for Nabilatuk and drove the 30 miles south to my new station, where I was welcomed by the very leave-happy John, the present OC and self-styled 'Baron' of Nabilatuk.

The OC's house is one of the two brick buildings in Nabilatuk, with the usual concrete floor, covered with Cardinal Red floor polish, and the standard PWD-issue furniture made in Kampala of *mvule* wood. The other house is 50 yards away and is currently occupied by a junior Assistant District Commissioner and his wife. Between us is the radio uniport, which has the only electrical generator in the sub-district. A line was laid from it to my house to supply just enough power for the lights, but no more; hence the paraffin fridge and a battery radio. Cooking is done on a wood-burning oven and there is a concrete stand outside for a 40-gallon drum of water over a wood fire to heat it up for baths and washing.

The police lines consist only of the usual aluminium uniports with thatched roofs as living quarters and a couple for stores and an office for the barracks sergeant. There is no police station building. The OC has to do his work on the verandah of his house. Between the house and the radio room is the OC's pit latrine in a small hut. About 30 yards south of the house is the River Nabilatuk, at present an empty river bed full of loose sand with the roots of trees sticking out from the eroded banks.

Tuesday 12 January

John and I spent the day in one of our three clapped-out Land Rovers, which are equipped with radios. These seldom work because of the continual shocks from driving through the bush or on very rough tracks, much to the despair of the vehicle and radio police workshops in Mbale, which is about 150 miles away to the south, where major repairs are carried out.

We are starting on a series of safaris to visit the six Nabilatuk out-posts plus looking in at some of Moroto's posts on the way round; also the border posts along the boundaries with Teso and Bugisu. Today we went to our three eastern posts at Kailikong, Koromoch and Moruita, which are manned by a corporal-in-charge, or in some cases a senior constable, and two or three constables, supported by three or four Karamojong Tracker Force constables, who wear uniform but, because of a lack of education, receive only a very basic training locally. In fact, they don't need training in the skill for which they are employed, which is tracking stolen cattle and cattle thieves.

At Koromoch post they reported that they had had to take spears and kill two crocodiles which were preventing them from getting at the only water-hole for miles around. It takes a whole day to visit the

169

three posts because, once one is on the Watershed road, newly built from Moroto down towards Mbale, each post is on a separate and unconnected long track off the road so it is necessary to go back and forth instead of just following a single route.

Sometimes one of the constables who has been on patrol will arrive at Nabilatuk to pick up supplies and mail, and can then be carried back with his items to the post if the OC is going that way. All police posts in Karamoja have radios and make reports at fixed times on the Moroto net, but addressed to the parent station – Moroto, Nabilatuk or Kotido, in the north. At other fixed times the operator switches to the Kampala Radio HQ net to pick up messages from there. The operators are trained radio constables with a radio corporal-in-charge at Nabilatuk.

Wednesday 13 January

When checking through the badly typed Nabilatuk stores inventory today, I came across an odd item which said: '10 Slaves'. I've checked and there are definitely no slaves at this station. The barracks sergeant told me that they are in fact ten shelves and that of those, eight are in the stores uniport and the other two disintegrated after the white ants got to work on them. So there go my cotton-picking plans.

This evening John said that we had been invited across to our neighbours, the ADC and his wife. He warned me not to express any surprise at the way they speak to each other as, so he said, they are very modern and trendy which means that they abuse and swear at one another constantly and in the most extraordinary, and apparently fashionable, way. I've never heard of such and was most surprised at their behaviour and the slovenly way in which their house is kept. The ADC's conversation was all of rugby football, a game which clearly is the centre of his life and in which I have no interest or knowledge whatsoever. I can't see our social relationship expanding.

Thursday 14 January

Today we went southwards through rolling plains of very long elephant grass, thorn bushes and acacia trees, and visited our posts at Moruita (again), which is situated under the marvellously rugged Kadam Mountain in the Debasien Range and Game Sanctuary. Then eastwards across to Moroto's larger post at Amudat in the territory of the Suk, the permanent enemies of the Pian, who are the Karamojong clan in the south, which is my kingdom. Back to our post at Namalu, where there is a rest camp that I shall be using and a prison with an excellent prison farm where I can purchase fruit and vegetables at very reasonable prices.

The government is trying to encourage the Karamojong to take up farming instead of being cattle nomads. The area here is black cotton soil and pretty well anything will grow in it: fruit, vegetables, maize, cassava and so on, with several crops a year. It has never been cultivated before, so all the goodness is there to be exploited, though so far very few of the Karamojong have shown any interest or enthusiasm for such work.

Then we drove westwards deep into the bush to Kopenek in the game sanctuary, where the grass was long and dry and the landscape dotted about with giraffe, ostriches, eland and other buck. It's also lion country though none was visible. The long grass hides them very effectively. A tiny dik-dik, the smallest buck, about the size of a small dog, ran straight into the Land Rover before it could be avoided. John dumped its body in the back to take back for a meal. He commented: 'They're always doing that. No road sense at all.' Another tasty source of food is guinea fowl, which are everywhere in this area but difficult to catch alive; which is better, so that they can be kept like chickens until they are wanted for the pot. The Karamojong are so fleet of foot that they actually chase and catch them. Nobody else seems able to do this. Then they bring them round to the house and have learnt to sell them for 1 shilling each.

Kopenek is right out in the bush. Their accommodation, apart from two thatched uniports, is mud and wattle huts. There is plenty of very long grass available for thatching, at which the Karamojong are skilful, so they are relatively cool inside. On such visits one brings them their mail and such supplies as they've requested over the radio, plus occasional uniforms and equipment replacements and the monthly pay. Sometimes a wife and children returning from a visit to the home village are brought or a man collected to go on leave. The OC also checks the Station Diary (SD), the Occurrence Book (OB), any patrol reports, and listens to any complaints or requests and has a look around the compound to see that it's clean and tidy.

Friday 15 January

Out today due westwards through the bush on a very rough and seldom used track to Napak Mountain, below which is our post at Iriri on the Teso/Karamoja boundary. Just to the north is Akisim, a vertical-sided outcrop of rock which forms an unmistakable landmark. We had a bad puncture trying to cross a very rough, dry wadi with sharp stones, rocks and a fallen tree in it, which delayed us considerably as it was difficult to use the safari jack to remove and replace the wheel in a steep dip with no level ground to work on.

We then drove out of our area into Teso on a liaison visit to the station at Katakwi and boundary posts at Okoboi, Adachal and Palam, which are also on our radio net because of frequent Karamojong cattle raids across into Teso. After that we drove to Moroto, where they were giving John a farewell party at the club. Much later, I took over the driving back to Nabilatuk in the dark as John was well past it, having enjoyed a most convivial and boozy last evening in Karamoja.

Saturday 16 January

We've now covered the whole area and, in between, John has been packing his kit and saying his farewells. Today, after we had piled everything into his car, he drove off southwards in a flurry of dust and shouts of glee as he headed for Kampala and UK leave. This leaves me just where I want to be – out in the bush and completely in charge of my own station. It's mine, all mine! And, best of all, a very long way from Police HQ.

Monday 18 January

Nabilatuk is a very small trading centre. There is a mixed general store run by a Somali, with the sort of basic stuff that Karamojong are beginning to buy if they have money; like *shokas* (black or brown sheets for wearing), blankets, bowls, beads, paraffin, salt, sugar, maize flour, tea, dried beans, Pepsi-Cola and a few tinned items. His main customers come from the families in the police lines and from our outposts. He also has a hand-operated petrol pump, which is very useful. Most Karamojong, however, are naked and so without pockets for money, even if they had any, so they don't do a lot of shopping.

There's good soil around my house, close to the river, so I have already planted tomato and lettuce seeds as well as pawpaws and some maize for corn cobs. There's a young Karamojong who comes daily and fills a 40-gallon drum with water from the borehole and rolls it to the house to fill the tank to supply the kitchen and bath water and also for the plants in my *shamba*.

Sunday 24 January

This last week there have been very serious tax riots in Bukedi District, which is south of Teso, and a number of chiefs and others were killed and a great many buildings burned down. The police had to open fire several times and eventually the KAR were called in and assisted in quietening the area down. The people were stirred up by political agitators, led by one Balaki Kirya*, against the chiefs, some of whom were being rather arbitrary about the way they assessed and collected graduated tax.

Monday 1 February

The bearded Charles Potts, Force Welfare Officer, visited us last week and I took him round the posts. Apart from dealing with family problems, he is concerned with recreational matters, so I urged him to get us a supply of books, games, cards and so on, or cash to purchase them. I told him I'm planning to put up a recreation room in the lines, which we will build with local materials, mud and wattle and thatching, since there's no money for a permanent building. But we must have basic equipment, which needs money.

At the moment the posts only have a welfare radio each, which works by battery and only picks up Radio Kampala. They are very simple saucepan radios made by Pye and constantly being put out of action. This is often because some of the men are not used to handling delicate mechanisms and they tend to operate switches with too much force, thus breaking or disconnecting them.

On Saturday I informed Moroto that I was leaving my station and drove down to Mbale, calling at Moruita and Namalu posts on the way as both have broken radios. In Mbale I went to a hardware shop and purchased a soldering iron and solder so that I can carry out the sort of simple repairs that these radios constantly require; mostly reconnecting wires with solder.

Wednesday 3 February

I was up in Moroto this morning, and on the police station verandah I met Godfrey Binaisa, who has been serving out his political rustication here since July. He has to report to the police station every day, which he'd just done, so we had a chat. I reminded him that we had met at Police HQ last year and he said he was quite enjoying his holiday away from Kampala and it gave him plenty of time for reading.

Friday 5 February

On my small battery radio at home I heard on the BBC shortwave overseas news that the British Prime Minister, Harold Macmillan, has been visiting South Africa and, in Cape Town, he addressed their all-white parliament and spoke of how the present trend of nationalism

---

*Later a minister in Obote's government and subject of a treason trial.

is going to change Africa. He said: 'The wind of change is blowing through this continent.' I bet that was not too well received down there.

Wednesday 10 February

Last month I put in a request for a proper station building here as I don't consider the verandah of the OC's house to be either suitable or proper for such use. On Monday a PWD lorry arrived and deposited the parts of an aluminium structure in our compound. It was definitely not new and had seen better days elsewhere. The workers sent from Moroto soon had the parts assembled and, using nuts and bolts as in the uniports, quickly erected it over the cement floor they had put down early the previous morning. Then I recognised it as my old traffic prosecution office from the former CPS compound, come here to haunt me four years later. It has three tiny rooms, with aluminium shutters for covering holes as windows. The tracker constables under their sergeant got busy thatching the roof, otherwise those of us who are to use it would soon be baked alive inside this metal oven.

Now we've got somewhere to keep the books and files as they also sent us a small filing cabinet. I can't think why this simple job wasn't done long ago instead of leaving the station in such an unnecessarily primitive condition. The other two small offices are occupied by the barracks sergeant and the station sergeant in charge of investigations. We have no detectives or CID here and he uses whatever uniformed constables and trackers are available at any one time. Most of the time he has to deal with cattle theft and associated killings in these raids.

Friday 12 February

The Police Air Wing pilot, Chris, flew up yesterday in his yellow Cessna and we had to clear the goats and children from our rough grass airstrip before he could land. My predecessor, John, called it Nabilatuk International Airport, but it's used more often for grazing animals and an occasional football kick-about. Chris wanted to practise message pick-ups, which he described as a piece of cake. Where have I heard that before? The idea is that two men hold long poles upright while standing about 10 feet apart. Each thin pole has a slit in the top end through which a length of string is threaded, without being tied or wrapped round, and stretched across from one to the other, with an empty soup tin containing the written message – such as: 'Help! Send more soup' – tied exactly at the centre point of the stretched string. The aircraft then swoops almost to ground level, dragging a hook on a long line, like a flying fisherman, which snatches the tin and string from between the cleft poles, leaving the two constables holding the sticks up and trying to get over the shock of being nearly swept away.

It's fairly primitive but, with no radio contact between the aircraft and the ground, it's apparently the best they can think up. I suppose it's better than standing on the aircraft wings semaphoring with flags. But somehow I don't think there will be a rush of volunteers to hold up the sticks now they've watched the first effort.

While he was here I went up with him to fly over my area for a bird's-eye view of it. I saw a lot of empty Africa below, and in a few minutes I was flying over outposts which take hours of hard driving to reach on the ground.

Monday 15 February

This morning I made my weekly visit to Bengt, the large Swede who is drilling boreholes in various parts of the district. For some time he's been in this area near the Watershed road, where his very noisy drilling machine is at work all day. He has a large caravan to live in and seems to be quite happy in the bush by himself and, like a factory worker, doesn't appear to notice the continuous sound of his drill. At least he is well supplied with whisky, for which he says he needs a permit in Sweden. Water is a great problem in this dry thorn desert area and, if the women from the *manyattas* have a borehole nearby to go to for their water supply, instead of spending hours walking miles for it and having to carry it that distance on their heads, it will make a considerable difference to their lives.

Wednesday 24 February

The tracker constables have been out following the tracks of a herd of cattle stolen from the Pian living near here and heading eastwards, so the thieves are Suk. It's really amazing when one looks at the endless mass of bushes covered with 4-to-6-inch-long thorns. These tall, naked warriors, wearing only giraffe hide or car tyre sandals and carrying 8-feet-long spears, drive the stolen cattle at a steady running pace in a straight line towards their destination. They completely disregard the long, sharp thorns and the damage done to their skin.

Once we find out which *manyatta* they have come from, we can go in and seize the cattle, or replacements, and drive them back to act as both a fine and compensation for the theft. Sheep and goats seized at the same time are usually combined in a list and classified as 'shoats'. And so it goes on, backwards and forwards. It's all a game really. Unfortunately, the small boys who herd the cattle are almost always

1960

speared to death in a raid and, if the raid is on cattle in the *kraal* of the *manyatta*, all those living in there, old or young, are put to the spear as well, if they don't escape into the bush in time.

If we can pick up news of an imminent raid in time, we can take men in the Land Rovers to stop it. Otherwise it's a clearing-up operation afterwards. When the annual DC's *baraza* is held, with the Karamojong and Suk chiefs present, the total number of persons killed on each side is totted up and the balance of blood money, paid in cattle, is worked out and agreed.

It's an endless game and nothing is solved. This is why the authorities are trying to persuade the Karamojong to send their children to school and to cultivate the land instead of being merely cattle keepers and thieves.

It's bad enough down here in the south, where only spears are used; but up in the northern part of Karamoja and across the border into Turkana in the Northern Frontier District of Kenya, they are becoming more sophisticated and obtaining guns from the Sudan and Abyssinia and increasingly using them on their cattle raids. Karamoja is a closed district and, because of spear carrying cattle raiders, the police up here are armed with rifles and do not move about alone, but always in twos or threes on patrol or other duty.

Wednesday 26 February

Police Standing Orders provide for camel and donkey allowances in Karamoja. Camels are no longer used but there are still a number of donkeys about, no doubt the descendants of those used to carry loads when there were no vehicles up here and the dirt roads were just narrow tracks. This afternoon a moke wandered casually through the open compound of my house and, when I asked it where it thought it was going, answer came there none as it plodded off into the bush; maybe visiting Pooh or Piglet.

Tuesday 8 March

A naked Karamojong came into the station today, carrying a piece of paper in a cleft stick. I was intrigued as I hadn't actually seen this before except in films about Africa. With no pockets, I suppose it's a sensible way of carrying messages, letters or even money. The message came from his chief to report that there had been a Suk raid on their cattle and, as usual, the herdsboys had been speared to death. I went out in the Land Rover with the station sergeant, a constable and the messenger as our guide. We had a long and bumpy ride over tracks and then into the bush, dodging around thorn trees, until we reached

176

the *manyatta*, where we picked up the father of the two herdsboys. More miles of bush until we could take the vehicle no further. From there we went on foot and eventually saw vultures in the distant sky circling round and pinpointing a kill.

When we reached the site there were the bodies of two small boys, probably aged between ten and twelve, lying sprawled on the ground. They had been dragged around by hyenas, wild dogs and vultures, which had all feasted on them, leaving little more than skeletons with just a few pieces of flesh attached to the skulls, shoulders and feet. The father had brought a whole dried cow skin on which he placed the two bodies, rolled up the skin and set off quickly with it on his head, back to the Land Rover. He had earlier told us that his other two sons had been similarly slain last year and these two were the last of his children.

The cattle and the Suk raiders had long since gone, of course, but the chief knew from the tracks which *manyatta* they had come from, as they had been raided by them before, and vice versa, no doubt. Although nobody could identify the actual killers or thieves, the usual seizure of cattle will be carried out for compensation and a fine. The vultures, kite hawks and marabou storks squawked their disappointment as we departed with the remains and further away the long-necked giraffes peered curiously in our direction and a warthog scampered across in front of our vehicle followed by its young.

Friday 11 March

Our clapped-out, short-wheel-based Land Rovers are early models and the seats for the driver and passenger are hard and uncomfortable. After driving for miles over bumpy tracks and bush one frequently develops 'Land Rover back', which causes considerable pain and discomfort when one gets out of the vehicle and tries to stand and straighten out the cricks in the spine.

The sound of the Land Rover's engine in the empty bush appears to be a considerable attraction to the giraffes and they seem to enjoy stretching out at full gallop alongside as we drive up a track. There's an almost tame eland that occasionally appears and trots beside the vehicle on the road into Moroto; but most small buck, like the duiker and dik-dik, foolishly try to cross in front of a moving vehicle and they don't always make it if they misjudge the speed. The constables riding in the back then joyfully leap out and grab it to take it back and share for a meal.

The Karamojong are wonderful runners and, with their thin, wiry body frames and long legs, they can run fast and far for hours without stopping. They live on a mixture of cattle blood and milk, which seems to be a remarkably nutritious and healthy diet. Clearly they would do well as marathon runners and probably make good sprinters and long-jumpers. Training at Uganda's minimum altitude of 4,000 feet would also give them an additional advantage over those who train and race at sea level. It seems odd that nobody has yet tried them out. I must speak to the athletics officer in Kampala.

Yesterday while driving along a track I saw a Karamojong with a spear, which they are not allowed by law to carry when walking about peacefully – of course, they ignore the law when on a cattle raid. This one's spear was without the usual thong of rawhide protecting the sharp blade, so he meant business. I was alone in my car so I stopped and got out to take it away from him. We had a spot of silent tug-of-war and he tried to use his ring knife, a sharpened circular and flat piece of metal mounted upright on a finger ring like a bladed knuckleduster, which he waved in my face. I grabbed his arm and tried to trip him and we struggled, then he broke away and ran into the bush. Unwisely, I ran after him and, remembering my hurdling days, thought to cut him off by hurdling over a lowish thorn bush. As I was coming down on the other side he turned with his spear pointed diagonally up towards me so that I would land on it. Somehow I managed to swerve in mid-air but fell over a tree root as I landed. As they used to say in adventure stories – with a bound he was free and away. There was no hope of catching him. My revolver was in the Land Rover under the seat where I always leave it; but I wouldn't have used it anyway.

Tuesday 15 March

The men have done a good job at the barracks and our new recreation room is up in all its mud-and-wattle glory, with a hard earth floor and a wooden door made from planks. The fancy thatching was done by Tracker Sergeant Owiny, an Acholi-Labwor from western Karamoja on the boundary with Acholi. They are regarded as the experts in decorative thatching all over the north.

The Force Welfare Officer has been helpful and sent up packets of playing cards, indoor games like ludo and *mweso*, colourful posters for the walls and even, at my special request, a blackboard and easel with a large pressure lamp. I've started giving English lessons on two evenings a week for those who wish to sit for the next Force literacy exam, and there's been quite a good turnout. We have no furniture, so each man brings his own chair or stool. I've donated some old books and a bundle of magazines as a start and I'll try and obtain more and some extra games as we go along. At least now the off-duty men have somewhere to relax and meet together; but this should have been done long ago.

Monday 21 March

I drove down to Mbale in my car on Saturday morning to have a night in the hotel and go to the small local cinema for a break. I'm allowed to leave the station each fortnight for this purpose – either going to Mbale or across into Kenya to Kitale, where there's an even smaller cinema. The shops in Mbale are not bad and one can get most things on the shopping list there. One shop I went into had a toy counter which attracted my attention and I spotted a tiny toy cap pistol with quite large caps; so I picked it up and put a cap in. At the other end of the shop the OC Police Mbale was making a purchase with his back to me. 'This is a stick-up,' I said, and fired the cap gun. It went off with an impressively loud bang and the Indian shop-keeper dropped something with a crash as the OC Mbale leapt into the air and spun round.

'God!' he cried, 'What on earth are you doing? Nearly gave me a heart attack.'

I said: 'Sorry, just trying out a new secret weapon to use against rustlers on the border.'

He departed quickly, muttering to himself about 'these madmen from Karamoja,' and I added the toy gun and caps to my purchases.

'OC quite jumpy, isn't it?' said the shopkeeper as I paid.

Wednesday 6 April

The missions are eagerly seeking to tempt reluctant Karamojong parents to send some more children to their small schools. I hear that a certain amount of pupil-poaching is going on. Some miles away there's a Protestant mission school on one bank of the river and an RC mission school on the opposite bank. Both at first had about equal numbers until a short while ago when the Italian brother who is headmaster of the RC school announced that they would give their students a daily free lunch meal. In fact the Karamojong, like most village Africans, tend to eat one main meal a day, in the evening. But this offer of free food, at any time, was definitely a winner. All the pupils at the Protestant school deserted and crossed the river to join the RC school. I think the brother must have had his tongue in his cheek when he claimed it as a miraculous conversion. More likely it was a case of rumbling stomachs. The headmaster and chief God-botherer on the Protestant side of the river now has to dream up a plot to retrieve his lost souls.

179

Tuesday 19 April

Last week a radio message from Police HQ addressed personally to me stated that an old friend of the Governor's was driving from Entebbe to Nairobi in a hired car and HE had suggested that he should divert on the way, visit me and have a look at Karamoja and take photographs. He's a wealthy British businessman from South Africa whom I met at Government House in 1957. I sent a signal that he should be advised to come via Soroti and I would meet him at Iriri, the easiest route up. All went well and he duly arrived in a large, dusty Mercedes Benz limousine. I transferred to it and drove him down to Nabilatuk, followed by the Land Rover and driver. It was a very comfortable drive after bumping about in our vehicle. In the two days he stayed with me I took him round some of the posts and he photographed Karamojong and animals, and complained of Land Rover back. He went down to Kenya on Saturday; I drove his car to Kitale, where we stayed the night in the hotel. Next day he set off to Nairobi and I returned to Nabilatuk in my own car, in which a driver had followed us.

This morning I was at Moroto prison and the Superintendent told me of a Karamojong recently released from Luzira prison, Kampala (where he'd been transferred), after serving eight years of a twelve years sentence for manslaughter during a cattle raid. At the main gate, clutching his travel warrant, he asked to see the Superintendent again. There he said: 'Sorry, *Bwana*, I've forgotten where I used to live.' They checked their records and questioned two other Karamojong convicts and managed to establish the approximate location of his *manyatta* and sent him happily on his way.

Wednesday 11 May

This being cattle country, it is alive with ticks, which manage to get everywhere. I have been de-ticking Blister regularly every week and plucking them off whenever seen in between. Unfortunately, the inevitable happened and he caught a bad dose of tick fever, so I needed to take him to Moroto for an inoculation from the District Veterinary Officer. The poor dog was completely listless. I received a report of a cattle raid near Namalu and someone had been speared, so I had to go down there immediately, in the opposite direction to Moroto. I put Blister into the other Land Rover on a thick blanket and gave the driver a chit to take to the OC Moroto Police asking him to do the necessary with the vet. When I returned here this evening after dealing with the aftermath of the raid, I was called to the radio and Mac told me that Blister had died in the Land Rover before reaching

Moroto. He was such a wonderfully loyal friend and so enjoyable and amusing to have around. I shall miss him very much.

Sunday 22 May

The southern Karamojong clan here, the Pian, were last Wednesday raided by the northern clan, the Jie, armed with spears, who took away a considerable number of cattle. Next morning, PC Mpanuka, from one of Moroto's posts, followed them with four other constables all armed with rifles. With them was a sub-chief and two unarmed ALG Police *askaris*. They eventually caught up with the herd and managed to seize some of them, at the same time arresting one of the raiders who had dropped back. Then a large group of Jie arrived on the scene with more stolen cattle. The Jie immediately became hostile and advanced towards the constables and the chief, with spears upraised, while shouting challenges and taunts. The chief ordered them to disperse and they responded aggressively by throwing their spears at him but without hitting anyone. Mpanuka then ordered his men to fire two shots over their heads to get them to disperse, but they ignored this and charged in a mass towards the small group. He then ordered two volleys to be fired at them and they broke up and ran off, leaving one raider dead. Blood trails indicated that several others were wounded but they all escaped, taking some of the cattle with them. Mpanuka* and his men then brought the recovered cattle back.

Monday 23 May

Meanwhile we had our own troubles. A group of Suk raided the Pian north-east of Koromoch post, where pursuing Pian caught up with them and there was a pitched battle with spears. The report from Koromoch was that there were a lot of bodies at the scene. I drove there in a Land Rover with the station sergeant and a constable and found the battleground right out in the bush well away from any tracks, with the usual vultures circling overhead. Some had flopped down on to the ground too full to fly, while others were perched in the thorn and acacia trees. There were 16 bodies lying around the area and the birds and beasts had already feasted and left only skeletons. All the wounded had gone off with their comrades, and the spears of the dead had been taken away too. One small Land Rover would not normally hold so many bodies but, in their skeleton state, they were piled in the back.

   To make more space after hearing the initial report, I had not brought

*He was later awarded the Queen's Commendation for Brave Conduct.

181

a driver, and the two men squeezed into the passenger seat. I drove to the Watershed road and then north to Moroto Hospital mortuary, where we unloaded the bodies on to the grass outside. A doctor came over, looked at the skeletons and said: 'They're all dead,' and signed the forms. Nobody would claim them or identify them, for that would lead us to the other raiders. There was no clothing or property. As far as the Karamojong and Suk were concerned, they should have been left in the bush to be disposed of tidily by the carrion-eaters, friend and foe together. If they'd not been skeletons I'd have had the unpleasant duty, as investigating officer, of attending 16 full-scale post-mortem examinations; something I was quite glad to avoid.

If possible we collect the owners of the stolen cattle and surviving herdsmen and take them over to the raiders' area to help search for and identify their stock. But many of them fear for their lives in enemy territory and decline to go, preferring to join a group on a retaliatory raid that will be planned immediately to make good their losses. However, if we manage to pick up groups of stolen cattle and bring them back, then they will identify them. Sometimes, with the Suk, the colouring and style of head-dress of a dead raider may indicate his clan and so help to locate the raiders or the cattle or both. The Suk custom requires a widow to wear a thin strip of goatskin round her leg, just below the knee, with the white hair showing, for one month after the death of her husband. Observing such a sign when checking a *manyatta* during investigation of a recent raid can sometimes help to pinpoint from where the raiders came.

Friday 10 June

Nick sent a telegram from home to Police HQ, which was passed to me on the police radio an Monday afternoon, to say that my father had died. It was cancer and he was in considerable pain. I do not understand the indifference of a God that makes good people suffer great pain and die such an ugly death. For a couple of hours I wandered disconsolately into the thick thorn bush desert until, realising that I was lost, I had to do some serious backtracking to find my way out. My leave is not due until January and I gather I'll be of more use at home if I wait until then.

Saturday 18 June

There was a blood-drinking party outside Nabilatuk yesterday evening. The Karamojong lit a huge fire of dry branches and then dragged the chosen bull into a clearing by a thong tied to one hind leg and held there by a couple of men. A spear was driven straight through the bull's heart and, when it fell to the ground and was still bleeding, the chest cavity was cut open with spears. The men lined up in order of seniority, elders first, and one by one knelt down, put their heads deep into the bull's chest and drank the warm blood as it gushed out. Each then stood up, grinning broadly, with blood running down his chin and chest, and stepped aside for the next man. Next the bull was dragged whole on to the fire and removed after only a few minutes when the hair had been singed off. An elder removed the bull's intestines, took the dung from them and handed round a small portion to each man, who smeared it on to his chest as insurance against bad grazing and non-productive women. The carcase was then cut up with spears and portions distributed according to social status in the clan. While they devoured the meat, songs were sung and the women in their cow-hide skirts kept up a rhythmic stamping, clapping and chanting. The younger men commenced solo jumping straight up and down, some reaching impressive heights. Others faced young women and they bobbed up and down alternately.

No drums or musical instruments were used, just a long horn blaring and honking out a single monotonous note giving the time to the stamping feet. The songs are usually about the prowess of the men and their courage and daring in battle – they are not at all modest about this – and about the big bulls of the herd and how the men resemble them in strength and so on.

Sometimes these feasts precede a cattle raid, but this one, I hope, was merely a peaceful party. They certainly drank a lot of *pombe*, a thick porridgy beer made from millet. I noticed that all our Karamojong trackers were taking part, also a couple of constables from eastern Teso, where many of them are related to the Karamojong.

Saturday 25 June

Four days ago a large raiding party of Turkana came across from Kenya into Karamoja north of Moroto. Two constables with Tracker Constable Aisu were sent to locate the whereabouts of the raiders. A group of about 40 Turkana attacked a *manyatta*, killing eight of the inhabitants and taking the cattle. Three of the Turkana, armed with rifles, became separated from their main party. They met a group of Dodoth, a northern clan, who were looking for them, and fired at the Dodoth, who then pursued the fleeing raiders.

The three constables on patrol heard the shooting and went to the scene, where they found the Dodoth. The Turkana by then were hidden in very long grass and thick bushes at the bottom of a gully. Aisu and one of the Dodoth followed the tracks leading to their hiding place and one of the Turkana shot and killed the Dodoth. Tracker Constable Aisu* stood his ground and exchanged shots with the Turkana until he ran out of ammunition.

Ron Weeding, a recent ASP (Cadet) and a very fine all-round sportsman, had come out from Moroto with the OC Police and they approached the area. Weeding was lying on the ground observing the position when a bullet fired by one of the Turkana penetrated his body and he died on the spot. The OC then took his body back to Moroto. I'd have thought that some effort would be made to capture the three Turkana, but I was not the officer on the spot at the time, so I'm not really in a position to criticise. A unit of Special Force has since been sent there from the Police College and they are engaged on a large-scale cattle-seizing operation, but it seems as if the killers have got clean away.

Thursday 29 June

I hear that Jack Hayes, the Assistant Commissioner in charge of Traffic and Communications at Police HQ has just left for home on retirement. He's the chap who used to come into my office at HQ and tell long, boring stories about the war and Lord Trenchard. The story goes that, some time ago, an officer who was extremely upset and annoyed with Hayes carefully placed on his desk blotting pad a tin of Haze Remover for motor vehicles, as a sign of his disapproval. It didn't work.

Wednesday 6 July

I was driving on the Watershed road back from Kailikong post yesterday behind a dangerously overloaded lorry that was speeding; so I pulled out in front and stopped him and warned the driver for court here in Nabilatuk today, as he lives here. In fact we have no courtroom, so the ADC performed his magisterial duties by sitting in the back of his Land Rover with a wooden box to write on.

The driver stood at the tail-board and pleaded not guilty. I played the parts of prosecutor and only prosecution witness. This was enough for him and he changed his plea to one of guilty and was duly fined. As that was the only case listed for hearing at this sessions, the court rose, or rather climbed over to the driver's seat of the Land Rover, and drove off for lunch.

*He was later awarded the Colonial Police Medal for Gallantry.

Friday 8 July

We've had very heavy rains. The water pouring down from Moroto Mountain has caused a flash flood which has swept down our wide, dry river bed, bringing with it whole trees, bushes and debris of all sorts moving higgledy-piggledy in the turbulent water rushing past my house.

I'm told that a group of young Europeans decided to camp overnight in one of the dry river beds near here some time back. They were caught by a bore from the mountain and swept away with their vehicle, tents and all their kit; and it didn't do them any good at all.

Monday 18 July

On Saturday I decided to drive down to Mbale for the night. I had rigged up a length of rubber hose to the exhaust pipe of my Standard and tied it to the roof as a snorkel device. I was thus able to drive through the first of two flooded rivers to the Watershed road with some ease. But the battering of the swiftly moving water caused it to come apart and I got stuck in the middle of the second river, and the water was rising rapidly. The constable who had cadged a lift with me to Mbale quickly got out and waded to the bank and away. He came back soon with some Karamojong, whom he ordered to push the car as I steered it out of the water.

Much of the road to Mbale is hard *murram* interspersed with black cotton soil. I lost count of the number of times the car stuck in the black mud. I had sacks and lengths of wood in the car to put under the wheels and a *panga* to cut bush branches at the roadside. It was a tiring and frustrating process, getting stuck, unsticking, moving on, getting stuck again, over and over. The whole day was passed in this delightful fashion and it was evening by the time we arrived at Mbale. I felt quite embarrassed walking from the hotel car park to reception covered from head to foot in black mud. However, when I said I'd just driven down from Karamoja the receptionist nodded and said: 'I expect you want a bath then.'

The return journey on Sunday afternoon was not so bad as it hadn't rained again and the sun had dried many parts of the road. So I only got stuck three times and drove through both rivers with aplomb and a snorkel, much to the surprise of the men in a Moroto Police Land Rover who were stranded on one bank waiting for the water level to drop. Before I crossed I showed the driver my snorkel device and he said he'd get one fixed. He then had a demonstration of how it worked as I went on my way.

I notice that our replacement drivers who are sent up here from

Kampala these days are all wearing the cloth belts that I started the HQ drivers on over a year ago. Evidently it has at last been realised that they are more comfortable and suitable for people who sit folded up in a driving seat for hours at a stretch.

Thursday 28 July

The news from Kampala is that, with the opening of the magnificent new Parliament building, surrounded by an ornamental garden, Police HQ has moved into the top three storeys of that building; which also houses the Ministries of Education and Labour. Only the radio HQ section remains in the previous HQ building for the time being. The old LegCo building has reverted to being just a town hall again.

Monday 1 August

In some administrative reorganisation the ADC has been withdrawn from Nabilatuk and posted elsewhere. There's no indication that there will be a replacement, so the house remains empty.

I was over at Moruita post this morning and found that they had arrested two Suk who had taken part in a raid. They could hardly deny this since both had open spear wounds on their thighs, which were deep and in need of stitches. Nothing had been done about these injuries and they just sat under a tree without showing any sign of discomfort or pain. I asked why first aid had not been administered and Corporal Abang replied with disdain: 'They are only Suk.'

I told a constable to bring the post first-aid box. His wife produced a bowl of hot water and I cleaned the injuries and put on antiseptic ointment and bandages. Then they were put into the Land Rover with an escort and I took them on a bumpy ride to Amudat and the RC mission clinic, where I deposited them under guard. I had several things to do in Amudat and, when I checked at the clinic later on, the sister told me that their visiting doctor had remarked that the treatment and bandaging were quite professional and that, apart from long scars, which they would not mind at all, they should eventually heal up nicely. Just in time to go to Moroto prison.

As the doctor was about to leave, I met him and had a chat. He told me of a young Suk he'd seen about three years ago after a raid in which the Suk had seen a spear coming towards him and had raised his giraffe-hide shield in protection. The very sharp spear glanced off the shield and went in just under his chin, the point protruding between his eyes and slightly above them. His whole face then came off as though on a hinge, held together by flesh and skin on the left side of his face. He crawled away into the bushes and hid until the battle was over. He put his face back in position with one hand and tied three long strips of grass round it to hold it in place, walked home 15 miles and, after that, came to the doctor's clinic to be sewn up. He recovered and lives on, though with a badly scarred face.

Wednesday 3 August

I've been taking photographs of the many varied Karamojong headdresses since I came here. There are some intricately worked skullcaps made of coloured beads and long fez-shaped head pieces with tufts, feathers or tassels attached. No two are alike. It's no wonder that they sleep with shaped wooden headrests supporting them in order to protect their fancy coiffures and prevent them from being crushed or damaged while asleep. The Suk also go in for these head decorations and display quite different patterns and shapes. Some of the designs indicate what clan or sub-clan they belong to.

Wednesday 10 August

Very early yesterday morning I was called outside and shown the dead body of one of our young constables lying on the path between my house and the police lines. He seemed to have been trying to reach my house and had collapsed only a few yards away. There were no injuries visible on his body but he had vomited and there was a curious discoloration around his mouth. I think it's possible he's been poisoned. I scraped some vomit and faeces into specimen bags, which I've sent with his body to Moroto accompanied by his widow and child. I've requested an urgent post-mortem examination at the hospital asking the doctor to look for suspected poisoning and to obtain various organs to be sent to Kampala for forensic testing. They will be taken by hand of a constable from Moroto and he will wait there to bring back the results.

The barracks sergeant tells me there's a rumour in the lines that he was bewitched by someone, but no names have been forthcoming. It's possible that someone may have obtained a poisonous substance from a witch doctor or some other supplier, but so far there's no evidence to support this theory, nor of any motive why anyone would want to harm the poor chap. The station sergeant questioned the wife and everyone in the lines and in the area and has been taking statements but, so far, without anything helpful. The constable was in his mid-twenties and has no record of any trouble or problems that we know of. His young wife was completely shattered and, unless she is a first-rate actress, can be ruled out as a suspect – apart from having nothing to gain. If it was self-administered nobody so far has produced a reason for it. He was working well and would have been considered for promotion fairly soon. So far there's no motive and no evidence of any family problems or quarrels and no sign of any *fitina* (grudges or feuds).

Monday 22 August

There was a radio call from the OC Moroto today to inform me that someone had messed up the specimen organs of the constable who died the week before last. According to the Kampala forensic people, they were put into the wrong preserving fluid at Moroto mortuary and were contaminated, so no useful tests could be carried out. Apparently the jars were not properly sealed while in storage. Also nothing suspicious was found in the specimens I sent in the bags, which seems rather odd. The PM report revealed no recognisable poison in the body, but I suppose it could have been something untraceable or unknown. It leaves us with nothing useful to go on; no suspect and no means. A complete mystery, in fact, and my little grey cells are telling me nothing. The men say it's *shauri la Mungu* (God's will).

Friday 27 August

I visited some of the Teso boundary posts today as there have been a couple of cattle raids there recently. When I reached Okoboi post in the early evening, the off-duty constables were sitting in a circle round a large pot drinking *ajou*, a millet-based alcoholic beverage which is very popular with the Iteso for social drinking. They sit back and each one sucks up the liquor from the traditional communal pot through long tubes made from hollow creepers called *ipiina*. They offered me some, but I've tried it before and I think it's pretty awful stuff, so I said sorry I couldn't as I had to stay sober to drive all the way back to Nabilatuk. They laughed and I drove off.

Saturday 28 August

There's a small recruiting team from 4 KAR in camp just outside Nabilatuk. They've been selecting a few suitable Karamojong as recruits. Tracker Constable Otehe came to the office today to request me to help him to be recruited. From the point of view of pay, conditions of service and future prospects, it would be a considerable step upward for him. He's not the usual tall, thin Karamojong but is about average height and stocky. He wears his uniform smartly and is generally well turned out, disciplined and reasonably intelligent; certainly enough to be a soldier.

I took him with me to visit the Scots major in charge of the recruiting team, who was not at all keen about Otehe. I pointed out that he had had a very basic mission school education for only two years, that we'd trained him in marching and rifle drill and he's smartly turned out. He was thus a considerable advance on the material they were collecting from the bush.

'What we want,' he said, 'are big laddies, good sportsmen and fighters. The sort of splendid fellers that we can rely on. I canna stand any of these namby-pamby mission-educated types. They're real wet weaks. Much better if recruits are uneducated and uncontaminated by priests. We can then mould them into our way of doing things in the Army and have much better control over them.'

'But in Kampala they're talking about self-government,' I said, 'so what's going to happen to these chaps when you people are no longer around to control them?'

He replied: 'Aye well, that's Kampala for you. It's not going to happen for a long time and then it won't be our worry, will it? Anyway, the important thing now is for us to keep up the strength of the battalion soccer team and, with luck, find a couple of potential boxers. Marvellous at sports these northerners, don't you think? Not the Baganda and other southerners, though. They're all politics, complaints and *matoke*.'

I pointed out that in the Police we have a champion football team, champion boxers, international champion teams of rifle and pistol marksmen, cricketers and athletes of renown – even taking part in the Commonwealth Games. In addition, we have African gazetted officers who are well-educated and intelligent and skilful investigators. The standard of our overall educational requirements for all ranks has been rising annually, so why couldn't the KAR follow suit?

He replied that they had a completely different approach and outlook as they had to train their men to use their weapons to fight as a unit in a war or a border conflict whereas the police are trained to use their heads and act individually to keep the peace. In the KAR they didn't want semi-educated types who thought too much and tended to act independently. 'We need men who work together as a unit and who do exactly what they are ordered to do, without stopping to think and argue the toss. Mission education's no good for that; we train them in everything they need to know.'

Still, in spite of his initial reluctance, the major accepted Otehe as a potential recruit. He came back to the lines with me and handed in his uniform and equipment and went off grinning all over his face. He was paid yesterday so all I had to do was send a radio message to Moroto to take him off the books and send me a replacement.

Tuesday 6 September

I've written to HE after hearing the news on Kampala Radio that Lady Crawford died two days ago as a result of an illness. He's going to miss her very much and I wonder if he'll stay on as Governor now; he has almost two years left of his governorship period.

Wednesday 7 September

The OC Moroto came on the radio on Monday to report that a case of theft by public servant which originated in Nabilatuk was coming before the RM for trial this morning. He added: 'It's your case, so you'd better come up here and prosecute it.' So I drove up to Moroto.

For some time the PWD had a gang of locally recruited Karamojong working on the road between Nabilatuk and Latome, to the north, filling in holes, digging drainage ditches and so on. The overseer was an Etesot and, as the result of a complaint made by two of the workers, we looked into the overseer's pay sheets and employees roll. The road workers were supposed to be paid 15 shillings each month but, in fact, he was paying them only 12. They were totally illiterate and, as is customary for such people all over Uganda, put their thumb-marks on the pay sheet whenever paid.

We found that there were more names on the payroll than actual bodies on the ground. The overseer clearly didn't understand the significance of fingerprints because he used his own thumb-print against all of the false names on each monthly roll. The same thumb-mark appearing several times on each payroll was an obvious give away. He pleaded not guilty and denied everything. So I trotted in my prosecution witnesses one by one. Each naked Karamojong came into the court-room, was told where to stand, and with some difficulty I obtained from him the number of months he had worked on the road and how much the overseer had actually paid him. They referred to him with a superior sneer as 'the fat man from Teso'. After five of these witnesses the RM asked me how many more I was going to call. I said that there were 24 altogether and they would all say the same thing.

'We'll take it as read,' he said, 'I've got the picture.' I then called evidence that the accused was employed by the PWD and was therefore a public servant; that he collected the monthly payrolls and cash and was responsible for paying out, and of the amounts he was supposed to pay out. Then there was evidence that several of the persons named on the rolls did not exist or were not employed by PWD; at which point he caved in and changed his plea to one of guilty on each count. Collapse of fat party, in fact.

Just as well, as I had nobody to call as an accepted fingerprint expert to compare the thumb-prints in court. In fact, an experienced eye in the course of investigation could easily see that the prints were the same, as we had, but in court that evidence has to be given by the gazetted fingerprint expert, who, at that moment, was probably sitting comfortably behind his desk in CID HQ in Kampala, far away. I would have had to ask for an adjournment to bring him all the way to Moroto to give that brief expert testimony if the accused had not changed his plea. Anyway, he's gone inside for a couple of years, which should give him something to think about. I don't suppose the road workers will ever see the money they were defrauded of, though.

Thursday 22 September

Yesterday afternoon Kopenek post in the south came on the radio with an urgent message. The senior constable there reported that a raiding party of over a hundred Pian had passed near the post heading east-wards, obviously out to raid the Suk. He had managed to arrest a strag-gler who had something wrong with his foot but, when questioned, he had refused to say which *manyatta* the raiders were going to attack.

So we had a bit of a problem. The raiders could attack anywhere in the east or north-east over a large area. There would be a lot of killing and huge cattle seizures with such a large raiding party. It was there-fore essential that I should know their intended destination in Upe county as it covers a large area and none of the eastern posts has enough men to handle such a situation. Consequently I had to reinforce the target area urgently with men from Nabilatuk. But there's only one of our Land Rovers working at the moment, and that with a very shaky radio. The other two vehicles are in Mbale workshops with their drivers. If we went to the wrong area, and there was a wide choice, we wouldn't be able to prevent the raid but would merely have to clear up the mess afterwards.

I could therefore only take as many men as I could squeeze into the one vehicle and make one journey to whichever was the nearest post to the planned raid, to collect more men and be there before the raiders arrived at their target. Everything, especially a lot of lives, therefore depended on our knowing their destination before we started out. So I called the Kopenek senior constable on the radio and said: 'I have to know which *manyattas* the raiders are going to attack. You must get me this information from the man you arrested and get it now. It is very urgent. So do whatever you have to do. It is my responsibil-ity.'

Shortly after this he called back and said that the raid was to be on the *manyattas* near Moruita post. By then the raiders had about 20 miles to run through the thorn bushes. It wouldn't take them long. I had a quick word on the radio with the OC Moroto to see if he could send down a few men, but his chaps were all out seizing cattle from the Jie in the north and he had none available. I told him what I was going to do and signed off. Then I told my radio corporal to call Moruita post and tell them we were on our way and to alert the other eastern posts. I jumped into the Land Rover, which was overloaded with armed men, and we set off along the rough track as fast as the old vehicle would go. The bouncing about soon caused the vehicle radio to become completely unserviceable and, by the time we reached Moruita post, it was early evening.

I ordered the station sergeant and the Moruita corporal to divide up their men into patrol groups and go out to the *manyattas* and blow whistles to warn the rest of us when the raiders came into sight so that we could converge on them. Fortunately there was a gibbous moon so we could see what we were doing. And so it worked out. By dawn we had rounded up a large number of the raiders and had collected a great pile of spears. There had been no deaths and no cattle stolen. The sudden sight of armed and alert police in unexpected places had a salutary effect on the raiders and they gave up without a fight. The small garrison at the post certainly couldn't have coped with such a large raid by themselves, especially as they could not have covered as much ground nor shown as much force as we were able to do.

Wednesday 28 September

When I visited Kopenek this morning to pay them, I asked the constable in charge how he had obtained the information from the Pian raider the other day. I hoped it was not going to be really bad news. He replied that his two tracker constables had previously been to the waterhole used by the people at the nearest *manyatta* and had found a half-grown crocodile there guarding it aggressively. They managed to catch it and, instead of killing it, they tied a rope round its mouth, as they didn't want to carry it, and they dragged it through the bush for a mile or so, which made it quite cross, and dumped it in the empty hut in the post compound. Shortly afterwards they received my order to question the Pian, so they decided to put him into that hut to encourage him to speak.

They untied the crocodile, pushed the man inside the hut with his hands tied and blocked the entrance. He had nowhere to go and there was nothing he could use as a weapon. He definitely didn't want to lose a leg to the very angry crocodile, so he hopped and jumped about and shouted out the information required. They then pulled him out of the hut. He was later taken to the sub-chief and handed over as they had nowhere to keep him at the post. Apparently they then killed and skinned the crocodile, which they had intended to do all along.

I congratulated and thanked them for doing a good job. No doubt there are people who would not approve of such actions. However, there are other people alive today in the Moruita area who would not have been but for their initiative and, as far as I'm concerned, that's what counts. It's much more important and useful to prevent crimes from happening than to detect and punish offenders after they've done the damage.

Friday 30 September

If it isn't one thing it's another. Yesterday morning the Nabilatuk medical assistant reported that he had to speak to the District Medical Officer in Moroto on the radio. A visitor from Teso staying with one of my constables has reported sick and the medical assistant has diagnosed the dreaded smallpox. I called up the OC Police Karamoja and suggested he might like to be present when the DMO was there, as I would be at this end, so that we could sort out and co-ordinate our arrangements without delay. The DMO listened to his assistant and said he would immediately send down another assistant with vaccine to help him to give jabs to everyone in Nabilatuk. Our own medical assistant and I are the only ones here who have already had smallpox jabs, so all the people in the police lines and the trading centre have to receive them. They will also do the same to people in Moroto and send someone round the outposts for the same purpose. More vaccine is to be obtained from Kampala and Entebbe for this purpose.

As it's highly infectious and we have to avoid an epidemic throughout the district, the present patient has to be isolated for six weeks and so does Nabilatuk. The men and their families cannot leave Nabilatuk, so no patrols can go out and the men in the posts can't come in. As the only one vaccinated, I am going to have to drive myself everywhere and visit the posts without escort; and deal with all other matters outside alone.

The NCOs have put up simple manned roadblocks, each of two men, on the roads outside the trading centre to prevent people from leaving or entering. It will also give the constables something to do during their enforced long confinement. Of course, it's easy enough to come and go via the surrounding bush and we don't have the manpower to surround the whole area, so I've ordered a foot patrol to move around between the roads. Most people use the roads anyway so as to avoid

193

the thorn bushes. Any wandering Karamojong will be seized and vaccinated, probably much to their puzzlement, so we'll have a couple of big chaps handy to subdue unco-operative customers.

We've put the patient into a hut in the lines by himself and his food is placed in the doorway. I've explained about thoroughly washing everything he touches in boiling water and left the rest of it to the medical assistant, who is a bright young Etesot who clearly knows his business.

Saturday 8 October

During the first week of our isolation I've been out first to the eastern posts, then to the southern, to check how things are going. Pretty quiet at the moment, fortunately. Just as well; if there's a raid Moroto Police will have to deal with it. They can go out and vaccinate all the raiders, too, if they are headed in this direction.

Today I drove on my solitary safari to check on Iriri post and then down the main road to Moroto to report in, collect mail, do some shopping and pick up the local gossip. It's a tiring business all this driving and Land Rover back is a bit of a problem. The thought of five more weeks of the same is best not thunked. Meanwhile our police lines are benefiting considerably. With all the staff at his disposal, the barracks sergeant has been using those not out on road block duty to carry out a very thorough clean-up of the whole compound and the uniports. Stones and rocks that have obstinately been a stone colour have been painted white and everywhere now, according to the sergeant, is very *malidadi* (smart). He's right; it is.

Friday 21 October

I went up to Moroto this morning, collecting mail and supplies, and called at the hospital to speak to the DMO about our smallpox situation. So far there have been no other cases, due to everyone's quick action. He said they've been kept busy carrying out eye operations for trachoma, which is very common here due to the particles of grass and dust being blown about by the constant high winds. I also enquired about a driver of mine who had had a complete mental breakdown for unknown reasons. He seems to be recovering slowly and I visited him in the ward and had a chat and left him some magazines to look at.

Saturday 29 October

All of yesterday and today I've been out on my lonesome driving the Land Rover round all the posts to pay the men. I was so tired today from the constant rough riding that, when I left Kopenek post, I drove off the track, which is now overgrown with long elephant grass, straight into a large and very hard termite hill. Fortunately I was going slowly but, even so, it damaged the vehicle and I was bruised, dazed and shaken from hitting the steering wheel rather hard. With much rattling and scraping of metal I eventually managed to reach Namalu Rest Camp, where I found an ADC from Moroto on safari. While I took a rest and a mug of tea he and his driver managed to straighten things out so that I could return to Nabilatuk; but the vehicle will have to be sent to Moroto or Mbale for repairs. I feel like being sent in for repairs myself. Because of this situation I haven't been able to slide off for the occasional weekend break at Mbale or Kitale and I'm getting bush-happy.

So far there are still no other smallpox patients. How such an infectious disease has avoided being spread around beats me. The medical people are surprised too. The earlier prediction had been for a fairly large number of patients.

Monday 7 November

I've been checking our smallpox patient daily throughout this period and he seems to have gone through the various stages of his sickness more or less according to the book. The pustules formed scabs which the medical assistant described as 'nice'. Not a word I would have used, but he was no doubt describing the progress rather than the appearance. At any rate, the scabs then separated and have cleared up and this was reported on the radio to the DMO yesterday. Today he came on the radio and declared us free of the dreaded plague, so we can now revert to our normal duties without ringing a bell and shouting 'unclean!'

Thursday 17 November

After a recent large *baraza* with the chiefs, which I attended, the DC and the OC Police Karamoja ordered a huge seizure of cattle from the Pian to be driven to the Suk in Upe and handed over at Amudat as compensation for past raids. So starting at first light yesterday, I arranged for relays of our men to drive the cattle in several herds at different times. It's a very hot and dusty job and, halfway along the road to Amudat, they were met by men from Moroto and Amudat who took over the particular herd and continued with it.

We still have only one working Land Rover as the one I damaged was sent to Mbale for major repairs, some of which had accumulated before the accident. So I've been collecting the men in the vehicle

195

after the handover and bringing them back to Nabilatuk to take out the next herd. After the first two journeys the driver, a new man here, packed it in, complaining of exhaustion and backache, so I took over and did the next three journeys. I also took out containers of water with plastic mugs for the constables and chief's men to slake their thirst on the dry and dusty walk. At the end of the afternoon, after more trips out, I sat on my verandah resting, flaked out and drained by the heat and dust.

The Police Cessna flew overhead and landed at the airstrip. I was too tired to go there as I normally would and transport the visitors. Apart from the radio room, all the men were out on the drive or other duties. My taxi service was suspended for the time being. Shortly after this a bespectacled European in neat, clean khakis appeared at my verandah steps and glared at me sitting stretched out. I'd never seen him before. He said quickly and angrily: 'What's this? Why didn't you come and meet us at the airstrip? Why are you idling here when there's so much to be done getting the cattle to Amudat? You should be out there in charge, not lying about in here.'

Just then Chris, the pilot, came staggering up carrying a crate of bottled beer, which he put down on the ground. I rose slowly and painfully to my feet and greeted him. Then I turned to the stranger and said: 'Look, I don't know who you are and I don't like your tone. I've been up since before dawn, I've had nothing to eat and I've been out on safari up and down that road all day and I'm just now taking a break. This is my station and as far as I'm concerned you can go to hell.'

He changed his tone then, gave his name and said he was a new ADC at Moroto. He offered to open some bottles of beer, which I don't drink, and set about doing so. Unfortunately for him, the beer was very warm and had been quite considerably shaken up during the flight in the Cessna and when carried to my place. As soon as he opened one bottle it burst in his hand and cut him rather deeply and he was carelessly bleeding all over the place. What a shame. Nobody tried to open another bottle. Chris performed first aid while I watched. I've got a chit excusing me from bandaging bumptious ADCs. He made a fuss and insisted on being flown straight back to Moroto to go to the hospital for stitches, so Chris shrugged and off they went. I then went out on a final trip and fetched the last lot of men back.

While we had been engaged on this work all day, the local chiefs and their ALG police had been busy rounding up and arresting suspected raiders from a number of *manyattas*. There is no lock-up in Nabilatuk and a large number of them were made to sit in the chief's compound, guarded by the ALG police. The overflow was put into a uniport with a padlock on the door. I told the ALG corporal to make sure his men stayed awake and alert during the night. At midnight I checked and all was well, so I caught up with some overdue sleep.

This morning the chief came to me and reported in great agitation that most of the prisoners had escaped in the night. I inspected the uniport, which had been packed tight with naked men with no tools or items of any sort. They'd had nothing to do, so some of them had played about with the nuts and bolts on the metal walls, which then came undone, dismantled themselves and collapsed. Thus they had made their great escape without even digging a tunnel. I've no doubt that the ALG police who were supposed to be guarding them were in fact asleep. They deny this, of course, but I ripped off the stripes from the corporal's sleeve and told the chief he was unfit to hold the rank, since I had warned him to watch the prisoners carefully. I then told them all to go out and look for the prisoners and bring them back.

Friday 25 November

In the mail collected from Moroto today was a letter from Police HQ. The senior superintendent who is now head of Traffic and Communications has written to say that he holds me responsible for 'the serious damage' to the Land Rover, when I was run into by a stationary anthill, and that consideration was being given to prosecuting me for dangerous driving. The man's a fool. I was in the bush, not on a public road, and nobody else was there to be endangered. I understand that he has never been to Karamoja as he's a permanent Kampala cowboy, so he probably has no idea of the situation here. It's no wonder his nickname is 'Snakey'. But I'm rather surprised and disappointed that the Northern Provincial Police Commander in Gulu, through whom the letter passed, did not immediately jump on the idea from a great height.

However, I've written a brief reply acknowledging the letter and stating that I shall require time to come down to Kampala to brief an advocate to defend me if a charge is brought, because I intend to fight it through every court. This time I hope the Provincial Commander gets a grip and slaps him down. It's his job to protect his officers from HQ harassment.*

Wednesday 30 November

A message from a sub-chief received this morning reported that a young girl had hanged herself from a tree near the *manyatta*. It was

---

*I never heard any more about it.

about 10 miles away and I drove out there with the station sergeant and examined the body, which had been cut down. Suicide is not common up here and it turned out that she was a Pian in her teens who had been about to marry a young man from a nearby *manyatta* who had recently been on a raid and got himself killed by the Suk. I decided that there was no point in taking the body in for a PM and gave permission for the parents to take the body for disposal according to their custom.

Tuesday 20 December

I'm coming to the end of my year here and leave is due, so my relief, David, arrived a couple of days ago and we've been going round the posts and the area generally. He carries a shotgun with him everywhere and from time to time shoots a buck, which provides meat for the house. The driver and escort get their share, so he should be very popular. It's something I could never do. He's an Oxford graduate with an athletics blue and a very keen type. Except that he's not at all keen to take over my regular English lessons in the recreation room. I showed him our station's excellent results in the last Force literacy exam in the hope of encouraging him to carry on, but he says he can't teach. Too bad.

When we were approaching Koromoch post we saw a group of about 20 Pian with spears about a hundred yards off the track, so we stopped and walked towards them. David had his shotgun and the escort his rifle and I fished out my pistol from under the seat. Seeing us thus armed, the men stopped and dropped their spears, which I then ordered two of them to pile into the back of the vehicle. We clearly needed help with so many prisoners so I told the driver to go to the post and bring the men there back with him. However, as he tried to turn the Land Rover in the river bed, it stuck in a drift of sand and the wheels sunk in until they almost disappeared.

We then organised the prisoners and they dug into the sand with their hands and heaved and lifted and pushed the vehicle until it came out of the drift. For some reason they seemed to enjoy doing this and there was much laughing and singing as they worked at it. In view of the fact that it was Christmas and I was about to leave the district and, furthermore, I didn't want to be lumbered with all these prisoners and nowhere to put them, I declared an amnesty on the spot. I warned them not to carry spears, which we were keeping, and told them to go home and behave themselves, as the police would be keeping an eye on them from now on. So off they went. At the post I gave the corporal their names and *manyatta* location, which the escort constable had noted down, so that he could have a word with their sub-chief on his next patrol that way.

Thursday 22 December

The radio hut, which is next to my house, has a 20-foot radio mast beside it. The mast is the usual Meccano-type construction, with a steel ladder fixed to one side up to the top where the aerial is attached. The radio constables climb this ladder occasionally to carry out repairs and maintenance. Recently, however, a swarm of hornets built a nest just where the aerial part starts and, in their comings and goings, the wretched creatures have taken to invading the radio hut below, much to the dismay and consternation of the duty radio constables.

So this morning I decided to take steps since nobody else was willing to climb up there. David made himself scarce by going off to shoot something and I made my preparations for battle. Knowing from unpleasant experience just how painful hornet stings can be, I put on a thick, long-sleeved khaki shirt buttoned right up and long trousers tucked into my socks. I topped this with a bush hat, the wide brim pulled down all round, and a mosquito net draped over it and hanging downwards from the brim so as to give me some protected working and breathing space. The radio corporal and his duty constable hastily took cover while I, clutching my small spray pump filled with DDT, climbed close to the top of the ladder and quickly squirted DDT into the mass of hornets and then slid down the ladder before they could recover from their aerial panic enough to attack me. Not long afterwards there were many dead or dying hornets around the base of the mast and I was able to climb up again and dislodge the nest, thus making the area safe for democracy and radio constables. And all without being stung.

Monday 26 December

David and I went over to Namalu prison farm two days ago with one of the corporals to select the bull which the prison has donated to the police for Christmas. Yesterday in the lines they all enjoyed a great feast of meat and *pombe* which ended in a dance started by the Karamojong trackers, who began their usual leaping up and down until, soon, most of the others joined in. Later Radio Corporal Uttu appeared at my house in a very smart suit wearing an elaborate Karamojong head-dress and carrying a West Nile harp-like instrument. He was looking very happy and well lubricated as he wished us Christmas greetings.

Friday 30 December

I handed over the station to David and departed yesterday. I shall be going from Kampala by train to Mombasa as I've decided to go home by sea, catching a round-Africa cruise ship that calls there on 13 January. First, I'm having a few idle days camping in Murchison Falls Game Park. My kit has already gone down by lorry to the PWD store in Kampala as I don't yet know where I shall be posted on my return. My cook, Juma, went with the kit and is then returning to Kisumu in Kenya. I'm taking with me in my car the luggage I shall need on the voyage.

I've really enjoyed my year in Karamoja and I'm so glad to have been able to sample the old primitive Africa of yesterday with safaris and camp-fires and walking through the bush in a dry, harsh land of rolling plains and grazing herds, both of cattle and wild animals, before it all disappears into some sort of development and modern life-style; as I suppose it is likely to do in the near future if the local politicians have their way.

These simple, warlike people, who are not concerned with clothes or possessions, other than their beloved cattle, are a complete contrast to life outside. I can't understand those types who regard Karamoja as a punishment station to be avoided like the plague. They don't know what they have missed, as almost anyone in the police or administration who has served up here would tell them. I'm certainly sorry to be leaving the district and hope to return sometime in the future.

I hear that down in Kampala everyone is on stand by as the Kabaka and the Buganda Lukiiko have declared that Buganda is to become independent from the rest of Uganda as from 1 January 1961. Just how they intend to accomplish this is a mystery to all, including themselves, since they don't have the capability in financial, economic or security terms. Consequently, all the police down there are on full alert, which is an excellent reason for me to remain up here in the game park, well out of the way of all such nonsense.

1961

Friday 13 January

Absolutely nothing came of the great Buganda independence declaration. The police were on stand by but, apart from a few beer parties, nothing actually happened; it just all fizzled out. The Buganda Lukiiko maintains that they have successfully seceded from the Uganda Protectorate but everything is going on the same as before, including day-to-day relations between the two governments. How utterly futile.

I drove down from Murchison Park and Paraa after a few days of idleness in camp and, when I reached the outskirts of Kampala, I was stopped by a couple of traffic constables. On safari I always carry a chuggle, which is a canvas drinking-water container that keeps water cool by evaporation through the thick canvas. It usually hangs from the rear door handle of my car and I'd forgotten it was still there. The constables said it was obscuring the rear number plate, which is a traffic offence.

The constables were unknown to me and I didn't bother to identify myself. I merely apologised and explained that I had just driven down from Karamoja, and I put the chuggle inside the car. So all I got was a verbal warning. I then had a couple of nights at the Uganda Club and sorted out various matters before putting the car into storage and departing on leave by this morning's train to Mombasa.

Sunday 15 January – At Mombasa docks, Kenya

The two days rail journey down to the coast was pleasant and uneventful. I arrived here in Mombasa before lunch, with plenty of time to go aboard the Union Castle ship *Kenya Castle*, which apparently does this round-Africa trip regularly. It's full of tourists and I hope that it isn't going to be an organised romp of the jolly Butlin's Camp type as all I want to do is rest and relax in some comfort. While finding my way about the decks I met John, who had been OC Kampala Traffic Branch when I worked there. He and his wife have chosen this way to go home on leave.

Wednesday 1 February – At Cape Town, South Africa

One good thing about this trip is that we stop for a reasonable length of time at each port so that we can go ashore and have a look round. From Mombasa we sailed down to the island of Zanzibar, where I wandered through the narrow streets with the scent of cloves everywhere and looked at the many intricately carved and studded huge wooden gateways and doors of the old Arab buildings. It was here and in Mombasa that the East African slave trade was conducted by and for the benefit of the Arabs around the Red Sea and the Gulf of Aden. Next we moved down to Dar-es-Salaam (Haven of Peace) for a day and then on to Mozambique, where we spent time in the two ports of Beira and Lourenço Marques. From there to Durban for a day and a half, where I had a swim from a magnificent beach and an evening at a cinema, after wandering around the old city. Then on a coach trip to the Valley of a Thousand Hills and the Nagle Dam, with a visit to what was claimed to be an authentic Zulu kraal with tribal dancing.

After that south to East London and Port Elizabeth, where it rained a lot; and round to Cape Town, where I am spending the two and a half days here ashore, staying at the home of HE's friend who visited me in Karamoja last April. He has driven me around the beautiful city and we've been up Table Mountain by cable car and generally seen the sights.

Sunday 19 February – At sea

We're going up the west coast of Africa now, but I was disappointed to learn that we are not calling anywhere on the mainland. Last Saturday we stopped at the island of St Helena and I went ashore and took a taxi trip round the small island, stopping at Government House and Napoleon's tomb and inspecting an ancient giant tortoise which was rampaging about the place. We also stopped at Ascension Island but, as nobody is allowed ashore because of defence installations and security, I presume we were only delivering and collecting mail and other items. On Wednesday we crossed the equator and started northwards to Las Palmas in the Canary Islands, where we've spent a pleasant day today, and were entertained on board by Spanish dancers. In town, before boarding the ferry back to the ship, I bought a large and colourfully woven Spanish blanket, which will decorate a wall in my next house.

Friday 24 February – Tilbury Docks, London

The crossing of the Bay of Biscay was not too rough in spite of winter weather, but it was very cold there, as it is here at Tilbury. From here I catch a train westwards and homewards. Fortunately there are no courses for me to attend on this leave.

Tuesday 14 March

I was up in London today, crossing the road outside Buckingham Palace, when I was almost knocked down by a large, black official limousine flying a flag. As I jumped out of the way I saw the familiar face, beard and black headgear of Archbishop Makarios, the President of Cyprus, sitting in the back, no doubt oblivious of the fact that he had almost ended my career. There's a Commonwealth Prime Ministers meeting going on here, and South Africa has just become a republic and decided to leave the Commonwealth.

Monday 27 March

According to the news from Uganda the LegCo elections were held last Monday to decide on a fully elected government for the year of self-government leading up to independence in 1962. However, the Buganda Lukiiko adopted its usual cut-off-the-nose-to-spite-the-face attitude and ordered a boycott of the elections in Buganda, so only 20,000 people bothered to vote there. But those few all voted for the Catholic traditionalist Democratic Party (DP) of Benedicto Kiwanuka. This gave him 19 seats unopposed and ensured that he was victorious over the Protestant Uganda People's Congress (UPC) of Obote. This was in spite of the fact that a total of 80,000 more votes throughout Uganda were cast for the UPC than for the DP. So it looks as if there will have to be fresh elections just before independence, with Buganda taking a proper part. It's a most unsatisfactory situation, resulting from the irritating belief by the Baganda politicians in the boycott as a successful political weapon.

Monday 19 June

I arrived back in Uganda yesterday, flying in a Britannia jet-prop of BOAC via Cairo. My new posting is most welcome to me as I'm now an instructor at the Police College, Naguru, on the Jinja road just outside Kampala. I have one of the staff quarters there and have taken on two Tanganyikans, John as cook and Mikairi (Michael) as *shamba* boy.

I knew the College Commandant, John, before as he and his wife are involved in KATS productions. He walked with me around the College compound, pointing out the various places. Outside the compound is the huge Kampala sewerage works. He seems to be fascinated by this and spent some time explaining to me how the system works. I was not able to share his fascination.

I'm sharing an office with Les, who is Chief Instructor in charge of the Training Wing. Mac, from Karamoja, is also here; now commanding Special Force, which is based at the College. I am to teach the law of evidence, one of the most difficult laws to teach and learn; also map-reading to promotion courses. Well, I don't mind that. Just to be teaching is good enough for me. Since Uganda is to become independent next year, I hope that I'll be able to keep this job at least until then.

Tuesday 20 June

There's a British policewoman, actually a sergeant, who came here in January, seconded from the Met as an Assistant Superintendent, to train and administer a section of women police. Apparently there are already eight recruits under training at the PTS. With women police, an air wing and a dog section, the Force is certainly being brought up to date and provided with the right sort of training and staff before we hand everything over. It also means that the quickened promotion of well-trained African policemen is even more necessary, so the job we're doing at the College is vitally important. It's a big incentive and my inclination, at present, is to try to arrange to stay on and work in Uganda after independence if this is possible.

Friday 14 July

Earlier I wrote to Dundori Kennels in Nakuru, Kenya, from where Blister's parents originated. I asked if they could let me have another wire-haired fox terrier and today he arrived by rail, a fine three-months-old puppy now named Kimbo. I'm very pleased with him.

I've started up English classes in the evening once a week here at the College for mixed students and staff who need extra tuition. I've also revived the weekly class over at Nsambya barracks, where even the first class was very well attended. The word has got around of how well the previous group of English students there did in the Force exams. With independence approaching, the men can see good chances of quick promotion coming up and the sensible ones are preparing themselves with the necessary qualifications. It makes teaching a great pleasure since they are so keen.

Sunday 13 August

It was Force sports day yesterday at Nsambya. Several records were broken, especially in the 100 yards and the 440 yards. In the 6 miles PC Wasagala, in his first attempt at such a distance, actually came only four seconds short of the Uganda record time. These chaps really can run and, with very little time and opportunity to practise or train, they can still run record times. With proper professional coaches and training they could produce some remarkable results, I'm sure.

Monday 21 August

Two of the courses were on the rifle range at Bombo today to fire their qualification. On the way there in my car, with a sub-inspector from the staff, we came on a traffic accident with a small schoolgirl lying injured after being knocked off her bicycle. I sent the vehicle driver and the witnesses to Jinja Road Police Station, while I took the child to hospital. On the way back I left her name and parents' particulars at the station so that they could contact them and inform them where she is.

As a result I was very late arriving at the range and incurred a certain amount of wrath as nobody knew where I had been. I couldn't ring from the station as there's no working outside line at the range. If only we had some sort of mobile radio communication it would be of considerable use in such circumstances.

Wednesday 23 August

John, my cook/houseboy, has just announced that he has converted to Islam and is now named Adam and would I please remember that when I address him in future. I gave no guarantees and signed nothing. It seems to have something to do with the fact that Tanganyika becomes independent in December this year, but I don't really see the connection yet.

Tuesday 29 August

Les, the Chief Instructor and now an acting superintendent, has ordered me to try the College Head Constable (a similar rank to sergeant-major) on charges of insubordination and disobedience of an order. Furthermore, he says I'm to convict and dismiss him from the Force. So I've got this nonsense once again.

Apart from the impropriety of giving me such an order, this man has served for 23 years in the Force and has been awarded both the Colonial Police Medal and the Colonial Police Long Service Medal and, by such a dismissal, would lose his hard-earned pension. Personally, I think he's a very fine example to the men. Also, although it's not relevant to the charge, he is the tallest man in the Force, which makes him special. Anyway, without making a fuss about it, I got on with the trial and found that, as I had suspected, what had happened was due to a misunderstanding and a loss of temper on both sides. I gather that they have clashed before at some previous station and there's a history of dislike and distrust. I dismissed the charges, which made Les furious and hopping mad; but, as I pointed out afterwards, he had made a fatal mistake when he tried to tell me what verdict to bring and sentence to award. That is something up with which I will not put, as old Winston used to say.

Wednesday 6 September

Extra promotion courses to step up the number of NCOs and sub-inspectors are now under way here; and today two squads of constable-to-corporal courses passed out. I was pleased that two of the men came from Nabilatuk as a result of my recommendations, and another two whom I had recommended came from other stations, but had served with me before. The courses are all working hard now as the incentive is easy to see. Most of the European officers will be leaving at independence, which means many quick promotions for Africans in the inspectorate, thus creating vacancies there and for NCOs who will also have moved up. The way up is wide open for those who are ready to seize the opportunities developing.

Jim Fleming, a district officer, now African Courts Adviser, has been given the task of starting a law school at Entebbe. The purpose is to train Africans as magistrates to replace and integrate the local customary courts with the central judiciary and also to replace outgoing European magistrates who were also district officers. The African courts at present are presided over by chiefs and elders with no training. These will disappear and a sufficient number of trained full-time magistrates will replace them.

He has commenced the first course and, naturally, finds he needs assistance, as there is a lot of ground to cover teaching the civil and criminal laws and procedures. A request came to the College for one of our instructors to give him part-time help on this first course. Apparently the Commandant asked Les to do it, but he, like many of our officers, doesn't like teaching. I know a number of them who actually dread a posting to the staff of the College or PTS because of their dislike of instructional work. So Les suggested that I should do it and, of course, I have agreed, being ready to seize any opportunity to teach at any time.

Monday 11 September

I drove to Entebbe last Friday and went up the hill to Nsamizi (it means 'Snake Hill') Training Centre, where the Ministry of Community Development holds residential citizenship and retail trading and similar courses for African men and women from all over Uganda and from every government department as well as from outside government. At present the Law School shares facilities with them but it is a separate department of the Ministry of Justice. Jim says they are going to put up a law school building with a classroom and a library across the road on this hill next to the playing field.

I went there again this afternoon and took the first lesson in criminal procedure, adjusting the approach to the point of view of a presiding magistrate rather than a prosecuting policeman. There are 26 in the class from different districts. Most are customary court judges, but others have been registrars or clerks in those courts, or teachers and so on, which means that they are not youngsters. I gather that once recruiting of potential magistrate starts, they will expect to be getting students in their mid-twenties to thirties, maturity being an obviously important requirement for this job.

The main reason that I enjoy teaching in Uganda so much is because of the lively interest shown by Africans in learning. They actively take part in classes and come up with searching and intelligent questions. One needs to be alert and ready to field all sorts of queries, not always relevant to the subject, arising from what has been said in class, or what they have read, or perhaps heard on the radio in the recreation room.

Wednesday 13 September

This government, led by Chief Minister Kiwanuka, is set on a frantic course of almost instant Africanisation of all government departments. Expatriates are beginning to depart or prepare to do so in increasing numbers. Promotion of African junior officials is going on at a great rate and obviously some are being ridiculously over-promoted so that they cannot cope with their new duties and responsibilities through no fault of their own. Another big problem that will arise later on is that many of the senior posts are being filled by young Africans who may be in that position for a long time, thus causing a blockage of promotion opportunities for those lower down, which could be rather discouraging for them.

No doubt Kiwanuka has a political agenda and he has to show that Africans are getting the jobs and promotions, otherwise he will be out at the next elections. But there are numerous important jobs for which no Africans are yet qualified or sufficiently experienced and he would do well to encourage some of the departing Europeans in such posts to stay on in shadow posts, passing on useful expertise and knowledge to the new substantive post-holders, instead of making so much noise about ridding the country of the colonialists.

A system of lump-sum compensation, which we all refer to as Lumpers, has been worked out according to one's final salary and length of service. After the initial lump sum has been paid, the rest will come in annual instalments. In the Force the talk among British officers now is all of Lumpers and what they are planning to do with it; such as setting up a business, buying a house, or whatever. It's clear that this government does not expect or want British police officers to stay on and most seem to be planning to leave this year or next.

I have no plans to leave and certainly no wish to do so. However, there's no point in staying in the police with no prospects of promotion but, as yet, I've no idea how to arrange something suitable that will keep me here for as long as possible.

Friday 15 September

Sir Frederick Crawford has already left, having given up the post of Governor without completing his tour of five years. So he will not see Uganda into independence. I doubt whether the new Governor, due in November, will be very long in the job since it's pretty obvious that they won't want to have a British Governor or Governor-General, for very long after independence. If the present frantic rate of Africanisation is any indication he would probably get the Order of the Boot fairly rapidly. I suppose London will find someone who is almost due to retire.

Thursday 28 September

The School of Anatomy at Mulago Medical School got word that a mountain gorilla had been killed by a leopard and the body was found in the forest near the Bufumbira volcanoes, so they arranged for it to be brought to Kampala for dissection. However, it was expected that it might not last too well, so the Identification Bureau at Police HQ was asked to obtain prints of its hands and feet on the spot before decomposition set in.

The body was taken to Mbarara Police Station, where two constables got to work with ink roller and white cardboard. They found that four fingers on the left hand were missing, probably the result of a fight a long time before, and, due to its resultant excessive use of the right hand, most of the ridge detail had worn away. However, they produced prints of what there was and they are now in the unique position to boast that they have fingerprinted a gorilla.

Wednesday 11 October

We had a visit from the Minister of Security and External Relations, Chris Powell-Cotton, whom I knew when he was Provincial Commissioner of Northern Province. He inspected the College and watched the increased training for accelerated promotion taking place.

The constable-to-corporal course, which I am responsible for overseeing at the moment, put on a display of a murder investigation. With the aid of plastic simulated wounds and lots of red ink we had a suitably gory victim lying under a tree. I had hidden the murder weapon and other clues in the grass around and the object was to demonstrate what to do on first arrival at the crime scene. An agitated student came and whispered to me that the Minister was standing on the murder weapon. So I turned to P-C, pointed at his feet and told him that, if he didn't shift himself, he was likely to be arrested for interfering with a murder scene. The Commandant looked aghast and obviously thought I was being insubordinate and flippant, but I know P-C well enough and he simply laughed and hopped out of the way.

Friday 13 October

In the class-room this afternoon one of the corporals on a promotion course asked out of the blue why there should be an official opposition in our Parliament. His point was that in a tribe all must recognise and obey their chief as leader and the tribe must not be split in any way, otherwise it would be destroyed. Any opposition to the authority in power must be suppressed in order to keep the peace and for the general security of the tribe. He said this must surely apply to the whole country. He could be right. It's all very well our introducing the Westminster pattern of government and politics to Africa, but such democratic ideas may not work here, where the average African recognises only the strong chief or leader and sees no need for any opposition but only danger in allowing it to exist.

In an earlier written test on homicides one student wrote: 'Suicide is not a good idea unless you want to die.' How true.

Sunday 29 October

Yesterday evening the Force Boxing Championships were held at Lugogo indoor sports stadium. As the Commissioner is on leave, the Deputy is acting Commissioner and so hosted the Kabaka, who had been invited to attend and present the trophies. Unfortunately, the Deputy doesn't much like the Kabaka, so he summoned me to HQ the other day and said: 'Look here, you know this Kabaka chap and how to deal with him, so I want you in attendance at the boxing and you can look after him for the evening.' It was clearly an order, not an invitation, so I said: 'Very well, sir.'

The officers attending the championships were all in mess kit but I decided to wear my converted army blue patrols with spurs and, when the Kabaka arrived in his Rolls, I found that he was wearing exactly the same uniform except for it being badged and buttoned as a captain in the Grenadier Guards. As we walked together into the stadium he remarked that he was very pleased that I had chosen to wear the same uniform but, he added, he found it a problem when dancing as the spurs caught other people and dresses and so on. Evidently nobody had told him the drill so I said: 'Well, the form is you either don't wear spurs for a ball or you remove them before going on to the dance floor.'

He looked at me and said: 'Ah, I see.'

Having sorted that little problem out, we went on and watched the bouts, which produced plenty of encouragement, applause and excitement among the audience before the Kabaka dished out the cups and trundled off in his Rolls.

The Deputy said: 'I think that went rather well.'

Saturday 11 November

Yesterday was a special occasion as the first squad of policewomen had completed their training and were passed out. We've been having very heavy rain in Kampala recently and the grass parade ground at the PTS is unusable as it is under water and therefore suitable only for passing out frogmen or frogwomen, as the case may be. So this pass-out parade was held at the College on our tarmac square, presided over by the acting Governor, who is George Cartland, who inspected and speechified. The new Governor is Sir Walter Coutts, who will be sworn in next week.

Monday 20 November

I recently completed my course of lectures on the Criminal Procedure Code at the Law School and then set and marked an examination for the magistrate students. Jim says he's very pleased with the results and with my teaching and he has asked if I would be interested in a permanent transfer from the Police to the Law School as a lecturer in law. He said it would mean my reading for the English Bar to become suitably qualified for a substantive appointment and I'm willing to do that, in spite of my dislike of studying for exams.

It would answer my wish to stay on in Uganda and do what I most like doing, and believe I do best: teaching. Straightaway I said I'd definitely be interested, so he's going to write to the Commissioner and the Public Service Commission to arrange the transfer as soon as possible. I believe that this is a heaven-sent opportunity and just what I need at this particular time. I just hope it can be arranged. Meanwhile I shall tell nobody.

Saturday 9 December

It is independence day for Tanganyika today and, since both of my domestic servants, Adam and Mikairi, are Tanganyikans, they naturally have the day off to celebrate this special occasion. They have put on their finery and, holding fancily carved walking sticks, have been duly photographed by me with Kimbo determinedly getting into the picture. Then they went off to celebrate with other fellow countrymen here in Kampala. We're next, and then not far behind, I expect, will be Kenya.

Tuesday 12 December

The letter to the Commissioner asking for me to be released to transfer to the Ministry of Justice and join the Law School has had surprising results. I had envisaged no problems but, in fact, for reasons not explained to me, the Commissioner has apparently taken exception to the idea. He not only wrote to the Ministry to say that I can't be spared as I'm doing an important job, but he then contradicted this assertion by ordering my immediate transfer from the College, where I was certainly doing useful work, to Nsambya barracks, where I am not. Instead I've been given the lowliest job of all here, that of OC Accommodation and Welfare, a post normally held by a sub-inspector, so there can have been no real need to transfer me.

I really cannot understand it. Nobody gains from this: the College loses an instructor at a time of need; the Law School doesn't get one at a time of need; and I get a useless job when I could be very useful elsewhere. What is the Commissioner thinking of? Other officers are leaving to go home almost daily, so why on earth should he object to my staying on transfer?

I tried to make an appointment to see him but was informed that he is unavailable, which means he won't see me. I phoned Jim at the Law School and explained the situation and suggested that the Ministry might bring some pressure to bear since the training of magistrates is a great deal more important than my acting as a Barracky Bill at Nsambya.

Saturday 23 December

As I am barracks welfare officer, I called a meeting of the men's welfare committee and suggested we should organise a Christmas dance in the recreation room here. The Police Band dance section agreed to play and we decorated the room and arranged for the canteen manager to supply soft drinks, as alcohol is prohibited in police lines by Standing Orders. I designed and produced some posters advertising the dance to be put up on the various notice boards in Kampala stations.

It took place this evening and I went along to see how it was going. Several other officers looked in from time to time and everyone seemed to be having a good time. The band played a selection from their growing repertoire of African-style rhythmic dance music arranged for their instruments. It was very effective and everyone I spoke to enjoyed it.

I have moved from my quarters at the College into the Officers' Quarters here at the barracks, so I usually walk down through the lines to my office at the other end of the huge compound. On the way down each morning I am usually ambushed and joined by a mob of toddlers, police children living here in the quarters, who dance along laughing and chanting '*Moojungoo!*' which is their version of *Mzungu* (European). Each *mtoto* grabs hold of one of my fingers or thumbs and hangs on until they are clustered around me, and those who can't find a finger just stay close. Passing NCOs and constables find considerable amusement in the fact that I am thus unable to respond properly to their salutes.

This regular morning Pied Piper ritual from these wonderful, funny little kids helps to make my day and to take away some of the disappointment of no longer having the interesting and useful instructing job at the College.

When I reached the barracks clinic this morning the African sister in charge came out holding a baby that was really black, rather than the usual brown; obviously from the far Nilotic north. She told me that the child was ill. 'Look,' she said very seriously to me, 'you can see how ill this child is: she is as white as a sheet.' I forebore from comment.

1962

Thursday 4 January

As a result of the recent rapid promotions, mainly from the inspectorate, there are now 60 African gazetted officers in the Force and nine of these are full superintendents and obviously headed for higher posts. Already five of them are in charge of up-country police districts and one has been put in command of Nsambya barracks, so he is now my OC, although only a short time ago we were of the same rank. This is happening all over, but the Asians in the inspectorate are not getting a share of these promotions.

The SSP at Buganda HQ called me to his office this morning and said that I was to act as the new superintendent's shadow and personally see to the administration and conduct the orderly rooms for him until he's ready to take it all over. In fact, I believe he's being groomed for a staff job at PHQ soon.* He added that if I do a good job for him the superintendent will then receive further promotion. Some incentive. Still, I'll do what I can. These chaps are being pushed upwards harder and faster than is really good for them and the Force, but it's not their fault and they need all the help they can get.

I was presiding over orderly room this morning and in one of the defaulters reports a sergeant wrote: 'On 11 November 1961 PC Okot came to me and said he wanted to go sick. So I gave him permission to go sick. When I later checked the sick report I found that he did not go sick; so I charged him with failing to go sick.' He was guilty of obstinately staying healthy.

Monday 15 January

The OC Stores here at the barracks is a cockney called Len who, before the war, was a private in the British Army serving in Egypt. Later he joined the Palestine Police as a driver. He's now marking time while, as he says: 'I'm waiting for me ticket.' He'll go home with his Lumpers and no job in sight and is probably too old now to start afresh easily. He idles around the barracks offices and usually pops into my office to gossip and to tell tall stories about 'the old days'.

This morning it was about when he was in Egypt as part of the British garrison in the Suez Canal Zone under the Anglo-Egyptian Treaty before the war. In those days there were still some British administrators and even magistrates working in the Egyptian courts. Len said: 'We was going along this road out of Cairo in an army *gharry* (lorry) when we collided wiv a big car full of Gyppo toffs and one of 'em turned out to be King Farouk. Well, our driver was taken before this British magistrate geezer for causing the accident and 'e told the magistrate that 'e was driving along when 'is truck was run into by this big car full of wogs. Well, the magistrate immediately stopped 'im and said 'e was not to refer to 'Is Majesty King Farouk as a wog. 'E said it was 'ighly improper, so 'e should start 'is evidence again. So the driver said 'e was sorry and goes on that 'e was driving along the road when 'is truck was run in to by a big car and then 'e sez to the magistrate: "'oo do you fink was in it? Well, it was 'Is Majesty King Farouk and a lot of other wogs."'

Friday 19 January

The Force Education Officer has gone on leave and he's coming back to do a last short tour before leaving Uganda. He asked me in his

*He later became Deputy Commissioner of Police.

absence to mark all the Force literacy exam papers from the recent English exam. Thus, I find myself with a huge pile of papers to read and mark. Quite a number of these are from my students or former students in Kampala but, of course, I can't identify them as they only show a candidate's exam number.

It gives me something useful to do while I'm sitting in the accommodation office. The actual work of allocating the quarters is done competently by a corporal and a constable. As far as I'm concerned it's an idiotic waste of time for me to be sitting here when I could be usefully employed at the Police College or the Law School at Entebbe.

Thursday 8 February

Somebody has done something at last. I've received a letter from the Public Service Commission offering me the appointment as a Lecturer at the Law School; adding that the effective date of my transfer would be by mutual agreement between the Commissioner of Police and the Solicitor General at the Ministry of Justice. The way I feel now, the sooner I get out of the Police the better. Then I can start my new career and do something useful and interesting once again.

As I was reading the letter and thinking about the future and now feeling considerably less cheesed off about the present, I could hear Len waffling on something about: 'So there was St Peter sitting at the Gate 'arping on 'is 'arp, when up comes this geezer...' Then he interrupted himself and pointed at a short, very stocky bugler who was walking past the office. Len said: ''Ere, look at 'im, ennee got fick fighs?'

Friday 9 February

The rains have not only been excessively heavy this season, but disastrously so. There's a very serious situation on Lake Kioga and the Nile rail services in the north are under water. Lake Victoria is still a good 4 feet above normal level and the pier at Entebbe is completely under water and out of use. Much sand on the beach there has disappeared under the rising level, which has caused the shore to change shape and the beach has been considerably foreshortened. There's no indication that the water levels are likely to go down anywhere. There are local mutterings that this is an omen about independence, but nobody seems able to explain the significance of the omen.

Thursday 1 March

The 1962 Uganda Constitution comes into operation today. The Chief

Minister becomes Prime Minister and the Legislative Council becomes the National Assembly, although everyone has already taken to referring to it as Parliament; so that members are supposed to be referred to as MNAs, but in fact, they prefer to use the British title of MPs.

Monday 12 March

Len sidled into my office this morning, sat on my desk and said: 'Oo, me afteritis this morning is playing up somink chronic. 'Ere, did I tell you about this mate of mine wot 'ad a canary wot got out of its cage? It flew into some chicken wire and broke a leg wot 'ad to be took off by the vet. Well, me mate tried to 'ave a little wooden leg put on the bird but it wouldn't stay on and it kept falling off. But the bird went on 'opping abart quite 'appy like on one leg. So me mate sez: "Well," 'e sez, "it don't reelly matter 'cos the canary's a singer not a dancer."'

Tuesday 13 March

Suddenly I'm very busy. The parliamentary elections to take us into independence take place at the end of this month. Large numbers of police have to be transported here and there to provide security at the polling stations. The SSP called me in and said I was to organise this transport as he knew I had done this sort of thing before. So I'm going to use the large sports field and parade ground at Nsambya for lining up the many vehicles in groups so that they can be loaded up with the correct number of men and sent off to the assigned polling stations according to the timing on my programme. I now have an office in Buganda HQ above CPS as well as at the barracks and I rush between branch offices like a bank inspector.

When I spoke on the phone to Jim a couple of days ago to ask about the delay in my transfer, he said that Police HQ now claims that my presence and services are essential for the elections period so they're holding on to me. In fact, of course, there are other officers around who could easily do this job. If the Commissioner goes on like this, inventing reasons to keep me here, somebody will have to put his foot down with a heavy hand.

Thursday 15 March

This time Buganda has decided to take part in the elections. No doubt someone has at last been able to get it into their thick heads in the Lukiiko that, with independence, or *uhuru*, approaching fast, if they persist in their pointless boycotts and sulks, they will be left out of everything and have no say in the new government of an independent

Uganda. So KY or *Kabaka Yekka* (The Kabaka Alone) has been formed. They claim that it's a movement, not a political party. This is so as to support their claim that they are above politics and politicians and wish to have nothing to do with them.

Now Obote and his UPC have worked out and effected what sounds like a most unlikely alliance with KY and, since it's obvious that most Baganda will vote for KY candidates, the alliance is pretty certain to succeed in the elections and so form the next government. The best Kiwanuka and his DP can hope for is to form a reasonably strong parliamentary opposition. However, the mass of people in Uganda see this election as the Protestants against the Catholics and neither the politicians nor the priests have made any attempt to disabuse them. Indeed, to a large extent it's probably true.

Wednesday 4 April

Len was lounging about in my office again, going on about his Army days: 'There was this sergeant, see, and 'e don't speak proper, see, and 'e was on Orderly Room giving evidence against Smudger Smiff 'oo was on a fizzer. 'E sez: "Sir, I sez to Private Smiff, I sez, strip that Lewis gun darn and clean it wiv an hoily rag, I sez. Then this ... I mean Private Smiff, 'e sez 'e ain't got no hoily rag, 'e sez. So then I sez: Two negatives don't make no infirmary, Private Smiff, I sez. And 'e ups and 'its me one in the stummick wiv the gun butt, sir."'

Before I could hear the rest of this enthralling tale of dreadful military crime I was called away to the office of the OC Barracks to deal with some men on Orderly Room, as our new superintendent still doesn't seem to be all that keen on undertaking this duty himself.

Friday 20 April

From the security point of view the elections went off reasonably well. We had no big problems but the men are tired after being moved hither and thither all the time and on constant stand by throughout. I spent several nights on a camp bed in my office because it overlooks the Nsambya parade ground and I could thus keep an eye on the transport and night movements.

The UPC collected 43 seats, DP got 24 and KY won 24 seats, which were all in Buganda, of course. The coalition between UPC and KY thus gives them a huge majority and makes Obote Prime Minister. Kiwanuka not only lost the election but he also lost his seat to a KY man. So he's not even got the consolation prize of being Leader of the Opposition. He won't like that. The Baganda bear grudges for ever and the Mengo hierarchy will never forgive him for ignoring their boycott of the first elections.

This has been my last duty in the Force and at least it's been more useful than fooling about in the barracks office. It has at last been agreed that I am to take up my duties at the Law School on 1 May, so I'll be moving my kit over to Entebbe by lorry the day before; after first taking a few days off camping in Murchison Falls Park.

Monday 23 April

The other day I called at the Band Hut at Nsambya to say farewell as I've kept in touch with them since our trip together to Hoima back in 1955. Ted Moon had earlier offered to put on tape for me a programme of marches to keep as a souvenir as I now have a Grundig tape recorder. So today I provided the circular blank reel of tape and listened as they worked through and recorded the programme of my choice. Then I thanked them all and took my leave and the tape.

I've taken my last evening classes in English at the barracks and the College, wished them all well in the next Force literacy exams and left them to it. They should now have a slightly better chance of qualifying, I hope.

I've enjoyed my seven and a half years of Colonial Police service and learned a lot. I shall keep in touch, of course, especially by continuing to contribute articles and cartoons to the *Habari*, which has now become a quarterly magazine instead of monthly, and has consequently grown in size.

Thursday 26 April

As always, I'm enjoying my brief camping trip away from civilisation. I was talking to an Assistant Game Warden today and he told me that one of their HQ staff was coming back from Wairingo with the mail on a bicycle through the park. His bike had no brakes and he was whizzing down a slope and found a pride of about 14 lions lying sunning themselves in the road in front of him. He couldn't stop or slow down and was moving too fast to jump or fall off safely, so he kept going by shouting and swerving from side to side to try and avoid hitting the startled lions. Some of them actually jumped right over him on his bike in order to get out of his way. When he reached the park office and recovered his breath and composure, he demanded to be paid danger money in future for performing this duty. He didn't get it.

217

2

The Law School: May 1962–February 1970

Tuesday 1 May

This is the day. Here I am, a civilian after 15 years in uniform. I've been allocated Senior Staff Quarter No. 1 at Nsamizi (Snake Hill). It's a fine three-bedroomed house on the far side of the hill from the Training Centre and Law School. There is fruit in the large garden: two lemon trees, an avocado tree and several pawpaws, with masses of flowering shrubs and trees all round. Lake Victoria can be looked down upon and seen in the distance through the trees. It's very pleasant and peaceful and I think I'll like it here.

Saturday 5 May

Jim suggested that I should visit his old station at Jinja, where he knew all the African district court staff. So here I am for three days being shown around various parts of Busoga. Today I sat in during several trials which were conducted in Lusoga, but the courts registrar whispered a translation into my ear. They seem to be reasonably well organised but these customary matters that they deal with, such as land disputes, dowry payment disputes, divorces, inheritance of property and so on, are all to be dealt with in the magistrates courts under the new system, which will replace local African courts of this sort.

Thursday 17 May

I've forwarded my application to become a member of Gray's Inn in London so that I can read for the Bar and sit the examinations. Jim is already a barrister and so was able to support my application. He has suggested that I start with just one exam in Part I to get the flavour of it. Then, at the next sitting, I can take two or more papers in other subjects as I feel ready. With my impatience about putting exams

218

behind me, this is not the way I would do it, but he knows more about it than I do at this stage, so I shall try it his way first.

I've started to prepare for the criminal law paper next month as I'm familiar with the subject, so it shouldn't take long to study. The civil law paper of tort and contract looks rather difficult; but constitutional law and legal history seem quite straightforward. I've taught evidence, but that's a Finals paper, so a long way off at the moment. Roman law is factual and a matter of knowing Latin, which I did at school.

Thursday 31 May

I hear that a week ago there was a great battle in southern Karamoja. Apparently the Suk had earlier raided the Pian and killed 22 people, so there was a massive retaliation raid organised by about 1,000 Pian, who assembled with spears from far and wide. In the ensuing battle 107 were killed and a great number wounded. However, there was a company of 4 KAR in the area on an exercise and the Pian foolishly decided to attack them and lost 60 more shot down. Fortunately, the KAR broke up the Suk pursuing force and sent them home. Independence is coming but they're still at it.

Friday 15 June

This year, and for the last time, the Queen's Birthday Parade was held at Entebbe sports ground instead of in Kampala, so I attended as a spectator. Although the KAR are around, they're otherwise engaged, so the parade was by the Police and the Governor took the salute. It went well but it's rather sad that we shall not be seeing it here again. A part of history now.

Wednesday 20 June

The magistrates on the course asked for a Law School tie to wear now and afterwards. Jim gave reluctant approval and I produced several designs and let the students choose one. Then I went to Wee Green's shop in Kampala, now owned by an Asian, and he arranged for a quantity to be made in the UK which he will stock for our future use. It has come out well: black and gold stripes on a rifle-green background. Most of the students are already proudly wearing them.

Friday 6 July

I collected my new car today. It's a royal blue Peugeot 403 estate car and, so far, I've driven 26 trouble-free miles in it. There's a new word out for the African fat cats, politicians and businessmen, who drive around in the obligatory and indispensable Mercedes Benz saloon cars so as to demonstrate their great importance. The locals call them *Wabenzi*.

Monday 16 July

I asked Jim why the school is called the Local Law School. I said it sounds as if it runs unimportant local courses of the citizen/trader type that Nsamizi puts on. He said that the Administration officials at the Secretariat, as it was then, had deliberately done this to keep it all at a low level so that nobody outside the administrative service would get above himself. It seemed to me that he agreed with this degrading policy and appeared to regard his association with the Law School as a mere passing phase in an administrative officer's career. I think it's completely the wrong attitude and I hope that it can be changed in the near future. I shall certainly try to do what I can in this regard and I am not going to use the word 'local' in any letter or document referring to the school.

Tuesday 31 July

I've been teaching the law of tort to the magistrates this term. I knew nothing about the law of civil wrongs before, so I had to read it up and make notes to make sure that I was keeping ahead of the class all the time. It's an exciting way of teaching and it certainly keeps me on my toes. It's also a subject I have to read for the Bar exams anyway.

The first magistrates course has ended and they've sat for all their exams. I set and marked the paper in tort and they did quite well in spite of it being more of a case of the blind leading the blind. They have had a graduation ceremony and certificates were presented by the Minister. Now they go back to their courts to continue as before while they wait for the legislation to be passed to amalgamate the customary courts with the central judiciary.

Meanwhile, the training must go on so that as many as possible will be ready when the time comes. We're starting the second course at the beginning of September, so I have August free in which to prepare for the criminal law paper in the Bar exams, which are also early in September.

Tuesday 4 September

Douglas Brown, another administrative officer, has taken over as head of the Law School and Jim has gone to the Ministry to be Senior Courts Adviser. The second magistrates course assembled, this time with 30 students, all mature types from government departments including some ex-policemen. More than half have experience in the customary courts but no special training. From the customary courts we have only been able to take those whose English is up to a standard sufficient to enable them to understand the instruction and to read and reasonably understand law textbooks.

Thursday 6 September

There's quite a lot of talk going on outside among Africans, no doubt encouraged by some politicians, about how the property of the 'rich' Europeans will be distributed and shared out after independence. Some people are naturally rather apprehensive about this, but I think it's all just talk. I certainly hope so, anyway.

Tuesday 18 September

There's a large photograph in today's *Uganda Argus* of a baby on the operating table at Mulago Hospital with the headline: A BABY'S LIFE IS SAVED. It describes how the baby son of a Mr and Mrs Kagoro was born with a severe and rare blood disease, which meant that its blood had to be drained and replaced to save its life. In the early hours of the morning the hospital phoned a European living in Entebbe who belonged to the required rare rhesus negative blood group. He raced to Kampala in his car and gave his blood and the baby is now out of danger.

Today I received a letter from the Director of the Red Cross Blood Transfusion Service to thank me for donating the blood. I registered with them several years ago but this is the first time that they've had to call on me for a special donation. So this little chap is going around with my blood in him and I shall probably never knowingly meet him.

Saturday 6 October

This is the big month. Today there was a special independence pageant at Entebbe sports ground, with a large crowd attending to watch schoolchildren of all races performing together in a display of exercises and dances. The Kisubi College Band played and marched up and down and then 4 KAR Trooped the Colour for the last time as they are about to revert to their original title of the Uganda Rifles. It was an excellent show. Tomorrow the Duke and Duchess of Kent arrive at the airport, ready for the independence ceremonies on Monday and Tuesday.

Monday 8 October

I received an official invitation to the Independence Tattoo at Kololo Stadium, Kampala, which is really the old airstrip on Kololo hill, at 9.30 p.m. today. When I arrived there were traffic police parking the large number of cars and others checking the invitation cards. As I passed some of the officers, I told them they were doing a fine job and several said rude things back. Once the Kents, the Governor and the Kabaka and other VIPs had arrived the show commenced.

The programme for the tattoo was very well planned and ended at midnight. The ceremonial trumpeters of the Police played a 'Fanfare for Freedom' composed by Ted Moon. This was followed by an amusing battle of the toy soldiers by the small sons of KAR soldiers. Then a display by 3 Regiment, Royal Horse Artillery, ending in shattering gunfire which made sure that everyone stayed awake. Next the magnificent *Bwola*, the very special Acholi dance that is the symbol of their chieftainship, the dancers wearing fine ostrich-feather headdresses, leopard skins on their shoulders, bells on their ankles and holding small drums. All of them tall, powerful-looking ex-KAR or ex-policemen.

The massed bands of the KAR, Uganda Police, Tanganyika Police and the combined pipes and drums of 1st Battalion Gordon Highlanders and 2nd Battalion Scots Guards was followed by the *ras*, a dance performed by the Ismaili Khoja Sports Club. An Army Air Corps helicopter put on a display of aerobatics and then the pipes and drums alone marched and countermarched, followed by sword dancing. A loudly applauded energetic Kiganda dance, the *nnankasa*, ended the general performance, with the dancers in *kanzus* and barkcloth and drums of various sizes being rapidly beaten and much ululating.

The finale was the ceremony of the Colour, when 4 KAR handed over its Regimental Colour and took possession of the new Regimental Colour of the Uganda Rifles from the Duke of Kent. The new Colour was then trooped, after which, at midnight, the British National Anthem was played as the Governor took the salute, and thus became the Governor-General, as the Union Jack was finally lowered in darkness with just one spotlight on the flag. Then Obote took his place and the new Uganda National Anthem was played as the Uganda flag was raised with the spotlight on it. This was accompanied by tremendous cheering from the huge crowd as the Protectorate era came to an end.

I must have been showing my feelings because an old, well-dressed African leaned forward from behind me and put his hand on my shoulder and said: 'Don't be so sad, we are all really very grateful for what you British have done for us and we thank you, *webali nnyo nnyo, ssebo.*'

Tuesday 9 October

The Independence Day celebrations took place at the same site at Kololo, starting at 10 a.m. today. It was very hot and an enormous crowd was present. As I walked towards the stands I passed a group of Uganda Rifles soldiers getting ready to fall in for the parade and, among them, I was pleased to see my former Tracker Constable Otehe from Nabilatuk, who joined the KAR in 1960; now wearing corporal's stripes on his smart new Rifles uniform. Our eyes met and we waved to each other, but he was on parade and there was no opportunity to talk.

The Duke, wearing the tropical dress uniform of the Scots Greys, inspected the 1st Battalion Uganda Rifles drawn up on parade with their kilted band. When they marched off, a flight of seven RAF jet fighters flew over in salute and there followed speeches and the signing of the constitutional instruments, which the Duke handed to Prime Minister Obote. The band played the Uganda National Anthem and the Duke and Duchess and other VIPs drove away as we all dispersed. Everything had gone well and the organisation was excellent.

There are other functions planned for this week: something at GH, a State Ball at Lugogo, a State Opening of Parliament; but, in my present lowly position as a teacher, I haven't been invited to any of them. I went back to Entebbe and enjoyed a restful day. This is the start of a new life for all of us in Uganda.

Tuesday 23 October

Obote didn't take long before flying off to the USA seeking aid. He's there now and yesterday was received by President Kennedy, who is rather tied up in the Cuban and Russian missile crisis at the moment and, I should think, has little time to spare for Uganda's problems.

With Obote is the Minister of Justice, Grace Ibingira. Before the latter arrived or was seen by the US press, some of them in their reports had mistakenly referred to the fact that Obote was bringing with him Uganda's first woman minister. I don't know why so many Catholics here give their sons names like Grace and Mary, but they do. It's a religious thing.

Wednesday 24 October

The Ministry of Works has commenced building the Law School here at Nsamizi. It shouldn't cost much as it's just a single-storey brick building with three staff offices, a reception area at the entrance where the clerk will work, and a library area that will double as a small class-room. We shall still use the large class-room across at the Centre for the magistrates courses; and the new course we are about to commence will use the library. This will be a small carefully selected group of about a dozen reading for the Part I exams of the English Bar. There's a need to provide senior qualified magistrates and more African advocates now. Makerere University College has no law faculty yet, so we shall have to fill that gap.

I've just heard that I passed the criminal law paper in the last Bar exams. But this idea of taking the papers one at a time doesn't suit me; it'll take far too long to get through them all so I'm going to sit for at least two or perhaps three papers in April and try to get rid of them as speedily as possible.

Thursday 8 November

A number of the less well educated Africans are very disappointed because their dreams of immediately taking over the cars and property of non-Africans on independence have not come true. There's also quite a lot of talk among politically-minded types and radical students of how they fought for their freedom. But, in fact, there was no fighting for it, hardly even what might truly be called a struggle. The hand-over seems to have come very easily and, perhaps, rather too quickly, due to the great pressure from the anti-colonialist elements in the UN and the USA and the British Labour Party.

Friday 9 November

A friend, now working in the Prime Minister's Office, tells me that, after the great battle between the Pian and Suk in Karamoja last May, while the KAR were mopping up, one of their two African lieutenants, Idi Amin, the boxer, took his platoon across into Kenya, captured three Turkana raiders and tortured them to death. The authorities in Kenya wanted to try Amin for murder and the KAR colonel wanted him court-martialled. A conversation took place between the Deputy Governor of Kenya and our Governor, Coutts, about this incident and Coutts then consulted Obote, who decided that it would be politically unacceptable to lock up one of his two African officers just before independence. Coutts suggested at least dismissal from the Army and warned Obote against keeping him in place, but Obote insisted that a severe reprimand would suffice. The whole matter has since been hushed up.*

Friday 16 November

Douglas and I were invited down to the AG's Chambers this afternoon as news has come through that our Attorney-General, Godfrey Binaisa, has been appointed a Queen's Counsel. The first Ugandan to become a QC. So they were throwing a champagne party there and every lawyer who could make it attended and helped to pour quantities of champers into Godfrey. When I arrived and greeted and congratulated him, I reminded him of our occasional encounters on the verandah of the Moroto Police Station, which he described as a 'pleasant rest cure'. I last saw him late this afternoon being carried shoulder-high by a group of European and Asian lawyers and, as they disappeared through a doorway, Godfrey was waving his arms and crying: 'Let right be done!'

Sunday 30 December

I've had a pleasant and quiet Christmas camping in the Murchison Falls Park. Animals of every kind all over the place; so many elephant herds and buck of all types. The Nile is still heavily flooded and the narrow falls couldn't cope with all the extra water, so a subsidiary falls has formed near by and may well be permanent, I'm told. The falls have thus changed their appearance, causing the original banks of the Nile to disappear, with the result that there are trees now standing well out in the water. The ferry across to Paraa had its landing stage submerged and, of course, it takes rather longer to cross the wider river now.

Further off, a large area of flat bushland stands desolately covered with dead standing trees, looking white and stark; the result of herds of itchy elephants continually rubbing themselves against the trunks and thus stripping the bark away.

My ninth year in Uganda is about to commence and, independence notwithstanding, I'm looking forward to and hoping for many more years here. This is where I want to be.

*Later Obote must have bitterly regretted this decision.

1963

Tuesday 8 January

We've started recruiting new potential magistrates in Buganda first as there are clearly not going to be sufficient suitable people to transfer from their customary courts. It has been decided that the minimum age must be 25 and we want someone who has held a reasonable sort of job first, such as teacher, clerk, policeman, medical assistant or similar. Those who have just left school are not mature enough for this job. Douglas and I sat with a co-opted member of the Public Service Commission as members of a board representing the Judicial Service Commission for these interviews. There has been a good response and some likely material among them.

Thursday 21 February

A very superior British woman professor, from social sciences I believe, came from Makerere College this afternoon as a visiting speaker to address the magistrates on the course. It was not my arrangement and I only looked in later because I was curious. I'm not sure what her subject was as I really couldn't understand what she was rattling on about, the language used was so high-flown and stuffed with academic jargon. The students sat politely still and without expression and, I suspect, with very little comprehension.

Afterwards, as she was walking to her car, I mentioned carefully that I doubted whether they had understood very much of her talk. She replied loftily that she was satisfied if any of her students understood even one-third of the contents of her lectures, as they were expected then to go to the library and find out and understand the rest by doing whatever reading and reference was necessary for that purpose.

Maybe this method works for her in the UK, though I'm doubtful about that, but it certainly is not my idea of teaching, either here or anywhere else. Because I have a very simple and non-academic approach to a subject, I always try to teach it by explaining the basics thoroughly and then building on that. I would never dream of the patronising conceit of aiming above their heads at any time, even if I could do so. Most of all, I try to make a subject as light and interesting as possible by introducing a little humour, as I've found that this goes a long way towards fixing facts in one's memory.

We are training magistrates to work in the district courts without libraries or other aids. The training must emphasise the practical side of the work. They need to know not only the applicable laws and procedures but how to apply them in actual cases and circumstances.

They must know how to work out and write judgments, how to come to decisions, how to deal with difficult people who are witnesses or accused persons, parties in civil suits, police officers, advocates, juveniles and so on. Airy-fairy academic musings won't be of much use to them when sitting in court alone out in the bush with people waiting for a fair decision from them. So I like to give plenty of time to explanations and examples and, later in the course, they each take it in turn to preside over a mock trial and produce a judgment.

Tuesday 19 March

Many Europeans tend to get upset when they help Africans, perhaps by giving them clothing or money or food or a scholarship, or just a lift in a car, and the African just accepts it and takes it and says nothing. The question then frequently asked is, why can't they be grateful?

But African languages generally have no words for saying thank you. It seems to be a foreign concept to them. In Swahili, which is not a proper Ugandan language – merely an import – words like *asante* and *shukuru* are used but, like much of Swahili, they are Arabic words transplanted, and even they only express pleasure. In Acholi, for instance, one uses the nearest word, *apwoyo*, which means 'I am pleased'. There is no actual word for thanks, and other local languages fall into the same category. However, at school here, African children are taught in English and so they naturally pick up English expressions of gratitude and use them early on in life, so perhaps this occasionally distressing peculiarity will become less noticeable in time. I recall some years ago when I said in English to a young chap in Kampala: 'You are under arrest,' he replied: 'Thank you very much, sir.'

Wednesday 3 April

In class yesterday the magistrates told me that they didn't want to receive certificates at the end of the course, as the first course did. They said any schoolboy can get a certificate and they were therefore not appropriate for this special type of course, so could they instead have a diploma in law? There was loud supporting applause from the rest of the class. So I told Douglas and said I also supported the idea, and he has agreed that I can go ahead and design a suitable diploma. I've produced an impressive-looking document which is to be signed by the Minister and the Head of the School, with a seal, and I took it to the Government Printer down the road. He has produced

227

some parchment from his old stock-room and is going ahead with the printing.

Saturday 13 April

Why anyone should want to have a zoo in Africa beats me, but they have now set one up in Entebbe. It's not a very good one, they seldom are, with small cages and little space. I went down to have a look because I heard that they have acquired a tiger. Everyone knows that there are no tigers in Africa, but here is one to prove the contrary. Apparently someone brought it in from India and it doesn't look too pleased about it. There was a lot of snarling and crashing around the cage. Since it's never going to be released into the wild here it would seem to have a pretty miserable future.*

Wednesday 24 April

I had a phone call from Police HQ yesterday. It was the PA to the Commissioner, a young African who has been promoted fast from sub-inspector. He was ringing about the Gazetted Police Officers Fund which, in the days when I looked after it, was mainly used to purchase farewell gifts to retiring or departing officers. Apparently it has been decided to close it down and use up the remaining money to provide a number of pewter beer mugs to present to the numerous officers who have left or are leaving the Force. The mugs are inscribed with the Force badge and the officer's name and years of service. Most have already been presented but, he said, he had been surprised to find that mine was still there and would I drop in and collect it when it was convenient?

Today I was in Kampala for other reasons so I called into HQ. The PA asked me to wait while he told the Commissioner that I was there as he felt sure that he would like to present it to me personally. I felt very doubtful about that in view of his unhelpful attitude when I was trying to transfer to the Law School. He had never explained why he had moved me from a useful job at the College to a dead-end job at the barracks and then delayed my transfer. Consequently I had not bothered to call in to say farewell when I was finally leaving the Force. I didn't really expect he'd see me now.

As I was sitting waiting in the empty office the Commissioner suddenly rushed past the open door and disappeared down the corridor. The PA came in looking rather embarrassed and gave me the mug

*It later attacked and killed its keeper and was shot.

saying: 'I'm sorry, the Commissioner had to go off on some urgent matter.'

I replied: 'What a surprise. Well, don't worry about it, I'll take it and go. Then you can tell him he can come out of hiding.'

Friday 17 May

The lake fly (midges) are swarming in their billions. Ordinary insect netting on the windows does not deter them, they are so small, and they leave an oily smudge when squashed. They get everywhere in the house because we are near the lake and they cover anyone out of doors as they fly in clouds from the lake to the land to breed and die.

Today I had to call the fire brigade. Kimbo was barking excitedly at the thick hedge dividing my compound from the road to the senior staff quarters. When I peered into it I saw a very large python stretched along inside the hedge doing absolutely nothing. After all, this is Snake Hill, so he's where he's meant to be. Hence the call, because it's the job of the fire people to deal with snakes and wild bees. For some reason they arrived in a large red fire engine dressed in fire-fighting kit, ringing their bell and needlessly alarming everyone on the hill. I would have thought that a couple of chaps in a van would suffice. Perhaps they were bored because nobody is burning things down these days. By now a small crowd had assembled, made up of domestic staff from the houses and whatever Nsamizi staff were not in class.

The fire officer in charge had a shotgun and quickly and efficiently despatched the python. The crowd applauded enthusiastically and the fire officer stuck his chest out and beamed proudly. His men then pulled the snake out of the hedge and stretched it along the ground, with Kimbo scampering about and getting in everyone's way. The coils were still twitching about even though it was dead, so Kimbo seized its tail and gave it a good shake, just to teach it a lesson and make the point that it was his snake; he'd found it. They then borrowed my measuring tape and announced that it was slightly over 14 feet long. This seemed to please everyone and there was more applause. Finally it was loaded into the fire truck and they drove off, taking my measuring tape with them. I wonder if they're going to eat it? The python, I mean, not the measuring tape.

Saturday 25 May

My cook, Adam, has a son now aged two called Msafiri, which means the traveller, because he was born in Uganda and his parents are Tanganyikans. This toddler wanders in and out of my house at will and is extremely fascinated by my record player. His favourite record

229

is one I have of a selection of old songs by the Cliff Adams Singers called *Sing Something Simple*; particularly one called 'Wheezy Anna'. He stands with his nose almost touching the revolving record and joins in with the group, singing his own version of the words, of which the only recognisable ones are 'Wheejy Anna'.

Wednesday 5 June

The BBC world news is full of a political scandal in the UK concerning John Profumo, the Secretary of State for War, whom I recall meeting when he visited GH in 1957. Apparently, he has had an affair with some woman called Christine Keeler who, at the same time, also happened to be the mistress of one Eugene Ivanov, the Soviet naval attaché in London, who no doubt is being made to appear as an evil Russian master spy. There's also a popsy called Mandy Rice-Davies involved somehow. It seems the politicians are taking this farce very seriously and resignations are in the air.

Friday 7 June

I'm up in Gulu with the new Senior Courts Adviser, interviewing local applicants for appointment as magistrates in Acholi. We're very short of northerners in the judiciary and there's a need for quite a number of them. Most young men here want to join the army, police or prisons service and it's rather a new idea for them to consider sedentary jobs like this. Still, we've spotted one or two possibilities. We're going to Lira after this for the same purpose.

Friday 28 June

Earlier this month I sat for some more papers in the Bar exams and am waiting for the results. Meanwhile, we've been marking the final exam papers of the second magistrates course, which has been very satisfactory and some of them have done exceptionally well. The students also heard quite a number of outside speakers from other departments such as the courts, prosecutions, police and prisons. They made outside visits to various of these departments to see how they work and to broaden the scope of their knowledge, with particular regard to those organisations related to the work of the courts.

Wednesday 3 July

We had the course graduation ceremony on Monday and various VIP visitors admired our new building, which we've been occupying since March. The students have gone away now for some leave before taking up their new posts as magistrates grade III in the districts. I'm off tomorrow on home leave as our tours out here have conveniently been reduced to two years instead of three as formerly, before independence.

Friday 20 September – In London

While doing some studying in Gray's Inn library, I met a Ugandan from Toro, Miss Elizabeth Bagaya*, who, if she qualifies, will be the first Ugandan woman barrister. There's been no thought so far about recruiting women magistrates, which is hardly surprising, perhaps, as we have yet to put together an African magistracy, which almost certainly will start off by being all-male staffed. Later, perhaps, things may change; though it could be rather slow to do this in such a male-dominated society.

Thursday 10 October – In London

The news from Uganda is that yesterday, 9 October, the first anniversary of independence, Uganda became a republic within the Commonwealth and the National Assembly elected the Kabaka, Sir Edward Mutesa II, to be the first President of Uganda, with Sir Wilberforce Nadiope, the Kyabazinga of Busoga, as Vice-President. Government House now becomes State House.

The Ugandan High Commissioner in London, Timothy Bazzarabusa, held a celebratory reception yesterday evening at the Commonwealth Institute in Kensington High Street, which I attended. Most Ugandans who were in the UK studying and so on also attended, as did quite a number of Britons who had formerly worked in Uganda. The well-padded wife of one of these, who knows me slightly, and who tends to get her facts wrong, saw me and, as she opened her mouth to speak, there fell one of those peculiar silences that sometimes occur at a gathering of many people, when inexplicably everyone stops talking at the same time. Into this sudden silence the penetrating voice of this woman addressed me: 'Tell me, are you still soliciting these days?' A number of startled heads nearby turned in my direction, much to my deep embarrassment, and I wished I was elsewhere. Then they all swivelled back and resumed their animated conversations.

Sunday 13 October – In London

Yesterday evening I met Luke Ofungi, now an Assistant Superintendent of Police, and currently attending a Special Branch course in London

*Later she used the title of Princess Elizabeth of Toro.

organised by the Metropolitan Police, and we exchanged news over a meal. As I had predicted and hoped, he is well on his way upwards now. It will be interesting to see just how high he goes.

While walking near Regent's Park this morning, I stopped to watch a convoy of Territorial Army armoured cars go past. They were led by an officer standing up in a Land Rover. A small cockney boy shouted at him: 'Yah, where's the war then, mate?'

Friday 22 November – In London

As usual, earlier this evening I was having a meal at a pub across the road from my apartment at Regent's Park. They do quite good hot meals there and the coffee's excellent. There was the usual hubbub and the chap behind the bar suddenly called out loudly: 'Here, look at this, everyone,' and pointed to the small black and white television set fixed to the wall. The news coming through was of the shooting of President John Kennedy in Dallas, Texas. We were all silent and shocked. How could such an awful thing happen? Here was a young leader seen all over the world as a good man doing a good job, trying to make the world a better place, and he's struck down in this appalling way, in what is supposed to be the leading democratic country. In the words of St John: 'He was a burning and a shining light: and ye were willing for a season to rejoice in his light.'

Thursday 12 December

Kenya became independent today, with Jomo Kenyatta as Prime Minister. A large number of white settlers have already left Kenya and moved down south to Southern Rhodesia or South Africa, where they hope to feel more at home, especially in view of the threats and promises made by the politicians to hand their farms and plantations over to Africans.

I've sat for some more papers in the Part I Bar exams while I'm here. There's even one paper in African law, which is nonsense, of course, since there is no such thing; any more than there is European or Asian Law. A certain professor at the London School of Oriental and African Studies has been very persuasive and, as a result of writing a couple of books on so-called African law, has not only obtained the introduction of the paper as an alternative choice in the Bar exams, but also secured the setting and marking rights for himself. Nice work if you can get it. I've read his books and, although I don't agree with some of his views, I'm well aware that in such cases it's necessary to put that aside and give the examiner what he wants to read. It's a part of examination technique which I also drill into the students here, since the object of the exercise is to pass the wretched exams.

I took it as one of my choices and found it was possible to write a sufficient load of convincing guff to persuade the examiner that I apparently knew something about his subject and thus secured a pass; which is all I wanted. A piece of cake, as old Kamoga used to say.

1964

Tuesday 7 January

I returned to Uganda from leave yesterday, glad to escape from a cold English winter. I gather that some of our few remaining Europeans have been rather foolish. On 12 December a party was held at a private house on Tank Hill just outside Kampala on Kenya's independence day. All those present were Europeans, including three of the few remaining police officers. At one point they played a rather drunken charades and some of them dressed up as Africans with the odd fez and *kanzu* and so on, and strongly racially abusive remarks were made amidst great laughter. The African domestic staff present were deeply offended and reported it to the authorities. A group of UPC youth-wingers then attacked the house and burned it down. All of the Europeans who attended the party, including the three police officers, were speedily deported. This is now referred to as 'the Tank Hill party'.

Thursday 9 January

The start of the second term of the present course for magistrates has had to be delayed because Nsamizi is full of Belgian refugees who have fled from Rwanda as result of a recent invasion by *Inyenzi* (rebel tribesmen from across the border with Burundi) attempting to take over the country. Arrangements are being made to fly off those who wish to go back to Belgium, so we should soon have the place back to normal, we hope.

Friday 17 January

It seems that in Zanzibar there have for some time been continuing troubles between the Arab and the African population. There has now been a revolution led by one self-styled Field Marshal John Okello who, oddly enough, is a Ugandan from Lango and once served as a constable in the Kenya Police. He seems to have succeeded in overthrowing the government and taking over with great violence. Something like 5,000 Arabs on this tiny island were killed and many others have fled to exile in other Arab countries. No doubt many grudges were settled by Africans at the same time.

I have heard that I've passed the remaining papers in the December Bar exams and so have completed Part I. I must now get through the Finals as quickly as possible. The Attorney-General, Godfrey Binaisa, has been most helpful and has written several times to the Council of Legal Education in London. He has succeeded in getting me excused from keeping terms (eating dinners at my Inn of Court, which I nevertheless had to pay for) and attending the Council's compulsory lectures in London for a year, on the grounds that I'm needed here full-time training magistrates and so cannot be spared.

Monday 20 January

In my absence the third magistrates course has started; also our first course to study for Part I of the English Bar. This consists of nine students, including one woman, all with a higher school certificate and three who are Makerere graduates. So I'm now teaching Bar students before I've even qualified myself. About par for the course with me.

Monday 27 January

There has been a series of mutinies in the former KAR throughout East Africa; mainly about replacing British officers with Africans and also increasing the pay of other ranks. They commenced in Tanganyika with the battalion there. They forced the British officers out of their beds at night and put them on an aircraft to the UK, some still in their pyjamas. They were not permitted to take any property with them.

This was followed by the Kenya battalions, and now the Uganda Rifles at Jinja have joined in. It's like wildfire spreading. The new pay rates here had only been for officers and NCOs, which was the main reason why the men mutinied. They seized Onama, the Minister of Defence, who was visiting the barracks to explain the new pay awards. Obote decided that he didn't want the newly Ugandan-officered Police Special Force to fire on Ugandan soldiers, so he requested British help to do the dirty work. The 1st Battalion South Staffordshire Regiment and a company of the Scots Guards have come up here from Kenya. The Guards are staying at Entebbe Airport and guarding that. The South Staffs are billeted here at Nsamizi and their Battalion HQ is in the Law School building, which we have had to vacate temporarily. An arrangement has been made for us to continue with our Bar course at Makerere, which means driving over to Kampala every day. The few students are being accommodated there and we have the use of the senior common room.

Friday 31 January

The South Staffs had no trouble in rounding up, disarming and arresting the trouble-makers, and a number have already been dismissed from the Army and sent home. Since the whole lot mutinied and they have been disarmed, I think this is the best time to follow the proper course and disband the regiment and either start again or, better still, do without. A unit that has mutinied once could do so again. Uganda has no external enemies who might attack, and all the border problems and internal security matters could be adequately dealt with by an enlarged Police Special Force. The Police Force has for long demonstrated its capabilities in dealing with ceremonial duties and parades, so that part is covered as well. But I doubt whether African politicians would agree; they probably feel the need for an army to bolster their image among other African leaders. At any rate, it seems that Obote has decided, or been persuaded, to allow the Uganda Rifles to continue in existence. Let's hope he doesn't regret it.

The last time there was a mutiny in the Uganda Rifles was in 1897, when it was by Sudanese troops who had been recruited into the Rifles during the reconquest of the Sudan by Lord Kitchener after the Mahdi rebellion and the killing of General Gordon in Khartoum.

Monday 3 February

The Prime Minister's Office has been dishing out the Uganda Independence Medal to various people. The medal has the Queen's head on it and the ribbon is in the national colours of black, red and yellow. The printed slip in the box I received said: 'In recognition of his outstanding service and loyalty to the country before and up to Independence Day, 9 October 1962.'

At the School we have received a government-issued framed photograph of the President/Kabaka in his Grenadier Guards service dress uniform, which all government departments are now required to hang in a prominent place. We put it up just inside the entrance.

Wednesday 12 February

The British Tutorial College (BTC) is a private firm with its head office in Nairobi and branch offices all over East Africa. They provide correspondence courses in a long list of subjects. The Director, Mr Lee, is currently visiting the Kampala branch office and he wrote to me a short while back asking to meet me. The Force Education Officer had approached them, asking if they could produce a correspondence course to prepare police officers for the Force law exams, which they now need to pass before being promoted. This is the result of the policy of continually raising the educational standard of recruits. My name had been suggested to him as the possible author of the lessons in the correspondence course, so he invited me to a meal at the Imperial Hotel to discuss this, as I had already indicated that I thought it was an excellent idea to provide such a course, and I'm certainly willing to produce the lessons and mark the test papers.

In order to keep the course manageable and not too expensive, we agreed on 20 lessons covering the five exam papers and subjects of criminal law, evidence, criminal procedure, general laws (traffic, firearms, inquests, prisons, police, extradition, vagrancy, markets, dangerous drugs, etc.) and police duties and procedure (covering Police Standing Orders). Each lesson will conclude with an eight to ten question test paper, and the model answers to each test will be sent to the student with the marked answer paper. The students will send or deliver their answer papers to the Kampala BTC office, which will forward them to me for marking.

So there will be four lessons on each exam subject and I shall have to pack in the information and explanations in the briefest and clearest way possible. With the experience of teaching law that I have acquired here and in the Police, plus my own simple non-academic approach, I feel reasonably able to reduce subjects to basics and to simplify explanations to the level necessary. Hopefully, this will help many more policemen of all ranks to qualify and to understand and use the laws. It should also improve the standard of their work as well as providing them with much better chances of promotion.

Saturday 25 April

It's been a fairly exhausting week as each day I've driven over to Kampala to sit for the Bar Finals papers at the local examination centre, which is the High Court here. Candidates are supposed to sit for the Finals in London, but the AG once again stepped in and obtained special permission from the Council of Legal Education for me to sit them out here. Thus I've been the only examinee in the room. There were papers every morning and afternoon, between which I had a swotting lunch at the Uganda Club. I had writer's cramp from gripping my fountain pen all day – it's simply not done to use a ball-point pen in such exams; the examiners would regard it like wearing brown shoes with a dinner jacket. Yesterday afternoon, after completing the last of the papers, the relief was so great that I have no recollection at all of driving back to Entebbe. The Bar Council seems to be testing one's stamina and mental determination as well as one's knowledge of the law.

Monday 27 April

Yesterday Tanganyika and Zanzibar joined together to became a united republic and they are to be called Tanzania. Both governments are extremely socialist and very much influenced by the large number of Chinese 'advisers', who seem to be more like controllers and directors. The Chinese nowadays are competing fiercely with the Russians in acquiring areas of influence in Africa, where socialism is all the rage and, in Uganda, Obote seems to be getting more left-wing every day. He calls it 'scientific socialism' but it's just an African form of communism. It's certainly discouraging outside investment here. I'm no economist but I wouldn't have thought that was a particularly good thing to do.

Monday 4 May

For some reason that I don't know, the designation 'Commissioner of Police' was changed some time ago to 'Inspector General of Police'. Since both titles have imperialistic connotations that can't be the reason; maybe it just sounds grander.

Obote would have liked one of his fellow tribesmen to take over the Force, but there is no Lango senior or experienced enough, nor in any way suitable for the post. Langi tend to be too politically inclined, controversial and undisciplined to make good policemen. The only northerner with enough seniority and any possibility of being considered is Oryema, an Acholi. He was an Assistant Superintendent when I was in the Force and one of the earlier African gazetted officers. He wouldn't be my choice, but I suppose that it was a case of *faute de mieux*.

In order to acquire some administrative and executive experience, he has been acting as shadow to the Commissioner, now IG, for some time, with the object of taking over substantively. Last Friday it was announced that he has now actually done so and the Force has its first African head. The former Commissioner has become a civilian 'Chief Police Adviser' and so continues in the background to keep an eye on things and tutor the new IG. I hope it all works out. A strong, well-run police force is vital for the security of Uganda now and in the future.

Friday 5 June

The three high ministers of Buganda are the Katikiro (Premier), the Omulamuzi (Chief Judge) and the Omuwanika (Treasurer) and they, with the 20 *saza* chiefs, constitute the Great Lukiiko. The Omulamuzi is head of the Principal Court of Buganda, where their judges preside. They have more powers under the Buganda Courts Ordinance than the customary courts in the other provinces and kingdoms.

The Judicial Adviser, Buganda, has always been a district officer from the office of the Resident, Buganda. The present holder of the post, Andrew Stuart, is also reading for the Bar, and is off on leave, with nobody left in the rapidly dwindling Resident's office to take over. So I have been appointed to act part-time in that office as from today, while still continuing to work at the Law School.

One of the Judicial Adviser's jobs is to oversee the training of Buganda judges and magistrates, which seems to me to have been rather neglected in the past. But the main part of the work is to hear first appeals from the criminal and civil decisions in the Principal Court. So it's really more of a disguised judicial appointment. I went to see Andrew the other day to be briefed before he departed on leave. He is a very tall chap, about 6 feet 4, I would guess, and, when I sat down to be briefed in the small courtroom in the Resident's block of offices, he stood on a dais. Thus his head was about 10 feet above the floor and I had to move my chair back to avoid getting a crick in my neck looking up at him as he loomed over me and spoke from his lofty altitude.

There are a number of appeals pending and it's been suggested by Jim, the Senior Courts Adviser, that I should leave them until Andrew returns from leave in a few months. Jim seems to be rather nervous and unsure about my ability to deal with such matters and keeps emphasising that it is only a temporary arrangement. Ignoring this nonsense, I told Andrew that I would like to have a go at hearing appeals and I thought that I could handle them. He said: why not? and showed me the files. I shall say nothing to Jim and just go ahead and fix the hearing dates. There's no way I'm going to hold a post and not do the job. The trouble with Jim is that he still thinks of me as a police officer and he has to excess the traditional administrative officer's low esteem for policemen.

There are numerous land disputes over *mailo* land (freehold), dowry payments, cattle ownership and trespass, refusing to perform *bulungi bwansi*, which is 'voluntary' community work building and maintaining roads, water ponds, etc., and a considerable number of criminal cases. No great problems.

I've told the clerk I shall come in once a week, every Wednesday, and I've fixed hearing dates for the first batch of appeals. He will do the paperwork and arrange to inform the parties involved. He also acts as interpreter. The Principal Court records are all in Luganda and have to be translated; but a number have already been done, so I'll get on with those as a start.

Friday 12 June

The news is that I've passed the Bar Finals, so that is over at last. I've written to Gray's Inn asking for dispensation regarding eating their miserable dinners and requested to be called *in absentia*. I don't have the time to fool around in London and certainly have no wish to dress up to attend Call Day. I went through this Bar business solely to ensure my appointment at the Law School and to secure the salary of a qualified lecturer, as so far I've merely been paid my last salary in the Police with nothing extra. The AG has also written to Gray's Inn supporting my plea for dispensation and I think they will do what our Attorney-General requests. It's all in a good cause, after all.

Thursday 25 June

I hear that about 800 sub-inspectors, NCOs and constables sat for the Police Law exams at the beginning of this month; the highest number so far. Quite a lot of them have been studying under the BTC course which I wrote. It seems to be very popular. There was a waiting list assembled for the course while it was being printed. No doubt the BTC is making quite a good profit from it, which is all right since, at the same time, it's filling a much needed requirement in the Force.

Wednesday 1 July

A report about our Law School Bar exam results was published in the *Uganda Argus* this morning, showing that we had an 80% success rate as eight out of ten students passed in each of the two papers sat. Since the London pass rate is less than 50% of those sitting for the exams, we can't be said to be doing badly. It's also a great financial saving since it's not necessary for them to go to London and be kept there. They will have to go over for the Finals, though, for which a scholarship will be awarded.

Friday 3 July

I hear that they've obtained a computer in the Ministry of Finance to deal with the salaries of government employees. Two of their staff are being trained to use the machine by a visiting expert. So far salaries have been competently prepared by hand and typewriter by a small army of hard-working and excellent Goan accountants. Now it's all to be done on this machine, we're told. I suppose it's progress, but, knowing how things are here, with frequent power cuts and probably not very competent maintenance, I can't help wondering what happens to all the information and calculations in the machine when it goes wrong or loses power. I hope it's not going to be used as an excuse for not paying us on time.

Friday 17 July

The third magistrates course final exams have been taking place. When I was setting the criminal law paper I couldn't think of a last question. All I could produce at first was this:

> Q – People take money out of banks all the time. Bank robbers also take money out of banks, and where does that money go? Probably back into banks. So they are merely helping to move money around. This means that they are a useful part of the country's economy. Discuss.

No, it wouldn't do.

Sunday 16 August

Today I drove eastwards to Mbale, where I'm staying at the hotel all week while running a refresher course for the district sub-court magistrates who attended our earlier diploma courses. The object is to bring them up to date on changes in the laws and recent relevant case decisions in the High Court as well as to discuss problems they have come across while working in the field since leaving the Law School. I believe this type of exercise will be quite interesting and useful both for them and for us, and I expect we'll be holding more of these refresher courses in the other districts in future whenever we can fit them in between diploma courses.

On the way here today, a few miles outside Mbale, I encountered a noisy procession consisting of a small number of Bamesaaba youths who were clearly circumcision candidates. They were dancing along the road clad only in shorts with traditional strings of seed beads crisscrossing their chests, hide belts sewn with cowrie shells round their waists and rattling bells tied round their thighs and calves. They also waved colourful handkerchiefs presented to them by girlfriends, and their bodies and faces were smeared with a white paste which is made

240

during the process of brewing the large quantities of millet beer in their home village as part of the celebrations. Accompanying them on their running and dancing around their area were a number of relatives and friends and hangers-on. The purpose of this gadabout is to announce formally that the young men are ready to be initiated into manhood and also to receive presents from relatives whom they visit on their way. The Bagisu are the only tribe in Uganda that holds circumcision initiation rites.

Saturday 22 August

At the crack of dawn I left the hotel and walked round to Pat's government quarter, from where we set off to climb Mount Elgon. Pat is the magistrate here and a former superintendent in Police SB who read for the Bar while he was still in the Force. It's his sub-court magistrates who have been attending the refresher course.

We started as it was getting light and, after quite a bit of mountain walking, but nothing too strenuous really, eventually reached Nkokonjeru, a 7,000-feet spur, where the Bagisu take advantage of the climate at that altitude to grow large quantities of vegetables in their *shambas* and sell them down in Mbale market. We sat and ate our breakfast of sandwiches and coffee which we had brought with us, then started back down. I left Pat at his home and returned to the Mount Elgon Hotel, where I'm staying, and found a noon session going on with several of the remaining European police officers taking part. They asked me to join them and I stayed for a while before going for lunch.

Friday 28 August

I was in Kampala this morning and met Nakkaka, a senior police driver who had been a Headquarters staff car driver when I was there. He's now driving the Nigerian Chief Justice, whom they have brought in as Obote decided he wanted an African to head the Judiciary but he couldn't find a suitably qualified Ugandan. It seems that Nigerian judges behave rather differently from what we're used to here.

Nakkaka told me that all the senior drivers have taken a turn at this job and got out of it quickly, and he was fed up too, as this CJ punches and kicks them when he is annoyed and calls them 'East African rubbish'. A northerner might have hit back but he's a Muganda and merely submits while taking great offence. He said he has already put in his resignation from the Force as he has found himself a much quieter and better-paid job as driver to a British bank manager in Kampala. Apparently all sorts of perks go with the job. I've heard before that ex-staff car drivers from the Force are eagerly sought after by commercial bigwigs as their chauffeurs because of their driving skill and safari experience.

The Ministry sent us a Nigerian law lecturer some time back; an Ibo barrister who frequently boasts of his three (British) university degrees and various academic prizes. He's very well qualified academically, but a hopeless teacher. He is a short, stout man with a loud, penetrating voice and an enormous ego, and he makes no attempt to hide his utter contempt for Ugandans and all East Africans. What makes these west-coasters consider themselves so superior is beyond me. He is loud-mouthed, boastful, abusive and totally out of sympathy with the students, who do not hide the fact that they dislike him intensely. Not what we need here at all.

Saturday 29 August

Obote has declared the UPC/KY political alliance at an end. Perhaps he feels he doesn't need them now as he's well in control and KY has been very awkward and embarrassing from his point of view, particularly over the dispute between Buganda and Bunyoro concerning the so-called Lost Counties.

The heavyweight boxer, Idi Amin, is now a full colonel and deputy to the Army Commander, Brigadier Opolot. Amin's career does not seem to have suffered at all as a result of his part in the Turkana incident in May 1962 and the army mutiny in which he was closely involved in January this year.

Sunday 30 August

Some of the very many sons and daughters of the Western Province Rulers have recently started to call themselves prince or princess, although it's rather doubtful that they are so entitled. There's even a porter working at the Entebbe Ministry of Works who insists on calling himself Prince something, which seems absurd. We've just commenced the fourth magistrates course and, as I checked their names when they gathered in the classroom after arrival, one of the students from Toro said he was Prince something. I replied: 'Nonsense, all magistrate students here are Mister and even that is dropped in the classroom.' And that's how it is.

Monday 14 September

The first Bar course has ended and it has been most successful, so we shall start another one soon. I have taken off as usual to the game park for recuperation. This time to the Queen Elizabeth National Park in Toro. Christopher, a 17-year-old schoolboy who is earning his school fees by working in the garden and house, asked to come along and see the park, so he is cook and everything is fried. Near the entrance to this park is a sign that says:

QUEEN ELIZABETH NATIONAL PARK
ELEPHANT HAVE RIGHT OF WAY

I don't think that anyone would argue with that.

There's plenty of game around, though it's quite dry and hot at the moment. This afternoon we drove past a large herd of elephant and on to some open country and Christopher asked me to show him how to drive a car. The track was fairly wide and not too rough there, and we got as far as chugging along in first gear when I glanced in the mirror and saw a huge bull elephant with long tusks charging along the track towards us at a considerable speed. Its large ears were flapping and it seemed very annoyed about something. It was also catching up with us and getting quite close and I had no wish to be flattened but, at the same time, with a learner driver at the wheel, I had to be careful not to startle and panic him so that he stalled the car. We had to keep going and increase speed so as to outdistance our pursuer.

We hadn't reached gear changes yet, so I couldn't try that. I said as calmly as I could manage: 'Christopher, look straight in front of you and push your right foot down hard on the accelerator pedal where it is now and try to keep it right down.' He did that without a query but the elephant was very close now, looming up behind us, as we started to pull slightly away. He kept his foot down, fortunately without looking in the mirror or behind him. As soon as we reached a thick belt of trees alongside the track I said: 'Now turn left off the track and keep going as you are towards the trees.' He did this and we moved behind the trees and, once we were out of sight, the elephant stopped, trumpeted angrily, and turned away. I heaved a sigh of relief.

'Was that all right?' asked Christopher.

'*Bulungi nnyo nnyo*,' I said (very, very good). He grinned happily.

Thursday 17 September

My weekly excursions to Kampala, heavily disguised as the Judicial Adviser, continue satisfactorily. I've heard a number of criminal appeals already and found the Principal Court judges generally to be arbitrary and harsh in their judgments and sentences. Most of the evidence against the accused is inadequate, very conflicting, or simply non-existent; the accusation often resulting from an old grudge or unpaid debt. In several such cases the judge would record in his judgment: 'If he is not guilty the *gombolola* chief would not have sent him before us,' and then awarded the usual harsh sentence, frequently of ten years in prison for some alleged minor offence. This seems to have been going on unchecked for some time.

So far, I've found very few verdicts acceptable; some judgments have to be reversed, and usually the sentences in the others have to be reduced. If they ever received any training it clearly hasn't worked. In the Buganda set-up it may have been difficult for a European adviser to try to train already established judges; especially as some are untrainable or not amenable to training because they think that it would be demeaning when they have been appointed by the Kabaka. The usual requirement for such appointments is membership of the right clan or having relations in powerful positions in Mengo, rather than merit or potential. Probably none of these will be coming on our magistrates course as they are too old for conversion to the new system; apart from the fact that their poor English and low educational standard would preclude them. They probably wouldn't agree to attend anyway and they will have to be retired when the Buganda courts are integrated.

Friday 25 September

Macoun, the former Commissioner of Police, now Chief Police Adviser, is leaving Uganda, and Oryema is in sole command of the Force. There was a farewell party this evening, to which I was invited. This is the first time we've spoken since before I left the Force over two and a half years ago. There were a lot of people there and we only exchanged a few words. He mentioned that he had seen a report in *Habari* that I had passed the Bar Finals and offered congratulations. I spoke to a number of officers whom I'd known in quite lowly ranks who are now very senior types.

Friday 30 October

Douglas is shortly leaving Uganda and going to the UK to work. I've applied for the vacant post and been interviewed. So, too, has our Nigerian lecturer, who pointed out scornfully that I haven't a hope as I'm not yet qualified, whereas he has three degrees as well as the Bar and so on. I merely remarked that my call to the Bar is just a formality now.

I've heard that the Buganda Principal Court judges have petitioned for my removal as Judicial Adviser on the grounds that I've allowed too many appeals against their judgments 'and clearly do not appreciate the importance and the excellence of their work in the Kingdom'. So it looks as though I'm doing something right. My concern has been to get people out of the *gombolola* gaols who should not be in there. They can do what they like about it. And they probably will.

Friday 6 November

Wednesday was polling day in the Mubende Lost Counties referendum, which is taking place in the two counties of Buyaga and Bugangazi to decide whether they wish to remain in Buganda or be transferred/returned to Bunyoro, to which they originally belonged. The Kabaka's scheme to restore *ebyaffe* (our things) by resettling Baganda *kawonawa* (ex-servicemen) in the area, so as to fix the poll in Buganda's favour, has not worked as they were not allowed to vote. The result has been announced and the two counties will revert to Bunyoro by an overwhelming majority vote. The Baganda are not happy.

Wednesday 11 November

The Baganda are very upset about the recent Lost Counties poll result and the Buganda Government of Kintu has resigned, no doubt on the Kabaka's orders. A new one has been formed, still all KY followers, but different faces, under Mayanja-Nkangi as Katikiro. He had just resigned as a minister in the UPC/KY government of Obote.

The Constitution is being amended to effect the change of status of the counties as from 1 January 1965. It's a great pity that this wasn't sorted out by the British administration before independence; but it was regarded as such a hot political potato that nobody wanted or dared to deal with it.

Thursday 12 November

Yesterday I was appointed to act as Head of the Law School pending a substantive appointment; and at the same time told that I shall actually be getting the job. Our Nigerian academic is grinding his teeth in rage and disappointment.

Cuthbert Obwangor is Minister of Justice and, at the moment, he is attending sittings of Parliament in Kampala. He wanted to meet me, so I drove over and sent him a chit by parliamentary messenger to say I was waiting outside. He came out and we had a long chat about the future of the Law School as there are changes I want to make. I brought up the status of the school and myself. I pointed out we are the only law school in East Africa and I suggested we rename it the Uganda

Law School instead of the absurd Local Law School and that my position be redesignated as Principal rather than Head, as it's an institute of higher education. Both changes would be more impressive and sound better outside, and he agreed and asked me to let him have it in writing so that he could have it gazetted immediately.

Tuesday 24 November

Quite a day. I was promoted to be Head of the Law School and, far away in London, I was called to the Bar in Gray's Inn *in absentia*. Naturally, I'm very pleased about all this, but I've never bothered with celebrations of so-called achievements, or anything else. As far as I'm concerned, passing exams and qualifying is the same as completing a crossword puzzle; once it's done you put it aside and forget about it. I've had a quiet evening at home reading and listening to music.

Thursday 3 December

In the *Argus* today was a report, which I'd supplied, of our students' recent Bar exam successes. Nine students sat for exams in September, of whom six have now completed the Part I exams and are shortly off to London on scholarships to read for and sit the Finals while they keep terms at their Inns of Court. The other three passed all but one paper to complete Part I, so they only have to repeat that one and should be going next time. Meanwhile, back at the ranch, I've asked to terminate my appointment as acting Judicial Adviser as I need to spend all my time at the Law School.

Saturday 12 December

I've just received a letter from the UK to say that I'm now an Associate Member of the Society of Public Teachers of Law, which is quite a mouthful. While here I've been appointed a member of the Uganda Law Reform Commission and have also accepted an invitation from Kenya to be on the editorial board of the *East African Law Journal*. Not a bad record for someone who doesn't usually join things.

We are roofless. We had a very heavy storm last night, with exceptionally strong whirlwinds and an awful lot of rain. The result is that the flat concrete roof of the Law School building has been torn off and we are exposed. It looks as if inferior cement was used. Fortunately, most of our books in the library were on shelves behind glass doors. Those that were not have got rather wet. We've been spending the morning rescuing our stuff and moving it all across the road to one of the Nsamizi classrooms until we're fixed up again.

Meanwhile, the Ministry of Works people have been tut-tutting and scratching their collective heads over our decapitation. Restoration work commences tomorrow, I'm told.

I've just been marking some papers containing some of our students' thoughtful offerings. In one I'm informed that 'a reasonable person is a person whom a reasonable person thinks is reasonable'. I suppose that's reasonable.

Sunday 27 December

In the garden this afternoon I watched a three-horned chameleon using its long extended tongue to lap up a line of ants marching along one of the few branches on the pawpaw tree. On the next branch down a large brown praying mantis was disposing of a small caterpillar with evident relish as it crunched it up. I waited a while to see their reactions on meeting, but each one kept to its own part of the tree, perhaps by mutual agreement.

I've been struggling with James Joyce's *Ulysses*, and struggle is the word. It's almost as unreadable as his *Finnegan's Wake*. In spite of what the pseudo critics say, I think this 'stream of consciousness' stuff is talentless, pretentious rubbish – as much a confidence trick as most so-called modern art.

Wednesday 30 December

Our Minister, Cuthbert Obwangor, has done the trick for us. In the latest issue of the *Uganda Gazette* it states: 'The Head of the Local Law School is redesignated as Principal of the Uganda Law School.' Thus the rather belittling attitude of the pre-independence administration has been demolished. A satisfactory way of ending the year.

1965

Sunday 3 January

For some time a young Indian has been attending Bar course classes here. He's not a member of the course but a private student who asked me if he might also come to our classes. Having a rich daddy, he is driven over from Kampala in a large car and is quite an intelligent chap. It's no problem as far as I'm concerned and costs nobody anything. He provides his own books and stationery, so nobody is deprived.

He invited me to a family new year party at their large house in

247

Kampala yesterday evening. One of the guests was an American Peace Corps girl with a thick Southern accent who works in the Sudan and had come down to Kampala for a holiday break. Someone asked her what she does in the Sudan and she replied that she teaches English. I was shocked and obviously showed it, because she turned to me and said: 'Waal, ah call it English.'

'I didn't say anything,' I said.

'No, but you looked,' she replied.

Friday 4 February

Field Marshal John Okello, who escaped to Kenya after being detained in Zanzibar following his successful revolution there in January last year, is now in Uganda, having been thrown out of Kenya. This has alarmed the authorities here, just as it did in Kenya, since someone who has successfully overthrown one government might try to do the same in another place. He's thus not welcome anywhere. Apparently he went to Lira to visit relations there, but it's believed he's now in Kampala and Special Branch is hunting for him. He'll probably 'disappear' and we'll hear no more about him. In fact, there are rumours and suspicions that it has already happened.

Thursday 25 February

I must be a glutton for punishment. In order to balance my professional qualification as a barrister with an academic qualification, I've decided to take an external law degree with London University. I can sit all the papers here by arrangement as the Ministry of Education provides an examination centre in Kampala for all London external exams. So I shall sit the first part, the Intermediate LLB, in June this year. As I did for the Bar exams, I shall do the necessary reading in the evenings and weekends.

Wednesday 10 March

I went into Kampala this afternoon to see Obwangor, the Minister of Justice, to discuss with him a report I had written about our Nigerian lecturer, whom I had been obliged to suspend from teaching duty. I explained that a deputation representing the whole of the present magistrates course had appeared before me to announce that they flatly refused to attend any more of his classes.

They said that he not only abused them constantly for being stupid, ignorant, bush Africans, but also had physically struck several of them in class for giving what he called 'stupid answers'. The magistrates are all mature men, not schoolboys, and some have been sitting in the customary courts for years. Others are former chiefs, teachers, policemen and so on, and they made it clear that they are definitely not prepared to accept such shameful and degrading treatment.

Obwangor agreed that such conduct was unacceptable. He added that bringing in some qualified Nigerians to various posts where there were no suitable Ugandans available had been a political decision designed to have Africans in place as quickly as possible and to demonstrate African solidarity. He added that there had already been some murmurings about the behaviour of the Nigerian Chief Justice, as I may have heard, but it would not be politically possible just to send these people away before their contracts expired. We have to be very careful.

The man has just five months of his contract left as he's due to finish in mid-August. I've told him to spend his time in his office on research and work on 'the important book on the law of evidence' that he claims to be writing. He'll still be paid and he has no choice, unless he decides to resign, which would be immediately accepted. Meanwhile, I'll take over his classes in addition to my own and I'll keep my eyes open for a possible Ugandan replacement. All this was agreed with Obwangor.

Sunday 14 March

I attended a reception at the Prime Minister's Lodge here in Entebbe yesterday evening. The last time I was at that house was over eight years ago when it was the Chief Secretary's residence, occupied by *Kali* Charlie. It has a pleasant and still well-kept large garden where the reception was held. The visitors were Princess Margaret and the Earl of Snowdon (or Tony the Mountain) who had arrived that morning. Everyone was fluttering around in best bib and tucker in the presence of Royalty and the ladies were in gloves and large hats. I was wearing clean socks.

A few of us were chatting with Lord Snowdon, who looked very pale and unwell. He explained that he disliked flying and he was still feeling uncomfortable from their long flight to Entebbe. On the other hand the Princess was positively sparkling and radiant and obviously enjoying herself. They are here for ten days and will be touring the game parks and visiting Jinja Dam and various parts of the country. That will keep the police busy.

Tuesday 30 March

The BTC correspondence course in police law is going well. A large number from the Force signed up for it and I've been receiving and marking their test papers as they come in. There's already a noticeable improvement in the answers as students progress through the lessons and see from the model answers just how to deal with the questions. I also write helpful comments on each answer paper marked, and deal with any queries that some of them add at the bottom.

On one I added a query of my own. The student had shown his name as Adolf Hitler Ogwal. I asked him why he was using the name of such an appalling dictator and murderer. At the foot of his next answer paper he wrote that he was born in 1944 and his father had greatly admired what he had heard about Hitler, a very strong leader, so he gave his son the name.

Tuesday 20 April

There's a fire engine at the bottom of my garden. It has been there all over the Easter weekend. Nsamizi is on a very steep hill and on the slope below the senior staff quarters there's a thick growth of trees and long grass, all very dry at the moment. In the trees live some very active vervet monkeys which constantly invade our gardens and help themselves to fruit and vegetables growing there. Each year someone comes from the Game Department and shoots carefully selected leaders of the monkey band and, for a while, until they hold their next leadership elections, they become less active and troublesome.

However, all this has nothing to do with the fire engine. On Thursday morning someone down by the road behind the hill either accidentally or deliberately set fire to the dry grass, and the trees caught and it started to spread upwards towards our houses. So I called the Entebbe Fire Brigade and they came up in their one and only fire engine and decided to tackle the fire from the top of the hill rather than from the road at the bottom. We occupants of the quarters and assorted domestic staff provided the necessary interested spectators for the show.

The driver brought his heavy vehicle into my garden and then moved down the slope so as to get nearer for the hoses to reach into the trees. Fortunately there was no wind blowing at the time and they soon got the fire under control. However, when they had packed all their equipment away, they found that the vehicle had adopted a sharp angle and sunk into the now very wet ground around it. When the driver tried to move it uphill the wheels dug in hard under the considerable weight and it stuck fast and tilted over some more. So they cheerfully abandoned it and left it in my garden as an Easter present.

250

When I came back from the School at the end of this afternoon I found that, with the use of a heavy breakdown truck, they had managed to winch it up to level ground and were just driving it away. They left the garden in a bit of a mess, though.

Wednesday 21 April

We have started the second Bar course. There are ten students and, as with the first course, one of them is the best student from the previous course for magistrates. By getting such chaps qualified, we can help to provide already trained senior magistrates. The word seems to have gone out and there were plenty of applicants wishing to attend the course, so I was able to select only those with the best potential, both for passing the exams and as future advocates or magistrates.

Thursday 20 May

We've had some good speakers from various government departments and outside organisations. When they appear I nearly always let the Bar students sit in with the magistrates so that all can benefit. Today we had a European prisons social worker, sent to us by the Ministry, who turned out to be a left-wing, trendy type, as I suppose most social workers are. Near the conclusion of his talk he was going on about what he considered were all the wrong methods and attitudes adopted by the British when running the prisons here in Protectorate days. He said he was now apologising for this and was, himself, speaking as 'a deeply repentant ex-colonialist'.

After he had left I had a couple of announcements to make and then one of the magistrates asked about something that the prisons speaker had mentioned. In reply I started: 'Well, speaking as a totally unrepentant ex-colonialist...' and there was a tremendous burst of laughter and applause from the whole class.

Saturday 29 May

I was invited to St Mary's College, Kisubi, an RC mission senior secondary school just outside Entebbe on the road to Kampala, for their annual sports day yesterday. Some of their athletes were of a high grade, trained by a brother who's a very keen sportsman. It's a first-rate school with a very high academic standard. It's run by the Verona White Fathers but all the staff are brothers, so not priests. I recently was invited to judge their inter-house debating competition, which was of an impressive standard. I've also spoken to their senior boys about

251

the legal profession and studying law, as I have at other similar schools around Kampala.

Saturday 12 June

I'm just back from a useful refresher course for magistrates which I held in Jinja for one week. It was for the magistrates in Busoga who have attended the three previous diploma courses. A very helpful way of keeping in touch and finding out their problems in the field. We also discussed recent changes in the laws and various case decisions in the High Court that are likely to affect their work.

Tuesday 15 June

The Bar students have suggested and requested that, like Makerere undergraduates, they should be able to purchase and wear students short black gowns. Since that's what they want, and I've certainly no objections, I've already spoken to the tailor in Kampala who provides the Makerere students red gowns and asked him to prepare for us sufficient black gowns with green facings to make them distinctive. This is for the present and future courses. After all, when they go to London for their Finals and they keep terms at their Inns of Court, they will wear black gowns for dinner, so they may as well wear them here for classes. The school ties are still popular with both courses and the Law School and its reputation is becoming quite well known around Uganda now. I'm all for encouraging the development of some pride in the School, especially as this is clearly what the students want.

We've just assembled the fourth course for magistrates here. Most of the former older magistrates transferred from the customary courts have now attended courses and these new students are mainly younger chaps whom we have interviewed and selected for appointment. They therefore don't have previous experience in any court. One of them has recently escaped from an RC seminary where he was training for a few years to become a priest. He has now decided that he wants to be a magistrate and smite the sinners in a different way. But he still has to be restrained from delivering a prolonged blessing at the start of each class.

Tuesday 20 July

In our western neighbour, the former Belgian Congo, now the Democratic Republic of the Congo,* a certain General Mobutu, for-

*In 1971 renamed Zaire and in 1997 Democratic Republic of Congo again.

merly an army corporal, has taken power in what is described as a bloodless coup and ousted President Kasavubu and Prime Minister Tshombe. Many of the remaining Belgian civilians living there have fled and taken refuge across the border in Uganda. A number of them arrived here at Nsamizi in lorries and we have had to send the students home for a week until the refugees can be sent by air to Europe.

The Uganda Army sent up some men to 'guard' the refugees and these so-called soldiers have become rather a nuisance. I saw two of them force a teenaged boy to run full tilt down the steep hill for their amusement. One of the men fired a rifle shot in the air close to the boy and they then chased after him with a bayonet. He was naturally frightened out of his wits.

They brought a light anti-aircraft gun up the hill and set it up near the staff quarters. It was a Chinese-made gun and, having served in a light anti-aircraft regiment at one time, I was curious to see it closely. But as I walked up to it the soldiers in the detachment became very agitated; perhaps they thought I might steal their toy, so I left them to it, as these fellows tend to be rather quick on the trigger nowadays.

Monday 26 July

I've just spent a few days at Gulu with the Senior Courts Adviser carrying out some more interviewing and recruiting of magistrates as we still have vacancies in Acholi. It's not easy to find enough in a district where they still prefer to join the Army, Police or Prisons Service. Some of the more educated are beginning to consider more sedentary careers. My Acholi's a bit rusty now but I managed to have a fairly simple conversation or two.

Tuesday 3 August

The Dean of the Faculty of Law at Harvard University, Dr Erwin N. Griswold, has just been on a visit to Uganda. Ever on the watch for interesting outside speakers, I contacted the Ministry, where they were making a programme for his visit, and found that he was already down to come and speak to the law students here. He came on Thursday and gave us quite a good talk.

On Friday I attended a garden party given in his honour by the Chief Justice at his residence and then a lunch yesterday given by the Minister of Justice. Later there was a reception in the senior common room at Makerere given by Y. K. Lule,* the Principal of the University

*President of Uganda for about two months in 1979.

College, and a former Minister in the Protectorate Government. I'm now suffering from a surfeit of lawyers.

Thursday 12 August

We had a very interesting visitor and speaker today: Sir Kenneth Diplock, a Judge of the Court of Appeal in England. When he was a QC in practice he was also UK legal adviser to the Kabaka and was one of those who travelled with Mutesa when he came back here from exile in 1955. His importance to us, in addition to being a very distinguished judge, lies in the fact that he is also chairman of the Bar Examinations Committee of the Council of Legal Education. I had a long chat with him and he was very interested in our Bar courses. I made the point that whereas in West Africa they have flooded their countries with half-baked lawyers, here I've been combing the country for possible talent and potential on a much smaller scale in order to find and train some first-rate lawyers, and in the process build the School's reputation for excellence as well as producing a high pass rate in the Bar exams. He said that he had already noticed how well our students have been doing in the Bar exams and he was very pleased about it.

I brought up the Inns of Court and Council's very high entry standards, which were giving us an occasional problem because one or two of the very bright Africans whom I had talent-spotted didn't have the required basic educational qualifications for admission, but I was satisfied that they could cope with the exams without any great difficulty. He said that, in view of our exceptionally high record of success in the Bar exams, he would personally arrange that anyone in that category recommended by me as a special case would be admitted and allowed to read for the Bar. This is a very helpful and valuable offer of which I shall definitely be taking advantage.

I then took him into the library and introduced him to the Bar students. We sat round the table with tea and biscuits and he chain-smoked and chatted to them about their studies and prospects and told them about his own work as an appeal judge. The students then invited him to join them in a group photograph that they'd arranged to commemorate his visit, which clearly they had all enjoyed. I think he did too.

Monday 16 August

Our recalcitrant and useless Nigerian lecturer has at last departed back to Ibo land, which thankfully creates a vacancy and I can now set about filling it with a Ugandan replacement. I've already spoken to a couple of possibilities working in the Attorney-General's Chambers.

Wednesday 1 September

I've just received a letter from the Solicitor-General saying that he has had a letter from Sir Kenneth Diplock containing this paragraph:

> I was particularly impressed with what the School of Law is doing at Nsamizi. To have scored 12 passes out of 12 with two second classes in Part I of the Bar Examinations is a record for any overseas centre and much better than we manage to do in London. I hope that we shall continue to welcome Ugandan students at the Inns of Court (particularly the Middle Temple). If you can maintain the present standard there need be no fear for the administration of justice by the new generation of judges and magistrates.

Wednesday 29 September

For the second time I had to make a night dash into Kampala to donate blood at Mulago Hospital for a blood change in a baby, European this time, needing my rhesus B negative blood. I don't know the name of the parents this time and, when I asked the sister, she replied quite shirtily that it was not their policy to divulge such information. Could be a Russian; there are plenty around now. Well, it doesn't matter; but I'd have liked to know, all the same.

Thursday 7 October

In the *Argus* this morning there's a report supplied by me that our Bar students have passed 21 out of 29 papers sat for in the Part I exams. This actually means that of the eleven candidates who sat, all passed in something; four in one paper each; four in two papers each and three in all three papers sat; which is not bad at all. I'm very pleased with them. It could be better, except for the last three, who excelled. They don't all sit for the same number of papers as they don't work at the same speed, so I leave it to them to decide how many they feel ready to tackle at any one sitting. Of course, I advise them, but the decision is theirs.

I've also just heard that I passed the LLB Intermediate exams so I'll try Part I of the Finals next time.

Wednesday 27 October

The Ministry today sent over a couple of Parliamentary questions connected with legal education in Uganda with a request that I should draft the Minister's replies. It seems that the politicians are taking notice of what we are doing here and this will be a little useful publicity for the School.

Wednesday 3 November

For some time the Solicitor-General (SG) has been talking about what he calls the need to move the Law School to Kampala, where he and the Ministry are both located. The problem as he sees it is that he is the permanent secretary of the Ministry of Justice, and the Law School is the only department in the Ministry which is not in Kampala and directly under his eye and control. This does not suit him and he wants to be able to interfere in various ways, particularly in the selection of Bar students. He thinks that the Baganda are not getting a fair share of the places, by which he means that they should be the majority on each course; whereas I've been looking for talent first, regardless of tribe, and also trying to find it outside Buganda, which already has more than its fair share of lawyers in comparison with other tribes. I want to try and make sure that we produce advocates from all over Uganda so that when they eventually go into practice, they will mostly do so in their own districts and the clients will then not have to go to the trouble and expense of travelling to Kampala when they wish to consult a lawyer. It will also assist the local magistrates courts, and the High Court when out on circuit, if there are local advocates available to take cases on the spot. Having to bring advocates from Kampala is very inconvenient and expensive and it adds to the problems when the courts are trying to fix trial dates and dispose of cases without too much delay.

Since the SG's office is in the same corridor as the Minister's, he is in constant contact and, it seems, he is getting his way. I was summoned to Kampala yesterday to attend Obwangor on a ministerial visit to a piece of land in Kitante Valley, between the museum and Kitante Hostel, at the far end of the golf course. This place, so Obwangor explained, was to be the site of a new, large Law School with library, classrooms, students rooms, staff houses and offices. No expense spared; so where's the money coming from, I wonder?

The new Uganda Television section of Radio Uganda was present in the person of a scruffy little European called Bob Astles, so I'm told. He had a camera on his shoulder and walked backwards in front of us as Obwangor and I walked solemnly over the empty patch of grass. An African assistant, carrying something like a battery in a satchel with a wire leading to the camera, trotted beside him, occasionally reaching out to steady the cameraman as he stumbled backwards over the lumpy ground.

Friday 5 November

Fame at last. Apparently I'm a TV star. Several people have phoned me at the School to say that they saw me on the Uganda TV news yesterday wading through some long grass with the Minister of Justice as if we were on an expedition searching for something. I gather that TV reception for the very short period that it's on each evening is occasionally not too bad in Kampala, but snowstorms on the screen are fairly common. I suppose it will gradually improve in time, but I don't think I'll bother to get one.

Meanwhile, I must continue the struggle to keep those greedy hands off the Law School, whether or not we have to move to Kampala; otherwise we shall end up with a bunch of dim students with the right Mengo connections but little chance of passing any examinations.

Friday 12 November

Yesterday Ian Smith and his all-white Rhodesian Front Party unilaterally declared independence, or UDI, as they call it, from Britain in order to stop moves towards ultimate African majority rule. They have also replaced the British Governor and ended judicial appeals to the Privy Council. I hear that in the UK Prime Minister Fatty Wilson is hopping mad and threatening all kinds of trouble and reprisals for the Rhodesians.

Sunday 28 November

I was invited to a dining-in night at the Police Officers' Mess in Kampala yesterday evening. Prime Minister Obote and the Minister of Internal Affairs, Basil Batiringaya, and various other VIPs were guests. Obote gave them a complimentary and inspiring speech in payment for his supper and, afterwards, went through the motions of conducting the Police Band at the invitation of the IG Oryema. I enjoyed the evening meeting and exchanging news with many old friends.

Monday 13 December

I've managed to persuade a young Acholi lawyer named James Obol-

257

Ochola, who is a law graduate from Dar-es-Salaam University, to transfer from the AG's Chambers to the Law School as a lecturer. The problem is finding a house for him in an already overcrowded Entebbe. While that is being sorted out by the housing authority he is going to caretake my house during my UK leave, for which I depart tomorrow.

1966

Friday 25 February

I arrived back from leave yesterday morning and, later that day, heard that Obote has removed the Kabaka from the post of President of Uganda and has suspended the Constitution. It's a political coup. The Baganda in their usual contumelious fashion have been demanding too much of the cake. In addition, the Kabaka has become tired of being an ignored constitutional head of state and he has made it clear that he wants to be an executive president. All this became too much for Obote and, after first breaking off the liaison with KY, he has now taken a more drastic step. It looks as though he plans to eliminate the opposition in Parliament and perhaps run a one-party state, as happened in Kenya in 1964. He doesn't seem to be very keen on democracy.

Thursday 3 March

Yesterday it was announced that the Prime Minister, Obote, acting with the advice and consent of the Cabinet, had declared that the duties and powers of the executive authority of Uganda should be vested in him rather than the President or Vice-President. Meanwhile, they are drafting a new constitution to replace the 1962 Independence Constitution produced in London. The Baganda are very unhappy but don't know what to do about it; probably waiting for a sign from the Kabaka.

Thursday 24 March

I appeared on Uganda TV again yesterday. Some producer rang me to ask if I would take part in a TV series in which each week they inter- view 'a prominent or interesting personality in Uganda' and talk about his or her work in a half-hour programme. UTV is in black and white only and I still haven't actually seen it yet. It was a 'live' show, not recorded, so I couldn't see it later. I had mentioned it at Nsamizi, where they now have a TV set in their common room, and I was told that some staff and students would be watching and would tell me how it went.

The Uganda Radio and TV studios are now located in the former European Hospital on Nakasero hill and it wasn't easy to find the correct room at night. The studio room was completely closed up, windows boarded over in an attempt to soundproof it. There was not even an electric fan in the stuffy room, which became unbearably hot when they switched on the very bright lights. I was wearing a suit and tie and felt as though I was melting. The interview was otherwise easy and I had no problems talking about the Law School courses, selection of students, results so far and future plans.

Today, in the common room during morning coffee break, those of the staff who had watched it said it had gone very well. Some of our students who also watched told me it was 'interesting and exciting' and they enjoyed it. However, nobody has asked for my autograph yet.

Saturday 16 April

Yesterday the Interim Constitution came into effect, replacing that of 1962, and the President becomes executive and replaces the post of Prime Minister, which disappears, and the present holder automatically becomes President. That is what the Kabaka wanted but it's Obote who got it, just as he intended. The Baganda are unhappy but quiet at the moment. To the ordinary up-country peasant, far from Kampala, working in the fields or herding cattle and goats, it can hardly matter really who calls himself president.

Friday 22 April

On Wednesday evening we held a debate with the National Teachers College at Kyambogo, just outside Kampala. The students on both law courses have combined to form a debating society and they arranged this with their opposite numbers at Kyambogo. I was invited to chair the debate so I went with them in the Nsamizi minibus. It's good practice for them in public speaking and in preparing cases.

The motion to be debated was that 'Laws make Criminals'. They had sensibly arranged that a Law School student and an NTC student spoke for it, and similarly one of each spoke against it, making it just a friendly debate and not inter-school. They all did very well and we had an enjoyable evening. The motion was carried and they even arranged for a short report on it to appear in the *Uganda Argus*.

On the magistrates course they are doing their mock trials and each one takes a turn presiding over a trial, in which I've briefed the witnesses and accused on what to say and do and the student is left to control the trial and produce a judgment. Our ex-seminary student delivered his judgment this afternoon in which he convicted the accused and, before he could be stopped, rose from his magisterial seat in the mock court and delivered a full blessing upon the accused and the court, moving his right hand about in true Papal style. This was followed by loud applause and laughter from the students. I've been trying to get him out of this habit but those Jesuits, or whoever they are at the seminary, really hammer home their teachings into their recruits, rather like Guards drill sergeants.

Thursday 28 April

At a meeting of the Law Reform Commission I suggested that we should abolish the death penalty for murder as they have done in the UK and elsewhere. I was immediately shot down by the AG, however, who said that it couldn't be considered as Uganda's not ready for it and Parliament would never agree. Everyone else on the Commission either concurred or remained silent.

We did, however, get rid of the tedious and time-wasting procedure for Preliminary Inquiries (PIs) which for years magistrates have been required to hold in all criminal cases triable by the High Court. Since it involved recording in longhand the depositions of all witnesses, it took up much of the magistrates' precious time and caused inordinate delays to trials in the High Court. It also gave the unfortunate impression of there being two separate trials of each serious case.

Two of us on the Commission had had experience of army courts martial and so, between us, we worked out a procedure similar to the preliminary proceedings for a court martial to replace PIs and turn them into a paper committal proceedings. Thus, some of the evidence, such as that of arrest, identification of the body, movement of exhibits, post-mortem examination reports and other technicalities, as well as the testimony of those witnesses which will not be contested, can now be admitted by both sides in advance of the trial, thus saving much of the trial court's time and that of the witnesses involved.

The third matter concerned the crime of robbery, which is very much on the increase in Uganda. In Parliament the members were echoing the loud demands of their electorate to make armed robbery a capital offence. The Commission was asked for its views on such proposed legislation. Several were in favour. I spoke against the idea on the ground that murder is already a capital offence; therefore, if anyone is killed in the course of a robbery the charge will be murder and the death penalty applicable. However, robbery in other circumstances carries a heavy prison sentence. If we make robbery a capital offence then robbers will soon reason out that they can't be hanged twice for the double offence of robbery and murder. Therefore, the best way to enhance their chances of escaping altogether would be to kill the robbery victims and other eyewitnesses at the scene. Consequently, more robbers will escape conviction and more victims will die.

The AG, Binaisa, said: 'Yes, we here accept that, but the fact remains that Parliament and the people are demanding the death penalty for armed robbery and they are going to get it in spite of your recommendation, even if I put it forward as the Commission's.' Unfortunately, he was right and the legislation has now been enacted.

Wednesday 18 May

The Law School Debating Society organised another debate this evening; this time against the Nsamizi students, on the subject of whether the white Rhodesians were right to declare UDI. One of the Nsamizi African staff members was in the chair and I sat at the back of the all-African audience, taking no part at all in this one. When the time came for the audience to vote on the motion, it went overwhelmingly in favour of the white Rhodesian UDI, which was a bit of a surprise.

Friday 20 May

Today we received the framed official portrait of President Obote with instructions from the Ministry to hang it in place of that of the Kabaka. So we did.

Saturday 21 May

In the *Uganda Argus* this morning there was a photograph of the seven recently successful Part I Bar students in their gowns, with me in the centre seat, which they had arranged to be taken prior to their departure to the UK to read for their Finals.

Sunday 22 May

The Buganda Lukiiko members have reacted to Obote's latest constitutional changes by passing a resolution to the effect that they no longer recognise the authority of the Obote Government as it has abrogated the 1962 Constitution. Consequently, the Lukiiko has ordered that the Central Government of Uganda must get out of Buganda and find somewhere else from where it can govern the rest of Uganda. Yet another typically futile gesture similar to that in December 1960 when they announced Buganda's secession from the

Uganda Protectorate. They live in a world of their own up in Mengo and never seem to learn anything at all from their constant policy failures.

Monday 23 May

There have been riots in various parts of Buganda following the Lukiiko's trouble-stirring efforts. These have involved violent attacks on several police stations and posts in which a corporal and two constables were killed; one each at Nagalama, Buikwe and Luwero. One of them was tied up and thrown into the back of a truck filled with dried thatching material which was then set alight and the poor chap burned alive. Reinforcements have been sent out and arrests made, including three Baganda chiefs who were busily stirring things up; no doubt on orders of the Lukiiko.

Tuesday 24 May

I was driving into Kampala this afternoon and near the fire station saw four army lorries, apparently coming down from Mengo, filled with bodies and trailing blood from the tail-boards. Apparently there has been a battle at Mengo, where Colonel Idi Amin led some troops in an attack on the Kabaka at his palace, resulting in the slaughter of most of the Baganda living and working in that area. Presumably, Obote sent him there on this mission, since he wouldn't do something like that on his own initiative.

Saturday 28 May

During the attack on the Lubiri there was a very heavy rainstorm which enabled the Kabaka to hop over a back wall and escape on foot unseen in spite of there being swarms of Uganda Army troops milling about the place. It's believed that he obtained help outside and travelled westwards, probably crossing the border into Rwanda or Burundi. Since the point of the attack was to capture, or more likely, to kill the Kabaka, the operation can hardly be described as a success; which is scarcely surprising with the ham-fisted Amin in charge. I hear that the Uganda Army troops have been rampaging around Kampala and outside, shooting at people and making thorough nuisances of themselves. Here at Entebbe it has remained relatively quiet, although there is an army roadblock on the outskirts of the township. At any rate, the news is that the Kabaka reached England safely and is once again in exile, thanks to his and the Lukiiko's efforts against Obote's Government.

No doubt he will resume his heavy drinking and generally dissolute life-style.

Friday 10 June

Last week we finished the final exams in the fourth course for magistrates and today was the graduation ceremony. It has been an exceptionally good course and for the first time we've awarded four first-class diplomas, and nearly all the others received second-class diplomas. The first four are easily suitable and eligible candidates for a later Bar course, which will enable them to become senior magistrates.*

The Chief Justice and the Attorney-General both attended the graduation and made encouraging and complimentary speeches. In my own short speech I took the opportunity to say: 'We've heard a lot recently about the three scourges of Uganda – poverty, ignorance and disease – but I suggest that a fourth scourge has also to be banished and that is injustice... We here must do all that we can to instil into each law student a sense of justice so that he will always try to do what is right for any person no matter who he is.'

This was all written up in today's *Uganda Argus* with a front page photograph of the AG, Godfrey Binaisa, chatting to me outside the building.

Tuesday 14 June

On my return from the School this afternoon Adam, my cook, reported that the cooking clock was sick. It turned out that he had dropped the kitchen timer on the floor and broken it. It probably doesn't matter a great deal as I suspect he has unexplained reservations and fears about using it and has sabotaged it for the sake of his own peace of mind. However, he then moved on to the more serious business on his agenda and requested some rubber medicine as he has a cold in his knees. In fact, he wanted some liniment to put on a stiff leg which he had bruised when he fell over the lawn-mower on returning last night from a *pombe* party. I pointed out that, as he's now a Moslem, he's not supposed to drink alcohol. Adam replied that he hadn't actually drunk any alcohol, but had merely watched the others drinking and he was overcome by the fumes. I believed him, of course.

Friday 24 June

Yesterday I finished the Part I of the Finals LLB exam in Kampala and today I drove up to Soroti, where I'm holding a week-long

---

*Two of them eventually became High Court Judges.

refresher course for the Teso magistrates who attended earlier courses at the Law School to bring them up to date and to explain relevant parts of the new Constitution.

Thursday 7 July

The fifth magistrates course and third Bar course have both assembled and commenced, keeping us fully occupied. Most days I'm in class all day long. It's exhausting but very rewarding work and I enjoy it.

One of our new Bar students is a magistrate who came top of his earlier diploma course here. He has only a primary education followed by just two years in secondary school before money for school fees ran out. But he has a first-class brain; so I took advantage of Sir Kenneth Diplock's offer and presented him as a special case with a certainty of doing well. Consequently he has been admitted as a Bar student to the Middle Temple, Sir Kenneth's own Inn of Court.

I've been trying for some time to persuade Oryema, the IG Police, to agree to release selected police officers to read for the Bar. I feel it would help to raise standards if, say, the future Head of CID, the Director of Training and the commandants of the Police College and the PTS are legally qualified. They could be given the necessary study leave and I will arrange for their scholarships, so it would cost the Force nothing financially. But he won't have it. He has not answered my letters or my request to meet him to discuss this proposition.

Police officers who are interested in this idea have told me that he insists that any officer who successfully applies to the Law School for a scholarship to read for the Bar must either forfeit it or resign from the Force. Two first-class officers have already done this and will probably go into private practice as advocates after qualifying, which will be an unnecessary and considerable loss to the Force. There are other officers who have approached me with the same intention.

Monday 18 July

Apparently the recent attack on the Kabaka's palace by Colonel Amin and his merry men has helped to save Amin from yet another crisis in his career. An Acholi MP, Daudi Ocheng, who oddly enough belongs to KY, accused Amin in Parliament of embezzling about £17,000 from the Congo nationalists who were fighting Tshombe. Ocheng produced and waved in the air Amin's bank statements in support, and the MPs duly passed a motion suspending Amin from duty pending an inquiry. Obote, who was said to be implicated, was away up in Lira while the matter was being discussed in Parliament. It seems that the Congo nationalists need weapons so they handed over stocks of gold and ivory, abandoned by the Belgians, to Amin to use for purchasing arms. He did this for them but, at the same time, creamed off large sums of money for himself. In spite of this Obote, on his return, has appointed Amin to be the Army Chief of Staff, which gives him very considerable control over it. Amin seems to have as many lives as a cat.

Saturday 30 July

With the new Constitution now in force, Buganda is at last brought within the Magistrates Courts Act and consequently the Principal Court and its lower customary courts are turned into ordinary magistrates courts, as in the rest of the country. Accordingly, I fitted in a special course for the selected Baganda magistrates and have been cramming them with facts, notes, procedures and practical advice on this crash course, which we held for three weeks at Makerere University in between our main courses; one of which they will have to attend eventually.

Monday 29 August

I've just managed to squeeze in a week's refresher course at Gulu for the magistrates in Acholi, followed by a relaxing two days at Paraa Lodge in Murchison Falls Park. While in Gulu I decided to visit Francis Onyona, who was my driver in Karamoja until he left the Force and took up farming. I had a rough idea where he and his family lived, about 3 or 4 miles outside Gulu on the road to Anaka and Pakwach. So I drove along until I reckoned I was near and then decided to use some of my rusty Acholi to make enquiries. After locating Francis, we exchanged news and I was taken on an inspection tour of his farm, which had been started by his late father. I also met his seven daughters and Francis said he is looking forward to acquiring considerable wealth as a result of eventually receiving a good dowry for each of them.

While speaking to some old friends in the police in Gulu, I heard that in a recent operation against armed cattle raiders in Karamoja, where they now carry guns instead of spears, one of the tracker constables shot a raider who was armed with a rifle. Assuming he was dead or dying, the Karamojong tracker ran forward to jump over his body in order that he might not be attacked by the spirit of the dead raider. But the man was still alive and ready for him. Both men then fired at the same time, instantly killing each other and falling down side by side.

Tuesday 4 October

Earlier this year I purchased a silver grey 'E' Type Jaguar in England and arranged to have it shipped out to Mombasa and put on the railway to Kampala. Unfortunately, when the suppliers delivered it to the London Docks the dockers immediately came out on strike; not because of my car but because they are always on strike about something. So it sat there for months, but now it's here at last. All the formalities have been completed and the local agents prepared it and put it on the road. I collected it the other day and drove it back here, with admiring stares from everyone around. It's the only one of its kind in Uganda. Because our roads are not so good and it has a very low-slung chassis, I've had a strong metal plate fixed under the engine to provide protection. Several people have asked me to park it outside their houses as they say it lends tone and distinction to the place.

Tuesday 11 October

In today's *Uganda Argus* there's a report of our recent Bar exam results from London, which show a 100% pass rate, of which we're all very proud. The 12 students on the course sat for a total of 24 papers and passed in all of them. The magistrate who came to the Bar course in July as a special case, with the assistance of Sir Kenneth Diplock, decided to sit for three papers at his first attempt, after studying for them for only three months. He not only passed in all three but gained a good second-class in one of them. A really remarkable effort by someone with only a basic educational background who would never otherwise have had such an opportunity.

It's this kind of result from my talent-spotting efforts around the country that I think makes our work worthwhile. Unfortunately, in spite of such results, according to the SG, I am selecting 'the wrong people' by bringing on such 'peasants' from outside Buganda. If he can get us moved to Kampala and control the selection, then the 'right people' with the Mengo connections will receive the scholarships. He hopes.

In addition to these excellent results, three of our students who went to London to prepare for the Finals only 11 months ago have passed them at their first attempt and are now qualified. One of them was a police officer who had wanted to stay in the Force but was required by the IG to resign. A fourth student obtained a conditional pass in the Finals and so has to repeat only one paper to qualify. I'm very pleased with them. The bonus is that I've heard I passed the Part I of the LLB Finals.

Friday 21 October

There is an obligatory paper on Roman law in the Bar Part I exams. This is no great problem for those who've done Latin at school, especially the students from RC mission schools or seminaries. But there are one or two from other schools where it is not taught. In these cases I have to teach them sufficient Latin to enable them to cope with this paper.

I've received congratulatory letters from both the AG and the SG regarding our recent triumph in the Bar exams. I hope this is remembered when they proceed with their plans to move us to Kampala, especially with regard to the selection of students, but I suspect that nothing has really changed.

Friday 25 November

I was asked to lecture to a promotion course at the Police College this morning and, because of other matters to attend to, left Entebbe rather late, so I had to speed up a little in my Jag in order to reach Naguru in time. On one stretch there was a car going quite slowly. Although there was a continuous white line along the centre of the road, at that point the road ahead was quite clear and I decided to overtake. As I did so, out popped a couple of constables from the side of the road and signalled me to stop. They were not known to me and they said quite rightly that I had committed a traffic offence. I said I was sorry but I was going to be late to give a lecture at the Police College. The senior constable said: 'Oh well, if you are teaching the police, that's all right. Please go on and thank you, sir,' and snapped up a smart salute.

Tuesday 29 November

I usually take Kimbo for a walk in the early evening along the lake shore at Entebbe beach. He enjoys rushing in and out of the water, fetching pieces of wood that I throw in for him. Today, after doing this, we went up on to the bluff and through some heavy undergrowth. There was a tremendous scuffle inside a thick bushy area, with Kimbo barking and jumping about excitedly. Out came a large Nile monitor lizard about 5 feet long and obviously extremely cross at being disturbed by a troublesome small dog. In typical terrier fashion Kimbo kept barking and making threatening and aggressive mock attacks around the lizard as it opened and closed its jaws. It then turned tail and fled into the deep bush behind it and I seized Kimbo and put him on his lead before he could follow after it.

267

1967

Saturday 3 December

I drove into Kampala yesterday morning to pick up some boxes of law books for our library from the British High Commission. The labels on the boxes read: 'Presented by Britain under the Special Commonwealth African Assistance Plan'. I had earlier submitted a list of books that we needed. I then decided to go to a shop in Kampala Road but, as I was about to turn into the road I was stopped by a Brit coming from that direction. His car skidded to a halt and he said: 'Don't go down there! The UPC Youth Wing thugs and Makerere undergraduates are demonstrating against the British for selling arms to South Africa, and beating up any Europeans they can find and smashing their car windscreens.' So I diverted and got on to the Entebbe Road via side streets and skedaddled back to Entebbe. I gather that one of the cars they smashed up, after beating the two white men in it, turned out to be carrying Russians who have been encouraging Obote and his youth-wingers in such unpleasant carryings-on. Perhaps we all look alike to them.

Tuesday 27 December

I've spent Christmas in camp down at the Queen Elizabeth National Park in the west. A game guard told me that a man had been eaten by a lion at one of the fishing stations here last month. He said that he and another game guard went out and found only parts of the man's legs. They tracked the lion down and shot it and found the man's head close by. He added that there had been two people eaten by lions there in the last five months and they were all hoping that it was by the same lion, which is now dead.

1967

Friday 6 January

There is a pair of swifts parked in my garage. Without asking for permission, they have built a mud nest on top of the electricity meter fixed to the wall and hatching has commenced currently, to coin a phrase. We have an unspoken arrangement: I leave the garage doors open all day and close them for the night at exactly 6.30 p.m. when it's dusk. The birds seem to know this and fly in from their all-day foraging for insects at that time. If I'm a minute or two early and see that they're not home yet, I stand at the doors waiting. They then fly in with a quick cheep as they zoom past my head and I close and lock the doors. First thing in the morning the *shamba* boy opens up to wash my car and out they fly.

Thursday 9 February

I've managed to recruit as lecturers two more Ugandans. George Kanyeihamba, a Mukiga,* has been teaching law at an institute in Southampton. He listened to my plea that he is more needed here and agreed to return and start this year. Francis Ssekandi, a Muganda,† has transferred from the Attorney-General's Chambers. I've made it clear at the Ministry that I do not want the expatriate staff they've offered from time to time, but only Ugandans. I want this to be their effort and achievement as far as possible.

Sebastian, the Law School clerk, came here three years ago as a young, unqualified and untrained typist. He is now expert in shorthand and speed typing as a result of using some Pitman's books that I brought back from the UK for him. I was also able to get him a place on a recent government clerical and shorthand course so as to obtain a recognised qualification. He did so well on that course that he's now fully qualified to be a personal secretary. As soon as I'd informed the Ministry, so as to adjust his salary accordingly, they snatched him away to be the Minister's personal secretary in Kampala. Our loss, but very much to his benefit. Fortunately our office messenger's a bright lad and he's now learning to type and should do well enough as a replacement.

Saturday 18 March

Last year I was given a Siamese kitten, which has now grown into a beautiful smoky-grey cat with dark markings on the face and legs. The trouble with this is that the vervet monkeys living in the trees below my house have almost exactly the same markings and colouring. This afternoon there was a commotion outside the front entrance of my house, where there are steps as it's on a slope. Looking down, I saw that three monkeys had cornered the cat by the steps and were trying to get close enough to attack. But Siamese are very fierce little creatures and mine was putting up a frightening display of claws, snarling and spitting and so holding them off. However, they were bigger and it was clearly only a matter of time. So I picked up two large pots of cacti and dropped them on to the monkeys, which quickly made off uttering cries of anger and disappointment.

*Later Minister of Justice/Attorney-General in 1979 and 1987.
†Later High Court Judge then Justice of Appeal.

Wednesday 22 March

Colonel Amin is now a Brigadier. He's moving up fast and I wonder what Obote thinks he's doing. It may be that the President has become so unpopular politically with his harsh treatment of anyone who opposes or disagrees with him that he's becoming more and more dependent upon the support of the army. Just how much he can rely on them is a big question, especially in view of what's been happening with military coups in West Africa.

Friday 28 April

The township weekly rubbish collection truck came up to the staff quarters today as usual and, when passing my house, for some unknown reason, Kimbo dashed out and was struck by the hub of a rear wheel. Although there were no external injuries he was dead when I got to him. The men in the truck were upset and worried but I told them they were not to blame and sent them on their way. I've enjoyed his companionship for the last six years and I'm going to miss him, especially as he often walked across the playing field with me to the Law School. He has sat quietly through so many classes that I recently told the students that he had probably qualified for a diploma.

Saturday 13 May

Some time back at a Ministry reception I had a chance of a few words with Obote, who remarked that he had heard we were doing good work at the Law School. So I asked him if he would agree to attend one of our graduation days. He said he would like to do so and I went ahead and arranged with his office for him to attend yesterday's graduation of the fifth magistrates course.

Two days before the ceremony something came up and the President couldn't make it, so I was told that he was sending the Vice-President, John Babiiha, to represent him. Babiiha's a nice old boy but this was a considerable disappointment. We went ahead and the Chief Justice and Attorney-General attended, with a crowd of the students' relatives and friends. There was a UTV cameraman and someone from the Ministry of Information. The lecturers and I wore gowns, as did the Bar students, thus making it a more academic-looking occasion.

Naturally I had sent an advance copy of my speech to the President's Office and I assumed that the VP would be given the President's speech to read out. However, this apparently was not done and, instead, some idle creature in the VP's Office had simply rehashed my speech with nothing original added. The poor chap realised this when I had finished and he rose to speak and found he was merely repeating what I had just said. He had constantly to interject: 'as the Principal has just told us' and 'as we have just heard'. He was obviously embarrassed and so was I. It was certainly not what I'd been hoping for and said little for his staff.

In addition to diplomas, we award book prizes for each subject studied and examined upon during the course. Law books as prizes are now donated to us each year by the two main London law publishers, Sweet and Maxwell, and Butterworths; also locally by the Uganda Law Society, the Uganda Bookshop, the AG's Chambers as well as the Law School itself.

During refreshments after the ceremony, the students mixed with the VIPs, who included prominent advocates, the IG Police, the Commissioner of Prisons and the SG. Today's Uganda Argus gave us a good write-up too.

Thursday 8 June

Brigadier Opolot has been removed as Army Commander and is now detained in Luzira prison for some unstated reason. Brigadier Amin has been promoted yet again, this time to Major General, and has been appointed to the new post of Chief of Defence Staff. Just what all this means we haven't been told, nor do I suppose we will be. Whatever's going on, it seems that Amin's star is very much in the ascendant at the moment. I wonder why.

Friday 16 June

Although I no longer have a dog to take me for a walk, I still go along the beach each day after work. Yesterday as I walked beside the water's edge deep in thought I was suddenly stopped with one foot in the air. How this happened I can't explain but, when I looked down, there directly under my raised foot was a large coiled cobra with its head down and obviously resting; which it wouldn't have been if my foot had lowered itself another few inches on top of it. I carefully slow-motioned my movements backwards so as not to disturb it and moved well out of range. The cobra stayed put and snoozed on. A couple of Africans approached from the opposite direction and I warned them to stay clear. When I mentioned this rather odd incident to Maggie, my Irish part-time secretary, this morning, she said: 'It's because they are not ready for you yet. You haven't finished the task you've been given.' Well, maybe; but one task which I hope is finished is the last part of the LLB Finals, which I've just written in Kampala.

271

Wednesday 28 June

I've just spent the last ten days in Mbarara, first for the Judicial Service Commission interviewing potential recruits for the magistracy; then we held a refresher course for Ankole and Kigezi magistrates. I was also invited by the headmaster to speak to the senior boys at Ntare Senior Secondary School in Mbarara. It's a fine school, with a reputation for academic and sporting excellence, and the students I spoke to asked some sensible and intelligent questions. They were also very interested in my 'E' Type Jaguar, which they inspected afterwards. One of them, who had been to a Kampala cinema, declared it to be a 'Jemis Bondi car'.

Tuesday 4 July

We have commenced the sixth year-long magistrates course. The students are those selected as a result of various up-country interviews on behalf of the JSC, and it looks as if we've got a very bright group. The fourth Bar course has also assembled. On it there are four magistrates who obtained first-class diplomas on their earlier courses; and one police officer who, as usual, had to resign from the Force to take up his scholarship here. The magistrates will stay in the Judiciary when they qualify, and be promoted to grade I, so they have a very considerable incentive.

Monday 31 July

I'm rich! I've just heard from the bank that one of the Premium Bonds that I purchased in the UK a few years ago has won for me the gigantic prize of £25. The idea of all this wealth makes me dizzy.

Friday 4 August

Obote held a press conference today to explain about his new Republican Constitution, which is currently being debated in Parliament. He said that the abolition of the four kingdoms and their rulers was no bad thing as they had encouraged tribalism, the enemy of nationalism. He added that Uganda is now one national entity and its people have to be encouraged to think of themselves first as Ugandans and, a long way second, as members of a particular tribe. He added that squabbles and disputes between tribes are not helpful in building a new nation. He's right about that.

Wednesday 30 August

This afternoon I was driving to Kampala and in front of me was an estate car driven by a nun, or White Sister, or whatever. A lorry driven by an African came shooting out of a side track straight on to the main road without stopping. The nun swerved to avoid the lorry, left the road and came to a halt in the bush. I stopped and walked over to her car and asked if she was all right. She was gasping with shock at the very near escape and said with an Irish accent: 'Glory be, I thought our blessed Father was going to get me then.'

I couldn't help thinking that she shouldn't sound so reluctant about that. After all, it's where such religious people claim they want to be anyway. I waited until she said she was OK and had driven off and then continued on my way. The lorry driver had long since departed without stopping.

Wednesday 9 September

The new Republican Constitution was passed in Parliament and came into immediate effect yesterday. Provisions have been made for the former rulers to retain some privileges such as a pension, one residence, staff and cars; but they have no authority or powers.

Obote is finding increasingly that his scientific socialism, like Nyerere's flirting with Chinese communism in Tanzania, is not making much headway with the majority of Ugandans. It's directly opposed to the way they feel and their tribal life patterns. They are used to a feudal system and some, like the Baganda, have hereditary chiefs and an inner ring of nobles and counsellors with a mass of people who simply obey them. It's an accepted pattern and it seems to suit them. Communism and socialism with their alleged dictatorship by the masses are anathema to a relatively unsophisticated people. Generally the educated African tends to have capitalistic inclinations. The economy of Uganda, with all its potential, has been considerably damaged by Obote's nationalisation policy, which has been followed by dangerously incompetent and corrupt management; and has also succeeded in driving away much potential foreign investment.

Sunday 13 September

Yesterday I attended a wedding at Rubaga (RC) Cathedral. I knew Freddie when he was an inspector on the staff of the Police College in 1961 and we've kept in touch since. He's now an ASP and was married according to custom, with dowry paid, some years ago. They have several children and, like many others, have been saving for years so as to make a big splash with a cathedral marriage followed by a large reception for many friends, which, in Kampala at any rate, costs a great deal. Everyone was dressed to the nines and it all went very well. There were a number of his police colleagues there and I was able to catch up with the latest Force news.

Tuesday 10 October

Yesterday was the fifth anniversary of Uganda's independence. I didn't attend any functions and I hear that in Kampala the Baganda didn't turn out in large numbers to watch the usual celebrations at Kololo airstrip. With the loss of their Kabaka and their special kingdom status, they could hardly be expected to be in a celebratory mood. The sprinkling of spectators shown in the newspaper photograph told its own tale.

At least I have something to be pleased about. I heard today that I've passed the LLB Finals. As far as I'm concerned that is the last examination that I'm going to sit for. I shan't bother to go to London to attend the graduation ceremony. I wouldn't even if I could spare the time, which I can't. There's too much to do here. They can cap me *in absentia*.

Thursday 23 November

Today the Uganda Argus published our recent Bar exam results showing 26 passes. Six of the students passed three papers each at their first attempt. Mary Ilero, our first woman Bar student, has passed her Finals in London and is the second Ugandan woman barrister. Our second woman Bar student, Annie Ogaino, has completed Part I and will now go to London for the Finals. We have two women on the present course, so it cannot be said that they are being neglected by us as far as legal training is concerned.

Some of these students, when they have qualified, will become government lawyers in the AG's Chambers or other departments; others will go into private practice and, of course, those who are magistrates will take up senior posts in the Judiciary, where the way will be opened for them to go right to the top. I hope I shall be around to see that happen.

Sunday 17 December

Yesterday evening I drove to Kampala to see a film at the Norman cinema. Afterwards in the cinema car park I found a horrible little VW Beetle had been thoughtlessly parked or abandoned very close to the front of my posh Jag, thus blocking the way out since I had parked it against a wall and there were other cars on either side. Fortunately a group of young Asians stood admiring the Jag, so I asked them to assist and we all gathered round the VW and, with a cry of: 'Everybody together – up!', picked it up and dumped it some yards away, and I drove off with a wave of my hand amidst shouts and laughter from the Asians.

1968

Thursday 4 January

I spent Christmas and the New Year quietly and restfully down at the coast, staying at a small hotel with beach cabins just outside Mombasa. I relaxed on the beach, swam in the warm Indian Ocean, strolled around Mombasa and examined the old fort and watched the Arab dhows load and unload in the ancient harbour. I drove down and back in my Jag, covering about 1,800 miles altogether. The car went very well, apart from the twin exhaust pipes having to be fixed back in place after a bad stretch of road in Kenya.

Tuesday 20 February

I had another unpleasant session with the SG today. He is still eager to take control of the Law School, and of course its reputation, in his own hands. He accused me of being a dictator because I alone run the school, select the Bar students, award them their scholarships, and decide on the contents of all courses. He may be right but, as I pointed out, our results to date can fairly be described as excellent and so justify my actions, so what's his complaint? He agreed that he cannot fault the work I'm doing here and the results, but he still wants control and, presumably, the credit for those results. In addition, he brought up his earlier complaint that I'm selecting 'the wrong kind of students' for the Bar courses: ordinary, common people from peasant families and other tribes. Not the Mengo elect from Buganda, he meant. I said I was only concerned with their ability and potential, not what tribe they belong to nor whether their fathers were peasants or chiefs. Furthermore, we have to provide for the whole of Uganda, not just Buganda or Kampala. Fortunately, the AG, Binaisa, although a Muganda, is more broadminded and strongly supports what we are doing.

1968

Thursday 29 February

The BTC law correspondence course is still going well, judging by the number of answer papers I receive for marking each month. I'm informed that the pass rate in the police law exams has increased noticeably these last few years, so it's proving to be as useful to the individual police officer as it is to the Force generally.

Friday 8 March

The district and administrative officers are all Africans now, of course, and they are still required to pass the law exam for administrative officers as in the past, although district officers long ago ceased to be magistrates. Since there is nobody to coach them, and they don't get any court experience in the field as the British DOs had, I offered to hold a short preparatory course of one week each year just before their exam, which, in fact, I also set and mark for the Administration, since there is nobody else to do it.

I've just held the course for this year; going over the type of questions in each paper, the main subjects to watch for and how best to answer them. So it's mainly examination techniques really, and dealing with their queries. They are all graduates, some from Makerere, others attended the universities in Nairobi or Dar-es-salaam.

Monday 11 March

I've just lost one of my lecturers, George, who is moving on and upwards in the academic world, as he has been appointed a law lecturer at Makerere University College. It's my policy here, as it was in the Police, that if someone's doing a good job and has potential and is given a chance of promotion or moving up and onwards, he should be encouraged and assisted to do so, not hindered simply because it's difficult to find a suitable replacement. Fortunately I've located a recent law graduate in the AG's Chambers who wants to do some teaching. He is Francis Butagira, a Munyankole,* who is moving over here to commence work this month.

Wednesday 13 March

The President visited King's College, Budo, this afternoon and they arranged a big day, with student science lab and other school work demonstrations. There were many parents there and other VIP and old boy visitors. The Headmaster sent me an invitation so I drove over,

*Later a High Court Judge, then Speaker of Parliament 1980–85.

276

taking Karemu with me. He's a Bar student who is an old Budonian so he was happy to go. It was a pleasant and well-organised afternoon. Obote made a good speech and in it asked the Headmaster to stay on for another year instead of retiring to the UK as he had planned. So he could hardly refuse, although he told me he had packed all his kit and sent some of it home already.

Friday 15 March

A short while ago I received an invitation to attend the World Assembly for Human Rights in Montreal, Canada. According to the information supplied, it's for non-government-sector members in countries throughout the world, with the aim of preparing proposals for consideration by the UN Conference on Human Rights, to be held in Teheran in April. The co-presidents of the Assembly are Trygve Lie, the former UN Secretary-General, and Chief Adebo, who is Nigeria's UN representative. Sean McBride, Secretary-General of the International Commission of Jurists, is one of the co-chairmen.

So far, whenever invitations to attend overseas law conferences have come to me, the SG has snatched them away. His view is that these invitations are meant for Ugandans, usually himself, the only ones who can properly represent Uganda, so I never get a chance to go. Since he controls the finances, there's nothing I can do about it; besides, I suppose he's right. This time, however, the letter came as an invitation to me by name and referred to the reputation acquired by the Law School. They are paying my fare and hotel accommodation; so I quickly accepted and I'm going. The SG may be grinding his teeth with rage, but too bad. Just to make sure, I informed the *Uganda Argus* and there is a report in today's issue under the headline: LAW SCHOOL PRINCIPAL TO ATTEND ASSEMBLY. It's in the paper, so it must be true.

Sunday 23 March – Montreal, Canada

It was a long, tiring journey; first a flight to London and then, my first across the Atlantic, to Montreal. We flew over Greenland, Newfoundland and huge frozen wastes which seemed to go on for ever. The posters say: BOAC TAKES GOOD CARE OF YOU, but they lost my suitcase, which was very inconvenient. It's freezing cold here, with snow everywhere, though the roads are clear, of course, but not the buildings. We are all staying in the Queen Elizabeth Hotel, which is also the Montreal Hilton, right in the centre of town. The conference rooms are directly under the hotel, as are some shops and an underground railway station, so we don't have to go out into the cold at all for the conference. Most of those attending are law professors from universities all over the world, with a few government officials, such as Tanzania's Attorney-General and Kenya's Solicitor-General, and some UN people who apparently spend all their time at conferences. What an awful doom.

Monday 25 March

My luggage eventually turned up and I was able to change my shirt. Half a dozen of those of us attending were asked to take part in a discussion on the local radio, CBC. The other five could all properly be addressed as professor or doctor and the producer was upset to find that I'm only a mister. He said: 'That won't do, I shall address you as professor.' So that's what I am in Canada. He said so and it's on the radio. We were taken in the dark by car from the hotel to the studio and back; it was freezing outside and I had no overcoat. The Canadians say it's almost spring and the St Lawrence is busy defrosting. Nevertheless, it's a bit of a shock coming straight from the equator to this.

I was appalled to hear that there are several Arab countries in North Africa which are still taking and selling Africans as slaves. It's time those in the UN and the noisy black politicians in the USA concentrated on getting some effective action to put a stop to this awful trade, instead of abusing those who are trying to help Third World countries.

Yesterday I managed to overcome my wretched shyness in public (except in the classroom) and made a modest contribution to the subject under discussion but was immediately afterwards publicly abused by a very aggressive Nigerian who declared that I was a neo-colonialist and imperialist lackey of the South African racist, fascist regime. I was a bit surprised, as I'd said nothing that could justify such an outlandish accusation. At the coffee break afterwards I asked him why he had attacked me like that since he knew nothing about me. He grinned and said: 'I was just playing politics, that's all.'

We finish at lunch-time on Wednesday so I've booked a coach tour of Montreal in the afternoon and I return to Uganda on Thursday. It's interesting here, but there's far too much talking and overlong flowery speeches, especially from the French-speaking delegates.

Friday 12 April

Obote has been travelling around Uganda on 'meeting the people' tours. Using aid money, he has also had hospitals built in each district, well outside the district HQ area or capital town, in an effort to show that the government cares about people in the villages.

Unfortunately they can't get the staff for these hospitals, so most are empty and unused. Even if there were sufficient trained medical staff they would almost certainly refuse to work in them because they are located right out in the bush. Nowadays people want to work and live in cities or towns so that they can enjoy the bright lights and leisure time at bars, nightclubs, cinemas and so on. There's not a lot of that sort of thing in the bush.

Monday 22 April

I recently produced a comprehensive set of specimen criminal charges from the Penal Code, which were then typed on to stencils and printed. I've issued them to the magistrates at the School and on refresher courses outside. Today I received a letter from the court clerk at Kinoni court in Ankole which reads as follows: 'I would like to have a copy of Space Man from you so that I can learn much about flaming charge sheets and learn all the charges that are found in the Spinal Code.'

Monday 29 April

I've just received a copy of the book *An Introduction to the Law of Uganda*, written by Douglas Brown and myself, and published by the London law publishers Sweet and Maxwell in their current *Law in Africa* series. I wrote the chapters on contract, tort, criminal law and evidence, and the Law School clerk, who has now qualified as a typist, typed the whole manuscript. Douglas, who was previously Head here, is now lecturing at the Birmingham College of Commerce.

I gave a copy of the book to the SG and asked him to allocate funds to purchase sufficient copies for it to be used as a textbook for our students. However, he refused, although there's nothing to use in its place and it would be really useful to them, which is why it was written. But it has my name on it so it won't do. Nevertheless, most of the magistrates on the present course have since bought copies, which I obtained for them through the Uganda Bookshop in Kampala. The Bookshop manager told me that a number of undergraduates at Makerere had bought or ordered copies and he has sent for more from his suppliers. I suggested that he should keep a reasonable stock as our future students will probably want copies.

Friday 7 June

We have held the final exams, followed by the graduation ceremony for the sixth magistrates course and I'm now clear to set off to the UK on leave. Instead of going straight to England I've arranged to stop over for a few days in Athens and Rome and plan to visit Delphi, the Vatican, Naples, Pompeii and Capri. I was hoping to add Paris to my itinerary but I've been advised to give it a miss as the air traffic controllers are about to come out on their annual strike. They wait for the tourist season to do this as a form of blackmail to get pay increases; or maybe they just don't like tourists.

Thursday 4 July – In London

For some years I've been a member of the Royal Commonwealth Society. They have a convenient residential club building near Trafalgar Square which is useful when I'm in town; and reasonably priced too. This year the RCS is celebrating its centenary with various social functions. Last week there was a Royal Garden Party at Marlborough House, which the Queen and the Duke of Edinburgh attended. I had obtained tickets and went along with my mother, brother and sister-in-law. The weather stayed fine and we had a very pleasant afternoon. Yesterday there was a cocktail party at the Tower of London followed by a conducted tour of the Crown Jewels, which was very interesting. The Duchess of Gloucester attended and, as she moved around the room and approached where I was standing, a large overweight American woman came from behind, pushed me aside braying loudly: 'I simply gotta meet this Princess,' and went up to her, seized her hand and started talking to her in a loud grating voice. An exhibition of arrogance, rudeness and ignorance in equal proportions. The Lady-in-Waiting moved in and quietly disengaged the Duchess from the awful woman and steered her safely away across the room. I turned aside, only to find myself facing Edward Heath, the leader of the opposition Conservative Party. As I have absolutely no interest in politicians, and he has this most appalling fake accent, I moved on.

I think it's disgraceful. The miserable Prime Minister, Wilson, has ordered the cancellation of the UK passport of Sir Frederick Crawford, our former Governor, who, after his wife died in Uganda, retired to live in Southern Rhodesia. It's shameful that he, with a lifetime of service in the British Colonial Service, should be treated in this spiteful and vindictive fashion by that dreadful little politician. He's now unable to visit his relations in Britain. Apparently a photograph was published in a Rhodesian paper showing Sir Frederick at a government reception shaking hands with Clifford Dupont, a government minister. It was alleged that Sir Frederick was thus showing sympathy for the UDI cause of Ian Smith's Government. What thinking.

Friday 13 September

I returned from leave ten days ago and we have been assembling the students this week for the seventh magistrates course. While I've been away the SG has been very busy and I now find myself faced with a coup in the department. He has somehow secured Cabinet approval to set up the Law Development Centre (LDC) in Kampala to replace the Law School, which is to close down. A High Court Judge, with no teaching experience, has been designated to be the Director of the LDC and will take over my staff and library, except for me. There's apparently no place for me in this new set-up.

How he has succeeded in persuading all these people to agree to this, in view of our well-publicised record of success in training magistrates and Bar students, is a puzzle. Why would they agree to shut me down? I would have expected the AG, at least, to have fought this one. How very disappointing. I feel like one of those people who complains about lack of gratitude. It's particularly annoying that they waited until I was out of the country on leave to do all this, so that I could not protest or even be consulted.

They've even found a building for this LDC. Close to Makerere there's a fine building put up by the International Labour Organisation (ILO), very well designed and built. The ILO was expelled from Uganda some time back for offending the politicians in some way involved with union formation and their building seized as government property. It has excellent classrooms, offices and some rooms for students to live in. The Law School building is to be handed over to Nsamizi Training Centre.

The English Bar courses, which have been so successful and have started to help fill the gaps in the Judiciary, the Attorney-General's Chambers and in private practice left by departing non-Africans, are to be stopped. This on the ground that Makerere has opened a law faculty. But it will be four years before they produce any qualified people and, if the Bar courses were to be kept going until then, there would be no gap. Now there will be.

All this is to happen at the end of this year, so I have a little time in which to sort myself out. I can't prevent this from happening because it's a Cabinet decision based on the advice of their senior legal officials and I'm merely an expatriate with no real authority, who hasn't been consulted.

Thursday 10 October

We are continuing with the current magistrates and Bar courses at the Law School while these people go on with their plans and arrangements for our replacement, though I'm told nothing. At least I've managed to obtain agreement that my three lecturers will keep their jobs and the students now on courses will be able to complete them at the LDC. There is a waiting list for next year's Bar course, which has now became a popular choice for Higher School Certificate holders instead of going to Makerere. I have written to the persons on the list to tell them regretfully that they must now look elsewhere for higher studies.

I spoke to the Judge/Director of the LDC to ask why I had been excluded from the staff. He was somewhat embarrassed and unable to explain and eventually agreed to ask for me to be appointed as his deputy. But, somehow, I didn't get the impression that he's all that keen on the idea. Yesterday I called at the Ministry and looked in on the AG, Binaisa. He said he would try to arrange the deputy appointment or 'something else' for me. There was no explanation of why this step has been taken nor of how it will improve the position. I'm certainly not begging for anything. It's known what I can do and it's up to them to find me a suitable appointment or ask me to leave. I've merely made it clear that I would be very happy to stay and work here if my presence is desired.

As I came out of the AG's Office the SG was coming along the corridor to his office. 'Ah, you've been trying to save your precious Law School have you?' he sneered.

I said: 'Of course,' and walked past, feeling sad that he should have built up such unnecessary animosity. Perhaps we were too successful and had to be brought down.

Wednesday 20 November

A letter arrived from the Institute of Administration in Kampala inviting me to come and speak to their students on 'The Law Regarding Youths in Asia'. I rang the Director and asked why on earth I should be asked to speak on such an odd subject, about which I knew nothing at all. He asked me to read out his letter, which I did. Then he laughed and said he had dictated the letter to his secretary and signed it later when in a hurry and without reading it first. The subject was supposed to be 'The Law regarding Euthanasia'.

Thursday 28 November

In the latest Bar exam results, reported in today's *Uganda Argus*, three more of our students have passed the Bar Finals in London, one of whom is a magistrate, and six others have now completed Part I and will be off to London for the Finals, greatly relieved that they are not to be cancelled or withdrawn by the SG and his miserable plans.

Because of my uncertain future I thought it might be a good idea to apply to become a member of the Uganda Bar, for which I am qualified; so I put in my application for admission to the Chief Justice. I was summoned to the High Court on Tuesday and appeared before the Chief Justice in a hurriedly borrowed wig and gown. My sponsor for the ceremony was the AG, Godfrey Binaisa, and it went off quickly and well. That, too, was reported in today's *Uganda Argus*. Nothing has yet been published about the new LDC set-up.

Saturday 14 December

For two days lorries from the Ministry of Works have come over from Kampala to collect all of the Law School office and library furniture and bookshelves and over 5,000 books, many of which I obtained through British aid. Most of the others are sets of Uganda laws and textbooks in quantities for issue and loan to students attending our courses. I sent two lecturers over to the LDC to organise the reception and unloading of the lorries and I stayed here with the other lecturer and some men borrowed from Nsamizi to load the stuff aboard. There are excellent staff houses at the LDC and even I have been allocated one since nobody has yet decided, or told me, what is to happen to me. We therefore handed over our Entebbe quarters and moved our kit to our new houses before starting on the School property. The students have all been sent home for the Christmas break and have been instructed to return and report to the LDC to continue their courses, which I hope nobody is going to mess about with. By 3 p.m. today I was standing in a completely empty Law School building with just a telephone on the floor. I then locked up and took the keys across to the Nsamizi Bursar's office and drove sadly off to Kampala, after a most enjoyable period in Entebbe lasting for almost seven years, and wondering what I shall be doing next year.

Monday 30 December

Once again I drove down to Mombasa for Christmas and the New Year, determined to have this relaxing break regardless of the disastrous end to the year. The LDC Director seemed surprised when I told him I was off, as it was booked and I'm entitled to the local leave. Perhaps he thought I should ask his permission, although I'm not a subordinate nor even on his staff. I've moved the Law School and set up the LDC for him without anything being done about my position. I just hope that something suitable will appear soon.

In Kenya I paused in the Rift Valley to look at the thousands of pink flamingo on Lake Nakuru as they feasted on the tiny larvae which appear when the flood waters spread over the soda flats. Beyond was a vast plain with a series of small green craters leading up to the distant Mau escarpment.

1969

Tuesday 7 January

Last November the SG, who has a Cambridge degree, brought out three law professors from Cambridge, London and Yale to produce a report on legal education in Uganda. They stayed for only a week and interviewed various people presumably selected by the SG. In spite of the fact that the only legal education current here is at the Law School, I was not at first on the list of those to be seen by them. Having heard of their presence, I asked to meet them and they condescended to give me a half-hour of their time. However, they seemed to be more interested in my qualifications than my work and results. Being a barrister with an external degree impressed them not at all. Only the London professor showed some slight sign of friendliness or interest and he admitted that the London law degree examinations are considered to be more difficult to pass than those of Oxford or Cambridge and, he added, the external law degree is even harder to obtain than the internal. But alas, shaking his head, it just doesn't have the academic status as far as they were concerned since I hadn't actually attended a university. I pointed out that I had been working full time and studying in my spare time. I suppose that, from their point of view, attending a university is an education whereas sitting for an external degree is merely obtaining a qualification. But that was all I wanted for the job and neither type of degree would have made me a better teacher anyway.

Their report has at last arrived, recommending that Makerere should now open a law faculty and the Law School should be moved to Kampala and be confined to the training of magistrates under the more direct control of the Ministry of Justice. The English Bar courses should be discontinued as Makerere will produce law graduates (who will by no means have a professional qualification) and our outstanding success in the Bar exams was disregarded. They went further and said that the courses were unsuccessful – a blatant lie. In spite of the excellent results produced while I've been Principal, the professors consider that I'm not adequately qualified to teach because I did not attend a university. All this is exactly what the SG wanted and it provides him with the ammunition he requires to give me the push. It's all very disappointing but not really surprising. My efforts over the years to produce really good results and to gain for the Law School some sort of status and reputation locally, and even internationally, appear to have been treated as being of little value or interest. There was no other way in which I could have worked and, to put it mildly, my prospects here look very gloomy now. I have written to the AG pointing out the many inconsistencies and inaccuracies in this report, but I doubt whether it will do much good. It's all much too late; they knew what the report would say and have already acted on it even before the professors came out here.

Monday 13 January

The LDC Director told me that he didn't want anything to do with the two existing and continuing Law School courses. 'You started them, so you can finish them,' he said, doing an effective Pontius Pilate act. Well, that suits me. I certainly don't want anyone meddling with them; especially someone with no teaching experience. I can't help suspecting that the reason the post of Director was not advertised, as all government posts are supposed and indeed required to be, was so that I could not apply for it. They might have found it rather difficult to say that I was unsuitable for the job in the light of the outstanding and well-publicised success of the Law School students and courses. But the SG had the support of his professors' report and my absence on leave also made it easier for him.

Thursday 13 February

This morning the Director came into my office holding a piece of paper between finger and thumb as if it were infected. 'I think this is a waste of time but perhaps you'd better deal with it,' he said, with considerable distaste. It was a letter from Army HQ requesting us to hold a series of courses on the laws of Uganda for army officers so that they would be in a better position to carry out their duties when dealing with civilians. It was signed by the Chief of Defence Staff, Major General Idi Amin. I think it's a good idea. It will give me the opportunity I've been hoping for to explain to them that they are not above the law in their behaviour towards civilians, which is a deteriorating situation each month. I rang up Army HQ, which is not an easy thing to do as they don't publish their telephone numbers for absurd and exaggerated security reasons, and managed eventually, I hope, to make an appointment to see the General to discuss the proposed courses.

Friday 14 February

A year or so after the attack on the Kabaka at Mengo in 1966, the Army took over and occupied the fine New Bulange building there as its HQ. I haven't been in the building since I was acting as Judicial Adviser five years ago and I was wondering what state it's in now. However, it appears that I'm not going to find out. I was called into the Director's office this morning, where I found his visitor, the large uniformed figure of General Amin, sitting in silence. As I was being introduced he said: 'Oh, I know him, the policeman.' I didn't bother to say that I left the Police seven years ago.

Apparently he had decided, or was persuaded, that it was not a good idea for me to be wandering around their so secret HQ, so the mountain came to Mahomet. He was wearing a smart British Army-style service dress uniform with red tabs and two rows of medal ribbons, which struck me as odd. I knew he had joined the KAR as a cook in 1946, a year after the end of the war, and earlier photographs showed him wearing the ribbons of the two medals to which he is entitled: the East Africa General Service Medal (awarded for anti-Mau Mau service in Kenya) and the Uganda Independence Medal. Now, however, he was also wearing 1939–45 war medals, including campaign stars for North Africa and Burma and even the Military Medal, awarded for bravery in action, to none of which he was entitled.

I suppose it's a natural and automatic thing for a soldier, or ex-soldier, to look first at a man's medal ribbons to see and assess where he's been and what he's done. Amin noticed where I was looking but said nothing and didn't appear to be embarrassed at all. I said nothing, of course.

His English is not too good and he speaks quietly but he made himself understood well enough. He wants his officers to be given short courses on the laws and Constitution to make them better citizens and to improve their relationship with the public, which is certainly needed. In answer to my questions, he said he wanted all of his officers, even the two brigadiers, to attend the course, and he thought that there would be 60 to 80 officers available from around Kampala but, of course, they could not all be spared from their duties at the same time. I suggested that we run three courses well apart in order to cope with this.

He added that he wanted an individual report on each officer at the end of his course. This gave me the opportunity to bring up the delicate subject of literacy or lack of it. Most of his senior officers were promoted NCOs with little or no education (like himself, in fact, though I didn't say this). I said the courses would have to be in English and they might find it rather difficult to understand, let alone to write answers in an examination. Amin replied that he knew this but he wanted an accurate confidential assessment in writing, addressed to him personally; so that's what he'll get.

We fixed the first course for next month, with the lieutenants and captains and a few majors attending. The second course will be in August for the most senior officers such as the brigadiers, colonels and senior majors; and the third course a month later, for all remaining junior officers. I suggested that the course for senior officers could be spread over a longer period but in the mornings only, so that they could continue to keep an eye on their commands meanwhile. He agreed and toddled off.

Thursday 27 February

The SG called for me to go and see him in his office. His latest complaint is that I've been continuing to use the title of Principal in my letters. It wouldn't do; it was unacceptable; it must stop; an end must be put to it; the Law School no longer existed.

I replied that I'm doing the same work at the LDC, that I haven't been given any other appointment there, in spite of my several requests, and that I was appointed as Principal of the Law School by the President in the Gazette and therefore that is what I am and I will continue to sign myself as such until the President decides otherwise. He dismissed both this and me with the sneer: 'You are Principal of nothing. I have seen to that.'

I came away thinking that it's odd that I should be expected by the SG and the Director to continue organising and teaching these courses and giving outside lectures, and yet neither has taken any steps to establish my position or abolish it. They want my work but not me. It's very unsatisfactory. I want to stay and work in Uganda but I don't like this uncertainty at all.

Thursday 6 March

Yesterday I went back to Nsamizi for the first time since leaving there three months ago, to lecture to a course for community development youth assistants on the Uganda legal system. It's rather embarrassing though when people ask about my present position. I don't want to talk about my problems at the LDC with the SG as any gossip springing from that would not help matters at all.

287

Saturday 22 March

Yesterday we finished the first army law course, which started on the 10th. There were 28 junior officers, lieutenants and captains, mostly with some education. Some of them were quite bright and we had some lively discussions in class. I took most of the classes, so as to let the other lecturers get on with our regular courses, and explained Uganda's legal system and the elements of criminal law, and I asked one of the lecturers to speak about contract and tort and outline court procedure.

I set a comprehensive test paper, with plenty of choices, at the end of the course and I've just marked them. Most are reasonably good and it's clear that, generally, they paid attention and, I hope, have benefited from this added knowledge. I particularly made a point of explaining about the powers of arrest and detention and made it very clear how limited they are when dealing with civilians. I just hope some of this sinks in.

Tuesday 1 April

I went over to the Institute of Public Administration yesterday afternoon and again today to lecture to the newly appointed assistant secretaries. They are all recent graduates who will work mainly in ministries or departments. Yesterday I spoke about the Uganda legal system and today the subject was 'Human Rights and the Rule of Law'. A bright lot, full of interest and with plenty of questions. I really enjoy these away sessions, no matter how busy and involved I am with our regular courses.

Thursday 17 April

Recently for five days I held my usual course for administrative officers preparing to sit for their law exams which, as usual, I shall set and mark; though I wonder who will do this in future. This afternoon I was over at Nsamizi again, this time explaining the legal system to some theological students who are attending a civics course. Their questions, as I expected, tended to be much concerned about the sanctity and secrecy of confessions to priests. They were not at all happy when I explained that, although conventionally this is observed in the courts, when you get right down to it, the law is silent on the matter and there is no legal protection, just as with journalists regarding their sources of information, or doctors or bankers for that matter. All can be compelled by the courts to reveal information and sources or go to prison for contempt for refusing to do so. It's just that priests never are expected or asked to tell. Of course, lawyers are protected; but then they would be, wouldn't they? It all makes for excitement, rising blood pressures and stimulating argument in class.

Thursday 24 April

Yesterday the results of the SG's recent efforts were revealed. Apparently he got together with the Minister of Public Service and the Chairman of the Public Service Commission (PSC), and between them they have cooked up a letter to me. It's based on article 127 of the new Constitution, which provides that when a qualified local candidate is available to replace a remaining expatriate (former Colonial Service) officer, and when that officer is called upon to retire to make a vacancy, he shall do so.

In their letter it states that under the Constitution the PSC has Africanised my post and I am accordingly required to vacate it and to leave Uganda before the end of three months from the date on the letter. For a while I was just shocked, but then I had a good think. The letter is full of legal errors and yet the SG is not only a Senior Law Officer of the State but also a former law lecturer at Dar-es-Salaam University. Yet he has made a nonsense like this, and to another lawyer, at that.

First: if my post of Principal of the Law School no longer exists, as he maintains, then how and why has it been Africanised? Second: even if you translate my post of Principal into Director of the LDC, the present holder happens to be an expatriate, so it still hasn't been Africanised. Third: the first words of article 127 of the Constitution are: 'If the President is satisfied that there are more local candidates ... he may select officers ... and by notice in writing ... call upon the officers to retire from the public service.' Consequently it is only the President who can do this, or at least approve it, not the PSC and most certainly not the SG. Furthermore, my appointment as Principal was by the President in the Gazette, not by the PSC, which only makes recommendations.

Yesterday evening was the St George's Day dinner at the Kampala Club. I've been a member of the Society for years and usually attend the enjoyable annual dinner as a tribal ritual. The Chief Justice, Dermot Sheridan, was there (the Nigerian CJ having at last departed) and I had a quick word with him early on. He agreed with my views and that I should fight it if I really wanted to stay on.

Friday 2 May

I decided not to write directly to the President about the PSC letter as

I believe it can be tackled indirectly. Obote's cousin, Akena Adoko, is a lawyer and is presently the Head of the General Service Unit (GSU), which is a sort of secret police/intelligence outfit which not only keeps Obote informed about what's going on but also carries out whatever dirty work is thought to be required. He also happens to be Obote's chief adviser.

I've met Akena before and get on well enough with him, so I've written to him, setting out what has been happening to the Law School and to me, and attaching a copy of the PSC letter and mentioning the deterioration in the working relationship between the SG and myself. I added that I'm willing to continue working in Uganda if so desired, but, of course, will leave if required to do so.

He asked me to call in and see him today and we discussed the situation. He agreed that the PSC letter was unconstitutional and said he'd spoken to the President about it and he's directed that I should ignore it as he wants me to stay on, since he recognised that I'd been doing very useful work. I pointed out to Akena that, in any case, I'm finished with the Ministry of Justice as I clearly can no longer work with the SG; but I want to stay and work here, teaching if possible. I had heard that they had lost a number of expatriate headmasters from senior secondary schools, so perhaps I could take on one of those jobs. He said he'd get back to me after considering the situation and examining the possibilities.

Sunday 11 May

I went to the Odeon cinema yesterday evening and parked my car in Kampala Road opposite the cinema. It was a western and, as usual, the Africans and Asians in the audience were cheering on the Red Indians. Near the end of the film a message was flashed on to the screen asking for the owner of my car number to see the manager. I went out to the vestibule and he pointed silently across the road. A Volkswagen Beetle was parked on the roof of my beautiful 'E' Type Jag with a very drunk driver sitting in the gutter alongside. He must have driven up the low rounded back of my car and then stopped. It was neat but unconventional parking and I was glad he hadn't been driving a lorry. The driver was in no state to question and just burbled rubbish. A young assistant inspector arrived with an older constable who looked familiar. I asked the AIP to check the driver's pockets and find out his insurance particulars and let me have them so that I can make a claim for the damage repairs to my car roof and back door. I was somewhat surprised when the AIP said that it was against the law for him to give me such information. I told him that was not so and

290

explained the relevant traffic law to him. I added that if I didn't get this information I'd have a word with the IG of Police about his lack of co-operation and ignorance of the law. He said I shouldn't speak to him like that. The constable whispered something to him and I caught the words Police College and Law School. He then quickly changed his tune and was very ready to help. The constable looked through the driver's pockets and fortunately found both his driving permit and his insurance certificate. I copied down the details and, with the assistance of some grinning passers-by, we lifted the VW to the road without causing any more damage to my car. By then the film was over and people were coming out. I don't know how the film ended.

Friday 30 May

Yesterday I met Akena Adoko again and he told me that they are still trying to fix me up with a suitable new job. He also mentioned that he was present in the office with the President when he carpeted the Minister of Public Service, the Chairman of the PSC and the SG and tore them off a most tremendous strip for writing that letter, and especially for usurping the powers of the President as well as trying to throw me out of Uganda.

Akena said that 'those people won't bother you any more', and he hoped I would just carry on for the moment at the LDC until they could arrange something better for me. He mentioned that the judiciary has two vacancies for chief magistrates and, if I would like to consider applying for one, he could assure me that the application would be accepted and the appointment made by the President without any delay. He added that, a year after starting the job and acquiring some judicial experience, I would be moved up to the High Court. He said that they considered this would be more appropriate than the headmastership that I had suggested. I replied that I was most grateful and I'd have a think about it and let him know. In fact, I'm not at all keen to sit in judgment on others and to listen to and sort out their problems. It cannot be as interesting and rewarding to me as teaching. On the other hand, I don't want to leave Uganda, so if that's what it takes to stay here, I'll probably have to do it.

Sunday 29 June

On Friday we held the graduation ceremony for the seventh magistrates course at the LDC for the first time. At my suggestion the Director had invited the President to attend and he had agreed to do so. I had contacted the police to make arrangements for parking vehicles and general security and a number of VIPs, including the ambassadors and high commissioners, were invited. Previously at the Law School for these functions I had always put the VIP guests in the front two rows of the audience but, when I brought this up, the Director said he didn't like it and everyone invited should be left to find a seat anywhere in the hall. I said they wouldn't like that especially as the more important ones always make a point of arriving at the last minute, which meant that the front rows would be filled by then, but I was overruled. As it was the last of the Law School magistrates courses, though they will continue to be held at the LDC, I was pleased that the Director otherwise left me to conduct the ceremony for, as he rightly said, it was my course.

I had arranged for the Bar students to escort invited guests to their seats while I, as always on these occasions, met VIP guests at the main entrance, but this time had the unnecessarily embarrassing business of telling them that no seat was reserved for them so they could sit anywhere. I thought it was so discourteous. The British High Commissioner quite happily found a seat in the centre of the hall, but I was approached by the French and Russian ambassadors, who together protested angrily about not being seated at the front. As diplomatically as I could, I indicated where the British HC was sitting and said that I was sure that he would be pleased if their excellencies would sit beside him, and fortunately they replied: 'Of course, we would be delighted.' So that was all right, but I silently cursed the Director and his silly decision.

At that point the Director approached me, looking rather harassed, and said he'd had a phone call from the President's Office to say that Obote was unable to come as something urgently requiring his attention had come up and the new Minister of Justice/Attorney-General, Lubowa, now occupying this combined post since Godfrey Binaisa's recent resignation as AG, was to stand in for him. Lubowa was already present and had been going to be one of the speakers anyway (I was the other) so, when we told him, he quickly agreed. The prizes and diplomas were to be presented by the acting Chief Justice Jeffrey Jones as previously arranged, so there was no other problem, but it was rather disappointing. However, apart from this, the ceremony went off very well.

The report in the *Uganda Argus* on Saturday refers to me as 'the Principal of the Centre', which probably made the SG gnash his teeth in rage when he read it. In my final speech in this job I pointed out that there are now 192 trained magistrates with law diplomas working in the courts all over the country; and it was principally to train and set up this Ugandan magistracy that the Law School had been started eight years ago. Photographs were taken and, so I'm told, on

Saturday evening UTV news showed quite a long extract of the ceremony.

The first five magistrates on this course have done so well they would be excellent Bar course material and would provide some useful senior magistrates later. However, now that the SG has abolished the Bar courses, they will not get that chance, which they had been very much hoping for; and they are naturally bitterly disappointed. I've made some enquiries on their behalf at Makerere and I'm hoping that some of them will be accepted there in due course on the mature age entry scheme, though the university seems to take very few on it. Still, it's their only chance now. I really cannot see how the Judiciary or the country gains by this arbitrary ending of a useful course and qualification for no good reason at all.

The students on both courses organised a dance in the LDC hall on Saturday evening and I was able to persuade the Police Dance Band to play. Actually they could hardly refuse because, although he was unable to be at the graduation on Friday, the President had kept his promise to attend the dance with his wife Miria. At one point all of our group were on the floor dancing, except for Obote, Miria and myself, all sitting in silence. What do you say to a silent president? Have you detained anyone interesting recently? Which foreign-owned business are you planning to nationalise next? Suddenly Obote spoke: 'Dance with my wife, Mr Allen.' A typical northerner speaking; no request; no consulting his wife; just an order.

I said: 'Certainly, sir.' She said nothing at all and we moved on to the floor. Neither of us was much good and I had to apologise for treading on her feet. I have no small talk and could think of nothing to say except an idiotic: 'Do you come here often?' which I just managed to stop myself from asking. The music stopped, I escorted her back to her chair and we still hadn't spoken. Then she made a faint murmuring noise which may have been polite, but was probably more like: 'Thank God that's over.'

Friday 25 July

Last Sunday I heard on the radio news that Neil Armstrong and two other US astronauts had landed on the moon in Apollo 11. I gather that it was shown worldwide on television by some clever means or other. The landing was a tremendous feat and final proof that the moon is not made of cheese after all, which will be disappointing to some.

This week I've been twice to Nsamizi, speaking first to a National Union of Youth Organisations (NUYO) course on the new Constitution and then a prison welfare staff course on the Uganda legal system.

There are always plenty of questions at these outside talks, generally reflecting the interests and work of the particular group of students. They never fail to show a lively interest and appreciation and I'm going to miss the enjoyment of giving such talks and, of course, of teaching generally. That is a needless loss I'm not looking forward to and for which I cannot forgive that miserable SG.

Saturday 2 August

We've just had a visit from Pope Paul VI – Pappa Paulo, as they call him here – lasting two days. There is a large black and white TV set in the students common room here and most of us watched the various ceremonies and events on the screen. Also visiting at the same time are four Presidents, Nyerere of Tanzania, Kaunda of Zambia, Kayibanda of Rwanda and Micombero of Burundi. There are 7 cardinals and 45 bishops and archbishops plus 12 new bishops just consecrated by the Pope.

Obote, though a Protestant, received a papal knighthood and papal medals were distributed. A well-attended public mass took place and gifts were exchanged. When he toured Kampala he visited Mulago Hospital near here and drove past the LDC compound, so we all went out and watched him passing very close, standing up in an open car. He went to the Martyrs Shrine at Namugongo to pay tribute to the 22 young Christians who were killed by Kabaka Mwanga in 1886 because they refused to give up Christianity. The boys were wrapped in mats of reeds, placed on a pyre of faggots and roasted to death.

At the Grand Hotel, where most of the Pope's retinue of cardinals and bishops are staying, a waiter toured the crowded foyer with a large sign on a stick reading: CARDINAL WHO WANTS TO GO TO PRISON, which rather bewildered the other guests there. One of the eminences stood up and was shown to a waiting car to take him on a prison visit that he had requested.

Monday 11 August

The eighth course for magistrates has commenced. This will be the first LDC course, although I've been organising it, as I did with all the others at the Law School; but I don't expect to see this one through to the end.

Tuesday 19 August

In the *Uganda Argus* today there's an advertisement headed: 'Youth Director required by Help the Aged'. A geriatric teenager, perhaps.

Yesterday we started the second law course for army officers. This is for three weeks, but mornings only, as we have 14 of the most senior officers on it, including both brigadiers and a bunch of colonels. As I have the afternoons available for the magistrates and Bar courses and outside talks, I am taking nearly all the classes on this military exercise. But it's a struggle; the brigadiers and some of the colonels have hardly any English, so I have to keep everything very basic.

In spite of their ages and seniority, like all Ugandans that I've taught over the years, they are respectful and very polite and show great interest in class. In return, as always, I put everything into each session and give them the best I can. It's certainly not a waste of time.

Thursday 28 August

The law course for senior army officers is going well and we have achieved a reasonably good rapport. In the afternoons they are busy elsewhere and so am I. This week I've been twice to the Police College to give talks on the Constitution and the legal system. I'm happy to keep up my contacts with the police and it's useful to them, I believe, since they have nobody there who can deal with these subjects competently.

In return I persuaded the IG, Oryema, to come and speak to our students on both courses this afternoon. Long ago, before he joined the Force, he was a schoolteacher, so he has the necessary knack. He was a bit misleading on one or two points concerning the Judges' Rules, dealing with statements to the police by accused persons, and I shall have to put that right in class soon, but otherwise it was good value.

Saturday 6 September

We ended the law course for senior army officers yesterday. I gave them a simple test as required by the General, but it was difficult to find anything worth any marks in the illiterate efforts of Brigadiers Okoya and Hussein, both of whom are pleasant, friendly old chaps, but not much upstairs. Hardly surprising really since neither has had any schooling. Anyway, I've typed my confidential reports on each officer and will send them over to Army HQ for General A on Monday. Nobody else at this end will see them.

Tuesday 16 September

I've just concluded a series of lectures to labour officers and labour inspectors. As they have to be able to prosecute offenders under the labour laws in the lower courts, I went through the court procedures, typical types of evidence, prosecuting techniques and the general role of a prosecutor, and gave them some specimen charges of offences under the labour laws which I had prepared for them.

Thursday 25 September

I was asked to attend the Judicial Service Commission today to go through the motions of an interview for the post of Chief Magistrate, although it has already been arranged, since the President's Office initiated the process. Still, the formalities must be gone through, I suppose, though I haven't bothered to inform the SG of this arrangement or interview. I certainly don't want him to foul it up, though at this stage he can't do much.

Friday 3 October

A short while ago I received a letter from the Secretary of the Makerere University College Law Society, formed by their first students in the new law faculty, inviting me to give a public lecture on the subject of 'How the Public looks at a Lawyer in East Africa'.

I accepted and we fixed it for yesterday evening at 8.30 p.m. So I drove across the road to the nearby campus and found the Arts Quadrangle Theatre, where it was to take place. As always, I arrived five minutes before the time fixed and, what a surprise, there was nobody there. Eventually, nearly ten minutes after starting time, a chap came up and introduced himself as Kasule, the Secretary of the Students Law Society. Treating him as I would any of my law students, I blasted him for not having the courtesy to be present on time to meet a visiting speaker, something I've always been very particular about. He was a bit shell-shocked and managed an apology, and we went in. The talk appeared to go well; as usual I kept it light and introduced some humour and the audience seemed to enjoy it. I dealt with their questions and departed after the usual vote of thanks.

Saturday 4 October

Karemu, one of our Bar students, has a schoolmate from King's College, Budo, now reading law at Makerere and he pops across the road to visit him now and again. After class today he came up to me and said he met his chum yesterday evening and he had mentioned the talk I gave them on Thursday, adding that he wished they had someone in the faculty who could explain things so clearly and interestingly.

When I was discussing my situation with Akena he mentioned the possibility of a post in Makerere; but I'm not an academic, just a practical teacher, and delivering learned lectures is not for me. I've no real interest in academic research and writing learned papers for law journals. What I do now may not be impressive academically, but I believe it's useful and necessary. It's within my limited ability and I very much enjoy doing it.

Monday 24 November

The Kabaka died in London last Friday, it is believed of alcohol poisoning. He was a heavy drinker before and, since his escape from the army attack, he'd become an alcoholic. The Baganda are dreadfully upset, of course, and refuse to believe the alcohol-poisoning theory, saying that he was poisoned by enemies, by which they mean Obote's Government, probably the GSU.

I met him on a number of occasions, particularly when I was at GH, but I only knew him slightly. I always found him pleasant and friendly, but I think he was driven hard by this Kiganda heritage business and very badly served and advised by the Lukiiko and his senior ministers with regard to their unnecessarily antagonistic relations with Central Government, both Protectorate and post-independence.

Friday 28 November

I've managed to fit in two talks at Nsamizi this month: to rural training centre wardens and to prison welfare assistants, both on the legal system. I've given this talk to many different courses because I think it's important that as many people as possible know something about their country's courts, how they work and how people can make use of them, as well as clarifying puzzling matters about lawyers and laws. I always invite questions and there are plenty asked every time and much lively interest shown.

There is a report in the *Uganda Argus* today that seven of our Law School Bar students have been called to the Bar in London, including another woman and three magistrates. Two others received conditional passes so they have only one paper to repeat before qualifying.

Saturday 6 December

We have just completed the third and last law course for army officers which lasted for a week, full-time, for 20 officers varying in rank from lieutenant to major. It has gone well, with some quite bright chaps among them. I've been writing their individual reports today. I think it's been a useful exercise. It was certainly time someone told these people how limited their powers are in law and just what the courts and laws are basically all about. It's just a form of citizenship really.

Monday 15 December

A letter was delivered to the LDC by hand from Army HQ, signed by General Amin, to say thanks for running the law courses for army officers and that he was very pleased with the results and the reports supplied. Another satisfied customer.

Saturday 20 December

Yesterday Obote attended an evening meeting of his party, the Uganda People's Congress (UPC), at a hall in Kampala to announce his new 'Move to the Left' policy, which means even more socialism. When he left the hall a shot was fired at him from behind a tree at a range of about 10 to 12 feet. There were supporters cheering him and he was turning his head from side to side acknowledging them. The bullet entered his jaw and exited through his open mouth, taking out two teeth and cutting through his lower lip. No other shots were fired but a grenade was thrown at him, which failed to explode. A bungled assassination attempt, it seems. Meanwhile Obote is in Mulago Hospital unable to talk, which must be agony for a politician.

Tuesday 23 December

My informant told me this evening that General Amin was not at the meeting although he was supposed to have attended. Consequently he is strongly suspected and soldiers have been sent to arrest him at his residence, but he has disappeared and gone into hiding. It seems that Obote was not seriously injured, although rumours have been going round Kampala for the last couple of days that he is dead. However, Obote was able to write an order for Akena's GSU men to go with an army officer to General Amin's house to tell him what had happened. But Amin had apparently already heard of the attempt on Obote's life and must have believed that he would be blamed – a guilty conscience perhaps – so he climbed over the high barbed-wire fence at the back of his compound and went into hiding, after getting a lift to Bamunanika, about 30 miles from Kampala, where Amin has a special unit of trusted men, mostly Nubians.

He turned up at Army HQ the next day while a meeting of senior officers was going on to decide what to do. His story was that he thought those who came to his house had come to kill him and he had fled, although he always has armed guards there. This was not believed and some of the officers were angry and others jeered at him and said that he should be called 'Dada' from then on. *Dada* is, in fact, a very common name among the Kakwa in the northern part of West Nile and, indeed, Amin's father is named Dada. However, they were talking in Swahili at the time; in which language it means sister or elder sister, and it seems it was meant to be a jeering reference to his lack of manhood when he ran away from his duty.

Apparently Brigadier Okoya, Amin's number two in the Army and my recent student, was so annoyed that he told Obote that Amin is not fit to command the Army. Amin then described Okoya as his 'best friend' since joining the army and admitted that he had made a serious mistake by running away at a time of crisis.

Friday 28 December

Following the attempt on Obote there are army and police road-blocks on every road out of Kampala, causing the greatest possible inconvenience to everyone, and they are treating anyone they suspect of anything, or just don't like, very roughly indeed. Already about a dozen have been shot, maybe more. It's a good time to keep off the roads.

1970

Monday 26 January

Last night Brigadier Okoya and his wife were shot dead at their village home of Koro, just outside Gulu. At the moment it's not known, or nobody's saying, who was the murderer, but I'd put my money on General Amin being involved after their recent controversy. Okoya was a nice old chap and we got on well during the law course for senior officers last August. There are many Acholi in the Army and they won't be at all happy about losing their most senior serving officer and will, no doubt, be looking around for vengeance.

3

Chief Magistrate: February 1970–September 1973

Friday 20 February

Akena Adoko rang yesterday to tell me that the Chief Justice has agreed to my appointment as a Chief Magistrate, and the President has consequently made the appointment effective from 4 February. So I am now a Chief Magistrate, but as yet without a court or area to administer. I'll have to sort that out with the CJ. I've completed 15 years in Uganda now and am about to commence my third career here. I hope it's going to last. I saw the CJ today and he welcomed me to the Judiciary, after swearing me in as a magistrate. I suggested to him that, as the post of Deputy Chief Registrar is vacant, I could perhaps take it and, while working at the High Court, I could continue to monitor and assist with the present courses at the LDC. He said he would think about it and let me know. As I'm due for leave in June I also suggested that, instead of waiting until then, I should go off on leave right away so that I start work in the Judiciary for a full tour rather than breaking off for leave just after commencing at a particular station. This was agreed and I shall now take my earned leave plus some accumulated leave so as to start in my new department completely from scratch.

All government transfers, postings, promotions and appointments have to be gazetted otherwise they don't exist. After the SG's denial of my existing appointment as Law School Principal, he has untruthfully published in the *Uganda Gazette* my transfer to the Judiciary by referring to me as a principal state attorney, which I've never been. At least he has admitted that I'm some sort of principal, which is something, even if it's nothing.

Tuesday 24 March

I was in town this morning, collecting a parcel from the main post office, where I met two police NCOs whom I have known for a long time. They were both from Teso and evidently not supporters of Obote's Government. Their conversation was full of complaint and discontent. One of them said quietly that there was a lot of trouble brewing and he had heard that there would soon be a coup to remove Obote. I didn't ask how they knew this and left them to their grumbles and rumours.

Thursday 26 March

Today is my last day at the LDC as this is Easter weekend and I'm away on leave on Sunday. I took my last classes with the magistrates and the fifth and final Bar course, said farewell and wished them all the best. Afterwards they surprised me by presenting me with a Parker 51 fountain pen, to write my judgments with, they said. This has been a most enjoyable and worthwhile job; for me teaching is more pleasure than work and I shall really miss it. People learn better when they're happy and comfortable and I've tried to make my teaching interesting and, whenever possible, amusing, so as to fix facts and ideas more firmly in the mind. The Chinese say: If you are planning for a year, sow rice... If you are planning for a decade, plant trees... If you are planning for a lifetime, educate a person.

Sunday 14 June – In London

Yesterday was the Queen's Birthday Parade and Trooping the Colour on Horseguards, for which I had obtained two tickets. I took one of my godsons, eight-year-old Stephen, for his first view of this wonderful old ceremony. Afterwards we went with the crowd to Buckingham Palace to see the Royal Family come out on to the balcony and wave to us. We had a snack lunch in the Buttery at my club off Trafalgar Square and then wandered around looking at the sights and crowds of summer tourists until it was time to catch our train back to his home.

Monday 29 June

I've heard from Uganda that there's been another failed attempt to assassinate Obote. He had been visiting Luzira Prison and was passing through Kampala on his way back to State House in Entebbe with a police escort car leading the way. The Vice-President, Babiiha, was in a similar convoy about a mile behind and the assassins evidently mistook his car for the President's and opened fire with automatic weapons. The bullets went straight through the rear side passenger window and out through the other side without hitting anyone. The VP was unhurt but very badly shaken. Fortunately for him the assassins exhibited their incompetence by not continuing to fire and not adjusting their aim. A large car with a blue light on top, moving at normal speed at close range, should not have been a difficult target to hit.

I wonder if Obote is getting the message that both he and his extreme left policies are not very popular. It looks as though those two I met in Kampala last March were telling the truth when they spoke of a probable coup attempt. Of course, plenty of others may have had similar ideas.

Thursday 23 July

During this four months on leave I have made frequent weekend visits to London to collect various of our Bar students who are reading for the Finals. I fill my hired car with them and off we go to see places that they would not otherwise get a chance to see while stuck in London, with very little cash and much studying to do. So we've been to such places as Oxford, Canterbury, Windsor, Brighton, Worthing, Herne Bay and Whitstable. I take a camera with me and afterwards send them each copies of the photos so that they have a record of it all to show people when they return to Uganda. It's been a pleasure seeing them and visiting these places with them. I've also been able to speak to staff at the Council of Legal Education and some of the Inns of Court as well as the Overseas Students Hostel in Kensington to find out how they're getting on here. Altogether it's been a useful and enjoyable exercise, even though I'm no longer their tutor.

Monday 3 August

I arrived back in Uganda at the end of July and saw the Chief Registrar, who told me that the CJ has decided against my being appointed Deputy Chief Registrar on the quite reasonable grounds that I should go up-country and acquire some experience of court work and the running of district courts first. The CR then offered me the choice of Gulu, in charge of Acholi District; or Mbarara, in charge of Ankole and Kigezi Districts. Unfortunately, my 'E' Type Jaguar, being so low-slung, is wholly unsuitable for up-country safaris and travelling around visiting sub-courts, which are often well off the main roads and along rough tracks. I would like to have taken Acholi but, from what I know of the roads, I've decided on Ankole.

Tuesday 25 August

I have moved to Mbarara and taken over the very fine, large residence of the Chief Magistrate here, which is on the side of a hill looking towards Ntare School and Kamukuzi, the location of the local government HQ and what was the palace of the Omugabe, who is now an ordinary citizen, except in the eyes of the Banyankole. At the palace is the *Bagyendanwa*, the Royal Drum House, where the ancient drums and regalia of past Abagabe are kept.

The court-house is located in the *boma* close to the District Commissioner's office and other government offices. It was not built as a court but is actually the Galt Memorial Hall, built for the use of the people of Mbarara in memory of the District Commissioner called Galt who was murdered here by Banyankole in 1905.

At the beginning of this century this area was known as Muti and there grew here what in the Runyankole language is called *mburara* (cow grass) so they changed the name of the area to Rwemburara. The European administrators came and, as a result of mishearing or mispronouncing the name, called it Mbarara and it became a township and administrative centre of Ankole District in 1906.

Friday 11 September

There are 14 grade II and III magistrates scattered around this large district of Ankole in the sub-courts; some with more than one court to cover. The acting District Commissioner, called Toskin, comes from Sebei in the far east of Uganda. I get the impression that he does not approve of a European coming here as a replacement of the African magistrate who was my predecessor. After our initial meeting we have had no real contact.

I don't mind. There's so much to do here that I've no time for anything else. My predecessor was a happy-go-lucky Muganda who spent most of his time here on the local golf course, the first tee of which is conveniently just outside the court-house. Very little work was done over the years in a busy station. Consequently, the floor of my chambers is covered with piles and piles of court case files that have not been attended to or, in some cases, even looked at.

I called in the police inspector who prosecutes in my court and discussed with him the quick disposal of the mountain of traffic and petty crime cases. If we sat for 24 hours a day we should never catch up with the hundreds of pending cases, and more coming in all the time. The only thing to do is to close a large number of those which have been pending for the longest time and the most petty of the recent cases. He is to produce his long list of suggested prosecution withdrawals and I'll go through them and stamp 'withdrawn' on all those that I agree with. I've made up a rubber stamp for the purpose from an old printing outfit which, with an ordinary office date stamp and my signature, will put them to rest.

Meanwhile, I'm having all the more recent cases fixed for pleas in large batches. There should be plenty of guilty pleas and the rest I'll fix for hearing before the grade I and II magistrates who are based at Kamukuzi and using local government rooms for their courts. The more serious cases of manslaughter, robbery, rape, serious assaults will be tried by me.

The civil cases, particularly appeals from decisions of the sub-court magistrates, are also in a sadly neglected state and many are pending from years back. So I've decided to spend one day a week hearing those appeals, again in batches, at speed, with no time wasted. I've spoken to our three locally based advocates and they are clearly relieved that many of their cases are at last going to be dealt with. They've agreed to reduce the time-wasting long addresses to the court to the minimum, so that I can give them verdicts and decisions as quickly as possible.

In addition to this I have a lot of administration to deal with as I'm responsible for visiting and overseeing and checking the sub-courts and all matters concerning staff personnel and pay, leave, transfers, replacements and so on. But I have a first-rate chief clerk/higher executive officer who really knows his job and between us we can deal with this and I can make the necessary decisions without having to refer to anyone else.

Saturday 10 October

Yesterday was the eighth anniversary of Uganda's independence. Obote had invited Presidents Kenyatta from Kenya and Nyerere from Tanzania to a ceremony at Makerere at which the university college became a fully autonomous university and Obote was installed as its first Chancellor, complete with an honorary degree of doctor of laws. He is now referred to on the radio and in the newspapers and elsewhere as Dr Obote.

Saturday 17 October

Friday is the day fixed for plea day when the court is overflowing with those whose pleas of guilty or not guilty are recorded in all the new cases. Bail applications are made either by remand prisoners brought across the road from the prison opposite, or by those in new cases. Those already on bail have it renewed and may be told a date of trial if it has been fixed. It is thus a very busy day and I go through cases at considerable speed once I've got started. The word has already gone round that I am lenient with those who save time by pleading guilty. When fining the customers I ask from where they've travelled and always try to leave them sufficient cash to get back home. We certainly don't want vagrants hanging around the court or in the township, so the answer as I see it is to fine them reasonably and send them on their way.

This morning when I asked one of the accused persons his name he kept repeating: 'I am innocent, I am innocent.'

I said: 'Well, maybe so, but I need to know your name before we get to that.'

He said: 'I am innocent.'

The prosecuting inspector intervened: 'It is his name, your Honour.'

So I asked him and he replied: '*Eee, ssebo*, I am Innocent Musoke.' Named after some Pope. Didn't do him much good as I later found him guilty.

Thursday 29 October

I go down to Kabale in Kigezi once a week, usually on Thursdays, to check on the other half of my kingdom. There's a grade I magistrate stationed there, one of the magistrates who qualified as a barrister at the Law School, who deals with the everyday work. Fortunately it's not such a busy station as Mbarara and he's been working hard and has kept the case-load under control. The mountains all around seem to keep most of the people on the straight and narrow path and they have plenty to do to make a living from their contour farming on the slopes and fighting against erosion. There are tall eucalyptus trees by the roadside, some with barrel-shaped beehives hanging on them, and occasionally one can see a rare sakersia tree with its pink saucer-shaped blossoms.

There are serious crimes from time to time, usually rape or robbery, and I always fix one of these for trial each week and deal with any other cases and administrative matters that crop up. I drive down very early in the morning on an excellent tarmac road. It's cold and misty on the heavily forested mountain roads and cattle, sheep, goats or baboons tend to make sudden appearances on the road so one has to be alert. Most hazardous are the children, who often have long distances to travel on foot to school and so are usually come upon running along the middle of the road in groups or twos. They never seem to acquire much road sense; perhaps the small amount of traffic is one reason. I lunch at the attractive White Horse

Inn, which has a large fireplace as it gets chilly in Kigezi, especially after dark.

Tuesday 3 November

The formerly illegal *waragi*, a highly potent spirituous liquor distilled from *matoke* (green bananas) was, some time ago, turned into a government commercial enterprise and is now manufactured and sold like gin. The old locally made illegal brew continues to be produced in the villages and is now referred to by its Luganda name of *enguli*, which it is an offence to produce, possess and drink.

I dealt with a case today in which the police had arrested a man for possessing two bottles full of *enguli*. He pleaded guilty and I said I wanted to see the exhibit to make sure it was *enguli*. The inspector produced two bottles which were almost empty. I asked where was the *enguli*. The inspector replied: 'The police exhibit storeman told me that it had evaporated while it was kept in the store, your Honour.' A likely story; I remembered from my time in the Police that this sort of thing frequently happened when the storeman had acquired a taste for the hard stuff.

'And you believed him?' I asked.

'Oh, yes, your Honour,' replied the inspector, 'he is too reliable.' 'Too' is invariably used to mean 'very' in African English.

I couldn't resist adding: 'And too thirsty, no doubt.'

Tuesday 24 November

There's been a huge pig wandering loose around the area and coming into people's compounds and gardens and eating growing vegetables and plants and trampling about generally. It has been a great nuisance. I asked my court interpreter about it and he told me that it belongs to the Town Clerk of Mbarara and nobody dares to complain about it. So, two weeks ago I wrote an official letter to him, pretending that I do not know who the owner is and pointing out that it is an offence under the Townships Rules to keep such an animal within a township. I requested him to put his enforcement officer on to the matter, discover the owner and prosecute him accordingly, and I would see to it that he was punished appropriately. I received no reply, of course, but the wretched pig has not been seen wandering round since.

Thursday 26 November

I've just received a copy of Douglas Brown's second edition of *Criminal Procedure in Uganda and Kenya* published in Sweet and

Uganda Police H.Q. security staff and drivers with Staff Officer (P.A.) and police dog Blister

On top of Mt Kilimanjaro (19,565 feet) with Outward Bound course 1959

Uganda Police identification parade, Kampala 1959

P.A. on a cattle seizure operation,
Karamoja, North Uganda 1960

Investiture at Government House, Entebbe 1957, P.A. standing left

Karamojong (Pian) Warrior at Nabilatuk,
Karamoja, North Uganda 1960

Sir Frederick Crawford, The Governor of Uganda, at the Mayor of Kampala's garden party (visiting the police bandstand). P.A. on right, 1957

Queen Elizabeth National Park, Western Uganda

Magistrates course graduation, Uganda Law School May 1967. Left to right: Vice-President Babiiha, Chief Justice Udo Udoma, Attorney General Binaisa, P.A.

Amin with three newly appointed judges at State House. The Solicitor General is on the left and Chief Justice Wambuzi on Amin's right. P.A. is on the extreme right

Entebbe Airport raid: the bullet riddled building which held the Israeli hostages seen after the raid and rescue

Amin with some members of the Defence Council. Malyamungu is at left rear and Ali Fadhul is extreme left in front, next to Nyangweso, Chief of Staff. Ozo is on extreme right.

Amin with family and friends 'praying' over the body of his wife Kay whom he killed and then had beheaded and dis-membered. Two of her children are by the bed; August 1974

Chief Justice,
Kampala 1985

The Chief Justice (P.A.) after swearing in President Museveni at Parliament building, Kampala 29 Jan 1986

P.A. with his mother and brother at a Buckingham Palace investiture, Feb 1987

Maxwell's *Law in Africa* series. I had read his manuscript and made some suggestions and provided a few up-to-date case references and suchlike and am mentioned in the preface. It will be a useful textbook for the students and police.

Saturday 5 December

Since I came to Mbarara in August I've been working every day without a break to sort out the station and reduce the great backlog of accumulated cases. I suppose it caught up with me at last. Yesterday was the usual plea day and the court was crowded. I had woken up earlier feeling awful and unable to eat breakfast. I went to court and started work feeling even worse. After I had dealt with several pleas I found that I could no longer hold or control my pen and I felt very faint. The room started to spin and I managed to get out the word 'adjourned', and staggered to the door behind me leading to my chambers, where I collapsed.

When I recovered consciousness I was in a hospital bed across the road from the court. My chief clerk had taken me there in his car with the help of other staff members. He visited me later and told me that the grade I magistrate (another ex-Law School Bar student) had come over from Kamukuzi and dealt with the rest of the pleas and bail applications. The doctor came and looked at me and said sternly I had been overdoing things and must rest. For the rest of that day people from the court or sub-courts staff in the area, plus odd policemen and others in the township, popped in at about five-minute intervals to see how I was. I thus got no rest at all. They were killing me with kindness, so I told one of them to ask the chief clerk to bring his car and take me home. I discharged myself, went home and climbed into bed, after telling my houseboy not to let anyone in until Christmas.

Monday 7 December

After a weekend resting in bed I felt surprisingly better and decided to go back to work this morning. Everyone seemed surprised to see me but I had remembered that the High Court sessions in Mbarara were due to start today and, although all the arrangements had been made and, as usual, I had to vacate my court while the judge was using it, I wanted to check that all was well. I walked into my chambers and the judge was sitting behind my desk. He said: 'I heard that you were dying, but you look quite fit to me.' I told him that rumours of my imminent demise were exaggerated and that I hadn't got time to be ill and would be working in one of the uniport offices beside the courthouse which provide us with some of the extra space we need for staff and records. There is so much to be done that I can't take time off while the judge is using my court, so I'm just continuing with hearing my cases in the cramped space of the uniport. Expiring is for later.

Friday 11 December

This week I had to send to prison the *gombolola* chief from Bumbaire for stealing money collected as graduated tax; and an executive officer from the Kamukuzi education office who helped himself to over 20,000 shillings of his department's salaries. The embezzlement of public funds by government officials is becoming more and more common now, particularly as the quality of appointees and their lack of experience and competence deteriorates throughout the service. Too many are political appointees and others relatives of chiefs and other officials who were looking for jobs. Integrity, honesty and competence are not essential, apparently.

At the end of a criminal trial if I acquit the accused and order his release, all his womenfolk who are in court, his wives, mother, sisters and so on, leave their seats and come forward in the courtroom and kneel on the floor in front of the bench and, with their palms pressed together, sway from side to side chanting: '*Weebali nnyo, ssebo! Weebali nnyo, ssebo!*' giving thanks for the court's benevolence, mercy, judicial skill and, if he's really guilty but has got away with it, blind ignorance.

I find this performance extremely embarrassing and have tried unsuccessfully to suppress such outbursts. The court clerk merely shakes his head and says: 'It's no good, sir, they won't stop doing it. It's the custom too much.'

Saturday 19 December

Yesterday evening I was invited to attend an Mbarara branch Lions Club dinner for members and their wives as guest speaker. I was not too keen to go, especially as I was asked to speak to them about the Uganda judicial and legal system, which is hardly a suitable subject for post-prandial entertainment. I tried to make it as light as possible but all the members are Asians and I'm not well tuned in to their type of humour, whatever it is. After the fairly heavy meal I suspected that most people would want to doze off. At any rate the majority of the Indian women in their colourful saris were clearly not greatly interested and some were soon snoozing away. I couldn't blame them and so made it as short as I could get away with and escaped soon afterwards, clutching my certificate of service to the Lions Club, which their local leader thrust into my hands with several flattering but undeserved remarks.

Tuesday 22 December

Even now, over eight years after independence, nobody seems prepared to take the blame for things going wrong here. In and out of Parliament the politicians in their speeches blame the wretched British colonialists and imperialists for everything that's gone wrong or hasn't been accomplished since they gained independence. In Makerere the very politically inclined undergraduates do just the same, encouraged in this particularly by the political science academics as well as by the politicians. It's pathetic and achieves nothing, of course.

1971

Friday 15 January

President Obote is at present away in Singapore attending the Commonwealth Heads of Government conference. Apparently he is making a lot of noise harassing British Prime Minister Heath over the sale of arms to South Africa and is threatening to demand the expulsion of Britain from the Commonwealth. He's getting a lot of support from other African and Asian heads and, of course, a great deal of publicity here and everywhere else, which is, no doubt, what he wants.

Sunday 17 January

Grass fires are burning all over Ankole. An airliner flew overhead and an old Munyankole walking with a young boy pointed to the long contrail left in the sky behind by the aircraft and remarked: 'Look, my son, God is burning his grass just as we do.'

Monday 25 January

This morning I was in court hearing a case and all was apparently peaceful. When I resumed this afternoon I noticed through the court windows that many vehicles passing the *boma* had leafy branches from bushes or trees tied to the front parts, a traditional celebratory gesture; so something had clearly happened. I finished the hearing at 3.50 p.m. and, soon after, one of the advocates came into my chambers with a small battery radio. He said there had been a coup in Kampala this morning and switched on his radio. There was just martial music playing. At 4 p.m. it stopped and a man speaking poor English said he was Sergeant Major Wilfred Aswa and he then read out an 18-point announcement explaining why the Army had taken over and removed Obote from power. These included detentions without trial, lack of freedom of speech, widespread corruption, failure to hold elections, high taxes, high unemployment and so on. Quite a long list of complaints.

He then explained that they only wanted unity in Uganda not bloodshed and that the men of the armed forces had taken over this morning and they have now decided to 'hand it over to our fellow soldier Major General Idi Amin Dada and we hereby entrust him to lead this our beloved country of Uganda to peace and goodwill among all'. The Christmas message was no doubt still in mind. It seems that this started as a takeover by the lower ranks in the Army and then they realised they needed someone to run the country for them, so they've asked Amin to be the leader. Oh dear, what a choice.

At home I listened to the radio, which repeated Aswa's statement several times. Then this evening General Amin was announced and he read out slowly and uncertainly a very short speech or statement which I suppose was written for him. He said:

A short while ago members of the armed forces entrusted the affairs of government to me... I am not a politician but I am a professional soldier... Mine will be a purely caretaker administration. I assure you there will soon be a return to civilian rule and for that purpose free and fair general elections will soon be held... Political exiles are all free to return to Uganda and all political prisoners now being held without charges will soon be released...

My cook tells me there's a lot of rejoicing and celebrating going on down in Mbarara township. The Banyankole are very politically minded and there was a considerable amount of opposition to Obote in this area. The latter's supporters have no doubt already gone into hiding or have fled.

Tuesday 26 January

At the court today we all carried on with our normal duties just as if nothing special had happened yesterday. Court staff, advocates, the parties in cases and witnesses turned up as usual and work went on. Presidents fall and rise, governments change, but here in the Mbarara court two old men, Butirima and Katараiha, are before me concerned only with continuing their many years of litigation and disputing over the boundary between their *bibanja* (cultivated plots).

Sunday 7 February

After discussing it for two weeks, the Army decided that Amin should be called President of Uganda and yesterday he was sworn in as such on Kololo airstrip, where the 1962 independence ceremonies took place, in front of a huge crowd of cheering, happy people. Afterwards, Obote's political detainees were brought in a lorry from Luzira Prison and greeted, congratulated and released by Amin. The newspaper report states that the British High Commissioner attended the swearing-in, which means that the UK has already recognised Amin as President. Surely they could have waited a while to see how things work out? Probably due to the usual half-baked advice from the BHC staff.

In his speech yesterday Amin promised that 'the military government will end in much less than five years', which is rather different from his earlier statement on 25 January that 'elections will soon be held'.

Friday 19 February

As there are no ministers left in government, Amin recently appointed all the permanent secretaries of the ministries to be the actual ministers. In order to give the appearance of a military government he has also appointed all of them to be officer cadets. They may not yet realise this but they are therefore now subject to military discipline and law, which makes it easier for the military to deal with them if they step out of line.

He has also removed Oryema from his post as IG of Police and given him the innocuous post of Minister of Mineral and Water Resources, which seems to indicate that Amin does not entirely trust him. After wearing the uniform of the IG of Police for years, he cannot be too happy about exchanging it for the plain khaki uniform with no rank badges on it worn by an officer cadet here. In fact he still seems to be wearing his police uniform. I was most disappointed to see that the SG has now been elevated to Minister of Justice/Attorney-General, which gives him considerably more power in the legal area, particularly with the Judicial Service Commission.

Saturday 6 March

In a blatant attempt to appease the Baganda, Amin has had the Kabaka's body flown from the UK to be buried at the Kabakas' Tombs at Kasubi, outside Kampala. The funeral took place today, with all the traditional Kiganda ceremonies plus Amin taking part and making sure that he was seen to be in sympathy with them, in spite of being the one who led the attack on the Lubiri and thus causing Mutesa's second exile. Amin tried to get round that one by having the effrontery to claim publicly that he had saved the Kabaka's life by allowing him to escape. Tell that to the Marines.

However, that sympathy has not so far extended to allowing them to select and crown a new Kabaka, nor is he likely to do so. It looks as if they can take it that the abolition of the kingdoms in 1967 is a permanent fact now.

Tuesday 9 March

On Radio Uganda news yesterday evening it was announced that the huge explosion heard all over Kampala a short time before came from the Lubiri barracks, where the Army was destroying a damaged bomb and, as there are other damaged bombs to be destroyed, there will be more explosions and people should not panic.

This evening my informant dropped in and told me that Amin had arranged for 32 Acholi and Langi senior army officers to be brought out of Luzira Prison, where they were being detained, and taken up to a room in Malire barracks which had been wired with a large quantity of explosive, which was then detonated and they were all killed. These were the 'damaged bombs' to be destroyed, but there had been overkill by the incompetents who arranged it and too much explosive had been used. Hence the fact that everyone in Kampala had heard it and a lot of panic ensued in town. He said that Amin has ordered a different method to be found for disposing of his 'damaged bombs'. Many of the Acholi and Langi soldiers who were either stationed around Gulu or on leave in the area after the January coup were hunted down and shot in that area. Amin is apparently using units made up of West Nilers and Nubians to do this grisly work.

Tuesday 13 April

Amin obviously has close friends at Simba army barracks situated just outside Mbarara, as he so frequently visits them. The Commanding Officer, Lieutenant-Colonel Ali Fadhul, spends a lot of time with him in Kampala, leaving the Simba battalion to be run by its unpleasant second in command, Major Juma Aiga. This morning, instead of visiting by car, Amin dropped in by helicopter – a newly acquired toy that he's obviously delighted to play with. It was Mbarara's first sight of such a machine and, before going to the barracks, it landed on the golf course just outside the court. The noise of the rotors made it impossible to continue hearing evidence in the civil case before me. But, anyway, everyone promptly ran out of the court building to gaze at this wonderful machine and the Big Man. So I was left sitting in an empty court-room.

I looked out of the window and saw Amin step out of the machine and wave to the people who were rapidly assembling from around town. A moment later he climbed back inside and it took off and flew away towards the barracks. Those people involved in the case before me, including the two advocates, came back in and we continued with the hearing.

This afternoon the local wide boys have been outside digging up the turf where the chopper landed and, so I've been told, selling lumps of it to eager and gullible locals, at the same time claiming that the soil on which Amin and the chopper stood would, as a result of this wonderful contact, bring the possessors of it considerable good luck and would also cure all sicknesses, impotency and so on. Thus unfortunately proving that here you can fool many of the people most of the time.

Tuesday 20 April

I believe that African wild bees are among the largest and fiercest bees in the world and it certainly pays to exercise great caution when anywhere near them. Their stings are extremely painful and a number of them can cause one to suffer considerable shock from the combined multiple pain and poison. An angry swarm can cause the death of a grown person, let alone a child. They are not docile creatures and tend to attack at the slightest provocation.

A large swarm has built a nest in the roof over the garage which is attached to the house. I've carefully left them alone for the experts to deal with. Two men from the Town Clerk's office came at dusk as the bees arrived back from their daily business. The men donned special thick clothing and masks, then climbed a ladder and sprayed some poisonous fluid that effectively finished off the swarm. From under the roof they then extracted a large comb and cut away the outside portion, which was spoiled by the sprayed liquid, and their reward was a good-sized mass of sticky, dark-coloured honey. My cook produced two large jars for our share and they went off happily with the rest and my thanks.

Friday 23 April

Ankole is very much a cattle area, with large ranches scattered around the district. The magnificent Ankole cattle with their distinctive long, wide, curved horns are kept in large herds carefully looked after by

Bahima herdsmen. There are also many farmers with their cultivated *bibanja* and so there is a constant war, often moving into our courts, between the cattlemen and the farmers, very much like the stories of the American West. The cattle need grazing land and must have access to water. The farmers don't want herds of large cattle trampling over their land and through their crops, so they put up fences. Then the ranchers come to court complaining of the blocking of their traditional rights of way to the water.

Often both sides have a good case and it's not easy to find a satisfactory practical solution. Cases start in the local sub-court and are appealed first before the Chief Magistrate and then sometimes to the High Court. Several years later, when there are different judicial officers in each court, they start all over again. The parties are seldom if ever satisfied. Some of the disputes are inherited from earlier generations. Like the Baganda, the Banyankole are very argumentative and litigious and many would probably feel rather lost without having pending cases in the courts to sustain their disputatiousness.

Thursday 29 April

Those wretched bees again. This time they invaded the roof of the court-house and became quite a nuisance, as we must have the windows open all day trying to keep cool with all the hot air around generated by the lawyers and their clients.

Some members of the public attending a trial two days ago panicked and started slapping out at the bees which had come into the court-room, upsetting the bees considerably. I said: 'Leave them alone and they won't hurt you.' As I said this a bee landed on my right eyelid and stung me. The pain was intense and my eye rapidly closed up. I've had to wear sunglasses these last two days as it looks as if I've been in a brawl. An urgent message was sent to the bee destroyers and they came yesterday evening and did the necessary; though there had not been time for the bees to produce much honey.

I was informed today that I've been appointed a director of the Mbarara branch of the YMCA. Someone had somehow discovered my name on the original list of members of the YMCA foundation committee in Kampala back in 1959; so I was invited to take up this post. I pointed out that I've very little spare time from running all the courts in two districts, but I'll do what I can.

Wednesday 12 May

Amin has just issued a decree allowing, among other things, for the detention of persons without trial; which was one of the reasons given by the army for overthrowing Obote in January. So what has changed since then?

Thursday 20 May

The former Prime Minister, Ben Kiwanuka, has gone back into private practice as an advocate and last week appeared before me in a civil suit. He arrived in style. I was already sitting in court and he was late, so I dealt with some applications in other cases. Then a large black limousine drew up at the open double door of the court-room. A driver got out and opened the back door and out stepped Kiwanuka in black Homburg hat, black jacket and pin-striped trousers, clutching a rolled umbrella and brief-case. He walked slowly and majestically into the court, followed by his driver carrying a pile of files and books. The locals in court gaped at this apparition, while I totally ignored him and got on with the applications.

I then heard the civil suit in which he represented the plaintiff. I wasn't very impressed by his advocacy but it was a fairly straight-forward matter and his efforts, as is often the case with advocates, made little difference to the outcome. I said I'd deliver judgment on Thursday (today), which seemed to surprise him. He said: 'But that's only a week, I don't think it will be convenient for me, your Honour. In Kampaia we normally wait a month or two for judgments.'

I said: 'Mr Kiwanuka, this is not Kampala. I've a great amount of work to do and many cases to deal with, so I can't afford the luxury of wasting time. I always give judgments a few days after trials in order to get them out of the way and so that parties know the result quickly. If you can't attend court next Thursday then ask one of our local advocates to take the judgment for you, because I'm not pre-pared to delay it.' In fact, he turned up for judgment today, going through the same impressive arrival rigmarole, and was probably not surprised that judgment was in his client's favour, though he probably thought it was due to his advocacy rather than merely that the facts and law happened to support his client's case.

Monday 24 May

I gave judgment this morning in a criminal case against an Acholi woman called Supia Lamunu, who had been charged on two counts: doing a rash or negligent act and, secondly, practising dental surgery without being registered or licenced. She was performing operations upon infant children and removing their lower teeth. In the present case the child was only two months old and he had to be admitted to Mbarara Hospital afterwards for treatment. A doctor testified that the injury done could be classified as dangerous harm as deep cuts had been made and the teeth grubbed out with a blunt instrument, without anaesthetic, causing considerable damage to the gum and jaw-bone. He said he had recently seen and treated over 40 infants between the ages of two months and nineteen months who had been operated on in this way. Twenty-three were admitted as in-patients because of their serious conditions. Of these nine had died as a direct result of the operation.

Lamunu claimed that she was acting according to Acholi custom and believed she was curing some unspecified disease. Her motive was therefore a good one and the parents in their ignorance brought their child to her voluntarily, as did all the other parents, but she had subjected them to terrible pain and danger and it could not be overlooked. In my judgment I pointed out that this highly dangerous operation was completely unnecessary as it cured no diseases at all, but often caused permanent damage to gums and jaw-bone. I sentenced her to imprisonment for one year on each count concurrently.

It might seem odd that an Acholi custom was being practised in Ankole, so far away, but there are quite a lot of Acholi in the district, mostly working in the Police, Prisons Service and the Army, but also in other government departments. The wives are usually uneducated and often prefer to trust customary methods rather than modern hospitals.

Wednesday 26 May

After judgment has been delivered in a civil suit or appeal, the winning party submits to the court a bill of costs containing an account of the cost of bringing the case to court, which is then taxed by the court; that is, the court has discretion in allowing or disallowing the claims for the expenses involved, which are sometimes inflated or imaginary. For instance, in Kiwanuka's bill of costs, which I received today, he was claiming on the High Court scale whereas he should have used the lower scale for magistrates courts, and his enormously bumped-up fees for so-called research and preparation were absurd for such a simple case in a magistrates court. I have therefore taxed his bill vigorously and very much reduced the amount to be recovered from the defendant. This will be sent to Kiwanuka in Kampala as I have no time to hold taxation hearings. I simply tax all costs while sitting alone in my chambers and send the result to the advocates concerned. The local advocates appreciate this time-saving method because they know it will be a fair taxation and promptly done. In any case they know they can always come to me and complain, or even appeal the taxation to the High Court, though none has done so up to now. By working together like this, during these last nine months we've disposed of a large number of outstanding civil suits and appeals, to the advantage of all concerned.

Wednesday 2 June

When Amin took over and abolished Parliament, no further Acts of Parliament could be passed; but even he needs laws, so they had to decide how his one-man government could make them, and it was decided to call them Decrees. They are signed by the President and printed by the Government Printer as before, but they don't get debated first. It's certainly quicker.

Tuesday 8 June

Previously confessions of accused persons in custody made to police officers below the rank of corporal were inadmissible in court. This has just been amended to cover all confessions made to any police officer. This became necessary, unfortunately, because of the large number of confessions obtained by torture and other improper means which the courts were constantly having to reject. However, the fact that some items were found as a result of statements by accused persons, such as murder weapons or stolen property and the like, can be given in evidence, but without mentioning the confession part of the statement. For one who expresses a genuine desire to confess to an offence, the police can take him before a magistrate in chambers, who will send the escorting constable to wait outside. If the magistrate is satisfied after questioning that it is entirely voluntary, he records it in writing, using an interpreter if necessary, and it will then be admissible in evidence at the subsequent trial.

Thursday 17 June

In a traffic accident prosecution before me this morning a lorry driver, whose first name was Friday, was charged with drunken driving. His lorry was hired in Kampala by the relatives of a dead man to transport the body in a coffin to a village just outside Mbarara for burial. Various relatives and friends of the deceased living in Kampala were also travelling in the open back of the lorry with the coffin. It was a long, hot journey and they had brought refreshments to enjoy on the way. These included gourds of *mwenge* and bottles of *enguli*. As more and more of the alcohol was consumed they all became boisterous and merry. Friday had his share and his driving became erratic and

317

wayward. Just outside Mbarara, on a sharp bend, he drove straight ahead off the road and into the bush. The lorry overturned, spilling the laughing drunks all over the place. There were a number of cuts and bruises but, with the usual luck of the very drunk, no serious injuries. The lorry was badly damaged and the coffin had been thrown out on to the road, and the body now sprawled half in and half out of it. As a result of a garbled report received at Mbarara Police Station of a dead body at the scene, it was wrongly recorded there as a fatal accident. Friday now has to pay a large fine and has been disqualified from driving for a long time, which means he loses his job. The funeral was slightly delayed.

Friday 9 July

Amin, in his dictatorial way, has recently issued a Decree appointing Kiwanuka as acting Chief Justice. The Decree does not reveal what is supposed to happen to Dermot Sheridan, the actual Chief Justice. I gather he has no choice but to accept this and leave Uganda on 'retirement'. I suppose Amin was persuaded that a former VIP like Kiwanuka ought to be given a high post now that he is free of Obote's efforts against him; but he has never held any judicial position before. Well, he won't be appearing before me again.

His first act as CJ was to summon all magistrates in the country to a meeting and conference in the Conference Centre at Nile Mansions today. So everyone had to abandon their cases and find a means of travelling quickly to Kampala. Some were very late, and all the courts were left unmanned. We sat in the full hall, with all the Chief Magistrates in the front row. I am the only Brit in the magistracy and I was thus sitting in a prominent position. Kiwanuka came in and started by saying that he already knew many of us. Then he pointed to me and said: 'Especially Mr Allen, who was extremely strict with me recently and afterwards taxed my bill of costs very harshly in my case before him.' The whole hall exploded with laughter and applause – almost all there had been students of mine at one time or another. Kiwanuka smiled ruefully and said: 'I see you all know him too.'

Sunday 11 July

The Army has a barracks in or near every town or district HQ and many of the troops in each barracks were recruited from the Acholi and Langi. On Amin's orders, those belonging to these two tribes are being slaughtered all over the country, including at Simba barracks here in Mbarara. In a recent announcement Amin said that 70 officers and 600 other ranks were killed by the Tanzanian Army, but there has been no battle of any sort down on the border with Tanzania, which is to the south of us here. He has used troops from other tribes to carry out this killing – from West Nile and also from the Western and Eastern Provinces and, of course, his Nubians. It's very sad that Ugandans have sufficient tribal hatred or lack of concern that they are apparently willingly killing each other in large numbers. Information about this is difficult to obtain but there was certainly a massacre here recently and there has been another at the huge Jinja barracks.

There's a report that two American journalists are missing after they walked into the Simba barracks seeking information about the killings that had taken place there. This was an exceedingly unwise and foolish thing for them to do since, whatever went on there was carried out under the orders and approval of the commanding officer, Lieutenant Colonel Fadhul, and Major Juma Aiga, his second in command; and these were the officers they went there to question about it. So it's hardly surprising that they have disappeared. The police here would not dare to go to the barracks to make any such enquiries; they'd be shot on sight probably, or at least disappear. Perhaps these rash Yanks thought that their white skins would protect them. But it's not so.

Sunday 1 August

As a result of Amin's visit to the UK last month, a British Army Training Team (BATT), consisting of a colonel and two majors, arrived a few days ago. They are here to discuss the possibility of setting up and initially staffing an officer training school for Uganda Army officer cadets. Amin is taking them on a tour of military installations and, on Saturday, brought them to his favourite watering hole, Simba barracks, which he so enjoys visiting. In the evening he gave a party in their honour, and senior officials and prominent local residents were invited to what the invitation card called 'a dinner and dance' at the officers' mess. I wasn't very comfortable about going into that barracks, or any other Uganda Army barracks, at this time, but I thought it might be interesting to find out what they are up to, so I went along there.

Simba barracks covers a large area surrounded by wire-mesh security fencing. At the main gate, just off the main road to Kampala, is a brick guardroom. On its wall facing the road is painted a large, brightly coloured lion, the *simba*. At the guardroom door I saw a scruffy, untidy-looking soldier leaning on the doorpost with his hands in his pockets. A fine sight to see at a military barracks being visited by the Head of State and other senior officers. I held up the invitation card but he was not interested, and probably couldn't read it anyway. I drove

319

around the compound unhindered and eventually found the mess built on a hill, but the doors were inhospitably closed and locked. A subaltern came past and told me that guests were expected to go down the hill at the back to wait until the President had finished an important conference with senior officers in the mess. I walked down the slope towards a group of civilians and army officers. There were no glasses and people were drinking straight from the bottles – a disgusting habit, especially as many were chipped and heaven knows what, if any, cleaning processes exist at the local bottling factories. The choice of drinks was limited to beer or Pepsi-Cola, neither of which I drink, so I declined. After about an hour of hanging about we were told that food was ready. The dinner in the mess to which I thought I had been invited turned out to be food dished out by cooks in dirty aprons standing behind a field kitchen and slapping rice, *posho* (maize meal), brown beans and very tough stewed meat on to plates held out by the line of guests. It reminded me of my early days in the Army and looked just as unappetising. There was nowhere to sit except on the grass and it seemed a strange way of dining with the President, who was not even present to enjoy it with us. It turned out he was inside, comfortably enjoying a proper meal in the mess while his guests were pigging it outside. As I had no appetite I didn't bother to join the food queue; I could get something at home later.

When it was dark someone came down from the mess and said we could now go in there, and herded us up the slope like a bunch of unruly cattle. In a large hall there was the usual African layout of chairs lined up all round the walls and we sat there while an army jazz band treated us to a deafening display of amplified music. The instruments were attached by wires plugged into wall sockets, perhaps to prevent them from escaping. Conversation was impossible and, when I scanned the seats on the opposite side of the hall, I found I was sitting opposite the Big Man himself. Our eyes met and he turned and spoke to one of his officers, who came across the hall and said that the President wished to speak to me. The cacophony ceased for a while and Amin said something complimentary about the army law courses that I had run for him back in 1969 and asked how I was settling in and enjoying my new job. He then introduced me to the three ministers who were with him. One was his brother-in-law, Wanume Kibedi, a young and only quite recently graduated lawyer, whom he had appointed as Minister of Foreign Affairs; also Lieutenant-Colonel Obitre-Gama, Minister of Internal Affairs; and Abu Mayanja, Minister of Education, whom I had helped to arrest for political agitation back in 1959; which neither of us mentioned. Apart from exchanging greetings, I had nothing to say to any of them, so Amin then introduced me to the three British Army officers and we had quite a long chat whenever there was a lull in the ear-splitting music. One of the majors, in answer to my question, agreed that they had very poor material to work on here and that most were untrainable as officers or anything else.

At one point an attractive and exotically dressed girl came sashaying up to us before giving a special dance performance for the President and his overseas guests. The other British major, who was well lubricated by then, stood up and joined the girl and they both swayed and shimmied to the throbbing music and the considerable pleasure and applause of those around. Next came Amin's party piece; the band stopped playing and Amin moved over to the stage, where he was handed a small accordion, upon which he played competently a couple of swinging dance tunes, followed by tremendous applause, of course. It was actually quite well done and had the right touch. Then the band got going again and the noise seemed to increase as the liquor flowed and it looked as though they were set for the night, so I slid off quietly and drove home.

Monday 9 August

The acting Chief Justice, Kiwanuka, recently asked for individual reports on each magistrate and I have compiled them for Ankole and Kigezi, and have added some comments of my own about the magistracy generally. I've suggested abolishing the grade III, except for those in training, and weeding out the dead wood and leaving an all-grade II establishment in the sub-courts. In addition, I've suggested the creation of a small cadre of senior grade II magistrates with increased salaries and wider jurisdiction. For the scheme to work there would have to be increased salaries, vehicle loans made available, and houses allocated. These houses exist already but they are occupied by the clerks of *saza* and *gombolola* chiefs who are not entitled to them; but the chiefs won't move them out.

Friday 27 August

The BATT team of three officers whom I met at Simba barracks at the end of last month has now been expelled from Uganda. In his announcement Amin accused them of having been sent to Uganda to spy on his military might. In fact, Amin was greatly upset at some recent uncomplimentary reports about him in the British press and, in retaliation, he has thrown out the military team. He has thus foolishly thrown away the chance of making some much needed improvements to his miserably inadequate army.

Friday 10 September

A High Court judge, Jeffreys Jones, has been appointed by Amin to be a one-man Commission of Inquiry into the disappearance of the two Americans, a journalist and an academic, in Mbarara. This is a thankless task; indeed it could be a dangerous one, since the Army is so closely involved, and they cannot really want the truth to be revealed. I suppose the American Embassy has been pushing hard for it.

Wednesday 15 September

In the *Uganda Argus* today there is a report on one of my recent judgments. A Kabale businessman named Wakuze was charged with having given false information in April to one Lieutenant Opus, an army officer at Simba barracks, that two high ranking police officers planned to assassinate Amin during his recent visit to Kigezi. In his defence Wakuze said that he reported the information in answer to the President's appeal that whoever undermines the security of Uganda must be reported immediately. He said he received the information from a woman whose identity he didn't know. The two police officers were the Kigezi District Police Commander, Superintendent Simba, and Inspector Rweibengeya, the OC Kabale Special Branch. They were arrested but the information was found to be false, so Wakuze was also arrested. He denied fabricating the story and he had no grudge against either of the police officers or the army officer.

The section requires proof that the accused, when he gave the information, knew or believed it to be false. There was no evidence of that here and Wakuze stated that he did not know whether it was true or not, he merely passed on the information as he believed it was his duty to do so. This was not refuted so I acquitted him. No doubt, as is so often the case, there was much more behind this matter than came out in court.

Tuesday 28 September

Michael Kagwa, a Muganda, was the first African Crown Counsel, and afterwards became Chief Registrar of the High Court when the Nigerian, whom he greatly despised, was Chief Justice. He was then appointed as President of the Industrial Court. He was also a very wealthy businessman and he drove around in a white Mercedes Benz sports car. His girl-friend, Helen Ogwang, caught the roving eye of Amin, ever on the look out for female companions. As usual in such situations, Amin would have the boy-friend permanently disposed of by his Nubian thugs so as to leave the way for him to move in. The other day Kagwa was seized by Amin's Nubian bodyguards at the Kampala International Hotel and he was taken to Mengo, near Namirembe Cathedral, tied to the steering wheel of his sports car and shot, then, after locking the car doors, they set fire to the car. Of course nobody has been arrested for this murder, nor will they be.

Friday 1 October

I've received notification that I've been appointed to chair a Commission of Inquiry into a trade dispute between the Kampala City Council (KCC) and its employees. They had a strike recently and have accused the Town Clerk, the City Engineer and his chief assistant of corruption, nepotism, tribalism, favouritism and unfair practices. In addition they complain about their terms and conditions of service, poor salaries and fringe benefits; none of which had been dealt with in spite of years of complaining.

The members of the Commission are three police superintendents and three army and air force officers, with an assistant secretary from the Ministry of Labour as secretary of the Commission. As this inquiry has to be held in Kampala it's going to mean a lot of commuting between Mbarara and Kampala, 150 miles each way, because I still have to keep my courts working in Ankole and Kigezi.

Wednesday 6 October

I held a preliminary meeting in the Mayor's Parlour of the KCC building, which is the location of the old Town Hall and LegCo, and met the other six commissioners. I already knew the three in the Police but had not come across the three lieutenants, Bigo and Nnaku in the Army, and Mutono, a pilot in the Air Force. I also met the Town Clerk, Kaduyu, a Musoga; the City Engineer, Luba, also a Musoga; and the Chief Assistant Engineer, Ibale, all of wham have been suspended from duty.

There are many employees of the Council, over 4,000 group employees alone, and it would take for ever to hear them all; so I asked each department or group to select a spokesman and representative, with an assistant, to bring before us the complaints and testimony from people within their own department. Meanwhile, anyone may send in written submissions at any time and some have already been received. We decided to start our hearings on Thursday 14 October and from then on we would sit on at least two days each week and three days when we could fit them in. Since the police and army commissioners are free of other duties it is really for me to decide this.

Thursday 14 October

There was no chance of starting to hear evidence in the KCC Inquiry today, due to the activities of the advocates involved. The Town Clerk, Kaduyu, is represented by Godfrey Binaisa QC, and the two engineers by L. Da Costa. I announced that the hearings will take place in the Mayor's Parlour, not in the main council hall, and that they will be *in camera*. I explained that if the public and press were present and serious accusations and imputations were made, as they will be, which might well prove unfounded, it would be grossly unfair and damaging to the suspended officials to have it all bandied about in the newspapers and elsewhere in public. But, particularly, I wanted everyone to feel free to speak out to us without fear of publicity and quite possible subsequent retaliation. I thought they would do so more readily and freely in the relaxed atmosphere of a small private room rather than in a large public hall.

It's a matter for the Commission to decide whether or not to take testimony on oath and I ruled that there was no necessity to take sworn evidence. I have never really put much faith in the efficacy of the oath. Anyone who decides to be truthful will be so regardless of whether he is on oath or not. As for those who tell lies, they generally seem to do so whether or not they are on oath or affirmation, so it really makes no difference. In this instance we are conducting an inquiry, not a trial. We just want to hear what people are complaining about, and what they suggest should be done about their situation. As the Americans say: 'It's a different ball game.'

However, the lawyers had very different ideas and they had to appear to be earning their fat fees. They gave the impression that they were bent on delaying or even preventing the inquiry from getting under way. They raised preliminary points and objections to everything, including the procedure and venue. They even asked me to rule that the Commission itself was illegally appointed and constituted. I said that it had been set up on the direct orders of President Amin, so perhaps they might like to go and tell him he had acted illegally, if that was what they believed; I certainly had no intention of doing so. The other commissioners smiled and the advocates looked worried. I added that, as far as I could see, an inquiry was very badly needed here and it would be to everyone's benefit if it was carried out promptly and with maximum co-operation and minimum obstruction. Having heard

324

my rulings, the advocates evidently found them distasteful because, instead of wasting hours of useless wrangling, they withdrew and swept out of the room, with the departing threat that they would take up their objections with the convening authority. And the best of British luck, I thought. If they reckon they are going to get anywhere arguing with Amin about it, they're welcome to try.

Saturday 30 October

We've been going ahead with the inquiry hearings and there has been no sign of the advocates returning, I'm relieved to see. I've heard nothing of their complaints to the convening authority; and the suspended officials, being intelligent, well-educated men, seem quite capable of looking after themselves. They attend all sessions and can question anyone who makes submissions. Furthermore, they're in a better position to do so than outside lawyers since they know the staff and all the workings of the KCC. Their questions and comments are consequently more pertinent and useful to them and to us. In addition, witnesses are not harried and badgered by niggling advocates and so feel more comfortable just sitting down talking quietly to the Commission as if at a meeting. We are certainly learning a lot about the work and the goings-on in the KCC. The spokesmen and representatives from each department are, on the whole, bright young chaps who are co-operating well and producing the people who can tell us what has been going wrong in their departments or sections without wasting too much time with needless repetition, which I had warned them against early on. I have encouraged them to carry on like this, emphasising that the sooner we can produce our report the sooner steps can be taken to rectify things. In addition, I'm endeavouring to keep the proceedings as informal as possible while, at the same time, taking a firm line with any attempt to speechify or harangue us, or make obviously absurd or rambling accusations.

Lieutenant Bigo, who works at Army HQ at Mengo, told us that when Amin is considerably displeased with an officer he calls him in and proceeds to bounce him off the walls of the office with well-directed punches. Apparently the Big Man prefers this method to going through the palaver of a court martial.

Sunday 31 October

There have been one or two clashes with Tanzanian troops on the border about 35 miles south-east of Mbarara. In one the Tanzanians arrested four Ugandan soldiers who had strayed across the border, probably looking for loot or women. They may have wanted them to exchange for a group of Tanzanian villagers living in the area who had been arrested by Ugandan troops for some unknown reason; probably as alleged spies or some such nonsense.

There followed a border skirmish during which the Ugandans shot the local Tanzanian police commander, a half-caste with a German father and African mother, called Hans Poppe. Because of his yellowish skin and mixed-race facial features, Amin decided to use his body for propaganda purposes and had photographs taken of the corpse and published in the newspapers, claiming that he was a Chinese colonel fighting with the Tanzanians. In fact, he looked nothing like a Chinese, but most Ugandans wouldn't know that.

Thursday 25 November

I was cruising merrily along in my Jag at about 85 m.p.h. on my way to Kampala for the KCC hearings and, as I approached Masaka, out stepped an African 'from the bush at the side of the road. He was so drunk he could only just stagger and so close to my car that I couldn't do anything to avoid him. I whistled past and he must have been about 6 inches from the side of the car as he lurched into the road. The special saint assigned to watch over drunks and fools ensured that, although I could do nothing, he was held back the necessary inch or two, and I passed on my way. I looked in my mirror and he was still staggering about in the road, apparently so drunk that he was unaware of his narrow escape. I certainly wasn't and I heaved a great sigh of relief.

I stay overnight in Kampala for my twice-weekly hearings, at the Kampala International Hotel. It's full of tourists and most of the Israeli military training team live here, as do any visitors concerned with aid to Uganda, so that travelling up and down in the lifts is like being in the UN. I'm leaving the Jag in Kampala for some engine repairs and the arrangement is that I shall from now on use the large black Mercedes Benz limousine and driver formerly used by the now defunct Mayor of Kampala; since mayors of towns, being political creatures, were abolished by Amin some time back.

When I arrived at the hotel today, there were two large groups of obviously American tourists in the wide reception area. As I passed them one of the broad-beamed, blue-rinsed elderly matrons called across to another in the second group: 'Say, Mildred, did ya enjoy ya trip up the Nile?'

The other replied: 'Yeah, Harriet, the view from the top was wunnerful.'

Thursday 16 December

In a recent speech Amin has once again lashed out at the Asians in Uganda. Back in June he ordered a head count of all Asians in Uganda, which must have made them rather apprehensive. Now he has accused them generally of currency racketeering, smuggling, undercutting and cheating African businessmen and, worst of all in his view, refusing to allow their daughters to marry Africans. He said that there were 12,000 pending applications by Asians for Ugandan citizenship and they would not now be considered.

In the towns Asians run four out of five businesses and are usually the landlords of the buildings (which they can own, but usually not the land) and some, but by no means all, are guilty of tax evasion and overcharging and illegal foreign exchange deals. Their refusal for years to bring Africans into their businesses and train them and give them experience in managerial skills has been a complaint for a long time. The Asians, most with large families, prefer to keep their businesses in family hands and control, or employ other Asians as managers, accountants, cashiers and so on. They do employ Africans, but generally for manual labour or as lowly clerks, drivers and porters. As for intermarriage, there has never been much of that and little desire for it; practically none by Asians. So it's not really an important issue except perhaps to Amin himself, with his insatiable desire for women of all kinds, colours and races.

Wednesday 22 December

The frequent unreliability of witnesses is particularly well illustrated in traffic accident cases – whether they are prosecutions or civil suits for damages, usually referred to as running-down cases. I noticed it first when I was prosecuting in the Kampala traffic court in 1956 and now again when I'm trying cases in this court. It's a universal fact that several independent witnesses at such a scene, no matter how honest and truthful, do not see or recall the same things. Sometimes one wonders if they were even at the same incident.

Witnesses tend to describe what they thought they saw or what they thought they ought to have seen, or even what they think probably happened, just as if it actually and definitely did happen. No doubt this is often due to the fact that their mind or attention was elsewhere at the time – perhaps on family or financial problems or difficulties at work or thinking about other people – when their attention is attracted by the noise of a collision or squealing brakes or whatever. But this, of course, is after it has actually happened, so they tend to infer or assume what they think must have happened before that and, by the time they come to court, actually believe that is what they saw. Thus, very careful questioning is required to sort out the wheat from the chaff.

Another problem is with colours. For some unexplained reason East Africans in their languages seem to recognise only three colours: black, white and red; any other colour can only be referred to by comparison with something of that colour. So, in Swahili a red object is *nyekundu*, which covers all shades from pink to purple. A black person is *mweusi* and a white person, including an Arab, is *mweupe*. Sometimes *safi* (clean) is used to describe a white object. In Acholi black is *col*, which really means 'dark', and red or brown is *kwar*, while white oddly enough is *tar*.

To refer to other colours in Swahili 'the colour of...' is used. Thus, yellow is *rangi ya kimanjano* (colour of turmeric), green is *rangi ya majani* (colour of grass), blue is *rangi ya samawati* (colour of the sky) though blue washing powder is called *buluu*, brown is *rangi kama ya majani makavu* (colour of dry grass) and grey is *rangi ya kijivu* (colour of ashes). In Acholi they also use 'colour of' so that green is *atworo* (sisal colour), grey is *buru* (ashes), yellow is *ocwak* (the yellow weaver bird) and they simply use *bulu* for blue.

In court, and in the Police, where descriptions of persons and objects are constantly required, I long ago learnt that simply asking 'what colour...?' is not enough. A grey car may be described as blue, white or green, and stripes and spots on clothing are constantly confused. I usually ask the witness to point to an object or piece of clothing in court that is of a similar colour or pattern, but many people seem unable even then to distinguish between colours and designs.

Wednesday 29 December

The *People* newspaper today featured half a page of reports from Mbarara, including one that I had sent yet another *gombolola* chief to prison for one year. He was chief of Rubare in Kajara *saza* and was formerly the headmaster of Rubare Primary School, where he had helped himself to almost seven thousand shillings in school fees which he had collected just before leaving the school and taking over as chief.

1972

Thursday 6 January

I was able to take ten days off over Christmas and the New Year and drive down to Mombasa for a pleasantly relaxing break. From Mbarara it was roughly 1,000 miles to the coast, which I did in three stages, stopping overnight at Tororo (as one cannot cross the border at the Malaba post into Kenya after dark these days) and Nairobi. It was worth it just to get away and rest.

Saturday 29 January

I woke up this morning in Mbarara to find the house shaking in a rather alarming fashion and my bed sliding across the floor, which had been highly polished with Cardinal Red, of course. The heavy wardrobe was also on the move and I heard a crash outside and a rumbling from far below, which wasn't my stomach. The many birds usually responsible for the dawn chorus were silent for once.

It was an earth tremor, which we feel occasionally on account of being not far from the volcanic Ruwenzori mountain range and the Rift Valley. While the bed was in motion I stayed put, but once it stopped I hopped out and pushed my bed back against the wall, hoping that it would be all for the time being and that nothing more drastic was to follow. Outside in my terraced hillside garden I found the long, low brick wall supporting the top terrace and flower bed had collapsed across the flower bed next below it, severely bending most of the flowers there.

The house walls looked all right; there was no sign of large cracks or imminent toppling. Inside I saw two short faint cracks low down near one corner but nothing serious. Some books had fallen from one of the bookcases and the cat looked as if she was about to put in an application for a transfer to somewhere safer. I headed in the direction of breakfast.

Friday 4 February

I've had a very busy day drafting the KCC Inquiry report. Yesterday I went through the 186 complaints and reports with the commissioners and we made a finding and suggested recommendation on each one. Now I'm putting it all together. Of course, this is supposed to be the job of the Commission secretary, but there's no way that I'm going to let someone else write a report with my name on it, particularly as he's had no experience of this kind of thing. Our two typists will then put it on to stencils for duplicating.

Friday 18 February

Amin has been on a visit to Tripoli to see his hero Gaddafi. Apparently, he has been offered lots of lovely money by Gaddafi if he breaks off

329

Uganda's relationship with Israel and joins the struggle against 'the evil Zionists'. However, he needs the Israeli military training team to train Ugandan pilots to fly Russian MIG fighter aircraft and to drive and fire Russian-made armoured vehicles. But he also wants the money. He's fair flummoxed.

We've been printing the confidential copies of the KCC Inquiry report this morning and putting them together in spring-back binders. There's one copy for the President, one for the Minister and one I shall keep. The members of the Commission will have copies stapled together in folders. An official handover will take place on Wednesday. The two army officers are both also celebrating their promotions to captain. I don't know if being on the Commission has helped them to get it, but they are intelligent and well-educated and have made a useful contribution.

Wednesday 23 February

This morning we all trooped along to the office of the Minister of Public Service and Local Administrations, Byagagaire, and handed over the KCC Inquiry report as he wants to be the one to hand it to the President. Photographs were taken and very brief speeches made, but not by me. I was hoping then to slide away and drive to Mbarara, where I have a lot of work to deal with; but the Minister announced that he had arranged a party for this evening in our honour, so I have to attend. Curses be upon him.

Sunday 27 February

It seems that when massacres of Acholi and Langi soldiers are to take place anywhere in Uganda, Amin first leaves the country, as if he needs an alibi. Having first given the orders, he then scuttles off. My informant tells me that, while Amin was in West Germany seeking aid at the beginning of this month, a large group of military and police and GSU detainees, somewhere between 600 and 800, was moved from Luzira Prison down to Mutukula Prison, which is a most remote prison down south of Mbarara and less than half a mile from the border with Tanzania.

The group included the three senior police officers who investigated the murder of Brigadier Okoya two years ago. In their inquiries they were getting too close to Amin as the instigator. They questioned some men who had been arrested for robbery, who told them they had earlier been hired by an air force officer called Captain Guweddeko to shoot Okoya. When the police arrested Guweddeko he implicated Amin as having given the original order. To put a stop to this investigation Amin had the police officers detained. One of them was Hassan, the only Asian senior officer and Head of the CID, and his assistant, Senior Superintendent Festus Wahuyo, who had served with me in Traffic Branch in 1956 when he was a station sergeant.

Apparently, these detainees were slaughtered at Mutukula over several days by shooting, explosives and bayoneting. Only 23 survived and managed to cross the Tanzanian border to safety. Many of the others tried to escape but were shot down while running the 500 yards through the bush to the border. Hassan was too ill, as a result of his detention, to try to escape and he was dragged outside and shot and buried with all the others.

For some reason Amin felt the need to explain this incident and he described it as an escape by 15 former GSU detainees who overpowered their guards and escaped to Tanzania. He added that he was grateful 'that the Tanzanians comprehended (sic) the escapees and handed them back'. However, Tanzania then officially denied this, saying that 23 Ugandans escaped to them and definitely would not be handed back. Later Amin stated that the detainees were guerrilla supporters of Obote.

Monday 27 March

It looks as if Amin has made up his mind about the choice between getting financial aid from Gaddafi or keeping Israeli military training staff here. Today he issued a statement over Radio Uganda that all Israeli personnel have been ordered to leave Uganda within three days. This will include a number of Israeli civilian experts working on buildings, roads and other constructions. Amin also has an executive jet aircraft which they lent him. I wonder if he will return it.

Tuesday 4 April

The former Omugabe of Ankole, Sir Charles Gasyonga, no longer a Ruler and so no longer immune to civil suits in court, is now causing constant headaches as those to whom he owes much money are bringing actions in court against him. He simply won't pay his debts, although he can afford to do so. For the second time I've ordered the seizure of his cars for failure to pay up as ordered in court. He and one of his sons came in his aide's car to the court this morning to see me to complain about the latest seizure. I told him politely that if he wants to stop the auction of his cars, he must cough up the money and settle his debts as ordered by the court, or else. There's no way I can let him off this one, as he seemed to think I could. He's got the money, or can raise it from his huge herds of cattle, but he just doesn't want to be parted from it. It's a hard life being an ex-Ruler.

Thursday 27 April

A Banyankole married couple, both well into their seventies, came to court last week, each petitioning for a divorce from the other. Neither was represented by an advocate. They accused each other of all kinds of unlikely activities, considering their ages, but neither called any witnesses in support. They had been married in church and I asked why they now wanted a divorce. Both said they wished to marry again. I pointed out that, since neither had brought any proof of the allegations they made against each other, they could not hope to succeed, so why not go home and try to sort out their problems with the help of their families. Both insisted they wanted a divorce and made some more unlikely accusations.

I explained that if they really wanted a divorce, one should make the accusations and the other not offer a defence. I could grant a divorce then if there was no collusion. But neither was willing to admit the other's accusations nor allow them to go undenied. I suggested they go and see a lawyer but this was rejected too. Their stubbornness and obstinacy defeated their aims, so there was nothing for it but to dismiss both of their petitions and send them away very dissatisfied customers.

Sunday 13 May

A friend from Kampala dropped in this afternoon and mentioned that in Kampala there are certain people going around offering to pay anyone 100 shillings if he goes with them and converts to Islam. I suppose Amin's getting worried as, in order to obtain financial aid from Libya, Saudi Arabia and Egypt, he's been putting it about that Uganda is a Moslem country whereas less than 6% of the African population is Moslem. Hence the recruiting drive in a very highly Christianised country; the result of the enormous efforts of missionaries earlier in the century. No doubt they'll now get a number of 'converts' at that price who will probably change back again when this regime is over. But he'll never reach convincing figures.

Friday 19 May

One of my sub-court magistrates came and reported that Major Gowon, the present second in command at Simba barracks (a Nubian former tractor driver), was interfering with land disputes already decided by the court. In one case the losing defendant had approached Gowon and persuaded him to assist. Gowon ordered this magistrate and both parties in the case to meet him at the site of the disputed land and, when there, he declared that the magistrate's decision was wrong and should be ignored as he (Gowon) would give his decision in the matter later in the DC's office. He then went to the DC and instructed him to write and inform all those concerned to meet in the DC's office on yesterday's date. The magistrate was given a copy of the letter to bring to me with the requirement that I must also attend.

I gave the magistrate strict instructions that he was on no account to attend such a meeting as it was illegal. Gowon has no authority to interfere in court cases and neither of us must appear to lend any support by attending. The DC was also well aware of this but perhaps afraid to say so. To protect the magistrate from Gowon, I gave him my instructions in writing.

Yesterday morning I was in one of the uniports checking some old files when a clerk came and told me that Major Gowon was on the DC's phone demanding to speak to me. I instructed the clerk to tell him that I was very busy and, if he wished to see me, he could come across to my office. The clerk reported that he had passed the message, but I've heard no more from Gowon. I wrote a report of this to the President's Office, complaining in strong terms about Gowon's unacceptable interference in court matters in my area and stating that I could not allow any of my magistrates to attend such unlawful meetings. I referred to the President's recent speech to military personnel telling them not to meddle with the work of the courts. I also sent a copy to the CJ and the Commanding Officer of the Simba Battalion, Mbarara. Now I'm waiting for the sparks to fly.

Wednesday 31 May

At the beginning of this month King Feisal of Saudi Arabia made a state visit to Uganda. A great deal of fuss was made of him as Amin was hoping to extract large sums of oil money from him for purchasing military items, and for building a proposed Moslem Supreme Council HQ in Kampala and the odd mosque here and there to prove how Islamic we are. He also wants to build a Moslem university in the West Nile. In return for all this assistance Amin assured Feisal that Uganda is rapidly becoming an Islamic state.

My informant told me that he was present at the VIP suite in Nile Mansions where Amin was sitting with Feisal surrounded by his retinue in their Arab robes. Refreshments were brought to them by a team of girl waitresses in miniskirts who generally look after

Amin and his parties. When Feisal saw them approaching he became agitated and upset and waved them away saying: 'Send them away, send them away, they must not approach me dressed like that.'

He then told Amin how much he disapproved of this dreadful and wicked Western fashion and that it was absolutely necessary that all females in attendance upon him should follow the Islamic custom of being covered from head to feet. Until then neither Amin nor his soldiers had ever objected to these girls in miniskirts; but Amin was desperate for the money, so he suddenly found that he fully agreed that such dresses were evil and he promised he would immediately pass a law forbidding the wearing of them throughout Uganda.

A few days later he signed a decree to that effect, banning not only miniskirts but also brief shorts (for females and males over the age of 14) and maxi-dresses with slits up the sides. His decree says skirts and shorts have to be no more than 3 inches above the knee line; an anatomical part that has not been defined. The newspapers have published letters from various Moslems praising Amin for ridding Uganda of these evil Western ways. They certainly haven't objected before this; but that's what bandwagons are for. The police received their instructions and started rounding up offenders, mostly youngsters, and taking them to the courts.

I believe that this type of personal interference is not only totally unnecessary but also contrary to the Constitution because it is not the business or function of government to tell people what they can or cannot wear. It's an unwarranted interference with their freedom of choice. Any disapproval can surely be expressed without making it a matter of law.

Some have been brought before me here but I simply cautioned or discharged them, warning them to be careful not to be caught again. I don't see why they should be fined or sent to prison for a non-criminal act. A few days ago I instructed the prosecuting inspector not to bring any more such cases as I don't consider they have committed any offence. So they've stopped charging them and so far there have been no repercussions. According to newspaper reports some magistrates have been sending miniskirted girls or youths wearing brief shorts to prison and ordering the confiscation of the offending clothing. No doubt pleasing to the military authorities but grossly unfair to those with little money and when clothing items are in short supply.

A lot of women and girls possessing miniskirts have extended the length of them by joining on another piece of cloth. Others have gone back to wearing the traditional *gomesi*, *basuti* and also *bodingis*, which are Victorian-style dresses, with a yoke at the neck, which reach to the ground. These were originally introduced very early this century by an extremely strict British headmistress of Gayaza Girls High School, just outside Kampala. The school was the first boarding school for Ugandan girls and the word *bodingi* originated there; it was the African version of 'boarding'.

Sunday 4 June

My former Law School clerk, Sebastian Kigonya, who went off to be personal secretary to a minister, and then to several ambassadors, has kept in contact. Today his son was baptised at the Uganda Martyrs Cathedral Chapel at Kyambogo and I was asked to be the boy's godfather, which I agreed to, but by proxy as I cannot leave the station at the moment. Sebastian rang me this afternoon to report that all went well and the boy has been named Peter Allen Kiyina Kigonya and a photograph is on the way.

Tuesday 6 June

In a traffic case before me this morning the police witness related how he saw a lorry being driven at some speed with the bonnet up and a man in overalls sitting under it, carrying out repairs to the engine as it moved along. So that's what is meant by running repairs. The driver pleaded guilty to carrying a passenger in a dangerous position and driving without due care and attention.

Saturday 10 June

Amin's speeches are always broadcast in full on Radio Uganda. In one today he said: 'African and Arab leaders must sit down together and consider what to do to destroy Israel and the Zionists in the Middle East.' That should please Gaddafi and Amin's other Arab bankers.

Sunday 11 June

Amin is considerably mistaken if he believes that giving Ben Kiwanuka such high judicial office as CJ will effectively restrain him from indulging in all political activity. BK's a politician and always will be. Most weekends he drives down to his home town of Masaka and spends a lot of time moving about the town and the district, with occasional excursions into Ankole that I hear about. A judge visiting a district on judicial or other official duty as a courtesy normally calls on the chief magistrate of that district. But BK doesn't call on me when he comes into Ankole because he's not on judicial but political business. He seems to be out busily improving and renewing his political contacts and building up a strong political following in both districts. He's clearly too much of a politician and too ambitious to let it all go. Rumour has it that he's hoping and planning to be the next President if and when the military's removed or hands over power. His movements are hardly disguised as he is well known and he invariably wears the same 'city suit' that he wore in my court and that he wears daily in the High Court. Even Amin's incompetent intelligence service, the State Research Bureau (SRB), and his many Moslem supporters who live in and around Masaka, must have some idea of what is going on and will surely report to Amin that BK is being politically active. With Amin's deep suspicion and distrust of politicians in general, he will hardly ignore it.

Thursday 29 June

I was reading yesterday evening when I detected a movement out of the corner of my eye across the room; near the door a fairly long snake was making a series of 'S' shapes as it slithered towards me on the highly polished floor. I fetched a metal grass slasher from the kitchen store and set about discouraging the slippery target. It didn't do the polish much good, though.

I haven't heard anything regarding my report about Major Gowon's interference with court cases and perhaps now I won't. But I saw an item in the *Uganda Argus* about some army activities in Karamoja and it included a mention of the fact that Major Gowon had recently been transferred to Moroto barracks as second in command. It's either a coincidence or somebody, presumably Amin, took quiet action to produce a solution. It's certainly a relief.*

I'm off on UK leave tomorrow and, as I haven't been told otherwise, I presume I'll return to Mbarara when I come back, so I'm leaving all my kit in the house, with the servants to look after it. Nobody's been named to act in my absence so I expect things will just pile up until I return.

Monday 3 July – In England

This is very annoying. Some fool has changed the British currency when my back was turned. Now I've got to learn about New Pence. But I notice in the shops and market that they still refer to half-a-crown, five bob and ten bob, even though these amounts no longer exist officially.

*Four years later Amin made Gowon a Major-General and Chief of Staff.

Friday 21 July

The Olympic Games at Munich will no doubt long be remembered for the dreadful massacre of the Israeli team by Palestinian terrorists and the inept and incompetent way in which the West German authorities dealt with it.

The good news from there has been the first gold medal to be won by a Ugandan, John Akii-Bua, a policeman, in the 400 metres hurdles in the world record time of 47.82 seconds. If only we had athletic coaches and trainers I'm sure that more Ugandans would reach Olympic standards. Northerners, especially, tend to be extremely fleet of foot. Let's hope there will be others who will get the big chance.

Monday 31 July

I've received two newspaper cuttings from friends in Uganda. The first is a report about the government findings in our KCC Inquiry report. Most of our recommendations have been accepted, including the setting-up of a special court for magistrates to deal with KCC enforcement cases, which was my particular contribution. They haven't accepted our recommendations to increase various pay and allowance structures, which are badly needed, as they say they want time to consider them – although I put the report in five months ago.

The second newspaper cutting contains the full report in tiny print of the inquiry into the two missing Americans from Mbarara barracks. Jeffreys Jones, the judge who carried out the inquiry, obtained a statement from an army officer clearly implicating the then CO and second in command of Simba Battalion, Ali Fadhul and Juma Aiga, in the killings and burning and disposal of the bodies afterwards. He even managed to locate the Americans' VW car, which had been hidden in the bush down a ravine near Fort Portal, 150 miles from Mbarara.

Jeff Jones did all this in the teeth of open opposition by Amin and others who did not wish the truth to come out. Ali Fadhul is a very close friend of Amin's and they spend much time together. I gather that Jeff Jones wrote his report, then left it on his desk with his resignation, drove to Entebbe and boarded the next flight to the UK, such was his apprehension of trouble resulting from numerous threats received by him. Amin has referred to him as having 'a prejudiced mind' during the inquiry. It's extraordinary that Amin allowed the report to be published in full; it is so damning of his friends at Simba barracks. But he does inexplicable things like that.

Thursday 10 August

The British newspapers are full of Amin's latest nonsense. In Tororo he made a speech and, copying Martin Luther King, he claimed he had had a dream in which God had told him to expel the 50,000 Asians from Uganda within 90 days. This number includes about 23,000 with Uganda citizenship and passports and 14,000 with UK passports. There's a certain amount of panic at this end as the British Government worries about what to do with the coming influx, since nearly all will be coming to the UK, regardless of passports or nationalities. Whatever it is that Amin's up to this time, his latest effort will effectively destroy the economy of Uganda at one blow.

Friday 8 September

Amin is taking advantage of this Asian departure to order the removal of all non-Ugandan Africans and most of the remaining few Europeans working for the government. The Africans come from Rwanda, Zaire, Sudan, Kenya, Tanzania and Burundi mainly and their total of 180,000 is much greater than the Asians. However, the international press does not seem to be very interested in this; probably because they will be returning to their own African countries, not to Europe. I hear that the few remaining Europeans in the Police and Prisons Service have been told to go. As they are engaged in training this will no doubt have some effect on future standards.

I am due to return to Uganda on 10 September, in two days time, and today I've received a telegram from the Chief Registrar at the High Court stating that, in view of the departure of all non-Ugandans, he advises that I should not return. However, there is no way that I would accept the CR's opinions or instructions in such a matter. As we both know, I've long had many doubts about his competence and ability and have said so, and being a Muganda he will never forget that, so he would be happy for me to depart. But it's not a matter for him to decide anyway. I've sent off an urgent airmail letter to the President's Office explaining my position and what the CR has told me. I've also mentioned that, if indeed I am to leave the service, I need to return first in order to collect my property, which I left at Mbarara in the belief and hope that I should be returning there to work.

Saturday 23 September

I've heard from the news that a small group of Obote's supporters invaded Uganda across the southern border from Tanzania, south of Mbarara, on 17 September. They reached as far as Mbarara pretty well unopposed and the so-called elite Simba Battalion fled into the bush in the direction of Kampala, abandoning their women and children as well as their weapons and equipment. But, as a result of the usual bad planning and lack of transport and petrol, they ran out of steam and broke up into separate groups to try and escape back over the border.

When reinforcements eventually arrived from Masaka and Kampala, they could only mop up a few stragglers and arrest and shoot quite a large number of civilians who were pointed out to them as having openly celebrated their believed deliverance from military dictatorship too soon. So ends another pointless effort which merely emphasises the military planning and operational incompetence on both sides.

Monday 25 September

A few days ago some men, probably from Amin's SRB, arrived at the High Court in the morning and went straight to the chambers of the Chief Justice and arrested Kiwanuka. They made him remove his shoes and marched him in his shirt-sleeves out to a waiting car. He was taken away and, so far, nothing has been heard of him. Nor is it likely to be, in these circumstances. I hear that the remaining expatriate judges, on seeing or hearing of this incident, adjourned their courts, locked their chambers and went home for the day, refusing to work their courts in this situation.

Thursday 28 September

Amin loves sending cables full of nonsensical advice or admonition to other Heads of State. He has just sent one to the UN Secretary-General, Kurt Waldheim, saying: 'Hitler was right about the Jews, because the Israelis are not working in the interests of the people of the world, and that is why they burned the Jews alive with gas in the soil of Germany.'

The West German Chancellor, Willy Brandt, has denounced Amin's statement as 'an expression of mental derangement'. That won't deter Amin, who has an extremely thick skin and, in any case, he loves all publicity about himself, even adverse.

Monday 16 October

Last Monday was the tenth anniversary of Uganda's independence. Amin took the opportunity to praise 'the magnificent fighting qualities and great courage' of his soldiers in 'defeating the recent cowardly invasion of Uganda'. He has distributed a large number of new medals that he has had designed and manufactured. The Defence

Council (which means Amin) has awarded him the three top medals, called the Victory Cross (VC), the Distinguished Service Order (DSO) and the Military Cross (MC), for unspecified acts of gallantry in leading the defeat of the invaders. No doubt he achieved this by bravely staying in Kampala well away from the shooting.

Following the cutting off of aid to Uganda, last Thursday the British High Commissioner, Richard Slater, was ordered out of Uganda and the Ugandan High Commissioner in London was recalled. Amin has received a very bad press recently in the UK and on the BBC and he blames the British Government for not controlling the media properly, as he does himself, and making sure that such a great revolutionary Head of State as himself is not insulted by these mere journalists. He can never understand or accept the idea of an independent press and radio. In addition, he has claimed that Britain was behind the recent abortive invasion from Tanzania.

I've just received a letter from the President's Office stating that there is no reason why I should not return to duty in Uganda, and adding that no order was given that I was not to return. Trust the CR to have got it wrong. It may have been wishful thinking or even mischief-making on his part, though. He certainly wouldn't mind seeing the back of me.

Tuesday 24 October

I landed at Entebbe yesterday with no problems on arrival. I was collected at the airport and driven to the Imperial Hotel for the night. After independence Obote changed the hotel's name to Grand Hotel as he considered the name Imperial was too imperialistic and so distasteful. But Amin, in his unpredictable way, said he preferred the previous name, so it's the Imperial again.

Today I drove back to Mbarara in a car hired by the High Court and I am to continue working there, which suits me. Being well away from Kampala these days looks like a good idea. The vacant office of Chief Justice has been filled by appointing one of the first group of Ugandan judges, Sam Wambuzi, a Musoga. He's young for the job, but suitably serious and hard-working.

Thursday 26 October

When I arrived back at Mbarara, I found a military road-block just outside the township and my car and luggage was searched, though I don't know what they thought they were looking for. I'm told that, since the September incursion, the military have been very active around here and all of Obote's known supporters have been killed.

Amin has ordered that any civilian found in possession of any type of military equipment is to be arrested. There's a report that a youth was arrested in Kampala because he was wearing a fake leather cowboy belt with a large metal buckle stamped in the shape of a revolver. The idiot soldiers seizing him insisted that it was a weapon. I have several old items of army webbing, including my binocular case and a small pack that I use to keep the safari first aid kit in. So I dug a hole in the garden and buried all the webbing when no one was around. No point in taking any chances.

Friday 10 November

There's a large grass-covered space in front of my court-house, with the DC's office over to one side. This space is used for public meetings and other local events. Last month a self-styled sculptor from the Uganda Army set to work in the centre of the square and put up what was referred to as 'a monument to the gallant soldiers who gave their lives fighting for Uganda'. Unfortunately his sculpting was extremely amateurish and lacking in artistic merit. The result is a brightly painted and rather grotesque statue of a soldier in the uniform of a lance corporal. In style and proportions it looks more like an unattractive cartoon rather than a serious representation of a human figure. All in all it's an unsuitable memorial of a best-forgotten incident. As it's situated directly opposite the large open entrance of my court-room, I have the additional misfortune of seeing this eyesore daily before me every time I look up from where I'm sitting in court. Even the birds leave it alone.

Thursday 14 December

The poor press that Amin has been continuing to receive in the UK, plus unfriendly reports on the BBC and a possible trade boycott by Britain, has caused Amin to respond in two recent speeches. In the first, at the end of last month, the former *Uganda Argus*, now renamed the *Voice of Uganda*, reported:

The General also said that there are many people who are ready to buy Uganda tea. In fact the British have been deceiving people.

If one goes to Britain and one asks for tea, they will say that they are serving him with British tea when in fact it is Uganda tea which has been grown here in Uganda.

He reiterated that he does not intend to take Uganda out of the Commonwealth and he intends to remain friendly with the British. But what he does not want is people to go to Britain to bring the British here under cover of aid. If anyone wants to bring assistance to Uganda, let him go and bring money...

Yesterday, while addressing the management and senior staff of the parastatal corporation called Uganda Hotels Ltd, which took over all the non-African-owned private hotels in Uganda, the *Voice of Uganda* reported yet another of Amin's many hopelessly inaccurate and unrealistic predictions:

> General Amin said that the tourist trade will increase tremendously once the Asians have gone. The increase would be to such an extent that they will only be limited by lack of accommodation.
>
> He added that in a few years time he wants Uganda to be an example to other African states where everything in the country is completely controlled by blacks. He told them that he has Ugandanised the whole army, police and prisons services.
>
> The British, he pointed out, apart from making useless propaganda and confusing people, will never give good advice to anybody.

Saturday 16 December

On Thursday an attempt was made to assassinate Amin. He was visiting down here at the Tanzanian border near Mutukula, observing a military exercise taking place in the area. When he headed back on the track leading up to the main road to Masaka and Kampala, his car was ambushed by (probably) ex-Army men armed with automatic weapons who opened fire on his car. The soldier driver was killed and so was the large NCO in the rear seat. Amin had followed his usual careful habit, which they ought to have taken into account, of switching cars and putting the big soldier in the back of his as a decoy. Meanwhile he drove safely away in another vehicle, following a different route back to the main road.

Tuesday 19 December

A short while ago I had to visit the new Indian dentist at Masaka hospital. He is apparently only recently qualified and at one point in our session, when nothing was happening, I looked over my shoulder and saw that he was busily looking something up in a large textbook. He then removed my front upper middle tooth and three weeks later I collected a single false tooth, which proved to be loose fitting, so I quite often don't bother to put it in. I was wearing it in court this morning and, while busy recording an order I'd made on a case file, I suddenly gave a tremendous sneeze. The tooth shot out and its trajectory carried it over the bench and down to the front row of the public seats, where it struck a young man on the forehead. He picked it up, examined it closely, and brought it up to the bench and handed it to me. I thanked him and he solemnly bowed and returned to his seat. I finished writing the order in silence, looked up and said: 'Now then...' and everyone, advocates and public, suddenly burst into laughter.

1973

Tuesday 9 January

Amin is now flirting with black American groups and has convinced himself that they have the interests of Ugandans at heart. The leader of the Congress of Racial Equality (CORE), Roy Innis, has visited Amin and suggested he could recruit black Americans to fill the gaps left by the departed Asians in professional occupations.

Innis has persuaded him that whites have exploited American blacks for too long and they now wish to establish links with the original African homeland. He disregards the fact that slaves taken to the Americas were from West Africa not East Africa, which was the province of the Arab slavers. According to the *Voice of Uganda* Innis said that he 'noted that the Uganda armed forces was all black Ugandans. From now on the entire world should know that the black-man is capable of anything, if not better than other races. The Economic War Uganda has fought will radiate the world over and the world will once again learn that the blackman is a genius on this planet'. He added: 'CORE wants to unite the thirty million blacks in the USA so as to talk with one voice and strike a blow at the capitalists and imperialists.' Yes, well.

Monday 5 February

I've been a subscriber to the British magazine *Punch* for some years. The issue dated 24 January, which I've received by airmail, contains a double-page spoof purporting to be the front page of the notorious French newspaper *France Dimanche* with the headline: ANNE OF ENGLAND ELOPES WITH IDI! and the sub-headline: 'Elizabeth Shocked: Philip Files For Divorce Again', with composite photographs of Princess Anne and Amin apparently together.

Amin receives copies of most British newspapers and magazines and, when he saw this, he did not realise that it is a typical *Punch* spoof. At the end of January the *Voice of Uganda* ran the story as a serious report, no doubt on Amin's instructions, and the front page headline was: SHE JUST CANNOT BE UGANDA'S FIRST LADY. The article started with: 'A military spokesman yesterday described as fictitious a story in a British magazine *Punch* that President Amin was going to marry Princess Anne of England, as "an appreciation of the General's victory over the British; that is why they are donating a Royal Princess as his fifth wife. General Amin is right when he says he loves the British as his best friends. The President will be happy to receive her in Uganda."'

Wednesday 7 February

In the *Voice of Uganda* today there was a report of my judgment in a case of defilement. The accused man Koya was 54 years old. At a beer party a man named Kato offered his nine-year-old daughter Florence to Koya as a wife on payment of 300 shillings dowry. This was agreed and Kato went away, leaving Florence with Koya. A week later Kato returned and told Koya that he had changed his mind about the marriage deal and wanted his daughter back. Koya refused to return her and unwisely reported the matter to the *gombolola* chief, who promptly arrested him and took him to Mbarara Police Station. Before me, Koya, a first offender, pleaded guilty to defilement of a girl under 14 years of age, a crime that carries up to life imprisonment with or without corporal punishment. I gave him a year inside.

Monday 19 February

Early in January Amin announced that he had discovered that the chiefs of all grades throughout Uganda are unreliable and not performing their duties properly or competently. He claimed that this was because they had been appointed by the previous political government and so they didn't have the 'right attitude' and they were consequently obstructing and preventing the country's 'progress at supersonic speed' which his military government had initiated. Therefore he has dismissed every chief from office and, until new chiefs are appointed, all such posts would be held by NCOs and private soldiers, which, he said, would mean that the work would now be done 'in a highly efficient military way'.

Understandably, this news has been received with dread and despair by the civilian population. The ordinary people have from time immemorial relied heavily upon their own local chiefs for help and guidance as well as leadership and local administration. Now Amin's awful soldiers have moved in and replaced their familiar chiefs and are there all the time in their midst with their guns and their bullying and general harassment. There's no escape anywhere from them and, unlike their own chiefs, these military replacements are not fellow tribesmen but 'foreigners'; some literally so, since they come from the Sudan and Zaire. The general feeling is that such chiefs won't have their precious tribal and communal interests at heart.

Already the soldier chiefs have interfered in every local activity, frequently threatening people with their guns, which they carry all the time, and occasionally shooting someone as an example, and generally disturbing the normally fairly peaceful trend of rural life. None of them has any idea of administration and their efforts in this direction tend to be both ludicrous and dangerous. Offers of advice and suggestions are just brushed aside or ignored as they know it all. The most worrying thing is that nobody knows for how long this state of affairs will continue. No time limit has been set and it's a realistic fear that it could be a permanent arrangement.

Meanwhile, people with personal grudges have found ways of making use of these chiefs for the purposes of obtaining revenge and causing trouble by making malicious reports about their rivals and enemies. The soldier chiefs are ever ready to display their authority and use force without troubling to make enquiries first. Those complained against are often locked up as trouble-makers after publicly caning them outside the chief's HQ while the villagers are required to look on. No offences are charged and they are not brought before the magistrate in the local sub-court, nor are the police allowed to deal with them. They are denied even basic forms of justice.

Others benefiting from such baleful activities are losers in land disputes which have been through the courts. If they can persuade or bribe a soldier chief to act, he usually goes to the site of the disputed land with both parties and announces that he has decided to reverse the court's decision because the magistrate was corrupt or ignorant, and he hands back the land to the complainer. Several magistrates from Ankole sub-courts have called in and reported such instances to me. One of my magistrates reported that the local chief has ordered him to hand over all his court files in land disputes so that he, the chief, can review and revise them as he sees fit. Total ignorance of the law and how to decide disputes doesn't for a moment cause these soldiers to display a lack of confidence in their own abilities.

Since the integration of the courts system in 1964, the chiefs have had no judicial functions and are merely required to execute all lawful orders given to them by a court. This usually concerns the service of summonses and other court processes, such as eviction orders and property attachments (seizures). They certainly have no power to interfere with court work or see court files.

I've instructed the magistrates in writing on no account to produce any files to soldier chiefs nor to give them access to any. I've written a report to the CJ giving the names of the soldier chiefs complained about and sent a copy directly to the President's Office, taking care to stress the fact that Amin has in several public speeches directed that soldiers must not interfere with the courts; and asking for the named chiefs to be dealt with.

Friday 23 February

I was in my chambers at court this morning when I was informed that two soldier chiefs were outside demanding to see me. I told the clerk first to remove the two chairs for visitors from the other side of my desk and put them into the court-room. People don't linger if they can't sit down, and I didn't want them to be comfortable anyway. When they entered I saw that both were in their early twenties and dressed in civilian clothes, brightly coloured sports shirts and fashionably flared trousers. One of them said in English: 'We are army officers and we want to speak to you.' That didn't sound very polite to me so I asked for their ranks. The spokesman said he was a lance corporal and his friend a private. So I replied that this meant they were not officers and they should not claim to be so. I asked what they wanted and he replied: 'We are chiefs and the magistrates in your area are not co-operating with us when we want to check their files. They say you ordered them not to let us see any court files.' I said that was correct and that the magistrates were merely obeying my orders about this as court files are confidential and chiefs are not entitled to see any court files or records. I added that I would not allow them to interfere with my courts in any way; they were required to obey the orders of magistrates when they want chiefs to serve summonses or property to be seized on the court's orders. I asked if they understood that and he replied arrogantly: 'We have the authority of the President to check the work of the courts.'

I said: 'Rubbish. You have no such authority or powers. You will keep away from my courts. I have already sent a written report to the President about you chiefs interfering with my courts here and I expect he will soon deal with you in his usual way. He has said many times that soldiers are not to interfere in any way with the courts. Now I'm very busy so you can go.'

They stamped out and one of them said angrily: 'You can't talk to soldiers of the Uganda Army like that. You will see.'

Monday 26 February

Last month Amin decided to try to suppress any further ideas of over-throw or opposition to his regime by making a few salutary examples throughout the country. It was announced that a group of guerrillas had been rounded up and that they would be tried by military tribunal and then shot; the verdict was already decided. Amin then added the final twist by stating that each guerrilla would be publicly executed at the district HQ of his home district and everyone would be required to attend to witness it.

The military tribunal was chaired by the grossly fat and extremely ignorant Lieutenant-Colonel Ozo, and the so-called guerrillas were very briefly 'tried' and convicted and sentenced to be shot by firing squad. They had been selected so that there were representative 'guer-rillas' from every district, so that nowhere would be left out of the exercise. The whole ghastly business was obviously carefully orches-trated and the victims chosen from among the many already held by the SRB or military police in their detention centres.

Arrangements were completed and the chiefs everywhere were directed to round up as many people as possible from their areas and ensure that they attended at a fixed time throughout the country at the relevant district HQ site last Saturday; which was declared to be a pub-lic holiday so that nobody had an excuse to be absent. Instructions were sent to the schools to take their students to watch the executions carried out by the local army unit.

Mbarara's share of the victims consisted of a young man named Karuhanga, aged 24 and a junior lecturer at a teacher training college in Kampala. The site was among some trees near the *boma* just off the grass space which was in front of the court. On Saturday I stayed at home and wrote a judgment. I could see through my windows large groups of boys from Ntare School walking towards the *boma*. They were in no way subdued and there was much loud talking and laugh-ter, both on their way to the execution and on the way back shortly afterwards. It did not take long.

Today the *Voice of Uganda* published photographs of the executed victims from all over the country. They were tied to trees with black hoods over their heads and white 'targets' pinned over their hearts. In the paper there was much praise for Amin for ridding Uganda of 'these danger-ous people' and reports of huge enthusiastic crowds attending at each place with many cries of: 'Kill them! We don't want guerrillas here.'

1973

Saturday 3 March

When the Asians were thrown out by Amin there followed a certain amount of chaos and many opportunists grabbed whatever they could lay their hands on; especially those in the army. Allocation committees and subcommittees have been set up, mostly of military personnel, and people invited to apply for whatever they wanted. Most of the businesses and properties have gone to members of the security forces and their families and the rest to Moslem civilians, including the Moslem Supreme Council, which has taken a large share of what was going. A few other people have managed to obtain smaller businesses or offices.

In spite of Amin's assurance that everything would go to Ugandan Africans, some of the property has gone to Nubians from southern Sudan, and even Palestinians, who came here at Amin's invitation, have been. given land and buildings. These are even less Ugandans than the Asians who were thrown out, many of whom were born in Uganda. However, none of this worries Amin, who has been riding on the crest of a giant wave of popularity not only in Uganda but also in many other African and Third World countries. Ugandans themselves are ecstatic at the idea of so much valuable property going free and up for grabs. The Asians generally were not popular among Africans so little sympathy is wasted on them. The country's right behind him and he's even more popular in the Army, where even private soldiers have obtained motor cars and lorries and buses and installed their wives or girl-friends in shops; mostly without the slightest idea of how to run a retail business.

Stock found in these shops was very quickly sold off or removed and, as hardly any of them had thought about restocking, or indeed knew how to go about it, many shops now have empty shelves and a number have already been locked up and abandoned, or converted into living quarters. Factories and other industries are now in the hands of people who have not the faintest idea of how to keep them going and, through ignorance, mishandling, carelessness, irresponsibility, lack of proper maintenance or just plain theft, the machinery has ground to a halt, production has ceased and the economy is sagging alarmingly. In no time Uganda has achieved zero growth.

Amin has passed a decree setting up the Departed Asians Property Custodian Board, with various administrative functions as well as to assess the value for compensation, which Amin has declared will be paid to the former Asian owners (another tale to be told to the Marines), and to collect rent on the many buildings which his government allocated to itself for this purpose. The new occupants are sup-

348

posed to pay to the government the assessed value of the business, or whatever they have acquired, though nobody has done so yet. I'm sure none of the military personnel will bother and there's not much that can be done to force others to do so either.

In my view this whole business was totally illegal and unconstitutional and any laws made to enforce or administer it are themselves contrary to the constitution and should not be enforced. But nobody's going to challenge them in the courts as, apart from fear, too many in high places have benefited so very much from this wholesale looting of the Asians' property.

Sunday 18 March

The Foreign and Commonwealth Office and the Ministry of Overseas Development have combined to send a small team to Uganda to meet the few remaining Brits still working here and advise us on how to depart as soon as possible, since British aid is no longer forthcoming to pay for us. Those officials and the British High Commission people are not encouraging any of us to stay on. Most are working in schools around the country and several are here at Ntare School. We were invited to meet the team yesterday at the hotel for an evening drink and a chat. When it was my turn I rather upset them by saying that, as I have decided to stay on, I was not really interested in their departure arrangements; I just came for the drink.

The BHC official looked rather peeved and pointed out that everyone else is going, the BHC is in the process of being reduced to a bare minimum and it was thus unlikely that any protection could be offered in future. Well, I said, so be it, but I'm still staying.

Tuesday 20 March

Here in Ankole there are many Banyarwanda; some are recent refugees from Rwanda and others have lived here all their lives. So far, without exception, when they appear in court as either witnesses or parties or accused persons, they seem to find it extremely difficult to tell the truth. Even when it would clearly be to their advantage, or affect their freedom, automatically they avoid the truth when answering a question. Generally their lies are so obvious and childish it's difficult to understand why they bother to do it. Time after time I've asked a witness why he is so obviously lying and the answer always is: 'I'm not lying.' It's very irritating and time-wasting. Someone told me that they will never tell the truth to anyone in authority. Now I groan when a Munyarwanda witness or accused appears as I know it's going to be a long, tedious job trying to extract the truth.

Wednesday 28 March

The departed Asians left many motor vehicles abandoned all over the country, which were seized by those who came across them; particularly military personnel. Someone must have pointed out to Amin that these many vehicles were together worth a great deal of money so Amin issued an order that such abandoned vehicles were not to be registered or licenced until they had been properly purchased at public auctions, and the sale and purchase of each has first to be certified by a magistrate.

When I came home for lunch a few days ago I found two army officers waiting for me in my sitting room. One was Lieutenant-Colonel Ali Fadhul,* commanding the Simba Battalion, and the other his adjutant, who had come to translate as Fadhul doesn't speak English. I told him this was unnecessary and we conversed directly in Swahili. Fadhul said that a number of his officers were worried because they already possessed cars which had belonged to departed Asians and, as a result of the President's order, they couldn't licence or register them or record the change of ownership. He said he wanted me to provide each of them with the necessary certification of purchase so that this could be done. I replied that the President's order was very clear and that I, for one, was not prepared to ignore it, especially as his men here had obtained the cars improperly.

While he was asking what could be done about it, I had a quick think and came to the conclusion that whatever was decided his men would almost certainly not agree to hand over the vehicles, nor would it be practical or possible to recover them. So I decided to obey the spirit of the order rather than the letter. They were not going to get away easily. So I said firmly that, in view of the President's order, the vehicles would have to be paid for otherwise I could not issue the certificates. Therefore he should collect from each of the soldiers concerned an amount in cash which they might have been expected to pay if the cars had been publicly auctioned, and then pay it all into the court, with a list giving details of the men and the vehicles. I would then certify the sale and purchase of the vehicles and authorise registration and licensing.

Rather to my surprise, he immediately agreed to this arrangement and today a big bag of money was brought to the court with the lists. It wasn't entirely satisfactory and the amounts paid are probably less than a genuine local auction might have raised, but at least they are not getting away with the vehicles for nothing, as they had originally expected to. In any case, it's all profit to the Treasury since the

*Later a Brigadier, a Provincial Governor then a Government Minister.

vehicles did not belong to the government in the first place. The only losers are the original Asian owners, whom I can't help anyway.

Thursday 12 April

Amin convened a one-day conference at the International Conference Centre in Kampala for all members of the Judiciary and we all duly travelled in and reported there yesterday. This has effectively closed down the country's courts for at least three days. The Minister of Justice and the Chief Justice chaired the conference and we were told that Amin would put in an appearance 'soon'. The magistrates brought up all the usual complaints, because nothing has yet been done about any of them since the integration of the courts in 1964. These include lack of transport, no housing, pitifully small salaries and the lack of court buildings. They all still need urgent attention but there's no reason to hope that anything will be done about them; just the usual meaningless promises to look into them.

At the end of the morning there was still no sign of Amin but we were told that he had been delayed by 'urgent affairs of State' and we were all invited to lunch with him. He had chosen Lutembe Beach as the location for the meal. It's several miles along the road from Kampala to Entebbe and then off along a rough track for a few miles down to the beach on the west shore of Lake Victoria, where there's a small marina and restaurant. Those of us with transport gave lifts to others without and we eventually reached the place, only to find that we had to stand about in the hot sun for a couple of hours waiting for our tardy host and for lunch. In due course he and his entourage of ministers, senior army officers and other hangers-on arrived in a stream of cars and they all promptly entered the only building there, which had been kept closed until his arrival.

We, the guests, watched from outside as they sat down and were immediately served with lunch, which they looked as if they were enjoying. After quite a long wait containers of hot food were brought out to us and ladled on to plates. There were no chairs or tables and we sat on a low wall or on the ground. It wasn't very hospitable treatment and I thought it displayed a rather derogatory attitude towards the country's Judiciary. Perhaps this jaundiced view is the result of experiencing two of these peculiar meal invitations. I must try to avoid attending any more.

After the excitement of this lavish hospitality had subsided, I returned to the Imperial Hotel for the night. This morning, before returning to Mbarara, I walked along Kampala Road, where many shops are now boarded up and locked. It's no longer the pleasant, busy shopping street I used to know. The largest shop, Drapers, just below the High Court, is now closed up. Outside I was stopped by an air force captain, who seized my hand in welcome. It was Addy Mutono, who was one of the commissioners on the KCC Commission of Inquiry. He said he'd been hoping to meet me again as he wanted to tell me about his son, who was born just after the inquiry finished. He told me he had named his son after me and he hoped I would one day be able to meet Allen Mutono.

Saturday 14 April

I was awakened after midnight by a faint scratching noise coming from the window in the short corridor at the back of my bungalow between two bedrooms. The window has vertical steel security bars and a fine net mesh on a frame covering the whole window to prevent insects from entering when it's open, as it was then. I moved quietly up to the window, which has a curtain over it so I couldn't see what was going on outside, but the noise was definitely coming from the window frame, where it sounded as if someone was unfastening the screws holding the netting in place. There's a locked and bolted door alongside the window, so I supposed the object was to reach in through the window bars and unlock the door, before effecting an entrance, as they say.

At first I thought I'd wait until he had his hand through the window and then thump him with my walking stick; then I changed my mind and merely swept aside the curtain and crashed my walking stick against the bars with a loud shout. He seemed a bit surprised and departed in some haste without even a greeting. As he ran up the hill past the servants' quarters, my cook came out and called out something. I went outside but he'd disappeared (the thief, not my cook).

Monday 30 April

The latest problem involving a military chief is considerably more serious and worrying. Yesterday one of the magistrates from the western end of this area came to me and nervously produced a criminal case file that he had dealt with, in which the accused young man was his own court messenger and summons server. Apparently a certain man had quarrelled with the messenger over a sum of 40 shillings that the man demanded should be paid to him. The messenger refused and denied the debt. The man next went to see the nearest soldier chief and told him that the messenger had stolen the money from him. Without making any enquiries, the chief arrested the messenger and, in spite of his denials, caned him publicly in front of the chief's office.

When the poor fellow persisted in denying any knowledge of the money, the chief made him dig a large hole and stood over him with a gun while he did it. He was then told to get into the hole and the watching villagers were ordered to fill the hole with soil. They protested at first but, when the soldier threatened to shoot them, they threw in the earth and buried the victim. By the time that the wretched man's head only was showing above the soil, he was screaming for mercy and agreed that he had taken the money. He was then dug out, caned again and taken at gunpoint to the nearby magistrate's court.

There the soldier ordered the magistrate to write out a charge sheet alleging theft and to deal with the case immediately. The messenger was now in a fearful state and he pleaded guilty to stealing the money and was promptly convicted by the magistrate, who was very well aware of the illegality of the proceedings. However, he could make no protest because, he said, the soldier had a gun. The magistrate then sentenced his own process server to imprisonment for five months and he was taken away to the local jail.

Yesterday the magistrate felt it was safe to come and report this, five days after the incident, and ask me to sort it out for him because he was too frightened to do any more. I told him he had not done at all well. He should at least have tried to explain to the soldier that it was better to hand the man over to the police and let them deal with him. He might not have succeeded in this, but he should have made an attempt to do things properly instead of feebly giving way from the start. The sight of the gun had been too much for him, so perhaps he could not be entirely blamed, but there was no excuse for his having delayed several days before reporting the matter to me.

I instructed him to sit down and write out a full report of the incident and sign it. I kept this and his court file and gave him a written order personally to go to the prison, taking care that the chief knew nothing about it, and to collect the messenger and bring him before me by the quickest available means.

This morning the messenger was brought before me in chambers and I questioned him and then recorded his version of what had happened, which he then signed. As Chief Magistrate I cannot revise and countermand the lower court order in spite of it being unlawful, so it has to be sent to the High Court for a judge's order. However, I'm satisfied that the plea of guilty was involuntary and the conviction and sentence were both illegal, so I formally released him on bail bond and arranged for him to be transferred today to the eastern end of my area, furthest away from where the unpleasant incident occurred. Having hopefully secured his safety, this afternoon I gave the file with my report and the statements to a clerk to take on the bus to Kampala to deliver by hand to the High Court for a revisional order to be issued. Knowing how very long it takes to get any action out of the High Court, I also sent a separate copy of the file and statements to the President's Office with a request that the soldier chief be removed immediately as he is a danger to the court and to the public.

Tuesday 8 May

I was awakened in the very early hours of this morning by a bright light shining directly into my eyes. It came from a powerful torch held by someone standing outside one of the windows on the other side of the bedroom. I jumped out of bed and yelled something, and the light disappeared as the holder of it took off at some speed down the hill towards the entrance to my driveway. I reached the window and saw him passing under a street light on the road and moving fast until he disappeared into the darkness. It seemed rather pointless. If he had intended to break in, why wake up the sleeping householder first, I asked myself. Possibly he was a Pooh-type Burglar of Very Little Brain.

Saturday 19 May

Three days ago in the township the wife of a British teacher at Ntare School was shopping. When she took out her money to pay for her purchases she produced a 20 shillings note which, as usual, had Amin's portrait on it in uniform. Then she noticed that the two eyes had been pierced by some pointed object and she unwisely said to the shop-keeper: 'Oh, look! The President's eyes have been poked out!'

When she left the shop, a soldier who had been in there and had overheard her, followed her outside and arrested her and took her to the barracks. Later a group of soldiers went to Ntare School and asked for her husband. They were told he was in class teaching, so they went to the classroom and, without explanation, said he must go with them. The students all called out: 'Don't go! Don't go!'

However, the soldiers seized his arms and took him to the barracks. From there the two were taken to Kampala and then to Entebbe, where they were put on an aircraft departing to the UK. They had nothing with them, only the clothes they wore. There has been no announcement of this deportation nor of what offence they are supposed to have committed. Not only have they had to leave behind all their property in the school staff house and their car, but the wife's mother had just arrived on a visit from the UK and she had no idea what had happened to her daughter and son-in-law, until the headmaster managed to find out and tell her.

I wonder what goes on in the tiny minds of people who can see a threat in such an insignificant incident. I suspect they believe that some sort of witchcraft is involved in defacing Amin's portrait by piercing the eyes. Amin himself is certainly primitive enough for such credulity and his West Nile home district is a hotbed of such beliefs.

Tuesday 29 May

When I arrived at the court this morning, I found the staff milling around like a disturbed ants nest. Last night someone broke into the court exhibit store by forcing open the large padlock. Many of the exhibits held in past or pending cases have been stolen. Some of the stuff was recovered stolen property being retained while an appeal was pending or awaiting collection by the owners in completed cases.

The old man employed by us as nightwatchman declared that he had seen and heard nothing last night and he tried to pretend that it had never happened. Of course, if he had been drunk or fast asleep or just absent from his place of duty – any of which is possible – then he may have told the truth when he said that he saw and heard nothing. On the other hand he may simply have been in league with the thief or thieves and either assisted or turned a blind eye. Whichever it was, he did not do his job and the result is a considerable inconvenience and trouble for the court and numerous others concerned; consequently I sacked him and handed him over to the police, who placed him *in durance vile*. Meanwhile, a replacement is being sought. I have had a word with the OC Police and he agreed that he would arrange for the dog and handler, at present here on temporary loan from Kampala, to visit the court building and my house when they go out on night patrol.

Saturday 16 June

A short while back I decided to take action against a number of local people who had lost land disputes in the Ankole sub-courts and then had incited or bribed soldier chiefs to put them back in possession of the land. I collected the facts in various cases of this sort reported to me by several of my magistrates, whom I instructed to arrange for the arrest of those losing parties. They were to be brought to my court under escort as soon as possible. This was quickly done and, as they were brought in, I remanded each of them in prison custody on a holding charge of contempt of court.

In order to make the maximum impact, I decided to deal with them together in as public a way as could be arranged, so that word would quickly spread around the district that this type of activity had to stop.

Friday morning is the best time for this as it's plea and bail day and not only are many accused persons brought in from the prison and by the police, but also their relatives and friends are in court, so it's always crowded and therefore ideal for what I had in mind.

Having left the seven men concerned to cool their heels in prison on remand for two weeks, I had them produced before me yesterday morning and they sat and waited in a packed court-room while I dealt with a few of the more important cases first. Then I told them to stand up and I addressed them, through the interpreter, though it was actually intended for the benefit of everyone present, and pointed out that they had each lost land disputes in my sub-county courts, but instead of appealing against the trial court decisions to my court, which they could easily have done at little cost, they had chosen to go to the soldiers and persuade them to interfere with the court decisions. They had thus recovered the land which a court had already decided was not theirs.

I added that it is the law in Uganda that issues that have once been brought before the court for a decision can then only be dealt with by the courts until they make a final decision, and nobody at all outside the courts has any right or authority to interfere in the matter. Thus, they would not be allowed to keep the land which they had unlawfully obtained in this way. In addition, by asking soldiers to intervene in their cases, they were all now guilty of the serious offence of contempt of court, for which they could be sent to prison by me for a very long period. I asked if they understood what I had explained to them and gloomily they said they did.

I asked each man if he had enjoyed his two weeks in prison on remand and each replied that he had not. I said that they had better understand that if they went back to prison it would be as convicts and for a much longer time, and life would be even more unpleasant. They all assured me that they definitely did not wish for that to happen and would I please tell them what to do to avoid it?

'Well,' I said with a display of reluctance, 'I think I shall give you a last chance. First you will each now apologise to this court for all the trouble you have caused and you will promise never to do such a thing again. In addition, you will not interfere with the disputed land in each of your cases and I am instructing the police to keep an eye on your movements and activities from now on.'

So each publicly apologised and promised as required and then begged not to be sent back to prison. I replied that as they appeared to have learnt their lesson I would not punish them further and they were free to go home. They could also now file appeals in my court in their land disputes if they wished, and I would hear them.

They should also advise their friends and neighbours not to cause any similar trouble. They then trooped out of court looking suitably chastened.

Tuesday 19 June

So many complaints about the appalling behaviour of the soldier chiefs from all over the country reached Amin's ears that he finally realised that he would have to do something about it. Recently new civilian chiefs have been recruited in each district, vetted by Amin's men, of course, and then appointed by the government. It was announced that they were first to attend courses in administration and chiefs duties, to be arranged in each district by the DC. Each area chief magistrate is required to arrange for lectures to be delivered to the new chiefs courses on basic law and procedure and the legal duties of chiefs. In Mbarara the other senior secondary school has been used for the course for Ankole chiefs. There were so many that they had to be organised by the DC into two streams, so it meant a double dose of lectures on each subject.

I told the DC that I would give the law lectures myself and seized this excellent opportunity to explain how chiefs must work with the magistrates and assist the courts. They seemed to be quite a bright lot in general and they showed considerable interest and raised many questions, which we've discussed as fully as time allowed. It's been a very useful exercise as well as a great relief to everyone concerned now that the courses have been completed and the soldier chiefs have handed over to the proper civilian chiefs and returned to their barracks.

Wednesday 18 July

The *Voice of Uganda* reports that Amin has sent a telegram to US President Nixon wishing him a speedy recovery from Watergate. That must have made his day. On another page there's a brief report that 'the American star of many monster films, Lon Chaney, has died in California'. It adds: 'His most famous role was as Lennie in *Of Mince and Men*.' It must have been a meaty part.

Monday 30 July

The chief clerk has a small car in which he normally takes the staff salaries around the sub-courts at the end of each month. However, his car is in for repairs so I took him round in my Jag. Today I was driving to Bushenyi court and carefully trying to avoid the rough patches, when we came to a primary school not far from the court. The children were all out lining the road and waving flags and cheering. There was nobody else on the road in front or behind me and I was puzzled at the unexpectedly effusive reception. Rather than ignore it, I told my passenger to wave back and look pleased. At the sub-court I was told that they were expecting a visit from the Minister of Education (an uneducated brigadier) who was on a tour of the district. Perhaps they were bored with waiting around and decided to practise their reception on us.

Friday 24 August

It's now two and a half years since the military takeover and, in that time, many people have gone missing; simply disappeared. Usually those who fled the country into exile have managed to send word back to their relatives or friends that they are safe, but there have been many who did not manage to leave Uganda in time to avoid the usually fatal consequences of having annoyed or upset Amin or any of his henchmen, often in some quite minor way. Such matters might have concerned political, religious or tribal affairs, or a dispute over land or other property, or perhaps a business, a debt or a woman. Whatever it is, the common method of dealing with opponents or rivals, or removing persons believed to be obstructing or frustrating them, has generally been final and permanent.

Amin rarely bothers to detain people by locking them up for long periods; usually for a short time, until they can conveniently be disposed of. He prefers more drastic action and people have learned that if someone is collected and taken away, often in the boot of a car, the choice usually left to relatives is to wait for news from outside of a successful escape or to go and look around for the body on the shores of one of the lakes or in Namanve Forest. The latter is the big dumping ground for the bodies of Kampala victims. It's a forest area about 9 miles from Kampala where people fearfully search for the remains of their lost relatives.

Although Amin has previously denied that many people have disappeared, he has now had to recognise it publicly as a fact because it became necessary to make some legal provision for the disposal of the remaining property of such missing persons so that their desperate families could make use of bank accounts and businesses for their support. As a result, a few days ago he signed the Estates of Missing Persons (Management) Decree; the purpose of which is to make provision for the administration of the estates and maintenance of dependent relatives of anyone who has not been heard of within a period of six months. The courts can now grant applications and make orders to enable one or more of the approved relatives to manage such estates. This has provided some relief to those concerned.

In addition, the Decree provides that, where a period of three years has elapsed from the time of the disappearance, that particular missing person is presumed to be dead. This allows for probate or administration of the estate to be granted by the courts in the normal way after a death. But this official recognition of such great need for these legal requirements and provisions unfortunately has not halted or reduced the rate of disappearances.

Monday 27 August

There are a few Asians scattered round the country who bravely stayed on, but not many. In a speech the other day Amin decided to send them a message of useful advice. He said: 'Some Asians in Uganda have been painting themselves black with shoe polish. Asians are our brothers and sisters. If anyone is found painting himself with black polish, disciplinary action will be taken against him.' So there goes any chance of a visit by the Black and White Minstrels.

Monday 10 September

At Kabale each week I find the most common serious crimes awaiting trial by me are rape and defilement. There is also a lot of indecent assault, but I leave those cases to be dealt with by the resident grade I magistrate as they come within his jurisdiction. The incidence of this type of crime is very much higher here than anywhere else in the country and it has been puzzling me why it is so. I've asked the OC Police, the probation officer and the sub-court magistrates, all of whom come from this district, but none could suggest any likely explanation or reasons for it. I cannot remember a single week so far without its quota of these offences and most of the accused are teenagers. They never plead guilty, but either deny the offence completely or insist that the usually very young girl consented and was willing. At least there are not so many homicides or robberies as elsewhere.

When I was training magistrates at the Law School I recall several of the older magistrates, who were from the customary courts, would insist that there was no such offence as rape committed in Uganda. They maintained that the girl or woman was, by tribal custom, always required to be willing and to consent, but in some areas she was expected to put on a show of reluctance so as to comply with local custom in that respect. Perhaps that explains why other areas don't appear to have so many such cases reported and prosecuted. Amin certainly expects and requires willingness and consent from the many women he takes a fancy to, or woe betide them.

4

High Court Judge: September 1973–August 1955

Friday 14 September

I was sitting in court hearing an application in a civil suit on Wednesday afternoon when a clerk brought in a note asking me to come to the telephone and speak to the Chief Registrar urgently, so I adjourned for a few minutes. The CR told me that I should leave for Kampala immediately as I was due to be sworn in as a High Court judge by the President at ten o'clock the following morning. As it was then four o'clock, I returned to court and, finished the application and then dashed home, grabbed a small suitcase of overnight things and a suit and drove at some speed to Kampala, arriving in just under three hours.

After a night at the Imperial Hotel, I reported in dark suit to the High Court and travelled with the other two potential judges to State House, Entebbe, where Amin administered the Judicial Oath, which is the same as that for a magistrate; so that, in fact I was merely repeating it for ceremony's sake. I have been a Chief Magistrate for three and a half years now, which is rather more than the one year's wait to get to the High Court promised by Akena Adoko in the previous regime, but still not bad really at the age of 43.

Afterwards there was a small open-air reception in the State House garden for the legal luminaries present, and Amin moved about chatting with each of us and photographs were taken. Amin, as usual, was in uniform, and I noticed that he's still wearing the Israeli parachute wings above his medal ribbons in spite of all the vitriol he pours out about the evil Zionists.

He came to me and said that if I now liked to apply I could have Ugandan citizenship straight away. I replied that I would think about it (for about five seconds). Bearing in mind what happened to those non-Africans who held Ugandan passports and citizenship and were nevertheless expelled after their passports were torn up at the mere whim of Amin, I said to myself: 'You must be joking.'

The three new judges are an African academic, an Indian chief magistrate and myself. This sample of all races looks like an attempt at *rapprochement* with Britain and India now that almost a year has passed since throwing out the Asians and other non-Ugandans, most of whom went to the UK or India; though I doubt whether it will make the slightest difference really. On the other hand, some notice has clearly been taken for I heard my name mentioned this morning on the BBC Overseas Service news and on the Voice of America news programme. B. B. Asthana, the Indian judge, said he heard it on the Indian radio news, so perhaps it is of some significance after all.

Tomorrow the only other Brit left on the High Court Bench, and in the whole Judiciary, departs on retirement. He has given me his wig and robes and I now remain as sole survivor. Having had no intimation that this promotion was in the air, there had been no time to finish any part-heard cases in the Mbarara or Kabale courts. This is typically Amin's way of doing things. Fortunately, I'm up to date and there are only three judgments, already written, awaiting delivery, one in Mbarara and two in Kabale; so I asked the grade I magistrates at each court to read them out in court on my behalf.

Saturday 15 September

Back at Mbarara, I've been packing my kit into boxes, which will be collected by a lorry on Monday. My cook and his property will then travel with it to Kampala, where I'm in the process of taking over a house on Kololo hill next to the old airstrip where the independence ceremonies were held. My successor here has arrived with his family and I've been handing over, which was easy. The court and administrative work is all up to date and in good order, with various trials fixed for future dates, which he will deal with. It's quite unlike the chaos and disorder that I took over when I came here.

I found an invitation for me to attend yesterday afternoon the inauguration of the General Idi Amin Charity Fund for the purpose of providing relief to the poor, the infirm, the needy, the sick and the aged, so the preamble says. For some reason he chose Mbarara as the site for the ceremony; perhaps because he wanted to spend time afterwards with his chums at Simba barracks. As there were one or two people I wanted to see before leaving Mbarara, and they would be there, I decided to go along. Before doing so I wrote a cheque to the fund, which I expected to drop into a collecting box at the end of the proceedings.

There was a large crowd present and, as usual, Amin was several hours late arriving and we all had to sit there waiting, another of the reasons why I usually avoid such functions. However, my main purpose was to see various people before moving to Kampala, and I was able to do this. Eventually he arrived and there followed some verbose and boring speeches in which several dignitaries told us what splendid and virtuous persons they were for being associated with such charitable works and how they all supported Amin's 'brilliant' idea in setting it up. Then, round about the time that it was beginning to get dark, a point was finally reached where we were all told to pay up. It was announced that the drill was for each contributor to approach the dais and hand over his cheque or cash, whereupon his name and the amount contributed would be announced to the world over the loud-speakers. The President would then shake his hand and he could go on his way to the sound of applause. A long queue quickly formed and the procedure commenced. The mere thought of such a public display of charity horrified me and I knew that there was no way I could take part. I'm not a religious person and I believe that any business that I have with the Almighty can be conducted with the minimum number of appearances at his HQ. St Matthew, chapter six, says it for me: 'Take heed that ye do not your alms before men, to be seen of them' and 'When thou doest thine alms, do not sound a trumpet before thee, as the hypocrites do...'

Since there was nothing to be done about it and I couldn't leave my cheque without going through all the public rigmarole, which I wouldn't do, I quietly withdrew from the proceedings towards the court at the back of the crowd, and drove up to the house to get on with my packing.

Sunday 30 September

I've now settled in here at Kampala. The Kololo house was built in Protectorate days and is fairly large, with three bedrooms, good servants' quarters and two garages. The garden compound is spacious and someone in the past planted lots of flowers and shrubs. At the High Court I have chambers on the ground floor at the east end of the old colonial building with thick walls and pillars at the main entrance. Each of the chambers has two or three framed prints of cartoons of English judges early in this century by Spy and more recent ones by David Langdon. There's a large expanse of grass on the slope down to Kampala Road and the trees and thick hedge along the sides and bottom help to deaden the sound of passing traffic.

Yesterday evening the Uganda Law Society organised a reception at the Imperial Hotel to mark the appointment of the Chief Justice some time back, and the three new puisne judges. There was the usual speechifying, of course; lawyers are never happy or comfortable unless they are on their feet making a speech, either in court or elsewhere. There were several former Law School Bar students, now with a number of years in successful practice or working in the AG's Chambers, with whom I had a chat.

Sunday 21 October

Apparently Amin has been receiving complaints from chiefs and others in the West Nile District that it's a long time since the High Court has visited there on circuit. This happens to be true and Amin has told the CJ that a judge should now be sent up there. So I've been given the files for seven murder cases awaiting trial there. The court has hired a large Mercedes Benz and driver to take me with my police constable orderly/bodyguard (armed with an AK-47) and my box of files, books, stationery, robes, etc. I asked the driver who was the owner of the car. He replied that it originally belonged to one of the wealthy Asian businessmen thrown out by Amin. So here I am, a High Court Judge on circuit in a looted car.

It took the whole day to drive up to Arua as we found the roads in West Nile were very wet and muddy, which slowed us down considerably. It's some years since I was last up here and I see that there are now far more permanent buildings around and the women have taken to wearing dresses instead of the bunch of leafy twigs fore and aft that I saw on previous visits. But some things have not changed. I saw several young girls with beer bottles containing paraffin, each with a bottle carried perfectly balanced upright on her head as she walked gracefully and confidently along the paths. A schoolboy was carrying a small suitcase full of books flat on his head.

Wednesday 24 October

The High Court here is not divided into divisions as in England and there are no specialists. Each judge deals with whatever criminal or civil matters come before him. He records the evidence in longhand and writes his judgment. There are no juries and the whole burden of the decision rests on the judge. On the whole I think that it is a good system. Juries are never required to give reasons for their decisions, no matter how irrational and prejudiced they sometimes appear to be, and I consider this to be unsatisfactory. I believe that everybody who comes to court is entitled to know exactly why a decision has been made against him or in his favour. It also makes it less easy for arbitrary and unreasonable decisions to stand on appeal, since the higher court always has a written record setting out the reasons and findings which can be attacked or supported when considered openly in detail.

In the seven murder cases before me, five of the accused have pleaded guilty to manslaughter and, with the agreement of the prose-cuting state attorney, these were accepted and they have been sent to prison. One of the two trials was quite interesting as it concerned some local customs. The accused, Omani, was alleged to have stabbed to death with a spear one Karemela, the sister of one of his father's wives. She was returning from market at the head of a single file of six women, each carrying her purchases on her head. When they were crossing a stream Omani came up behind them and pushed past until he reached Karemela, whom he then stabbed with his spear several times. The police investigating officer did not reach the scene until five days later and the post-mortem was carried out two days after that. In this very hot climate the body had decomposed considerably by then and it may not have been possible to ascertain the number of stab wounds. The PM report didn't say and the doctor could not be ques-tioned in court about this as he had since 'disappeared', so his report was put in by consent of both sides.

Apparently Karemela had abused and mocked Omani because all his children were dead. The local belief is that one must have plenty of live children to prove one's virility and importance and to ensure one's security in old age. She called him a fool and said she would kick him and stamp on his legs and stomach. One of the local asses-sors explained that this indicated that there had been a dispute between them which would eventually be resolved by the death of Omani, when she would kick and stamp while dancing on his grave. The defence was that Omani was greatly provoked by this and he stabbed her as a result of that provocation. This is only a partial defence since, if suc-cessful, it reduces the offence from murder to manslaughter; but it also means prison instead of hanging, so it's an important defence. I accepted it and sentenced him to five years, in addition to the year and a half he had already spent in prison waiting for trial.

Monday 29 October

I finished the Arua sessions on Thursday morning and then drove across to Gulu, where I had six murder cases to deal with. Since the northern tribes are warrior types, they are generally proud of their killing prowess and so pleas of guilty are the norm, together with state-ments like: 'Of course I killed him; wouldn't you if he spilled your beer/took your woman/insulted your manhood, etc?'

So I dealt with four of these cases on their pleas. In the next the accused had escaped from prison two days before I arrived and was believed to have disappeared across the border into southern Sudan. The prison warder on duty at the time was his 'brother' and was being dealt with.

In the last case, where the accused had pleaded not guilty, his defence was an alibi. He claimed that at the time in question he was at home listening to his battery radio. He said he had switched it on to the BBC World Service and the announcer had said: 'It is now twenty hundred hours quinishing time.' I asked what quinishing time was and he replied: 'They always say it on the BBC. I think it's a special time.'

Of course. 'Surely you mean Greenwich Mean Time, then?' I asked. 'That's it,' he said.

It was very hot in court; there was no power on locally and so the ceiling propeller fans didn't work. Sitting in court all day in the heat wearing long red robes, a stiff wing collar and a wig, one tends to melt. The court clerk/interpreter earnestly assured me that it wouldn't have mattered if the power had been on, because the fans are not working anyway. Some working or electrical part has to be replaced and they've been waiting several months for it to be sent from the Ministry of Works in Kampala.

Wednesday 31 October

In Kampala Amin has just announced that a joint force of British, American and Israeli commandos is being assembled in Nairobi to invade Uganda. This scare has given him the excuse to send some army units to the border with Kenya and thus keep them busy hunting for non-existent enemies and harassing and shooting civilians accused of aiding foreign invaders.

Thursday 15 November

Somehow a few months ago Amin secured the agreement of the Kenyan Government that they would return Ugandan refugees or exiles accused of crimes in Uganda. The Kenya Police have been bringing them to the border to hand back, and even allowing Uganda Police or SRB personnel to enter Kenya and pick them up. By agreeing to this the Kenyan authorities are sending these people back to their deaths, and they must be aware of this.

Tuesday 11 December

I've received the latest issue of the Police *Habari* and in the editorial there's a complimentary mention of my High Court appointment and the fact that I have contributed to the magazine since 1955. But I notice that the standard has fallen quite a lot recently. There are just a few contributors trying to maintain the high standards, but gradually there is creeping back a succession of the old childish talking animal stories that I got rid of 18 years ago.

Thursday 13 December

It's so boring reading the insistent and perpetually dreary wailing and gnashing of teeth emanating from the British newspapers, magazines and radio concerning what they regard as the ever present economic plight and imminent collapse of the UK. Amin receives all of these papers and, I suppose, someone reads them to him. He has now announced that he's offering to provide financial and other material aid to his 'best friends' the British. He went on to claim in his usual boastful style that by his declaration of the Economic War he had rescued Uganda from the economic crisis which is being suffered in the West and he had thus set the country firmly on its feet again. He recommended that all other developing countries should follow his brilliant ideas. It would be difficult to find a more effective and speedy method, short of war, of destroying the economy than has been adopted by Amin.

However, he has now generously offered to feed the whole population of Britain, which he fatuously declared Uganda could easily do. He's asked Ugandans to send in food parcels and old clothes, to which would be added generous donations of money, all of which will be flown to his poor and needy 'best friends' whom he is determined to save from starvation and poverty. Thus he declared open his great 'Save Britain Fund' and everyone laughed. I doubt whether we shall hear any more about it. As Lewis Carroll put it:

> He only does it to annoy,
> Because he knows it teases.

1974

Sunday 20 January

My local godson, Peter Allen Kiyima-Kigonya, was two years old on the 17th and I was invited to attend a special Mass for him this morning at the Church of Christ the King. On arrival I was informed that in fact the Mass was for both Peter Allens, senior and junior. It was in a mixture of Latin and Luganda. Whatever it was all about, I suppose we both need it. Everyone was very smartly dressed. Afterwards I had lunch with Sebastian and his wife and friends and photographs were taken in all directions.

Friday 25 January

Luke Ofungi, whom I have watched climbing the ladder of promotion in the Force since he was a recruit in 1955, has been appointed Inspector General of Police. I had hoped and expected that he would eventually get to the top, but it's a pity it's while Amin is in power. Luke is an Alur from West Nile so he comes from the 'right' area, which probably helped a little.

But there are a few evil men around in the police and the worst is a Nubian Moslem named Ali Towelli, who somehow reached the rank of assistant inspector before Amin took over. He was never competent or intelligent enough for that rank and should have been discharged long ago. Standards in the Force deteriorated considerably during the years that Oryema was IG and unsuitable people like Towelli were not weeded out. He showed his eagerness to support Amin in 1971 by killing various senior people at the time of the coup and he was quickly promoted on Amin's orders to the rank of senior superintendent of police. Since then he has headed the Public Safety Unit (PSU), which was originally formed as a mobile anti-robbery unit. He has turned it into a torture and murder squad that carries out special assignments for Amin, who protects it so well that it is above the law.

The bad news is that Amin has just promoted him to Senior Assistant Commissioner and Director of Operations. He still controls the PSU and, in addition, now has considerable power and control over the whole Force.

Saturday 26 January

There was a judges meeting at the residence of the CJ this morning to discuss all sorts of things, particularly the need for official cars. At the moment we are following the old Protectorate system of using our own cars with an official driver supplied. Since I don't allow anyone else to drive my Jag, mine just sits beside me as I go to and from the court. I'm told I'm known as 'the Jaguar Judge'. Because of having to carry a load of court and personal kit plus a police bodyguard on circuit, a car has to be hired for me and this is expensive and not entirely reliable. Clearly the best solution is to provide official cars with drivers.

There were also complaints about the salary and allowances for judges. The CJ afterwards complained to me about the fact that, although I'm one of the newest judges, I'm the best paid of them all, including himself. This is because I receive not only a local judge's basic salary but, in addition, a British inducement allowance, paid in sterling, called 'topping up', to bring it more into line with British salaries and to take into account that Uganda is considered to be a hazardous posting. I just grinned and said: 'I see you've been doing your homework.'

Tuesday 5 February

There is a court usher assigned to work with me, though we all still use the old Protectorate title of office messenger for them. He's an ancient Muganda named Kikambi, known to everyone here as *Mzee* (old man). He comes into court with me and carries the files and books. He also goes to the post office and bank for me and is supposed to unlock and clean my chambers before I arrive each day. I estimate that this part of his duties takes him about half a minute each morning. He clutches an old rag, waves it about in the general direction of my desk, causing loose papers to float to the floor. Then he strikes each of the pictures hanging on the walls a blow with the cloth. This leaves them all hanging askew; firstly to show that he has passed that way and secondly because he knows it annoys me to see pictures out of alignment. He gleefully derives what he thinks is secret entertainment from watching me go round the room straightening the pictures.

As the only remaining Brit in the Judiciary, I feel I have to make some sort of gesture in view of Amin's constantly expressed anti-British attitude. So I have a large print of the Annigoni portrait of the Queen hanging on the wall. The official portrait of the President hangs in the CJ's chambers, and fortunately individual judges have not been issued with them. Some of my colleagues have expressed trepidation and advised me that it's unwise to display the Queen's portrait in this way. However, as I tell them, the Queen is Head of the Commonwealth and Uganda is still (just) a member and, furthermore, Amin himself has her portrait hanging in at least one of his offices, where he has been photographed sitting in front of it.

This morning I arrived at my chambers and found a colleague sitting waiting to speak to me. I strode past him complaining: 'That wretched *Mzee* is always knocking the Queen about.' He looked at me startled, but by then I had reached her portrait and, as I straightened it I said: 'I'm fed up with him, he always leaves her looking skew-whiff. It's treason.'

Friday 1 March

I've just spent most of February in Mbarara on circuit. It was pleasant to be back in my old court again, with the same interpreter working with me. I had a pile of files, both criminal and civil cases, to deal with and spent the evenings at the hotel writing judgments.

Sunday 3 March

I first met Lieutenant-Colonel Michael Ondoga, a short, stoutish Lugbara from West Nile, at a reception in Mbarara in 1971 when he had just been appointed Ambassador to the USSR. He had some education but his main qualification was that he was a cousin of Amin's second wife, Kay. In mid-1973 he was recalled from Moscow and Amin appointed him Minister of Foreign Affairs. Now, for some reason, Amin has taken a dislike to him and moved on him a couple of days ago at a graduation ceremony at Makerere University. I was invited too, but I did what I usually do with invitations to official functions these days, and dropped it into the waste-paper basket.

However, my informant was present and came to see me this morning. He said that all the ministers and diplomats were in attendance on Amin as required, so it was ideal for his purpose. Also present was the lawyer Elizabeth Bagaya, who now prefers to be known as Princess Elizabeth of Toro. Amin was attracted to her and, unusually, his advances were rejected, which would not have pleased him. But he is clearly still trying. Amin rose to speak and, ignoring the real purpose for which he was present at the university, he called Bagaya to the rostrum and said he wanted to announce that he had fired Lieutenant-Colonel Ondoga, and introduced Bagaya as the new Foreign Minister. Neither of these had been informed of this decision in advance. Ondoga was sitting only a few feet away and no doubt was greatly embarrassed at this public humiliation but could do nothing, of course. He should have been very apprehensive since firing by Amin is usually followed by more drastic action.

This is what concerns my informant at the moment; because he's of the same tribe as Ondoga and a friend of his. He said that he and other Lugbara friends have warned and advised Ondoga to get out of Uganda quickly as the Big Man is obviously after him. The official announcement in yesterday's *Voice of Uganda* stated that Ondoga has been assigned to special duties, which is always ominous.

Wednesday 13 March

On the Radio Uganda news yesterday evening it was announced that

Ondoga's body had been found in the Nile. Amin claimed that he had been kidnapped by imperialists. My informant dropped by this evening and I asked him about his friend Ondoga. He said that Ondoga ignored their warnings to get out and made no attempt to do so. He took his small daughter to school as usual on 6 March and members of Amin's Nubian bodyguard seized him outside the school, beat him up, and took him and his car away. His head and ribs were battered, he was shot and stabbed and his body was then dropped into the Nile from a helicopter. And it wasn't by imperialists.

Sunday 17 March

A short while ago Amin proudly announced that he has at last been able to persuade his main Arab backer and his 'best friend' Colonel Gaddafi of Libya to pay a brief visit to Uganda, where, he was told, everyone was longing to meet him. Today was to be the day, but the visit was to be only as he passed through on his way elsewhere, so it would take place at the new international airport still under construction at Entebbe. Invitations were sent out and I received one, which I proposed to ignore as usual. However, for no good reason I allowed a colleague to talk me into going there with him on this hot Sunday afternoon.

On arrival at the airport we found a large area of open tarmac runway had been roped off and hard seats set out, upon which we sat in the blazing sun for an hour or two. There was a wavering heat haze rising from the hot tarmac and several of the sensible ones had brought umbrellas and dark glasses. The rest of us sat in suits and sweltered in the heat. Eventually the Libyan Air Force jet could be heard and seen making its landing approach. A young man from the President's Protocol Office immediately started to round up VIPs to be lined up for introduction to the visitor. As he came to us two judges he said, I thought, rather rudely: 'Oh no, we don't want you.'

'In that case,' I retorted, 'why were we invited?' But he just passed on his way, selecting and urging the chosen diplomats, sheikhs, khadis and senior security officers to join the welcoming line. I suppose I could hardly complain since I didn't want to meet the man anyway. If I'd had my own car I'd have departed at this stage, but the other judge wanted to stay. The aircraft was brought to a halt near a red carpet and the two national anthems were thumped out by a Uganda Army band and a guard of honour inspected. As Gaddafi was taken along the receiving line, I noticed that he was carrying the leather cover swagger-cane that he had acquired after seeing and admiring British officers carrying them when he attended a course for army signals officers at Catterick in Yorkshire in 1961.

Both Amin and Gaddafi were wearing tropical uniforms with short sleeves and, in addition, Amin wore a webbing belt with a pistol holster, as is his habit. Amin's speech of welcome fairly oozed with praise and hero-worship as he gave every possible assurance that both he and all Ugandans fully supported Gaddafi's words and deeds. Gaddafi then delivered a long harangue in Arabic over the screeching loudspeakers, with impatient glances at the nervous interpreter standing beside him. With much arm-waving and hatred, he poured out his usual diatribe against the imperialists, Zionists, infidels and all other poor, miserable creatures who have the misfortune to have earned his disapproval. He could have spoken in English but probably preferred to refrain from using an imperialist language, thus doubling the length of time we had to sit in the sun being cooked. After this Amin took him to show off his new airport, and while that was being done I managed to persuade my colleague that enough was enough and we drove back to Kampala.

Monday 25 March

There's been some sort of mutiny in the Uganda Army. On Saturday night there was a battle at Makindye Military Police barracks. It may have been a coup attempt. Apparently it was a fight by Ugandan troops of Malire Battalion, led by Brigadier Arube, the Chief of Staff, and Lieutenant-Colonel Elly, both from Amin's Kakwa tribe in the West Nile, against the almost entirely Sudanese military police. They took Radio Uganda and were searching for Amin at the Command post, his residence at Kololo, not far from my house. They were also looking for the dreaded Nubian policeman, Ali Towelli, who has gone into hiding. Apparently a part of the army has at last got tired of the constant killings by murder squads from the Sudanese military police and Towelli's PSU.

Unfortunately, as usual, it has mostly gone wrong due to their general incompetence. Arube was shot dead, Elly was arrested and a lot of soldiers killed and wounded. Amin has announced that Arube committed suicide (very unlikely) and that Towelli has been dismissed (great relief everywhere); and that Brigadier Marella, the Sudanese commander of the military police, has been retired with full benefits. He added that Lieutenant-Colonel Elly is to be tried by a military tribunal. Amin has also divorced three of his four wives as he suspected them of sympathising with Arube's recent efforts.

Sunday 7 April

Apparently Amin paid attention to the request by the judges for official cars. A fleet of brand new Mercedes Benz saloons arrived last week, one for each judge. My driver was very pleased as he now has a car to drive instead of being driven around by me. I've put it to immediate use as I was due to go on circuit to Bunyoro, so today we drove to Masindi, where I'm holding criminal sessions.

Friday 12 April

Masindi is in the north of Bunyoro, close to the boundary with West Nile district, and quite a lot of Alur from that district are settled in and around Masindi. The murder case in which I gave judgment this morning involves these people and, as usual with West Nilers, it also involved witchcraft.

Two Alur, called Semukwa and Loronga, were accused of murdering Ozunga, who was Semukwa's father-in-law. The reason for the killing was because of the death of Semukwa's baby daughter from measles shortly before. This disease is a frequent cause of infant mortality in Uganda but, like most West Nilers, Semukwa was unable to accept that the illness killed the child; it could only be the result of witchcraft. In court Semukwa blamed his daughter's death on his father-in-law, who, he alleged, had bewitched her, though he could give no reason why the deceased had done this.

The child's funeral was attended, as custom required, by all the members of the extended family as well as close friends and clan members. While the ceremony was going on, the two men seized Ozunga and tied him up in a Semukwa's hut. He was an old man and didn't resist. They took sticks and beat him unmercifully until he collapsed unconscious. The victim's small daughter, Thorach, came into the hut and watched and later testified clearly what she had seen. Several people came into the hut and sat and watched, according to their evidence, without interfering or helping the old man, who was then still alive. Ozunga told them the old man had caused his child's death, which they instantly believed, and so would not have dreamed of lifting a finger to help him.

When Semukwa saw that the old man was unconscious he went to the village chief, a Munyoro, and reported that his child had died as a result of being bewitched by Ozunga and that he, Semukwa, had been informed of this fact by a local witch doctor whom he had consulted immediately after the child's death. He told the chief that Ozunga was at that time in his, Semukwa's, hut, but he didn't mention what condition he had left him in. The chief went to have a look,

373

stood around doing nothing, except to notice that the man was still alive and could talk. The village chief decided it was too much for him to deal with so he told people around to untie the old man and carry him to the sub-county chief, which the onlookers refused to do.

After much discussion, the village chief walked 2 miles and reported to the sub-county chief, who ordered him to bring the victim to his office. Back he walked and after much more heated discussion they agreed to carry him there. Meanwhile, absolutely no treatment, not even a drink of water, had been given to the old man. On arrival at the sub-county chief's HQ that chief merely told them to take him to the hospital at either Hoima or Masindi, both many miles away. There was no transport available, as the chief well knew, so they sat around having another long discussion until one of the men came and spoiled it for them by reporting that the old man, left lying on the verandah without any treatment or assistance, had died.

The child's internal organs were sent to the Government Analyst in Kampala and his report merely said that there was no sign of poison. Since the case had nothing to do with poison, his report was unhelpful and I ignored it as irrelevant. The PM report said the child died from measles and the old man died from a ruptured spleen and considerable internal bleeding. I took into account that the two accused were apparently genuinely convinced that Ozunga had bewitched the child, that they had reported soon afterwards to the chief and there was some doubt about an intent to kill, so they were convicted of manslaughter and I gave them six years each to ponder on it.

Saturday 27 April

I arrived back from the Bunyoro circuit just in time for a judges meeting this morning. All the usual complaints were trotted out, mainly about money, or lack of it. Then our bright judge from academe produced the brilliant suggestion that, like the ministers, we should all be given military ranks and uniforms and issued with pistols to carry around with us. There followed an animated discussion, more than half serious, about what would be a suitable senior rank for judges, and they decided that we should all be brigadiers and the CJ a major-general. I had taken no part in this idiocy until then, so I interrupted and pointed out that the Judiciary is a civil institution with its own controlling laws. If it was turned into a military organisation it would be subject to military law and become involved in Amin's military tribunals and courts martial and very liable to unpleasant interference from his Sudanese Military Police and other nasty types. Was that what they really wanted in return for wearing some badges on a uniform?

I added that none of them knew anything about firearms and that guns in the hands of amateurs are very dangerous weapons to everyone around, including themselves.

'Well, you could train us,' said our keen militarist.

'Oh no, I couldn't,' I replied, 'because I won't be staying around here if you accept this idea and put it forward to the President. I have served in the best army in the world and I've no intention of now serving in the worst.'

After a silence they came to their senses and decided to drop the idea and, as it was my turn to keep the so-called 'confidential' minutes, which would certainly be seen and passed on by one of our resident SRB types, I decided it would be wise not to include any mention of it in them. It should never have been discussed.

Saturday 11 May

Christopher called in this afternoon. He had worked for me back in 1962 as a schoolboy earning his school fees. He was looking very shaken and upset. He said he'd travelled by taxi from Entebbe and on the way they were stopped at a military roadblock and told to get out of the taxi. Just at that moment there was a disturbance as a car stopped, followed by another one. Out of the second car jumped the dreaded Lieutenant-Colonel Malyamungu,* one of Amin's most feared psychopathic killers. He was in uniform and Christopher recognised him as he'd seen him before.

Malyamungu ordered the soldiers to take the people out of the car he'd been following. There were five young men in it. They were told to lie face down on the grass at the side of the road. Malyamungu then took out his pistol and, without a word, shot each man in the back of the head as he lay there. He then said to the soldiers: 'Get rid of them,' and jumped back into his car and drove off. Everyone else had run off and Christopher and the other passengers quickly got into their taxi and the driver drove away as fast as he could. Nobody tried to stop them.

Saturday 25 May

My cook frequently greets me after work or on arrival after a long and dusty safari with a recital of the latest household disasters. He never seems to be short of a calamity to announce and it's always done with polite smiles and much laughter. It might be that there is no electricity or no water, sometimes both, or perhaps the *shamba* (garden) boy

*His name means 'Wealth of God'.

375

has left suddenly without finding a replacement, or the chickens have died of some sudden plague, or there's no food because he forgot to ask me to leave some money for shopping. Whatever it is, he clearly enjoys the role of harbinger of doom and he makes the most of each dramatic incident, harbingering away the more gleefully the worse the misfortune and always ignoring the fact that gloom-laden tidings are not welcome. It's no wonder that in ancient times bearers of bad tidings were often executed. I sometimes feel like despatching the cook with a quick left and right after receipt of the latest bulletin.

Yesterday evening he nearly succeeded in despatching me. He said he'd heard me remark that I liked curry and so he had put some curry powder into the meat and gravy prepared for the evening meal. As usual I was reading while I ate, and shovelling it in without paying much attention. But very soon I was gasping for breath and my throat felt raw and burning. I swallowed a couple of glasses of cold water in an attempt to quench the conflagration.

Staggering into the kitchen, I croaked: 'What did you put into the food? Show me the curry powder packet.' He produced an empty packet which was clearly marked: WHITE PEPPER.

I asked how much he had put in and he replied: 'All of it.' If I'd had a fire extinguisher handy I'd have used the contents on myself first and then beaten his brains out with the container.

Monday 10 June

I gave judgment today in several criminal appeals from convictions by the Kampala magistrates. In one case a man called Kakuba had been heavily fined on a charge of corruption of a police officer. The allegation was that he had offered a bribe of 10 shillings (a ludicrously small amount) to a constable to excuse him from prosecution for various petty traffic offences.

The prosecution case was that three constables in a patrol car claimed they suspected him of undefined offences and followed his car and stopped it and arrested him for petty offences (for which there is no power of arrest) and then brought him to CPS and sat outside in the station compound instead of going inside. They went through the motions of writing down particulars and it was then that they said Kakuba offered the pitifully small bribe.

In his defence Kakuba said he had been pulled from his car and beaten by the constables who accused him of traffic offences. While this beating was taking place his wallet fell out of his pocket and one of the constables picked it up and kept it. They then put him into the boot of the patrol car and took him to the station, where he was allowed to get out of the boot and he demanded his money back. The constables replied that he had given it to them as a bribe to release him, which he denied.

The trial magistrate accepted the constables' version as he said he could not believe that 'responsible policemen' would beat a motorist, put him in the boot of their car and drive him to the station in daylight 'where their bosses would see them'.

The appellant's advocate, himself a former senior police officer (and ex-Law School) submitted that the magistrate's assumption that all policemen were responsible was alarming in these days and that he must be living in a world of his own if he was unaware of the fact that some police officers had been convicted of taking bribes. Furthermore, it was a notorious fact that people had been carried off in car boots by various officials, including some irresponsible police officers, and nothing was done to those carrying out these terrible acts. This was true and I repeated it in my judgment. It was also a brave statement for an advocate to make in open court these days with someone usually around listening to what was being said.

In my judgment I expressed surprise that the magistrate was so impressed with what he called 'the indisputable truthfulness' of the three constables in court. I pointed out a number of inconsistencies where they disagreed with each other on most of the important facts in the case. They failed to produce the alleged bribe money in court and the magistrate failed to ask for it, nor did he refer to it. Altogether it was unsatisfactory and there were unresolved doubts, so I allowed the appeal.

Friday 21 June

Amin's ban on miniskirts and shorts two years ago is still in force and he has now added a ban on the wearing of wigs and long trousers by women; though women serving in the Army, Police and Prisons Service are allowed to wear long trousers. This is a result of the black American leader of the Congress of Racial Equality (CORE, which is not about equality at all), Roy Innis, who has been getting at Amin again, unfortunately. This time he has persuaded Amin that all such wigs are made from the hair taken from black American soldiers killed in the Vietnam War. Of course, Amin believes anything of this sort that he's told by someone like Innis, hence the ban. However, court wigs worn by barristers are permitted. Amin has also banned the use by women of facial make-up, including the very popular and much used skin colour lighteners. A rather difficult law to enforce, I suspect.

A piece of extra bad news is that the dreadful Ali Towelli has been forgiven and reinstated in his senior police job by Amin, who evidently finds he can't do without the fellow's murderous operations.

Tuesday 25 June

Foreign newspaper and magazine reports, editorials and articles have become increasingly critical of Amin and his military regime, and Amin continues to blame their respective governments for failing to control them. He just cannot believe that journalists anywhere can be independent and uncontrolled by governments. He has now issued a ban on all foreign newspapers and journals, which is not at all popular. Many people buy Kenyan newspapers in the street to find out what's going on in Uganda; now even these are banned. I subscribe to various British magazines and am continuing to receive them and renew my subscriptions regardless. I've merely asked the suppliers to enclose the magazines in brown envelopes so that they can't be identified.

Sadly, it seems to be the end of the Police *Habari*. The editorial in the June issue, the only one to come out this year, explains that earlier issues were not possible as no contributions were received. There has been a considerable loss of interest and drop in sales, and spiralling inflation has increased printing costs beyond what could be afforded.

Another probable cause is the tremendous fall in morale in the Force since Towelli and his murder squads have taken to killing off the British-trained police officers with long service, presumably with Amin's agreement. This, together with a huge fall in recruitment standards, in order to bring in many illiterate West Nilers, Nubians and Moslems, some of whom have criminal records, has resulted in little interest being shown in the Force magazine and a reluctance to report on station goings-on in case such reports are misinterpreted and result in unpleasant reaction.

At the bottom of the last page of the June issue of *Habari* in capital letters is printed: THE END OF POLICE HABARI. For me this is a particularly sad message after 19 years of association with the magazine and my many contributions to issues over the years. I can only hope that sometime in the future, after Amin's regime is over, someone will take steps to revive this useful, entertaining and morale-boosting periodical.

Friday 5 July

The East African Court of Appeal is based in Nairobi and it visits each territory: Kenya, Uganda and Tanzania, three or four times a year, hearing civil and criminal appeals from the decisions of the various High Courts. The Court has just been here for two weeks and the Court President, Sir William Duffus, has announced that it is his last visit as he is retiring in September. They concluded their hearings yesterday and in the evening Sir William gave his farewell dinner to the Uganda judges at the Kampala International Hotel.

When I arrived there I couldn't find which room in the large building had been allocated to the party. The usual notice-board was not visible and the receptionist to whom I spoke could not be bothered to help. So, feeling rather fed up, I strolled around in the large foyer, seeing nobody I knew and wondering if I had perhaps got the date wrong. Then I met a European woman similarly wandering about looking as if she was searching for something or someone. She looked lost and harassed so I approached her and, with my usual marvellous tact, asked: 'Are you looking for this awful dinner party too?'

She replied: 'No, actually I'm Lady Duffus, the hostess. I'm just looking out for the guests to show them where to go.' Oh dear.

Tuesday 16 July

At the end of June I was obliged to sack my cook finally. I had, in fact, dismissed him on several previous occasions but he had refused to go or he had unilaterally reinstated himself and I had feebly let him do so. This time, however, he had gone too far, no doubt taking advantage of my apparent reluctance to let him go. I could not overlook a theft that was more than just exercising a perk and, after some unpleasantness, he left. It was most inconvenient as I go on leave tomorrow, but I've just managed to find a replacement in sufficient time to install him to look after my house and property in my absence. I hope.

Two nights ago I was awakened by a faint noise in the sitting-room, which I assumed was my cat knocking picture frames off the bookcases on one of its periodic furniture-hopping circuits of the room chasing house lizards or moths or whatever. Yesterday morning I discovered my mistake. A thief had entered the house and taken a selection of my property. I suspected my ex-cook because entrance was by the kitchen window, which he knew to be insecure and easy to force, though it doesn't look it from outside. Also all the items taken were carefully chosen by someone who knew exactly where to look for them without making the usual thief's messy search. Most were electrical goods, such as the kettle, iron, radio, record player and so on, each in a different place yet taken without any disturbance to other items.

Most of all I was concerned about my brief-case, which had my

379

passport and air ticket and keys in it. However, on the floor below the kitchen window which had been forced open, I found the passport and air ticket placed neatly together against the wall. The thief (my ex-cook?) evidently decided not to delay my departure and left me this consolation prize. I doubt whether an ordinary thief would have done that. Police from Jinja Road station came and bumbled about and later declared that they'd found my former cook's fingerprints everywhere, which was hardly surprising since he'd worked here for years. But there's no sign of my missing property, so I'm going on leave with an increased shopping list.

Thursday 18 July

Using the new international airport for the first time, I joined the line of departing first-class passengers at the desk of the passport officer, forgetting that as I'm now a judge I'm entitled to use the VIP lounge. In front of me were four Europeans, apparently business executives from Kenya. As each of them reached the passport officer he was asked how long he had spent in Uganda and the answers came: 'two days', 'three days', 'two days', and 'four days'. Then it was my turn and I handed my passport over and the official, without looking up, asked: 'How long have you spent in Uganda?'

I replied: 'Nineteen years, three months, two weeks and three days.'

He looked up startled and then seeing who I was, said with a gleaming smile: 'Ah, you are very welcome. Thanks for your work and come back soon please.'

Friday 11 October – In England

Yesterday was general election day here and the awful Wilson has got back in again, this time with the huge majority of three. Amin always keeps his beady eyes on what's going on in the UK and is never backward in offering his useful advice to other heads of government. He has sent a telegram to Wilson, which was featured prominently in the newspapers today. After congratulations he added:

I call upon you to seriously consider granting freedom and full independence to Scotland, Wales and Northern Ireland, whose people have repeatedly demanded and have demonstrated at elections their respective eagerness and wishes to become independent of London. Each of these countries should be permitted not only autonomous self-government but full sovereign independence with their own flags and thus limiting the Union Jack to England only.

What nonsense. Surely, if there's no longer a union there would be no need or justification for a union flag? However, I have much more serious matters to consider. This morning I was in town standing on the pavement edge trying to remember the location of a certain shop when my arm was seized by a lollipop lady and I was hustled across the road. 'There you are, dear,' she said, and bustled away to interfere with someone else.

What does it mean? I thought their job was to help children and old folk across the road, using their circular STOP sign on a stick. Perhaps she thought I looked so old and decrepit that, like a small child, I needed assistance to cross the road. On the other hand, I didn't want to cross the road. The shop I was looking for was now on the other side. So why did I feel guilty as I waited for her to move out of sight before I sneaked back across the road?

Friday 18 October

I'm back from leave, and what a flight. I shall never travel by Air France again. I had a doubly confirmed first-class seat on their flight from Heathrow to Entebbe and Nairobi yet, when I checked in, the woman behind the counter said that the flight was full as far as Athens and there was no seat for me, not even in the tourist section. Totally unhelpful. I went across to BOAC and they quickly put me on their flight to Athens which was about to leave, an hour before the Air France departure time. Then back to the Air France counter and, very reluctantly, they agreed I could catch their flight from Athens to Entebbe provided I signed away my right to a first-class seat and if their people in Athens agreed when I arrived. Having no choice at this stage, I flew comfortably to Athens by BOAC, where I had to walk across the broad tarmac landing ground lugging my two very heavy suitcases and my cabin bag and raincoat. Unfortunately there was nobody to assist and no trolley for the luggage. It was a very hot night and the other departure hall was a long walk. Halfway across I was stopped by a large plain-clothes Greek security type, with a shoulder holster bulge in his ill-fitting suit. He said that he must search my suitcases for bombs. So I had to put them down on the tarmac in the dark and he opened and searched them, leaving me to repack them. Fortunately, I had forgotten to pack any bombs, but I was pouring with sweat by the time I had finished repacking and had staggered across the rest of the runway. In the second terminal Air France said '*non*' to my first-class ticket and I found myself stuck in the smoking section of tourist class, choking over the dense fumes from French passengers determinedly smoking themselves into an early grave. Never again, *mes amis, au grand jamais*!

Thursday 31 October

The news on the radio and also on the TV, for the comparatively few who have a set, is of the fight last night in Kinshasa, Zaire, between Muhammad Ali and George Foreman in which Ali regained the world heavyweight boxing title from the holder. What an odd place to hold it. I hear the 'organisation' has been shambolic.

Friday 8 November

Luke Ofungi has resigned as IG of Police. He didn't last long, with the dreadful Towelli constantly objecting to his decisions and openly countermanding his orders. In addition, Luke protested strongly to Amin about recent killings of Acholi and Langi police officers ordered by Amin and carried out under Towelli's direction, and said that he could no longer carry out his duties in the present situation. It's a great pity as the Force needs a leader like him but, on the other hand, it would clearly be most unsafe for him to try to continue. In a clash between him and Towelli Amin would almost certainly support the latter, just as he has now, in fact.

Tuesday 26 November

Due largely to the efforts of Towelli, the Police Force has become incompetent, inefficient, disorganised and with morale at rock bottom. Most of those with proper training and experience have been removed; either killed, retired or fled the country. Police prosecutors and the CID are not producing the necessary evidence or conducting their cases in court competently. Even with a reasonable amount of evidence available, incapable prosecutors are making such a mess of their cases that a much greater number than normal of guilty persons manage to escape punishment.

The ordinary members of the public, seeing what is happening, have come to the conclusion that there's no longer much point in taking offenders to the police and the courts when, in so many cases, they are quickly set at liberty again for lack of evidence, and then come looking for those who reported them. Consequently many people have taken the law into their own hands and, even more than before, the long-established African custom of thief-beating has increased enormously. Civilians and soldiers openly deal promptly and summarily on the spot with those caught stealing or merely suspected or accused of it. A number of grudges are also settled in this way since it's very easy to summon a crowd of eager thief-beaters by making an alarm and making an angry or righteous false accusation.

The courts have been acquitting many accused persons for lack of evidence and releasing others on bail to await trial. Most people, especially the ignorant soldiers, cannot understand this and they blame the judges and magistrates and have complained to Amin demanding action 'to stop the courts from releasing known criminals'; which means all accused persons as far as they're concerned. Amin, ever eager to please and satisfy his troops, summoned the Chief Justice and the Minister of Justice and called a press conference, without first making a few enquiries to obtain some facts. Surrounded by the Defence Council, he proceeded to harangue the CJ and Minister.

The *Voice of Uganda* reported that Amin said he had received many complaints from soldiers and public all over the country that some judges and magistrates were receiving bribes to release criminals and he warned that 'no judge or magistrate should behave as a God and think he is indispensable because the Military Government could not kneel down before anyone and would dismiss anyone who was corrupt and against Government policy'. He declared that 'the Government has a big file about judges and magistrates who have imposed improper fines or sentences on offenders'. He alleged that those who awarded lenient punishments were 'siding with the *kondos* (armed robbers) and smugglers'. He then went on to give two examples, which turned out to be the real reason for this outburst. The first was irrelevant with regard to the complaints of the public as, so Amin thought, it involved a criticism of him and his government. In fact he had completely misunderstood the words used by a chief magistrate, which were also misreported in a newspaper. Again there had been no checking or enquiry first before venting his fury on the luckless magistrate, whom he had suspended.

Amin's second example was said to be the case of a corrupt former district commissioner in Masaka who was arrested collecting money illegally from the people, he said and added: 'Even the Provincial Governor knew well that the man had stolen the money but, when he was taken to court with all the necessary evidence, he was released by a corrupt judge.' That meant me, since I was the judge who released him. But Amin had all the facts wrong.

The Minister of Justice then spoke and, instead of standing up for the Judiciary and trying to explain how things worked, the miserable creature sycophantically told the President that the Judiciary wanted more help from members of the security forces to track down judges and magistrates who were corrupt. What nonsense. The Judiciary certainly does not want any interference from the ignorant and dangerous security forces. The fool then went on and said he 'will keep an open eye on bad elements and remove them at once when they are found out'. He then obsequiously assured the President that 'with more help from the security forces the Judiciary will improve'.

The newspaper report said that the CJ spoke briefly, saying that if the Judiciary was corrupt, judges and magistrates could not command respect, and he promised that they were determined to handle the issue and deal with the culprits and he would welcome any help in tracking down the culprits. Again no attempt to defend the Judiciary or explain the reasons for the releases. The weakness and feebleness of the statements by the CJ and the Minister was very disappointing and most unhelpful to everyone concerned.

I was particularly annoyed about being accused of being corrupt because of allowing the appeal from conviction of the ex-district commissioner, which had received considerable publicity, so many people know that I'm the judge referred to. The DC, Wanyama, had been accused of demanding a bribe from a Moslem trader in Masaka so that he could be appointed the local agent for a government-controlled textile company. The police made a nonsense of their trap to observe the handover of the money as they hid where they couldn't see or hear anything of what went on. The whole case smelt fishy to me, although the magistrate had convicted Wanyama in spite of the inconsistencies and doubts raised in the prosecution evidence. For instance, the shifty-looking trader had placed the marked money under the blotting pad on the DC's desk on the side where he, the trader, was sitting, and that was where the police found it. If the DC had received it, as the trader alleged, he surely would have put it under his own side of the large blotter. He would hardly go round his desk and hide it where he couldn't get at it and where someone else was sitting. Furthermore, the DC denied ever seeing the money, let alone receiving it, and there was no evidence of this apart from the trader's word. The police observers were supposed to supply that evidence but they hadn't placed themselves properly for this purpose, through sheer incompetence. So I threw the case out and released the DC on appeal.

This evening my contact dropped in and, when I mentioned my annoyance at the matter, he told me what was behind the case. Apparently the military governor of the Province had quarrelled with Wanyama, the DC Masaka, over some official business in which the governor was illegally involved for his financial benefit and he'd threatened to 'fix' the DC and this frame-up was the result. So it was as fishy as I had suspected. My decision and the publicity that it was given annoyed the governor so much that he went to the President and told him that the judge who had released Wanyama was corrupt. Amin usually believes what his army officers tell him, and it coincided with the other complaints against the courts, so there followed the attack on the Judiciary.

Thursday 28 November

The courts are generally supplied with two Bibles for swearing in witnesses, a Protestant and a Catholic version. I think the missionaries originally insisted on this – I can't imagine anyone else being so pedantic and divisive. Many of the magistrates courts are without a Koran for the Moslem witnesses. Consequently they are treated in the same way as pagans and atheists and simply affirm that they will speak the truth; with the right hand held up while making the affirmation. This has prompted one indignant Moslem to write in complaint to the editor of the *Voice of Uganda*. The letter appeared in today's issue, protesting that the courts are discriminating against Moslems because Christians are given their Bible to swear on whereas 'we Moslems are made to swear in the air'.

Friday 29 November

One of the many consequences of throwing the Asian businessmen out of Uganda has been that those persons with outstanding claims filed in court against Asians or their businesses are now unable to obtain satisfaction. Even if they could obtain a judgment in their favour, or if they already have one, it can't be executed since the Asian no longer has assets in the country. Most business names have been changed, usually to be appropriate to Amin's Economic War, and some premises are being used for quite different purposes, making it difficult to trace the former business. In any case the new owners are not liable for the debts and actions of the former Asian owners.

Last December Amin signed a Decree establishing a special tribunal with exclusive jurisdiction to deal with all claims still pending for the recovery of a debt owed by a departed Asian; thus removing this jurisdiction from our courts. But this tribunal has still not been set up and there is also no provision for dealing with the large number of claims already filed and pending in our courts. There is no mention of such cases in the decree. A firm of advocates with a pile of such files recently brought one before me as a test case in order to obtain a ruling.

Kazibwe was injured while working in an Asian-owned factory in 1971 and his advocate filed a claim for injury compensation in the High Court. This claim and the company's defence to it had both been filed by Asian advocates who had left Uganda, so Kazibwe was the only one involved left. Earlier this year Kazibwe went to his present Ugandan advocate requesting assistance. An advocate for the State-owned National Insurance Corporation, the insurers of the former Asian company, also appeared and asked for the same ruling as they have a number of similar claims pending.

There's no easy answer because whoever drafted the Decree didn't think it out first in order to cover all likely possibilities. It was absurd to take away the court's jurisdiction without immediately establishing the tribunal as it leaves all such cases floating, which might then be affected by the Limitation Act. I said it appeared that Kazibwe would have to withdraw his suit against the former Asian company in this court and file his claim before the tribunal if and when it came into being. He might also try applying for an order of *mandamus* in the High Court to require the relevant Minister to appoint the tribunal. But I was not happy with this decision and very much regretted that I couldn't offer a better solution in the circumstances.

However, it seemed to provoke a little reaction as the Decree has now been amended to abolish the useless and non-existent tribunal and restore the jurisdiction to the courts. But it still doesn't solve the problem of collecting damages or debts from departed Asians or their defunct companies. Probably the only reasonable solution would be for the government to pay the amounts due; but it's most unlikely since it hasn't yet paid any of the promised compensation to former owners for property and businesses seized from them. Nor is it ever likely to do so.

Tuesday 3 December

Child witnesses in court often provide some amusement as well as problems. With small children it's not practicable to put them into the wooden-panelled witness box since they simply disappear from sight. I usually have them up to stand beside me so that I can talk to them and ask questions in a normal tone of voice in order not to alarm them. In fact, small children often seem more confident and less inhibited in court than many adult witnesses.

Today I asked one little girl how old she was. She smiled sweetly and replied: 'I am six; how old are you?' Her testimony was quite clear and useful and she didn't appear at all nervous. At one point I was writing down her answer when I heard titters coming from the public seats. On looking up I saw that she had sidled right up alongside me and was peering over my arm at what I was writing. The advocate who had been taking her through her evidence remarked that she was probably checking to see whether I had recorded her evidence accurately.

Sunday 8 December

Earlier this year 200 British soldiers belonging to 38 Field Regiment, Royal Engineers, went to the southern Sudan as part of a British aid project to reconstruct a bridge over the River Tonj. This would replace a pre-war bridge which had become very unsafe. Working in the blazing sun for six days a week, these Sappers completed the project in three months and provided the area with a free stone and steel bridge which was built to last 50 years. It was opened by Sudanese Vice-President Abel Alier at a ceremony in which he said that it was one of the few times in history that armies of sovereign states had worked side by side for peace and progress.

At the prompting of his Russian advisers, Amin has just received a delegation from southern Sudan consisting of members of the Umma-Communist alliance, who are opposed to Sudanese President Nimeiri, whom Amin has been persuaded to regard as an enemy of 'Revolutionary Africa'. These people told Amin that the British Army had entered the Sudan 'in their hundreds' disguised as engineers who, in fact, were there to help exterminate revolutionaries like themselves. They added that Nimeiri has also selected and appointed to his government and army some former *Anyanya* members (southern rebels) with the object, they alleged, of deceiving northern Moslems into believing that Nimeiri also has southern support. They also claimed that Nimeiri was using former *Anyanya* as his bodyguards. For that matter Amin, too, has recruited many former *Anyanya* into the Uganda Army after the rebellion in southern Sudan ended in an settlement. He believes them to be more loyal to him, and thus more reliable, than the majority of Ugandans in the army. It's the loyalty of mercenaries to their paymaster. The military police, who are known for their malevolence and brutality, are nearly all Sudanese.

Amin usually refers to such goodwill visits by the British Army units to the Sudan and Kenya as being preparations for a invasion of Uganda. He frequently uses these imaginary threats when railing against the British generally and when he feels the need to divert the attention of the population and the dissenting groups within his army from the miseries and general unpleasantness of life in Uganda, with its failed economy and its incompetent, ignorant and greedy military government.

Friday 13 December

I've been on circuit to Mbale all week, dealing with several murder cases that were left over from a previous sessions. In yesterday's case the accused was alleged to have killed his aunt because he thought that she had been bewitching his mother. He said that he was speaking to his aunt when something just came over him and he could not remember what happened or how he came to kill her. The defence advocate told the court that the defence was one of automatism; that the accused had acted while in a state of unconsciousness and so he was unable to control his movements or be aware of what he was doing. To support this the advocate declared that he would be calling medical evidence to the effect that the accused was suffering from 'motor cycle epilepsy'.

I've never come across this one before and I was looking forward to hearing about it. It sounded like some sort of traffic madness; a fit of the Hondas, perhaps. In fact, rather disappointingly, it turned out to be psychomotor epilepsy.

Wednesday 18 December

At Amin's request Gaddafi has been sending some Libyan doctors to assist in our very short-staffed hospitals. Unfortunately they do not seem to be really qualified; more like paramedics or even just first-aiders, and often without much English. They don't stay long; a year is about all that even they can stand of conditions here.

In an Mbale murder case today the Libyan medical officer who had gone through the motions of performing a post-mortem examination of the victim had left the country several months before and the written PM report was, as usual in these cases, put in by consent. The cause of death was shown on it as 'Sub dwal haen wrihge' which looked rather odd at first. But by now I've got used to deciphering their peculiar medical reports and so read it as 'subdural haemorrhage'.

In the same case an English-speaking witness being sworn in said: 'I solomonly swear...' which the pedantic court clerk could not accept and he tried several times unsuccessfully to get the witness to say 'solemnly'. After three more 'solomonlies' I told the clerk to leave it as he was near enough and it didn't really matter. The clerk looked shocked.

I had a problem with this same clerk when he was interpreting in a rape case before me earlier in the sessions. He is one of the *Balokole* (Born Again Christians) and very strait-laced, which doesn't help when translating the sort of intimate questions that have to be asked of the woman complainant and the medical examiner in rape cases.

He actually stood up in court and protested to me about the need for such questions and declared that they were improper and immoral and he therefore couldn't bring himself to translate them. I had to adjourn and ask the chief magistrate for another interpreter.

Friday 20 December

I finished the Mbale sessions with the final judgment delivered this morning in a case in which a woman was charged with murdering her husband. He was a violent drunkard who had constantly assaulted and brutalised her over a long period until, during a particularly vicious beating with a thick stick, she had summoned the strength to push her cooking knife into him. In the circumstances I reduced the offence to manslaughter and, since she had been in the *chokey* awaiting trial for about eight months, sentenced her to be imprisoned for one day. This in effect meant that she stayed in custody at the court and was then released when the court rose for the day, which in this instance meant at lunch-time since that was the last case in the sessions. I had then been hoping to slip back quickly to Kampala. However, I was caught by the Chief Magistrate, who is a member of the local branch of the Lions Club, and invited to their monthly lunch at the hotel today. The members these days are all African businessmen and professionals dressed in smart suits and ties.

The only other European there turned out to be a visiting fireman, an ancient bishop who had served in Uganda many years ago and was on a short visit to see old acquaintances. He was their guest of honour and extremely doddery and for some reason I was seated next to him, although we had never met and I had nothing to talk to him about. I usually avoid priests.

He stood up to make a speech in answer to one welcoming him and told a long, rambling and boring story of long ago when he was in Uganda. I didn't pay much attention until he came to his concluding sentence which was: 'Well, I thought the chap did very well – for an African, that is, of course.' He then sat down beaming around him and obviously expecting wild applause or laughter or something. Instead everyone looked highly embarrassed and bemused and there was only a brief scattered clapping and clearing of throats. I was so embarrassed and annoyed by the old fool's glaring *faux pas* that I just wanted to disappear under the table. Who on earth did he think he was talking to?

1975

Sunday 5 January

Late yesterday evening I was at home writing some letters when I was startled to hear a rifle shot outside my window. As it was very dark I decided to make a cautious enquiry first before going out to investigate, in case the police sentry was feeling trigger-happy. I called from the window and he replied that it was all right, he had made a mistake. So I went to inspect his mistake.

He had been sitting on a chair in the garage beside my Mercedes Benz official car. He sheepishly explained that he had accidentally pulled the trigger. In answer to my questions he admitted he'd earlier put a bullet 'up the spout' and then left the safety catch off. He had sat on the chair holding his rifle across his lap and soon fell asleep with his finger on the trigger guard. In the course of his sleep he had slipped or his finger had twitched and pulled the trigger. There's no proper weapon training nowadays. I searched around the garage with my torch and soon found that the bullet had passed right through the boot of my car, cutting the wiring of the rear lights but fortunately just missing the petrol tank. I gave the constable a severe ticking-off for his carelessness as a sentry and for the mishandling of his firearm and pointed out to him that he was lucky not to have shot himself or been slightly immolated by an exploding petrol tank. Wilson, my driver, went spare this morning when he came in to drive me to court.

Wednesday 15 January

It's now four years since Amin took over and, during this time, the Army has taken control not only of the government and administration, but also of most of the economic structure of Uganda. And what a mess they've made of it all. The one branch of government that they've had no success in penetrating and taking over is the Judiciary. Here their influence is very small and this clearly annoys them. They do so wish to interfere with the courts and so make sure that we lock up all those whom they want put inside.

This evening my contact dropped in to see me, after phoning first so that I could warn the police sentry to let him in. He said he had a rather important matter to discuss with me. He'd been asked by Amin and the Defence Council to obtain my unofficial reaction to a suggestion that they were considering for implementation.

Their proposed scheme is to appoint one air force and two army officers, all captains, to be High Court judges and thus ensure, so they hoped, that they had an effective say in the running of the courts to the satisfaction of the military. I asked if the officers selected were legally qualified and the answer, of course, was no. They had chosen three officers who had attended, but not completed, secondary schools and spoke some English; which they considered to be a sufficient qualification. I was horrified at the idea and said so. He's well aware of how strongly I feel about maintaining high standards and the independence of the Judiciary and I added that it would be a great mistake to do this. Most of the judges would probably resign rather than try to work with such impossible colleagues whose whole outlook and standards would be so very different.

No doubt it would be followed by more such appointments of lower ranks as magistrates and it would be the same as when they were made chiefs: utter chaos and unpleasantness for all concerned. It would mean the disintegration of the Judiciary, which would be a great loss to the people of Uganda. I pointed out that we still had a good working judiciary and it was pointless to destroy it in this way. I certainly would not want to be part of such a set-up and no doubt many of my colleagues would feel the same way.

I mentioned that such a move would not be received at all favourably by the outside world and it would certainly result in bad publicity for Amin. Not that I cared a fig about that, but I wanted to provide him with some convincing arguments to take back. I asked him to try to persuade Amin to drop the idea as unworkable. It sounded to me as if there existed some doubt there already, otherwise it would, as usual, just have been announced on the radio as having happened, without this unusual consultation.

Tuesday 21 January

My contact called in this evening and brought me the news that Amin had dropped the plan to infiltrate the Judiciary with his military officers. A slight victory. However, he has moved to Plan B. An earlier Decree gave military tribunals power to try offences against the State, such as treason, for which the penalty is death by firing squad. Now he has produced the Economic Crimes Tribunal, which is also a military tribunal. Its purpose is to try 'certain crimes damaging the economy' which, so Amin claims, cannot properly or effectively be dealt with by the ordinary courts. So hoarding, overcharging, embezzlement, smuggling, corruption, thefts by clerks and other government servants, business officials and agents, foreign currency offences and even the banned hunting of elephants have all been included. All these have been removed from the jurisdiction of our courts, which now cannot even remand such accused persons nor release them on bail. People are just slung into prison and left to await the arrival of a tribunal in that area. It could be quite a long wait as they don't sit very often. Each tribunal has a lieutenant-colonel or major as chairman and a grade I magistrate as legal adviser, to whom they pay no attention. He is not a member of the tribunal and is required only to advise on law and procedure. There are some very odd characters on these tribunals who tend to call themselves by eccentric names like Captain No Parking and Captain Kill Me Quick. There is provision for a Military Appeals Tribunal for appeals against their arbitrary decisions, but it has not yet been set up. It's just a paper court.

Wednesday 5 February

There was another failed attempt to dispose of Amin last Saturday. He was in the last of three cars travelling together, having cunningly moved out of the centre car just before they started. They were ambushed after dark at Kibuye, just outside Kampala. Two cars were caught in heavy machine-gun fire, but the last was hardly touched. A bullet broke the side window and a piece of glass cut his upper left arm slightly, but he just drove off safely. The sheer incompetence of these attempts is breathtaking. It takes years of practice to be so useless. After each attempt Amin laughs and boasts that 'they' will never kill him. He often claims he knows when he is due to die – he and God only – and it isn't for a long time yet. Is there no justice? Maybe only spontaneous combustion will rid us of this man.

Monday 10 February

I drove to Masaka yesterday afternoon to start the western circuit, and opened criminal sessions here this morning. On the outskirts of town we passed the body of a man with his hands tied behind him lying partially in the road. I rang the OC Police on my arrival at the hotel and asked why it had not been collected, and he replied that it was an army *shauri* and they would not allow anyone to move it. It's raining hard and the temperature is down. In fact it's really chilly here on the equator. We even had large hailstones yesterday afternoon just after I arrived at the hotel. Another unusual event was that there were actually two guilty pleas to manslaughter today. This is very unusual in Masaka, where normally nobody admits anything and there has to be a trial gone through in each case.

Friday 21 February

All the murder cases and the one armed robbery case have been completed and yesterday I commenced the civil sessions with appeals first. There's no water in the hotel nor in the whole of Masaka. It's very awkward in the hotel. The staff bring in the odd bucket of water for washing, which I suppose they get from outside since it's been raining every day. The food is pretty awful, but that's normal in Uganda's hotels these days. Whenever the rain stops and the sun comes out, the roads start to shimmer and waver in the sudden intense heat and clouds of steam rise from the road surfaces as they rapidly dry off. Each change from cold rain to burning heat is quick and impressive.

Friday 7 March

I gave judgment in a civil appeal concerning a claim for damages by one Kakoza for the seduction and pregnancy of his 14-year-old daughter, Nantongo, by the headmaster of the primary school she attended. Such claims are for loss of the girl's services in the home, which, if not otherwise proved, are presumed to be the normal participation in household affairs and the performance of ordinary domestic duties. Since there was no allegation that a servant was employed and paid to replace Nantongo while she was pregnant, the loss of services could be taken as only nominal.

The sexual intercourse and subsequent pregnancy were not disputed but the headmaster maintained that it was his brother, Senyondo, a Makerere University undergraduate, who was the father. The headmaster agreed that he gave her gifts to help her during her pregnancy, but insisted that he did so on behalf of his brother. Kakoza testified that the headmaster had admitted to him responsibility for her pregnancy and the man's own witnesses did not support his allegation about his brother, whom he also failed to call as a witness at the trial. It was clear that the girl had in fact been the headmaster's mistress (or headmistress?) for quite a long time, since this was her second child by him, so it was not easy to believe that she was seduced against her will. The trial magistrate found the headmaster to be an unsatisfactory and untruthful witness and had given judgment against him.

Kakoza had asked for damages covering searching for Nantongo and caring for the child; but he gave no evidence of making any search. The magistrate allowed an amount for diminution of future bride-price, which would have been correct, except that Kakoza had failed to ask for it in the claim in his plaint, drawn up by his advocate; so I cancelled it, as you don't get what you don't ask for in civil matters. An amount had also been allowed for dishonour to Kakoza's family, but I found this negatived by Kakoza himself allowing the girl to continue at the school after learning of her first pregnancy (the headmaster

393

should have been prosecuted, of course). Clearly at the time there was no dispute between the parties; it came later.

As usual in these cases, a claim was made for the cost of the girl's education up to the time of her pregnancy. They always claim this and, as always, I found it unacceptable since the girl had had her education and it was not a loss to her or her father. I also reduced the amount of damages awarded on the ground that Kakoza was a negligent and imprudent parent.

Thursday 13 March

I finished Masaka sessions today and shall return to Kampala tomorrow and prepare for the Mbarara sessions, which will be next on this circuit. The last judgment that I delivered today at Masaka was in a running-down case, a claim for damages as a result of death or injury sustained. in a traffic accident. This was a good example of a false claim.

Even in genuine claims the injuries are usually exaggerated, sometimes to an absurd extent, and in some the claimant has never been injured at all and someone else's medical report is used; or perhaps the claimants are not the real relatives of the deceased victim. Questions of identity thus frequently arise and the lack of birth and marriage certificates in the majority of cases adds to the difficulty of trying to sort out the genuine from the fraudulent. It's not often easy to discover whether the children brought into court are really the children of the deceased as claimed and, from time to time, it becomes obvious for various reasons that they could not have been.

In today's case Kibirige had filed a claim on behalf of the estate of his deceased wife, whom he said was knocked down in a traffic accident and then had died later in hospital. However, the plaint on the court file was a claim by one Haji Sadi Baliirakumpapula, a Moslem, who claimed to have been married to the deceased, called Restituta Najjembe, a Catholic, which looked unlikely. So who was Kibirige? His advocate said that an amended plaint had been filed later, but there was no copy on my file. I asked him why a Christian had been substituted for a Moslem and he replied that the original plaintiff had had a power of attorney to file the case on behalf of Kibirige. I said it did not say this in the original plaint and, furthermore, it claimed he was the husband, not someone acting an his behalf. The advocate said it was a mistake.

Then there was the dead woman. The plaint and the police accident report showed her as Restituta but Kibirige denied this and said her name was Yowanina, not a name that could be written or mistaken for

Restituta. The dead woman's father, Ssonko, testified and I asked him for the correct name of his daughter and he said he had forgotten it! Her nephew was the next witness and he said he had never known his aunt's first name. Nor did he know the first name of her husband, his uncle, the present plaintiff. When I asked why he didn't know their names he replied that he was a Catholic and they were Protestants so he couldn't know their names. There seemed no end to this rubbish. It was like *Alice in Wonderland*.

I demanded evidence of marriage. Kibirige claimed they had been married in Kasozi Catholic Church, thus contradicting his own witness, who had said they were Protestants. But Ssonko, the father-in-law of Kibirige, denied that his daughter had ever married in a church. He insisted that it had been a customary marriage with the usual tribal ceremonies and payment of dowry. He added that his daughter had had two children, his grandchildren, but he didn't know their names. He could not explain this odd ignorance.

The plaintiff, Kibirige, said his wife had been looked after in hospital by her sister-in-law, whose name he didn't know, of course. He also referred to an eyewitness to the accident as Joseph, but the man himself said his name was Petero. The wife died as the result of a miscarriage a week after being admitted to hospital. There was no medical evidence that her death had anything to do with any traffic accident injuries. I declined to assess any damages in the case as I said I didn't believe any of the witnesses and considered the whole case to be an extremely incompetent fraud and a total waste of the court's time.

Monday 17 March

It's St Patrick's Day and 20 years ago exactly since I first set foot in Mombasa on my way to Uganda. A lot of interesting things have happened since then. I certainly don't regret coming out here to live and work.

However, the news on Radio Uganda this evening has spoiled my day. Amin has been promoted to the rank of Field Marshal 'by popular acclaim of his army' so we are told. Thus the boxing sergeant I met in 1956 has got his baton. That's what 19 years of incompetence, ignorance and viciousness can accomplish. His number two, the awful, illiterate lorry driver, Adrisi, has been promoted to full General.

Monday 24 March

I drove to Mbarara yesterday afternoon to open a fairly long and busy criminal sessions, which will last about a month, I expect. Before I went to court this morning the Deputy Chief Registrar rang to report that my house was broken into last night by forcing a front window. He's a sensible chap, a former Law School Bar student, and has already arranged for a day watchman in the house compound as well as getting on to the OC Jinja Road Police Station, whose police sentry had not reported for duty at my place last night. He has also arranged for the window to be repaired and tells me that the cook says that only the electric iron and my small radio are missing. I shan't return there until Thursday for the long Easter weekend, as there's too much to do here.

Wednesday 26 March

There was no court today as Amin declared a sudden public holiday and we're all supposed to spend the day mourning his paymaster, King Feisal of Saudi Arabia (who didn't like miniskirts), who was shot by an assassin yesterday.

Thursday 3 April

This morning I gave judgment in a criminal appeal in which three men, Police Constable Mubiru, Prison Warder Kagwa and a so-called military intelligence officer, who didn't appeal, were convicted by the local magistrate for the offences of theft, wrongful confinement and demanding money with menaces. The three planned together to relieve a civilian named Kasara of a large sum of money. During the incident the constable and the warder wore their uniforms as if on duty. The third 'intelligence officer' wore civilian clothes. They travelled in the warder's car, which he had obtained after it was abandoned by a departing Asian in 1972. When they reached Kasara's house just out-side Mbarara, they demanded a large sum of money in exchange for not putting him in the boot of the car and disposing of him. Kasara handed over 700 shillings, which was all he had in the house. They took it and said they'd be back for more on the next evening.

Kasara had recently bought a second-hand bed, which they told him was stolen and he must pay them 2,000 shillings or go to prison or possibly be shot by firing squad, so he handed over the money. Three days later they came back and demanded more money but he had none left and said so. He added that they might as well cut his throat and finish the matter. But they told him to get into the car. During the ride further demands for cash were made, but he said he had none. Kasara asked them to take him to the police station but they drove past it and stopped outside the military police barracks, where yet another demand was made, to save him from prison or death, they said. He repeated he couldn't pay and they could do what they wanted. When they saw that he was not going to produce any more money they stopped the car and let him get out. He went straight to the police station and reported the matter; something he should have done several days before.

For once, the case had been properly investigated and prosecuted and I dismissed their appeals against conviction and the concurrent terms of three years imprisonment on each count, and remarked that they had been treated too leniently, bearing in mind that they had abused the trust placed in them by the government and public.

Sunday 20 April

I finished the Mbarara sessions and returned to Kampala this weekend. My contact visited me this afternoon and told me what had been going on a few days ago only a few miles south of my court in Mbarara, on the Tanzanian border. A unit made up of Ugandan troops who were neither Nubian or Kakwa, from West Nile, was sent down to the border on the usual pretext that Tanzania was about to invade Uganda. The Nubians and Kakwa in the unit already down there killed all the newly arrived soldiers, using heavy machine-guns.

He also told me the sad news that a magistrate called Mawagi, a former Law School student, had been shot and killed outside Masaka after he had been heard complaining in public about military oppression in Uganda.

Thursday 24 April

When he was in Kigezi recently, Amin's attention had been drawn to the existence of the old British memorial there on a hill commemorating the first British administrative post established there in May 1909.*

In a speech made a couple of days ago Amin dutifully praised the PLO and reviled the wicked Zionists and asserted that the Uganda Army is ever ready and eager to go and fight alongside their Arab friends in the cause of returning the Holy Land to them. This time he hit the headlines with his announcement that not only must Israel be wiped out, but also that Hitler definitely had the right idea about burning the Jews. Amin added that he greatly admired Adolf Hitler, most especially because he had killed over 6 million Jews; but, in Amin's opinion, he ought to have finished off the job. Amin said he now proposes to remove the British memorial in Kigezi and build on the

*See entry for 20 June 1959.

same site a large and fitting memorial to Hitler 'in recognition of his praiseworthy efforts to solve the Jewish problem'.

Amin loves making these startling announcements so as to make sure his name appears frequently in the headlines of the international press. In addition, he no doubt feels that this particular effort will convince his Arab friends of his continued rabid anti-Zionism. However, as usual he spoke first before considering the significance and possible consequences of his words. He overlooked, or was ignorant of, the fact that his other 'best friends', the Russians, had suffered very great losses in their Great Patriotic War, as they call their part in the Second World War, against Hitler's Germany and that, consequently, the Russians have absolutely no liking or admiration for Hitler and what he did.

Since the Russians are supplying Amin with most of his weaponry and providing training assistance, they are in a strong position to influence him and exert pressure on him when they feel it necessary. I hear that, after Amin's speech in praise of Hitler, the Russian Ambassador called on him and made it very clear just what the Kremlin thought of Amin's latest 'brilliant' idea. So the great Hitler memorial idea has been dropped quicker than a hot plate and I doubt whether Amin will make any further mention of Hitler in his future speeches. In one of Amin's favourite expressions nowadays: he is a 'gone case'.

Wednesday 23 April

One of the many disastrous results of Amin's Economic War has been the disappearance of even basic commodities from the shops and the consequent development of a thriving black market. The closing down of very many shops once they couldn't be restocked has very considerably reduced the sources of supply to the ordinary citizen. Amin doesn't appear to be greatly concerned about the mass of people, although he often claims that he is; but he decided that it was necessary to keep the top civilian echelons of government going somehow. He certainly doesn't want to see foreign diplomats withdrawn because of the unavailability of basic foodstuffs and other essential supplies.

Consequently a government corporation called Foods and Beverages Ltd was formed earlier in the year for the purpose of bringing in necessary supplies and distributing them to defined customers. This firm runs the Duty Free Shop, also known as the VIP Shop for diplomats, government ministers, judges and permanent secretaries. The army has its own system of canteens and shops, which are very well stocked and used by all ranks from the highest to the lowest. Their stocks come in from the UK on what is known as 'the Whisky Run' from Stanstead Airport and are sold to them at barely profitable prices in an attempt to keep the soldiers happy and loyal.

Membership cards with photographs attached are issued to those of us allowed to use the VIP shop and we are allocated one day each month on which we can collect the full ration of sugar, rice, salt, milk powder, cooking fat or oil, margarine, flour (usually weevil-riddled), toilet soap, washing soap and washing powder, which are the items defined as essential commodities. These are sold at fixed prices considerably below those of the black market paid by the general public. I always share my monthly allocation with my domestic staff, driver and one or two friends who are in need.

The black market, which is actually the only generally available market, is known here as *magendo* and those involved in selling at high prices as *magendoists*. Everyone complains about it but it's become an established fact of life and no amount of official denunciation in speeches, or complaints by those writing to newspapers, has made the slightest difference. Indeed, some of those who shout the loudest against the evils of *magendo* are among the worst offenders.

A recent correspondent in his letter to the *Voice of Uganda* complained of '*magendoists* living a comfortable life of sausages'. Such ordinary items as bacon, sausages, butter, steaks and so on are now luxuries only to be brought in, usually smuggled, from Kenya by those with plenty of foreign currency. For almost everyone else such items are simply unattainable and can only be regarded with nostalgia for the past plentiful times in Uganda. The big problem now occupying much of one's time is how to obtain the bare necessities for oneself and for those for whom one has responsibilities.

Monday 28 April

In court before me, the accused, who was in his middle thirties, was on a murder charge and he had applied to be released on bail because his trial had been so long delayed, as usual. I wanted to know if he had a surety to stand for him and he indicated an oldish man wearing a Moslem white cap who stood up. I asked the old man if he was related to the accused and he replied: 'Yes, he is my father-in-law.'

I looked doubtfully from one to the other and said: 'How can that be? He's much younger than you.' There were some titters from the public.

'That's so,' he replied, 'but I took his daughter as my third wife and married her last year.'

1975

Wednesday 30 April

I was processing from court in the usual way this afternoon, led by my constable orderly in full dress uniform, then myself in red robes and wig, followed by Mzee, the usher, carrying my books and files. Suddenly the constable stopped and dithered. We were in a fairly narrow corridor leading to my chambers and another constable was sitting, or rather lounging, in a chair fast asleep, with his long legs stretched straight out across the corridor and blocking the way past. Without thinking about it my military training came back to me and I barked out: 'Move yourself, you dozy idle creature!' Thereupon the half-asleep constable levitated straight up in the air in the sitting position and came down and hit the ground standing quivering to attention. It was very well done and various members of the public and other constables nearby were falling about with laughter at the amazing sight. Meanwhile we processed solemnly on our way.

Friday 2 May

There was some talk by Amin of his attending the present Commonwealth Heads of Government summit in Kingston, Jamaica, and several Commonwealth Prime Ministers made it clear that he would not be welcome. Those from African countries didn't seem to object to him, though, apart from Nyerere of Tanzania, who hates him, and Amin wavered this way and that. Finally he announced that, as the Queen would not be there, he would not attend either. No doubt there was a sigh of relief from most of those present.

Monday 5 May

I opened Kampala criminal sessions this morning. What a shambles. Some accused were not produced from the prison as they couldn't find them; some advocates had not been informed and many witnesses not served. There was much wailing and gnashing of teeth as I descended on all concerned from a great height until things were sorted out.

My interpreter proudly told me that he has taken the name Ssalongo, which means 'father of twins', so I congratulated him. The Baganda consider such an achievement to be especially praiseworthy and commendable, thus requiring the taking of the additional name. The mother becomes Nnalongo.

Monday 26 May

My temporary *shamba* boy at the moment is Andrew, a 17-year-old schoolboy, currently studying for his O levels. In return for the

400

occupation of a rent-free servant's quarter, he attends school in the afternoon stream and is supposed to cut the grass and do the weeding in the mornings.

Friday morning I sent Wilson, my driver, from the court to fetch a book from my house. It appears that he parked in the drive, leaving the ignition key in place while he went inside his own quarter. Andrew left his weeding, got into the car and started to 'drive' it. He has never driven a car but he has watched with interest as Wilson starts the car each day and, he explained afterwards, he was absolutely confident that he could drive it. Instead, almost as soon as the big, heavy car got under way, he lost control and it shot around the drive towards the gateway, went over the cutting in the embankment beside my house, which is on the side of Kololo hill, and collided hard with the bathroom outer wall. Wilson heard the car start and gave chase and switched off the engine, grabbed hold of Andrew and pulled him out of the car, which was considerably damaged in front and along one side. Andrew was shaken but unhurt. My cook telephoned the court to report that my car was very sick and would I come to view the remains, which I did.

After the car had been separated from the wall, it was towed away for repairs. Andrew had been carted off to Jinja Road Police Station before I arrived on the scene. There he was put into a cell and left to contemplate his fate. Yesterday his mother, whom I had not met before, came to see me and begged to have her only son released. I was sorry for her but not for Andrew. However, I wrote a note to the OC Police at Jinja Road, pointing out that, since the boy is a juvenile, he cannot be sent to prison and, as he has no money, he cannot pay a fine – and I have no intention of paying the fine on his behalf in the circumstances. There doesn't seem to be much point in proceeding against him; so I said I would agree to his being released with a severe caution so that he can get back to his exam studies at school.

At lunch-time today he reported back here, looking very embarrassed and woebegone. I gave him the benefit of an unexpurgated opinion of himself and his future prospects if he is not more careful. I noticed that the police caution had been more than spoken and must have been delivered with a rather heavy hand, for his left eye was swollen and closed up. I think he'll keep well clear of the car now.

Thursday 12 June

A military tribunal has today sentenced to death by firing squad Denis Cecil Hills, a British lecturer at a teacher training college. He was arrested two months ago because, in the manuscript of a book he's

401

writing called *The White Pumpkin*, he refers to Amin as a 'village tyrant'. Just how the authorities became aware of what was contained in the manuscript has not been revealed, but it may perhaps have been due to the information having been supplied by someone close to Hills.

I'd say this was an inapt description of Amin and mild compared with some of the things already written about him in other publications outside Uganda. However, Amin has chosen to appear to become exceedingly angry about it and he has construed the expression somehow to amount to treason, although there's no legal basis for this, of course. First he declared that Hills would be tried in court on the treason charge, but his legal advisers for once got through to him and convinced him that the charge did not stand a chance in the courts. He next announced that the trial would take place before a military tribunal, where tiresome legal technicalities are irrelevant, and Hills will then be shot by firing squad after he has been found guilty. There was no doubt about the verdict from the start since the members of the military tribunal would not risk the dire consequences of Amin's wrath by declaring that he was wrong. In any case such a possibility would not arise since they are in agreement with Amin in these matters.

There are no British advocates still practising in Uganda, so Hills asked, through the British High Commission, for one to be brought from Kenya. He was P. J. Wilkinson QC, who had a practice in Uganda in Protectorate days. He was allowed into Uganda at the beginning of the month and even as far as the room where the tribunal was sitting, but he was then told that he would not be given permission to appear and defend Hills since the tribunal had decided that it was not necessary for him to be legally represented.

The whole trial was a farce stage-managed by Amin, who, throughout it, periodically made public announcements that Hills would be shot at the end of it. What the evidence amounted to was not made known to the public and it probably didn't matter since the conclusion was foregone anyway. The magistrate assigned as legal adviser to the tribunal (another of my former students) told me he had been ignored throughout the trial and, towards the end, he and the members of the tribunal, the witnesses, police and others involved were all taken in military vehicles to a place outside Kampala where there were some trees. A dummy figure was tied to a tree and they were told that it represented Hills. It was demonstrated how the execution would take place and they were all then taken back to town. The purpose of all this rigmarole was not explained to them.

Today Radio Uganda announced that the tribunal had found Hills guilty, though it's not clear of what, and has sentenced him to death by firing squad. Amin has stated that the execution will take place very soon. Clearly no appeal is going to be permitted and it wouldn't change things in the circumstances. No tribunal appeal court has been set up, anyway.

The tribunal chairman in this case was Lieutenant-Colonel Juma Ali, by far the worst among a bad bunch. He's a merciless psychopathic killer and an illiterate of such low mentality that he is known everywhere, including among his military colleagues, as 'Butabika', which is the name of Uganda's only mental hospital here in Kampala. There is no hope for anyone unfortunate enough to be brought before him in a tribunal or, for that matter, anyone who by chance upsets him in any way outside the tribunal. His usual reaction is to use his pistol, which he always carries with him. In the compound of his house, on the Bombo road outside Kampala, he keeps goats and chickens and, if he sees any passer-by daring to turn his head to look inside his compound at his animals or anything else, he is likely to open fire immediately. At petrol stations and shops which he chooses to patronise nobody is foolish enough to risk the consequences of asking him to pay for his 'purchases'. He's a small, cocky man, originally a band-boy in the Police Band. His father was chief executioner for years at Luzira Prison. The trait appears to be hereditary, for Juma Ali has become one of Amin's chief executioners, though he has a certain amount of competition in that line from others who are just as blood-thirsty.

Sunday 22 June

I don't know whether Amin realised that outside opinion about the Hills case was bound to be unfavourable, but he has been startled at the uproar in the world's press and the loud protests from so many countries and governments; even from some of those still quite friendly to him. At first he was adamant about carrying out the 'lawful' sentence of the tribunal, but he has now come to realise that it just won't do, and he's looking for a way out.

As usual he has managed to manoeuvre himself into a corner with his firm assertions and at present it seems he can't see any way out without a very considerable loss of face. Now he has announced that he will only pardon Hills if the British Foreign Secretary, James Callaghan, himself comes out to Uganda to collect him. It's not much of a solution because Callaghan has refused to come. Various heads of state or government have sent messages or emissaries to Amin begging him to relent or be forgiving and release Hills, though they kept pretty quiet while he's been killing off thousands of Ugandans. The

Queen has now been dragged into the matter and, as Head of the Commonwealth, she has sent a personal message to Amin by hand of Lieutenant-General Sir Chandos Blair.

Someone in London is obviously paying attention because Amin has been publicly declaring his great love and admiration for the Scots and all things Scottish. He has claimed to have received letters from several Scotsmen and Scottish organisations asking for his support in their desire for autonomy and home rule away from England. On several occasions Amin has boasted that he has been invited to become King of Scotland. He has even had some of his soldiers trained by Scottish pipers of British Caledonian Airways to play the bagpipes, and they now dress in full Highland uniform with kilts. They are produced proudly at all official functions, where they perform, though how competently I cannot say, as it all sounds the same to me. Amin has taken to wearing a glengarry when in uniform and it's rumoured he has a vast kilt, although I haven't seen any pictures of him wearing it, and I don't know what tartan. The Black Watch, perhaps?

Recently I made one of my very infrequent appearances at an official function and Amin in his glengarry was moving around speaking to the guests. When he reached me he chatted in his quiet and friendly way for a few minutes and then he asked me from which part of the UK I come. I suspected he was hoping I would say from Scotland so that he could go into further raptures about how he and the Scots admire each other. So I said I'm English and proud of it. The expression on his face changed from interest to total blankness, a danger signal with many Africans, and without a word he turned and walked away.

The choice of General Blair as Queen's messenger was obviously the result of careful thought. He's a Scot who was commissioned in the Seaforth Highlanders and is now GOC Scotland and Governor of Edinburgh Castle. I recall meeting him briefly in 1960 when he was a lieutenant-colonel commanding 4 KAR, which was then on a training exercise in Karamoja. He therefore had been Amin's CO and has returned to Uganda several times since. Amin announced that he was his 'best friend'.

That didn't stop Amin from publicly humiliating him. As soon as Blair arrived and sought audience with him, Amin flew by helicopter to his home district in West Nile, where he had ordered the erection of a typical Kakwa chief's hut, which is circular without a door or wall; the thatched roof slopes down to within 3 feet from the floor all the way round. Amin sat inside in solitary state on the only chair waiting for his visitor. When Blair was brought to the hut he was told to go inside and meet Amin. The General's a tall man and, while newsmen took photographs, he had to stoop almost to his knees to enter the hut and deliver the Queen's letter. That's what comes of being Amin's best friend.

Thursday 26 June

Yesterday evening Amin held a reception to celebrate the handing over of the report of a Commission of Inquiry that he had ordered into the disappearances of a large number of people in Uganda. It's his answer to the many complaints and reports in foreign newspapers and from organisations like Amnesty International and the International Commission of Jurists. Of course, he's already aware that most of the disappearances are the result of the well-known efforts of his murder squads from SRB, the PSU and the military police. Proving this is an almost impossible task, however.

The judge who chaired the inquiry had a very difficult job and met with considerable difficulties and obstructions, together with a natural reluctance by surviving witnesses to come forward and testify. He has now produced his report, and some names of those accused of causing the 308 disappearances of which he received evidence are mentioned in it; but Amin was exonerated from personal involvement and blame. Nobody was likely to testify against him anyway, not unless he was feeling suicidal.

The reception was a very small one for diplomats, judges and the Defence Council only, and it was held on the flat roof of the house where Amin lived on Kololo hill when he was army commander in the 1960s, which he has since called the Command Post, in 25th January Drive (formerly Prince Charles Drive) about 250 yards from my residence. I was very reluctant to attend the reception as I could see nothing to celebrate; nor do I think the report will make the slightest difference or stop the disappearances. Also I don't approve of the insulting way in which he treated the Queen's letter and General Blair, so I felt in no mood for a friendly chat with Amin. However, the CJ said that all the judges were required to attend, so I went.

At the gate to the Command Post compound I met the Russian Ambassador and we walked together up to the entrance of the building. He was wearing a smart Western-cut grey suit with a really horrible, shapeless 'worker's' cap perched on his large head. I was not feeling diplomatic so I asked him why did he keep giving General Amin all the weapons, tanks, aircraft and so on that he asked for. He laughed and said: 'Oh, we don't give them to him. He has to pay cash on the spot,' and walked off chuckling to himself without having answered my question.

I don't know why the Russians supply Amin with the military hardware required for his oppression and suppression except, perhaps, out of mischief-making because Amin is a small thorn in the side of the Western powers. It also gives them a toe-hold in East Africa, though rather a precarious one since Amin is by inclination a capitalist and a right-wing fascist dictator without even the faintest pink-hued socialistic tendencies. His massive business takeovers cannot be described as socialist nationalisation; they were simply the grabbing of economic control by Amin and his cronies and sharing out the spoils among themselves afterwards for their own benefit. Clearly it was private enterprise. The ordinary people received nothing at all out of it. Perhaps the Soviet Union supports him because he brings the chaos and havoc they seem to consider necessary before a successful revolution.

When Amin arrived at the reception he moved about the roof-top chatting and, every now and again, his two kilted pipers would commence huffing and puffing away on their bagpipes. The noise of strangling cats was ear-splitting as the small space on the roof prevented one from moving to a place of safety. It certainly killed any conversation that was going on. As the pipes wailed to a halt Amin reached me and asked: 'How do you like my expert Uganda-Scottish pipers?'

I told him that, speaking as an Englishman, I could only agree with Sir Thomas Beecham's remark that 'bagpipes sound exactly the same when you have finished learning to play them as they do when you start'.

Waving that seditious remark aside, he went on to explain that he had been ready to step down from the Presidency and submit himself for trial if he had been found to blame for any disappearances of people by the Commission of Inquiry. I could not recall that he had ever publicly revealed this readiness before the Commission had made its report, so he was on safe ground mentioning the 'offer' now. I merely made a non-committal sound in reply. 'Well now, Judge,' he went on, 'I want you to help me to persuade Mr Callaghan to come to Uganda and discuss with me about Denis Hills so that I can arrange to release him soon.' I replied that I regretted that I would be unable to assist because I didn't know Mr Callaghan and he certainly didn't know me. Amin looked somewhat displeased with this answer, but I don't know what he was going to say next because his infernal pipers let loose again and Amin just shrugged his massive shoulders and walked off.

Friday 11 July

I've been in Masindi all week conducting civil sessions and I arrived back in Kampala late yesterday evening as the car engine gave trouble all the way here. The *Voice of Uganda* is full of the visit yesterday of the Foreign Secretary, Mr Callaghan. Evidently there was some second thinking in London and he decided to come here after all. There are photographs of the Highland McAmin handing over Hills, who doesn't look too much the worse for wear. A friend who was at Entebbe airport yesterday afternoon told me with amusement that when the official farewells had been exchanged, and photographs taken, Callaghan and Hills covered the remaining yards of tarmac to the waiting RAF transport aircraft at a rather undignified trot. They were no doubt fairly eager to be on their way; and who can blame them?

Wednesday 16 July

I'm just back from Fort Portal, where I conducted a quick civil sessions; mostly closing a number of very old cases involving Asians and others who are no longer with us, and hearing a few appeals.

In the *Voice of Uganda* it's reported that, before he left Uganda, Hills signed a statement addressed to Amin which, among other things, asserted that all of the Britons still in Uganda customarily act as spies for the British Government and they have always done so. I've no idea whether Hills actually wrote this or, if he did so, whether it was voluntary and in his own words. Amin has announced that, in view of this statement, he requires the SRB and the soldiers to keep a constant watch on all Britons and to report anything suspicious to him personally. I can't say that this news makes me feel either happy or secure. Curse Hills and his miserable book.

Tuesday 22 July

On Sunday I came all the way here to Kabale to hold a criminal sessions but no state attorney has yet arrived to prosecute. I rang the High Court and, after considerable difficulty, got through, asking them to chase up the DPP, but nobody has appeared. There are several accused who have been on prison remand for a long time awaiting trials who now wish to plead guilty to manslaughter. This morning I managed to get through to the DPP on the phone and I suggested he appoints a local advocate to act as state attorney just for the purpose of taking those pleas and disposing of the cases. There is even a former state attorney here in private practice now who could and would do this, so he tells me. However, for his own reasons, the DPP stubbornly refuses to agree to it. So I have to return to Kampala tomorrow having achieved nothing here; and the accused must go back to prison for a further long wait until another criminal sessions can be arranged. All this time and money wasted because one obstinate official won't agree to a simple solution.

Wednesday 23 July

At the last meeting of the Organisation of African Unity (OAU) it was agreed that Uganda would host the summit meeting due this month, so it followed from this that today Amin, to his great delight, has become the Chairman of the OAU for a year. He has already unsuccessfully offered to be permanent chairman but has decided to make the best of it and the title 'Current Chairman of the OAU' appears prominently after his name now on all official invitations and in news items and speeches referring to him, as an addition to all his other titles. He has also made it clear on several occasions that he is ready and willing to take his turn as Head of the Commonwealth; a title which he maintains should also be rotated.

Great preparations have been made for the summit in Kampala, and the new International Conference Centre and affiliated hotel, Nile Mansions, have received much attention and expenditure. Fleets of brand-new Mercedes Benz limousines and smaller Fiats have been purchased and imported for use by those taking part. The police have received large numbers of special white motor cycles with radios and other gadgets attached, and many drivers have been recruited for the cars. The accident rate so far has been high and a number of vehicles have not survived for use at the summit.

The new drivers were recruited hastily without checking their records and backgrounds; just so long as they could produce a driving permit, which, however, was not always their own. So it's not surprising that cars have been smashed in accidents and others have disappeared with their drivers across one or other of the various borders around Uganda, and no doubt disposed of very profitably.

The roads in Kampala have at last been repaired and decorations put up and shopkeepers have been exhorted to paint and decorate their premises. Amin has had a field marshal's uniform made in sky-blue of such magnificence and with so many medals and stars attached to it that even Hermann Goering would have been envious. Kampala is now full of African luminaries and their retinues, and cars flying all sorts of flags zoom around the city.

Friday 1 August

At a reception for OAU delegates yesterday evening, four disgustingly sycophantic Europeans carried Amin shoulder-high sitting in a large chair supported by long poles on their shoulders with the Uganda flag hanging below. A fifth European walked behind holding up a large golf umbrella over Amin. There was much laughter and cheering as Amin waved to the crowd. It was supposed to be a joke based on the White Man's Burden but, in present-day circumstances, it seems to me to be a joke in rather bad taste.

Today the OAU delegates were driven about 6 miles outside Kampala to a place on the Lake Victoria shore which Amin has named Cape Town View. Here they, with members of the Defence Council, Ministers and sundry VIPs, were supposed to watch a demonstration by the 'invincible Uganda Air Force' carrying out an attack on a small deserted offshore island which he has named Cape Town. Amin's object was to show his distinguished guests and locals just how his magnificent fighting men, under his expert guidance and leadership, were going to destroy Cape Town by bombing it.

In fact, his long-obsolete MiGs are only capable of firing rockets and machine-guns, not bombs, but the Field Marshal believes that any aircraft delivering explosive missiles is dropping bombs. Amin duly appeared in his battle fatigues with pistol holster on his belt and waited proudly and boastfully for a successful outcome to the demonstration which he announced was designated 'Operation Cape Town'.

Not surprisingly to most of the rest of us, the exercise was not an entire success as the 'bombers' completely missed the island with their rockets – not even a single hit. The missiles merely disappeared into the lake and dismembered a number of fish which could hardly be blamed for apartheid. Amin stalked off from Operation Shambles looking very disgruntled and an amused crowd promptly dispersed. Apparently, and not surprisingly, Brigadier Guweddeko, the Air Force commander, has been dismissed.

Saturday 2 August

Several of Amin's military henchmen, including General Mustafa Adrisi and Colonel Malyamungu, have recently had huge, lavish and well-publicised weddings at the taxpayers' expense; Adrisi taking as his fourth wife a girl young enough to be his granddaughter and Malyamungu, the multi-murderer, having the gall to marry in a church.

Having in one year become Chairman of the OAU and a Field Marshal, Amin decided to complete his hat trick. He, too, recently married again, this time to a pretty young dancer named Sarah Kyolaba. So he arranged to repeat the flamboyant ceremony as today's grand conclusion to the OAU meeting before a vast crowd of guests and the television cameras. For this occasion he wore his new sky-blue field marshal's uniform and about a ton of assorted medals and stars fastened all over his tunic. Sarah looked very attractive in a white bridal gown and train that had obviously not been made locally. The Chief Khadi intoned interminable prayers and advice in Swahili and the members of the Diplomatic Corps and other foreign visitors tried to look as if they knew what was being said.

We were all required to attend, and afterwards, in the large gardens of the Conference Centre, there was a long line of dignitaries, notables and others moving up one by one to congratulate the couple. I noticed that Sarah was not looking exactly overjoyed, but perhaps she was finding it rather a bore having to go through an action replay of the whole proceedings in front of people who were mostly strangers to her. On the other hand, she could have been thinking about the fate of her predecessors as wives of Amin, who has proved to be a combination of Bluebeard and King Henry VIII. There was also the fact that her boyfriend, with whom she had been living and by whom she recently had a child, was murdered by SRB men on Amin's orders so that he could have her for himself. He now even claims to be the child's father.

Whatever she was thinking, I know that I had these things in mind as the line grew shorter in front of me, and I could think of nothing appropriate to say to them at this rather absurd farce without being hypocritical. So, when my turn came, I merely shook hands, offered a quick 'congratulations' and walked away to find my car and go home.

Sunday 24 August

Vice-President Adrisi was, it seemed, a little peeved at having his recent huge and lavish wedding ceremony and reception upstaged by Amin going through his wedding twice, and on an even grander scale. So Adrisi retaliated by holding a repeat of his own recent Kampala wedding yesterday up in Arua. He could not exceed the magnificence and publicity of Amin's performance so, instead, he arranged for it to be held as far away as possible. Thus all those officially required to attend, diplomats and senior officials and so on, were put to the maximum amount of inconvenience and travelling. That did not bother Amin for he did not attend it. Neither did I.

Tuesday 26 August

Every day I send my driver, Wilson, to the industrial area to collect three packets of milk. I still use the old fridge that I had in Karamoja but it doesn't keep things fresh for long now, so I have to make daily purchases. Sometimes Wilson takes quite a long time to carry out this small errand but he usually explains that the milk production was delayed, which does happen.

Today he came to my house very late and was followed into the drive a minute later by another Mercedes, which drew up at the front door and out jumped a strange civilian wearing dark glasses. He looked like trouble and, as he walked towards my driver, I went outside and spoke sharply to him: 'Just a moment, who are you and what are you doing in my compound?'

He replied that he was the Secretary for Research, another name for the Head of the State Research Bureau. So it seemed that the big guns had been turned in our direction. I said: 'Identify yourself, please,' and he produced an official identification card. He explained that he had pursued my driver because he was involved in a big milk racket. He was alleged to have been filling the boot of my car with milk packets and then selling them at a profit to the lads at the local police stations, of all places. The supply of milk is certainly irregular and seldom sufficient for everyone's needs, but surely this wasn't really much of a racket.

I didn't know what Wilson might have been up to, but it could explain his frequent lateness in bringing my own milk supply. He had been quite evasive when I questioned him about it on previous occasions. However, I said nothing of this to the man, as I can never see any good reason to assist the SRB. Wilson, of course, denied the allegation and he opened the car boot and revealed nothing but my three packets, which proved nothing anyway. The chief spy looked rather unhappy and muttered to him: 'Well, you had better look out because we shall catch you soon.' With which awful threat he climbed back into his car and drove off at high speed, scattering gravel behind him. I pointed out to Wilson that he was being extremely stupid to get entangled with the SRB and, by doing so, endangering both of us, so his little racket must cease forthwith. But what a trivial matter for the dreaded head of SRB to bother about.

Wednesday 10 September

There are now very few British permanent and pensionable officers left from the former Colonial Service still working for the Uganda Government, and the British High Commission here has sent each of us a printed letter to the effect that supplementation of our basic salaries by HMG will cease on 31 March 1976 when the current supplementation agreement expires. This is paid as part of overseas aid through the Ministry of Overseas Development as an inducement to work in developing countries.

In the case of Uganda, following Amin's expulsion of Asians in 1972 and the seizure of their property, HMG decided to restrict the level of aid to Uganda and no new aid projects have been undertaken, while existing commitments including us survivors, were being wound up, run down, and written off. The staff of the High Commission has been reduced considerably to acting High Commissioner level. So we have six months warning of this action. We can continue after that working for the Uganda Government as permanent civil servants, but without British supplementation and overseas leave facilities; which means on local terms; or we can try to switch to expatriate contract terms with the Uganda Government, which would at least provide for a return passage for home leave. I want to stay on, if it can possibly be arranged, so I wrote today to the Minister of Overseas Development, Reg Prentice*, as well as to the New Forest MP, Patrick McNair-Wilson, and to Lord Diplock, as he now is, a judicial member of the House of Lords whom I met at the Law School back in 1965. My object was to point out that the continued supplementation of the small handful of Britons who are willing to stay on would cost very little and that, as schoolteachers, a surgeon and a judge, we are giving some much needed help to the ordinary citizens without in any objectionable way supporting the military regime.

Friday 19 September

I toddled along to the Ministry of Justice this morning to see the Minister, Godfrey Lule, about staying on. I wanted to find out if they really want me to stay or not before I take steps. He said the Government does as I'm doing useful work. He has agreed that I should be offered an expatriate contract if I apply for it. That's good, but I'll wait and see if anything else crops up first. Apart from that, we've had heavy rainfall every day this month so far. My ancient fridge has finally broken down and so has my record player. Life gets tedious.

Thursday 2 October

Amin recently decided that it was time he addressed the UN and gave the world the benefit of his wise and lucid thoughts on various subjects. Yesterday in New York he laid the foundation stone of a 14-storey building for housing the Uganda Mission. Presumably his Arab friends are paying for it; Uganda certainly can't afford to do so. The stone is engraved: 'October First 1975. Laid down by His Excellency

*He defected from Labour in November 1977, later became Tory Minister of Social Security for two years in Mrs Thatcher's first government.

Alhadji Field Marshall [sic] Idi Amin Dada VC DSO MC President of the Republic of Uganda and Chairman of the Organization of African Unity 1975 and 1976.'

He wore his light-blue Field Marshal's uniform and large quantities of medals and stars for his address to the UN. Amin showed his infinite superiority to all other Heads of State by remaining silent and having Uganda's ambassador actually reading out his speech for him as he sat there brooding in all his glittering glory. Actually this backfired somewhat as most of the delegates thought he either couldn't read or he couldn't speak English, or both. The speech was full of his usual bombast. He called for the expulsion of Israel from the UN and its extinction as a state. He said: 'Zionists have infiltrated the CIA and turned it into a murder squad.' Well, he knows all about murder squads. The US Ambassador, David Moynihan, has called him a 'racist murderer'. At the UN, thanks to Amin's visit, the polite art of diplomacy seems to have reached its highest level.

Thursday 9 October

I've celebrated Uganda's thirteenth anniversary of independence by sacking my cook, Lawrence. Actually he hasn't been with me long and he really is an excellent cook. His pastries, cakes and bread are really out of this world. But, unfortunately, he seems to have a complete aversion to soap and water and his pungent aroma when he brings food to me immediately puts me off eating, apart from problems of kitchen hygiene. I call him Lawrence of Effluvia. And the desert would be the best place for him.

Monday 13 October

We've had a lot of rain this month and yesterday at lunch-time there was a hail-storm with large hail-stones hitting the window panes and damaging the plants in the garden considerably before quickly melting. This was followed by the appearance of swarms of mosquitoes trying their best to break and enter my house. It's some years now since Kampala ceased to be mosquito-free as the careful precautions for their suppression are no longer taken by the public health department of the city council.

I started a long criminal sessions in Kampala last month and it's still going on, with numerous cases of murder and armed robberies to be dealt with. Witnesses can be very trying, particularly unsophisticated village peasants who insist on doing things in their own way, which includes never giving a straight answer to any question. Even

413

an elementary and introductory matter such as obtaining the age of a witness can cause headaches. Typically it goes like this:

Prosecutor:	Can you say how old you are?
Witness:	Yes.
Prosecutor:	Yes what?
Witness:	Yes I can say how old I am.
Prosecutor:	Well, how old are you?
Witness:	I am about twenty years old.
Prosecutor:	About twenty years? I thought you knew your age?
Witness:	Yes, I am twenty.
Prosecutor:	When were you born?
Witness:	I don't know the date.
Prosecutor:	Then how do you know your age?
Witness:	My parents told me.
Prosecutor:	When did they tell you?
Witness:	A long time ago.
Prosecutor:	On what date?
Witness:	I don't know dates.
Prosecutor:	Well, what age did they say you were when they told you?
Witness:	They said I was twenty years old.
Prosecutor:	But, if they said that you were twenty years old such a long time ago, how can you still be twenty now? Surely you are older?
Witness:	I am twenty years old.
Prosecutor:	But you must be more than that by now.
Witness:	I am twenty. My parents told me; what do you know about it?
Prosecutor:	But that was a long time ago, you said. Do you agree that you get older each year that passes?
Witness:	Yes, I agree.
Prosecutor:	Good. So, do you know what age you have reached this year?
Witness:	I don't know it, but I am twenty years old.
Prosecutor:	But...?
Me:	This all seems to have been the usual waste of time. I have already recorded the age of this witness as about thirty-five years, which is what he appears to be from my own observation. Can we now get on with the evidence?
Prosecutor:	As your Lordship pleases.

Sunday 26 October

The East African Court of Appeal is still a part of the already crumbling East African Community organisation and it provides a useful final court of appeal for the three territories. Previously the judges were all expatriates but now there are Africans appointed. The British President of the Court is due to retire and it's clearly time for an East African to be appointed to the post. The Vice-President would normally move up, but he's also a Brit so he won't get it. Amin has offered our Chief Justice Wambuzi for the post and it can't be denied that Uganda is long overdue for such an appointment from its Judiciary since no court president has come from here for many years. In addition, the CJ is a first-class judge and ideal for the post so it's not surprising that his nomination has been readily accepted. So now Amin has to appoint a new CJ and there's considerable speculation about whom he will choose.

When I answered the phone this afternoon I stumbled over my number, which for some reason I can't seem to remember, and I heard a chuckle on the line and immediately recognised my contact, who asked if he could come round and see me. When he arrived he said that the 'Big Man' is concerned about the very bad state of relations between Uganda and the UK at the moment and he wants to do something about it. Consequently Amin had said to him: 'Ask your friend if he would be interested in being appointed Chief Justice as such an appointment would be appropriate now and I consider he is suitable,' or words to that effect. So that's what he was doing. I can't believe that I am his first choice and I think he's just shopping around before making a decision. Still, it is a surprise and it presents a tricky problem. I appreciate the offer and I'd certainly like to be CJ, and I think I could make a reasonable job of it, but I've no wish for such an important, high-profile job while Amin is in power. For one thing, I'm sure it would be only a short time before I inevitably clashed with Amin or one of his senior henchmen over matters of human rights or military interference with the courts, or in regard to military tribunals or something of that sort, and then I shall be out. I can't pretend to approve of or act disinterested in matters about which I feel strongly, and there seems little point in the almost certain chance of an early dispute and inevitable booting out without achieving anything useful. I think it's better if I just plod on as I am and help where I can from time to time by working in the background and keeping to my usual very low profile.

Amin is a great one for having a large entourage and he likes to have most of his top people hovering close to him in fairly constant attendance at his various comings and goings as well as for his speeches and public appearances. That's something I want absolutely no part in at all. I work for the people of Uganda not for Idi Amin and I've no wish to appear to be closely associated with him or with those around him. Over the last five years I've deliberately avoided attending most official functions and being seen in public except in court, when I'm effectively disguised in wig and robes. In this way I reckon I'm in a better position to do what little I can to give some useful assistance.

So the answer has to be no for the present; but, of course, my friend needed convincing reasons to take back with him so as not to anger the Big Man by my apparently disagreeing with him. I suggested that after having two Ugandan CJs it might appear to be rather a retrogressive step to appoint a European once again and it could result in unfavourable comment from leading Africans outside Uganda as well as internally. I also said I really prefer to work in the background as much as possible and I wish to avoid all the publicity that his appointing a British CJ would inevitably produce. A pity to chuck away such a job, but there it is.

Monday 10 November

I commenced criminal sessions in Arua, West Nile, last week. There are only three murder cases but we started late because no defence advocate arrived until the third day. He said he had transport problems – the usual situation these days. For once there were no long delays at military road-blocks and we reached here in just under six hours. A very hot, dusty and tiring safari on roads that got progressively worse as we came northwards.

In two of the cases the accused pleaded guilty to manslaughter and only one came up for trial. This involved a soldier, Lance Corporal Onenchan, who was accused of murdering one of his father's wives, not his mother, called Nyalango. Prior to this the six-years-old daughter of Onenchan had died in hospital after suffering from the very common measles, and her body was brought back to the village for burial at the home of Onenchan's father.

On the day of the funeral several local village men started to dig a grave in the garden for the burial, but Onenchan said: 'If you keep on digging the grave and if you bury the child in this grave I am going to kill somebody. I want the body of the child to stay out for three days before burial.' He did not explain why he said this but just left them and went into a hut where a number of women relations were sitting, including Nyalango. Once inside, he tried to close the door but the women objected because it's contrary to Alur tribal *desturi*, custom, to cry and mourn with the door closed. Onenchan was in army uniform and, when the women tried to prevent him from closing the door, he took out a bayonet and flourished it. Nyalango asked why he was behaving like this.

Onenchan replied that he wanted to kill somebody because his daughter had not died naturally, but by witchcraft. He then pushed Nyalango against the wall and stabbed her with the bayonet in the back and the neck. She ran from the hut bleeding copiously. One of the women went up to Onenchan, who was just standing there doing nothing, and took the bayonet from him and he said: 'I have killed the wizard who killed my child.'

At his trial Onenchan admitted everything except the actual killing, which he didn't mention at all. As he chose to make an unsworn statement, he could not be cross-examined about it. There was clear medical evidence that the child died of measles but, as usual in the West Nile, the accepted belief is that nobody dies naturally; and this has to be taken into account. In my judgment I said: 'The accused knew well what had caused his daughter's death as he had a death certificate. However, it's also possible that he believed her death had resulted from witchcraft because he is uneducated and this is a common belief here among the peasants. Consequently he may have been provoked, as he claims, by his mistaken belief that the deceased woman had caused her death by some form of witchcraft.' I gave him the benefit of the doubt and convicted him of manslaughter rather than murder and sentenced him to six years in prison.

Tuesday 18 November

Yesterday I drove to Gulu for criminal sessions. I usually travel on Sundays so as to start court on Monday morning, but last Sunday there was a dinner for judges to say farewell to the CJ before he leaves for Nairobi to take up his new post as President of the East African Court of Appeal.

There were numerous army road-blocks on the way north from Kampala. Most are permanently in position, thus defeating their purpose, if they have any, since the people with reason to avoid them know in advance their location and use a track through the bush or a side road to get round them. I always tell the driver to drive past any line of waiting vehicles and go up to the barrier, where it's the police orderly's job to tell them that I'm a judge on circuit and get us through. Even if we stop, I refuse to allow a search or to unlock my court box. These bullying so-called soldiers love harassing and terrorising civilians and expect them all to cringe and grovel to them, which unfortunately most people do. I believe that the better answer is to bully them back and so I speak sharply and with authority to them, although some of my brother judges don't agree with this approach. Other useless creatures causing obstructions on the road are the odd herds of goats left to wander and stray by careless herdsboys, and groups of baboons that seem to have acquired a liking for sitting on the hot tarmac or dusty *murram* roads. I never speak to any of these.

At the hotel I found the usual SRB types lounging about in dark glasses and flashy clothes spying on the few visitors and terrorising the hotel staff when there was nobody else to torment. These are a fixture everywhere now. Unlike bath and basin plugs, which have been stolen from all Uganda hotels by staff or visitors. I always carry a bag of spare plugs of various sizes.

Friday 21 November

There were only four murder cases to try in Gulu and three of those turned out to be acceptable pleas to manslaughter, so there was only one quite short trial, which resulted in an acquittal. The Army and others who protest and object when what appear to be obviously guilty criminals escape justice by being acquitted and released by the courts are generally unaware of the strict legal requirement for proof of guilt beyond reasonable doubt. Unfortunately it's a fairly common practice among prosecution and other witnesses to give the court what they think is necessary or required by embellishing what was perfectly good prosecution evidence, often so much or so obviously that it renders the whole of their testimony unreliable or doubtful and so ends what might well have been a straightforward conviction in an unexpected acquittal; as happened in this mornings case, much to the astonishment of even the accused himself.

Before leaving for Kampala I went westwards out of Gulu to call on my old acquaintance Francis Onyona and his family, found they were all right, left them a few things and then sped southwards to Kampala. It's not worth going into Murchison Falls National Park these days. There are no tourists to keep the place going, the lodge is no longer in good condition and there are very few animals to be seen, due to the army having made constant forays into the park to shoot down whole herds of all types with automatic weapons for meat, or just for the pleasure of killing them.

Friday 28 November

The Uganda Law Society gave a farewell party for the CJ last Tuesday evening and this Tuesday another was given by the Judicial staff. It was announced that Mohamed Saied is to be the next Chief Justice. He's a Kenya-born Asian Moslem with a British passport, and a first-rate judge and administrator. A good choice, in fact.

I received a letter from my mother today. She celebrated her eight-ieth birthday two weeks ago and was lamenting the fact that she can no longer call herself 'middle-aged'. She wrote: 'I suppose I must say I'm old now. I don't like it at all.'

Thursday 4 December

In addition to hearing appeals from cases in the magistrates courts, the High Court receives monthly returns of cases completed from each lower court. These are shared among the judges who peruse them and can call for any file in which no appeal has been filed, for the purpose of inspecting it to see whether an error has been made; and correct-ing the error by means of a Revisional Order. This is useful in cases of wrongful imprisonment, excessive sentences of imprisonment or fines, or some error of law or procedure.

I dealt with several of these today. In the first a magistrate at Mbale had convicted a 15-year-old girl, Nandutu, of wearing a miniskirt and fined her 100 shillings or, if not paid, one month in prison. I called for this file because persons under 18 cannot be sentenced to impris-onment by a magistrate. In addition, an order had been made to for-feit the dress, which was not even produced in court as an exhibit, so the magistrate didn't see it. This is a common order nowadays in such cases, but I maintain that it is wrong and unnecessary in these days of shortages and high prices. The dress could be lengthened somehow or handed down to a smaller sister, perhaps; or just kept in a drawer until this nonsense is over. At any rate, I set the order aside, removed the fine and illegal prison sentence and substituted a caution.

There were also two files from different courts in which prison sen-tences had been passed on the two accused persons who had attempted to commit suicide, which, unfortunately, is still regarded as a crimi-nal offence here. In one the accused man was sent to prison for six months after explaining to the court that he had been very disturbed by people accusing him of being a thief when he was not one, so he tried to cut his throat. In his judgment, the magistrate commented that cases of this sort caused anxiety in society because the police had to spend time and the taxpayers' money investigating the case. It didn't seem to me to be a very useful or relevant comment in the circum-stances.

The magistrate in the other case did not record how or why the man had tried to kill himself. He wrote: 'There is no proper punishment for this offence and about three months imprisonment will help the accused to reform.' Just in what way he was expected to reform was not explained. I wrote in my revisional orders to both cases, setting aside the prison sentences and ordering their release, that I am unable to see how imprisonment or, indeed, any form of punishment can be considered appropriate in this type of case; it won't give the man the will and desire to live and it won't necessarily prevent him from having another try at killing himself. In my view such a person should not be considered to be a criminal at all, but rather treated as a person who quite obviously is in desperate need of help. Perhaps put on probation with an order for medical or psychiatric attention, though the latter is in any case not available.

My secretary's on maternity leave again; she's unmarried and already has three children by different fathers. Not unusual these days.

Monday 22 December

It has rained and rained right through this month so far and we seem set for a miserable, wet Christmas. Yesterday I went for Christmas lunch to the private residence just outside Kampala of Francis, one of the judges and a former lecturer at the Law School. His wife told me that he had been rushing around the room before I arrived, straightening up the pictures on their walls as he knows how I feel about them hanging askew. I have a vague theory that many Africans find it difficult to put things in a straight line or parallel, possibly as a direct result of being born in circular huts. Maybe the reverse is why most Europeans can't draw circles. I expect the theory needs some work done on it. My theories usually do.

1976

Tuesday 27 January

The Uganda Army Sports Officer, Captain Serwagi, a Muganda, is an exceedingly stupid man; one among many in the army. Last Friday he went to the campus at Makerere University and ordered the undergraduates to attend his 'lecture'. He spent some time abusing them all generally and particularly the female undergraduates, saying nonsensical things such as that he had had intercourse with all the women students; that he could marry any whom he chose; that most of them had gonorrhoea and that universities were training grounds for fools and idiots. The soldiers who had accompanied him to the campus all laughed and cheered and applauded everything he said. The students did not. It sounds to me very like a frustrated student speaking. I suspect that Serwagi at some earlier time applied for admission to Makerere and didn't get it.

He then moved to Kololo Senior Secondary School and delivered more abuse there and had his face roundly slapped by a senior student for speaking to them like that. He pulled out his pistol to shoot the schoolboy but all the students mobbed him. Then he managed to open fire and killed one boy and wounded several others before driving off at speed.

A letter of protest at Serwagi's behaviour was written by Makerere undergraduates and signed by many of them. It was sent to Amin, who responded yesterday by announcing that Serwagi had been promoted to the rank of Major as 'he is a reliable and hardworking officer'.

Tuesday 3 February

I came to Mbale yesterday afternoon to open criminal sessions. It was a hot journey which took three hours due to so many army road-blocks. The Mount Elgon Hotel is nowhere up to its fine standard in the old days. I'm well used to this nowadays and, in my safari kit, apart from basin plugs of various sizes, I carry soap, a glass tumbler, a torch and various other useful items.

There's an old custom still carried on of providing a police guard of honour, complete with bugler, for the judge to inspect if it's the opening of the first sessions of the year for that particular district. Because of my dislike for public appearances and general pomp, especially when wearing these high-falutin red robes, I usually cancel such parades if I discover in good time that one is being planned. I think that the police should be giving their whole time to crime prevention and investigation, which is so ineffective and needs all their attention these days.

The Chief Magistrates in the districts know how I feel about this so they generally don't arrange such parades for me, though I believe that most of the other judges expect them to take place. However, the Chief Magistrate here, a former Law School Bar student, while well aware of my dislike for such ceremonies, considers them a necessity and was determined that I should have a guard of honour; so he craftily arranged it all and only told me when it was too late to cancel it.

In the P3, medical examination report, on the woman complainant in the first case, a rape, the Libyan medical officer, who had already left Uganda, wrote in his findings: 'Rape very likeable'. I wondered aloud whether this was a medical opinion, a personal opinion, or whether he meant to write 'likely'.

Tuesday 10 February

Having completed the Mbale criminal sessions at my usual speed, I was able to open the civil sessions today. I dealt first with several preliminary applications and in one, where I granted only a part of what the advocate had applied for, he sighed and said: 'Oh well, beggars can't be losers, I suppose,' and sat down.

Thursday 19 February

At the hearing today of one of the Mbale civil suits, a witness was a young woman who was nursing an infant. While she was giving her evidence the child kept yattering on in baby talk at the same time. It was rather distracting so I stopped the woman and said: 'I cannot listen to two people speaking at the same time. The baby must be taken outside the court and I'll hear the woman's evidence first and the baby's evidence afterwards.' The interpreter, with a perfectly straight face, duly translated this, and a younger sister of the witness came up and took the baby outside.

Wednesday 25 February

Having finished at Mbale, I opened civil sessions at Tororo today. There are a few appeals and several suits, some of which won't get off the ground. We continue until the end of the month and then move on to criminal sessions here. The Rock Hotel in Tororo is even worse than the Mbale hotel. The food is really awful and the service either non-existent or very slack.

Wednesday 10 March

I opened the Tororo criminal sessions at the beginning of this month and this afternoon adjourned to visit the prison here on inspection. I always make this a part of criminal sessions up-country.

The enacting of the Economic Crimes Tribunal has given the army a lot of powers that should have remained with the police. They constantly arrest people for overcharging in shops, regardless of the fact that prices are not fixed by law except for only a very few items. As the military tribunals are very slow and seldom bother to sit up-country, the prisons are grossly overcrowded with 'offenders' awaiting trial by tribunal whom we in the Judiciary cannot deal with nor interfere with in any way; no matter how illegal the original arrest or non-existent the offence charged.

The prison authorities are given no warrants nor anything in writing to explain or authorise these arrests and detentions. Nobody investigates the cases – the police can't touch them – and many people have not been told why they are locked up. The soldiers bringing them in know nothing of legal technicalities and care even less. I always try to have a word with them on a prison inspection visit although there's nothing I can do except write to the Attorney-General, who's supposed to arrange the prosecutions in tribunals, and provide details of those being illegally held in the hope that he will arrange their release, but so far he's done nothing at all.

The prison superintendent showed me the hole where, during the previous week, about 15 detainees awaiting military tribunal had broken through the wall of their dormitory in the night and had cut the outer wire fence and disappeared into the bush, presumably over the nearby Kenya border. My only comment was: 'Well, good luck to them.' He looked rather startled at that. He has only been here a few days, having taken over when the previous superintendent, who was in charge when the escape took place, was collected and taken away in a car boot by soldiers.

Friday 12 March

I was standing at the entrance to the Tororo Rock Hotel waiting for my car to be brought round to take me to court, when an African drove up in a car and asked me: 'Do you know where I can find a lady waiting for a car to pick her up?'

I replied: 'Yes, it's probably my mother in Hampshire. You'd better hurry; she doesn't like to be kept waiting.' He gave me a rather odd look and then went inside the foyer to speak to someone at the reception desk. A sensible move, I thought.

Monday 22 March

Following the letters I wrote in September last year concerning the proposed cessation of our British overseas supplementation at the end of this month, I've just heard in the nick of time from London and from the High Commission here that, because there are so few of us left in Uganda, the supplementation will be continued to be paid to us for a further two years, until the end of March 1978. This affects the remaining six of us – four head teachers, a surgeon and myself – and gives us time to make plans for the future.

Sunday 4 April

This morning I drove my Jaguar to town to post some letters and, as I was passing the golf club to go back up Kololo hill, a car came from the opposite direction. The driver was alone – it was Amin in a bright sports shirt. He waved, so I waved back and we went on our way.

What an opportunity for someone to get him; but they always seem to try when he's escorted, and I think he knows this. I've often seen him driving alone on Sunday mornings. Probably going to visit one of his many girl-friends.

Monday 5 April

I've been hearing criminal appeals all day. A tiring business listening to all the excuses why various villains should not be incarcerated. In the second case after lunch the appellant's advocate rose unsteadily to his feet to address me. He rambled on vaguely about the evidence in the trial court, with much waving of arms and solemn emphasis of the more irrelevant points. He then confused his appeal with a murder trial and declared that his client should not be convicted since there was no proof of 'a malicious afterthought' and that consequently – a word with which he had to struggle – his conviction resulted in a 'serious carriage of misjustice'.

With that, he threw his arms wide apart and collapsed back on to his seat. I asked him if he had been drinking and he replied that he had taken only a glass or two for lunch. So I admonished him and said I'd give judgment tomorrow and he'd better be in an improved condition by then. But he was already asleep.

Wednesday 14 April

Amin has announced that as a result of his recent summit meeting with his 'best friend' President Mobutu of Zaire, they have agreed to rename Lake Edward, through the centre of which runs the border between Zaire and Uganda. Our half is to be called Lake Idi Amin – what a surprise – and their half will be Lake Mobutu. This dramatic and world-shattering news has caused everyone here to be overwhelmed with massive indifference and apathy. No doubt those who live around there, and anyone else concerned, will continue to call it Lake Edward.

Friday 23 April

This morning I was handed a chit sent in by a witness in a case I am hearing. It read: 'Sorry I cannot come to court today because of my eyes. So I have gone to see the special eyelist. I hope to see you some-times.'

Saturday 1 May

Amin recently made the next move in his hobby of collecting titles and arranged to be 'elected' an honorary doctor of laws of Makerere University, insisting that he is henceforward to be addressed as 'doc-tor', with all his other titles, of course. Fulsome speeches of praise for Amin's 'great achievements' were made by his supporters and syco-phants at the university when Amin, in his robes as Chancellor of the University, went there to receive his doctorate. I received an invitation to attend but, as usual, filed it in the waste-paper basket.

Afterwards Ugandan doctors, physicians, surgeons and specialists, had the courage to come out on strike. It was a brave act because it's an almost certain invitation to have armed troops move in forcibly and roughly. They have very good reasons to strike because they are extremely seriously hampered in their important work by an almost total lack of drugs, medicines and medical equipment due, they are repeatedly told, to the great shortage of foreign exchange. This much used and abused excuse never seems to prevent Amin and his military ministers from embarking on frequent and very expensive trips abroad with plenty of foreign currency in their pockets for shopping.

The doctors insisted on meeting with Amin and he agreed and has just been to see them as there's been a complete breakdown in the hospital system. Amin stood before those experienced and highly qualified professionals and had the effrontery to say to them: 'As you know I am a doctor just like you, so I already fully understand all your problems.'

He said that he was working on solving their problems as soon as possible but meanwhile they must go back to duty. In fact, most of the drugs and medicines coming into the country are allocated auto-matically to the military hospitals, where the army doctors sell or use them for their private purposes. Amin probably knows this but he can't afford to change this arrangement as he must try to keep his military satisfied, so it's unlikely that there will be much in the way of improve-ment.

Tuesday 4 May

Yesterday I drove up to Moroto for a short criminal sessions. The jour-ney by car took the whole day with a stop at the Soroti Hotel for lunch and to give the driver a break. We then drove eastwards to the Karamoja border. It was hot and dusty on the *murram* roads but they were in fair condition so we were able to maintain a reasonable speed. When we reached the Iriri police post at the Karamoja boundary it looked exactly the same as when it was one of my posts in 1960, sixteen years ago.

We were met by an armed police escort in a Land Rover, as had been arranged in advance. There are the usual intertribal clashes and cattle raids still going on and, the day before, some over-exuberant tribesmen had attacked a police patrol with spears and a gun not far away from Iriri. One constable had been killed and the District Police Commander was taking no chances on my 50 miles drive to Moroto from Iriri, so the escort vehicle was filled with armed men. Fortunately it was an uneventful journey.

The court hall in Moroto is just a roofed-over, but unwalled, brick-built meeting hall used by the magistrate and by the district administration for *barazas*. Because of its open sides it's reasonably cool to work in; though not so much if one is encased in wig and robes as there's no overhead propeller fan. Another problem is when the occasional powerful gust of wind comes down from Mount Moroto behind the little township and is funnelled through the court hall. Away go loose papers, files and smaller books; advocate's robes billow out like parachutes.

It's the rainy season and both wind and heavy rain tend to arrive suddenly through the open sides, as it did this afternoon, and court was adjourned and cleared in record time; members of the public having a flying start since they had nothing to take with them, followed by witnesses, accused and prison warders, police and interpreter. I tried to exit with some dignity, though I felt like lifting my robes and sprinting for cover like the rest.

Some things are much the same in appearance as when I was stationed up here all those years ago, but there have been a few changes. In Moroto people now walk about wearing clothes and more of the cases coming before the court are killings by shooting rather than by spearing.

Wednesday 5 May

The OC Moroto CID called on me at the Mount Moroto Hotel. We had served together in the Police before independence when he was just a corporal. He gloomily informed me that this was a punishment station for him. Apparently he had dared to question the recruiting methods and policy of the dreaded Towelli. He and Towelli had long ago served together as assistant inspectors and, trading on this, he had unwisely asked him why he was recruiting so many illiterates as policemen these days instead of following the old policy of attracting only those with at least some secondary education. Towelli's reply was absolutely typical of him. He said: 'Education is not necessary; I never had any and look where I am now.' Towelli's reaction to this criticism was quite mild in comparison with his usual murderous or violent response, possibly because of their earlier association, and he merely transferred him to Karamoja.

Thursday 6 May

Both cases resulted in manslaughter convictions followed by another heavy downpour of rain. This afternoon I visited the prison. Previously the inmates were inside mainly for manslaughter, cattle-raiding and assaults. Now there are many for theft of property besides cattle. Inevitably the Karamojong have acquired more interest in material possessions so that thefts of bicycles, radios, clothing, bedding and money are quite common. Of course, cattle-raiding still continues but they tend to use firearms these days.

I wanted to see something of Karamoja after all these years and thought it would be a good idea tomorrow to drive down the Watershed Road and then on to Mbale and back up to Soroti for sessions there. A roundabout route but it would enable me to see something of my old area in southern Karamoja. However, the OC Police advised against it, first because of the heavy rains, which would make it difficult for a Mercedes to get through the muddy roads. As I well knew, a Land Rover is the best vehicle for use there. The second reason is the security situation here, with a number of trigger-happy gangs around the area, it would mean detaching enough of his much needed manpower to provide an adequate escort all the way down to Sebei. So, of course, I said I'd go out the way I came in and straight back to Soroti.

Thursday 20 May

I've been holding both criminal and civil sessions here at Soroti this month and we've been able to clear up a large number of outstanding cases. The civil sessions should finish next week and this afternoon I took a break from court and paid my usual inspection visit to the prison here. I like to walk around prisons with the superintendent, looking at the buildings and occupants on a normal working day with nothing special laid on. Out of courtesy I always inform the superintendent in advance when I'm going to visit and this time, when I arrived at the main gate, the double doors were flung wide and I found the long entrance drive lined on both sides by prisoners, who commenced clapping in rhythm. This is the sort of thing done for visits of Ministers and it really embarrassed me. It was definitely not what I expected. I asked the superintendent what it was all about and he replied that the prisoners were also planning to make speeches and to sing and dance for me. I said I was very grateful but I could not possibly agree to this as I was there only to make a quick working inspection and hear complaints, and then I had court work to get on with.

I knew from experience that once the tribal dances and songs began they would go on for hours and I just didn't have the time to spare for it. Moreover, it's the sort of reception accorded to people like the President or their own Minister, and if distorted word of this reached them, as it probably would, it might be thought that I had asked for such treatment and was getting a bit above myself. But mostly I just wanted to carry out an ordinary working inspection and then leave. It was quite obvious, though, that they had all put quite a lot of effort into the preparations and so I felt that, as a courtesy, I'd have to submit to some of it otherwise they might feel offended and upset. So we quickly compromised and I agreed to listen to one song and watch one short dance before inspecting the place.

I was given a large chair placed in the centre of a semicircle of seats occupied by all the prison staff and we watched the prisoners thoroughly enjoying their own entertainment of songs and dances accompanied by drumming. I felt rather conspicuous being the only European sitting there in undeserved splendour and I thought: I feel like Sanders of the River. I must have spoken this aloud because the superintendent said: 'I beg your pardon?'

'I said the dancing is very good.'

He replied: 'Yes, they've been practising all week for this. Would you like to watch another dance?'

I said I would very much but I simply didn't have the time as I had to get back to the court. However, before I could escape from the prison, as it were, they craftily managed to slip in a speech by a 'senior' prisoner (he had killed two people) who baffled me by declaring how happy they were to see me. After all, I had put some of them in there. Then he presented me with a quite roughly carved, but clearly identifiable, fish eagle cut from a block of wood and about 14 inches high. I thanked them and said I had been delighted by their entertainment and went off to have a quick look around the buildings before departing. I suspected that they were rather more pleased than I because it had provided them with a very enjoyable break in the dreary tedium of prison life and, after all, who can blame them?

Tuesday 8 June

While I was in court here in Kampala this morning and my cook was shopping at the Owino market, someone broke into my house and stole my bedding, radio and various other items. I called Jinja Road Police Station at lunch-time and a mere detective constable eventually arrived, but he said that, as there's no transport available at the station, he can't go out to make enquiries. Nowadays they won't go out on foot or by bicycle as the police used to do in my day. Then he had the cheek to say he needed to borrow my official car to use for his investigation. I gave him the short answer. No doubt he wanted to use it for his own purposes. So I'll just have to write the stuff off as usual; I'm sure that Jinja Road won't produce any results.

Thursday 10 June

I attended a meeting at the British High Commission this morning to discuss various matters and then went off to visit the only dentist left in town, as a back tooth has been playing up for several days. He removed it with some force and there was quite a lot of blood. In some pain, I then returned to court to continue with a part-heard case, but nobody could understand what I was saying until feeling was restored to my mouth.

Friday 11 June

There was yet another failed assassination attempt on Amin yesterday evening. The Annual Police Review took place at the police sports ground at Nsambya at 4 o'clock. I had been invited to attend but I had a trial in court and, anyway, Amin and his gang were going to be there so, as usual, I decided not to break off the hearing and go there, although I generally try to attend police functions.

He left just before 7 p.m. in an open Land Rover and, at the last moment, decided to drive it; so he changed places with the driver. He seems to get these last-minute premonitions and always acts on them. As he left the ground two grenades were thrown, which halted the escort car following him and injured his own driver sitting beside him. Two shots were then fired somewhere and Amin accelerated away and took his driver to Mulago hospital, where he died as the splinter from the grenade had penetrated his brain. He was sitting where Amin should have been sitting, but these people never seem to learn. The sheer incompetence of these attempts is incredible. They never take into account Amin's common habit of changing seats at the start of a journey; nor do they follow up any attack to ensure success.

Monday 21 June

Following the recent assassination attempt, it has been announced that the Defence Council has proclaimed Amin as President for Life and he's now to be addressed as Life President, plus all his other titles. What a jolly thought. Looks as if we've got a long wait for elections.

Last Wednesday I was invited to sit on the Court of Appeal for the first time. We High Court judges are all *ex officio* members of the Appeal Court and can be called upon to make up their numbers. The criminal appeal involved a senior police officer who had earlier been a member of the Commission of Inquiry with the present CJ, when he was the judge/chairman, inquiring into the disappearances of many people. The CJ felt it improper for him to sit on an appeal involving someone he'd worked with; so I got the job instead and naturally I accepted.

The case involved Detective Superintendent Esau of the CID, who had been charged with murder but was convicted by the trial judge of manslaughter and sentenced to imprisonment for ten years. A man called Mujuisa had been arrested at Kabale on various charges arising out of some bomb explosions and other incidents which occurred in Kampala in 1975. Superintendent Esau travelled down from CID HQ in Kampala in order to interrogate him. Esau first took him from Kabale Police Station by car in order to search his house. A police driver and two inspectors went with him and, when they reached a point about 3 miles outside Kabale, Esau ordered the driver to stop and they all got out. Esau told Mujuisa that he must now tell the truth, but he replied that he had nothing to say. He was told to lie down on the ground and Esau fired two shots from his pistol at the man, who died on the spot.

Esau's defence version was that, at the time, the man was trying to escape and had ignored his shouted order to stop, so he fired a warning shot into the air and then two more shots at the man when he kept going. However, Esau on his own admission was very drunk at the time, having consumed large quantities of a mixture of beer and *enguli*, and this was believed by the trial judge, although the two inspectors and the driver testified that he was not drunk when he fired the shots.

One of the prosecution witnesses was Towelli, who, as Director of Operations, had ordered the arrest of Esau, no doubt with considerable satisfaction because, as Esau testified, when he told Towelli of the incident in Kabale and the circumstances in which he shot the deceased, Towelli said: 'Don't try to deceive me, I know too much about the case. As a member of the Commission of Inquiry into

Missing Persons you caused me to be tried by the Military Tribunal. Now it is your turn. I am going to do much investigations into this.'

Esau's appeal counsel naturally made much of this and claimed that the investigation and subsequent prosecution testimony was biased and unfair to Esau because the police officers concerned had been subjected to undue pressure from above so as to ensure a conviction. This may have been true but, unfortunately for him, it was not put to the prosecution witnesses at the trial and it's doubtful whether any of them would have dared admit to such pressure even if it had happened, for they knew the risks of incurring Towelli's displeasure and revenge.

But, apart from that, Esau did shoot the man twice in the back and he was not trying to escape at the time for he was lying on the ground. Even if he had been escaping, there were four policemen present who could easily have pursued and recaptured him. The two Appeal Court judges felt that he was very lucky not to have been convicted of murder in the circumstances. Nevertheless, I was extremely unhappy at the idea of being in any way involved in assisting Towelli to obtain his revenge. Unfortunately Esau seemed to have placed himself in an impossible situation by his own actions and behaviour. I did suggest that perhaps the sentence might be reduced, but the other two judges could not agree and repeated that he was lucky not to have been sentenced to death for what was clearly a murder. I had to admit that this was probably true and the appeal was dismissed.

Tuesday 29 June

On Sunday an Air France Airbus, Flight 139, was hijacked by Palestinians on its way from Tel Aviv to Paris with 106 Israelis on board. It was forced to fly to Entebbe airport and landed there yesterday. Amin has been to visit them today and photographs were taken of him reassuring the passengers that they are safe. It's very noticeable that the hijackers are friendly with Amin and let him do as he likes; though it's not surprising really, since Amin has permitted additional automatic weapons and explosives to be handed over to them.

The hostages are being kept in a room in the old airport building, which is not far from the new international airport where they landed. They are guarded by Uganda Army Marines, mostly Nubians, who mingle freely with the hijackers. Meanwhile on Radio Uganda we are told that Amin is conducting negotiations with them for the release of the hostages. But there's little doubt that Amin has no intention of releasing them. It would suit both the terrorists and him to make a big gesture at this time by blowing up the Airbus and shooting the Israeli passengers. Amin could thus prove beyond doubt to Gaddafi and the Palestinians that he is their strongest and most active supporter in Africa, which he probably is.

Thursday 1 July

Amin has again had himself photographed by his own Presidential Press Unit in uniform, still wearing his Israeli parachute wings, addressing the hostages as he walked among them, stating that he will personally arrange for special food to be provided for the young children and medical treatment for those who need it. The French non-Jewish passengers have now been released and flown away. He also directed that the elderly passenger, Mrs Dora Bloch, be taken to Mulago Hospital in Kampala, although there is a suitable grade A hospital in Entebbe. Clearly he would not have been allowed such free access by the terrorists unless they were convinced that he was at one with them in their scheme.

Amin's main problem has been exactly what information to put out over the radio and in the press. He obviously wants to appear to the world as a responsible, competent and concerned negotiator who is determined to effect the release of the hostages. At the same time he very much desires to make it clear to his Arab paymasters that he is one of them and that the cursed Israelis are not going to get away with anything. The two ideas are so contradictory and so far apart as to be irreconcilable, so that even a clever and intelligent person could not convince anyone that he is on both sides. Amin's efforts in this direction are pathetic and it's obvious to those of us listening anxiously to the radio news reports just which side he is really on. There's no doubt that the release of the hostages occupies no place in his plans or intentions. The bulletins with their clear indications of imminent disaster, and the impossible demands of the terrorists for the immediate release of over 50 Palestinians held in several different countries, all point inevitably towards a ghastly massacre this weekend. It's an appalling prospect, but what can anyone do about it?

Saturday 3 July

Amin reluctantly had to leave his hostages and fly to Mauritius yesterday to hand over the chairmanship of the OAU to the Mauritian President. He now has no further interest in the OAU and he didn't bother to stay. He flew back this afternoon after making the excuse that he has to attend to the hostage negotiations. It looks as if the hostages are about to be shot. There are no negotiations, nor will there be, and there's no way he's going to release them now. Events seem to be carrying him towards a nasty climax.

Sunday 4 July

Wonderful news. Last night, only about four hours after Amin returned from Mauritius, a brilliantly planned and executed rescue raid was carried out by Israeli commandos on the old Entebbe airport and they have taken off with all the Israeli hostages except for Mrs Bloch, still in hospital. Apparently they killed the Palestinian and German terrorists and, so Amin says, 20 of his marines; so it was probably considerably more. They also blew up the dozen Russian MiG 15, 17 and 21 aircraft and the two ancient DC Dakota planes belonging to the Uganda Air Force which were parked at the old airport. Amin was at State House at the time, probably hiding under a bed. The Israelis may have thought he was still abroad; if they had known he was there they might have taken him with them. There are many people here who wish they had done so. State House overlooks the airport – I lived there in 1957 – and he must have heard the shooting and explosions as his 'elite' marines were dealt with; most of them took to their heels, I hear. Just as well, they wouldn't have stood a chance against Israeli commandos. Unfortunately, the commander of the commandos, Lieutenant-Colonel Yonni Netanyahu,* was shot dead by a sniper in the airport control tower, but his body was taken back to Israel.

Tuesday 6 July

There's a strong rumour that Mrs Bloch, the elderly woman hostage left behind in hospital, was removed from Mulago by SRB men and taken away and murdered. A local freelance photographer named Jimmy Parma apparently found her body near some trees outside Kampala and took photographs. Later SRB men killed him too, so there will now be no evidence.

Wednesday 7 July

Amin declared yesterday and today to be public holidays so that we could all mourn the deaths of 'the brave Ugandans and Palestinians who died in the cause of freedom'. I haven't seen anything of any mourning going on. The people I've spoken to are all very happy and relieved that the hostages were rescued and Amin thwarted of his massacre. As for Ugandans being killed, the marines are a bunch of

*Brother of Benjamin Netanyahu, who was Israeli Prime Minister in 1996–99.

murderous Nubians from the Sudan and nobody much cares what happens to them.

Amin has announced that the airport is closed and there will be no flights in or out. This is typically closing the stable door after the chicken has crossed the road and is up the creek without a paddle. Amin also said that a number of senior army and air force officers were guilty of cowardice and negligent failure to prevent the rescue operation from succeeding and so they have been 'permanently discharged', which we take to mean executed.

Monday 12 July

This closure of Entebbe airport has presented me with rather a problem as I'm due to fly home on leave on Wednesday and I definitely need to get away for a break after another two years of Amin's madness. I contacted the Minister of Justice and, with his help, managed to obtain a permit signed by the Army Chief of Staff and addressed to the officer commanding the marines at the airport, instructing him not to hinder my departure. Although the airport is closed to all flights, I've been informed that the East African Airways flight on which I'm booked to travel will in fact be allowed to land at Entebbe at 1 a.m. on Thursday on its flight from Nairobi to London. That's a relief.

Thursday 15 July – Somewhere in England

Because of the situation, I decided that it would not be a good idea to arrive at the airport so late last night and I left Kampala early in the evening. It also enabled the driver and the Deputy Registrar escorting me to get out of that dangerous area and return to Kampala at a reasonable hour; but it meant a very long wait for me at the airport. However, I could cope with that by taking a book to read, so I was not particularly worried.

We drove through the perimeter of heavily armed and anxious-looking marines, who suspiciously pointed their guns in our direction but who could not read the letter I carried. It's true that illiteracy can kill you. I was left to sit in the VIP lounge in solitary splendour being, in fact, the only passenger in the whole airport last night. There were no other flights arranged or allowed either in or out except the one London flight, which was apparently coming in merely to pick me up.

The night dragged slowly on and 1 a.m. came and passed with no sign of my flight arriving. I dared not sleep in case the flight came and went without anybody bothering to come and tell me, as there were no visible airport staff on duty and I hadn't seen anyone for hours. Nearly four hours overdue, the aircraft touched down and a chap came and helped me with my luggage, which I had kept with me all the time as there was no check-in, and I climbed on board with a sigh of relief and we departed.

The first-class cabin was empty except for an EAA captain travelling as a passenger and a Queen's Messenger surrounded by sealed bags. On arrival at Heathrow the spare captain went first to the flight deck and then left the aircraft. He returned shortly afterwards and came up to me and said that some members of the press had got wind that there was a passenger from Uganda aboard and they were eager to interview me about the recent Entebbe raid. Did I want to see them? I said that I was feeling very tired and anxious only to reach home as soon as possible and, in any case, I had no wish to speak to journalists as I intended to return to Uganda after my leave. The captain said: 'You'd better come with me then, and we'll dodge them.' He took me out of the aircraft through the aircrew door and into the terminal building, where we went along an empty passage with various labelled offices. In the end one we met an immigration officer, who took a quick look at my passport, and from there I was able to escape unnoticed. I thanked the captain and went on my way.

Wednesday 28 July

Yesterday it was announced that Britain had broken off diplomatic relations with Uganda; all aid, apart from the six of us, has already been withdrawn, so that it has little effect. But I think it's a mistake and I've written to the FCO to say so, as this is an unprecedented move and a possible political mistake to break with a member of the Commonwealth; especially when the UK is still dealing with foreign regimes that are as bad, or worse, in Latin America, Russia and Asia. I offered to come up to town to discuss it with anyone there interested and to give any assistance I can as I feel it's very dangerous to stop talking to Amin. He might well do something appalling in retaliation.

Saturday 7 August

I've heard nothing from the FCO but I'm in town for a couple of days for other reasons. At lunch-time I was passing Uganda House in Trafalgar Square, where the Uganda High Commission is located, when someone shot out of the front door and called my name. It was Mukasa, who had been the secretary of the KCC Commission of Inquiry with me in 1971, now bearded and disguised as commercial attaché at the High Commission. He said he's happy to be in London and out of Uganda these days. He added that if he's recalled he'll stay here as a refugee. There are, in fact, quite a number of Ugandans scattered around London.

The other day I was asked why I stayed in Uganda and worked for that monster Amin. I replied that I don't work for him but for Uganda and its people, regardless of who is head of state. The Judiciary is there to provide law and justice for everyone, not to support political or other leaders. It's true that many highly qualified and skilled people have had to flee or have just chosen to abandon Uganda. But if everyone of principle had gone then the country would be left almost entirely in the hands of the incompetent and corrupt who are destroying it. Fortunately, others stayed in their country and have tried to carry on against all odds. The few of us expatriates left can't do much but we can do something to help the ordinary people there from time to time. I believe it was Edmund Burke who said that for evil to triumph all that is necessary is for good men to do nothing.

Monday 11 October

A couple of weeks ago I stayed with George Kanyeihamba, formerly a lecturer at the Law School, and his family at Coventry, where he's teaching these days. He found he had to leave Makerere and Uganda some time back and came here to work. He now has a doctorate and seems to be doing well. I was glad to see him as it's several years since we last met and exchanged news.

I'm due to fly back to Uganda on Wednesday and, two days ago, I at last received a brief acknowledgement of my letter to the FCO in July. It is to the effect that they are grateful for my offer of assistance in discussions concerning the situation in Uganda but the murder of Mrs Bloch, who had a British passport, had ruled out any alternative course of action to that they had pursued. They then strongly advised me not to return to Uganda as it is not safe to go there while grave threats from Amin hang over the British community which might not have dissipated by the time I return. Today I received a similar letter from the Ministry of Overseas Development saying that although there has recently been a welcome lowering of the political temperature, Amin is unpredictable and any UK citizen travelling to Uganda risked finding himself in trouble and HMG's ability to help in such a situation would be limited. So what else is new?

Saturday 16 October

Having disregarded the advice of the FCO and the ODA, I arrived back in Kampala on Thursday. This morning there was a judges meeting to discuss the programme now that Amin has at last agreed to come and meet us here at the High Court. There are problems of security, finance, housing, court buildings and so on, which the Ministry of Justice has done nothing about for years. I urged that we should bring to his attention the truly appalling state of the Police, with especial regard to investigations, prosecutions and long remands of accused persons while their cases were being investigated. Some judges did not support me in this; they said it was not our business to interfere. But of course it is; the real reason, which I can well understand, is that they fear the dangerous reaction of Towelli, who as Director of Training and Operations is responsible for the situation in the Police. He certainly will not welcome criticism about it from us to the President.

However, I'm convinced that it's necessary to seize this opportunity, probably our only one, to speak out about such matters. I went further and said it's our duty to do so and, incidentally, to try to move Amin from his mistaken belief that the courts are solely to blame for the many acquittals and long remands. In my opinion there is no good reason why we in the Judiciary should remain silent and thus apparently agree that we are to blame for all that is wrong in this regard. Since there was this understandable reluctance to bring up such matters at the meeting and I feel so strongly about it, I suggested that I should make the criticism myself and point out that I am speaking only for myself and not on behalf of my brother judges. There was still considerable reluctance to agree to this, but I'm going ahead.

Saturday 6 November

Late yesterday evening my cook came in and disturbed my reading. He announced with great satisfaction that the police sentry outside had been bitten by a snake and was about to die. I went out and the constable reported that he had been sitting in a chair beside my car in the garage (and had obviously been asleep) with his hand hanging down near the ground when an unfriendly snake came along and bit his wrist. He showed me the two distinctive marks and he was shivering and looked very ill.

I knew from experience that it would be a waste of time to ring his station at Jinja Road as they never have any transport and, in any case, you can't get any sense out of the dozy night duty staff there. So I phoned the CPS Operations Room on 999. They sent a Land Rover and took him off to Mulago Hospital. He left behind him in my care his cap, belt, AK-47 and a spare full magazine, which I locked in a cupboard. This morning I rang the OC Jinja Road station from my chambers and inquired about the constable. I was told he'd been given an injection of serum and was now off duty, recovering. I mentioned that I had his gun and uniform items at home and we arranged that someone would call there and collect them at lunch-time.

Tuesday 9 November

A very hot safari to Soroti yesterday to hear a bundle of civil appeals. I have to return to Kampala after I finish court tomorrow afternoon for the big day on Thursday. I certainly don't want to miss that.

Thursday 11 November

Amin visited the High Court this morning – arriving late as usual – and we gathered outside the main entrance to meet and greet him on arrival. Before that, various senior police officers and one or two ministers arrived and we all stood around chatting. one of the arrivals was Towelli and, when he started to greet and shake hands with the judges, I moved quickly away behind some other people so as to avoid having to speak to him or shake the murderer's hand.

Amin then arrived and went off to the CJ's chambers for a private chat before joining us in the judges common room. We had envisaged a fairly private meeting with him and the Minister of Justice but, instead, the common room was crowded with assorted police and prisons officers, Ministers and permanent secretaries and other hangers-on standing all round the walls while we sat at the long table. I found myself sitting close to Amin, with Towelli standing ominously just behind me. Amin told us that various matters, including those that I wished to speak about, had already sufficiently been discussed between him and the CJ and the Minister at their preliminary meeting. It was suggested that we should now talk about other matters. But I had nothing else worth bothering about and I was determined not to be deprived of having my say in this obviously premeditated arrangement.

So I spoke up and said that I didn't know what had been said before our meeting started, so it might be possible that I could add something concerning the police. I reminded Amin that I had been a police officer and had spent some time as an instructor and so I had a good idea of what training should be given to police officers as well as how their duties should be performed. I briefly outlined the defects in the investigation and prosecution work and the reasons for long remands and I added that the main cause was hopelessly inadequate training and little or no supervision by officers. I could hear Towelli shifting about behind me and muttering: 'No, no,' to my remarks but, nevertheless, I carried on.

When I finished, Amin glanced at Towelli and remarked that any bad training was the fault of those in the past who had all been 'imperialist agents and we have now got rid of them all'. To which I remarked that I had been one of them. Amin gave a slight smile but said nothing. I wonder if any of it has sunk in; it certainly doesn't seem so with that last remark of his, but he doesn't always say what he's thinking. Maybe I haven't done any good at all. We shall see.

Saturday 18 December

The CJ was invited to present diplomas and give an address at the graduation ceremony yesterday of the latest magistrates course at the Law Development Centre. However, he has to be with Amin at some other function at the same time so he asked me to stand in for him. Fortunately he knows me well enough not to give me a prepared speech to read out for him. Instead he left it to me to say whatever I felt to be appropriate in what he described as my 'usual trenchant style'.

I greatly enjoy teaching or lecturing but I dislike making speeches, or listening to them, so I usually try to avoid them whenever I can. In this instance I decided to make it brief and, hopefully, to the point. Presumably there was little other news because my speech was featured on Radio Uganda and Uganda TV in the evening. In addition, it is front page news in today's *Voice of Uganda* under the headline: SENSE GUIDES MAGISTRATES' NOBLE TASK.

I had only one typed copy of my speech, in note form on one sheet of paper, which was snatched and carried off by the *Voice of Uganda* reporter immediately afterwards, so I have to rely on his report to remind me what I said. It seems I told them that to be successful a magistrate requires common sense and initiative because every case he comes across needs a different approach. So he must be alert and ready to adjust and adapt in order to deal effectively with unexpected crises and the surprising things that crop up. I advised them not to be afraid of admitting that they need time to look up a particular point in a book, as this enables them to give correct decisions in law and to avoid mistakes and blunders.

I spoke of the need for a sense of humour to overcame the tiresomeness and frustrations of the job. I warned them to watch their conduct in and out of court and advised them to behave with a sense of responsibility, modesty and dignity; at the same time not to think that their position made them superior within the society they serve. They should exercise tolerance, fairness and consideration for others and keep on with their reading so as to make sure that they are up to date with laws and procedures.

Monday 20 December

Amin has sent one of his multi-page telegrams to the Prime Minister of Israel protesting about a film recently made in Israel about the raid on Entebbe airport. He described it as 'false propaganda' and added that he allowed the French Airbus to land at Entebbe 'purely on humanitarian grounds'. He said he believes 'firmly in the just Arab cause and the Palestinian struggle'. He added: 'Uganda is not weak and we are not cowards but, because of our strong belief in saving innocent lives and promoting international understanding, we did not take action at Entebbe airport. The Israeli soldiers came purposely to destroy lives of innocent people, including the hostages.' He added: 'I personally did everything to save the lives of the hostages [like Mrs Bloch?] but all this hospitality was abused... Uganda will not be taken by surprise again... Those who are rejoicing will one day suffer and some of them will come and kneel before me for mercy...' and so on. Copies of the Aminagram were sent, as usual, to other Heads of State such as Castro of Cuba, Tito of Yugoslavia, Gaddafi of Libya and various other members of the dictators club.

For some time now I've had disquieting information from people abroad with whom I correspond that some of my letters have been tampered with in the post. I've made a few inquiries here and it seems that the miserable SRB types who sit around in the post offices, as they do in all public offices and buildings, watch out for outgoing letters addressed to people overseas and open them to see whether anything has been written about Uganda or Amin. So I never put my name and address on the back of envelopes. It means that one must be rather careful when making comments – just another headache.

Wednesday 22 December

In court this morning I dealt with a case in which the losing defendant had failed to pay the damages awarded to the plaintiff. I asked him to list what property he owned and he replied: one hut, two cows, five goats and a wife. When I pointed out that a wife is not property as people cannot be and have not been owned since the abolition of slavery, everyone in court – the defendant, the plaintiff, the court interpreter and others, looked at me aghast at such nonsense. I could see that they were totally unbelieving and clearly thinking: of course a wife is property – is she not purchased with bride-price, which itself indicates her value? There was a short silence and I said: 'Well, I say she's not property, anyway, and that's what matters.'

It's very difficult to get domestic servants nowadays. Even those who are experienced seldom stay long in one place. The present nomad-like urge to move on seems to be irresistible. It's tied up with security or, perhaps, insecurity. My present cook is not much good, especially with pastry. He persists in making rock cakes but they turn out so hard as to be inedible. However, he's keen and I haven't the heart to tell him he's a rotten cook, so I just keep throwing them away when he's not looking. The birds in the garden gave up on them long ago, due probably to broken beaks and indigestion. In a hundred years time an archaeologist will come on one of these cakes and it will give him something to think about. Today, as usual, I had tea on the verandah and casually flung the daily rock cake over the high shrubbery. There was a sharp cry from the other side and Douglas, my new *shamba* boy, emerged from the bushes rubbing his noddle and looking distinctly disgruntled. He shouldn't have been there anyway. Now he'll probably give the game away to the cook. *Shamba* boys these days are better educated but still as work-shy as ever. As far as I can see, he sits on a large tree stump most of the day reading his Luganda version of the Bible. I suppose he'd claim that he's going about his work religiously. I call him my Garden Gnome.

Wednesday 29 December

I was hearing criminal appeals today and in one case I had previously ordered a production warrant to bring the appellant prisoner to court from Luzira Prison. He didn't appear today as ordered; instead the sergeant warder handed up the production warrant, on which had been endorsed the words: 'Prisoner has now been transferred to Paradise.'

I asked: 'Does this mean what I think it means?'

The sergeant explained that a senior army officer had been allocated a broken-down beach resort on Lake Victoria by Amin. On it he's now building a sort of lido with beach huts and a restaurant for weekend picnickers, swimmers and fishermen and people like that. No doubt in order to get cheap labour, he demanded that some prisoners be brought out and based there to do the manual work. Thus, they had been required to transfer some prisoners there for a few months, including the man I had called for. The place is called Paradise Beach; hence the endorsement on the warrant.

1977

Monday 31 January

I've spent this month in Mbarara on criminal sessions, with nine murder cases and an appeal to deal with, followed by civil sessions. Not a very exciting collection of cases and it has rained every day. Some miles outside Masaka on our journey back to Kampala yesterday the road was blocked by a Mercedes Benz which was on fire. There was no sign of the driver. A few villagers were standing around enjoying the sight of one of the *Wabenzi*'s property going up in smoke, but nobody was doing anything positive. My driver was reluctant to drive past on the narrow road because he feared that the petrol tank might explode as we got alongside, and he added, rather irrelevantly, he hadn't yet been paid this month. He may have been influenced by American film-makers who show every vehicle collision or overturning as ending in an explosion. In fact, this rarely happens. In the police, I had attended many such traffic accidents and a number of burning vehicles but I had never seen one explode. We were not carrying a fire extinguisher and there was no water anywhere near. 'It won't explode,' I said, but I was outvoted by the driver and the police orderly; so we diverted on to a muddy track and, after slowly twisting and turning and skidding for a couple of miles, arrived back on to the road only a little further along from where we had left the conflagration. We stopped and looked back and saw the Benz still burning away merrily without having exploded. We now had a very muddy car and a lot of time wasted. 'There you are,' I said, 'I told you it wouldn't explode.'

The driver shrugged and said: '*Tugende, ssebo,*' (let's go, sir) so we did.

Friday 18 February

Since the beginning of this month I've been holding criminal and civil sessions in Masaka. When I came back to Kampala this afternoon I was told that the Anglican Archbishop of Uganda, Janani Luwum, an Acholi, was killed two days ago, together with two Ministers, Oryema, the former IG of Police, and Oboth-Ofumbi, Minister of Internal Affairs, in an apparent traffic accident. Actually Amin suspected them of possessing a store of concealed weapons and ammunition and plotting a coup against him, so they were shot and the 'accident' between two vehicles staged for photographers to record. Nobody is deceived by this fake accident story and the real facts seem to be widely known in Kampala. So now he's killed a Chief Justice and an Archbishop. Clearly nobody is safe from this evil creature.

Thursday 3 March

At the end of February a massacre of Acholi civilians was carried out by Amin's soldiers and murder squads in and around Gulu. A High Court criminal sessions was scheduled to be held there just now and the judge designated to go there decided that the situation in that area, from the reports available, made it too unsafe and he understandably declined to go. Nobody could blame him for that. However, the Gulu Chief Magistrate managed to get through on the phone and reported that the Gulu police believe that they can bring in the required witnesses for the criminal trials in spite of the situation. The CJ discussed it with me and I offered to go and find out the position and proceed with the sessions if I found it feasible. As usual, Barkis is willin'.

When I arrived in Gulu at about lunch-time last Monday, I found it to be a ghost town. The shops were all closed and shuttered and nobody was about. It was completely silent, with no traffic at all. After a while a few women and girls started to move about, but there were no men or boys to be seen anywhere. Some of the shops had been smashed in at the front and many were bullet-riddled. There were pock-marks on many walls where bullets and grenades had struck them. I thought it might be difficult to hold sessions after all, if nobody was going to turn up. However, I was pleasantly surprised to find the district court still working, though with only a skeleton staff. The police had somehow managed to round up and bring in the necessary witnesses for the cases. Perhaps for once police protection had saved them from becoming victims. The two local magistrates described what had been happening in the town and outside. They said that any Acholi males, young or old, seen walking about had been attacked and killed. Even at the schools those staff and pupils who had not managed to flee into the bush in time were slaughtered. It was an appalling story and nobody seemed to know what had started it or why. Since all the accused and witnesses were available I decided to commence the sessions.

Yesterday Amin sent the Vice-President, General Adrisi, up here to Gulu to tell the soldiers to cool down and stop killing people. It seems he has received numerous urgent and pitiful complaints about what was going on from chiefs, elders and other prominent Acholi and their friends, so that even he felt he had to take action to bring it to an end. Unfortunately, far too late. Adrisi came up by helicopter and was driven straight from the airfield to the army barracks, escorted by heavily armed guards although there is nobody to be seen on the roads or around the area.

I was in court all morning and, as usual, it had been very uncom-

443

fortable and hot with no ceiling fan working as the power was off. I was glad when it was time to break off for lunch so that I could return to the hotel and have a cool wash and rest before resuming in the afternoon. However, on arriving at the hotel, I was waylaid by a very worried-looking manager as I was on the way to my room. He told me that the Vice-President had arrived at the hotel and had insisted on using the VIP suite, which I was occupying, and he was there having his lunch and a rest. I was hot and tired and in need of my own lunch and a rest, so not in a good mood. I expressed my displeasure bitterly and bluntly about being turned out of my room by this miserable creature and what these dreadful people had been doing to the Acholi. The manager recoiled from my anger and indiscreet observations, as Adrisi was only a few yards away, and he rightly pointed out that he could have done nothing about Adrisi's demand for the room. A refusal or show of reluctance in the matter could have been fatal for him. I knew this and apologised for biting his head off and asked where I could go for a wash and lunch. He replied that he had already prepared a room and took me there.

The room was at the front of the hotel and, after lunch, I heard a commotion outside at the front entrance. Through the window I saw a closed-in military ambulance backed right up to the front steps. It was surrounded by armed soldiers who looked as if they expected an imminent attack. A bunch of officers then emerged from the hotel and I caught sight of Adrisi's frightened-looking face in the centre of the group. He was hustled into the back of the ambulance, where he crouched on the floor as the doors were closed. It immediately drove off at high speed, accompanied by heavily armed men in Land Rovers leading and following. Again the roads were completely empty and no soul was to be seen for miles. He was obviously a very scared little man and no doubt feared that the Acholi would be after him for what his soldiers had been doing up there.

When I went back into the suite I found my clothes had been thrown on to the floor in the corner of the bedroom and my toilet articles had been swept off the bathroom shelf and lay in a heap on the floor. I called the manager and showed him and he clucked in sympathy and called a room servant to pick things up. I returned to court unfortified by my lunch break. However, the sessions was completed this afternoon with three convictions for manslaughter and two acquittals; so it's back to Kampala tomorrow.

Saturday 5 March

Apparently after Adrisi returned to Kampala the other day Amin issued a statement deploring the killing of 'a few people around Gulu by some drunken soldiers' who, he said, had already been dealt with severely. That should provide solace to all the new widows and orphans in Gulu.

Monday 7 March

The second leg of the northern circuit is Arua, West Nile, which I discussed this morning with the CJ. He's worried about it because there's been no contact with Arua court for some time and apparently the Chief Magistrate has disappeared. The CJ asked me to get through to him by phone and report my safe arrival and what the situation is. I had intended to travel up there today and start the sessions tomorrow but, as usual, the DPP has failed to produce a prosecuting attorney and it's useless going there without one.

Wednesday 9 March

After persistent chivvying, a state attorney was found to prosecute and I travelled up to Arua all day yesterday; a long, hot and dusty safari with only one puncture on the way. On arrival I went to the district court to make the call to the CJ because the hotel telephone stands on the reception counter and any conversation on it can be overheard by SRB personnel hanging about nearby. The Chief Magistrate is not here and, in his absence, the local grade II magistrate is in charge but without any power to do very much. He told me that the Chief Magistrate, an Acholi, had fled because he had been warned in time that some SRB men were on the way to collect him. He's in hiding somewhere in the bush.

I told the magistrate to book a call for me to the High Court but he said he couldn't do so because they were out of touch with Kampala as the High Court administrative staff have neglected to pay the court telephone bill for many months. Post Office HQ reacted, perhaps on orders, by instructing the postmaster in Arua to cut off the court's telephone communications. This present sessions had been arranged through the police radio, which is also monitored by the SRB, so I didn't want to use it. The cutting-off of communications, the disappearance of the Chief Magistrate and some threats made to him, had upset and frightened the magistrate and he had not dared to send a report by letter, as he thought the mail would be intercepted; and he was probably right.

The OC Police called into the court to pay his respects, so I asked him to go across to the post office with an intimidating-looking armed guard to bring the postmaster before me without delay. When

445

they arrived I told the postmaster that I had instructions to report directly to the Chief Justice and I required to be connected to Kampala immediately. He replied that he could not do it as his instructions to cut off the court line had come from his superiors at Post Office HQ in Kampala. I tried to persuade him but he still refused, so I switched to Plan B and offered him a choice; he could either reconnect the court line straightaway and leave it open while I'm here or, if he still refused, he would be put in the police cells for obstructing the High Court sessions, which amounted to contempt of court, and he would stay inside until I decided to release him. To soften the blow, I added that I would speak to the Chief Justice about the telephone bill and I assured him it would be paid immediately, so he need have no fear about any consequences on that account from his HQ.

He promptly complied and obtained a line through to Kampala quite quickly. I made my first report to the CJ and he agreed to see that the bill is paid. He asked me to ring each day to keep him in the picture. I said I would not be able to say much on the phone as it's not sufficiently private, but I'd give him a full report in writing on my return. There's almost certainly an SRB man at the local telephone exchange.

The magistrate brought to my attention a most disturbing matter when he produced his court files. It seems that a certain Sergeant Dralega of Malire Mechanised Regiment in Kampala had quarrelled here in his home town with a man called Invule over some shop goods which the sergeant coveted for himself. A few days ago he arrested Invule and took him at gunpoint to Arua Police Station, where he ordered the police to type out a charge sheet alleging that Invule had committed shopbreaking and theft. He insisted that Invule should be kept in custody. When Invule was later brought before this magistrate by the police he pleaded not guilty and applied for bail and was released. The sergeant heard of this and went to see the magistrate and angrily demanded to know why Invule had been released contrary to his orders. The bail procedure was explained to him but he refused to agree to it.

He then went to the shop and re-arrested Invule, again at gunpoint, and he also arrested Invule's father, who had stood surety for him, and three other relations who just happened to be there at that time. While he was in the shop Dralega took the opportunity to help himself to many of the shop goods and some of Invule's personal property. Dralega took these people to the police station, where he insisted that all five should be included as accused persons on the charge against Invule. Since Dralega was waving a gun about, the assistant inspector told me that he felt he must comply, although there had been no report of an offence and no police investigation and there was no supporting evidence.

Dralega took all five men and the police officer to the court, where, still openly displaying the gun, he ordered the magistrate to take pleas from the 'accused persons'. Two of Invule's relatives were so intimidated that they pleaded guilty and the magistrate was required to convict them and sentence them to six months imprisonment. The others were remanded in custody after the sergeant had instructed the magistrate to cancel Invule's bail and warned him and the assistant inspector that they would be shot if any of the men was released for any reason. The magistrate afterwards recorded on the court file:

> The Accused were made to confess before me at gunpoint. I consider that was not proper and I maintain their previous pleas of not guilty. I was also threatened to be kidnapped because I allowed the first accused out on bail. For this I reserve the case for the Chief Magistrate when he returns.

I ordered the five men to be brought before me from the prison this afternoon and had their statements recorded and translated. I've also obtained written reports from the magistrate and the assistant inspector of police. Obviously the five men ought to be released from the prison because they are inside unlawfully but they told me, and I believe them, that their lives would be endangered, as would that of the magistrate, if they were released. So I've decided that it would be safer for them to remain in prison until the sergeant can be dealt with and satisfactorily neutralised. However, I've given the prison superintendent a written order directing that the convictions will eventually be confirmed as quashed by me and that, for the time being, the men are to remain in prison only for their own safety and must be treated like remand prisoners.

Saturday 12 March

I've been getting on with the Arua sessions – there are eight murder cases to hear – and this morning I was sitting in the Chief Magistrate's office writing a judgment when the magistrate came in and said quietly that the wife of the Chief Magistrate was outside at the back. She didn't want to show herself to the staff or anyone as the SRB are still looking for her husband, but she wished to speak to me.

I know the Chief Magistrate well; he's a former Law School student, but I hadn't met his wife before. Not surprisingly, she was very nervous as the SRB might easily decide to take her in for questioning. I asked about her husband and she said he's safe at the moment and hiding out in the bush and she knows where he is. They are planning to go to Kenya soon. There are some arrangements that need to be made about his salary and one or two other matters that I agreed to deal with in Kampala for them.

Monday 14 March

The sessions are making good progress, with six convictions for manslaughter and one acquittal so far. In one case the accused has been on remand awaiting trial for four years, which naturally affected the standard of testimony from the witnesses, who were illiterate. Some were very unintelligent and others were understandably let down by their memories after so long.

Apparently there was beer party and a group of people were taking part in a traditional dance near the drum. They were interrupted by another group led by a man carrying a ceremonial axe called a *koyo*. The accused, Manganga, was in this group and he alleged that a bystander called Atilio had bewitched the dance and a drunken quarrel ensued. This turned into a fight and stones were thrown. A man called Otera, with others, intervened and the group leader cut Otera on the neck with the *koyo*. Seeing this, Manganga then stabbed Otera with a knife, also in the neck. He was unable to explain why he did this. Too drunk and excited at the time, I expect.

The post-mortem report showed deep wounds on both sides of Otera's neck severing the windpipe and carotid artery, which bled into the open windpipe, causing him to die from asphyxia and shock. The group leader fled over the border into Zaire, which is very close, and only Manganga was arrested by the *Mukungu* chief. For various reasons I convicted Manganga of manslaughter. He's aged about 50 and has spent four years in prison on remand, so taking that into account today, I gave him another three and a half years.

I phoned the CJ late this afternoon and told him I'm returning to Kampala tomorrow and will report in full on arrival. Thankfully there's been no sign so far of the unpleasant Sergeant Dralega.

Wednesday 16 March

After a long drive back yesterday, I showed the various statements to the CJ and pointed out that as long as the sergeant is free and able to obtain a gun, either from the barracks in Kampala or Arua, as he easily could, then nothing can safely be done regarding the case and the men concerned. I said that I want the sergeant first discharged from the Army so that this dangerous threat can be removed and I can then release the men.

This morning the CJ called in the DPP to discuss possible action. The DPP, whose opinion I generally regard as useless, said we must approach General Adrisi, as Minister of Defence, and ask him to deal with the matter. I immediately objected and stated that I have absolutely no faith in Adrisi or his ability to act effectively, or even in his willingness to do so, as he has never shown any sign of being in support of law and order. I insisted that only Amin could and would sort out the matter, and it was agreed to approach him. So I put together my report and the various statements for the CJ take to Amin.

Friday 25 March

The CJ told me yesterday that Amin had agreed with the course of action that I suggested regarding Sergeant Dralega and he has already been discharged from the Army. That's a relief. I sent a telegram to Arua court ordering the release of the men, and arrangements have already been made to transfer another chief magistrate up there. I hope the other chap managed his escape safely with his family.

In the *Voice of Uganda* this morning there's a report that Amin addressed a large gathering of soldiers from all regiments attending some inter-unit basketball finals. In his speech he spoke of this incident, without mentioning names, and warned that 'all soldiers must respect the law of the country and uphold the legal system'. He added: 'Instead of the unnecessary interference in the course of justice as I have told you happened in Arua, soldiers should assist the law courts to ensure the highest degree of justice in the country.'

Thursday 14 April

I opened criminal sessions at Jinja on Monday. There are eight murder cases and one aggravated robbery. The hotel is even more awful than usual; there's no water except what is fetched in buckets, no proper room service, the food is appalling, there's been a considerable leakage of water through the ceiling, the mosquitoes are bothersome and the noise at night by the numerous drunken soldiers and SRB men using the hotel makes sleep very difficult. A fairly normal situation, in fact.

Wednesday 20 April

The sessions continue at Jinja, with no improvements in the ghastly hotel. There is a very old and locally much respected Indian advocate named Bhatt, who has been in practice in Jinja from the beginning of time. He didn't leave with the other Asians five years ago because he said he was too old and had no family left and nowhere to go, so they let him stay on. It's his invariable custom to raise a multitude of preliminary points and objections before the commencement of any trial in which he appears. Unfortunately over the years the courts have indulged him in this excessively time-wasting hobby. Most of his objections are so absurd they can quickly be dismissed, but he still takes hours on his feet explaining tediously and boringly at great length why he is making them and it's very difficult to get him to stop, except for the frequent need to adjourn for a few minutes at his request so that he can totter out to the loo. A criminal trial in which he's defending counsel takes twice as long as it would with anyone else. As there are so many pending cases and so little time in which to deal with them, I groan with despair when I see his name down for the defence. In addition, in spite of all his years of experience, he's really not much good at the job.

Tuesday 26 April

I finished the Jinja sessions today with the last of the judgments, making a total of five convictions, three acquittals and one withdrawal from prosecution. I then drove back to Kampala, glad to be out of that dreadful hotel at last. There were masses of white butterflies along the road, which runs for miles between the thick Mabira Forest. Perhaps the road is the only open space where they can cavort. The windscreen of the car was soon heavily spattered with them. As usual we stopped on the way to fill the car boot with oranges and the driver's *matoke*. The green oranges that grow here are excellent for squeezing and making orange squash and they can be purchased from the roadside stalls very cheaply.

Tuesday 10 May

The Military Governor of Central Province, which includes the City of Kampala, is a certain Major Nasur. As an army private he was promoted to sergeant when he was appointed football coach. He is uneducated, vain, conceited, immensely arrogant and has become fat, which is regarded here as the outward and visible sign of accumulated wealth and power. He is also an inveterate meddler and, since he became Governor and realised what power he had or could seize for himself, he has established a reputation for arbitrary and often extremely unpleasant behaviour with the civilian public; most especially with those who have the misfortune to displease him in any way.

At this time of great shortages when, among many items, shoes just cannot be obtained anywhere, he has issued an absurd order that nobody is allowed to wear plastic slip-on sandals, called flip-flops, in the city. These are the cheapest form of footwear available and within the price range of the ordinary person. Many can afford nothing else and so the order is often ignored. It's a risky thing to do, however, because Nasur likes to roam about 'his' city and if he spots anyone wearing such sandals there can be unpleasant consequences. I'm told that recently he ordered two such people to eat their flip-flops.

In a recent speech Amin asserted rather sanctimoniously, but quite truthfully, that a lot of senior government officials are drinking too much. Nasur was present for that speech, of course, and he evidently decided to act on it, perhaps to ingratiate himself with Amin. Last Sunday afternoon, Nasur went along to the Standard Hotel, formerly the exclusive Kampala Club, and in his usual heavy-handed way, arrested eight people, including a magistrate, whom he found drinking at 3.30 p.m., took them to CPS and ordered the police to lock them in the cells.

They were taken to court yesterday morning and charged before another magistrate with consuming liquor on licensed premises outside the permitted hours. They agreed that they had been drinking but explained that they had been playing or watching tennis on the courts next to the hotel and they were members of the tennis club, which had become a part of the hotel so that it could have access to a bar. The magistrate nevertheless convicted them 'on their own pleas' and fined them. Perhaps he was not willing to risk upsetting the Governor. Because Nasur was involved the case was splashed all over the local newspapers.

When I read this I directed the Registrar to call for the court files from across the road for my perusal. When I read them my initial suspicions were confirmed that both the Governor and the magistrate had acted unlawfully. Although the hotel bar licence doesn't permit the sale and consumption of liquor at that time in the afternoon, the associated tennis club had obtained a special club licence which allowed club members, such as all the accused, to drink liquor at that and other times. So they had committed no offence. I contacted the DPP and he agreed and I quickly made revisional orders in the various cases, quashing the convictions and setting aside the fines. I remarked in my order:

Even if they committed an offence it was only a minor one and did not justify the arrest of persons of substance such as the accused. They could have been warned to attend court by summons. The arrests and subsequent detentions were unlawful and unnecessary. At the very least the police should have released them on bail with instructions to attend court instead of keeping them in custody. This seems to have been an example of using a large sledgehammer to crack a very small nut.

So far there's been no reaction from Nasur.

Thursday 19 May

I've just dealt with an application by the DPP for my opinion on a point of law. A simple theft case in which one Kibwire was charged with theft by servant of a few boxes of matches belonging to his employer. Unfortunately this minor offence has been dragging on for a long time, with many quite unnecessary adjournments in court. Thus, it was still pending when Amin signed the amendment to the Economic Crimes Tribunal Decree which made a number of offences exclusively triable by military tribunal, including this offence of theft by servant.

Consequently, when this case came before the magistrate for continuation of his prolonged trial, the police prosecutor submitted that as the offence was triable only by a military tribunal, this trial could not continue. The magistrate didn't know what to do so he passed it to the chief magistrate, who invited the resident state attorney to appear and make submissions. But he didn't know what to say so he got rid of it by applying that the question of law arising should be reserved for the opinion of the High Court. It's called passing the buck.

I'm particularly keen to keep as many cases as possible out of the tribunals and it seems that the DPP, who is responsible for prosecutions before them, feels the same. He mentioned that there are a number of cases in a similar position, so it would be useful and helpful to have a High Court opinion.

This was not a question of a new offence being introduced but of a different court and procedure with harsher penalties, thus adversely affecting the rights of individuals concerned. The many adjournments which brought this case into the tribunal frame were not the fault of the accused and I could see no good reason why he should be made to suffer for the inefficiency of the prosecution and the court. I held that cases commenced before the amendment to the Decree were not affected by it and they should continue to be dealt with by the original trial court, which should take urgent steps to finalise the particular case.

Friday 27 May

Yesterday I spent interviewing, on behalf of the Judicial Service Commission, law graduates who wish to be potential magistrates grade I. There were one or two reasonable possibilities but the rest received a thumbs-dawn. The big problem is that the low salary offered in comparison with what even a duffer can earn in private practice does not attract the best applicants.

This morning there was a judges meeting and the main subject discussed was the number of complaints of corruption in the Judiciary; some of which are probably justified, but many others are made by losing parties in cases. There is a persistent complaint from several advocates that a certain judge is corrupt, but nobody names him. My contribution was that he knows who he is and obviously he should do something one way or the other to end the speculation. Resignation or retirement would seem to be a way out.

Tuesday 31 May

Yesterday I drove to Mbale for criminal sessions with eight murder cases to hear. On the way one of the car's rear tyres burst; not just a puncture, it disintegrated. We were moving fast but, fortunately, on a clear road between Tororo and Mbale and the driver managed to keep control until we stopped on a flat stretch of grass off the road. Since the tyre was quite new it looks as if it may have been defective. Somebody should be sued.

Thursday 2 June

I was about to go into court this morning when the phone rang and the Chief Registrar called from Kampala to inform me that my house was broken into again last night and, he said, it looked as though a lot of property had been stolen; in fact, he said the house had been stripped. I refixed today's case and drove straight to Kampala.

On arrival I found that all of the five outer doors had been forced, which seemed odd; and inside, most of my movable property had gone, including all my clothes, bedding, household items, radio and record player. There was a clear element of vandalism in addition to theft, which is unusual. For instance, why smash all the doors? In the garage large crowbars had been used to rip open the double doors with excessive force and then used on the rear door of my Jaguar, which was twisted and bent out of shape. The radio had been ripped from its moorings with considerable force. However, the very effective steering lock had prevented it from being removed. Two large crowbars were lying on the ground nearby, as if leaving a message.

Although Jinja Road station had been informed by the Chief Registrar, there was no policeman on the scene and nobody had come to guard my residence in my absence. When I queried this with the OC Police I received only vague, off-hand excuses. It would appear that the police were not baffled – they just were not bothered. Considering the excessive and deliberate damage done and the theft of many useless items in addition to valuable property, and some other signs I found around the house and in the compound, I have a strong suspicion that the police themselves were involved. Consequently I decided to ring up the Director of CID at Police HQ. I know him and, without mentioning my suspicions, I asked him to send someone to have a look around as Jinja Road was doing nothing about it. Two senior CID officers came soon after that and sniffed around. The older one, whom I've known for a long time, came up to me and said quietly that he strongly suspected that the job had been carried out by policemen, most probably from Jinja Road station. He would make further enquiries and report back. I then told him of my own similar suspicions and he suggested that I shouldn't contact that station about the matter nor ask them to send anyone to the scene. I said that it was in line with what I had already decided.

My servants claim that they slept through the whole incident and heard nothing, which I simply do not believe. The considerable noise that must have been made breaking all the doors, especially the large garage doors next to their quarters, should have been heard by them. Also at least one vehicle must have been driven into the compound to carry away all the property. Maybe they've been intimidated or bribed to keep quiet.

Saturday 4 June

I asked one or two of my own contacts to keep their eyes and ears open. Yesterday I was at home while the doors and locks were being repaired or replaced, and one of them called in and said that a fellow staying in the servants quarters of a neighbour was in possession of good quality imported men's clothing of a sort unavailable in Uganda. He's said to be a relative of a constable at Jinja Road station and was showing signs of being about to move away. I immediately contacted CID HQ on the phone and asked for the Director. I was told he was not available so I left a message asking him to ring me urgently. Nothing happened and I tried a few more times but each time I was told he was unavailable. I sent a note to him but again no response. In the present circumstances this meant only one thing.

It seems that the inquiry has been killed and the CID officers have been told to drop it. In the circumstances only Towelli could and would have been likely to have given the necessary orders to both Jinja Road and the CID preventing an investigation involving a High Court judge. It's possible that he has chosen this way to obtain his revenge and express his displeasure about my criticisms to Amin at the High Court meeting with the judges.

Well, we shall see. I'm determined that his victory won't be complete, so I've written a report to the CJ explaining that I cannot continue working here effectively without sufficient clothing and household property, and I've requested that the President be informed that this was due to the failure of the police to guard my property while I was up-country performing my duties as a judge. I've supplied a list of stolen property and values.

Wednesday 8 June

Yesterday was the Queen's Silver Jubilee and the Commonwealth Heads of Government conference opens in London today. For weeks Amin has been announcing that he will attend both events, even if he has to fly in secretly. Some businessmen and retired ex-service Brits living quietly in Uganda were somehow persuaded to accept reserve military ranks and form a special bodyguard for Amin's proposed UK visit. A photograph in the *Voice of Uganda* shows them all kneeling before him taking the oath of allegiance, normally taken while standing, with Amin and Adrisi standing there grinning with triumph at this shameful act. In a speech recently Amin said: 'I love the British people and I will be going there with two hundred and eighty people. I have a long memory of Britain and the Monarch. I even knew the Queen before Mr Prince Phillips.'

However, the British Government has made it clear that he isn't welcome nor will he receive any facilities or official recognition. Commonwealth Secretary-General Ramphal has indicated that in his opinion Amin could not and should not be prevented from attending if he so wishes. But then he's not only ignorant of the situation but also has this Third World view that tends to be divorced from the realities. Sometimes such a view may be attractive or amusing, but not in this case.

However, the message has finally got through to Amin that he quite definitely will not be welcomed or received in Britain and he realises that he would not be able to laugh that one off. So he has backed down and announced rather weakly that he's unable to spare any of his precious time to attend the conference because all his time and efforts are concentrated on fighting Uganda's Economic War. A sigh of relief all round, I should think.

Saturday 11 June

I've been continuing with the Mbale sessions and came back to Kampala yesterday evening to see how things are at home. My contact dropped in this afternoon and told me that apparently there was a plot to shoot down Amin's aircraft with a missile as it took off from Entebbe airport to take him to the London conference. When he decided not to go they decided to ambush him on the Entebbe road at mile 15.

Considering that the officers concerned had access to whatever weapons, transport and radios they needed, such a simple plan ought to have succeeded if it had been carried out with a modicum of competence. But, as usual, there was insufficient organisation and secrecy. Amin, as he has often done, scented danger and he simply used his old trick of changing seats with the driver of his vehicle so that he was driving, instead of sitting in the back, and the driver was sitting alongside him. He was thus on the opposite side of the car from the ambushers, who were not even on both sides of the road. He had two escort vehicles with him, both following behind and, when they reached the place, they came under automatic fire and several bodyguards were killed or injured.

A bazooka shell was fired at the nearside of Amin's car, where they thought Amin would be sitting, but it killed his driver, whose body partly shielded Amin from the effects. Even so, he was injured by fragments of the shell and the blast threw him out on to the road, where he lay stunned and only semi-conscious for a short while. This was the perfect opportunity for the ambushers to move in and finish off the job, for he was completely at their mercy and there was no opposition or protection. But, as usual, they failed to do anything positive or effective. Instead, for some unknown reason, they lost heart, or lacked the courage and determination to see it through, and they all fled.

Amin collected several small pieces of shell splinters in the upper part of his back, shoulders and arms. He was very shaken and shocked at his narrow escape and he went into hiding on one of the smaller islands of the Ssese group on Lake Victoria, where he has remained incommunicado. Rumours are flying about that he has died as a result of the ambush, or that he has been badly injured, or that he has fled the country. There is much speculation about who is likely to succeed him as President.

Monday 13 June

I returned to Mbale this morning to finish off the sessions. Amin has reappeared looking quite chirpy and has announced that he was not injured at all in the attack on him and that he merely went to the island for a rest and to plan the next stages of the Economic War. It has also been announced that the Defence Council has awarded Amin the CBE, meaning 'Conqueror of the British Empire in Africa in General and in Uganda in Particular' and, with his other decorations and titles, he is to be referred to as the Conqueror of the British Empire in future. This is apparently in retaliation for being kept out of the UK for the Commonwealth conference. What a buffoon.

There have been a number of arrests and executions of air force officers at Entebbe who were suspected of being implicated in the recent attempt on Amin's life. Sadly one of them who was shot was Major Addy Mutono who was on the KCC Commission of Inquiry with me back in 1971. I have not had the chance to meet his baby son who was named after me.

Wednesday 15 June

I was recalled to Kampala this morning as, for some unknown reason, the Vice-President, General Adrisi, was to address all judges and magistrates at the Conference Centre this afternoon. It sounded like a typical waste of time to me. There's nothing that cretinous moron can say that could justify closing down all the courts. Adrisi holds the portfolios of Minister of Defence and Minister of Internal Affairs now, unfortunately. It sounded rather ominous that Amin should be turning him loose on us.

Recently some printed leaflets have been circulating clandestinely stating that Amin has made a mess of running the country and the economy and advising that he should step down and hand over power to the Chief Justice until early elections can be held. Perhaps it was the mention of the CJ that prompted Amin and the Defence Council to suspect that the Judiciary is somehow involved or sympathetic and that, consequently, we are in need of a dressing-down. But it may be something quite different. Looking for logic or reasons behind many of the pronouncements and actions of Amin and his supporters is an unrewarding task. Adrisi has demonstrated what a mess he can make of the two security ministries, so perhaps Amin has decided to let him have a go at us. Ideas don't originate in the dim recesses of Adrisi's mind so presumably he's acting an Amin's orders.

We all congregated in the hall of the Conference Centre and awaited the arrival of the great man. He came accompanied by a string of army officers, including an interpreter, for he knows no English and very little of any other language, it seems. With him was Obura, now Commissioner of Police, the title having been changed back again, who previously succeeded Towelli as head of the notorious Public Safety Unit. He has recently converted to Islam, no doubt to further ingratiate himself with Amin.

It turned out not to be a meeting or conference at all, but merely an uninterrupted harangue by Adrisi. His very basic Swahili didn't make much sense, but his interpreter managed to do quite a good job of producing a string of accusations against the Judiciary. He may have been reading from a prepared script. We were blamed for being too lenient with criminals and for the excessively long remands of those awaiting trial. We were accused of being corrupt because we 'deliberately release known criminals' who had been 'arrested as a result of the efficiency of the Police and Army' and so on. It seemed clear that Obura had provided the brief for Adrisi and had seriously misled him, since the repeated theme emerged that the Police were carrying out their duties with highly commendable competence and efficiency whereas the Judiciary was spending all its time frustrating their noble efforts.

I could barely restrain myself from interrupting this nonsense and the CJ made several attempts to do so and to explain our side. Each time he tried to speak, Adrisi, sitting beside him, brushed aside his arm from the microphone and prevented him. It was a shocking exhibition of disrespect and sheer bad manners; though probably to be expected from someone like Adrisi. Eventually the CJ burst into Adrisi's rubbishy tirade and spoke quickly, making his points that the Police were largely to blame as a result of their almost totally incompetent investigations and inadequately prepared prosecutions. He added that to blame the Judiciary for these shortcomings was both unfair and undeserved. At this we all spontaneously burst into applause and support for the CJ and drowned the proceedings with loud clapping, cheers and table-banging.

Adrisi was completely taken aback by this; it had probably never occurred to him that there might be another side to the problem, even if he was able to understand it. He had expected us to sit quietly listening to his words of wisdom and to accept the blame that he said was ours. He was particularly upset because the judges sitting in the front row, which has a long curved table in front of it for microphones, were thumping the table vigorously in support of the CJ's words. Adrisi lost the thread of his harangue and, instead, kept on about how bad it was that we should dare to bang the table at *him*, the Vice-President no less, and nobody should show such disrespect. He kept repeating pitifully: '*Mimi Vice. Mimi Vice,*' (I am the Vice) like a frustrated child.

He could not grasp that he was not addressing a bunch of army recruits as ignorant and illiterate as himself (he cannot even write his name) but he was talking to a gathering of people trained in the law who could hardly be expected to hang respectfully on the words of a man whose sole accomplishment was driving an army lorry. As Mr W. Shakespeare put it:

> Drest in a little brief authority,
> Most ignorant of what he's most assur'd...

The meeting soon broke up when Adrisi saw that he was not having any effect on us and no apology to him would be forthcoming. He stalked out, muttering and bewildered, followed by a very disgruntled Obura. The CJ was naturally very upset at this attack on his Judiciary by one who was clearly representing the President and, when we judges gathered round him outside the hall and told him that we fully supported his words and action inside the hall, he declared that he could see no other course but to offer Amin his resignation. The general feeling of the judges was that we should all do the same, but he asked us not to, saying that his own should be sufficient to make the point in the circumstances.

Tuesday 28 June

When I called into his chambers to have a word with the CJ this afternoon, he told me that when he saw Amin and handed in his resignation Amin didn't refuse to accept it or try to talk him out of it, he merely said: 'Well, you know Adrisi's Swahili is very poor and he could easily have been misunderstood.' So what was the point in sending him to address us?

The accusations made against us by Adrisi were given maximum publicity on the radio, TV news and in the newspapers without mentioning what the CJ had said in reply or our reaction. Amin knows Adrisi so well and he must have realised that to allow such an ignoramus to speak to the Judiciary was bound to upset and annoy us. Perhaps that was what he wanted to happen, for some devious reason. Nobody appears to have gained anything at all from the incident, which has merely left a thoroughly unhappy and dissatisfied Judiciary with morale even lower than before. Meanwhile, Amin seems to have ignored the CJ's resignation letter and he continues to treat him as CJ.

The CJ handed me a letter from the President's Office to the Minister of Finance and copied to me, through the CJ, stating that my personal losses in the housebreaking incident earlier this month were, in the view of the President, the result of inadequate security having been provided while I was away on duty, and that government must accept the blame. The Minister of Finance was directed to pay me in sterling the total value of the missing items so that I can obtain replacements when I next go on UK leave. So it looks as though Amin wants me to stay on for a while.*

Wednesday 29 June

Another consequence of the housebreaking is that a 6-feet-high security fence has been put up all round the compound of my residence. The cemented supports have an angled top designed to face outwards to keep out intruders, or to face inwards to keep in prisoners or detainees. True to form, the men from the Ministry of Works have put mine in the wrong way round, while I was away at Mbale. Presumably this was done to prevent my escape. There's a high wrought iron double gate on the drive now with a wooden sentry box for the police sentry. No doubt the white ants will soon get to work on that (the box not the sentry).

Thursday 5 July

I opened Tororo criminal sessions today but I have to commute as I'm staying at the Mount Elgon Hotel in Mbale, 28 miles away. When I arrived at the Rock Hotel in Tororo yesterday, the manager told me that his whole hotel had been taken over by the military tribunal now supposed to be working in the area, and the military have refused to allow other people to stay there while they are in occupation, although there are plenty of vacant rooms. So he had transferred my booking; which made it very inconvenient and time-wasting, but it was the best he could do at short notice. I'm certainly not going to cancel my sessions because of those miserable people.

Monday 11 July

Mentally disturbed prisoners are supposed to be kept apart from other prisoners while they await transfer to the mental hospital at Butabika in Kampala. Occasionally in some prisons they are allowed to mix

*When I went on leave in April 1978 Finance gave me the sterling cheque.

with other prisoners, especially if they are considered to be harmless or, as usual, there's insufficient space; but it's against regulations.

This afternoon I visited Tororo prison and, as I was leaving one of the wards after inspecting it, I stepped outside followed by some prison officers. There was a small group of prisoners standing nearby, and a poor deranged fellow moved from the group and suddenly leapt at me and banged me on the top of my head with his fist. It was not a hard blow and I quickly pushed him in the chest and he overbalanced. He remained silent all the time. The prison superintendent and my police bodyguard just stood there smiling while the other prisoners laughed. But, like Queen Victoria, I was not amused as he might quite easily have been more violently inclined and holding something that could be used as a weapon. I pointed out sharply to my bodyguard that he was there specifically to step in and prevent any such attack on me, not just to hang about behind me gossiping to the warders.

I shall complete this Tororo sessions tomorrow when I deliver judgment in the fifth and last murder case. Sir Norman Birkett KC, who was a famous barrister until he became a judge, was appointed the UK alternate judge at the Nuremberg trials of Nazi war criminals in 1945–46. Afterwards he wrote: 'When a perfectly futile cross-examination is combined with a translation which murders the English language, then the misery of the Bench is almost insupportable.' I know exactly how he felt. Sometimes, though, the problem is to obtain an accurate translation rather than a mere interpretation.

Friday 15 July

There's an article in the *Voice of Uganda* about a mysterious illness in the south-west of Uganda that has manifested itself there in the last few years, especially in the Masaka and Ankole districts, that the doctors say they haven't yet been able to identify. It affects youths and young adults, mostly men so far, and causes them to lose weight rapidly and succumb very easily to various diseases that are prevalent. Already a number have died, mainly of pneumonia. The locals call it 'Slim Disease'. The Ministry of Health has issued a statement to say that there is no new disease and it's nothing for people to worry about. But the fact is they don't know what it is nor how to treat and cure it. Some photographs of very emaciated young men were printed with the newspaper article. They look like survivors of German concentration camps in World War II.*

*In the 1980s when this disease became known in the West it was called AIDS.

1977

Tuesday 2 August

I drove up to Moroto yesterday for a criminal sessions consisting of only one murder case. After we left Soroti and had been going for about 10 miles I had a feeling that we were going north rather than east, although the countryside looks very much the same all around. This new driver had said he knew the road so I had left him to it, but when I questioned him he admitted that he might have taken the wrong road. I always carry an OS map of the area I'm travelling in (left over from my police days) so I checked and found we were going north-westwards on a road leading to Lira. The map also showed a fairly rough road or track, which we then took through the bush to bring us back down to the road to Moroto.

The prosecution case today was pathetic. It wasn't helped by the failure to find the body of the deceased, although that wouldn't necessarily have been so much of a problem. But the witnesses were hopeless and I had to find that the accused had no case to answer. A pity there were no other cases as I'd like to have spent more time in Karamoja.

Monday 15 August

I went next to Soroti for criminal sessions after Moroto but, as often happens, there was no prosecuting state attorney available, so it was put off until this week. I enjoy visiting Soroti; it's a quiet little township, sleepy in the heat. The Soroti hotel is as comfortable as they can make it in these difficult days of power cuts and water shortages. After court at the end of each afternoon, I go for a walk from the back of the hotel, usually up to the odd outcrop called Solot Rock, on the top of which I sit and survey the flat country around; miles and miles of Africa shimmering in the heat haze with only the soft sound of doves breaking the immense silence. It's my Thinking Place. In and around the small town the local men sit outside their huts or homes drinking millet beer, called *ajono*, which they believe increases their potency and gives them the magic words to keep any woman spellbound and cause her to fall madly in love with them (they hope), especially when they dance the traditional *akogo*. If only all were as peaceful as it looks.

On the front page of the *Voice of Uganda* last Thursday we were told that Amin has announced that the Uganda Air Force is being prepared 'for an impossible mission with other friendly countries' which he refused to name. He told the pilots that they 'must now prepare for a suicide mission and their future is bright'. Such childish rubbish has to be solemnly repeated on Radio Uganda, UTV news and in the newspapers. It's pathetic.

Thursday 18 August

I delivered judgment this morning in the fourth of the five murder cases at Soroti. It involved a village chief called Ojakal, from northern Teso, who was accused of murdering a young man called Ocii, missing from his home since some time in 1976. Several prosecution witnesses were called to testify as they had earlier made statements to the police to the effect that they had seen Ojakal cut Ocii on the head with an axe. Unfortunately, in court they either denied or contradicted their police statements and clearly were trying to wriggle out of any involvement in the case. Some denied knowing Ocii and others asserted that they didn't in fact see what happened to him. It looked very much as if the witnesses had been got at and fixed somehow. Then there was the problem of the identification of the body. This was found buried, and exhumed about three months after the murder. By then, of course, it was only a skeleton, yet according to the PM report Ocii's uncle, Okwangale, identified the skeleton to the doctor, who examined the bones and recorded the identification without questioning it. I could not let this one go and I asked Okwangale just how he was able to recognise the skeleton as his nephew's bones. He couldn't explain and just obstinately and persistently maintained that he knew his nephew's bones. I said that was absurd but he stuck to it. There was no deformity or healed fracture or anything like that which might help identification, so there was no satisfactory identification at all. This, together with the very unsatisfactory witnesses, caused the prosecutor to throw in his hand and offer no further evidence. So I had to find that the chief had no case to answer and acquit him; although he may well have been the killer.

Monday 29 August

I finished the Soroti sessions last Tuesday. For the last two days I was feeling very ill and didn't eat at all, although I continued to hear the cases in court. I went straight to bed on arrival here at Kampala and, after spending a week in bed just feeling very weak and ill, I went to court this morning. I don't know what it is. As one of my uncles used to say: 'I'm bad in bed and worse up.' The CJ brought his Pakistani doctor friend to my house on Saturday to look at me and he said I'm run down and need a rest, which I already know. I think it's just a surfeit of Amin's Uganda after nearly seven years of his awful regime. In colonial days it was considered advisable for expatriates in the tropics to take a break of a week or so of local leave in mid-tour and it was included in our terms of service. However, Amin simply cancelled this on the ground that the few remaining expatriates should not enjoy any benefits not available to Ugandan employees. Anyway, I came in this morning as I was down to commence Kampala criminal sessions with nine cases to hear. I shall just get on with it.

Monday 12 September

This morning for the first time, after all the homicide cases I've heard, I sentenced two men to death for armed robbery. I have avoided this so far, since becoming a judge four years ago, by finding reasons to reduce murder to manslaughter or armed robberies to simple robbery. In the present case, however, I was left with no choice.

In November 1975, at Makerere, a gang of over 15 men forced their way into the house of the complainant, Rukyalekere, at about 1 a.m. by first banging on the front door and demanding entrance, saying that they were policemen. When the door was not opened they moved around to the back and broke in by that door. The house has electric lighting fitted, which was switched on, so the occupants were able to see the robbers clearly. Two were later arrested and brought to trial, but the others were not traced.

They beat up Rukyalekere with sticks and demanded that he should hand over 30,000 shillings in cash (worth about £2,000 then), which he said he didn't have. The first accused, Ssembajjwe, was carrying a *panga* (a large wide-bladed knife), which he raised saying: 'I'll kill you,' as he aimed a cut at Rukyalekere's head. The latter's wife, Angelina, aged 26, immediately put up her right arm to protect her husband and she took the blow from the very sharp *panga* on that arm. The blade sliced through the tendons, nerves, artery and bone and, when it eventually healed, the unfortunate young woman was left with a 'claw hand' which had lost all feeling and sensation and gave her no gripping power. At the time, she fell to the floor bleeding copiously and crawled under a bed clutching her baby.

The second accused, Kalule, was carrying a large hoe, which he used to cut the electric light wires in the corridor, but much too late to prevent their being seen and recognised. The gang then ransacked the house, forcing open locked drawers and cupboards and removing all the property. Some of it was later recovered by the police from the house of Ssembajjwe.

In court the two accused denied all knowledge of the robbery, but I was satisfied that they had been properly and credibly identified by Rukyalekere and his wife, who had had ample time to see them before the wires were cut and the lights put out. Unfortunately the young wife was crippled for life as a result of her courageous act in protecting her husband and saving his life; though in court he showed no sign at all of appreciating what she had done. In fact, he didn't even mention it until examined about it. Since she was so seriously injured and the robbers were carrying deadly weapons, the offence came into the category of an aggravated robbery, which carries the mandatory death penalty. So I convicted them and sentenced them to death, words which I found very difficult to say this morning. But they just stood there with completely expressionless faces.*

Friday 16 September

Back in July 1975 Amin produced his Community Farm Settlement Decree 'for the purpose of bringing together all persons who wish to engage in community farming and in farm industries as a way of life'. The idea was that all the unemployed able-bodied citizens of both sexes between the ages of 18 and 50 were to settle on such farms. They could volunteer or be directed by the provincial committees chaired by the provincial military governors.

A similar scheme, called National Service, had been proposed by Obote's Government in 1970 and it hadn't been received with any enthusiasm then. This was likely to be even less welcomed, since no doubt undisciplined groups of illiterate soldiers would be sent out with vague orders to round up the unemployed. They would just grab any-one passing who could not persuade or bribe their way out of it. No one in his right mind would actually volunteer for this exercise. There would be minimal organisation and administration; but, in fact, the scheme never got off the ground. No farm settlements were con-structed and no more was heard of it until Amin remembered it in April this year. When he discovered that nothing had been done about it, he decided to revive it. The main reason for this was because, as a result of his Economic War, trade and industry have collapsed in Uganda. *Magendo*, the black market system, is thriving, however.

The big men behind *magendo* are mostly senior army officers, ministers, provincial governors and some rich Moslem businessmen. They have taken to using as agents the many youths and boys now found hanging around the streets in the city and every township. These are great enthusiasts at creating artificial shortages and constantly pushing up the prices. These youngsters are known in Luganda as *bayaye*. This word is derived from both *muyayu*, a tame cat which has gone wild, and *muyaye*, a person who has done the same thing.

*Their appeals against conviction and sentence were later dismissed.

465

They are a menace as they roam about in gangs, robbing people and stealing property when not engaged in *magendo* and illegal currency-dealing. So many complaints have been made by the public that Amin decided to put a stop to it. He issued an amendment to his earlier Decree, specifying that the able-bodied persons eligible for farm settlement are now those between 16 and 40. It goes on to provide that those over 12 who have no visible means of support and cannot account satisfactorily for themselves, the *bayaye* in fact, are to be arrested and committed to prison – not by the courts though – and then settled on these farms. Just how they are to be kept there against their will is not explained; they would have to be prison farms.

The immediate result of this has been that soldiers and police have rounded up large numbers of youths who were unable to produce student identity cards and pushed them into the already overcrowded prisons all over Uganda. Since then I've been out on circuit each month at Mbale, Tororo, Soroti and Moroto. In each place when I visited the local prison the remand prisoners wards were grossly overcrowded with these indiscriminately rounded-up youngsters. The prisons can't cope with them and nobody knows what to do about it. The prison authorities have no extra money to use for feeding all these extra hungry mouths and nothing for the youngsters to do all day. No provincial committees have been set up and no settlement farms exist anyway.

At the prisons, I pointed out to the superintendents that the boys can only be kept in custody for 30 days and then they must inform the Minister of Internal Affairs (the egregious Adrisi). If the Minister failed to give instructions within seven days then the decree required that they be released. To those who expressed fear that the soldiers might object to such release I told them to show them the last page of the decree which says: 'Made under my hand and Public Seal this 7th day of April, 1977 AL-HAJJI FIELD MARSHAL DR IDI AMIN DADA VC, DSO, MC, Life President'. I assured them that the soldiers can hardly argue with the fact that Amin himself made the order, so they must obey it. In any case, I'm quite sure that the soldiers have lost interest in the matter and would neither know nor care what happened to the youths after rounding them up.*

Monday 19 September

Amin has announced that he has signed the Venereal Diseases Decree because there's a lot of it about; too much, in fact. He should know,

*That is what happened in fact.

he's had it twice. It's particularly rife in the Army and he has decided that he's worried about their state of fitness. He should be.

The Decree makes it an offence for anyone to refuse to tell a medical officer or health inspector the name of the person who infected him, or for failing to report for medical tests, spreading the infection, harbouring the disease, wilfully contaminating another person, and so on. In his announcement Amin stated that he has decided that the disease should not be known as venereal disease any more as he has renamed it 'Good Hope', and everyone is to call it that. How on earth did he think that one up? Surely it would be a better name for the treatment rather than the disease. It is the usual fallacy of the ignoramus that unpleasantness can be cured by legislation rather than action. This Decree will simply be ignored and forgotten like so many of Amin's so-called 'brilliant' ideas.

Monday 26 September

Amin has announced his decision to outlaw 28 religious organisations, mainly Christian, but also including one Jewish and one Islamic sect. He claimed that these societies, missions, churches and sects have been working against Uganda – which presumably means against Amin – as they were said to have been indulging in treasonable activities such as collaborating with guerrillas from outside and hiding weapons for them. The first three listed: the Seventh Day Adventists, the Salvation Army and the Bahai Faith, are probably the best-known among them. It's particularly sad to see that the Salvation Army is banned as they've been doing wonderful work in Uganda for many years, with especial regard to the care of orphaned infant children. No proof of any of the allegations made against any of them has been produced publicly or in the courts or the military tribunals. There's much been said everywhere about the rule of law prevailing but what about the rule of unjust laws? This one, for instance, deprives people of the right contained in the Uganda Constitution to freedom of religion or belief and 'to manifest and propagate his religion or belief in worship, teaching, practice and observance'. Is the rule of law, even unjust law, always sacrosanct?

Thursday 29 September

A recent letter from ODA has stated categorically that the remaining British aid, in the form of the supplementary salaries paid to us five still in Uganda, will definitely end on 31 March 1978. So, if I want to stay on here, I have to find another sponsor. I've written to Kutlu Fuad, a former judge here who is now Legal Director at the

Commonwealth Secretariat in London, to find out whether they can assist in any way.

Friday 21 October

I've just concluded a two-week criminal sessions at Mbarara. The standard of police investigation nowadays is still dreadfully low everywhere and many cases end in acquittals simply because proper inquiries haven't been carried out and there's often a failure to find and question key witnesses. Much of this is caused by the fact that trained and experienced CID officers are no longer around to oversee the investigations, due to the efforts of Towelli and his minions. The last case in which I gave judgment today was an alleged matricide. The accused young man was alleged to have killed his mother by cutting her on the neck with a *panga* after asking her why she had bewitched his family. The witnesses spoiled the prosecution case with absurd lies and by constantly contradicting themselves and each other. The investigation by the police was utterly feeble, and some searching questioning in court, mostly by me, revealed that the probable killers were two of the prosecution witnesses who were also relations of the deceased. I acquitted the accused.

Wednesday 2 November

For some months prominent Moslems in Uganda have been making large and much publicised donations towards Amin's fund for building the huge headquarters planned for the Moslem Supreme Council on Old Kampala hill. The Finance Minister, Brigadier Moses Ali, is the chairman and treasurer of the fund-raising committee, and there's much competition among leading Moslem businessmen to be seen to donate the most and so achieve the much sought after favour of Amin.

Haji Kalodo, a multimillionaire of Masaka, made headlines by donating one million shillings to the fund recently. In addition to the praise and flattery which he received, his donation attracted the unwelcome attention of others. One night towards the end of last month a gang broke into Kalodo's large house at night and tortured him until he revealed where his ready cash was hidden – he was apparently known to keep large sums in his house – saying that, if he could give a million shillings to the Moslem Supreme Council, then he could also give the same amount to them. Having obtained this amount from him they then killed him and disappeared with the loot.

A tremendous hunt for the killers has been mounted on Amin's orders, as no doubt he doesn't want others to be discouraged from making large donations. One of the main rumours flying about is that the killers were Catholics, and this seems to have been believed by the Moslems. Consequently, a form of witch-hunt is being conducted in and around Masaka, mainly by soldiers and SRB personnel, and there has been a great deal of noise and panic and shooting. Many local Catholics, prominent and otherwise, have fled from the area and gone into hiding. This includes some Masaka-based lawyers.

Criminal sessions in Masaka had been scheduled to commence on 31 October and go on right through November, as there are 13 murder and robbery cases to deal with. The judge assigned to that circuit, himself a Catholic, was most understandably reluctant to go. Being expendable, I was asked to take the sessions in his place and I agreed and came here.

On Monday it looked as if it was not going to be possible even to open the sessions, let alone try any cases, due to the absence of defence advocates. The sound of gun-fire can be heard from various parts of the town and armed men are moving about in vehicles. Considerable tension and uncertainty has built up among many Catholics in the District and the situation is unpleasant. Yesterday was the opening of sessions and, while I was robing in chambers, I received a phone call from one of the local advocates (ex-Law School) who had been assigned some of the State briefs for the defence. He said he was speaking on behalf of himself and two of his colleagues, all Catholics, and he assured me that they were willing to appear in court and defend the various accused persons but, due to the dangerous situation, they were keeping out of sight for the time being and they did not feel it would be safe to appear in court or in public for at least two days.

This seemed to me to be sensible in the circumstances so, instead of holding a sessions opening ceremony in court and then fixing the hearing dates of the various cases, I fixed the trial dates with the advocates then and there over the telephone. Unconventional and highly irregular procedure, no doubt, but I considered it better than abandoning the sessions. The prison staff already had the accused persons in court, so I went in and explained what I had done and informed them and the prosecuting state attorney of the dates arranged for the trials.

Saturday 12 November

So far the arrangement has worked well. Defence advocates have arrived on time for each trial, performed their tasks and then left immediately after each case has been completed. Obviously they don't want to hang about in the township for longer than necessary so, for once, there were no delays, no requests for adjournments nor any of the usual preliminary niggling. I decided to go back to Kampala this week-end and, after breakfast today, found that I had no driver. My police orderly went to make enquiries and returned with the Military Governor of the Province – a captain who, only a short while ago, was a private and one of Amin's chauffeurs. He spoke reasonable English and said that he had personally arrested my driver late on the previous evening because he found him driving my official car in an unsavoury area on the outskirts of Masaka (so what was the Governor doing there?). In the car with my driver were two *malaya* (prostitutes). The driver told the Governor that he had gone out to buy some aspirins for his headache. Hardly a convincing story.

The Governor took the driver to the police station and directed that he be taken to court and charged with using an official car without the owner's consent. Nobody checked whether I had given my consent; otherwise, the Governor had acted correctly and so I decided to leave the matter to the magistrate. The only problem, I told him, was that I could not hang around waiting for the case to be dealt with as I wished to return to Kampala without delay. He seemed eager to assist and offered the loan of his own official driver, which I promptly accepted. As a former chauffeur himself, I was quite certain he would have selected a first-class driver for his own car; and this proved to be the case.

My own driver, wisely in the circumstances, pleaded guilty to the charge, paid the fine and then reported back to the High Court for duty; only to find himself sacked by the Chief Registrar, who said that he'd received a message from the Masaka Governor that the man was not to be allowed to continue to drive for judges. The CR, who comes from Masaka, instantly complied. Ordinarily I wouldn't have stood for this sort of thing, but this driver has for some time been misusing the car in a similar fashion so I decided not to intervene.*

Friday 25 November

The criminal sessions is still going on in Masaka in spite of the continuing unrest in the area. The big problem is the lack of petrol caused by the Kenya Government, which doesn't like Amin and recently put an embargo on petrol and oil being transported through Kenya to Uganda. Petrol for Zaire, which has to pass through Uganda, has been allowed to come in and has been promptly seized by the military to keep their trucks going. This shortage has been going on for two weeks and is causing chaos in all walks of life. I've managed to keep my car

*He soon found another, better-paid, job driving in the private sector.

on the road with the assistance of the Masaka Governor, who has made some of his military stock of petrol available.

The East African Community has been rapidly breaking up due to nationalism, inter-state and inter-president quarrels and disagreements. Immigration, customs, income tax, railways, airlines and other useful combined services have already split up, and the East African Court of Appeal was among the last to go early this year. After a long hiatus the Judicature Act has been amended by Decree and Uganda's own Court of Appeal has been established as the final court. It's headed by the Chief Justice, but no appointments of appeal judges have yet been made. The CJ wants me on it and I want the job. I'm fed up with trial work and I much prefer hearing appeals. It would also give me time to do some lecturing outside, which I very much want to get back to doing.

Thursday 1 December

My Masaka criminal sessions is still going on, but I interrupted it to come to Kampala to hear a civil suit that I had fixed for today well before I knew about the Masaka sessions, which were not originally down to me anyway. Today's case was an unusual one of enticement, brought by a 70-years-old man named Yosofati, who sued Alifajjo, aged 80, for enticing Yosofati's wife, Kenkuha, to live apart from him. Normally African elders do not get involved in this sort of thing at all.

Yosofati claimed that he had married Kenkuha by customary marriage in 1956 and had paid dowry of one cow to her brother. They had a son born in 1960. Later a man named Nuru, who was a member of the wife's clan, moved into their home, apparently uninvited, and stayed there for a long time. Yosofati didn't object to this curious arrangement and said that he simply treated Nuru as his brother-in-law. In 1972 Nuru disappeared with Kenkuha and her son and, after making some enquiries, Yosofati traced them to the home of Alifajjo. Yosofati then accused Alifajjo before the sub-county chief and at the local police station, but he was advised by both to bring a civil suit in court, which he did, and this was it. He asked for damages from Alifajjo for enticing his wife from him.

When he was cross-examined Yosofati asserted that he had in fact lived with Kenkuha since 1946, not 1956 as he had earlier stated. He explained that she had been married before he met her but she ran away from that husband, and her brother had then 'given' her to him, Yosofati, in return for payment of a cow. He also claimed that he had sent their son to school up to the age of 11, when the boy and his mother left home.

471

The old woman, Kenkuha, told a different story. She declared that she had never married Yosofati nor had any dowry been paid. She agreed she had lived with him for about nine years, from 1946 to 1955, during which time they had no children. They then separated by mutual agreement and she went to live at the home of her uncle. Four years later, in 1959, she met and befriended Alifajjo and, as a result, the boy in question was born to them in 1961. She stated that Alifajjo was the father and it could not have been Yosofati because by then they had been living apart for over four years. This was confirmed by Alifajjo, who added that he did not marry Kenkuha nor did he entice her away from anyone. He found her living at her uncle's home and she never told him she had a husband. He said the boy, now 17, was living in his home and was definitely his son. Kenkuha's brother denied ever receiving any dowry from Yosofati and there was thus no proof of a customary marriage. It appeared that they had merely lived together for a while.

Even if they'd been married, it was for Yosofati to prove she'd been enticed away by Alifajjo, whereas, in fact, it had been Nuru who had gone away with her and there was no evidence that Nuru had acted for Alifajjo. There was no proof of a lawfully recognised marriage and no actual enticement by Alifajjo, so the claim failed. Both men claimed the boy, Sekamondo, and each asked for custody. As usual in these older cases, there were no birth or baptismal certificates produced. I could find nothing credible to negative the mother's declaration that she left Yosofati over four years before the boy was born, so I found he had failed to prove his paternity as well as the enticement.

Friday 2 December

The front page headline in today's *Voice of Uganda* is of the appointment of a new commandant of the Field Marshal Amin Air Force Base, as they now call old Entebbe airport, called Lieutenant-Colonel Gore – an apt name. Amin announced that he had sacked the previous commandant because 'he was not suicide enough'. Presumably he's still alive, which is rather unsporting of him. Amin urged Colonel Gore 'to be a little more suicide in his new duties in case of a bad situation'. One tends to wonder what Amin thinks the word means. Maybe they're all afraid to tell him. Can't blame them.

Friday 9 December

Surprisingly, it's all worked out well. In spite of all the trouble at Masaka I've completed the sessions, with all 13 criminal cases disposed of. However, six of the murders and the one robbery case all ended up as acquittals; caused to a great extent by incompetent investigation and lack of preparation for prosecution. This, in addition to the usual number of obviously lying witnesses, spoilt several cases that should properly have ended up in convictions. Looking back, I see that I've been out on circuit every month of this year and I feel very ready for a break after trying so many cases and having to stay in all those poorly managed and exceedingly crummy hotels; but my leave is not due until next April, so I'll just have to soldier on.

Wednesday 14 December

In another move to appease the Moslems, Amin has announced that the weekend must now include Friday, the Islamic day of prayer. But, in order not to lose working time, the weekend will now consist of Friday, Saturday afternoon and Sunday. So we're supposed to work on Saturday mornings in a split weekend. Of course, many simply won't bother but instead enjoy a three-day weekend. Africa wins again.

Tuesday 20 December

This year the CJ once again asked me to represent him at the magistrates course graduation ceremony at the LDC, presenting the diplomas and prizes and making a speech. This took place yesterday and a report appeared in today's *Voice of Uganda* as well as last night's radio and TV news. I said:

I know that it's very pleasant and satisfying to receive a diploma at the end of your sustained mental efforts, but remember that it is only the outward and visible sign of having reached a certain standard of knowledge and training. Your real work will start once you are in the field and it's then you must prove that, not only have you filled your heads with useful facts, but also that you can use them all to some practical and effective purpose. The test of a person's value to the community is his usefulness to those around him. Do not put too much value upon paper qualifications. There are some people with letters after their names whose true capacity and efficiency level doesn't rise above washing motor cars. Although such people have managed to cram a considerable amount of knowledge into their heads they have, at the same time, failed to acquire much in the way of common sense and the practical ability to make use of what they know. I hope that there's nobody like that here. If so then he'll be of little use as a judicial officer.

Do not become one of those magistrates who either ignores the laws or who is so ignorant of them that he constantly perpetrates acts of serious injustice to the great distress of those unfortunate persons who have to come before him for decisions in their disputes. We have one or two like that already and there are no vacancies for any more.

Working in court all day every day can be very tiring and frustrating. People everywhere can be irritating, stubborn and foolish and we get our share of them in the courts. It needs much patience and understanding and, of course, tolerance to deal with them fairly and justly; especially when they don't appear to deserve it. I'm sure that you will find that cultivating and maintaining a sense of humour is a great help at such times, otherwise you may well go quietly mad and be carried off in a strait-jacket. Abraham Lincoln once said about being President of the United States: 'With the fearful strain that is on me night and day, if I did not laugh I should die.'

A magistrate should be a respected member of his community; but respect is never just given away. It's like loyalty – you have to earn it by your endeavours and your behaviour towards those around you. All human beings have weaknesses and, if you will try to understand those weaknesses and treat all those who come before you with tolerance, understanding and mercy, then your efforts will certainly be much appreciated and rewarded.

Some magistrates try to make a good impression by earning a reputation for handing out harsh sentences. You are not supposed to spend any time trying to please a particular person or group of persons by the severity of the punishments which you hand out – no matter how loudly certain people may demand this sort of thing – and I know that they do. There are certainly instances when a severe sentence is appropriate and called for, but many others when it is not. You must temper justice with mercy. The Judicial Oath, which you will now take, requires that you do right to all manner of people in accordance with the Constitution and the laws without fear or favour, affection or ill-will. If I may quote from the Bible something that applies to us all no matter what religion or faith we may profess: 'What doth the Lord require of thee, but to do justly, and to love mercy, and to walk humbly with thy God?'

1978

Tuesday 10 January

This morning I delivered judgments in several criminal appeals. One of them concerned a police driver, Busingye, appealing against conviction for robbery.

On the evening in question Busingye was wearing civilian clothes and he went with another police driver, who was in uniform, to a bar owned by a Muganda in a village outside Kampala. Both drivers were members of the PSU and were in a private saloon car taken from one of the PSU's many victims. In the bar the drivers ordered everyone to lie on the floor while they beat them with sticks to intimidate them. They took all the cash in the till and then beat the bar owner for not having more money in it to be stolen. They also threatened to shoot him and dragged him outside and forced him into the boot of their car, saying he was to be taken to the PSU base at Naguru.

On the way they stopped and opened the boot and told the owner he could either give them 6,000 shillings or be killed. The owner begged to be taken back to his bar so that he could find the money for them. On arrival there he could produce only a few coins left in the cash box and the drivers angrily forced him back into the car, which they then found wouldn't start. A crowd gathered, fetched by others from the bar, and commenced throwing large stones at the pair. The uniformed driver was killed by the mob and Busingye, although injured, managed to run to the nearest police station, having dropped his driving permit (with his photograph attached) at the scene.

In his defence at the trial Busingye admitted being in the bar but he claimed that he had quarrelled with the uniformed driver over a girl and a hostile crowd gathered and beat them both, but he'd managed to escape. He denied demanding or taking any money and the kidnapping of the bar owner. The trial magistrate believed the testimony of the many eyewitnesses at the scene and convicted Busingye and sentenced him to five years imprisonment and twelve strokes corporal punishment.

Dismissing the appeal, I criticised the lenient sentence saying: 'The appellant, as a policeman, deserves a greater punishment than the ordinary person on conviction of a serious offence like robbery, since he was employed by the State at the taxpayers' expense to protect the public from crime and criminals. In addition, this appellant has a previous conviction for another robbery for which he is apparently now serving another sentence of five years imprisonment.'

In other words, Busingye was absolutely typical of the sort of criminal thugs recruited by Towelli for the PSU. The only remarkable thing about the case was that for once they had allowed one of their men to be tried in a court. It's certainly the first time I've had one before me.

Wednesday 18 January

There are shocking reports of atrocities committed here in Uganda. The tortures in military barracks used as detention centres are appalling. Many are the results of the efforts of and training by East Germans, North Koreans and Palestinians; they practise on detainees held by the SRB on Nakasero hill. Amin's Nubians have also come up with their own versions which are just as cruel. A common one these days, especially at Makindye Military Police barracks, is to tie the victim beneath a suspended vehicle tyre filled inside with petrol and set alight. As the rubber melts it drips on to the victim's face and body, causing dreadful burns and pain.

In the bush and some of the hidden forests victims are being forced into cannibalism by these Nubian maggots. They force starved Ugandan detainees to beat other detainees to death with clubs and then they are required to butcher, cook and eat them. Any refusal or show of reluctance by anyone merely makes him the next victim. Just what Amin and his military supporters think they can achieve by using such brutal methods on Ugandans is not known. In his speeches and in meetings with people from other countries he constantly reiterates how much his people love and admire him. Just who is he trying to convince?

Tuesday 24 January

I had a long talk with Matovu, the Minister of Justice, this morning about my future here. With British ODA supplementation definitely ending in March, in order to stay on I have to take a local contract or find an outside sponsor. It looks rather as if the Commonwealth Secretariat is going to step in with a contract for a single maximum period of two years, but it's not finalised yet. Matovu said the government wants me to stay on and they'll do what they can as regards a local expatriate contract. I mentioned how much I would prefer working in the Court of Appeal; but it seems I've impaired my chances by working hard and completing so many trials in the High Court. As he put it, if I move up to the Appeal Court, who will fill the gap and deal with the cases that I get through in each year? Rather more than any other judge, according to him. The conclusion seems to be: don't be indispensable. If you can't be replaced, you can't be promoted.

At the end of last October I wrote to the UK Minister of Overseas Development, Mrs Hart, in an attempt to persuade her to extend once again the supplementation for the handful of Brits still working for the Uganda Government as head teachers, a surgeon and myself. Her reply removed any hope of that:

> The 1976 renewal of supplementation took place in the context of an improvement in relations between Britain and Uganda which can now, in retrospect, be seen to have been temporary and short-lived. As you know, we now have no diplomatic relations with Uganda, and it is not easy to see how further renewal of what are in fact Government to Government agreements could take place, even if the desire to renew them existed on both sides. But in view of the continued massive violation of human rights in Uganda, H.M. Government is clearly obliged to disassociate itself in every way possible from the current regime and in these circumstances, even if a further renewal of the agreements were feasible, I can see no justification for taking this action. The number of British Supplementees now remaining in Uganda (8 at the end of September, is so small that it cannot be argued that they are making, nationally, a significant contribution towards the maintenance of reasonable standards; an argument which might have been advanced earlier, that we are helping to prepare for the eventual rehabilitation of the country when circumstances permit, no longer therefore carries conviction.
>
> I have no reason to doubt Mr Justice Allen's statement that he is himself still able to do useful work in Uganda, and the decision whether he should now stay on is of course one for him alone; but HMG's decision is clear, has been communicated individually to the officers concerned, and is I think the only one which could be defended publicly in Parliament.

Things generally in Uganda are not improving at all; in fact they are getting worse and nobody can doubt this. Thus Ugandans need all the help they can be given and I do not wish to desert them in their darkest hours. In spite of what Mrs Hart wrote – or had written for her – I can't agree that we few remaining Britons are making an insignificant contribution because, as I've been told time and again by various Ugandans, our very presence here is itself a sign to them that they have not been entirely forgotten and abandoned by their friends. At any rate, I intend to stay if I can arrange it.

1978

Thursday 9 February

Last Monday I opened Mbale criminal sessions. A sleep-starved week due to the constant noise at night in the hotel. The army and SRB types who stay here spend the nights shouting drunkenly at each other and frequently slamming their room doors. It's like this in most Uganda hotels nowadays.

Today I delivered judgment in an alleged murder of a local butcher by a police constable called Turyomugyenyi, one of those hundred-yard-long names from western Uganda. The butcher, Wamala, was known to suffer occasional spells of mental disturbance and some complaints had been made that, in the course of one of his fits, he might harm someone using the town council slaughterhouse, where he went for meat, although in fact he had never been violent. The Town Clerk decided to ask the District OC Police to arrange to collect Wamala and send him for treatment at Butabika Mental Hospital. For that purpose a medical report would be required and then Wamala would be taken before a magistrate for an Urgency Order to be made under the Mental Treatment Act. The OC Mbale Police Station was instructed to arrange for Wamala to be brought in for this purpose and the OC, not knowing Wamala, sent three armed constables to do this. They were the accused PC and PC Byakune (who was a prosecution witness) and PC Ajuga, who fled from the country immediately after the incident. Each was carrying a .303 rifle and ammunition and they travelled in a police car to the butcher's shop at Namakwekwe, about a mile north of Mbale on the road to Soroti. Wamala was not at his shop when they arrived there so they waited for him. Eventually he arrived on his bicycle and they told him that he was wanted at the police station. Wamala replied: 'All right, let me go and put my bicycle in the store.' He went behind the shop, dumped his bicycle on the ground and ran off. None of the constables had bothered to go with him nor did they chase after him, although Wamala was stoutly built and middle-aged and could easily have been caught by the young policemen. Instead they climbed into the police car and drove to Wamala's home, 3 miles away, and expressed surprise that he was not there. Just how they could have expected him to cover the distance on foot before they arrived by car was not explained.

Without any more effort, they decided to give up as it was all proving too difficult for them, so they started back to the police station in the car. On the way they saw Wamala waiting peacefully beside the road for a lift. They stopped and got out and, on seeing them, Wamala took off again, but this time pursued by the constables. For no explained reason, and quite unnecessarily, Ajuga and Byakune fired

478

their rifles in the air, which had the natural effect of frightening Wamala and he ran faster. Then he saw his brother, Ntambi, approaching and ran towards him and threw himself down at his brother's feet asking for help. Ntambi suggested to the policemen that they should allow him to bring his brother in as he would be more likely to come quietly with him. This was obviously a sensible way to do it but, instead, the accused PC raised his rifle and pointed it at Wamala, who was still on the ground. PC Ajuga said: 'Don't shoot him.'

But the accused replied: 'He has made us tired. Let me shoot him.' He took aim and shot the sitting Wamala in the groin. The bullet severed the femoral artery and Wamala quickly died from massive loss of blood. The three constables panicked and jumped into the car and fled to the police barracks without reporting back from duty to the station. One of them even left his uniform cap with his name in it at the scene. There was conflicting prosecution evidence as Ntambi testified that Wamala was shot through the front as he sat there, but the other prosecution witness, PC Byakune, agreed with the accused that Wamala was shot in the back as he attacked one of them.

As usual, the medical evidence was unsatisfactory and incomplete. The PM report merely referred to a bullet wound in the groin without any information about entry or exit wounds. The doctor could not be questioned about his meagre report because, as usual in these cases, he had already left the country and returned to Pakistan after staying in Uganda for only a year.

In his defence the accused PC claimed that Wamala had attacked PC Ajuga with a *panga*, though nobody else had mentioned it nor was it produced as an exhibit. He admitted shooting Wamala, but his version was that it was necessary to do so in order to save PC Ajuga. He had no supporting witnesses and Ajuga was out of the country. He was very evasive and unconvincing and it was a question of whether to believe him or Ntambi about what happened.

If the prosecution case, based mainly on Ntambi's evidence, was believed then the offence was clearly murder since the accused had shot a defenceless man sitting on the ground and no threat to them. The defence case was of arresting an armed and violent madman, so some force might have been necessary. But, of course, Wamala was not a criminal at all and he was not supposed to be arrested but only brought into the station for treatment, hopefully willingly. If the constables had gone about the business sensibly and properly, he could have been brought in with the aid of his brother and almost certainly without difficulty. Instead they had frightened him unnecessarily with their guns and generally upset him. The accused PC had certainly over-reacted, whichever version was true.

Even if Wamala had been violent, he could easily have been over-come by three strong young policemen, without the need to do much harm. I was satisfied that the shooting was unnecessary and unlawful whichever version was accepted and that the accused PC had gone too far. Since there was disagreement between the two prosecution eye-witnesses about what happened, this raised a slight measure of doubt regarding the accused's intention at the time, so I convicted him of manslaughter and gave him six years to add to the year he'd been on remand already.

Tuesday 14 February

This morning was a particularly trying one, in both senses, with a series of difficult, awkward, stubborn, evasive, unhelpful and exceed-ingly untruthful witnesses. When I adjourned for lunch and went into chambers to change out of my robes, the Mbale Chief Magistrate came in grinning and asked me if I'd had a hard morning. I replied that I certainly had and he said: 'I thought so; some while back an old man who is one of our local chiefs came out of your court and said to me: "That *mzungu* in the red blanket is very religious; he keeps resting his head in his hands and asking God to help him."'

Wednesday 22 February

I completed Mbale sessions at the end of last week and started at Tororo this week. Today I gave judgment in a nasty murder case with three accused persons; an old man called Asani Bosa and his two sons Nabulere and Mubala. Their victim was Bosa's estranged wife Maimuna, aged about 70 years.

Nabulere had announced that he was going to kill his mother because she had caused him to suffer pain from a disease by bewitch-ing him. In fact he had gonorrhoea. The old woman heard of the threat and reported it to the *Mutaka* chief, who was so lazy and incompetent that he didn't know what to do about it; so he did nothing. The three men went to Maimuna's hut on a bright moonlight night with *pangas*. She was sharing the hut with a young woman and a small boy. Bosa stood outside and said: 'Cut all these persons and finish them.' His two sons entered the hut and hacked their mother to death. The young woman recognised all of them and ran outside. She was attacked and badly cut on the head and arm but she managed to make an alarm, and the three men ran off. She reported what had happened and named the men to neighbours who quickly arrived there. This in spite of her serious injury, as a result of which her arm had to be amputated at the shoulder as it was cut right through. In their defence the three men denied everything and claimed that they answered the alarm and found it had all happened.

For once the prosecution evidence was very strong and corroborated and it was a very bad case, particularly because of the relationship between the victim and her killers. I convicted all three of murder and sentenced them to death.*

Saturday 25 February

On my return to Kampala I found a letter from the Commonwealth Secretariat offering to sponsor me here in Uganda on a single contract for two years after the expiration of my current tour. The financial aid is an improvement on my present British supplementation and the period is for long enough to give me time to find something else to follow on, or for the general situation here to change somehow. So I've written to accept their offer.

Some advocates stayed in my chambers for a chat yesterday morning after we had finished with various civil applications. One asked me hopefully: 'When are the British coming here to save us from this man?' I had to reply that the British public and press would never agree to its government spending large sums of money and risking its soldiers' lives upon such an enterprise. Apart from that, the politicians themselves would be so afraid of that nebulous thing called world opinion and the vociferous screams of protest that such an operation by the 'imperialists' would evoke from the UN representatives of so many states. So it wouldn't happen. I said that if Ugandans want to remove Amin then they'll have to do it themselves. They have the most to gain or lose and unfortunately hardly anyone else is interested enough to become involved, but, I added, they could take heart in the knowledge that nothing is for ever and even these dark days must pass.

Wednesday 1 March

In large headlines in this morning's *Voice of Uganda* it says: DR AMIN APPEALS FOR BLOOD. One's first reaction is – hasn't he had enough already? It turns out that he has launched a country-wide blood donor operation.

On the inside pages of this newspaper one constantly comes across advertisements put in by self-styled doctors and professors claiming to be astrologers, native doctors and instant miracle-workers. These people usually set themselves up in a room in a small hotel in Kampala and deal with the streams of customers and clients who willingly and

---

*Their appeals were later dismissed.

eagerly hand over their money for alleged cures, charms, placebos and predictions. Today's advertisement is very typical of this type. The spelling is all their own and the editor clearly prefers to leave them as received:

NATIVE DOCTOR
PROFESSOR MUSTAPHA

This is your Native Doctor and Astrologer registered in Uganda. What is your ploblem? None surpassis. Come to me for power medecine to cure madnes, hurt-felior, ashima and foming in the maut (epilezi), veneral diseasis including chasing away diomons e.t.c. Money back if not certisfied. Come for lucky charm to help you pass examnations and to be popular with your boss and fellow workers. Come for reproductif medecin. If your wife runs away come to me and I will bring her back – every day from 8 a.m. to 2 p.m.

COME ONE COME ALL

Monday 6 March

The Vice-President, General Adrisi, apart from being illiterate, ignorant and uncomprehending, is as greedy as anyone else around him and he constantly uses his powerful position to increase his fortune, as they all do. He takes a large share of any motor buses or lorries brought into Uganda as well as seizing businesses, factories and whatever else he can grab. Those unwise enough to object or obstruct him are promptly removed. He's also involved in the flagrant smuggling of coffee into and through Kenya, where a lot of the coffee sold as Kenyan is, in fact, Ugandan coffee. No doubt his minions are cheating him in all directions since he is incapable of checking the necessary paperwork himself but, in spite of this, he has become an extremely rich man.

There's always a shortage of foreign currency here, due mainly to the wasteful use of it for purchasing prestige products, luxuries for the soldiers and, most of all, large supplies of armaments from the Eastern bloc and Arab countries. There's also a great deal of extravagant travelling abroad by Amin and senior officials. More than others, Adrisi needs foreign currency for purchases for his two ministries of Defence and Internal Affairs because priorities go to them rather than to Health and Education. He also takes much foreign exchange for his own business use and for purchases. He constantly demands more and quite often has to be told politely by fearful Treasury and bank officials that this or that project has to be delayed because of lack of foreign exchange; probably taken by Amin.

His limited mental powers make it very difficult for him to understand or accept the slightest frustration, and the constant reiteration of the chant 'no foreign exchange' bewilders and exasperates him, as he doesn't know what it means. Recently he burst out in his severely fractured form of Swahili: *'Nani huyu forrin ixchinja? Lete yule mbele mimi. Natengeneza yeye.'* Which very roughly means: 'Who is this Foreign Exchange? Bring him before me and I will fix him.' As a result, grinning Ugandans refer to him as Mr Foreign Exchange.

Tuesday 21 March

Yesterday evening the armed police constable had just arrived to guard my residence for the night. I went to lock the padlock on the large double gates of the compound. It's the job of my cook, Douglas, to do this, but I knew he had gone out and would not be back until late because he had asked for an advance of salary; thus it was a safe assumption that he would come back very late and very drunk. The sentry was a new young constable who had not been on this duty before and unfortunately my mind was on other matters and I briefed him too light-heartedly. I said: 'My cook has gone boozing and will come back later. He has a key for this gate lock so don't shoot him when he opens it. All right?'

'Yessir,' with a face blank of any sign of understanding. Half an hour later there was a banging and thumping on the front door. I dragged my mind from the judgment I was working on and went to the door. The sentry stood there looking agitated and bewildered. He had evidently been thinking. 'Please, sir, why do you want me to shoot your cook?'

'No, no, I did not say that. You misunderstood me. I said that I do *not* want you to shoot him. It was a joke, of course. Do you understand now?'

He replied: 'Yessir.'

This morning at breakfast Douglas was looking his usual post-booze-up self: red-eyed, miserable and clutching his head and emitting loud groans every few minutes. These dramatics failed to move me and elicited no response or sympathy whatever. As usual I simply ignored the whole performance. I said: 'The coffee is cold again.'

'Yes sir, I forgot to take the milk out of the fridge in time. Can I have an advance of two hundred shillings, please sir?'

I said: 'Certainly not, you had an advance only yesterday. If you go on like this you will be paying me at the end of the month instead of the other way round. Anyway, what do you want an advance for?'

'I have to pay it to the *askari*,' he said gloomily.

'What *askari*?' I asked.

'The gate sentry last night. When I finished to reach here he said that you had ordered him to shoot me but he kindly decided not to shoot me if I would pay him two hundred shillings instead.'

'Good heavens, what did you do?'

'I agreed to pay him today if I could get an advance from you.'

'Definitely not. Out of the question. If he asks you again tell him to come and see me and I'll fix him. Whatever next?'

'Yes sir, but what shall I do if he decides to shoot me?'

'It will be a merciful release and good riddance; but definitely an unnecessary waste of ammunition. I have already told you that I will deal with him, so stop worrying. But, if it goes wrong, I shall certainly arrange a most impressive funeral for you. I might even attend it if I'm not too busy. You can invite all your friends.'

'Thank you, sir. Can I have the advance now?'

'The trouble with you, Douglas, is that you have a one-track mind. I have already said no. If I really had told him to shoot you, why should I also pay him not to do so? It does not make sense and neither do you. Now go away and do some useful work. The house is knee-deep in dust and dirt.'

When I reached the court a telephone call was put through to my chambers. It was the OC Jinja Road Police Station, which supplies the house sentries for the Kololo area. 'Very sorry to trouble you, your Lordship, but this new constable who guarded your house last night has reported that you ordered him to shoot your cook.'

Having sorted that out, I managed to get on with same work until a colleague stuck his head round the door of my chambers.

'Morning, Peter, I hear that you've been arranging to have your cook shot. Is he so bad? It's a bit drastic, isn't it? My own cook has a brother who can replace him. Shall I send him to see you?'

Towards the end of the morning a senior clerk tapped on the door and entered, looking very solemn, and delivered an obviously prepared speech: 'Your Lordship, we have heard in the Registry that your cook has passed away after being shot so we are making a collection towards his funeral. We are all very sorry to hear this sad news, my Lord, and we wish to express our profound condolences. One of our staff says he has a distant relative who can come and replace him and work for your Lordship, if you please, sir, my Lord.'

'Oh, God.'

'My Lord?'

More explanations. Then, while I was at home for lunch, the telephone rang. It was a friend at Entebbe. 'Is it true that your cook has been shot? How awful; what happened?' How does the word get around so quickly? There are no talking drums as in West Africa yet everybody always seems to pick up on the country-wide grape-vine what's going on very soon after it's happened, even if not always with any great degree of accuracy.

Friday 24 March

It's Good Friday today. Yesterday Amin decided it was time for him to interfere with religion and do some God-bothering as well as his usual people-bothering. He announced that people in Uganda have not been saying enough prayers. So from now on it is ordered that everyone must attend a mosque or church every week. How he proposes to enforce this he didn't say. I shall continue not attending.

Friday 31 March

Well, today is the last day of my permanent and pensionable service in Uganda, which has lasted for exactly 23 years. It's also the last day of the remaining British aid for those six of us still in Uganda (two others have left). Technically, then, I'm retiring. Good timing for me really, as I finish this tour on Tuesday and am then off to the UK. I expect to come back from leave as a Commonwealth Secretariat 'expert' on contract and no longer a part of British aid; but doing the same job, of course. There's still no news of appointments to the Court of Appeal. I'm hopeful but not expectant.

Sunday 2 April

I'm off to the UK tomorrow on leave and was hoping to use the whole of today to pack and make arrangements. Unfortunately, Amin inconveniently decided to throw a large party for the Judiciary and lawyers this afternoon and I was told that I had to attend. It was held at Lutembe Beach, a bay in Lake Victoria several miles by *murram* track off the road to Entebbe. It got its name because a huge old crocodile named Lutembe used to live here. It was believed to be over 200 years old and it was used by successive Kabakas of Buganda for disposing of human sacrifices and criminals. There was an official Muganda keeper who called the crocodile from the lake by ringing a bell. Lutembe was last seen in 1950, otherwise I'm sure Amin would be making use of him.

At the party there was the usual tribal dancing, which was followed by a surprisingly pleasant and un-noisy local pop group; and a lot of drinking, of course; it was a very hot afternoon. The inevitable, ubiquitous SRB men were there, well-dressed and wearing the obligatory dark glasses, trying to listen in to conversations that they could not understand. At one point, near the end, Amin stood up and made one of his long, rambling, off-the-cuff speeches wandering from one irrelevancy to the next, and my thoughts drifted off to my leave plans, when my attention was caught as I heard him say: 'Some people say that I am controlled by the imperialists – but,' sweeping wide his arms, 'do you see any whites here?' I heard a murmured 'yes' all round me and was embarrassed to see the eyes of many grinning faces looking in my direction – the only European present.

Wednesday 3 May – In London

I went up to town and had lunch with a chap called Howell, the Chief Personnel Officer of the Commonwealth Fund for Technical Co-operation (CFTC), during which we arranged my contract for two years and agreed a salary. Wonderful. So now I'm fixed up until mid-1980.

Saturday 27 May

In the newspaper today there's a report that the former Governor of Uganda, Sir Frederick Crawford, has died in Rhodesia. This wretched Labour Government never allowed him to return to England and I think it's sad that he died an unhappy and very badly treated man after a hard-working lifetime in the British Colonial Service.

Tuesday 27 June

I arrived back in Uganda yesterday from leave, which I had badly needed after the last two years of non-stop Amin's Uganda. It's a long time since I've done any teaching but I still keep my eye on my former Law School students and enjoy seeing them rise in their chosen careers. Each time I hear of a further promotion or success I quietly rejoice and take a little private pride in having had a small part in it. I've been hoping for some time that eventually one of those in the Judiciary would be appointed to the High Court as a judge. While I was on leave it happened and I've returned to find that George Engwau is newly appointed to the Bench. I interviewed him as a potential magistrate, taught him on his magistrates diploma course and later brought him back to do the Bar course. Since then I've watched him working as a grade I magistrate and a chief magistrate and now he is a colleague. He has shown the way and I shall be very happy if others follow on.*

Thursday 29 June

I brought back a T-shirt for Douglas with I HATE WORK printed on it. He reported that he wore it to the market today and an old man told him he should be ashamed.

I also brought a box of tea bags from the UK as I've not tried them before and they're not available here. Unfortunately I delayed in explaining to Douglas how to use them and, when I went into the kitchen for that purpose this afternoon, I found that he had already torn all 100 of the little bags and emptied the loose tea leaves into the container that I use as a tea caddy.

Wednesday 26 July

There is cholera in Kampala and the authorities are trying to hide the fact. There's been no public announcement yet because they are short of vaccine, apart from the other required medical facilities to deal with such an outbreak. David, one of the judges, has influence and took his teenaged son to the medical centre this afternoon for a jab and invited me along; so we all got jabs. I warned the cook, Douglas, that everything must be boiled, and today for lunch he produced my usual cold salad, but it now consisted of thoroughly boiled lettuce and tomatoes. That'll teach me to be more precise; I ought to know by now that everything is taken literally.

Friday 28 July

A very bad night last night; I had a high temperature and felt feverish and I couldn't sleep. There's a severe pain in my right side. Surely this can't be the vaccination; my arm feels OK.

Sunday 6 August

Not the best week in my life. Last weekend the pain in my side became so bad I couldn't sleep, eat or even rest. The CJ brought a Pakistani doctor to see me on Saturday and he said it was a spinal complaint and I must go into Mulago hospital on Monday for tests. But I was sure it wasn't that. I thought it might be appendicitis; the pain was constant and excruciating. I was very ill and weak on Sunday and asked Douglas to ring the CJ. He came and took me to Mulago in his

*Five others later became judges and three went up to the Court of Appeal.

car, which I got into with great difficulty. I can't recall much about going there, in fact.

Later I was lying on a bed in a private ward, still in great pain and without anyone having been to see me, when a chap came in and said he was Professor Saad, a surgeon from Egypt. He was passing and heard me groaning and offered to examine me, which he did. He is Amin's personal surgeon and he'd previously been surgeon to President Nasser of Egypt. He said I must have an immediate operation as the appendix had burst and I now had acute peritonitis, which explained the intense pain and fever. He offered to perform the operation unless I preferred him to call someone else in. I just wanted relief from the pain so I said: 'Please just do it. I have complete faith in you.' Later, on the way into the operation room, I was barely conscious when the CJ came and asked if he should send a telegram to my brother in the UK. I said: 'No thanks; only if I don't make it.'

When I recovered consciousness I felt completely trussed up. There was an I.V. tube in my arm, another tube up my nostril down into my stomach and yet another tube sticking out of a hole they'd made above my hip. I was given a series of hourly injections, making sleep very difficult. Yesterday they removed the various tubes and I was assisted out of bed and allowed to sit in an ancient armchair on the verandah. I felt pretty weak and still do. I seem to have lost about 2 stones in weight, and I'm not a bulky person. My legs look like sticks.

Douglas has brought my toilet things so that, when I get some strength back in my arm, I can shave and comb my hair. He has been given a mattress on the floor in a corner of the room. It's the custom in Ugandan hospitals for a member of the patient's family to move in and look after the patient, as there are never enough nurses to do this. I've arranged with the CJ to have telegrams sent home and to the CFTC to report my condition. I shall write letters later when I can hold a pen firmly enough.

Thursday 10 August

The hospitals nowadays are geared to feed Africans only as Europeans are not supposed to get ill, so they are unable to feed me with the sort of very light meals that I need and can cope with. However, the CJ and Mrs Saied are my principal benefactors and the Higher Executive Officer (chief clerk) at the court, Rugadya, and his staff arrange delivery of a meal each evening. They also bring jerricans of water as there's been no water supply in the hospital for some time. I can now walk very slowly to exercise my legs. I've been visited several times already by Protestant, Catholic and Moslem priests. I must look like a sinner in dire ecumenical need. There was even an evangelist two days ago who said it was time for me to be saved.

Saturday 12 August

I walked out of my room this morning and along a corridor for my exercise. On the hospital notice-board for this floor I saw a notice about ten days old referring to me. It said: 'The condition of Mr Justice Allen is improving and it is not hoped that he will die.' That was good news.

This afternoon I was sitting as usual on the verandah reading when I heard the commotion of many feet in the corridor outside my room. The door was flung open and I looked up to see the large figure of Amin crossing the room towards me, followed by a horde of medical staff and other hangers-on. I was occupying the only half-decent chair; there was also a metal-framed chair with broken strips of plastic wound round it to form a seat and a backrest. It did not look safe to sit on but Amin grabbed it and put it beside my chair and plonked himself down on it. Somehow it didn't collapse with him on to the floor.

He greeted me and said how sorry he was to hear of my misfortune. Then he apologised for visiting me while dressed in a track suit, explaining that he had been playing basketball, which his team had won, naturally; then he had called in to visit a senior officer who is a patient here and the staff had told him I was here. After a few more minutes chatting he went on his way, followed by the rest of the people who had filled up my room while we talked. I think it was kind of him to look in; after all, there was no special reason for him to do so. No photographers or pressmen were present to make anything out of it.

Friday 18 August

I've been in this hospital for three boring weeks now. The stitches were taken out this morning, leaving a 6-inch scar on my abdomen. Professor Saad seems very pleased with progress so far. He said that due to the delay in getting me to hospital, the peritonitis had advanced so far he had not really expected me to pull through. No wonder I've been feeling so weak.

I brought back from leave a large jar of multi-vitamins as such things can't be obtained out here, and I asked Douglas to bring them from my bedroom dressing table so that I could start taking them right away. When he came back he reported that he could not find them there or anywhere else in the house, although I know exactly where I left them. I'm afraid it's clear that he has succumbed to the temptation and has pinched them and sold them, as a very good price can be obtained for such a scarce and useful commodity nowadays. Of course, I can't prove it and there's nothing to be done. Any other time and it wouldn't matter much, but I really need them now.

Saturday 2 September

I've been exercising as hard as I can, which isn't very hard really. I just pace slowly up and down this room with frequent stops for a rest. But I'm so bored. I used the phone provided and managed to persuade the CJ, who reluctantly agreed, to send over some files from magistrates courts requiring revisional orders to give me something useful to do. My back is not in a terribly good state though, with occasional quite painful muscle spasms and no one available to massage or help overcome this.

Thursday 7 September

At last the Prof has agreed that I can go home after serving my six weeks sentence in this room. I'm still quite weak and have lost far too much weight, but at least I can move about. The Prof wanted me to go to the UK to recuperate but I said I've only just come back from there and I want to stay here now; so I've agreed to compromise by taking five weeks sick leave before returning to court. I shall do whatever work I can at home. The hole in my side has been closed but I still need to return to have the dressings changed a few times. It's no fun being took poorly.

Tuesday 10 October

Yesterday was Uganda's sixteenth anniversary of independence, a public holiday and the last day of my sick leave. I arrived at the court this morning and found that cases had been fixed for me to hear as I had requested. I've had enough of idling around the place.

Wednesday 11 October

Last week I sent my driver to Foods & Beverages to pick up this month's ration of essential commodities and he was sent away by some fool there who told him that as I hadn't taken last month's ration I was not entitled to any this month. Irritated by this absurd decision, I decided to go straight to the top. Since the VIP shop comes under the President's Office, I wrote there complaining about what had happened and stating that, as I'd just come out of six weeks in hospital, I now badly needed the commodities.

This morning I received a phone call from a very angry, loud-voiced woman demanding to know why I had troubled the President about this matter when I should have gone through the proper channels by writing first to her as General Manager of F & B. I know that she is Amin's sister – a large, fat, overbearing woman with no business knowledge or experience. The usual nepotism, of course. I remained silent while she ranted on, frequently using the words 'chain of command', which happens to be Amin's current favourite expression and so used constantly by his sycophantic followers. When she eventually paused for breath or ran out of words, no doubt expecting some sort of grovelling apology to a relation of the Big Man, I merely said that I thought the shop manager's response to my request was absurd and I couldn't continue working here without a regular supply of these necessities. Perhaps realising that her bullying approach wasn't working, she cooled down and said that if I'd send my driver round right away she would see to it that I received the stuff. And this was done – with even a few extras included.

Sunday 22 October

My contact called in this afternoon and brought me up to date on the recent Kagera incident. Earlier this month Amin decided to move against two of the battalions in his constantly unreliable army. One was the Chui (leopard) Battalion stationed at Gulu barracks. Apparently the President believed that many of its men were supporters of the Vice-President, General Adrisi, rather than Amin. As Amin has recently become very suspicious of Adrisi's intentions and doubtful of his continued loyalty, he despatched some of his murder squads from the military police and the SRB in Kampala to eliminate the suspected malcontents in Gulu.

However, before they arrived word of their mission reached the Chui Battalion and ambushes were laid. The Chui men, in spite of some initially incompetent preparations, did manage to dispose of most of the murder squads, who were not taking any precautions and whose own incompetence may perhaps have gone towards cancelling out that of the ambushers.

Amin's next worry was that he had learned of an alleged plot against him by some members of what had been the favoured Simba (lion) Battalion in Mbarara. Having failed to deal effectively with the northern battalion, he decided to try killing two birds (or beasts, in this case) with one stone by ordering the Chui Battalion to prove its

491

loyalty by moving against the Simba Battalion to put down what he called a mutiny at the Mbarara barracks. Possibly he was hoping and expecting that they would carry out his orders unquestioningly and thus slaughter each other, which would be a most satisfactory solution from his point of view.

However, both battalions quite easily discovered what was going on and decided to join together rather than attack each other. Amin then sent his 'elite' marines to disarm and deal with the two dissident battalions. Amin has frequently boasted that the marines, who are all Nubians, are the most highly trained and elite of his army, which is really saying nothing at all. In fact, they were quickly routed and driven off with a large number of casualties and desertions.

In desperation Amin turned to what he believed to be his only remaining reliable unit available, the Malire Mechanised Regiment in Kampala, which, with remnants of the marines, he sent to Ankole on a consolation mission. They were to cross the border into Tanzania at the trading centre of Mutukula, with orders to occupy the salient north of the Kagera River. This area is largely uninhabited and unimportant. It covers about 700 square miles used mostly to graze cattle, with some agriculture. The troops were told to help themselves to whatever they found there. In this way Amin perhaps hoped to save face with his soldiers and placate those whom he thought still had some loyalty towards him, as well as demonstrating that he was still in firm control of the situation.

The occupation of the Kagera salient was an extremely easy exercise because, apart from a small police post, there are virtually no Tanzanian security personnel in the area. Amin's men joyfully looted the area and killed civilians everywhere without scruples, morals or conscience; and herds of cattle and goats were driven into Uganda, as were lorries and other vehicles. These were soon sold or abandoned by the drunken and irresponsible troops. People from Kampala, Masaka and other places were heading towards Mbarara, where they had heard that these vehicles and animals were to be picked up at give-away prices.

The *Voice of Uganda* published photographs taken by the Presidential Press Unit, all of whom received medals for their 'bravery', of members of the Uganda Army posing in mock aggressive attitudes with their guns pointing uselessly and unnecessarily at the dead bodies of civilians, who were described as Tanzanian soldiers disguised as civilians, who had resisted the brave Ugandan troops. There was no explanation of why they were not in uniform and not armed, nor how they would have been able to resist anybody. They were civilians who had been deliberately slaughtered or who had got in the way of flying bullets. If there had been any resistance Amin's troops would have fled at the first sign of it.

Amin recently held a series of highly publicised briefing sessions at the Command Post for Ministers, VIP visitors, diplomats and others. At these he was photographed in uniform, with a pistol prominently on his hip and holding a long pointer with which he was apparently indicating Kagera to them on a large-scale map of southern Uganda as he explained what he called his grand strategy and the so-called justification for straightening out the border with Tanzania by removing the salient at that point.

Naturally there have been loud protests from many countries at this totally unwarranted invasion. Even a few African countries thought it was going a bit too far and added their criticism, which they have been reluctant or slow to do with regard to Amin's past activities. Kenya, which at the moment is unfriendly towards Tanzania, has remained neutral so far. The Americans have cut off oil supplies to Uganda from their three companies represented here – Caltex, Mobil and Esso. However, Agip, Total and Shell have continued with their supplies, which have not been sufficient to cope with demand.

Friday 3 November

Even Amin has realised that he has now no choice but to pull out of Kagera, and he has done so, leaving behind considerable damage to property and general devastation. The Tanzanians have moved back in and no doubt put same sort of garrison there to prevent a repeat of this nonsense.

Monday 6 November

Today I delivered judgment in a claim for damages resulting from a fatal traffic accident which actually occurred at Timboroa in Kenya. It concerned Lubega, a 30-year-old Ugandan bank accountant, who was travelling in a bus from Nairobi to Kampala. When it reached Timboroa the bus overturned and Lubega received severe injuries and died on the spot. The Kenya-based bus company ignored our service of the summons and the claim by the widow and filed no defence, so there was no explanation of how the accident was caused. This was the equivalent of their admitting negligence and liability. It was one of many such claims that comes before this court. The only thing special about it was that the accident occurred in Kenya, outside the jurisdiction of the court.

There was no record of any earlier relevant decision regarding the jurisdiction of the Uganda courts over civil claims of this sort, so I had to make a decision in a new matter of law. I found a parallel decision of the House of Lords in the case of a British serviceman killed in a traffic accident in Malta. The H of L held that an English court was competent to hear an action based on a civil wrong perpetrated abroad which was the sort that could normally have been tried in England if it had been committed there, provided it would be regarded as not justifiable according to the law of the foreign country where it was actually committed. I applied the same rule here and, in addition, found that the bus company has an operating office in Kampala. It was then just a matter of assessing the appropriate amount of damages to the widow and three small children.

Wednesday 29 November

For a change I've just dealt with a civil suit from the West Nile. We don't get many from there. In this one a man named Placid Willy Iga sued the Moyo Town Council for damages as a result of a fire which destroyed his shop and stock. The evidence revealed that the land on which his shop stood belonged to the town council and he had leased it from them but had never paid the rent, nor did he have a trading licence. The town council did nothing about either of these matters.

Iga alleged that a large swarm of dangerous wild bees had settled in a tree near his shop and, when council employees were sent to remove and destroy them by smoking them out, they somehow managed to set fire to the shop and destroy the building and property inside it. This version was quickly shown to be untrue and a load of rubbish. In fact, the swarm of bees actually settled in the shop itself in a space between the hardboard inner wall and the corrugated-iron outer wall. Iga then claimed that he didn't know the actual location of the bees and had been misinformed by his shop assistant. Since the bees were in place for two months and, as Iga claimed, he was in the shop daily, he could hardly have failed to know of their presence, especially as he was the one who approached the town clerk and asked for them to be removed. The only truthful part of his claim seemed to be that the shop had burned down.

He claimed a very large sum for destroyed stock, building materials and a flour-milling machine. When I asked how a solid steel milling machine could have been destroyed in an ordinary fire, he replied that it was only the rubber parts that were burnt, so it was not in working order – not destroyed. But he had claimed the full value.

The defence revealed a different story. The men from the council went there to spray the shop with a substance poisonous to bees, as they were not permitted to use smoke or fire in a building. Before they could start, Iga's two employees had insisted on removing the honey before it was poisoned, so they burned bundles of grass to smoke out the bees for this purpose. In the process they managed to start a small fire in the building, which they extinguished. The area was then sprayed and the bees destroyed. When the council men left all looked well; but in fact the remains of the fire smouldered on and flamed up in the night, causing the destruction and loss. Clearly the fire was caused by Iga's own employees and he'd just been trying it on when he claimed against the council. I dismissed the claim and Placid Willy wasn't.

Friday 1 December

My Mercedes was in the garage yesterday having an adjustment made to the gears. My driver waited until it was ready at about 6 p.m., and as he drove past the High Court he was in head-on collision with a lorry. When I was taken to see the car this morning it looked completely wrecked, with the driver's seat concertinaed right up against the steering wheel. I suspect he was drunk because the drunk often seem to have special protection enabling them to walk away unhurt from such a crash. Anyone else would have been squashed flat and couldn't have survived. But he ain't saying nuffin.

Wednesday 6 December

I'm now using a private Mercedes and driver hired by the court. Actually I suspect that it belongs to the CR or one of his family. On the way to court this morning we hit a cyclist and knocked him for six. I got out and helped him to his feet. Both he and his bike were undamaged but he seemed dazed, so I decided to test my theory and told him to report to the Chief Registrar at the court. On arrival there I informed the CR that he was probably going to have a visitor with his hand out and it was definitely the driver's fault. The CR later told me that he gave the cyclist some money and he'd gone off happily. I rather expect he'll be waiting for us in ambush tomorrow morning in order to be knocked down again.

Thursday 14 December

In a speech made a short time ago after complaints against the excesses of the notorious State Research Bureau had reached his ears, Amin stated that the work of the SRB was definitely not spying on or torturing people but only checking such matters as the price of sugar and suchlike. He added that they had nothing to do with police work or interrogations. This was yet another illustration of Amin's firmly fixed opinion that he has only to say something for it to be believed by everybody, no matter how false – the Goebbels syndrome. Nobody living here can have any doubt about what the SRB is really up to. It has full-time employees and informers planted in every government department and section as well as Makerere University and in private organisations throughout the country. Many are from West Nile or Nubians and Moslems, but there are some Baganda and some from other tribes, eager for the power and the perks. Their intelligence, in both senses, is minimal, inaccurate and misleading and often directed against people with whom they have quarrelled or have grudges or debts. However, the unreliability of their reports does not stop them from acting on them and detaining, torturing and killing countless numbers of people who have been unable to flee into exile in time.

There's nothing secret about them and they readily identify themselves and are easily recognisable as, like all third-rate spies and 'secret' police, they wear dark glasses all the time, indoors and out, night and day. Many women typists, secretaries, barmaids and prostitutes work for them and report on their employers, customers and clients. The few expatriates are constantly watched and I'm well aware that my telephone at home is tapped as I can hear the clicking of the clumsily worked three-way connection as the circuit trips in and there's a hollow-sounding line when it's being used. I warn callers and then make use of colloquialisms, slang, abbreviations and allusions in our conversation which hopefully make it incomprehensible to eavesdroppers. No sort of interference is permitted from anyone, no matter how senior, and the courts and police have no authority over them as they operate outside the law. Even Amin may not hear all of what they do, although he frequently drops in at their HQ on Nakasero hill, where most of the torturing takes place. But he knows and he's responsible for it all; he can't dodge that.

Wednesday 20 December

Reuben, a former Law School Bar student who eventually left the Judiciary and now has a very successful legal practice in Mbale, called in today and very kindly presented me with a huge live Christmas turkey. So I was stuck with a large, noisy rampaging turkey in chambers. I summoned assistance to have it removed and taken into custody before the advocates came in to make their chamber applications. The door opened and the turkey promptly shot out into the court corridor, followed by my messenger, constable orderly and several members of the public, all whooping and laughing. Sighing, I closed my door and left them to it. Later, at home, my domestic staff, driver and police orderly all carried off their shares.

1979

Thursday 11 January

Last evening my cook, Douglas, took his usual pleasure in causing me to let out a startled squawk when he materialised suddenly and silently before me while I was reading. He smugly reported that the police sentry had arrived and he was very drunk. Since Douglas is often in that condition himself, he had nothing to be so smug about. I went outside and found that the constable had sat down on the ground and then had fallen sideways in a deep drunken sleep. The smell of alcohol was strong enough to intoxicate the whole neighbourhood. It was necessary to disarm him as he had clutched in one hand an AK 47 almost certainly loaded with one round up the spout, as they all do these days, unfortunately. The safety catch was most probably off as well – it was hidden by his body – and I therefore wanted to remove the gun without causing him to wake up and react with his finger on the trigger. I told Douglas to stand out of the way behind the brick archway to the servants' quarters while I very carefully and gently loosened the sentry's grip on the gun and eased it slowly away from him. Fortunately he was well away and stayed like that, because he was a big chap and I wouldn't have liked to have to try to wrestle the gun away from him. I then phoned Jinja Road station and was lucky enough to catch the duty sergeant in the station. I explained the position and, after about half an hour, he arrived with a replacement and an escort for our sleeping beauty, who was dumped without ceremony into the back of the Land Rover. I handed over the weapon, which I had switched to safety and unloaded in case he woke up.

The new OC Jinja Road, Superintendent Oballim, back in 1957 was a corporal at Mityana when I was OC Police there, so he knows me well. He rang me in my chambers this morning and reported that the man had already been dealt with and discharged from the Force. He apologised for the incident and explained that the constable had come straight from his quarters to my place without first reporting into the station before going on duty, otherwise his condition would have been noticed.

Tuesday 16 January

The painters from the Ministry of Works arrived yesterday at my house. They are doing the inside first, then the outside. The house is long overdue as it hasn't been painted since 1973. When I came home at lunch-time today I found that, where there are bookshelves in a recess, instead of removing the books first, they had simply painted over the end books when doing the surrounding wall. I'm not entirely convinced that it's an improvement.

It's incredible the nonsense that is believed here, even by some in high positions. Amin recently announced that two British bombers of the RAF had flown from Kenya to attack Uganda but 'our brilliant radar' had successfully driven the aircraft back from the border. He seems to think that radar is an offensive weapon rather than a detection system. The latest is that a talking tortoise has announced its intention of walking from Jinja to Kampala (80 miles at high speed should take a few years) to call on the President and speak its mind about the current situation in Uganda. As a result of its boldness, we are told, it has been locked up in a police cell in order to prevent this confrontation. What next?

Sunday 4 February

At 8.30 p.m. last night there was a tremendous explosion somewhere in Kampala and all the electricity in the city went off. Apparently guerrillas of SUM (Save Uganda Movement), who have infiltrated from Kenya and Tanzania, blew up the power station. There are rumours that Tanzanian forces have already invaded Uganda across the border at Kagera in response to Amin's nonsense down there last October. Amin merely says he's watching the situation.

Monday 5 February

I'm supposed to have gone to Masindi today for criminal sessions but the CJ has cancelled circuits due to the commotion and strong rumours in Kampala of an invasion. I certainly don't want to be marooned up-country if we're under attack. The SUM guerrillas have blown up an oil storage tank in the industrial area and a huge black cloud of smoke is hanging over the city. Amin's troops are rushing about in a panic like disturbed ants, firing their guns aimlessly. It's best to keep one's head down right now.

Friday 9 February

Not a good day. There's been no water for three days and the army is carrying out house searches accompanied by a lot of violence all over the city. Radio Uganda is giving out no news except for Amin saying that nothing is happening, which means something is, and we should carry on with our duties; which we are doing, except for circuits, of course.

Thursday 1 March

The inside of the house has been painted and looks good but there's no sign of the outside painters. Maybe the rumours have scared them off. It's very difficult to obtain news as the Military Council is keeping very quiet, which is ominous. It would appear that the Tanzanians, who have no transport and are advancing slowly on foot all the way, have overrun Mbarara and Masaka. Amin continues to say he's closely watching the situation and nobody should worry. But he at least must be worried because he can't stop the advance. He has no reliable troops; they are militarily useless and are only effective when dealing with unarmed civilians. Armed opposition is unknown to them and, with no proper training and poor morale, they simply can't cope. In fact, the Tanzanians are not having to fight all the way to Kampala, if that's where they are headed, because Amin's troops are retreating so fast and the two armies are keeping so far apart that clashes occur only occasionally and generally unintentionally. It's a sort of dance done by a large number of military types moving together in the same general direction but keeping a prudent distance from each other while each side fires off a great deal of ammunition, mostly at random. Amin has just announced that 'very severe steps will be taken to stop people from mongering rumours'.

Tuesday 6 March

Business seems to be going on as usual. As a result of the release of some funds long promised for furnishing the residences of judges, an excellent new blue carpet was fitted in my lounge and bedroom today and a new sofa set delivered. I hope that it's not going to prove to be a wasted effort.

There's a rumour being mongered, which I heard seriously discussed by some senior people, that the Tanzanians are using a large bombing aircraft which can fly backwards and sideways so as to bomb a target accurately. They are not referring to helicopters because those are a familiar sight, being Amin's favourite form of transport. In fact neither side has any bombing aircraft.

Wednesday 7 March

A criminal case from Teso before me today for a revisional order involved three men who were sent by a chief to fetch an old man whom the chief had accused of stopping the rain from falling in that area, which, as often happens in Teso, was suffering from a drought. The old man was supposed to be the local rainmaker, so it seemed rather unlikely that he would have been doing just the opposite; unless perhaps it was some form of strike for higher fees.

When the men arrived at the rainmaker's house he was out at the market, so they decided to take his two sons to assist them in looking for him. They didn't find the old man, so the men proceeded to beat up the elder son for wasting their time. He reported them to the police but the magistrate, who is unknown to me, made a complete dog's breakfast of the case in court. The DPP could not support the convictions as a result. The magistrate also failed to go into what happened about the rain and the failed rainmaker, so it all remains a mystery. It's very worrying.

Thursday 8 March

Yesterday I commenced a special Kampala criminal sessions. There's only one case but it's going to be a big one with 22 prosecution and 4 defence witnesses. It's also most extraordinary as the accused is a police assistant inspector named Drajua, from West Nile, who is the staff officer at the Public Safety Unit HQ and Towelli's right-hand man.

He is indicted on a double murder charge and the victims were two Nubian privates in the Marines called Gogo and Moro. The PSU made a big mistake when they took those two into Naguru and killed them because they both happened to be related to Brigadier Taban, an illiterate Nubian who commands the Marines. He persuaded the Army Chief of Staff to order both Drajua's arrest and the CID investigation, which, for once, seems to have been properly carried out. No doubt the police concerned were glad to have this chance to deal with the PSU at last.

Friday 16 March

The facts in this case reveal that there were 12 men beaten to death at the same time by the PSU staff but only these two marines appear on the indictment. The other ten were civilians and nobody seems to care about what happened to them, including the commander of the Marines and the DPP. If it hadn't been for the two marines no action would have been taken, as in the very many other killings by the PSU.

Most of the prosecution witnesses were inmates of the PSU cells who were rescued from almost certain death and kept in a specially arranged protective custody at Luzira prison awaiting this trial. Since they were under the protection of the Marines commander, nobody dared to tamper with them. They each described the horrors of the

PSU where the Nubian staff carried out punishments, tortures and killings as ordered by their officers, all wearing police uniform, particularly Towelli. The murderous orders issued by Towelli were passed on to the staff by Drajua.

This case was a typical instance. The witnesses described how Drajua ordered the two marines and ten other detainees to be brought from the cells. They were handcuffed together in pairs and told to lie face downwards on the ground. The staff NCOs had a heavy iron bar 5 feet long and 3 inches thick and took it in turns to use it to beat each pair of detainees on the neck and back until they were dead. When one of the staff was tired he handed over the rod to another, who started on the next pair of victims. There was much shouting, screaming and huge quantities of blood spilt.

Drajua was the senior officer present and he stood watching the scene throughout. When all 12 were dead he ordered four other detainees to pile the bodies into the back of an open Land Rover and instructed the driver and escorts to take the bodies to the city mortuary and dump them there. No paperwork was done and no names of victims were given to the mortuary attendant, an ancient police corporal. He was a very nervous witness and obviously worried about giving evidence against the PSU. He described the arrival of the vehicle and bodies and he recognised the driver as one who frequently brought in unidentified bodies. He described the injuries to the bodies, which matched up with the method used to kill them described by eyewitnesses. Other detainees at the PSU described how they were ordered to fetch many buckets of water to wash away the large pools of blood in the PSU punishment yard.

Drajua ordered a corporal to record that the 12 detainees had escaped but, surprisingly, he refused, saying he knew nothing of any escape. The Brigadier testified that he thought that the two marines were being detained by the police on a genuine armed robbery charge – which they were until the PSU took them over – and, since they were relatives, he had been keeping an eye on the proceedings. When he found out what had happened to them at the PSU, he went to arrest Drajua and his immediate superior, Superintendent Farijala, who certainly knew and approved of what happened. However, in court Farijala placed the blame entirely on Drajua, who for some unknown reason was the only one indicted.

Monday 26 March

This murder trial has been going on for three weeks now and much horrific information has come out about the activities of the PSU at their Naguru base. As each of the 20 former detainees testifying for the prosecution completes his evidence, I have ordered his immediate release and watched him walk free out of court; for none was held for a validly legal reason. One of them is an assistant inspector of police whom I knew many years ago when he was a constable serving under me. I was glad to be able to set him free and on his way home. They all looked extremely relieved at this chance of Fate that has saved them from certain death at the hands of the murdering PSU staff.

In his defence Drajua denied being present at the killings and denied giving the orders; but he admitted that these sort of incidents occurred while he was staff officer at the PSU. He said that Amin gave the PSU special powers, above the law, so that beatings and killings could be carried out. As they were a special unit these acts were not regarded as unlawful. He repeated that he personally had never had anything to do with these or any other killings, he just worked in the office.

While this trial has been going on we've been hearing gun-fire and explosions outside the city every day and now at night as well. It seems that the Tanzanians have almost arrived. They are moving slowly on foot still. If they had been mobile this would all have been over long ago. The big question is – are we getting out of the frying pan into the fire?

Thursday 29 March

I delivered a long judgment today in the PSU murder case and convicted Drajua on both counts and sentenced him to death. It's a pity that Towelli and Farijala were not in the dock as well. But that would be too much to expect as they are well protected by Amin. Indeed, it's surprising that he has allowed this very public trial – in a crowded court – to go ahead since so much has been revealed.

One odd thing is that there has been no newspaper or radio reporting of it although journalists have attended court, so it looks as if some steps were taken to try to hush it up. Not very successfully, since the court has been filled by the public every day of the three weeks trial. I was wondering how Amin would react to my usually blunt judgment, especially where I said in it that the Public Safety Unit should have been named more aptly as the Public Danger Unit and that I would like to have seen Towelli and Farijala indicted as co-accused. However, as we all left the court this afternoon the gun-fire became heavier and shells were landing and exploding in the city. Everybody fled from the court area. From my chambers I watched Drajua being hastily put into a prison vehicle and driven off towards Luzira prison. This time I had no compunction about sentencing him to death.

As I drove home, the gun-fire continued from the south-west and increased in intensity. They seem to be firing some rockets as well as shells. There's a night-time curfew imposed and no lights to be shown from houses. But clearly a lot of Amin's people are ignoring the curfew and one can hear the sound of many vehicles of all types leaving at night. Even before dusk cars, lorries and vans loaded to bursting with furniture and personal and looted belongings can be seen heading northwards out of the city. Amin's supporters have paid no heed to his demand that they should stay and fight to the death. They are on their way out.

Friday 30 March

My contact rang this evening and congratulated me on the result of the PSU case. But he reported that when the prison van carrying Drajua to Luzira was passing Naguru, where the PSU is based, Drajua's friends ambushed the van and rescued him. It seems he has gone off northwards with them, probably to the Sudan.

Saturday 31 March

Yesterday was most unpleasant with rockets, mortar and gun shells landing all over the city, and quite a number on Kololo hill. At one point they seemed to have bracketed my house, but they're obviously firing at random as they have no artillery spotters. The roofs of several houses around here have been damaged. Fortunately they are not using heavy or medium artillery; and it's all fairly light stuff, as can be seen from the shallow craters in the roads and gardens. This morning I had no official car so I drove to court in my Jag, only to find the place deserted and the gates padlocked.

Tuesday 3 April

The gun-fire continues. I feel as if I'm in the siege of Mafeking. At night the flashes from the guns light up the sky to the south and west of the city. The only time we get any peace and quiet is when it's raining heavily, as it is now daily, and they stop firing their guns and take shelter. So we all pray for lots more rain. Amin and many of his senior officers have already left Kampala with all the loot they can carry in their vehicles. The city is wide open and the Tanzanians could walk in, but they sit outside firing unnecessary shells in at random. I suspect that they have no plans for taking Kampala and don't know how to set about it. Neither side has the slightest idea how to obtain and use intelligence information. It's all just banging away wildly like cowboys in a B film. I believe that Nyerere, infuriated by Amin's attempted occupation of the Kagera salient, sent his soldiers in to punish Amin and Uganda by doing as much damage as possible before leaving. This whole exercise is too half-baked to be a planned invasion and occupation, though it looks as though it's turning out that way due to the craven pusillanimity of Amin and his much vaunted army.

Some enterprising youth called at my house offering a duck for sale. He may well have looted it; I didn't ask. Food is running out and I need fresh meat, so I paid him and off he scooted. There are no shops or markets open these days. Fortunately I managed to stock up some tinned foods before the shooting got too close. As usual I have tomatoes, cucumbers, lettuce, bananas and pawpaws growing in the garden. Yesterday Douglas reported back from a food-foraging expedition and said that soldiers were going round the city in lorries rounding up the civilian men and youths they could catch. They say they're to be given guns to fight the 'enemy'. As each one was caught, his identity card was demanded and, on production, it was torn up and thrown away. It all seems rather pointless, but typical. Douglas was amused because the soldiers had been unable to destroy his identity card. I had made it myself from red cloth binding on thick cardboard covers with photograph and official rubber stamps. It looks very impressive. I had then completely enclosed it in a polythene cover, so it was no wonder they couldn't tear it. The soldier who tried threw it to the ground in disgust, and Douglas picked it up and ran off at the same time as a group of them made a break for it, scattering in all directions. The few soldiers didn't know what to do so they all got away. It was, in any case, a hopeless attempt to obtain reinforcements, for nobody seized was trained nor could they be in time, even if they were willing. Since most of them are Baganda they are certainly not supporters of Amin and his northerners and are not going to fight for them. Even his own men are deserting in large numbers daily and moving off, with their property and loot, well away from the scene of battle.

Thursday 5 April

The only traffic in the city now is military and there's not much of that about. Many of the Baganda have wisely left and gone to their home *kyalo* (village), where they feel safer. Others have fled northwards or eastwards where the roads are still open. The Tanzanians don't seem to have realised that they ought to have surrounded the city if they wanted to capture Amin's men; another indication that they made no plans for coming this far.

The few people out and about are those scouting around for food. The curfew at night and switched-off street lights seem to be more for the purpose of enabling Amin's people to escape unseen, though their vehicles can clearly be heard. Most diplomats and government officials live on Kololo hill and it's clear that they have already gone, heading for the Kenyan bonder in convoys of cars. Nearly all my neighbours have left. There are some Libyan soldiers sent by Gaddafi in response to Amin's urgent plea for assistance. But there's nobody to tell them where they are or what to do or how to recognise friend from foe. They look lost and bewildered without maps or guides. I suspect Gaddafi has sent us troops he regards as unreliable and expendable. Probably just as well.

With so many people departing from the city residential areas, a certain amount of looting has commenced and this morning I was sitting on my verandah reading a Penguin paperback book with a background of gun-fire, when I heard the unmistakable sound of a crowd of people chasing after a thief and coming in my direction. Suddenly a man came running into my compound and stopped breathless and panting on my verandah. He sat on the low wall and gasped: 'Help me, please.' He was closely followed by a bunch of about 25 people all shouting and waving sticks and *pangas.*

It was rather annoying being interrupted in this rude manner, so I stood up and said loudly: 'Get out of my compound, you unwanted visitors,' or words to that effect. At the same time I threw my Penguin book in their direction. As one man, they turned about and fled through the gateway out of the compound and along the road. I walked to the gates, which I had ordered to be kept closed at all times, and locked them, muttering impolite words about whomever had left them unlocked.

One of the crowd came back then and shouted: 'You are helping a thief.'

I replied: 'Then go and report it to the police station and don't come back here. You are not welcome.'

I returned to the verandah, picking up my book on the way and smoothing out the creased covers and pages, then sat down and continued reading. The fugitive had disappeared meanwhile. I thought to myself it would make a good headline: JUDGE DISPERSES MOB WITH PENGUIN. Douglas then came from the house out of breath and waving the Gurkha kukri that I keep hanging on the wall for decorative purposes. I took it from him and asked where the visitor had gone. He replied that he had chased after the fellow but he had escaped by climbing over the bottom corner of the compound fence and he had disappeared.

A short while after that Douglas came on to the verandah grinning and reported that he had been outside to see what the mob I had sent away was doing. They had met one of Amin's stray soldiers wandering along the road carrying his automatic rifle and looking lost. Some of them told the soldier that they had been chased away from a house by a *mzungu* with a gun. When he heard that, the soldier took to his heels and fled in the opposite direction.

This afternoon the sound of gun-fire increased and it's moving up the western edge of the city. There are still some random shells landing on Kololo, which is entirely residential and has no military targets. There's also some scattered and sporadic small arms fire from light automatic weapons around the city. As usual I took tea on the verandah while trying to drown the sound of war with some pleasant music. My neighbour, a Muganda doctor, approached and said that he'd decided to leave his government house and take his family to the safety of the *kyalo* (home village), where they will stay until it's all over. I asked if he'd like some tea. He just laughed saying: 'No thanks, I must go now. I've read about the English sitting calmly drinking tea while all around them is chaos and revolution; but I didn't think that it really happened. Now I've seen that it does. *Weeraba, ssebo* (farewell, sir).'

Friday 6 April

Those of us who are still around have been keeping in touch with each other by telephone. Oddly enough, the phones are still working, even the incoming international lines, but not outgoing. I went through my list several times, checking off who was still around and OK and who had gone. I think the CJ has already left for Nairobi as I can't raise a response from his number. A man from Reuters in Nairobi has rung up three times asking for information about what is happening here. I explained and then asked him to contact the BHC in Nairobi to pass on a message to the Commonwealth Secretariat that I am still in Kampala and safe so far. He said he would do so.

At 7.30 p.m. it was very dark and I heard the unmistakable sound of tanks moving northwards along the road outside. The Tanzanians have no armour, or, if they've captured some, they'd probably be blazing away with the tank guns in the same haphazard manner that they waste their artillery.

Saturday 7 April

Heavy rain has reduced the gun-fire for a while but still those timid Tanzanians haven't entered the city, which is empty now. There's a Libyan road-block down near the golf club, but that's all. Several people rang today whom I thought had left, including a friend in Jinja and the man from Reuters. Wilson, the surgeon, called in and very kindly brought me a chicken and some eggs. He is driving around in his white coat with a large sign in his car windscreen saying *DAKTARI*. It seems to work.

Most of the Tanzanian artillery and ammunition has been supplied by the Chinese and it's not much good. It's a relief that at least a third of their shells are defective and dud. There are many unexploded shells scattered around Kololo, but they shouldn't have been fired at or into civilian residential areas anyway.

Tuesday 10 April

I think I'm the only one left in this road now; everyone else seems to have left. I tried to get some sleep last night but the gun-fire was continuous and the sky alight with flashes. A shell landed in my neighbour's garden on the other side of the compound and exploded among the flowers. It didn't do them much good. Another, evidently heading for my roof, hit a tree branch overhanging close to the house and exploded, blowing in all the windows of my bedroom and bathroom. The blast flung me out of bed and everywhere inside was showered with broken glass, ceiling plaster and leaves and twigs from the tree.

I spent the rest of the noisy, sleepless night on the sofa in the lounge with my scramble bag at the ready – an old flight bag packed with my emergency escape kit. This morning I looked at the mess in my bedroom and found on the pillow, where my head had been, a small jagged piece of shell casing. Just as well I was blown out of bed before it landed. I checked outside and found that several other windows have been broken, some of them round the corner from the explosion and blast, which is odd. Many tiles have been lifted off the roof and are either broken or displaced. Fortunately for me the large tree beside my house took much of the force of the explosion and deflected some of the blast towards the abandoned house on this side. The occupants won't be too happy when they return, though.

The water supply and electricity are both off and it's alternately raining hard or very hot. Shells are still landing in the area and gun-fire is all round now. There's quite a lot of light automatic weapon firing in different parts of the city, but Amin's men left days ago. The Tanzanians don't know who is and who isn't one of Amin's supporters and, no doubt, many local grudges are being settled by those pointing someone out as one of them.

Wednesday 11 April

There's still a lot of small-arms firing, but mostly in the air, I think.

I've seen a considerable amount passing through the higher branches of the many trees in the area, taking off leaves and twigs on the way. I went out with Doc Wilson in his minibus to look around. Nearby, at the golf club roundabout at the bottom of Kololo hill, there are shallow craters in the road and the completely burned-out remains of a large Mercedes Benz limousine diagonally across the road. The fire had melted away the tarmac road surface all around it. Two other smashed-up cars were not far away. One had been hit by a shell and had then crashed into the high gates of a house compound at the road-side. The other had a row of bullet holes through it.

Some bodies were lying around, including those of two Europeans. The UN representative in Uganda – refugees department, I think – who has remained behind, came round and asked me if I could iden-tify them but I was unable to; they turned out to be East Germans who had left it too late for safe movement and they were shot while trying to get out at the last minute.

On another road we met a large group of men in civilian clothes walking along laughing and shouting. They looked very pleased with life and told us that all the prisoners had been released from Luzira prison by the liberators. My heart sank as I contemplated the security problem the authorities and public would now have to face following this emptying of the large prison and release of very many criminals on to the streets, especially if the Tanzanians do the same in the other towns they liberate. Except for political prisoners, it is highly irresponsible. At a crossroads on Nakasero hill we met a group of soldiers standing about rather aimlessly and looking lost. They seemed rather dazed by the fact that they were actually in Kampala and they told us that they were Ugandans who had been away in exile for between six and eight years. Clearly they were very glad to be back in Uganda.

Thursday 12 April

More people are coming out from where they've been hiding and already serious looting has commenced. There are many abandoned houses, shops, offices, factories and other buildings which were occu-pied by Amin's supporters or by people who have simply fled from the fighting. Furniture, fittings, personal property, kitchen and office equipment and other items are all being removed and carried away. Everywhere one can see hundreds of people looking like ants, carry-ing on their heads or backs whatever they can snatch and scurrying or staggering off in all directions. Almost everyone has joined in, includ-ing some senior officials and professional men. Some are looting the furniture and property of neighbours who have left for safer places. It's really appalling and pathetic as well as being a very deeply depressing augury for the future here.

My present *shamba* boy is from the West Nile so I told him to lie low and stay in the compound. People from Amin's district are obviously not popular at the moment and I've no doubt that any of them still around are likely to be made to suffer by both Tanzanians and Ugandans.

Friday 13 April

It's Good Friday and the looting continues all over the city. No attempt is being made by the Tanzanians to stop it; in fact they are taking part. I can get Radio Uganda now on my battery radio and it has been announced that a new government has been formed, made up of returned Ugandan exiles. But nothing was said about the looting.

During the morning I was, as usual these days, sitting on my verandah reading when I heard the sound of someone climbing over my locked compound gates. I walked quickly up to the gates and found a Tanzanian soldier climbing down on my side. Another stood outside holding an automatic rifle. Behind him was a small crowd of civilians. I angrily demanded to know what they thought they were doing and the soldier with the gun pointed it at my stomach and said in Swahili: 'You are Amin's man.'

'Don't be ridiculous,' I replied, 'I'm British.' Nevertheless they insisted on searching my house for Nubians, or *Nubis* as they call them. Since I couldn't prevent them I reluctantly agreed; but I spoke sharply to the civilians outside my gate and told them to clear off as they would not be allowed to enter. They were obviously hoping to loot the place and had no doubt brought the soldiers to assist them in doing so. I was shocked to see that the leader of the group was a very senior officer in the Ministry of Justice whom I know and who is well aware that I live here. He didn't look at all embarrassed.

The two Tanzanians walked around inside the house looking for Nubians by opening the drawers of my desk and poking about in cupboards, quite obviously searching for portable items to take away. I kept close to them all the time so as to frustrate such efforts. Then one of them noticed an old photograph of me wearing British Army uniform and asked: 'Were you an army officer?' When I replied that I was he looked at his companion and said: 'I think we should go now.' I agreed and escorted them to the gates, let them out and locked the padlock. When I returned to the verandah I found that one of them had pinched my new sunglasses.

509

Later, other looters came and tried to enter the place, but when they saw Douglas and myself patrolling the compound, each carrying a heavy club in a determined and unfriendly fashion, they soon decided to go elsewhere after easier prey.

Saturday 14 April

In the course of phoning various people this morning, I spoke to the Chief Registrar, who told me that Wambuzi has returned with the exiles (he has in fact been a member of the Kenya Court of Appeal) and is to be CJ now. He wants to meet any judges still here. I think most have stayed in Kampala.

The water and electricity supplies have surprisingly been restored in some parts of the city, including my place. Douglas went out and about scrounging and scavenging and obtained some vegetables and fruit, so we can manage for the moment. There's still some shooting around here and occasional explosions. It seems that our liberators are blowing their way into the banks and offices in the city and helping themselves. I spoke to the British general managers of Barclays Bank and Standard Bank and they have both been in to inspect their premises, only to find them severely damaged, and not in any battle or fighting, with most of the contents missing.

Looters are stripping all the shops and offices, and paper records in banks and government departments are being burned or thrown away. It's going to be an enormous headache sorting this lot out when all this nonsense dies down. This ineffective bunch of returned exiles – academics and businessmen – who call themselves a government of the Uganda National Liberation Front (UNLF) have done nothing to prevent or stop this stupidly wasteful looting and destruction. In these few days probably more material damage has been done and loss suffered in the city than in all the eight years of Amin's regime. The Asian exodus at least left most of their property intact. The Police Force has disintegrated and is ineffective at the moment but the invading forces are supposed to be under control and should have been used to stop the looting and destruction; instead they've all taken part in it.

Amin fled first to Jinja, from where he announced that he would fight to hold the dam (whatever for?) and then changed his mind and travelled north to Nakasongola, where he had an aircraft waiting on the airstrip which took him to his best friend Gaddafi in Tripoli. So he has got away. Not surprising really, with the tortoise-like slowness of the Tanzanian advance.

Sunday 15 April

The former American President, Harry S. Truman, was once described as an example of mediocrity enlarged by history. Perhaps, in a rather different way, it might also describe Amin. But in his case enlargement didn't imply that he became a better and more responsible, or even likeable, person and leader after his rise to power and fame. Certainly he expanded in many ways – including girth – and he was widely admired and acclaimed in many developing countries; most especially when he displayed his contempt for the leaders and policies of powerful Western countries and chided and derided those leaders in his speeches and volumes of telegrams.

Amin often used the word 'revolutionary' to describe himself and his actions. He also used it when endeavouring to explain away a multitude of errors and unwise and imprudent decisions. But in the true sense he was revolutionary for he brought about great changes – unfortunately for the worse – which have drastically affected the economy of Uganda and the way of life of its people and will continue to do so for a very long time to come. Recovery and rehabilitation will now have to take priority over progress in new fields for much of the foreseeable future.

I think most of us who met Amin would agree that he had considerable charm, when he wished to exert it, and he could put on a convincing display of earnestness and desire to do what was right. He earned much open admiration for his charisma, his machismo and his swaggeringly outrageous and exuberant style. It was his style that particularly caused him to stand out from among other shoddy, third-rate and uninspiring national leaders. It was his irresponsibility and his incompetence that made him inconspicuous among them.

His frequent descriptions of himself as being 'brilliant' and 'a genius' were expressions of extremely wishful thinking on his part and as inaccurate as they were immodest. His professional military training was as an ordinary infantry soldier, at which he was never outstanding. Although he understood the value of discipline he was himself poorly disciplined – he supported the mutineers in his own army in 1964. He also knew the value of loyalty but was frequently disloyal to those with whom he was associated and who relied upon him for support in their work and duties.

He had a broad sense of humour but little imagination and he could turn from laughing fat man to evil-minded sadist in a moment. He was reluctant to do even a minimal amount of paperwork and would tend to avoid it whenever he could by designating someone else to deal with it – which usually meant that it was much delayed or didn't get

511

done at all. Maybe it would have been better if he had appointed a civilian prime minister to relieve him of such work and to deal with the boring but necessary day to day work of the administration. However, that would have meant surrendering some power and Amin was never one to do that. Nor did he approve of his ministers and other senior officials acting on their own initiative. Thus, decisions publicly announced by one of them were easily and often reversed by Amin by means of a humiliating radio announcement, without first informing that official, and so publicly manifesting Amin's displeasure.

What has surprised many of us both inside and outside Uganda is that Amin lasted as long as eight years. Considering how extremely incompetent, unpopular and destructive the military regime was, I think most of us optimistically hoped and expected a much earlier overthrow. Amin's imminent fall was constantly and inaccurately predicted, but one had to recognise that the indecisiveness, incompetence and dilatoriness existed among both his supporters and opponents alike.

Monday 16 April

It's Easter Monday and after I'd had a late breakfast a battered-looking car arrived at my gate with a European and a Tanzanian soldier escort. It was a chap called Posnett, whom I vaguely remembered as an administration official in the office of the Resident, Buganda, before independence. He said he'd been sent out by the FCO to represent British Government interests, whatever they might be, and he needed a Union Jack to fly on his important car as he drove about. Why he should think I had one I don't know. All I had was one printed on a tea towel that someone had given me once and which I'd stuck on the wall as a mildly defiant gesture to Amin when he forbade the flying of the British flag. I pointed out the obvious fact that, if he found the keys to the High Commission, probably held by someone at the French Embassy, he could open up the place and no doubt find a supply of flags for important cars plus having a good base to work from. It's been closed for a few years and, with any luck, not looted. I added that if he can't find the keys I'm sure that a passing Tanzanian soldier will obligingly blow it open with his RPG (rocket propelled grenade).

The Tanzanians and returned Ugandan exiles are now referred to on the radio and in the press as *wakombozi* (liberators) and apparently we are expected to feel deeply grateful to them for coming here and liberating us by looting and blowing up the city. The Ugandan *wakombozi* address each other as 'compatriot' instead of using normal titles.

Perhaps they find 'comrade' a little too far to the left, or maybe they just want to be different.

Now that it's too late and everything in the city that's lootable has been taken, the UNLF Government has announced that the looting must stop. It should never have been allowed to happen in the first place. I gather that our glorious liberators had never expected or intended to take Kampala and so no plans were made for its occupation or policing. It's been announced that teams of Makerere undergraduates will be sent round the houses to recover looted property. What a nonsense. How would they they know what's looted and what not? Since they are unsupervised they will almost certainly collect items for their own purposes, as many of them will no doubt have done before the announcement. When a lorry-load of them arrived at my place this afternoon I refused to allow them to enter. They became quite arrogant and stated that it was President Lule's personal order. I informed them that they had no right to invade the residence of a High Court judge and they were committing a criminal offence and they could tell Lule that I had said so. I then ordered them to leave and they went off grumbling loudly.

Tuesday 17 April

I was informed on the telephone that the newly appointed Chief Justice requires my presence as he has called a meeting. A vehicle came today to take me to the court and we picked up two other judges from their houses on the way. As we drove along the roads near the Parliament building I could see that the grass and plants in the centre road islands had been dug up into a series of shallow two-man slit trenches, each covered with waterproof capes and manned by Tanzanians. The City Council gardeners will be pleased.

Also attending our meeting was a former exiled advocate now appointed Minister of Justice. I recall in the 1960s when he was a young advocate with what was then the standard beard of a troublesome radical politician, he came to the Law School asking to be appointed as a lecturer. I took one look at the beard and said – no vacancies. He doesn't look as if he's changed much; I wonder how long he'll last in this job. Apart from exchanging horror stories and accounts of the last few days, the meeting was pointless, though it established that only the two Pakistani judges had left the country. It will be no great loss if they don't return; both were idle and largely ineffective. Amin brought them here because he wanted Moslems in every department to prove his loyalty to his Arab paymasters. The main loss is the previous CJ, who was first class at the job. His replacement, Wambuzi, as a former CJ is experienced and now getting his second bite at the cake, but, this time he seems to be rather political, even attending UNLF cabinet meetings. Apparently he was also a contender for the post of President and somewhat disappointed not to get it, as were a number of other ambitious types in this mixed political bag. In the end they appointed a compromise candidate, the nonentity Y. K. Lule (formerly a junior minister in the Protectorate Government and then Principal of Makerere University College). Since he's a Muganda the Baganda are very happy, as it's the tribe that counts more than merit. I doubt he'll last; there's too much competition and, although he's a good person, he has all the charisma of a steamed pudding.

Wednesday 18 April

Many of the looted items have been abandoned on the roadsides, perhaps found useless to looters or too heavy to carry far. Filing cabinets, typewriters, calculating machines, sofas, empty shop tills, ceiling fans, refrigerators and the like can be seen lying about. They are gradually being collected in lorries and taken to police stations so that the owners can go and identify and collect them. An elderly British businessman back from Nairobi told me that he had been out in his pick-up truck trying to locate various items looted from his house in his absence. He found his fridge and one or two other things. Then he reached a place where there were thick bushes by the roadside. As he searched around the stuff lying there he came across two armed Libyan soldiers in hiding. They climbed into the back of his truck, which was covered with a canvas, and with a gun pointing at him told him to drive them out of Kampala. He reached a group of Tanzanians blocking the road and checking passers-by and they asked him where he was going. He explained that he was out searching for his stolen property. At the same time, keeping his hands in front of his body, he pointed urgently towards the back of the lorry and said very quietly: 'Ndani nyuma,' (inside the back). A slightly brighter one among them got the message and went quietly to the back of the truck, lifted the canvas quickly and without a word shot the two Libyans. This was rather a shock as he had expected that they would take them prisoner. Besides, if the shots had been even slightly badly aimed he could have been shot himself.

Friday 20 April

The judges and staff go to court each day but no cases have been fixed for hearing yet. This morning the Chief Registrar wanted some court files from the chambers of one of the Pakistani judges, who had departed leaving his chambers locked and taking the keys with him. When I walked past I found a chap from the Ministry of Works with a large chisel hacking away at the thick stone wall around the heavy *mvule* wood door. I asked what he was doing and the CR told me that he had called him in to break in round the door so as to enter the chambers. Obviously neither of them had a clue and there was going to be a great deal of needless damage done to the masonry. I told the man to stop and move back. I put my finger two inches to the right of the door lock and said: 'Just there, I reckon.' Then I stepped back, put my hand on the workman's shoulder to steady myself, and bent my right knee up to my chest and straightened it with all the force I could muster, kicking the door exactly on the point I had indicated next to the lock. It flew open and we were in. No damage to the wall or the door; merely a replacement lock required. 'There you are,' I said, 'and there'll be no extra charge for the breaking and entering.'

Another judge who had stopped to watch the proceedings asked: 'Where did you learn to do that?'

I replied: 'I was once a tough cop.' Actually, the only time that I did that to a door while I was in the Police was to my house front door after it closed and self-locked, leaving me outside with the keys inside.

The CR collected the files he needed and on the desk I found a pile of lower court files awaiting revisional orders that had obviously been there for some time. I picked them up, blew the dust off and said that I'd deal with them as it would give me something useful to do until he found more doors for me to force open. The MoW chap grabbed his chisel and went off muttering mutinously, having been deprived of his interesting demolition job. He had obviously not seen the right films.

It's been announced that we are now resuming the old-style weekends of Saturdays and Sundays instead of Amin's religious cocktail of a weekend. The Tanzanians are trudging towards Jinja and will then turn northwards. I doubt whether they'll came across much opposition on the way. Amin's men are all in the Sudan or Zaire by now and a new batch of political exiles will have gone through Kenya either on their way to Europe or south to Tanzania or Zambia. Apparently Gaddafi has already found that there's insufficient room in Libya for two mad military dictators and so Amin has had to move on to his miserable friends and bankers in Saudi Arabia, where he's been given a large place in Jiddah to house his family and loot.

A chap from Amnesty International called into my chambers this morning and, in the course of our chat, I passed on some information concerning certain people whom I had reason to believe the Tanzanians were improperly detaining and mistreating. He said he'd look into it.

Wednesday 25 April

I had lunch at the British High Commissioner's residence. On the way there were several shell-holes adding to the hazard of numerous potholes usually found in Kampala roads. Only drunken drivers drive straight along such roads nowadays. Posnett has now been appointed acting High Commissioner and wanted to discuss aid to Uganda with some of us. I emphasised that they must not hand over lump sums of cash as it will simply go into the pockets of the government ministers. I don't think I was believed and I suspect they'll disregard my advice. The lunch was all right, though.

Saturday 28 April

George Kanyeihamba called at my house this morning. He was a lecturer at the Law School for a short time long ago and is now Attorney-General. His family is still in the UK and, as he's flying there tomorrow, I gave him some letters to post there as our postal service is still not working. He came in a pick-up with an armed Tanzanian escort. He has acquired this returned exile notion that all of us who stayed and worked here are, by that fact, to be condemned as Amin's supporters and should be removed or locked up. I told him that was utter rubbish and he should know me well enough by now to understand why I stayed on.

Apart from those who genuinely had to get out to save their lives, many of the exiles had no real need to leave Uganda, but did so to avoid the hard economic life and because of the availability of highly paid jobs abroad in universities and the UN. In a few of them now there may, perhaps, be some unconscious feeling of a need to justify deserting their country in its time of need. Now they're back it's very much an 'us' and 'them' situation, and the exiles, or returnees as they call themselves, appear to think that all benefits and good jobs should go to them. Instead of the much-needed reconciliation and co-operation, we're getting this splitting into two camps and too much accusation and self-justification. To boost their egos and impress people with their intelligence, each member of the UNLF Government uses the title of doctor or professor; some are genuine titles, like George's; some are doubtful and others are entirely spurious.

The Tanzanians come from a country totally impoverished by their President Nyerere, whose extreme socialist policies have bankrupted his country and ruined its economy. They have nothing there and are finding so many items here in Uganda that they desire, so they're just helping themselves. Anyone wearing a watch, dark glasses, carrying a portable radio/cassette player or riding a bicycle is likely to be separated from this property by patrolling pairs of armed Tanzanians in the streets. There have been public complaints that the Tanzanian People's Defence Force (TPDF) is an occupying force in Uganda and should now leave. The obsequious UNLF Government has stated that the Tanzanians were in fact invited to Uganda by the government. This, of course, is nonsense. Amin certainly didn't invite them here and the UNLF Government didn't exist when they invaded. Nyerere sent the TPDF to punish Amin for his earlier invasion of the Kagera salient. Of course, they are invaders and occupiers and they are behaving as such, and the sooner they leave the better. Now that Amin has gone their job has ended and they should leave the running of Uganda to Ugandans, of whom there are many better qualified than Nyerere and his gang of economy-destroyers.

Thursday 3 May

I was collected in a car this morning to go to the court and on the way passing near the golf club I saw the familiar bald head and stocky back view of Godfrey Binaisa QC, walking in the direction of town. So we stopped and gave him a lift to the Nile Mansions, where the UNLF people hang out. He has come over from the UK and hopes to be a part of this government. They certainly need some sensible, intelligent and experienced chaps of his calibre to get things sorted out. At the moment the UNLF Government, which they now call the National Consultative Council (NCC), is a bunch of arguing, dissenting, ambitious politicians who only came together to take over from Amin and have very little else in common. Some are bright but are political opponents. Nyerere obviously doesn't trust them an inch. Every decision of the UNLF Government has to be referred first to Dar-es-Salaam for Nyerere to confirm or disallow. He has even sent one of his ministers to sit with Lule's puppet government to oversee all discussions and make sure everything really is referred to Dar. What a degrading situation.

I managed to send some letters to the UK yesterday via Frank McGinley, who was visiting from the BHC in Nairobi. He'll send them on from there. I rang the Kampala Head Postmaster today to ask when our local postal services will be resumed. He said he hopes to get them going next week but various post offices around the country have been looted and some badly damaged. After lunch a team from the British TV company Granada arrived at my house and asked if they could interview me about the Amin period. So we did this for about an hour and then they buzzed off.

Thursday 17 May

The other day my constable orderly, PC Outeke, reported that he was having trouble with his left arm. He lifted his sleeve and showed a lump in his upper arm. Apparently during the shooting in and around Kampala last month a stray bullet, which must have been almost spent in flight, struck his arm and entered the flesh, stopped dead and lodged just under the skin. I wrote a chit to Wilson (Dr Carswell) and sent Outeke off with it to have the bullet removed. He reported back yesterday with a small bandage on his arm and said it came out very quickly and easily and all is well now.

Tuesday 22 May

We judges were required to attend Parliament this afternoon as Lule was opening the Consultative Council and making a speech. It was more boring than uplifting. This was one of Lule's rare visits to Kampala. The timid fellow spends all his time at State House, Entebbe, and gives the impression of fearing Kampala. However, as far as the Baganda are concerned, he's one of them, which means that after many years of being ruled by northerners they are now on top, and so anything he does and says is all right by them. It's understandable, I suppose. At the reception afterwards I was chatting with a group of lawyers about where we had each been during the Kampala siege. Some said that they had gone back to the *kyalo* until it was over and others that they had been outside the country in exile. I remarked that I'd stayed in Kampala throughout. To this one opined: 'Then you must be strong-hearted.' Another said: 'You must have been mad.'

Friday 25 May

George, the AG, is back from the UK and he called in today and brought me a bag of apples. I had asked for them as it's many years since I had an apple in Uganda. The only apples sold here used to come from South Africa, which is the only part of the continent where the climate is suitable for growing them. But because of apartheid and the consequent ban on all goods from South Africa, we've been without such delicious fruit ever since.

Wednesday 30 May

Contrary to my advice, the British Government has handed over £1 million in cash to the UNLF Government. The Americans have given $1 million at the same time. Predictably, this government has announced that they regard these cash donations as compensation for their own hard life (!) in exile and they have openly shared out the whole of the two sums of money between them and put it into their overseas personal bank accounts. Not one penny has gone to Uganda or its ordinary people. This is where I say: I told you so. If any people had hard lives it was those people who stayed in Uganda, certainly not the exiles. This was open theft.

Tuesday 19 June

The UNLF Government has drafted a law for the trial of Amin's men who have been detained, such as former members of the SRB, the PSU and the military police. This law cuts out the need for legal evidential proof and normal court procedures. Most of the judges seemed to be fairly complacent about this so I requested a judges meeting and pointed out that these trials would be exactly like Amin's military tribunals and just as objectionable as a farce and injustice to all concerned, and a great discredit to the government and to Uganda's legal system.

Although several judges at first said we should support the government's proposal for special courts, eventually all agreed to sign a letter to the government setting out our objections to the proposal. When the members of the Uganda Law Society heard of our stand on this, they also supported us by registering their objections. One of the ministers said publicly that the judges are not supporting the UNLF Government and that this is unacceptable. Like other ignorant people, he doesn't understand that it's not our business to support any particular government but to remain impartial and administer the law equally to all. It's up to the CJ to explain this to them. After all, he's one of them and sits in their cabinet; so why didn't he and the Minister of Justice and the Attorney-General all object then? However, it seems that they are not now going ahead with setting up these courts and Amin's men must be tried before our courts.

Thursday 21 June

Yesterday afternoon Lule was given the boot by the UNLF Government. Even that lot has at last realised how useless he is. Binaisa has been appointed President in his place. This is great news. However, the Baganda are out in the town rioting, led by Makerere undergraduates all screaming: 'Lule! Lule!' Even though Binaisa is also a Muganda they hate him because he was once in Obote's

Government and they think, quite mistakenly, that he will try to bring Obote back as President. They haven't a clue about him really. He's probably the best of those around now. But it's easy to raise a shouting mob here and there's been a lot of violence overnight and gun-fire can be heard, also some explosions. The Tanzanians won't be awfully happy either because, unlike Lule, Binaisa will not bow down to them. I doubt whether he has much respect for Nyerere or any of that bunch.

Saturday 23 June

I spent the morning putting barbed wire up in a tangled pattern all over my iron gates to try to keep out unwanted visitors. I did the job myself, wearing thick gardening gloves; receiving curious looks from passing pedestrians. There are many burglaries and quite a number of shootings going on at night in this area and indeed all over Kampala so, with the Baganda all steamed up about the egregious Lule, precautions are necessary.

Tuesday 26 June

Yesterday the Baganda came out on strike in Kampala. If they think that will bring their beloved Lule back as President they're very much mistaken. It's rather like the childish efforts of the Kabaka and his followers when they couldn't have things their own way in Protectorate days, and later in Obote's regime. They don't seem to learn that obstinate petulance gets them nowhere. I went to court in the morning but only two or three of us were there. Nearly all the staff are Baganda and they stayed away. It doesn't make much difference at the moment as the courts are not sitting so there's very little to do. But Ugandans will have to get a grip on themselves and stop squabbling otherwise they'll never recover from all these disasters. They should be getting down to hard work and showing determination to get their country back on its feet again.

Wednesday 4 July

Most nights one can hear the odd bursts of gun-fire. These are robberies, drunken quarrels between soldiers over women, grudge murders and the like. The few police back on duty cannot cope yet and the TPDF soldiers roam about the city day and night, fighting over women and stealing property. They are poorly disciplined and very trigger-happy in an atmosphere where they are the victorious occupying army with many temptations in their way. Last night was sleepless, there was gun-fire from different parts of the city all through the night. It doesn't feel much like liberation, nor is it a great improvement on the Amin regime.

Stuart Kiwanuka, an old acquaintance, called on me early this evening. I've known him for years and he has recently become a qualified soccer referee. He told me that last night his home was broken into by Tanzanian troops who not only stole all his clothes and household property but also beat him severely with canes and their rifle butts. He removed his only remaining torn shirt and showed me his back covered with cuts, bruises and abrasions. He'd been to the clinic for treatment and they could only put some ointment on as they have no bandages. I gave him some clothes and other items with a tube of liniment, unobtainable here, and some cash for replacements.

There's talk of these wretched Tanzanians staying here for a year or even two years. But it's probably only the UNLF people who want this, not the rest of Ugandans, who will be glad to see the back of these arrogant, thieving visitors who have no interest in the rehabilitation of Uganda.

Thursday 12 July

An ancient file came before me today. A land dispute was decided by the former Buganda Principal Court in 1958 and an appeal was filed in the High Court in October 1963. Five years later, a judge ordered a survey of the disputed land. In December 1971 it came before another judge, who found that no survey had been carried out. In May 1974 it came before yet another judge who, for no good reason, simply adjourned it. Three months after that a fourth judge refused an application by the respondent to dismiss the appeal for want of prosecution, which he could properly have granted. In March this year a fifth judge directed the Registrar to take steps to have the appeal dismissed, and so it has come before me today.

I recorded that the appellant and his advocate, who were both absent from court, had taken no steps to have the appeal fixed for hearing in 16 years, which meant that the original judgment in favour of the respondent had been in abeyance for that time, which I held was not only grossly unfair to him but also a flagrant abuse of the judicial process. I dismissed the appeal with costs to the respondent, who was the only one who had attended court for each hearing over the last 16 years. But this should have been done long ago.

Wednesday 18 July

I had met Stephen Ariko, a former advocate in Soroti, before he went into exile. He is now Minister of Justice, having replaced the chap who, as I predicted back in April, didn't last long in the job. A short while ago I went to see Ariko to discuss the urgent need to establish law and order back under Ugandan control, which requires the revival of the Uganda Police and much necessary reorganisation and training. I said that they can ask for assistance from the UK police training teams. At his request I advised him that the best chap to take over the Force would be Luke Ofungi. I knew Ofungi was then in Nairobi and I urged Ariko to persuade government to invite him back and appoint him as soon as possible. I hear now that he's back in Uganda and it appears that they're going to do just that.

Ariko agreed with me that what Uganda doesn't need is an army. There are now no threats of outside aggression and African armies bring nothing but death and misery to their own countries all over the continent. A well-trained and equipped police force can deal with internal problems and minor border incursions of the sort that sometimes occur. Ariko's response to my views was: 'You're preaching to the converted.'

Saturday 28 July

On Saturday mornings I normally drive to Kampala GPO in my Jag to check my post-box. As usual there were two armed Tanzanian soldiers standing outside watching people passing. As I walked towards the rank of boxes one of the Tanzanians stopped a young Muganda and pointed to the wrist-watch he was wearing. I approached and heard the soldier say in Swahili: 'Nataka saa yako' (I want your watch) and he reached out to take it.

I kept on walking and, as I reached the young chap, who was a complete stranger to me, I seized him firmly by the upper arm and said: 'Hello, Joseph, how's the job? Not seen you for a long time. Have you seen your brother lately?' and kept on babbling fictions like this as I marched the startled chap away from the Tanzanians, who stood there with their mouths open doing nothing.

As we turned the corner of the building I released him and said: 'Sorry about that. But he was going to steal your watch. It's better to keep it in your pocket around town. That's what I do.' Changing to Luganda I said: 'Bulungi. Kakati genda mangu mangu' (Good. Go now quickly).

He grinned and replied: 'Webali nnyo nnyo, ssebo' (thank you very much, sir), and he moved away. Then he turned back and asked: 'But how did you know that my name is Joseph?'

Saturday 4 August

I had just gone to bed last night when a group of men in scruffy civilian clothes appeared at my bedroom window, which was open. They were carrying clubs and *pangas*, and their leader demanded to be let in. There are still no policemen available as night guards for judges, so they had climbed over the locked and barbed wired gates. I said loudly that they had better leave as I was calling the police. I picked up the phone and pretended to do so. It would have been a waste of time actually to ring them as they have no mobile patrols organised yet. Fortunately these characters didn't know that and they all scarpered.

This morning I rang Ariko in his VIP room at the Nile Mansions and reported what had happened, to emphasise my urgings about reorganising the police. He said he would arrange for sentries at my residence.

Monday 6 August

Yesterday evening two soldiers of the TPDF in camouflage uniforms and carrying the usual AK 47s turned up and said they had been sent to guard my house. Two hours later Douglas came into the house and reported that both he and the *shamba* boy had been turned out of their quarters, which were now occupied by the Tanzanians – one in each room with the doors bolted on the inside.

I went to the quarters and thumped on the doors, shouting in Swahili for them to come outside immediately. One of them came to the door. He'd taken off his uniform and had obviously been using the bed. The other one appeared in the same state. I said angrily: 'What do you think you're doing? This is not an hotel. You were not sent here to sleep but to guard me and my house. If you can't do that you're useless to me and I shall report you to your commanding officer in the morning.'

I thought they might start threatening with their weapons but instead the harsh tone of voice worked and they quickly got dressed and came outside and started to patrol the compound. So that they could hear, I said loudly to my servants: 'Go into your rooms and lock and bolt the doors and do not let anyone come in. I shall be checking up later.' I stood there for a while watching the sentries move around, then went inside.

Early this morning when the Tanzanians were leaving I went out and thanked them and said: 'Tell your OC I'm very grateful but there's no need to send any more sentries here.' I'd rather manage without added headaches. They're more trouble than they're worth.

Monday 13 August

A few days ago a Muganda called Musisi was brought before the Kampala Chief Magistrate on a charge of corruption of a public officer. His advocate applied for bail and the police prosecutor objected, saying that neither the police nor the court had jurisdiction because corruption is an offence listed in Amin's Economic Crimes Tribunal Decree as triable only by a military tribunal. The CM agreed and said that as that Decree is still in force, even though there are now no military tribunals, he was unable to grant bail or deal with the case in any way.

Since the police knew this in advance it seemed rather pointless filing the charge and bringing the man to court. Musisi's advocate appeared before me and said he wished to appeal against the refusal to grant bail. I pointed out what he should have known anyway, that there is no appeal against a refusal to grant bail. The procedure on being refused bail in one court is to file an application for bail in the next higher court. But, since the Decree mentioned gave exclusive jurisdiction to military tribunals, no such application could be entertained in the High Court. In fact the Decree does not permit any release on bail for those accused of tribunal offences. Obviously urgent legislation is now required to deal with this anomaly and get rid of all these tribunal Decrees and offences and procedures. Meanwhile, what to do?

Looking at the file, I pointed out that the police charge had been brought under a section of the Penal Code, which, in fact, had been repealed nine years ago, before Amin came to power, by the Prevention of Corruption Act, 1970. This had brought all corruption offences together into one statute. It was offences under this 1970 Act which had been later included in the Economic Crimes Tribunal Decree, and the police should have charged Musisi under that Act. Once again they were out of date with the law.

Fortunately for Musisi, they had charged him under a repealed section of the Penal Code, which meant that he was being held on a charge brought under a non-existent law. In other words, he was being held in custody unlawfully and there was therefore no need for an application for bail. Having held that his custody was unlawful, I ordered his immediate release. This should have been an obvious error to anyone looking at the charge sheet, so why wasn't it noticed by the Chief Magistrate, the advocate or the police?

Wednesday 22 August

The judges were invited to lunch with President Binaisa at State House today. It was very enjoyable as Godfrey Binaisa is such a fun-loving, pleasant character and the conversation was lively and interesting. At one point during lunch he became deliberately mischievous and quite improperly started asking judges about their political leanings. After two or three had dutifully answered 'left of centre', he suddenly noticed that I was looking aghast at him. He grinned and said: 'I see that Judge Allen doesn't approve, so we'd better change the subject.'

While we were taking coffee afterwards, the Minister of Defence, an earnest young Marxist political scientist called Museveni from Ankole, started spouting communistic rubbish. He had been heavily indoctrinated by Cubans in Angola and Chinese in Tanzania and others elsewhere and was declaring the great and urgent need to politicise the people and especially the army. He added: 'Even the British Army is strongly politicised throughout.'

I couldn't take that and I burst out: 'That's utter rubbish. No political activity at all is permitted in the British Army. I should know; I served in it for eight years.' Museveni, who doesn't know me, looked very displeased at the fact that he, a Minister, was being so abruptly contradicted.

'Oh good,' said Binaisa, grinning, 'let's have an argument.' So we argued about the need or dangers of politicising soldiers. As we were about to leave, Museveni came up to me and said that we must meet again and continue our discussion. When I said farewell to Binaisa he mentioned that he'd heard about the recent attempt by a gang to break into my house and he said he wanted to make sure that I had proper security. I'm to let him know if there's anything I need.

Wednesday 29 August

Mathew Opu, who was a judge when he fled into exile in 1971 with Amin's SRB pursuing him, has just returned to Uganda and has reported to the High Court to take up his judgeship again after eight years away. Another former judge, Emmanuel Oteng, a Lango, has also returned after some years in exile. A slight problem has arisen regarding their seniority as judges. One view (theirs) is that their years in exile should count, thereby making them the most senior judges. The other view is that only the years of actual service on the Bench should count, which would put them well down on the seniority list. Nobody knows the answer. But returnees usually get their way now.

George Engwau, a former Law School student, who has been a judge now for just over a year, has decided that he doesn't want his appointment to be confirmed as he prefers to return to his legal practice in Soroti, where his family is living. Being in Kampala is too far away and inconvenient for him and, with his large extended family, he needs the higher income from private practice. I'm hoping that another former Law School student will soon be appointed. Another former Bar student, Enos Sebunya, called in today to see me. He is now in legal practice in Canada, where he has spent several years in exile. I suggested that he could be of considerable use back here in Uganda, where his talents are needed, but it seems that he is now well established professionally and financially in Canada and only intends to return occasionally for family visits. Unfortunately, this is going to be the answer given by so many well-qualified and much-needed Ugandans now settled permanently abroad.

Tuesday 11 September

In an attempt to reduce the amount of night-time illegal activity, the government has ordered a curfew in Kampala from 8 p.m. to 6 a.m. At last the police have got together sufficient personnel to be able to provide house sentries for judges. A number of men have rejoined the Force after returning from exile or from their villages, to which they had been arbitrarily retired by Towelli. Luke Ofungi has called for all former police officers to return to duty if they so wish and there's been a good response so far.

George Engwau called in – he's down from Soroti for an appeal hearing – and he brought me a box of eggs from his farm. He says he's much happier now that he's back in private practice and is his own boss and with his family. Still, the years he spent as a magistrate and judge will prove to be very useful experience for him.*

Saturday 29 September

The painting of the outside of my house, which was not carried out due to the inconvenient arrival of the Tanzanian invaders in February, has now commenced and the work is going well. I thought they'd completely forgotten about it but the MoW chap in charge said he'd kept my name at the top of his list until they received fresh supplies of paint.

Friday 19 October

In the local newspaper *Weekly Topic* today there's a report about an application for a writ of *habeas corpus* before me. It concerned the arrest and detention of one of Amin's former ambassadors to Egypt, Lieutenant-Colonel Jack Bunyenyezi, who had been detained in Luzira

---

*He was reappointed a judge some years later, then moved to the Appeal Court.

prison for five months, simply because he was an Amin appointee, not for anything he was alleged to have done.

I found that he'd never been told why he was detained nor had he been served with any detention order. The AG's Chambers had no objection to his release, so I ordered it. However, the newspaper report says that he was rearrested outside the court by the police. The Minister of Internal Affairs and the Attorney-General need to get their act together. Amin appointed several senior army officers to be ambassadors abroad if he wanted them out of the way for various reasons. They were usually educated types who did not agree with his murderous military methods, so he sent them abroad where they were out of his hair.

Of the other six similar applications for release, I granted all of them, including one former senior police officer, and all walked away, although the paper says that one of them was later rearrested on a criminal charge. There are so many people detained in prisons these days, without being committed there by the courts, that we are constantly having to deal with *habeas corpus* applications for their release.

Saturday 20 October

Today is the start of the new currency issue and exchange of all the present currency notes which have Amin's big head on them. The exchange is to last for nine days and the replacement notes have neutral buildings and animals in their designs.

Friday 26 October

President Binaisa attended the graduation ceremony of a diploma course for magistrates at the Law Development Centre this afternoon. I was there with other judges. I must see if it can be arranged for me to do some lecturing there again. I miss teaching very much and there are different people at the LDC now who may be more co-operative.

Monday 12 November

Douglas and John, presiding over the kitchen and garden respectively, were both absent this morning. Apparently they were arrested last night for being out after curfew; so they spent the night in the nick. They reported back here at lunch-time after they'd been cautioned and released. They'd been out drinking, of course, but since Douglas has a watch that I'd given him, he ought to have kept a closer eye on the time. A pair of chumps. But Douglas is getting too fond of the booze and I warned him about this.

527

Tuesday 20 November

Binaisa has sacked Museveni as Minister of Defence and moved him to the less important post of Minister of Regional Development. But he's still quite powerful and dangerous. He has many Banyankole and other westerners supporting him.

Wednesday 21 November

There are two good headlines in the *Voice of Uganda*. On the sports page at the back it says: PRIESTS FLOG REFEREES IN CURTAIN RAISER (referring to a soccer match between RC priests and the Uganda Referees Association before the start of a league match). On an inside page it says: ENTEBBE TO HOST A GIANT YOUTHS SEMINAR.

Monday 3 December

The judges had a meeting today with the Minister of Justice, Ariko, at the International Conference Centre to discuss a number of problems covering salaries, allowances, buildings, official cars, courts, circuits and so on. It seemed fairly useful and was very forthright, but whether it will be productive remains to be seen. We can only hope.

Sunday 16 December

Two chums, one back from the UK and one from Nairobi, called in this morning bringing me boxes of various useful goodies for Christmas supplies and other items still unavailable in Uganda. Afterwards I got the Jag out and took it for a run as far as the main post office to check the mailbox. As usual the leper was sitting near my box waiting for a handout. We exchanged greetings and, as he has no fingers left on his hands, I placed some coins carefully on to one palm. He then brought his other palm across to hold the coins firmly while he transferred them to the gaping pocket of the ragged jacket he always wears.

We've been getting heavy rainstorms daily and it's quite unusually cool at what is normally the hottest time of the year; but with very dull and miserable-looking skies.

Thursday 20 December

Some time ago I wrote to the Law Society in London to ask them to collect out-of-date and replaced law books from solicitors to send out here to help us to renew our law libraries. Those of the chief magistrates up-country were either looted or destroyed in the fighting in the area and we have no allocation of foreign currency available to buy replacements. They have now informed me that they are collecting a quantity of books for us.

1980

Friday 18 January

Today is a public holiday for census day, and senior school students all over the country have been hired to go from house to house filling in the census forms. I found a student sitting on the front doorstep when I unlocked the door this morning at 8.30 a.m. For some reason he'd decided to start his area at my place. The nightly curfew still goes on but has been altered to commence at 10 p.m. since the beginning of the year. A considerable relief to boozers like my cook.

Tuesday 21 January

At last I've been back to the LDC on invitation to lecture to the present course for magistrates on court procedures and etiquette. I've missed teaching very much; when I'm in front of a class any depression, worries, colds or headaches disappear for the whole period as I put everything into it. Among the students I was pleased to see Didi, short for Didymus, a court clerk/interpreter who had worked with me in Mbarara when I was chief magistrate and later when I was there on circuit, and whom I had recommended for this course. The lecturers say he's doing very well.

There's been no piped water supply to the house for over two weeks now. The driver goes out with several plastic jerricans and fills them wherever he can find water. Not very convenient. When it rains we put out buckets and bowls to catch the water to use for washing clothes and flushing the toilets. Most days this month, though, it's been very hot and dry.

Wednesday 13 February

A few weeks back James Owori, the son of a former Law School Bar student, Reuben Owori, came to see me with a letter from his father. James is now a maths undergraduate at Makerere and badly needs a pocket calculator, which is one of the very many useful items unobtainable out here. I wrote to Sharpe in the UK and asked them to send one out to me urgently, which they have done. When James collected it today I warned him to be careful with it as, with the many shortages here these days, items like that are liable to be stolen very quickly, even in a place like Makerere or indeed anywhere. I had a brand-new book stolen from my chambers in the court a few days ago. There are light-fingered types everywhere now.

Monday 18 February

It's 20 years since I was stationed in Nabilatuk, Karamoja, and although I've been to Moroto on circuit a number of times, I've not been able to get down to Nabilatuk. Today, for the first time, I wrote a revisional order in a criminal case from the Nabilatuk magistrate. Nowadays the criminals there are more sophisticated, it seems, since the accused Karamojong, Lomilo, was convicted on three counts of cheating.

In the first one Lomilo told one Anyang that a Catholic bishop was going to visit Nabilatuk and he, Lomilo, had been sent by a mission father to collect contributions from local Christians towards making the visit a success. Anyang had then handed over 20 shillings. In fact, there was no such visit planned. In the second, Lomilo obtained 400 shillings from one Lamakol as advance payment for two crates of beer, a dozen exercise books and a box of radio batteries. The items were not delivered and were never intended to be.

In the third he told a woman, Miss Akello, that he had sugar to sell at the nearby RC mission at 15 shillings per kilogram. She gave him 160 shillings for 10 kilos (someone's arithmetic was a bit out), but when she went to the mission to collect the sugar they'd never heard of Lomilo or any stock of sugar. Lomilo was sentenced to concurrent terms of five, eight and six months imprisonment respectively, which he had already served by the time this matter came before me. The sentences were all right but I had to revise the convictions to obtaining money by false pretences on the first count and obtaining credit by fraud on the other two, as cheating was the wrong offence. There were no confidence tricksters up there in my day. That's progress for you.

Tuesday 26 February

The Commonwealth Secretariat CFTC director wrote to me to say that, as they only give single contracts, my contract with them will not be renewed when this one expires in April. Of course, I'm already aware of that. As HMG has recognised the UNLF Government and is already providing Uganda with aid once again, I wrote to ODA applying to recommence with them in April. This time it will have to be on two-year supplementation contracts which are renewable.

Wednesday 27 February

I gave judgment in an appeal in a civil suit in defamation between two chiefs today. In August 1977 the *Saza* chief of Kigulu county in south Busoga called a meeting of all the chiefs in his county. Lugogobe, a *gombolola* chief, stood up at the meeting and complained of pains and swelling in his feet, hands and legs and pointed at Lukungu, one of his *muluka* (parish) chiefs, and alleged that he was bewitching him and causing him to die so that he could replace him as *gombolola* chief. The chiefs sitting near Lukungu then all moved away from him and left him isolated. He was unclean.

At the trial for defamation of character, Lugogobe denied ever speaking at the meeting, let alone making the alleged accusation of witchcraft. Lukungu called five other chiefs, who testified that he had indeed been so accused by Lugogobe. The trial magistrate believed them and awarded damages to Lukungu. Lugogobe then appealed.

Practising witchcraft is a crime in Uganda and the accusation clearly should have been made to the police and certainly not at a public gathering of chiefs. Possibly a private meeting of the two chiefs with the *Saza* chief might have sorted it out. I agreed with the magistrate that it was defamation (slander) but I reduced the damages awarded as they appeared to me to be excessive and unjustified. Generally with appeals, if it's at all possible and appropriate, I like to give both sides something to feel pleased about, so that they don't go away empty-handed.

Friday 29 February

I was invited to lunch with the Minister, Stephen Ariko, today so I went to the reception desk at the Nile Mansions and asked for him. The receptionist, who is obviously a snob, said: 'Who is he? Is he an Honourable? We only have Honourables staying here. Everyone has to be an Honourable here.'

The man went on with this idiot babbling so I stopped him and said: 'Look here, Mr Ariko is the Minister of Justice. You should know that by now. What does it matter whether he's an Honourable or not? For that matter I'm a High Court judge, which makes me an Honourable too, so stop wasting my Honourable time and ring his room and tell him I'm here.'

Over lunch we discussed my contract arrangements as ODA need to have an official request from the Uganda Government for my retention as a judge and for my salary supplementation by them. I asked

531

him to deal with it through the British High Commission and he agreed to go ahead.

Friday 7 March

This morning I heard an appeal in a civil suit concerning a dispute over land. Before I entered the court Ssalongo, my interpreter, came to collect the files and books and, grinning, told me that one of the parties in the dispute had brought a witch doctor to court and he was sprinkling magic powder in each corner of the room to make sure that his client won. I asked him if he thought it would help and he replied: 'Well it's never too late for a stitch in time.'

So I said: 'Don't tell me now which party he's supporting. Let's just see if it works.'

It wasn't a complicated matter, for once, and I was able to deliver judgment later this afternoon. Afterwards in chambers I asked Ssalongo about the matter. He said that the business in court this morning hadn't worked as I'd given judgment in favour of the other party. But he added that it was not conclusive as the winner had afterwards boasted that he had previously consulted a more powerful and expensive witch doctor and so had obtained a much stronger bewitchment. Personally I didn't feel a thing.

Monday 10 March

A couple of months back, one of my former Law School Bar students, Peter Mpaka, called on me in chambers. His practice is in Mbarara and in the Tanzanian invasion last year his office and all his books had been destroyed by gun-fire and he had nothing left to work from or with. He was presently negotiating to rent a room in one of the surviving buildings there, but his big problem was the replacement of his law books, also a wig and gown, none of which could be obtained in Uganda and foreign currency would be needed.

I suggested that he should write to his Inn of Court, the Inner Temple, in London and explain what had happened and what books and items he needed as they would probably be able to find funds to replace them. I said I would write to them supporting his application for assistance and explaining the situation out here, including our foreign exchange problems. They were very helpful and have sent to me a very useful selection of books to work with. I had suggested that they could send them to me as the post office at Mbarara was very badly damaged and is out of action still.

I ordered and paid for a wig and gown from Ede and Ravenscroft in Chancery Lane and received them. Mpaka will pay me for them in

Uganda currency. Today he arrived, as he had a case in court here, and afterwards collected his goodies. He was very pleased.

Tuesday 25 March

Yesterday evening Douglas called me from outside one of the windows. He was standing in the dark and said he had been bitten by a snake. I unlocked the door and he came in and I saw on his forearm two sets of obvious snake bites close together. I fixed a tourniquet above them and cut into the bites with a new razor blade so as to make them bleed and hopefully extract some of the poison with the blood.

The curfew is still on, so one can't go dashing about safely and I'm still using a hired car which comes daily and is not left here overnight. So I phoned the police Information Room at the CPS by dialing 999 and explained the situation to the duty officer and requested transport to get Douglas to hospital urgently. While we waited outside in the dark, as there are no street lights working in this area yet, Douglas told me that, as usual, he had been out drinking after curfew and, on his way home, a military vehicle came into sight so he hid behind a convenient tree as he had no wish to be shot at. He put his left arm over a tree branch for support but that happened to be just where a snake was coiled and resting. It objected to this disturbance and reacted accordingly.

He appeared to be weakening and was becoming drowsy so I placed a large cushion behind him and a blanket round him. There's still no police sentry supplied so I had to leave him from time to time to check the road outside for the police vehicle, which had no way of finding us. I had arranged to stand in the road with my torch to indicate my whereabouts to the driver. A Land Rover with a blue light over the windscreen came hurtling up at full speed and I signalled to it and it screeched to a halt in my driveway. Some armed constables jumped out shouting: '*Nyoka wapi? Nyoka wapi?*' (where's the snake?).

'Never mind the snake,' I said, 'just get my cook to hospital as quickly as possible for treatment.' They were disappointed at having no snake to kill but I pointed out that, in any case, no sensible snake would stay around here with such a noisy crowd of people milling about. We lifted the now semi-conscious Douglas into the back of the vehicle and away they roared into the darkness, with the Land Rover rattling and backfiring and the constables shouting and laughing. I wondered if I'd be seeing my cook again.

I had expected that he would be kept in hospital for the night after treatment so as to make sure all was well. But at 2 a.m. I was awakened by a vehicle horn and shouting at the gates and went outside to find the Land Rover waiting there with Douglas. I opened the gate for him and thanked the policemen and they buzzed off. This morning Douglas seemed quite recovered and he told me that, when they arrived at Mulago hospital, the constables routed out the apprehensive and bewildered duty doctor, who found himself surrounded by heavily armed policemen all talking at once. Eventually it became clear to him that he was required at all costs to save the life of this valuable cook, otherwise the judge would have no breakfast. This was apparently regarded as a potential disaster.

So, while they all stood over him, the doctor nervously produced whatever snake-bite serums he had available and gave Douglas several different injections just to make sure. One of them must have worked because he then made a rapid recovery and they decided to bring him back. Consequently I had my important breakfast.

Tuesday 15 April

I started my leave today. Comsec had booked my flight on Sabena, which meant that I had first to fly to Nairobi to pick up their flight to Brussels and from there to Heathrow, where I discovered that one of my suitcases had gone missing in the change-over.

Monday 5 May

Like everyone else, my eyes were glued to the TV as it showed the SAS team enter the Iranian Embassy in London and rescue the hostages. That's the way to do it. Later there was a phone call from the ODA to confirm that they are producing a contract for me to return to Uganda as part of British aid once again. I'm glad that's sorted out at last.

Wednesday 14 May

The news is that Binaisa has been overthrown and replaced by a Military Commission chaired by the very dangerous Paulo Muwanga as Head of Government and with Museveni as Vice-Chairman. Apparently it was a palace coup when Binaisa tried to remove Museveni and the Army Chief of Staff, Brigadier Oyite-Ojok, a Lango. With Muwanga's help they acted first and overthrew Binaisa, who had also made himself unpopular with the pro-Obote faction by announcing that the elections later this year will be held under the umbrella of the UNLF and not on a party basis. This coup's definitely not good news for Uganda. In addition, I hear that a number of politicians are talking about 'getting rid of Amin's judges', so it's rather a worry.

Friday 30 May

I was in London yesterday to attend the Corona Club annual reception in the evening, for former members of the Colonial Service, at the Connaught. I had lunch at my club with Mohamed Saied, the former Chief Justice, who is now living in London and looking for a job. The taint of having held high office under Amin is proving difficult for him to overcome.* I wonder if I'll be in a similar position soon.

Monday 30 June

I've been waiting to hear from the High Court that my contract with the Uganda Government has been produced and when I'm to return to work there. Ten days ago I sent a telegram to enquire and two days later an attempt was made to phone me from Kampala but we were cut off a few seconds after being connected and before we could talk. I was merely able to establish that it was the Chief Registrar calling. I rang the ODA and was told that the Uganda Government had not yet signed the aid supplementation agreement, so the contract with them was not operative. The delays to both contracts are in Kampala. The Chief Registrar rang from Kampala today and got through this time. He reported that, although the aid agreement had not yet been signed, it's only a formality and it would be soon dealt with, so he's booked my return flight by Uganda Air Lines on 4 July. That's a relief.

Saturday 5 July

I arrived back at Entebbe late this afternoon instead of early this morning as the departure of the UAL aircraft was delayed for ten hours at Gatwick for unexplained 'technical' reasons. Probably needed a new elastic. At least they put us into a hotel there overnight.

Wednesday 23 July

After a week with my old fridge completely out of action, it having finally expired after giving me sterling service for 20 years, a new fridge was produced today by the Ministry of Works and put in place. All well and good but, as there's no power on, it still isn't possible to have it working. Murphy's Law is in operation as usual.

This morning the monthly rations were issued to judges and we received our rice, sugar, flour (full of weevils as usual) and toilet rolls, and our money for the same was collected. These simple items are still unobtainable in town except on the black market.

*He later became a judge in Hong Kong.

Friday 1 August

At last somebody has found a pen and signed the British/Uganda aid agreement. So now perhaps I can be put on the books and be paid instead of living on air. The electricity has come back on and maybe it will stay for a while, but there's been no piped water for the last three days.

Friday 15 August

I gave judgment this morning in a criminal appeal by one Corporal Warder Tigawalana, a Mukiga from Kigezi, who had been stationed at Kirinya Prison at Jinja. He was convicted with another warder of aiding eight prisoners to escape.

At the prison, in addition to 74 convicted criminals, there were 619 detainees who were ex-soldiers from Amin's Army. It was eight of those who had escaped. The corporal took over charge of them on the night of 9 September last. He claimed that they were not counted by him but the records showed that they were indeed counted according to regulations. Next morning when a check was made by a Principal Officer, it was discovered that eight were missing. There was no sign of a breakout so it was obvious that they had been assisted. The corporal was seen talking to the detainees late at night and a warder saw the gate, which was supposed to be kept locked, standing open. The other warder convicted, who did not appeal, had the keys that night and he admitted to the superintendent next day that he had released the eight detainees on the corporal's order. Apparently the two were to share 8,000 shillings which the detainees were paying for their release. There was also evidence that certain *wakombozi* soldiers camping outside the prison were involved in assisting the escapees afterwards. There was adequate evidence that the corporal was responsible and that the sentence of 20 months imprisonment was reasonable in view of his clean record and past service up to that time, so I dismissed the appeal.

Friday 12 September

Yesterday evening when checking my compound security fence I found that two holes had been cut in the wire mesh at some time. I spent the night patrolling the compound as there was clearly going to be a break-in. Nobody came, so I've closed up the two gaps with barbed wire today. It's very worrying as I'm obviously a target; they wouldn't bother making such preparations otherwise. No police night guards have been coming since last month as they claim there's a shortage of manpower, which is probably so.

Sunday 14 September

Well, they came last night. They were not put off by my repairs to the fence and they cut new holes in the wire and then smashed the french windows on the verandah. It was the noise of this that woke me up. There seemed to be about eight or ten of them. As they entered the house I started blowing my old police whistle and shouting orders to imaginary people. Although they were armed with various weapons, they fled when they heard all the noise I was making. I rang the police Information Room and requested assistance, but they made it clear that they didn't want to come if the gang was armed with guns. They were willing if I disarmed them first, it seemed. An hour later a Land Rover with six armed constables arrived and they ran around shouting, then they left. At my request one of them remained as a guard for the remainder of the night. But I couldn't get any sleep.

Monday 15 September

The MoW sent some men to fix my broken doors, windows and locks, which is all very well, but the place is just as vulnerable as before. I spoke to the OC Jinja Road Police Station and he promised to send a night guard regularly from now on. I hope he does.

Monday 29 September

It appears that the 'Slim Disease' we've been experiencing in the south-west of Uganda for the last four years or so is the one that is just now being referred to as AIDS in the USA. I wonder if it was taken to the States by their Peace Corps people or other US aid workers who have been down in those parts. Successive governments here have been very quiet about the disease and the number of victims who have died over the years. Maybe now someone will do something about finding a cure or some treatment.

Friday 3 October

Preparations for the General Elections are going ahead and various political parties are involved. As well as the old-established UPC and DP there is a new party led by Museveni, who calls himself the Interim Chairman of the Uganda Patriotic Movement. The party's publicity secretary is one Bakulu Mpagi Wamala and he has filed a civil suit against the five members of the Electoral Commission for various

537

alleged failures to make proper preparations for the elections, such as necessary amendments to the National Assembly (Elections) Act and the demarcation of constituency boundaries.

Wamala and his advocate came before me in chambers this morning, asking me to grant an urgent *ex parte* injunction restraining the Electoral Commission from proceeding with the registration of voters on Monday 6 October. I refused on the grounds that it was such an important national matter that the Commission must be given a chance to be heard. So I've fixed the hearing for Tuesday 7 October and ordered the members of the Commission to be served with hearing notices. As they are a government body they'll no doubt ask to be represented by the AG's Chambers.

Wednesday 8 October

I've had a painful toothache for the last eight days and yesterday morning the dentist extracted the tooth. His motto seems to be: When in doubt, take it out. I went straight back to court to hear the election application but was unable to speak clearly because of the after-effects of the injection and extraction. However, the hearing proceeded. I had been expecting the SG or one of his senior state attorneys to attend and argue the matter on behalf of the Electoral Commission, but there was nobody in court from those chambers. The Commissioners themselves did not bother to come to court as apparently their chairman told Wamala's advocate that the AG would handle their legal affairs, and washed his hands of it.

I instructed the CR to ring the AG's Chambers but there they claimed to know nothing about the matter, which was unlikely as it had been featured prominently in the local newspapers and on radio and TV news. In addition, there were several foreign journalists in court, so the matter was widely known. Having been told all this, the SG himself stated that he was unaware of the proceedings and showed no interest in either coming to court or sending a representative. It was most extraordinary that a vital matter concerning the first election in Uganda since independence 18 years ago, and a matter of very considerable national importance, was being treated in such a cavalier fashion. Possibly nothing has been done to amend the election laws and they have no wish to admit it openly, or maybe these senior civil servants fear a UPC election victory and hope that this behaviour will somehow cause an opposition coup instead. Perhaps someone said: 'Leave it in the hands of this *Mzungu*, then he can be blamed if things go wrong.'

So my problem was that I had no knowledge of whether amendments had been made to the election laws. I had received nothing in print and the AG's Chambers would not appear and tell me. If the laws have been amended the voter registration can proceed lawfully. If not, then it would be void and so should not be allowed to proceed, as Wamala was requesting. But it was not as straightforward as that. This is the first election in an independent Uganda after two decades of appalling governments, including the present awful Military Commission, which must be brought to an end as soon as possible for the sake of everybody here. A properly elected government could give Uganda its badly needed chance to start to recover and rebuild. These UPM people were doing Uganda no good at all by attempting to delay or stop the election. Their leader, Museveni, has stated that he is not afraid of the election and does not wish to delay it, yet he's doing this, so I wonder what his game is. In my ruling today I said this:

> At the moment I can see no great harm in allowing the registration of voters to proceed. If later it is held to have been carried out unlawfully, then the present registration can be declared void and this exercise can be repeated after correcting the legal position. It is to be hoped, of course, that this will not have to be done since not only the plaintiff/applicant, but all the other potential voters will be greatly inconvenienced as a result.

Thursday 9 October

My ruling has provided the headlines and front page news of the various newspapers and the radio news. The *Uganda Times* reports: 'A few hours after that ruling, the Interim Chairman of the UPM, Mr Yoweri Museveni, told a press conference that the Party's supporters should now go ahead and register as voters.'

The DP leader, Paul Semogerere, is also reported as having registered on the first day in spite of the fact that the DP, following its usual custom of boycotting everything and achieving nothing, had earlier said it was pulling out of the registration exercise. What possible good that could do is completely unknown. Even ex-President Lule has issued a statement from his hideout in Nairobi appealing to all citizens of Uganda to register as voters. So it looks as though I made the right decision after all.

As it is Independence Day, I decided for once to attend the government reception at 4 p.m. as I wanted to see how my ruling had been received. It seems to have been what people were hoping for, judging by the congratulations I received. I also had useful conversations with the Minister, Ariko, and with Luke Ofungi, who told me that he has been able to locate and reinstate a useful number of well-trained and experienced police officers and a British Police Training Team has been invited out here as I had suggested. This is good news.

I also spoke to Superintendent Oballim, OC Jinja Road Police Station, and mentioned that, once again, I've been getting no night guards at my house. He went off to telephone and came back to report that two sentries were now on their way there. So that's something, even if it's nothing.

Wednesday 29 October

A couple of months ago I was approached and asked if I would be interested in filling the long vacant post of Professor of Law at Makerere. I've had ten years in the Judiciary and would be only too pleased to get back to teaching, so I said yes. I was given some application forms to fill in 'as a formality for their file' as it was by their invitation not my application.

After this long wait I received a letter from the Registrar today to say that they were unable to grant my 'application' as the post was reserved for returned exiles and had been filled. Since I didn't initiate the business and I happen to know that the post is still vacant, I wonder what they're playing at. I suspect that the offer has been blocked by some returned exiles because I stayed in Uganda. It's the usual reason for their interference these days. I dropped the letter into the waste basket.

Thursday 30 October

Two weeks ago my cook, Douglas, cleared off with all my shopping money and went on a drunken spree, so I sacked him as it's not the first time and he'd been warned about it. So I've been doing my own cooking, laundry and so on while busy in court all day. It's not easy to find experienced and willing domestic servants these days. One villainous-looking bearded type came and applied and I turned him down immediately. The scruffy individual had probably been a guerrilla in the bush, by the look of him. I said: 'I never employ people with beards,' and he immediately offered to shave it off, as if it would change the sort of person he appeared to be. Today I've found an apparently suitable replacement, who unfortunately is also named Douglas. So he will be Douglas II and I'm giving us both a try-out for a month.

Friday 31 October

I gave judgment today in a civil claim filed by a man called Amos Yaya, a supervisor in the Ministry of Works. He had sued the government for damages for a trespass to his home and goods committed in Amin's time in 1977.

In June of that year there had taken place a failed attempt on Amin's life, mainly by members of the Air Force, and it was suspected that weapons were hidden in a small trading centre called Abayita Ababiri, close to the shore of Lake Victoria and about 3 miles outside Entebbe on the Kampala road. A large group of heavily armed soldiers suddenly descended upon the place in Land Rovers and lorries on a Saturday morning. They fired their guns into the air in order to frighten and intimidate the inhabitants and then they took over the homes of various people, including that of Yaya. The occupants were thrown out and, in the course of searching for weapons, of which they found none, several people were badly beaten and houses were stripped of all furniture and fittings and personal possessions. These were loaded on to military vehicles and taken to the nearby army barracks.

Some of the occupants, including Yaya's wife, were also taken there and detained for three or four days. The soldiers remained in and around the houses for the same time. When the civilians eventually decided it was safe to return to their homes they found them completely bare.

The AG's Chambers defends actions in court against the government but they were in the difficult position of trying to defend the actions of a previous government of which they totally disapproved. They claimed, without calling any evidence in support, that the soldiers were not acting in the execution of their duty at the time but were on a private illegal operation, so government could not be held liable. I decided that Yaya and his family had been wrongfully and unlawfully evicted from their home and that their property had been taken and removed by the soldiers. Since they were in uniform and carrying weapons and using military transport, without proof to the contrary, the presumption must be that they were on duty of some sort, whatever it was supposed to be, and so government was liable for their actions. I added that I considered the actions of the soldiers to be extremely high-handed and intolerable to innocent and peaceful citizens, and awarded exemplary damages as asked for.

Thursday 6 November

Fortunately a police sentry was on duty here for once last night. According to him, two armed men tried to climb the gates and he

541

challenged them and fired some shots. I went outside to see what was going on and he reported that they had run off when he opened fire. One of his shots had hit an iron upright of the left side gate and passed right through the metal. I don't think he hit anything else.

Monday 10 November

I was supposed to open the Kampala criminal sessions today – there are four murder cases to deal with – but the DPP failed to assign a prosecuting state attorney. I was asked to adjourn for a week and, on leaving the court, I felt extremely dizzy and walked straight into a wall.

Tuesday 18 November

For the last few days I've been having peculiar dizzy spells. Yesterday morning I was expecting to get started on the Kampala criminal sessions but I couldn't even get out of bed. The room was spinning and I fell down each time I tried. I felt awful.

Saturday 22 November

Wilson, the surgeon, called in last Tuesday and carted me off to Nsambya RC mission hospital, where his wife is a physician. I was in a bad way and had totally lost my balance. Apparently it's some sort of virus in the labyrinth of my ear. Very nauseous feeling and I've lost 14 pounds in weight as I couldn't eat. I was discharged and allowed to go home this morning on two weeks sick leave. There's some slight improvement but I've a deep and uncomfortable pain in my neck and can't move my head easily. There are tablets to take for this, and a string of kind visitors to commiserate with me; but really I wish they'd just leave me in peace.

Monday 1 December

Seth, one of our judges, has brought me a duck. His news is that already Wambuzi has been replaced by a new Chief Justice. It's the former Director of Public Prosecutions, who has no judicial experience. It seems though that he is very active politically and, like Muwanga, is a strong supporter of Obote and the UPC, which most people believe will win the elections. I don't know him at all, having done no more than exchange brief greetings on perhaps a couple of occasions. So whether this is a good move or not I've no idea. I can't say the news makes me feel any better, though.

There's been no piped water supply for the last four days and, being December and very hot and dry, it's not too comfortable.

Wednesday 10 December

Today was General Elections day in Uganda and everyone except me went to vote. A very quiet day, in fact. Because of transport problems outside Kampala and up-country, it has been announced that polling is to continue until 2 p.m. tomorrow.

Saturday 13 December

Everyone was waiting for the election results when, early yesterday evening, all hell broke loose in the area. Very heavy gun-fire could be heard all over the city. We all naturally feared it was another coup; but it turned out to be the military supporters of Obote celebrating a UPC victory in the polls by firing several tons of metal into the air.

Our former Chief Registrar, Sendegeya, and the former Higher Executive Officer (chief clerk) at the High Court, Rugadya, and a former judge, Butagira, have all been elected as MPs, the first for DP and the other two for UPC. At least this should rid us of the awful Military Commission and Muwanga.

Monday 15 December

Obote was sworn in this morning at the Parliamentary building for his second time as President. I felt just well enough to attend the ceremony and, at the reception afterwards, had a few words with him. He remembered me from Law School days. I also met the newly arrived British High Commissioner, William Hillier-Fry, and then had a word with our new Chief Justice and explained why I hadn't been able to attend his swearing-in last Tuesday, being still took poorly and consequently discombobulated.

Friday 19 December

Our new CJ called a meeting of judges on Wednesday and admitted he knew little of the work in the High Court. So why was he appointed? He said he'd come round to each of us in our chambers for a long talk to hear our views of the work and other problems. He came to see me this morning and we had a reasonably long chat. He has no useful experience for this job and was not an effective DPP. All we can do is to see how things go, I suppose. But this is a time for strong administrative leadership in the Judiciary.

My driver has managed to smash up my fairly new Mercedes

official car and it's going to be a long garage job, possibly even a write-off. So now I have to use a rather tatty little Datsun saloon which has been used by the staff as a general runabout and not properly kept or maintained.

Tuesday 23 December

The new MPs were sworn in at Parliament today and the former judge, Butagira, was elected Speaker. The awful Muwanga, having stepped down as Chairman of the Military Commission, is unfortunately now to be Vice-President. That is very bad news and does not bode well for us. It seems he's apparently too politically powerful to be kept out. Oh dear.

The UPM did very badly in the elections and won only one seat – in Toro. Their leader, Museveni, who was not elected, has announced in a fit of pique that he is taking to the bush and will fight a guerrilla war against Obote's Government. That's just what Uganda needs now. Instead of being able to use all our resources for the much needed rehabilitation and rebuilding of the country, we have a totally unnecessary civil war on our hands because of the personal political ambitions of one man. How many people are now going to die just for that? A very expensive sulk.

Monday 29 December

I've long been aware that there are some around who are rather too ready to take advantage after being given some assistance that may have been either fairly considerable or only slight. Such people then follow it by constant demanding, not with menaces of course, but nevertheless with great persistence as they take it for granted that you will always be there to bear their burdens for them. A little friendly assistance is one thing, but permanent dependence is something else.

Wednesday 31 December

My new cook has lasted exactly two months. When I came home from court for lunch today, I found the house locked up and the doors bolted on the inside, so my keys were useless. The driver climbed up and squeezed through the small pantry window and opened up. The cook has stripped the place and he must have brought a vehicle. All my clothes, bedding, kitchen stuff – everything is gone. And he took all the keys with him, so it means new locks yet again. What a pleasant way to end the year. He even took all the food in the house and left the rooms in a dreadful mess with dirt, torn paper and cloth all over the floors. I suppose it was planned, because there was no previous quarrel and he said nothing at all yesterday to indicate any dissatisfaction or change in the domestic situation. It seems rather odd because this is an easy job, reasonably well-paid and with plenty of spare time. Why on earth all the deliberate messing up and fouling of the house? Bother.

1981

Thursday 1 January

I spent the day at home cleaning up the house. Once again I have to look after myself until I can find a suitable cook/houseboy. Not easy these days. Very few want domestic jobs even though there's much unemployment. I've written a chit to Stephen Ibale, who long ago was a civilian education officer at the Police College when I was there on the staff. He's now General Manager of UGIL, a parastatal business which manufactures goods made from cotton grown in Uganda, such as clothing, blankets, sheets, curtains and the like. I need replacements of all these things as that fellow took the lot and left my house bare. Stephen rang to say he can supply me with some of the stuff right away.

Wednesday 7 January

Since the election we've had a spate of election petitions filed in court complaining of various offences against the election laws, each asking the court to declare the petitioner as the duly elected member rather than the candidate said to have won the election in that particular constituency. All, except one, are filed by losing DP candidates against UPC winners. The one I've been given is the exception in Luwero South in Buganda, where the DP won most of its seats. The petitioner is from the UPC, a vociferous and locally well-known Moslem called Haji Musa Sebirumbi.

As independent Uganda has never had an election before, there have never been any election petitions and nobody knows how to deal with them in court. So, naturally, dogsbody gets the first one to do and I'm asked to show the way and establish a procedure and set a pattern for the others to follow. I started this one today and it's going to take some time to hear as there are 14 witnesses and each will take a while to get through, especially as there are six advocates involved and, of course, each one will want to talk and examine witnesses.

The winning candidate is one Joe Senteza of the DP, who polled over 30,000 votes, and the loser Sebirumbi got just aver 4,000, so it can hardly be called a close-run thing. Sebirumbi alleged many electoral offences, including intimidation of UPC supporters; use of DP flags and symbols at polling stations; campaigning by DP while voting was going on; use of force and duress on UPC supporters; illegal prevention of UPC agents at vote-counting: counting outside proper hours; falsification and destruction of votes; lack of security and non-compliance with election laws; lack of supervision and misconduct by the Returning Officer. All these are also alleged *against* the UPC in the other election petitions.

Sunday 11 January

I spent the weekend washing some clothes and sheets and experimenting with cooking, including making some cakes, which came out quite well. There's no sign of a possible cook yet although the word is out. I don't enjoy this housekeeping stuff, though I can cope when it's necessary.

Wednesday 14 January

The new British High Commissioner, William Hillier-Fry, called into the High Court this morning and met and chatted with all the judges during mid-morning coffee break. Afterwards in my chambers the veteran advocate and Muganda politician, Mayanja-Nkangi, now an MP in the all-Baganda Conservative Party (a sort of resurrection of the Kabaka Yekka) came for an adjournment order and then stayed on for a chat. He was one of the early nationalist politicians in the 1950s and 1960s, working hard and earnestly for independence from the British and several times was in trouble with the authorities.

He surprised me when he sat back and said: 'You know, Judge, after all these years I've come to the conclusion that we were totally wrong to get the British out of Uganda. We would have been far better off and avoided all these dreadful horrors if you people had stayed on.'

I said: 'Well, it's a bit late for all that now. It has happened and it's history. But I recall that many Brits, including myself, thought at the time that it was much too soon for Uganda's independence. But the UN, the USA and all you politicians disagreed. It was the spirit of the times.'

Saturday 17 January

All the East African Presidents – Obote, Nyerere and Arap Moi – are meeting in Kampala for discussions. There is some talk of re-establishing the East African Community. It certainly would be a good idea for all concerned. The curfew has been lifted and the city has come to life at night again. I wonder if it's going to be allowed to last.

The election petition continues each day slowly on its way, much delayed by the activities of the many advocates involved. Lord save us from lawyers.

Friday 23 January

I don't know whether I'm doing the right thing here but desperate measures are required. I need a cook/houseboy as I simply can't go on doing these domestic things myself as well as my job. Now my earlier cook, Douglas the First, has returned begging for his job back, and I've provisionally agreed. But I really don't trust him and I'll have to keep everything locked up. Well, we shall see.

Saturday 31 January

The other day I was persuaded to buy a Dayton radio/cassette player to replace my stolen radio. The parts for these Daytons are manufactured in South Korea and assembled in Uganda by some enterprising local firm. The only problem is that they don't work. Between the assembly instructions written by some scatterbrained and incomprehensible Korean and the willing but incompetent efforts of the local assemblers, what we get is a soundless radio – no doubt designed for the totally deaf or for those who don't like radio programmes.

However, the Deputy Chief Registrar, Anthony Ochwo (ex-Law School, of course), always knows somebody who can do things, and he brought an earnest-looking character to my house with a screwdriver and soldering kit. This chap mumbled and muttered to himself about the uselessness of the Baganda assemblers and proceeded to pull the bits of wire out and then reconnect them in a completely different pattern and, hey presto, everything worked. He accepted my congratulations and then charged me 600 shillings, which was more than exorbitant, but I suppose I had little choice. Of course, it might all be a racket if he is in league with the radio assemblers and they deliberately ... well, no use thinking about that.

Tuesday 3 February

The election petition drags on as each witness is examined and cross-examined at great length by a queue of advocates who feel the need to look as if they're earning their fat fees. Their prolonged and often repetitious or irrelevant questioning followed by equally irrelevant and sometimes patently untruthful answers occasions the odd interjection from me, such as: 'Oh, do stop waffling and answer the question,' and 'Heavens above, must we go over all that again?' Situation normal, in fact.

There's been another week without piped water at home. The machinery at the main pumping station is very old, dating from Protectorate days, and poorly maintained, with no spare parts available. It takes ages to extract foreign currency from the Ministry of Finance for the overseas purchase of the necessary spare parts, no matter how urgent the need, so we have to put up with these constant breakdowns. After all, the Ministers need the dollars and pounds for their trips abroad, staying in luxury hotels and for their wives' shopping.

This evening I went to the house of the British Consul, George Anderson, who gave a party for a visiting British junior minister, Richard Luce, who I gather is Parliamentary Secretary in the FCO responsible for African Affairs. In my view anyone who claims to be responsible for African affairs has a lot to answer for.

Friday 6 February

Along with the lack of water supply, there's a considerable petrol shortage. Twice this week I've been unable to get to court because of no petrol for the car. I tried again today but we ran out half way to the court, so I walked the rest of the way and told the CR to send someone to rescue my car.

There was a judges meeting to try and select the new Chief Registrar and I suggested Zadok Ekirapa, a chief magistrate and a former Law School student (of course). Objections were immediately raised by those supporting other candidates. 'But,' I said in all innocence, 'he's a good chap.'

This seemed to amuse the other judges and the CJ said: 'Good chaps don't always make good administrators.' So that's probably that, but he's the best of the names put forward, in my opinion.

Tuesday 10 February

For the last three nights there have been explosions and gun-fire around the city. These are apparently caused by Museveni's guerrillas attacking various buildings. A very useful contribution to Uganda's recovery.

At last we've reached the conclusion of the election petition hearings. Now I have to write the judgment. It's going to be quite a long one, for once.

In the *Weekly Topic*, over an article to do with a fund for widows and orphans, there's an interesting headline which reads: SECRE-TARY QUITS OVER SHARP DIFFERENCES IN WIDOWS BODY.

Wednesday 18 February

The CJ wants to resume up-country circuits and, since I'm expend-able, he's sending me to Gulu and Lira next month to see what hap-pens. The Northern Province is still in a turmoil and Karamoja is overrun by roving bands of Amin's ex-soldiers. Most of West Nile, north of Arua, is in the hands of the Uganda National Resistance Front (UNRF), commanded by Brigadier Moses Ali, who claims he is no longer an Amin supporter but running his own show. Neither does he support Obote and the UPC, nor is he a friend of Museveni.

Saturday 21 February

Yesterday was judgment day in the first election petition and it's the longest judgment that I've produced for a long time, being 23 typed foolscap pages in which I considered all the objections and the evi-dence which, in fact, showed that the objections were nearly all groundless. On security I said:

According to the petitioner he travelled about the constituency during the election campaign with several armed bodyguards. For someone who claimed such great popularity as he did and, so he said, was among such a large number of his supporters all the time, he seems to have been strangely afraid of them. In addition, he appears to have the idea firmly fixed in his head that because the policemen on elections duty were unarmed there was conse-quently no security provided. To him security equates with gun power. I do not accept this idea at all. During an election the last thing that members of the public want to see is groups of men armed to the teeth. It's the sort of thing that is much more likely to encourage intimidation and violence than a few unarmed civil-ians merely shaking their fists.

The security during Uganda's previous three elections, all before independence, in 1958, 1961 and 1962, was also the responsibility of the Uganda Police and I recall that they effec-tively performed their duties on those occasions unarmed. Election duty is a part of normal police duty even though it doesn't happen very often here. The Uganda Police is a civil

549

police force and has never been an armed constabulary. I reject the petitioner's claim that no guns means no security and I reject his complaint that there was a total lack of security or indeed any significant lack of it. This is supported by the fact that voting took place uninterrupted at every polling station in the constituency and vote counting and the declaration of results occurred without undue problems.

I went on to dismiss the petition and declared Senteza, the DP candidate, the duly elected member for Luwero South constituency. Today the various newspapers spread it all over their front pages, no doubt especially because it was a UPC defeat. The loud-mouthed Sebirumbi, one-time Amin supporter, has been shouting that I was wrong and that he will appeal but, in fact, the Act does not make any provision for an appeal from election petition judgments. His lawyers have obviously told him this and perhaps that's one reason why he has announced that he has sacked them all, the other being because he didn't win.

Thursday 26 February

Although we've had the discomfort of no piped water for yet another week, at least I had the consolation of lecturing to the magistrates at the LDC on two afternoons this week. It's good to be standing in front of a blackboard again.

Wednesday 4 March

There has been an alarming increase recently in the attacks on prominent people in their homes around Kampala, and especially here on Kololo hill. Last night just along the road two of my neighbours were shot by such assassins, a veterinary officer and a doctor's son, both known to be keen DP supporters.

Wednesday 11 March

I was supposed to go up to Gulu for civil sessions on Monday but there was no vehicle for me and, in any case, no petrol available until this morning when I was able to leave. This is a test circuit to see if they are feasible and the CJ wants me to write a report on it, particularly regarding the security on the journey.

In fact we encountered five UNLA military road-blocks and the journey took just under four hours. At one road-block a soldier took the gun away from my bodyguard. I was most annoyed and severely berated the second lieutenant in charge. Then I reached out and took the gun from the soldier and gave it back to my constable. The soldiers were so surprised by this that they didn't know what to do. I gave them a good finger-wagging about respecting High Court judges doing their duty on circuit and said I would report their obstructiveness to Army HQ when I return. Then we drove off.

Friday 13 March

This week it's been very hot in Gulu, with some rainstorms. I've disposed of nearly 20 civil cases and, after finishing in court this morning, we drove back to Kampala. The journey was without incident except that at one barrier an army second lieutenant demanded a lift to Kampala. As this miserable little Datsun car was full with three of us and all our kit, he didn't get it. If he had asked politely instead of arrogantly demanding it, I might have made a little space for him. So hard luck.

Friday 20 March

Very late last night I was called out by my recently acquired *shamba* boy, who reported that Douglas, the cook, had been shot and was lying outside the locked gate. I unlocked it and found he was unconscious with a bleeding forehead where a bullet had apparently grazed his noggin. He appeared to be concussed as well as dead drunk. He probably felt no pain.

We carried him to his room and I cleaned his wound and put antiseptic ointment on it and bandaged it. Then I sat beside his bed, waiting for him to recover consciousness and answer some questions. Several hours later he woke up and didn't know if it was half past ten or Thursday. Mind you, he's always a bit like that. However, he must have had a rotten headache, what with the combined effects of the injury and the booze. I gave him some aspirins and water. He agreed he'd been out drinking after curfew but he had no idea who took a pot-shot at him, or even if he'd been the real target.

Monday 23 March

Today I went up to Lira for civil sessions. There were six military road-blocks on the way. At the last, at Karuma Falls, an army captain tried to turn us all out and commandeer my car for his own use. We had a bit of an argument about that idea and I told him very forcefully not to behave like Amin's soldiers, and that I would be reporting him to Obote and he should be prepared to take the serious consequences. He backed off and I drove away. One difficulty is that this miserable little car does not look impressive enough to keep these wretched military idiots at bay. High Court circuits just shouldn't be like this, of course.

Friday 27 March

I've disposed of ten civil cases at Lira. In one a man called Agom had obtained a divorce from a woman, Adongo, who had been married to Agom's brother. She was mentally ill and had killed her husband and child, and Agom, according to custom, had taken her over as if she was another wife. Later he went to the magistrates court and asked for a divorce from Adongo, which had been granted in spite of the fact that no marriage, customary or otherwise, had ever taken place. Indeed there was no proof of any original marriage to the dead brother either. There had been no dowry or ceremony. It turned out that the woman is now so mentally deranged that she has not been able to move from her parents' home, where she has lived for several years. Agom therefore was not looking after her as he claimed and indeed had assumed no responsibility for her. I made a revisional order setting aside the meaningless divorce granted by the magistrate, and that was that.

On the way back to Kampala we passed through eight road-blocks and there were irritating problems and delays at several of them. The situation is clearly not yet conducive to peaceful circuits, and in my report to the CJ I said so and I recommended that we wait awhile before they are restarted.

Monday 30 March

I've been marking a huge pile of exam papers from Makerere Law Faculty. They asked me to be an external examiner and I agreed, although it's taking up rather a lot of my time. I'm also making a keynote speech and opening a seminar for magistrates at the LDC tomorrow, which should be interesting.

Friday 3 April

I had a meeting this morning with some police types who called into my chambers to discuss their training. They were the Director of Training, Odyek from Police HQ, and the Commandant of the Police College, Francis Tibingana, who served with me as a constable at Mityana Police Station in 1957, and an officer from the PTS. We discussed various proposed courses and I offered to go along to the

College and talk to the students. I also suggested that they try to get funds to revive the Force magazine *Habari*, which died seven years ago. They asked if I would update the police law correspondence course that I wrote for the BTC back in the 1960s, and I agreed to do that as it would be once again very helpful to the Force.

Monday 6 April

Douglas went to the market to do some shopping this morning, leaving all the washing out on a line across his part of the compound. Before I returned for lunch someone had climbed over the security fence, pinched all the clothes and sheets, and disappeared with the lot. He must have been waiting and watching for a chance when Douglas was out.

Thursday 9 April

There's a tremendous shortage of petrol in Kampala at the moment and we are going into work only in the mornings these days. This morning I lectured to the magistrates at the LDC and on Tuesday I was at the Police College, talking to a promotion course about the legal system. The inspector from the British Police Training Team, for some reason, when he introduced me to this course said I had studied and obtained my law degree at Makerere. I said nothing at the time but afterwards pointed out that my legal qualifications are impeccably English and not from Makerere. He said he was sorry and he'd been misinformed about it. So I replied: 'Not to worry. The one thing this country is rich in these days is false information and rumours. Or is that two things?'

Thursday 16 April

This afternoon I attended the graduation ceremony for the latest magistrates course at the LDC. The CJ was there and in his speech advised that magistrates must not be involved in politics at all nor make public political statements. This from a judge who does both of those things openly and blatantly. Realising this, he then added that, of course, it is different for him as Chief Justice. He didn't explain how or why it is different, but it is no secret that he's an ardent UPC supporter. He attends their rallies and makes speeches at them. He can't seem to realise that he's supposed to be, and appear to be, impartial and unpolitical.

Tuesday 28 April

These last two weeks have been unpleasant, with sporadic gun-fire at night and a continual petrol shortage inhibiting movement and generally restricting work to mornings only. Last Wednesday I spent the morning lecturing on constitutional law at the Police College – they send a vehicle to collect me – and I went there again today to monitor and comment on some mock trials for potential police prosecutors in magistrates courts.

Saturday 2 May

Because of the curfew these days, most evening parties, sundowners, receptions and so on are off. The few that take place start at about 4.30 p.m. and finish before dark, when curfew starts, so that people can get home safely. Thus at 2 p.m. today, on a very hot afternoon, I found myself at a cheese and wine party at the British High Commissioner's residence. It was, for once, a very British affair instead of the usual guest mixture.

Friday 8 May

A large old tree collapsed across the drive in my compound. The white ants had been working on it for many years and had finally chomped their way through the roots and it subsided with a crash. Douglas promptly declared that it was a sign from God. So I asked what it was a sign of and he replied that he didn't know. Fat lot of help he is. That's Douglas for you – seer, oracle, clairvoyant and part-time chicken strangler.

The other day when I got home from court I found a cryptic note he'd left for me. It said: 'I was here and I found you not here.' Last week he left me another searching note: 'My Lord Sir, I have gone to wait for my mother because I don't know where she is and she doesn't know where I am.' Very poetic. Two lost souls wandering forlornly around in search of themselves. Kampala's a good place to do that in.

The previous week it was: 'Please sir I have gone to buy sauce as I don't have enough.' There are two schools of thought about that.

Monday 18 May

Really bad news. Obote has sacked Luke Ofungi as IG Police and replaced him with the strong UPC supporter Okoth-Ogola. This is most disappointing as Luke has done a great deal towards getting the Force reorganised and on its feet again. It's a political move, of course, as Luke is not an Obote man, but not particularly against him, either. He's a servant of whatever government is in power, which is a concept not widely understood in Uganda.

Friday 22 May

The front page headlines in the various papers today all concern my recent judgment on the seizure of non-Ugandan businesses by Amin. The civil suit was a claim made by the Departed Asians Property Custodian Board (DAPCB) for a large sum of money from the defendant, who had been allocated a textile business. Early in the judgment I said:

> I will say at the outset that I have no sympathy with the claims of either party in this suit. My view, which I have held consistently since early 1973 and have made plain in Court on a number of occasions since, is that the seizure of businesses and other property by the Military Government from Asians and other non-Ugandans was unjustified, inequitable and entirely contrary to the provisions of the Constitution (especially Article 13 thereof). This seizure was tantamount to theft on a huge scale and those who, like the defendant in this suit, became allocatees of such businesses and property, in my opinion placed themselves in the same position as knowing receivers of stolen property.
>
> I do not know why so far none of the real owners of the property involved has filed a suit for such a declaration by the Constitutional Court and for recovery of their property. They would have ample justification. In addition to that, a number of the businesses seized and allocated were in fact owned by Ugandans and I have in several such previous suits ordered the Board to hand back the wrongfully seized properties and wrongfully collected rents to the proper owners on their application. Typically the whole exercise of seizure was carried out carelessly and irresponsibly. This applies to the present case also.

This comment in my judgment has sent ripples of interest and alarm among the community. Nearly all prominent politicians, businessmen, civil servants, lawyers, even judges, have allocated property in their possession and they don't want to relinquish it. As I own nothing here, I'm one of the few who can be impartial about the matter.

Shortly after delivering the judgment a message came from the President's Office that a copy of it was required there urgently. I have since heard that the President has ordered a parliamentary bill to be drafted setting out ways and means for non-Ugandans to be able to apply to reclaim their property. This is exactly what I was hoping for when I flew this kite.

The day after the judgment a chap from the BBC called in and asked me to clarify a few points on the judgment for his report. That's good too, since the more pressure put on the government from all sides on this issue, the sooner something can be done to rectify the situation and perhaps encourage some business investment here to recommence.*

Tuesday 27 May

The prisons in Uganda and the Prisons Service itself are both in a complete mess, having been so misused for political and other detainees by successive governments. As part of British aid, a former senior prisons officer here, Bill Kirkham, has been brought back to reorganise the service and the administration of the prisons. One of the many things he's doing is to revive and re-establish the prison farms that used to be so productive and useful.

When I met him recently at a BHC party he offered to supply me with fresh eggs and vegetables from their Kampala farm at a very reasonable cost. So now I send the driver each week to collect these items. It all helps. We are still getting our monthly rations of essential commodities, such as sugar, salt, soap, flour and cooking fat/oil, which continue to be in short supply.

Friday 5 June

In the *Uganda Times* this morning and on Radio Uganda yesterday various judicial appointments and renewals of contracts, including mine, were announced. The 'good chap' and former Law School Bar student, Zadok Ekirapa, or Zadok the Priest as I call him, has in fact been appointed Chief Registrar, as I recommended at the judges meeting last February when this post was discussed, and when my suggestion was laughed out of court. So I suppose that proves something or other.

Friday 12 June

After lecturing at the Police College yesterday afternoon, I went on to attend the reception for the Queen's official birthday at the BHC. The cameras of UTV were there and, so I'm told, I was shown on the TV

*The Expropriated Properties Act (Act 9/82) followed and provided for the return of such property to the former owners on their application.

news chatting to the High Commissioner. I still don't have a TV set and have made no move to obtain one. It would merely provide the thieves with something else to steal and these days I keep such property down to a minimum.

Last night one of my neighbours, Mrs Kinani, a nurse, rang and asked for help. Her husband is away in the USA on government business and earlier in the evening someone had knocked at her back door. When her teenaged son answered the door, a man came from the darkness and stabbed the boy in the side with a knife and tried to enter the house. The boy had managed to close the door in his face and bolted it.

I called the constable on guard at my gate and we both went round to her house and searched the compound and surrounding area, after I'd knocked on her door and identified myself. Nobody was outside, so I sent the constable back to guard my place and I stayed and sat with Mrs Kinani in their lounge and chatted for a couple of hours to reassure her that all was now well. I checked on her son, whom she had bandaged efficiently and sent to bed, and spoke to him, but he had not recognised the attacker nor could he describe him. The knife wound had fortunately not been dangerously deep and he seemed to be all right for the time being. He could go to the hospital with his mother in the morning. When I left later, I told her to ring me again if she needed any help and meanwhile to stay locked and bolted and to open to nobody else.

Saturday 27 June

There's been a lot of shooting at night this month and last night there was a great deal of gun-fire. According to the radio, the Tanzanian police still hanging on in Uganda were sent out on an operation to round up prostitutes. It doesn't sound very likely. Just why such an operation should entail enough gun-fire for a Normandy landing was not explained; nor what they were proposing to do with the prostitutes when they were rounded up – but it is easy to hazard a guess, knowing the way these Tanzanians behave.

Several hundred Tanzanian police are left here but most of the TPDF have left, taking with them hundreds of stolen vehicles and much personal loot, such as radios, watches, clothes and the like. In spite of this being common knowledge and well photographed down on the border where they crossed, we are still told how very grateful we should be for the actions of these very ill-disciplined armed robbers in getting rid of Amin's equally ill-disciplined armed robbers. Out of the frying pan into the fire is what comes to mind.

Thursday 2 July

At a recent Judicial Service Commission (JSC) selection board, chaired by me, we selected some new law graduates for appointment as grade I magistrates. Afterwards, the CJ, who is the chairman of the JSC, found that a couple of his appointees had been rejected because of being below standard or otherwise unsuitable, and he tried to persuade me to add their names to the list. I declined to do so, then told the CR to send the selected names straightaway to the President's Office for the appointments to be approved and made public so that there could be no tampering with the list. There has already been too much nepotism practised in secretarial and clerical court appointments.

Today the new Isuzi saloon cars were received and distributed to judges by the CJ personally. One car was supposed to be for me but he has refused to hand it over, saying that he's keeping it for the next new judge to be appointed. Apparently he's using it himself, or his wife is, as a second official car.

Wednesday 15 July

I received a very nice letter from my neighbour, Mrs Kinani, thanking me for going to her assistance last month. She says her son is now out of hospital and recovering well from the knife wound.

Obote and his UNLA Chief of Staff, Brigadier Oyite-Ojok, both Langi, have embarked on a difficult and delicate attempt to prise the Acholi from key political and military posts. Since the Acholi include not only the Prime Minister, Otema Allimadi, and the Army Commander, Major-General Tito Okello, and the very powerful Central Brigade Commander, Colonel Bazilio Okello, the UPC and the Army could possibly split into two warring factions with devastating consequences. We really don't need this sort of thing. Tribalism is still Uganda's worst enemy and it isn't going away.

We've had no tap water for nearly three weeks. Today there was a heavy rain-storm, with large hail stones crashing around against the windows and playing havoc with garden plants. At least I managed to get all the buckets and bowls filled with water. Otherwise I exist on whatever my driver can find and fill into the collection of jerricans and containers he carries around in the boot of the car.

This afternoon I went in to see the CJ and once again asked him to hand over my new official car, which he has been retaining and is now using as a runabout and for shopping. Once again he refused and we did not part on good terms, and I'm left with this clapped-out old Datsun.

Friday 7 August

I came home from court at lunch-time to find that the house had been broken into once again and my radio, electric kettle, iron, typewriter, a suitcase, clothes and even the heating rings on the electric cooker have gone. The cook, Douglas, has gone too and it's pretty obvious that he's taken all these items to sell. The apparent breaking in is an unconvincing cover.

I have a heavy cold and feel unwell and very depressed. I think this is the fourteenth breaking or attempted breaking into my house or theft from it. Apparently those who take domestic jobs these days do so mainly to place themselves where they can steal at will. So I'm back to looking after myself.

Once again I've called in the MoW man to change the locks on the doors. The civilian watchman from Securiko that the High Court hired as a day guard said he heard and saw nothing. If he's not involved then he was either asleep or absent from his post at the gate. Totally useless. I'm beginning to wonder if I can go on like this.

Monday 10 August

This afternoon I dropped in to see Hillier-Fry, the British High Commissioner, at his invitation to discuss various topics, including the general security situation in Uganda. Returning to my chambers, I found two more parcels from my brother, Nick, in the UK. From time to time he sends several out to me containing much-needed small items unavailable here. These are a great help.

Thursday 20 August

I was invited to the BHC's residence this afternoon, where he had asked a few select friends to watch a video film on his large TV screen of the Charles and Diana Royal Wedding. It was very good, but everyone had to rush home immediately afterwards as it was dark and it's very dangerous to be out after dark nowadays. Stealing cars at gunpoint and then shooting the driver is one of the main hazards.

Wednesday 26 August

When I recently met my contact, who is in the President's Office, I mentioned the difficulty I'm having with regard to the official car. Today the CJ very reluctantly handed over the new car to me. In fact, it's in a filthy condition and has clearly been misused and mistreated. It wasn't handed over voluntarily and someone has clearly spoken to him about it. The old car I was using was in a very bad condition and

falling apart. In addition to its unsuitability for circuits, it made a very
bad impression, especially when I went lecturing to the Police College
or the LDC. My driver tut-tutted over the condition of the new car
and got to work on it right away. He'll soon have it looking very
different.

Monday 31 August

I've not found a new cook yet and there's been no piped water all
month. The heavy rainstorms we've been getting this month have
revealed several leaks in the house roof where the exploding shell damaged it back in 1979. I climbed up into the ceiling loft and have tried
to fill in and block gaps between the tiles but some of them are badly
damaged and ought to be replaced. The problem is that these special
roof tiles were made long ago in Protectorate days and purchased from
an RC mission in the former Belgian Congo. Nowhere else makes
them and, of course, they no longer do so either as the mission was
destroyed long since in some fighting in the area. Like so many things
in Uganda nowadays, they are unobtainable.

Wednesday 2 September

Since last month I've been lecturing to a magistrates course at the LDC
twice a week on the law of evidence. They have nobody on the staff
there capable of teaching this difficult subject, so I offered to take it
on. I fit in the lectures each week with my court work so that neither
interferes with the other. It makes a refreshing change for me to get
in a reasonable amount of teaching once more, and it's a vital subject
for these new magistrates to grasp.

Yesterday afternoon during a lecture we were suddenly shattered
by several very loud explosions from Wandegeya, just around the
corner and very close to the LDC. The students were understandably
disturbed and very nervous. I tried to calm them down and went
on with the lecture. There was no point in breaking off or going outside, where it might be dangerous. As soon as I finished they all
scattered and disappeared rapidly. I drove home slowly through
Wandegeya but couldn't see much sign of anything. But the area was
unusually quiet with hardly anyone moving about. It appears that, on
the day before, the Wandegeya police had arrested four UNLA soldiers for looting and there was a shoot-out in which the soldiers were
killed. So today some of their friends piled into an army vehicle and
drove to Wandegeya Police Station and shot it up and threw grenades
in there.

Saturday 19 September

Wilson, the surgeon, is back from UK leave and has brought me some shirts and trousers from Marks and Spencer as badly needed replacements for those stolen by Douglas. George, an architect, is back from a visit to Kenya and he brought me a new electric iron. Friends like these have been so kind and helpful in producing replacements of the stolen items.

Wednesday 30 September

I was invited to a function at the BHC but didn't go. There was a very heavy rainstorm which resulted in a simultaneous leaking through the roof and a flooding inside the house caused by a blocked toilet overflowing. The place was in a fearful mess and I couldn't leave it in that state. As I have no domestic staff now I had to stay and clean it up myself.

Monday 5 October

The CJ called me into his chambers this morning. These days we rarely speak to each other. He gave me the file for the Bob Astles murder trial and said I should hear the case next Monday. Astles, a Brit, was Amin's right-hand man and a sort of Mr Fixit for years. He was so useful to Amin that he gave him the rank of major in the Uganda Army and also gave him special powers for various purposes. The CJ said he is accused of various murders but, due to the lack of evidence, such as live witnesses, is only being indicted for one of them. He has been held in detention since 1979 pending trial. I'm rather surprised to be given this case as the government probably wants to obtain a conviction and I don't produce verdicts to order. At least he said nothing about that.

Wednesday 7 October

Yesterday there was an early evening reception at the BHC and, in the course of our conversation, the High Commissioner asked me which judge would be trying Astles. I said I had the case. He nodded and walked off, knowing that I couldn't discuss it. I didn't realise then that the CJ was also at the reception and, apparently, the High Commissioner afterwards said something to him about my being the trial judge.

This morning the CJ phoned and said I should bring the Astles file to him. When I went into his chambers he berated me for telling the High Commissioner that I was the judge trying the Astles case. I said that I was not aware that it was secret. Why on earth should it matter who knew which judge was trying a case? I pointed out that High Court Cause Lists are normally issued in advance to indicate which cases are coming before which judges; indeed, they used to be published in the newspaper. There is nothing confidential about them. I added that the High Commissioner was probably interested in the case because Astles is a British subject and the trial is for a capital offence; so it's his job to keep an eye on how it goes.

But he wouldn't have it. He insisted I had breached confidentiality somehow and that I shouldn't have told the BHC that I was the trial judge. What utter rubbish. He said: 'Give me the file. I'll allocate it to another judge. You wouldn't give us the result we want, anyway.'

This was an astounding thing for a CJ to say and absolutely unacceptable. I threw the file on to his desk and said: 'If that's your attitude I don't see much point in my continuing to work here now,' and left his chambers. I wish now I'd obtained that job at the Makerere law faculty and so escaped from this place and this CJ. I really don't need all this hassle.

Wednesday 28 October

Well, the Astles trial is over and Seth, who was given the case to try, has acquitted him. I had a browse through the trial evidence and judgment in Seth's chambers and, with the gaps and inconsistencies in the evidence and the clearly unreliable witnesses presented, there was no other conclusion possible. I'd have done the same.

No doubt it's better that he came before a Ugandan judge rather than a Brit. One might ask why the CJ didn't try such a spotlight case himself. But he has no trial experience and, in addition, most of the preparation of the prosecution file must have been carried out while he was still the DPP and officially in charge of the prosecution; thus he could not properly preside over the subsequent trial.

Friday 30 October

Sebirumbi, of the election petition in February, came up before me today for another judgment. This time it was an appeal against the taxation order made by the Deputy CR in his capacity as Taxing Officer. Taxation is a determination of the winning party's costs which the loser has to pay. In this instance the advocates for the winning respondent, Senteza, had filed a bill of costs amounting to well over 2 million shillings, which had been allowed by the Taxing Officer, and Sebirumbi had naturally appealed.

In my judgment today I went through the bill of costs item by item, slashing the amounts claimed. For instance, the advocates were claiming a million shillings for their instruction fee, alleging that the case was full of intricate points of law. In fact there were no complicated matters or points of law and the examination of witnesses was no more difficult than usual. As I pointed out, the whole of the burden of proof of each matter rested on the petitioner, Sebirumbi, and the respondent and his advocates had nothing to prove at all. It was just easy straightforward cross-examination. But it was certainly an important case and it did last for three weeks, so I said I would allow a fair rate for the work done, but no more. Groans from the advocates.

When I added up the amounts allowed at the end, it came to 170,000 shillings instead of 2.2 million which was a considerable reduction. Thus, although Sebirumbi came off badly before me in his petition, he was quite successful before me in his costs appeal, so he couldn't complain quite so much now.

Wednesday 4 November

I've been three months now without a cook and it's been very difficult. I interviewed a possible contender for the title today and am giving him a trial, to coin a phrase. He is Matayo, a Mukiga from Kigezi, and he's starting straightaway. I wonder how long this one will last.

Thursday 19 November

Whoever's responsible for training this present UNLA army is not doing a very good job of it; especially with regard to weapons discipline. All over Kampala there are military sentries guarding the residences of ministers and senior army officers. Constantly these sentries loose off shots from their weapons because they persist in carrying them around loaded and cocked. So, an accidental touch or pressure on the trigger and away the bullet goes often into the foot of the sentry; sometimes into a comrade while they are playing about with their weapons. There's a report in the paper of a foolish young recruit going on leave by train to Kabale who took a live grenade into the railway carriage and actually played with it on the journey, like an ignorant child. The pin came out and, in the resulting explosion, he and the other passengers sitting with him were all killed, including a young woman with a baby.

Apart from guard duties, the ever trouble-making UNLA has at last been officially banned from around Kampala, and most of the road-blocks around the city have now been removed or taken over by the police. This is a great relief to everyone else here, most especially to vehicle drivers and their passengers, who were being constantly harassed by the soldiers manning road-blocks with demands for *chai* (tea), meaning money.

I hear that in the Bombo area, about 30 miles north-west of Kampala, a large group of Museveni's NRA has been wiped out after heavy fighting. They were conducting guerrilla attacks in and around Kampala from their strategically placed camp there.

Tuesday 8 December

Yesterday I drove up to Soroti with a pile of files for civil sessions here. As the up-country road-blocks are generally being manned by police now rather than soldiers, it was not such a troublesome journey as usual, except for my back, which is playing up and makes moving about rather difficult.

Wednesday 16 December

The Soroti sessions is going well and the pile of case files is gradually diminishing. I gave judgment today in a second appeal in a divorce matter. As usual in these cases, the real argument is over the repayment of dowry. However, one of the advocates involved asked for guidance on a ruling made by a former chief magistrate here in another similar case: that divorce in customary marriages in Teso could not be entertained by the courts and such matters were only to be disposed of by chiefs and clan leaders.

I ruled that he was entirely wrong and had acted most improperly in trying to bar litigants from the courts in this way. Since chiefs have no judicial powers, they would be acting without authority and unlawfully if they interfered in such matters.

Friday 18 December

I've disposed of 20 cases in Soroti and, after delivering the last of the judgments, drove back to Kampala today. There were two cases of defamation against the *Uganda Times*. In each case the newspaper was accused of publishing the photograph of that particular Soroti resident in a batch of 24 portraits under the heading: 'Wanted: Police plea to aid investigations. The following people should report to the police to assist in investigations into some activities of the defunct State Research Bureau.' The names and Soroti addresses of each of the plaintiffs was shown under his photograph.

They were arrested and locked up by the police, and later the Deputy Minister of Defence, Colonel Omaria, met them and apologised on behalf of the the government for their unlawful arrest and detention.

Apparently the wrong photographs had been published. These had been found on SRB files, but as victims and persons put under surveillance, not as active SRB officials. The newspaper didn't bother to file a defence in either case and took no part in the trials. It was thus a matter of assessing the compensation due for their illegal detention and being publicly associated with the evil SRB.

Wednesday 23 December

For two nights there has been much shooting as Acholi troops in the UNLA fight the Langi and Iteso troops supporting Obote. The Acholi came off worst and for a short time General Tito Okello and Colonel Bazilio Okello, both Acholi, were placed under house arrest, but they have now been released.

There's been no electricity for almost three days but my cook expertly produced hot meals and coffee on the standby small pressure cooker.

Saturday 26 December

It's very hot at the moment. Yesterday was a quiet Christmas Day until the evening, when there was a lot of gun-fire and several explosions. Not a coup, as many people thought, but merely the drunken soldiers celebrating in their usual fashion. I've no idea what their casualty figures were, but a large quantity of lead was fired into the air and had to come down somewhere.

Since I came back from Soroti I've continued with my previous practice of patrolling my compound here at odd hours during each night whether or not a police sentry has turned up for duty. There is still a lot of unrest in and around the city and plenty of housebreakings and robberies in the residential areas and one needs to remain on the alert.

There are several large cacti growing in the garden and over the last few months I've been breaking off pieces and planting them around the inside of the compound security fence to reinforce the barbed wire as a further discouragement to intruders. The various pieces have quite quickly grown to a useful height and the sight of their long sharp spikes will hopefully make the less determined unwanted visitors think twice before attempting to climb over or cut through those parts of the fence.

I've also added to the barbed wire along the top of the gates, not only to discourage intruders but also to try to prevent the escape of my constable sentries. The present drill is for my cook to lock the large padlock on the gates after the constable sentry has arrived in the evening and then bring the key to me. But some of the more idle

565

sentries wait until they see the house lights go out and then they climb over the gates and return to their quarters at Jinja Road Police Station barracks for a more comfortable night.

Tuesday 29 December

An accused called Sseruga was convicted by a Kampala magistrate of theft and escaping from lawful custody and the matter came to me for a ruling on the second offence, the escape. A person arrested without a warrant must be brought before a magistrate within 24 hours. If this is not possible due to a weekend, public holiday, or no magistrate available, or something like that, the OC Police should release him on bond. If he has to be retained in custody he must go before a magistrate as soon as practicable. In this case Sseruga was arrested on a Sunday and should have gone to court on Monday, but the police kept him in the cells until the following Monday, which was a full week later and no good reason was given for this. This meant, in fact, that he was no longer in lawful custody at the time when he escaped from the police station. As I said in my ruling, I consider that it is not a criminal offence to escape from unlawful custody. Indeed a person has a right to do so, provided he can do it without breaking some other law in the process.

1982

Monday 1 February

To Soroti for yet another long civil sessions with a pile of accumulated civil suits and appeals to deal with. It's very hot up here but quiet and peaceful compared with Kampala. I always enjoy a visit to Teso; most especially because it's a long way from Kampala.

This afternoon a soldier in uniform wandered into court and, without thinking about it, I barked out: 'You there, that soldier – take your hat off in court, you horrible thing you.' He jumped back startled and whipped his beret off, to the amusement of the spectators sitting around.

Friday 5 February

I go back to Kampala for the weekends in order to check on security after having been a burglary victim so often. Today on arrival I found that my latest cook/houseboy has decamped, taking with him the few things left to steal. He lasted three months and seemed to be doing all right. Nowadays, though, even previously honest and trustworthy people seem to find it difficult, at this time of great shortages of everything, to keep their hands off any movable property left around. One can't lock everything up; things have to be available to a domestic servant in order to do his job. So he takes them. These days I get the cheapest available replacements.

Saturday 27 February

This month in Soroti I've disposed of 40 civil cases and I'm quite pleased with that. Many of these concerned disputes over land or cattle and, of course, the perpetual claims for refund of dowry. In one of the civil suits a chit was handed into court stating that a certain witness was 'unable to attend the honourable court today as he is decomposed'. I suppose that might slow him down a little. On arrival back in Kampala, however, I've found no piped water and the guerrillas have blown up the UEB power station, so there's no electricity either. What good do those people think they're doing? Just making a hard life harder.

Once again I'm trying out a new cook/houseboy. This one is Wilson Mwebasa, who says he's from Ankole, but he's a Tutsi and 6 feet 4 inches tall and insists on speaking French, so I reckon he's from Burundi. At least he seems to be an experienced cook. My French these days is just not up to household chatter though; or anything else, for that matter.

Thursday 11 March

For the last three afternoons I've been lecturing at the LDC but this afternoon when I arrived I found an empty classroom. Last night there was a lot of gun-fire and a number of explosions in the area and, it seems, the students have all gone to ground. This sort of thing happens in Kampala so often that I tend to ignore it, but these chaps from up-country are more used to the quiet life and it has been rather bad lately, so they can't be blamed for keeping their heads down.

Tuesday 16 March

There appears to be an unusual amount of trouble around Kampala at the moment and a lot of Baganda have been rounded up and carted off by people working in the office of Vice-President Muwanga, who seems to have set up a sort of secret police organisation. The thugs he uses are acting in the same way as those in Amin's SRB and quite probably some of them are the same people.

A Commonwealth Military Training Team (CMTT) has arrived to begin instruction on everything ranging from mechanics to ordnance and ambush techniques. But this is largely a waste of time in my view as the UNLA is an undisciplined, untrainable rabble and the best thing to do with it is to disband it.

Wednesday 17 March

Today I gave judgment in a claim for damages for an assault six years ago in a village in Bufumbira when the plaintiff Matiasi Muhutangabo was a juvenile. He found one Mwenderahe cutting down and stealing bananas from the family's plantation. The boy raised an alarm and chased after Mwenderahe, who turned on him and cut the boy on the left hand with his *panga*, slicing through three fingers. The tendons and nerves were cut through, affecting the function and circulation in the hand and remaining finger and thumb. A medical report five years later showed the damaged fingers extended and not flexible, considerably limiting his gripping capacity. This case first came before me in June last year and I then asked the surgeon whether an attempt could be made to give Matiasi more use of his hand. He said he was willing to perform a further operation to try to achieve this improvement. My view was that it would be more useful to do that than just assess the damages on what I had before me in court.

Matiasi is now aged 23 and an undergraduate at Makerere. He has had the extra operation that I requested and it excised the divided tendons, replaced them with tendon grafts from the right foot and left forearm, followed by intensive physiotherapy. He now has better flexion and gripping power, which he demonstrated effectively in court with books and pens. This is a distinct improvement on what I saw last year and worth the effort and the long wait, I believe. Certainly of more use to this young man than money alone. The operation cost him nothing as it was performed at a government hospital. Ugandans only have to pay for treatment if they go to mission hospitals.

Sunday 4 April

I'm off on leave on 15 April so I've been trying to stir people up to produce my air ticket and deal with immigration requirements. The BBC radio news is all of the recent Argentine invasion of the Falkland Islands. The Governor there, Rex Hunt, was previously a District Commissioner in Uganda. I met him a couple of times but didn't really know him.

Thursday 8 April

I saw the CJ about my leave and returning here afterwards. He doesn't like speaking to me these days (it's mutual) and clearly would be happier if I didn't return, so I'll have to make sure that he doesn't sabotage my chance of coming back, since I wouldn't want to oblige him.

There's still a lot of gun-fire at night around Kampala, and the Baganda are very unhappy so far with the second regime of Obote and the UPC Government.

Wednesday 14 April

I had lunch today with George Edmead, an architect, who had a visitor called Robin Hancox, who is a High Court judge in Kenya. I told him about the situation here and how unhappy and uncomfortable I feel with this CJ and he suggested that I might like to consider a transfer to the Kenya Bench as they are a judge short at the moment. I said I'd think about it. But it's the job I want to leave, not Uganda.

I went to the Immigration Office as I'd earlier applied for the usual re-entry permit for my next tour. However, it seems that my 27 years service has been noted and the President had authorised the issue to me of a Certificate of Life Residence, which I've collected. So now I'm entitled to live in Uganda for ever, working or not, and need not again be bothered about immigration entry and re-entry requirements.

Monday 14 June – Dorset, England

Today it was announced that the Argentinian forces have surrendered at Port Stanley, which is once again in our possession. The presentation of the Falklands war news by the BBC has been appalling. For some smugly left-wing trendy reason they've pretended to be neutral observers referring to the British forces as though they were as foreign as the Argentinians and casting doubts on our forces' success claims in a most despicably unsupportive way. What a contrast to the World War Two BBC's wireless reports referring to 'our' forces, 'our' aircraft and ships etc. with pride and patriotism.

Thursday 17 June – London

I called on B. B. Asthana, our only Indian judge, who is on leave. He has a house at Kingston-on-Thames. He's just been appointed to the Court of Appeal, the post that I was hoping for, and indeed expecting; but, of course, this CJ put the kibosh on it, as I thought he would, even though it would have meant I was no longer working with him.

569

BB said that a number of ex-Uganda Asians live in that area and that they, and many others now in the UK, display Amin's picture and regard him as a saviour since his action in chucking them out of Uganda had enabled them to jump the queue and move to the UK many years before they could otherwise have hoped to do so under the British Government quota system for Commonwealth immigrants. Most are now very wealthy businessmen, with their children at fee-paying schools.

Friday 2 July

I arrived back in Uganda yesterday morning with all my luggage intact and found my house and property, what little was left, all present and correct. I always bring my domestic and court staff presents back from leave – usually a shirt or something equally useful that's in short supply. Yesterday I gave my new cook, Wilson, his shirt and thanked him for looking after the house and property in my absence. This morning there was no breakfast and when I went out I found that he had packed his kit and left last night. Not a word to me or even to the *shamba* boy. Yesterday he seemed quite happy here and pleased with his gift and he made no complaints or important announcements. It's quite extraordinary. He didn't pinch anything either. So, back to square one.

Tuesday 13 July

I spoke to the CJ today. He appears to be rather unhappy that I've returned like a bad penny. When I asked about my chances of getting into the Court of Appeal he was unresponsive. Even though such a move would get me out of his hair he won't help because he knows it's something I want.

Wednesday 14 July

Looking at some copies of recent judgments on my desk, I see that the Court of Appeal has at last delivered its judgment in the appeal in the case in May last year where I stated that the seizure of Asian property by Amin was theft on a huge scale and those who applied for and were allocated businesses and goods had knowingly received stolen property. The Three Stooges in the Appeal Court have held that I was wrong. The whole exercise, they announce, was a legal nationalisation of the property with provision for payment of compensation under the law, and no article of the Constitution was violated. What utter rubbish. The property was stolen from the Asians and no compensation was ever paid. Even their personal possessions were stolen from them at Entebbe airport. Our appeal judges don't seem to understand that the word nationalisation means taking businesses into public ownership and administering them by government-appointed boards with the minister accountable to Parliament, or whatever. These businesses here were seized and given away to individual soldiers, Moslems and other people for their own personal use. They were not nationalised. The Constitution was very much violated in this as in almost everything that Amin did.

Still, the members of that court were hardly in a position to give an unbiased judgment, let alone a wise one, since at least two of them have been in possession of allocated properties or businesses and so were not properly able to make such a comment. Fortunately, the government is taking no notice of this absurd judgment supporting Amin's actions and is continuing the process of arranging for the restoration of the properties.

One of several reasons why I want to move up to the Court of Appeal is to help to ensure that the highest court in the land produces final judgments that can be respected and followed in similar cases in future. This will not be achieved by the present system of moving the dead wood up from the High Court. One of these appeal judges does not write judgments at all. His sole standard contribution consists of: 'I have read and agree with the judgment of — and I have nothing useful to add.'

Friday 13 August

I opened criminal sessions at Jinja on 19 July and finished today; it's been a long and tedious circuit, with a mixture of murders, robberies and rapes. The hotel is not in good condition yet and service and food are still way below standard. For once there were no pleas of guilty, so all the cases had to be tried. The only amusing incident was with a medical assistant who was a witness and came up with some nice malapropisms, for instance referring to the umbilical cord as the 'biblical' cord and claiming that the doctor 'diagonised' what was wrong with the victim.

There's not much change in Kampala these days. Still no water from the taps and insecurity is the name of the game. In various residences of diplomats and bank managers steel doors have been fitted internally so that, if armed gunmen enter at night, the inhabitants can retreat behind their armour plating. My police orderly/bodyguard, who is from Teso, has kindly presented me with an ostrich egg. It is a large one and it has a small hole drilled neatly at one end through which the contents were extracted. A knotted cord has somehow been fixed in the hole so that the egg can be hung up. The purpose of the exercise, he explained, is that by custom the hanging of this egg in one's house will henceforth prevent any more breakings or intruders from entering the house. Well, I hope what he says is true because I certainly need an effective preventative, so I've put it up straight away. Who knows? It might even work. Of course it's not going to be much use against thieving domestic staff already in the house. But what to do?

Thursday 16 September

At the hearing of a rather dull civil suit before me this morning one of the advocates kept saying the word 'counsels' when speaking of the advocates involved. Ever the English teacher I intervened and remarked that the word counsel is the same as sheep in that the plural is the same as the singular. The other advocate, who I suspect had been half asleep, suddenly jumped to his feet and said: 'I strongly protest, my Lord, at your Lordship calling counsels sheep.'

Sighing I said: 'No, Mr —, it was just a semantic interlude.'

'Oh,' he said, obviously completely baffled, and sat down.

Sunday 10 October

Yesterday was the twentieth anniversary of Uganda's independence. There was some sort of celebration organised but I didn't go, and I hear that it was not well attended. There's really not a lot to celebrate at the moment and the local population, being Baganda and very anti-Obote and his UPC, was simply not interested. In the evening there was heavy gun-fire all over the city – the usual undisciplined firing in the air and general wastage of expensive ammunition by the UNLA in some sort of celebratory mood.

In 1962 when Obote first came to power the country was in a fine state and the economy was booming; so he set to with zealous socialism to pull it down with unnecessary nationalisation and government controls. This time on his return to power he was faced with a totally shattered economy and a worthless currency, so he has abandoned all pretences of socialist financial and economic purism and practice. In return for badly needed financial aid, he has taken the advice of the World Bank and the IMF and raised the prices of Uganda's main products of coffee, tea, cotton and tobacco. The shilling was floated resulting in drastic devaluation, bringing down the prices of necessities. Foreign exchange is easier to obtain now, and consumer goods are slightly more available, though they are still much too expensive. But there's still no sign of any political conciliation between north and south.

Friday 29 October

We had a British visitor at the High Court this morning. He was Peter Archer, a Labour MP and former Solicitor-General who is now Labour's spokesman on legal affairs; on some sort of overseas swan disguised as a fact-finding expedition, I suppose. I wasn't interested enough to ask him. I left him chatting with the other judges as I was due at the LDC to give a lecture. Not a very impressive character, I thought. But then he's a politician.

Friday 26 November

Yesterday I gave judgment in a case against Grindlays Bank, which for three and a half years had, on the orders of the Minister of Finance, frozen the current and savings accounts of one Juma Kenyi, who was alleged to have been an Amin supporter. There was a certain amount of interest in the case because only the Minister of Finance can authorise the freezing and unfreezing (or defrosting?) of bank accounts – and President Obote himself also happens to be the Minister of Finance.

My judgment was fairly long and rather carefully worded since I felt bound to hold that the Minister had failed to make a proper freezing order, nor had it been gazetted as required by law. Consequently I held that the bank had acted unlawfully in refusing Kenyi access to his accounts and that the money in them must be released to him immediately. This evening my contact told me that Obote was not at all happy to hear of this and he has now made a proper freezing order. I wonder if Kenyi managed to clear his account before that was done.

Saturday 27 November

Today I received a letter from Lofty Wilson, my former very tall cook. It was written in poor French, which is the sort I speak, and posted in Zaire. He says that he wants to come back to work for me but still hasn't revealed why he departed suddenly after I returned from leave. I concocted a brief reply in fractured French telling him not to bother as there is no vacancy. My *shamba* boy, Vincent, has taken over as cook, and has soon proved he can cook anything, as long as it's fried.

Thursday 16 December

I opened civil sessions at Jinja on 1 December with a pile of cases to get through. At last they've done some work at the Crested Crane Hotel and produced a reasonably comfortable room; the service has improved too.

Today I gave judgment in the last of the Jinja cases. It was a second appeal in a dispute over a land boundary between two men who had been neighbours for 30 years and still hadn't sorted it out. The plaintiff, Gwina, said that the boundary was marked by a line of six *birowa* (barkcloth) trees on the other side of a path. The defendant, Lubale, and his witnesses said that the boundary was marked by a footpath which he had made for the purpose of carrying sugar cane from his *shamba* for sale outside. The trial magistrate, himself a Musoga, visited the disputed place and later gave judgment in favour of Gwina because, so he said, in Busoga customary land tenure trees are used as boundary marks because village paths tend to change from time to time. The first appeal was in 1978 and came before the acting chief magistrate, who was a Pakistani lawyer appointed by Amin. He declared that, although there was no evidence before the trial magistrate to the effect that a boundary cannot be a village path under Busoga customary law, this was so well known that it was not necessary to prove it. How he could say this I don't know, since he had then been in Uganda for only a short time and knew little or nothing of the customs. I had certainly not heard of it and was not prepared to accept it without proper proof from witnesses acquainted with the local customs. Furthermore, if the boundary in this case was in fact a footpath, it was of no consequence whether or not the boundary was fixed contrary to a custom. There is no law that requires such customs to be followed nor did it conflict with the law of the land. The defendant, Lubale, and his witnesses, all Basoga, not only denied that it was a custom, but firmly asserted that the footpath was in fact the boundary. One of those witnesses had actually allocated the land to the two men in 1952 and he had indicated it was the boundary. Consequently I held that Gwina had failed in his original claim before the trial magistrate and I allowed the appeal.

I received a letter from Difasi Sinane of Mbale today. He was a police corporal in Karamoja with me in 1960, after which I sent him on a promotion course. He has now retired in the rank of Assistant Superintendent and sent the letter by hand of his son, who was born when we were in Nabilatuk and whom he named after me. Now this P. A. Mabonga is training as a medical assistant in Mbale district and has just finished a short course in Kampala.

Monday 27 December

It's a public holiday today since Boxing Day was on a Sunday. As usual I went to the main post office to collect mail; for one good thing about the postal service in Uganda is that, when it is working, there is mail every day, regardless of weekends and public holidays; something that has not changed since Protectorate days. It's better and more frequent than in the UK. We have two deliveries to boxes every day and one delivery on Sundays and public holidays.

One thing that is definitely not so good, though, is the mosquito situation. The mosquitoes here are vicious and persistent creatures and, being *Anopheles*, are malaria carriers. Before independence and up until the late 1960s Kampala was a mosquito-free area, kept so by frequent and efficient malaria-control procedures. Unfortunately, these since became lax and eventually almost disappeared and the ever-waiting mosquito moved back into the area and proliferated again. One therefore needs to take anti-malarial tablets regularly or suffer the consequences.

Thursday 30 December

In a criminal appeal judgment today I dealt with an unpleasant fellow called Nsimbe, a Muganda, who said he was Youth Security Officer with the National Youth Executive Committee in the Office of the Vice-President, Muwanga. In other words, one of Muwanga's secret police recruited from the UPC Youth Wing known for their interfering and obnoxious methods.

He had gone with some armed policemen to a shop in Kampala belonging to one Sentamu and arrested him and seized 200,000 shillings in cash from the shop. They also arrested the shop assistant and three customers. Nsimbe claimed that he was acting against *mafutamingis* (fat cats, black marketeers) at the time. These people were taken to Jinja Road Police Station and detained. Nsimbe there threatened to cut off Sentamu's head and kill the son of one of the customers if they failed to pay him 1 million shillings each for their release alive. Nsimbe had no legal power to arrest people and the police should not have helped him to do so nor should they have accepted them as prisoners. But they did so, and so were responsible in law for their detention. They were quite obviously, and perhaps understandably, frightened of the people from the VP's office, just as everyone was afraid of the civilian SRB in Amin's time, which was not so long ago. Unfortunately the police had made a shambles of the charge sheet against Nsimbe as well as a botched prosecution. The trial magistrate, who should have corrected the errors, had failed to do

575

so and added some of his own, so I had, most reluctantly, to quash the conviction on one count and reduce the unlawful sentence on another count. The only relief was that he went back to prison to serve the legal part of his sentence.

1983

Tuesday 18 January

At the invitation of the British Police Training Team I spent the morning at the Police College speaking at a seminar for district police commanders (superintendents) who are being given a command course. It was interesting and went well; as usual there was a considerable amount of involvement and numerous questions asked. Most of these chaps had been constables in my police days. The BPTT is doing a good job and has been able to bring in some equipment which is being used for instructional purposes and will afterwards be handed over for general use here. There was an article about it in today's *Uganda Times* which gave them a good write-up.

Wednesday 8 March

Yesterday evening there was a party at the CJ's residence for the visiting CJ of Zambia, Annel Silungwe, who is also a regional bigwig in the Rotary (or was it the Lions? I can't recall) Club, which was his excuse for visiting Uganda. All the judges were invited, naturally, though I think our CJ would have preferred my absence, which is why I went. He wasn't very welcoming but that didn't matter. I had a long chat with Silongwe and suggested that their overseas members might be stirred into doing some useful work by collecting together many of the discarded and unwanted spectacles from the public and superseded artificial limbs from hospitals in Western countries and having them shipped to Africa, where there is a great need for them. The small local industry for making artificial limbs, providing employment for several limbless men, which was started just outside Kampala some years before independence, unfortunately disappeared sometime in the late 1960s.

Then a large flagged car arrived, with military escort vehicles front and rear filled with armed soldiers. It was Major-General Tito Okello, the Army Commander. He was introduced to us all round and I could see that the CJ was rather put out when Okello greeted me joyfully as *Mwalimu* (teacher) and announced that he had once been my student. He had attended the law course for senior army officers that I had run in 1979 when he was a colonel. His English is still poor and he hadn't done very well then, but he's a nice old boy and very friendly.

Monday 11 April

The newspapers are featuring my judgment in what they refer to as The *Panda Gari* Case. This locally well-known expression means 'get on the lorry' and is commonly used by soldiers when rounding up and arresting civilians in their various sweeps through the city. In this case Kityo, a lawyer, was about to go to work one morning in March last year when soldiers arrived in vehicles and started searching houses in that area. They fired shots at his house wall until he opened up. They claimed to be looking for guerrillas and illegal weapons and wanted to search his house. When he asked if they had authority to do so, they became abusive and threatened to shoot his barking dogs. They then demanded money, kicked him and threatened to shoot him and his family while they searched his house and stole what money they could find. When they left he heard more shooting and saw people being rounded up and put into the army lorries.

He reported the theft and assault to Central Police Station, where he was told that, as it was a military operation, it was not the concern of the police. The soldiers were all in camouflaged uniforms with their weapons and military trucks. The defence called no witnesses – none would have appeared from the army if he had tried. The State relied on the usual claim that it hadn't been proved that the men were members of the UNLA and they might have been other people wearing stolen uniforms and that Kityo ought to have reported them to the police. Since in fact he had done so and the police had said they were army and declined to help, this wasn't very helpful. In my judgment I said that if these men had not been UNLA then why did not the army and police move in and do something when they heard all the shooting in the area? It was clear from their uniforms, weapons and transport that they were in fact UNLA units and that 'these soldiers on official duty had behaved like criminals in uniform' – the newspapers eagerly seized hold of that phrase – and 'their action and behaviour was high-handed, oppressive and intolerable as well as totally undisciplined'. I added that soldiers are not paid out of public funds so that they can use their positions and weapons in order to rob and terrorise fellow citizens and consequently their disgraceful and violent behaviour fully justified the award of exemplary damages against them. I concluded that such searches should only be carried out by the police and not by clearly unsupervised military personnel. The newspaper headlines went to town on these remarks.

1983

Monday 18 April

A new British Police Training Team arrived a short while ago and has been busy at the College running courses for CID and senior officers. They called on me in my chambers this morning. The team is led by Assistant Chief Constable Brook of the South Wales Constabulary with a Detective Chief Inspector and a DI from two other county forces. Brook is a large man with the most enormous hands I've ever seen. A villain caught in his grasp would find it difficult to break away. We discussed the most urgent types of training required – just about everything – and various problems that they'd found so far, such as an almost total lack of equipment and transport. I offered to come along to the College, as I did before, and give whatever assistance I can as I regard the rehabilitation of the Police to be most important, particularly in reducing the role of the Army in civilian affairs.

At one point Brook several times mentioned that they had been teaching how to deal with 'verbals' and I said the expression was new to me. It apparently means statements made to the police by suspects and accused persons, usually confessions or admissions of some sort. He said those he'd spoken to here didn't seem to know much about verbals or how to record and deal with them. I said: 'But didn't they tell you that in Uganda confessions made to the police are not admissible in court?' I showed them the relevant part of the Evidence Act and they looked shattered. Brook said that they'd been giving instructions about the careful recording and handling of such confessions and then giving evidence in court about them, and nobody had drawn their attention to this law. I replied: 'Well, they were probably too polite, nervous or embarrassed to say you were wrong. Maybe they thought that the law had recently been changed and they hadn't heard about it; which is quite possible here.' In fact, I thought that the team ought to have checked the law on this before commencing instruction, so as to avoid any confusion such as would now have to be sorted out. Fortunately, there were no other problems of this sort.

Wednesday 20 April

Museveni and his NRA are very active in an area forming a triangle between the main roads from Kampala to Gulu and from Kampala to Hoima. In these hundreds of square miles, known as the Luwero Triangle, the NRA is in control and telephone communications between Kampala and Hoima, Masindi and Gulu have been cut for months. The power supply to Masindi and Hoima is also cut. All this is a great discomfort and inconvenience for the people who live there or who wish to travel to or communicate with the area.

It doesn't seem to matter to Museveni that his action of taking to the bush in petulance after being totally rejected in the 1980 elections has cost the country so much in lives and property and delayed or prevented Uganda's recovery and rehabilitation after the destructive years of Amin's regime. And what is it all for? It can't be a difference in policies. Any Uganda government must have the same aims of rebuilding and rehabilitating the country and people. So it just comes down to personalities and ambitions for power. How many people must suffer and die to satisfy this desire? And for how long? Nothing in Uganda is now better than it was at independence 21 years ago; indeed, everything is in a very much worse state and Uganda has merely achieved negative growth.

Even this present awful government would not be anywhere near so bad as it now is if it wasn't being constantly attacked and harassed by guerrillas and violent opponents. If everyone had the sense to put aside personal quarrels and political ambitions for the time being while rebuilding this beautiful country, they could do wonders. But there is no hope of that.

Friday 20 May

My houseboy Vincent has been carrying out the tedious task of taking out my books from the shelves and dusting them off. Over the years the hardbacks have been attacked and chewed by cockroaches and silverfish. There seems to have been something in the glue used in the binding process that attracts these insects. They love chomping on it.

I recall at the Law School in the 1960s I was given a liquid of some sort to put on the library bookshelves which either poisoned silverfish and cockroaches or discouraged them in some way. But such things are not available here these days and all one can do is spray insecticide around the shelves occasionally. It doesn't do all that much good.

Thursday 26 May

There are claims that Brigadier Moses Ali's Uganda National Rescue Front (UNRF) has disintegrated in the West Nile district. He is out of the country in the Middle East, where he has business interests, and his guerrillas have temporarily degenerated into a number of small groups of thugs and bandits with no present political aims. They're just operating across the Sudan and Zaire borders and looting. The UNLA in the area, meanwhile, continues to harass and terrorise the civilian population that they are paid to protect. We really don't need any of this.

The only ferry across the Nile to Pakwach at Laropi has been destroyed and sunk, allegedly by the UNRF. This is a typical piece of mindless destruction that benefits nobody. Large numbers of Ugandan refugees have gone into southern Sudan – a reversal of what used to be the case.

Monday 27 June

There's been no piped water all month and no power for several days. A mains water pipe has burst in Kampala and it seems to be beyond their power to repair or replace it.

Monday 4 July

I was supposed to go to Gulu on circuit today but, much to the CJ's displeasure, I refused to go. Nowadays everything has to be paid for in cash, even between government departments. No credit is given anywhere, mainly because hardly anyone bothers to pay their bills, either personal or official. On circuit we judges have to carry sufficient cash to pay hotel bills, purchase petrol and pay witness allowances. I was told by the CR that no cash was available for my Gulu sessions so I didn't go. I've no wish to be stranded up in Gulu waiting, probably in vain, for the cash to pay everyone which the CJ vaguely promised to send up by hand 'later'. Such assurances, particularly from him, are worthless in my opinion.

Wednesday 13 July

I was invited to the BHC residence for a late afternoon reception to meet Malcolm Rifkind, a Minister of State in the FCO. He's out concerning the future of the British Army and Police training teams, among other things. I spoke to the colonel in charge of the military team and said surely he must find these so-called soldiers untrainable since they never had basic discipline drilled into them and are irresponsible and uncontrollable by their own officers. The only effective way is to start all over again with completely new recruits strictly disciplined from the start. But he didn't agree. He said: 'No, we manage all right and we train them effectively.'

This is utter nonsense. One has only to see how they behave towards the civil population, robbing, looting and killing them indiscriminately. They are just producing more effective killers of unarmed civilians. He moved away when I put this to him.

The High Commissioner is a Scot and he has a French wife. Neither of them seems to like the English, but especially her. I'm the only Brit here in a senior government post yet each time we meet she asks me what I do in Uganda in a voice displaying complete indifference to my reply. This time I muttered: 'I'm a dustman; I clear up the rubbish,' and moved away to get a drink. I thought a diplomat's wife was supposed to put up a better show than that.

Thursday 21 July

I spent this afternoon speaking at a seminar for magistrates at the LDC. They have a lot of problems in their work these days and there was much to discuss and I gave what advice I could. But there are many things that are out of our control and solutions to these problems are difficult to find.

This morning I gave judgment in one of the many *habeas corpus* cases that we receive in connection with the very many, mostly illegal, detainees presently held in prisons by the government. In this instance one Byekwaso had been held in detention for the last two years without ever being interviewed, questioned or informed why he was being held. He was arrested by the military in September 1981 at a road-block on the Kampala to Mityana road. He said that they told him that, as he had a beard, he must be a guerrilla, so they took him into custody. Somebody apparently with the same idea about beards that I have. At Makindye army barracks a blank Presidential Detention Order, already signed by the Minister of Internal Affairs, was filled in with his name and the date.

The law requires that a Minister designated to act for the President in this matter has to receive sworn information justifying the detention before a detention order can be made out and signed. This wasn't complied with and, even worse, the Minister was (and maybe still is) issuing pre-signed blank detention orders for use and misuse by anyone possessing them. I declared the detention order null and void and ordered his release. He was rearrested outside the court as usual. This Minister controls the police and prisons and, in accordance with his orders, persons released by the courts for any reason are immediately rearrested and taken back to prison whether or not there is any lawful reason to detain them. It seems that nobody has the guts to allow released persons to walk away from the courts and so disregard the unlawful orders of a most unpleasant Minister. I've tried complaining about this Minister to the CJ but he also favours detention without trial so it's very difficult to secure any releases.

Friday 29 July

The BPTT under Vivian Brook is presently holding a senior command seminar for assistant commissioners and senior superintendents and I was invited along to spend this afternoon speaking to them and discussing problems covering a wide range of police and security matters. I suggested that it was time to get men back walking the beats again – something that has not been done for a very long time – as it seemed to have been forgotten that the main function of the police is to prevent crime and not just tag along reacting to crime and trying to clear up the mess after crimes have been committed. For years the constables have not been issued with notebooks and this absence often affects their evidence in court, which I've remarked on several times before. I suggested that this should now be rectified. Much must be done too to raise the morale in the Force and to provide better conditions of service and pay. I also mentioned the idea of reviving the Force magazine *Habari* to boost morale and *esprit de corps* and to provide inter-unit interest and entertainment.

Saturday 13 August

At last, after waiting for over four years, the Ministry of Works has sent some men to carry out repairs to the damage caused to my house by gun-fire in the 1979 Tanzanian invasion. The many window panes, which I had blocked with plywood or thick cardboard, are now being glazed. The side door has been replaced as it had rotted away at the bottom and was keeping nothing out, rain, rats, snakes or whatever. The faulty water supply to the servants quarters is being fixed and so is the leaking water tank in my roof. It's not exactly an express repair service but very welcome nevertheless.

Wednesday 31 August

I received an official letter on Monday from the CJ, just down the corridor, putting on record his complaint that my weekly lectures at the LDC and Police College have seriously interfered with my court work (without offering any proof of this) and that, as of now, I'm forbidden from doing any outside teaching. I don't actually see how assisting in the training of our own magistrates can be called outside teaching. As I've tried to point out to him in my written reply, I've never allowed my voluntary teaching to interfere in anyway with my court work and, as he well knows, I have continued throughout not only to deal with all my cases but, in overall figures, I generally dispose of more cases monthly than any other judge in the High Court. Since he still doesn't do any court work himself, he's hardly in a strong position to complain anyway. I added that, in spite of his order, I intend to continue my teaching as it is to the considerable benefit of the

Judiciary and the country to have well-trained magistrates and police officers, and I consider it my duty to use my long service and experience to assist in such training. I had my secretary make an extra copy of this letter and of the CJ's letter and on Monday evening I handed them to my contact to show to President Obote, as I think he should know what his Chief Justice is up to.

In direct disobedience of the CJ's nonsensical order, I went to the LDC this afternoon and delivered the first of a series of lectures to the present course for magistrates on the law of evidence. This evening my contact rang to say that he had shown the letters to Obote, who was very angry about the CJ's interference and wished me to continue to give assistance to the LDC and the Police as before. Apparently the President has already spoken to the CJ and torn him off a strip.

Thursday 1 September

Before the judges meeting this morning the CJ rang me and in a very subdued tone said that he had had second thoughts and had decided to withdraw his objections to my outside teaching as it was obviously useful and helpful. He added that he had not meant to stop me from teaching but only to make sure it didn't interfere with my court work. Well, well. Obote seems to have straightened him out quite effectively. The meeting itself went on all day, as the CJ's meetings tend to do, allowing endless talking and waffling at great length. I mentally switch off at these extremely time-wasting assemblies. We even had lunch brought in from an outside caterer.

Friday 2 September

It was a very busy out-of-court day. I was lecturing at the LDC in the morning and at the Police College in the afternoon to a senior command course. I even managed to fit in a couple of short matters in court in between. It was quite exhausting but worthwhile.

Monday 12 September

Obote's senior Lango army officer, Brigadier Oyite-Ojok, the Chief of Staff, is getting far too big for his boots. Although he's not the army commander he's driven around in a huge Mercedes with several heavily armed escort vehicles front and rear, sounding police sirens and flashing lights and pushing all other vehicles off the road to make way for the Great Man. I get rather peeved with Laurence, my timid driver, who immediately swerves off the road when Ojok's convoy appears. The other day I was delighted to see Ojok's lot going one way and

Vice-President Muwanga's very similar convoy coming in the opposite direction. Neither gave way and they hurtled past each other, flashing lights and sounding sirens to indicate their self-important passage. Any hopes of a tremendous security crash were not fulfilled though.

Thursday 20 October

I have been speaking to BPTT command and other courses for some time now and they have been interesting and productive. Today, however, I was asked to speak to a new type of course. They are all university graduates recruited as potential gazetted police officers.

I spoke of the Uganda legal system, and for the first time in the very many classes and courses I've taught over the years in Uganda there was no response whatsoever. No interest shown and no questions asked and there were no smiling faces. What was wrong? I asked the British Chief Inspector afterwards and he said that these graduates have been shanghaied into the Police against their will on government orders and they are not co-operating in their training, no doubt hoping to be chucked out as a result.

What a stupid idea; I gather it came from the Minister of Internal Affairs, which is not really surprising. You cannot force people to become policemen if they are reluctant. What possible use could they be to anyone by failing or refusing to carry out orders and policies and only half-heartedly performing vital duties? No wonder they were a silent class. I told him to cancel my second lecture to them. I'm not wasting my time taking part in an exercise clearly doomed to failure from the start.*

Thursday 27 October

While the workmen are at my house, I asked that they should build me a proper sentry box with cement blocks – thinking back to when I had that one built at Government House in 1957 – to replace the wooden one which, with the able assistance of the resident termites, is falling apart. They found a cobra living in the small thatched roof. If Ali, the daytime watchman, had known about that he wouldn't have spent so much of his time dozing in the box.

Ali is a great collector of useless rubbish. On his way here he picks up broken and abandoned objects and brings them to add to his world-acclaimed collection of trash behind the old sentry box. All this the workmen removed and dumped with the remains of the box. When

*This graduate training scheme was abandoned shortly afterwards.

Ali arrived he went up the wall at this cavalier dealing with his precious garbage accumulation.

Monday 31 October

For two days now we've had storms of large hailstones lashing down followed by heavy rain. It must be a sign of something. In view of that, I spent most of yesterday afternoon fixing a coil of barbed wire across the top of my gates to reinforce the strands already there. I'm still trying to prevent the police night sentries from escaping after dark. Recently one of them actually tunnelled under the wire security fence and made his escape. Must have seen one of those old wartime POW escape films. Makes me feel like the Commandant of Stalag Luft VI, except it's not supposed to be the guards who escape. But we're in Uganda, of course.

Tuesday 15 November

After court this afternoon I went to lecture to a senior police officers management course. The Deputy IG and the heads of CID and SB and other senior officers were attending, and the seminar was organised by Vivian Brook on the lines of similar UK courses. There was a group photo afterwards and time for tea and a chat. I had known most of them as very junior policemen and some had returned after being retired or exiled by Towelli's efforts.

Saturday 3 December

The UNLA was supplied by a Swiss-Canadian company with three Augusta-Bell 412 helicopters, one of which the Chief of Staff, Brigadier Oyite-Ojok, has been using as his personal aircraft. Yesterday he was out north of Kampala somewhere visiting a unit when the helicopter exploded, blowing to bits all those inside. Either someone planted a bomb in it before it took off or it was shot down by a rocket-fired missile. Whichever it was, there are not many people mourning the death of this very dangerous man who almost certainly had presidential ambitions; which could be a motive for removing him. Or it could have been done by UNLA Acholi soldiers or NRA guerrillas. He had plenty of enemies who did not wish him well.

Langi officers in the UNLA have been targets elsewhere recently as fears of Langi domination in the army rise. Two were shot dead in an incident in Old Kampala and six others were murdered on their arrival at Magamaga Ordnance Depot near Jinja, where they had been sent to take over the depot controlled by officers from other tribes.

1983

Wednesday 7 December

The CJ issued an instruction this morning that all judges should go along to pay their respects to Oyite-Ojok, who is 'lying in state' (even in death his hubris is overwhelming). The coffin apparently contains a hand with a ring on it, which was the only identifiable part of Ojok that was found. As I have no time for either the CJ or Ojok, and certainly no respects to pay to someone who'd earned none, I rang Zadok, the CR, and told him I had a heavy cold and, as I didn't want to share it with anybody else, I could not appear in public so I wouldn't be going along to pay my disrespects. He knows me well and just laughed and asked if it was a very bad cold. I said it was a diplomatic cold, which meant I would recover by the afternoon, when I would be back in court.

Monday 19 December

As my driver is on leave I was yesterday sent a new young replacement driver who, in fact, lasted less than a day. I don't believe he had ever driven anything much before and certainly not a large car. He had no idea of its width. On the way out, taking me home for lunch, he hit one of the court gateposts and at home failed to line the car up with the garage entrance and scraped it along one wall. When we were on our way back to court after lunch, he apparently couldn't find the brakes near the golf club and we ran into the back of another Mercedes, carrying a government Minister. Fortunately no damage was done, so I hopped out of my car and, ignoring his rather belligerent-looking bodyguard, said to the surprised Minister: 'Sorry about that. This new driver of mine doesn't seem to have much of a clue. I'll have to sort him out.' At the High Court I told the driver to report to the Chief Registrar, whom I then rang from my chambers and instructed: 'Get rid of this menace before he gets rid of me.'

Friday 23 December

I received a Christmas card from Luke Ofungi today. He's now a successful businessman again. I'm still hoping it will be possible to get him back in the Force later on. He's the only one who can really sort things out. The present IG of Police is Okoth-Ogola. He's a pleasant, hard-working chap but very much a political person who does not seem to stand up to his Minister and insist on certain things being done, or not being done. And the Internal Affairs Minister is so arrogant and self-satisfied that he needs to be stood up to occasionally. He and the CJ seem to be a pair – both apparently believe in locking up every dissident and potential opponent and throwing away the keys. Their version of the expression 'Rule of Law' puts all the emphasis on the first word rather than the last.

I'm glad to see that my suggestion last July that police notebooks be once again issued to all members of the Force has been attended to. Apparently the British Police Training Team then arranged for sufficient books to be sent out from the UK as part of their training aid scheme. The officers and NCOs will once again be able to check more accurately on the duties and reports of constables and all of them will be of more reliable assistance in court when testifying.

1984

Monday 30 January

Early this evening I went to the British High Commissioner's residence to meet Timothy Raison, a junior Defence Minister who's probably out here to see what the British Army Training Team are up to now that the rest of the Commonwealth Training Team have packed up and gone, having no doubt found it a useless task trying to train the untrainable.

I wanted to talk to him about this and the security situation generally but the BHC staff must have been briefed to keep us apart, as each time I approached him one of them intervened and insisted I should meet so-and-so. It's the usual foreign service story – they don't want anyone who might know something to give different information from the brief that they have provided. When I did get to him and started to speak, one of the staff quickly brought someone else up to him to be introduced and I was edged away. I had heard him say how impressed he was with the Minister of Internal Affairs, who was also present. He's a smooth, suave, well-dressed, intelligent type who is one of the main causes of our problems over trying to release people unlawfully detained, and our visitor should be told that anything he says has to be taken with a pinch of salt.

I'm fed up with releasing people on *habeas corpus* applications because they have been detained improperly and for no good reasons, only to find that each released applicant is rearrested outside the court and taken back to prison. When queried about this the prison or police officer concerned merely states that it is on the orders of their Minister. Such applications are heard in chambers and, on a couple of occasions after making release orders, I have sent the prison warder off on some pretext and then personally escorted the released prisoner down to a side door from the court and told him to scoot from there before he is seen and rearrested. I've also found that even accused persons in criminal cases whom I have released on bail are being promptly re-arrested afterwards. When I complained to the CJ about this his response was to berate me for releasing any criminals at all on bail. I pointed out that the law and Constitution allowed this and it is per-fectly proper, and he replied that, if I persisted in this, he would per-sonally get together with the Minister and draft legislation to abolish bail in High Court cases. 'Well,' I replied, 'I shall continue to release them in accordance with the law,' and walked out. It's quite incred-ible. I had to remind myself afterwards that the person I was speak-ing to calls himself the Chief Justice. What a mockery. So I wrote a letter to the President setting out my complaints about this matter of releases and rearrests and pointing out that police and prisons officers questioned by me all said that the order came from their Minister. Neither the police nor prisons have any interest in detaining people released by the courts as they merely act on orders, and only their Minister could give such orders. Of course, the original order might have come from Obote himself, in which case I'm wasting my time. I gave the letter to my contact to hand directly to Obote as I didn't want it to go through anyone else and be side-tracked.

A couple of days ago I received a letter signed by that Minister and copied to the President's Office in which he completely denied ever having given rearrest orders for anyone, and he went further and said nobody had given such orders. In other words, I was lying. Or he was. I left it like that. I have no personal interest in these matters and so have nothing to gain by telling such lies, and they know this. I'd reported to the President and I couldn't do more, especially with no backing from the CJ. It was up to Obote to decide whom to believe and what to do about it. Nothing, I suspect.

Tuesday 31 January

I gave judgment today in a divorce petition between a Ugandan called Mukiibi and a Chinese woman named Madam Xu Ping of the People's Republic of China. Mukiibi graduated as an engineer from Shanghai University and married Xu Ping in front of the mayor in the Huang Pu District of Shanghai 'in conformity with the stipulations of the Marriage Law of the PRC', said the certificate.

When they came to Uganda Mukiibi treated her in the usual way as an African wife/slave, frequently slapping and beating her. She had to get medical treatment from a Chinese medical team at the PRC

Embassy in Kampala. She wanted to go out to work but he refused and kept her as a servant at home, making her wait on him all the time in every way, constantly complaining about her work and denigrating her. He brought African girl-friends home and she often found him in bed with them.

She left him after a few months of this, and after complaining at the Embassy and getting advice there, and went to live with an African family she knew. Mukiibi stayed with his special girl, who became pregnant. It was an undefended petition as Mukiibi was no longer interested in what she did. The witnesses produced ample evidence of cruelty and adultery and there was no condonation or collusion, so I granted the divorce.

Friday 10 February

Nothing much happened today. The Soviet leader, Chairman, General Secretary, or whatever he's called now, who was the former head of the KGB, Andropov, died and my new carpets for the lounge and bedroom were delivered.

Friday 17 February

There are Red Cross officials from the ICRC trying to trace and register about 750,000 displaced people in the Luwero Triangle area. They are working with Save the Children and Oxfam, who are feeding and caring for 130,000 or more civilians currently being held in army and police-run so-called refugee camps, which are actually more like concentration camps.

Food, water and medicines are in very short supply and the death rate, especially among the children, is high. Anyone found outside the camps is liable to be shot on sight by the army as a suspected guerrilla or bandit. It appears that thousands of Baganda from Mpigi, Mubende and Luwero have been killed, mainly by the UNLA, but the NRA guerrillas have also done their share of the killing. The situation in the area looks worse than at any time during Amin's regime and none of this need be happening if the guerrillas ceased their operations, for then the government security forces would be withdrawn and the inhabitants would be freed from their desperate plight.

Tuesday 21 February

We are constantly beset by a shortage of stationery items in the courts these days. Some magistrates are recording trial evidence on exercise book pages, others are using the blank backs of court forms and warrants. Several times in the High Court judges have been unable to proceed with a trial because they have no paper on which to record the evidence.

Because nobody trusts anybody to pay debts, government departments have to pay cash to each other for services or supplies. We can only obtain paper and other stationery items from the Government Printer by paying cash. When the GP has no paper we have to purchase it from ordinary shops. Frequently, though, the funds allocated for such purchases have been diverted and misused and so are not available for their proper purposes.

We produce copies of our judgments by having them typed on to wax stencils for printing and duplicating, but stencils are in short supply also. Recently, in order to produce copies of my judgments required by advocates, I've had to ask them to produce stencils and paper themselves so that we could supply the duplicated copies they needed. It's most embarrassing, but they well know the position here and the cause and source of these shortages.

Wednesday 22 February

Today I gave judgment in an appeal against what was an appallingly badly investigated and prosecuted robbery trial conviction by the magistrate at Mukono, about 14 miles out of Kampala on the Jinja road. As usual, the arresting officer and the investigating officer were not called to give evidence, as they should have been. The identification of the accused man, Ofwono, was by the woman complainant, Nambirige, and her seven-year-old son Robert. Ofwono was not only an occasional visitor to their house but actually held a *tadoba* lamp, a small open oil lamp, in his hand to see and be seen in the house. The woman said he also held an axe, a knife and a stick in his other hand and then, in spite of his hands being so full, he managed to find two more hands with which to try to strangle Nambirige. Meanwhile, she struggled and he was apparently juggling with the lamp and all the weapons. The whole picture was absurd and farcical, but she insisted that that was how it was.

The amount of money reported to the police as stolen was later multiplied by five by the woman in the trial court. Nobody there bothered to ask the accused the vital question of where he was on that night although he had pleaded not guilty. There was an unexplained gap of four days before the police started to take statements in the case. The woman, Nambirige, said she couldn't give a statement until later because of her 'serious injuries', which consisted of a small bruise and two light scratches. She did not name Ofwono as the robber when her neighbours came to help, nor to her husband when he returned home later. She only mentioned the name to the police five days later. There was no way in which this could properly be called proof beyond reasonable doubt and I allowed the appeal against conviction.

Thursday 23 February

Last Monday about 200 of Museveni's NRA overran the town of Masindi in northern Bunyoro and captured the army barracks and all its weapons and ammunition. Although the UNLA garrison was expecting an attack, they were in a dozy state. The senior officer was absent on a visit to Kampala and his second in command was present but drunk. The NRA occupied Masindi for about seven hours and then cleared off back into the bush with the captured weapons and uniforms.

Thursday 29 March

I've heard that a Soroti advocate, F. X. Oliso, has been murdered up there. I've known him for many years – first when he was a police sub-inspector, then later, after he qualified in law, as an advocate. Apparently he had succeeded in a land dispute in court and the loser had friends among Vice-President Muwanga's gang of thugs, who came up and found him seated at his home on the outskirts of Soroti. They told him to go outside and he refused, saying: 'I know you will kill me if I go outside.' So they shot him where he sat in the house, in front of his family, put his body into a wheelbarrow and pushed it through the village and then dumped it. There are so many incidents like this nowadays and they seem to be on the increase.

Friday 30 March

I gave judgment today in a criminal appeal from Kumi in Teso concerning a charge of unlawfully administering poison. A woman called Kedi was married to Okurut but having an affair with a man named Ekue, who gave her a bottle of some substance to put into Okurut's food to kill him and get him out of their way. When she opened the bottle in the kitchen, the noxious fumes from the contents caused her to become unconscious and very ill afterwards.

According to the Government Chemist's report, which was put in at the trial without proof, the bottle was empty when it reached the Kampala laboratory. It had contained Diazinone, which he described as a very poisonous chemical used for the eradication of bedbugs and other pests. The report didn't state whether the poison was solid or liquid or dangerous to humans if administered internally or externally. In spite of these gaps in the report the magistrate found the substance to be poisonous to humans, which was the very essence of the case, without any supporting proof. Furthermore, it wasn't actually administered to the intended victim Okurut, so the magistrate decided that the woman Kedi was the required victim and he convicted Ekue. The state attorney quite rightly didn't support the conviction and I allowed the appeal.

Wednesday 4 April

Today I granted a divorce to an Italian who had married a Kenyan Maasai woman in Uganda. The co-respondent was a Brit now back in the UK. The son was born in Kampala but is now living in Kenya with his mother. The Italian pays for the boy's upkeep and has given the ex-wife a car for her use. So, fortunately, apart from the adultery, there was no unpleasantness and spiteful vitriol in this international case, which makes a change.

Thursday 12 April

There are bags of grain on open sale in Kampala shops stamped: UNICEF FAMINE RELIEF – FREE. These were brought in to be taken up to Karamoja because of the drought and the activities of the local banditry and the devastating army campaigns against them, which have left the ordinary Karamojong in a desperate plight. Unfortunately the military seize lorry-loads of this famine relief in Kampala on its arrival and sell it to the local traders. I don't know how much actually reaches Karamoja, if any. Even if it does it's probably looted up there as well.

Monday 16 April

A short while ago we judges had a special meeting to which the CJ was not invited. A letter was drafted to the President setting out the various reasons why we have completely lost confidence in the CJ and stating that we consider him totally unfit to hold that post and asking for him to be replaced. One of the judges took it to Obote personally, but we have had no reply or acknowledgement and nothing has been done thus far. I'd be very surprised if it has much effect. There are so many members of this government openly filling their coffers and generally misbehaving that none would want to be the one to throw the first stone.

The CJ has now got his threatened anti-bail legislation through after warning us (especially me) at judges meetings, followed by a circular objecting to the release on bail of any persons on capital charges. Some of those persons have been in custody on remand for years with no sign of a trial in sight because the investigation has either never been started or has not been completed; nor is it ever likely to be.

According to this disgusting piece of legislation, a judge cannot release a person on bail unless the DPP first gives his permission. So here we have a comparatively junior officer of the court, who is obviously biased because he represents one side, the prosecution, actually telling the judge what he can or cannot do. I've already stated in open court that I regard this as totally unacceptable and unconstitutional, and so I continue to release people on bail regardless of the DPP's protests and those of his state attorneys waving copies of the legislation. To be fair, some of them do not agree with it either, and they remain silent when I make a release order.

Thursday 17 May

I left Uganda yesterday to commence my UK leave. However, the flight was, as usual, late in departing and we arrived over Gatwick after dark. At Gatwick they only allow Uganda Airlines to land and take off in daylight. I don't think they have much faith in UA aircrew or aircraft. So we were diverted to Stansted airport, where apparently it doesn't matter if you crash, as it doesn't frighten the horses.

Thursday 19 July

As usual I came on leave with four suitcases, three empty and two of them inside the larger ones, since the thieves have left me with considerable replacement needs. Some people have given me shopping lists and other friends need all sorts of items, hence the extra cases.

Tuesday 31 July

I arrived back from leave this morning and found that someone at Gatwick had neglected to put my luggage on to the aircraft. There is also no electricity or water in the house. I hear that Wilson, the surgeon, who in his own time was researching the cause and spread of AIDS here, published the facts and figures revealing that there is a lot of it about. This upset the government and, after UPC youth-wingers had been round to his quarters and beaten up his domestic staff, he was ordered to leave Uganda.

Tuesday 14 August

My luggage has arrived at last after being in orbit for two weeks. I was in court all yesterday, hearing criminal appeals and bail applications. As before, I am continuing to release people on bail regardless of the CJ's disgraceful anti-bail legislation and protests by the DPP.

Monday 20 August

The replacement for the late unlamented Chief of Staff is another Lango, Brigadier Smith Opon Acak, whom I vaguely remember as once in the Police. As Obote wanted a Lango and none was senior enough, he had to be promoted over the heads of a number of disgruntled Acholi colonels. The CJ is still in his chair and looking pleased with himself, so it appears that our letter to Obote has had no useful effect. Why am I not surprised?

Wednesday 22 August

I needed a document from the British High Commission so I rang and asked for it to be sent over. I told the British secretary there that I was Judge Allen at the High Court. When the messenger arrived I saw that the envelope was addressed to 'George Allen'. You just can't get the staff nowadays.

Thursday 13 September

I arrived at Jinja ten days ago with a pile of files for a long criminal sessions here which will probably last into October. The hotel doesn't seem to have improved much and it's still very noisy at night. There's no water here and I've a rather upset stomach, probably resulting from eating contaminated food from the dirty kitchen. However, I'm continuing with the hearings.

I gave judgment today at the end of the trial of a former SRB man charged with kidnapping with intent to murder a man named Ali Banginagina, which occurred in February 1979, over five years ago. At that time the head of the SRB in Busoga was Captain Rwakaikara, whose cover job was as ADC/1 in the DC's office at Iganga trading centre. The accused, Kairugaru, was a one-armed army sergeant-major transferred to SRB whose cover was as an NCO in the District Administration Police. These two SRB men accused Ali of being in sympathy with Obote's guerrillas from Tanzania and of collecting funds for them. He denied this but the SRB brought three soldiers in civilian clothes to live in Ali's house and keep an eye open for visits there from guerrillas.

After a few days the accused arrested Ali, beat him and took him to the DC's office for interrogation. Others were detained there and they were all beaten badly with whips and sticks and tortured in various unpleasant ways. The only survivor, an Arab called Saidi, testified that they all felt sure they would not live to see their families again. All except Saidi were taken to Gaddafi Army Barracks in Jinja by the accused and were not seen again. The bodies of these SRB victims were usually thrown into the Nile below the dam for the crocodiles to consume. The accused admitted most of the events related but claimed that he was only a driver who had to follow his superior's orders. However, the evidence indicated otherwise and I convicted him. There is the death penalty for this offence but the court can pass a prison sentence instead, depending upon the circumstances. This accused had been on remand in prison for five years so I gave him another ten years to serve.

Thursday 27 September

Judgment today in yet another kidnapping with intent to murder case. This was not the usual SRB case but confined to the police. The accused, Sebbi, was an Assistant Commissioner of Police and Busoga Provincial Police Commander in February 1977, seven and a half years ago. The victims were senior police officers and so were all the prosecution witnesses, who secretly recorded the facts and their statements and preserved them for a future trial. Thus, although it happened a long time ago, the evidence given was much more factual and credible than is usual from the ordinary civilian witnesses. The open investigation was carried out in mid-1979 but there was no explanation of the delay of five years in bringing the case to trial.

Sebbi was typical of that time. He was a Nubian detective corporal in the police who was promoted directly to senior superintendent and then to assistant commissioner, without education, training or experience. Merit in Amin's day was irrelevant. What mattered was that he was the right tribe and religion and ready to initiate or carry out murderous assignments. The other officers involved, superintendents down to inspectors, were all experienced, well-trained officers who had attended courses outside and had earned their ranks.

On the day in question Sebbi instructed Superintendent Kiwoma, his staff officer, to summon all officers to attend an address by him (Sebbi) at 4 p.m. At the meeting Sebbi complained of lack of respect and discipline by the officers, who habitually referred to him as 'the corporal', which was what he had been when serving under them, before being promoted over their heads. While he was haranguing his officers a car arrived bringing four military police in civilian clothes. One of these was the warrant officer in charge of the Special Investigation Branch of the Jinja Military Police, with whom Sebbi had a private talk. He then called over Superintendent Odeke and Deputy Superintendent Esolo (who were the two who most often referred to Sebbi as 'the corporal') and told the military police that 'these are the people you wanted'. Sebbi ordered them to get into Odeke's car with the military police warrant officer. When they drove off, Sebbi followed behind in his car. They went first to Bugembe military police barracks, where the two police officers were held at gunpoint and Sebbi said: 'My part in this affair is finished.' He took away Esolo's office keys and instructed his own driver to take over and drive the two officers 'to Nakasero in Kampala', the SRB HQ, and he was not to stop on the way. The driver testified that he saw the two officers taken into the SRB building at Nakasero and they were never seen again. When the driver returned to Jinja he secretly told the officers (now witnesses) how the two had been very roughly treated on arrival at Nakasero. A month later Sebbi had the families of the two missing officers evicted from their government quarters and they were given no assistance to go back to their homes.

I convicted Sebbi on both counts but, luckily for him, decided not to sentence him to death although it was a very bad case. He had begged to be sentenced as 'a humble corporal' and not as a senior officer, which he admitted he ought not to have been. But that was not on, of course. He had been in prison custody for five years so I gave him another fifteen years concurrently on each count to serve, which was less than he deserved.

Friday 28 September

In contrast was the judgment I delivered today in a case against two soldiers and a civilian accused of a series of eight armed robberies in Naluwerere Village two years ago. At the start, the prosecuting state attorney withdrew five of the counts against the accused and asked for the remaining three to be reduced to simple robbery, which meant the case should have been taken before the Chief Magistrate here instead of the High Court.

The witnesses he produced all constantly contradicted themselves and each other and proved to be worthless. For instance, one woman victim testified that she had not been assaulted or injured nor had she been to hospital, after evidence had already been given to prove her injuries and medical treatment. The civilian accused was named and arrested ten months after the robberies although he lived in the same village and was known to all three victims. No explanations were offered for these and numerous other inconsistencies and contradictions in the prosecution case, so I threw it out and acquitted all three accused; though it doesn't mean they were innocent.

Friday 12 October

I finished the Jinja criminal sessions on Wednesday but was stuck here because the court failed to send up the cash for the October part of the hotel and court expenses until this morning. The extended time merely added to the bills, of course. Typical.

Thursday 25 October

Today I dealt with a divorce petition under the Hindu Marriage and Divorce Act. The parties were both Hindus and members of the Ramgarhia Sikh Society who were married at the Sikh Temple in Old Kampala in September 1958 when they were living in Mbarara. The petition, on grounds of adultery and cruelty, was brought by the wife and was not defended. The family left Uganda in 1972, when Amin expelled the Asians, and they remained in India for 11 years and returned to Uganda in 1983. However, the husband took to drinking *enguli* excessively and frequently became violent and beat her. He then stopped providing money and support for the family. When her parents visited from Kenya and gave her money he abused and quarrelled with them and ordered them out. Both parties were now occupying different flats in the same building in Kampala but they didn't visit each other. He had ordered her to have no visitors there, but the wife found him in bed with their African housegirl, who left her job shortly afterwards.

I granted the divorce but no alimony was asked for and, although the wife asked for custody of their five children, they were all, in fact, over the age of fifteen and so entitled to decide which parent they wished to live with. The adults among them, of course, could go their own way.

Monday 5 November

I'm to preside over a treason trial – apparently no other judge will touch it, so it has to be me. At first there were no advocates willing to undertake the defence of the six accused persons as they consider it to be too risky to represent them. This is understandable in the circumstances. I called in Henry Kayondo, the President of the Uganda Law Society, and asked him to assist. He was a Law School Bar student and, before that, a colleague in the police, so I knew I could rely on him.

I said that these people have to be defended. If not they'll just be taken away and you can guess what will probably happen to them. He agreed to defend one of them and managed to persuade five other advocates to join him and defend the other five. It's a very stout effort on their part.

Wednesday 7 November

I've already started the treason trial, which is going to be a long one. Apart from a large number of witnesses there are six accused persons, each with an advocate wanting to be heard and to examine and cross-examine the witnesses. Treason is a capital offence here and the Deputy DPP is prosecuting the case; which isn't saying a lot, since he's not much good. The first accused is Balaki Kirya, who has been a well-known politician in Uganda since Protectorate days. The second accused, Sajjad Soori, is a Pakistani and the other four are Ugandans.

We started off with an application to strike out two counts of treason against Kirya and Soori on the ground that this court has no jurisdiction to try them. The indictment alleges that within and outside Uganda they plotted by force of arms to overturn the Uganda Government, then lists eight overt acts supporting the charge, all of which occurred in Kenya in 1981 and 1982 and none in Uganda. If some acts are done in Uganda and some outside, it is still the offence of treason, but in this instance all the acts were done outside Uganda, which meant that, as submitted by the defence, the court has no jurisdiction to try them.

The prosecution was relying on an amendment last month to the Act granting jurisdiction in treason offences over Ugandans who committed such offences outside Uganda. If this is applicable then it would certainly affect Kirya, a Ugandan. But there is no proof, and not even an assertion, that Soori is a Ugandan or even a resident here. Apart from this, defence counsel argued that this recent 1984 amendment could not be applied retrospectively to acts done in 1981 and 1982. The prosecution argued that as it was merely a procedural amendment it could be treated as retrospective, which is so if it was. But I held that it was not procedural as it affected the jurisdiction of the court, which is a constitutional matter, and it created a new class of offence not existing before or at the time when the alleged acts were done.

Thus the two counts were defective for want of jurisdiction and I ordered them to be struck out. This leaves other counts outstanding against both accused, so the trial could then get under way.

The court-room is crowded each day with spectators and journalists from all the newspapers, the radio and UTV. There's a lot of interest in the outcome of this trial, and the six accused have many sympathisers.

Friday 16 November

The prosecution has been producing a string of witnesses who were themselves recruited as guerrillas in the bush, but then escaped or were captured, and are now employed as so-called security personnel in Vice-President Muwanga's Office. In each case they first claimed to be otherwise employed as traders, taxi drivers and so on, until I demanded identity cards. These were reluctantly produced after each spent a few hours in the cells. Clearly their employment by the VP was not meant to be revealed and I castigated the prosecutor for assisting in trying to hide these facts from the court. They have been given these security jobs and paid money to be prosecution witnesses in this case; and they thought they could hoodwink me.

The newspapers are lapping it all up since the trial provides them with front page material each day as each witness reveals what was going on in the bush. *The Star*, for instance, heads each front page: 'Kirya Treason Trial – Day 8 (or 9 or 10 etc)'.

The evidence of some of the prosecution witnesses of their recruitment, training and exploits in the bush is so absurd and nonsensical as to be beyond belief. Some of them, when questioned, don't know one end of a weapon from the other and confuse weapons and military terms in obvious ignorance. One described the NRA attack on Lubiri barracks in Kampala in February and said that none of those who took part in the attack had any ammunition in their weapons, in spite of which they managed to make a great deal of gun-fire noise, shot up the garrison and took it over for a while. Other witnesses contradicted this and said of course their weapons were all loaded.

When the many inconsistencies are put to them by any of the defence counsel, in terms of – how can you say this when you earlier said that? – the answer usually is: 'I don't know.'

Monday 19 November

One of the many problems in court these days when weapons are exhibited is that we have no ballistics expert in Uganda since Amin got rid of the last of the expatriate police officers. This makes it difficult when evidence regarding firearms and ammunition is required. Some years ago I gave a ruling that such evidence may be given by a police officer of some rank and considerable service who has handled and used the particular weapon regularly and frequently. But officers in this category are not easy to find now.

I often find in court that the prosecutor and defence counsel have absolutely no knowledge of firearms and just don't know what questions to ask, often leaving me as the only person there who has some knowledge of them. However, a judge has to be careful of making use of his own knowledge as it isn't evidence. So it becomes difficult at times, especially when I'm aware that a witness is mistaken, ignorant or lying in his evidence about a weapon and neither counsel is in a position to pick it up.

In this treason case, for instance, a witness yesterday was claiming to be an expert on the SAM 7 and to have been trained to use and fire it, and he had trained others. His credibility in this and other statements he had made had to be tested but there was nobody in court, or available to the court, qualified to do this. None of counsel knew a SAM 7 from a refrigerator. At the end of his examination and cross-examination no questions had been asked about this so I asked him to describe a SAM 7 and how to fire it. This Russian-made weapon is called a *strela* (arrow) in the USSR or, in the West, Surface to Air Missile 7 (SAM 7). It's small and one-man portable, carried in a sling. The launcher tube, missile and high-explosive warhead weigh only 10 kilograms complete and it's only a metre and a half long with a slant range of 3,500 metres. Its main use is to bring down low-flying aircraft.

This witness, however, insisted that it was a large, heavy weapon requiring four men to carry and fire it, with a range of 10,000 metres. All the information given by him was wrong but there was nobody else to challenge him. I put the correct figures to him but he totally disagreed and insisted that he knew all about the SAM 7. I said to him: 'Your description of the SAM 7 is all wrong and you have scored no marks out of ten for your efforts'; and made a note at the end of his testimony that his evidence was inaccurate.

Thursday 22 November

The trial continues with witness after witness all claiming to be ex-guerrillas taken from the bush. So far not one has given the appearance of being truthful or reliable as a witness. One claimed that the accused Pakistani, Soori, was their chief weapons instructor who was sent with a lieutenant to Entebbe to shoot down Obote's presidential jet aircraft with him in it. The take-off was delayed for some reason, which should have given them ample time to be ready to fire the SAM 7 missile but, when the aircraft did take off, Soori and his assistant couldn't find the firing mechanism on this simple weapon. Meanwhile the plane flew off. Some weapons instructor.

Thursday 29 November

A witness has been describing how he and Kirya were arrested in Nairobi, assaulted by the Kenya police and then handed over to Ugandan authorities. They were then taken to Tororo army barracks, where they were blindfolded and driven to Kampala and there detained in Luzira prison.

It's never easy to get a Swahili interpreter in the High Court. Most of our interpreters are Baganda and they are loftily disdainful of anyone who speaks Swahili, which they have always regarded as the language of *askaris* and domestic servants and therefore not worth knowing. So usually we have to make do with a policeman or prison warder who is unskilled in the art of interpretation, when a witness or accused chooses to speak Swahili.

Yesterday I used a prison warder as interpreter for such a witness and it didn't go too well. The warder's Swahili was even worse than mine and several times I had to correct him when he translated a question into something rather different. At the end of the afternoon I thanked him and added: 'I don't think much of your Swahili, though,' which caused some amusement among the advocates and police in court who had listened to us struggling through.

In various parts of Kampala for the last week or so there have been explosions, usually in the afternoons, as saboteurs plant bombs pretty well at random. Several have been in the Nakivubo area, where there are plenty of people but absolutely nothing of any strategic importance. Perhaps the object is to cause panic, unrest and instability. Shopkeepers have consequently increased the prices of ordinary commodities in their usual reaction to anything.

Wednesday 5 December

On Monday we came at last to the end of the prosecution case in the treason trial and the various defence advocates were required to inform the court whether their clients were going to testify in their defence. Four of them, including Soori, said they would make unsworn statements. So they can't be cross-examined on them. Counsel for Kirya and for the sixth accused submitted that their clients had no case to answer, so I had to deal with these two first and I gave my ruling yesterday morning.

After my ruling at the commencement of the trial, only one count containing one overt act remained against Kirya. This was that, as chairman of the Uganda Freedom Movement (UFM) from November 1981 to July 1982, he sent a large number of armed people from Kenya for the purpose of levying war against Uganda. The three witnesses relied upon by the prosecution to prove this count were not only discredited but none actually gave any evidence of activities relevant to the charge. For instance, there was no evidence of a planned invasion of Uganda from Kenya; only of guerrilla actions within Uganda. Furthermore, there was no evidence of Kirya committing even the smallest part of his alleged activities inside Uganda. Whatever he did, if anything, was entirely in Kenya and, following my earlier ruling on jurisdiction, I held that the prosecution had failed to make out any case of Kirya committing a treasonable act within the court's jurisdiction. Consequently I found that he had no case to answer and ordered his immediate release. A prison warder in the court then attempted to take him into custody as he was trying to leave the court but I quickly intervened and stopped that and blasted the warder, much to the amusement of the spectators, who were in a celebratory mood and loudly accompanied Kirya out of the court, where he was greeted with cheers and congratulations. Apparently he was then rearrested and taken away; just as one would expect with the present government.

I next decided that the sixth accused had a case of some sort to answer, not on account of the strength or credibility of the prosecution evidence, but merely because some witnesses had implicated him and I wanted to hear his explanation, if any. *The Star* made the most out of today with a front page headline: 'Treason Trial – Day 24: Acquittal Causes Drama in Court'.

The rest of yesterday I spent hearing the defence case, which didn't take long since all five of the remaining accused chose to make brief unsworn statements denying any involvement in the activities charged. I then adjourned until today for final speeches of counsel. As no defence witnesses had been called, the defence had the last word. Next I summed up the evidence for the benefit of the assessors and pointed out that all the prosecution eyewitnesses were themselves confessed guerrillas who were therefore not only traitors who could be convicted of this offence, but also dubious and unreliable since they had changed sides twice, in some cases, and had had no compunction about swearing loyalty to both sides. They could be taken to be accomplices of the accused and their testimony was thereby tainted and ought to be corroborated. Furthermore, as accomplices they could not usefully corroborate each other and we needed to look for independent reliable corroboration, which, in fact, had not been provided by the prosecution.

I pointed out that some of the witnesses who had claimed and emphasised that they had been forced into joining the guerillas in the bush had joined in the fight with so much enthusiasm that they had been promoted and had trained others, which hardly supported their assertions of reluctance to be involved.

After my summing-up, the assessors asked to be able to give their opinions on Friday morning as they had a lot to think about. As I have really no interest in the opinions of assessors and have always regarded them as a waste of time, since they are untrained and often illogical, like juries for instance, and I was already mentally working on my judgment, I only reluctantly agreed to the two days delay.

Friday 7 December

The court was packed this morning, with journalists occupying the front two rows of public seats. Outside, the court compound was surrounded by armed police Special Force personnel and armed prison warders. What a fuss. It looked as though something was up. As I opened my mouth to ask the first assessor to give his opinion, Kabega, the state attorney who has been assisting the deputy DPP, and doing most of the work, stood up and said: 'I have just received instructions from the DPP that continuing with this case is no longer in the public interest. The DPP has instructed me to file a *nolle prosequi* [notice of withdrawal of the prosecution].'

Definitely unpleased, I demanded to know why the sudden change of mind and why we had all wasted five weeks trying a case in which the DPP had no interest. Kabega was very embarrassed; it was not his fault, of course, and he said: 'Those are the instructions I was given this morning.'

I replied: 'Then you should have had the courtesy to come to my chambers first to tell me before I came into court.' I discharged the five remaining accused and told them they were free to go but, of course, they were rearrested outside by the police, as always.

Perhaps the government wished to avoid the embarrassment of the judgment and scathing remarks they knew they could expect from me after my preliminary rulings and the summing-up to the assessors, in which I had clearly indicated the way I was thinking about their miserable witnesses and the case generally. There had been an appallingly incompetent investigation and preparation of it for prosecution, due mainly to the constant muddling interference of the military and the Vice-President's security agents and Rwakasisi's National Security

Agency (NASA) in what should have been left to the police to handle. It was Kirya whom they were really after and hoping to get sentenced to death. So, when I released him, I think they lost interest and simply acted vindictively by taking the accused back into custody for no lawful reason.

Saturday 8 December

While I've been fully occupied with this treason trial other games were afoot. Apparently, before it commenced, the opposition Democratic Party leader, Paul Ssemogerere, claimed that he had got hold of a copy of a letter written by the Chief Justice to the President recommending that, before the Kirya trial commenced, various DP leaders, including Ssemogerere himself, should be arrested and detained. Of course, the CJ has no business dabbling in this sort of thing, but it seems quite typical of him. It appears that Obote then denied ever receiving the CJ's letter, which nobody believes. Ssemogerere next held a news conference and read out his own letter to the President as well as the CJ's original letter and stated that he had 'withdrawn his confidence in the Chief Justice of Uganda ... for failing to maintain the traditional independent role of Chief Justice'. He added that 'there could be no sustainable explanation as to why the head of the judicial service plots with government and police to deny citizens of the country due process of law'. Following this, Ssemogerere and his National Publicity Secretary, who is also a Democratic Party MP, and the editor of their Luganda newspaper, *Munnansi*, were all three charged with uttering and publishing seditious matter. This offence is triable by the Kampala Chief Magistrate, who has fixed the trial to start on 17 December and released the three accused on cash bail.

Thursday 13 December

At the judges meeting today, at which as usual I sat silent, the CJ suddenly turned to me and asked why I, as chairman of the library committee, had held no meetings this year. I dislike committees and meetings of any sort and avoid them like the plague, but this time I had a good excuse. I pointed out that, as he was well aware, the library had received no allocation of funds at all, let alone the necessary foreign exchange, so we were unable to subscribe to any British law journals or law reports or purchase any law books or even *The Times* for its excellent law reports. There was therefore no reason to hold a meeting for the selection of such items for the library, and the day-to-day running of the, thus, static library required no meetings. That shut him up. But it's all rather a pity as we're getting so out of touch.

Monday 17 December

The Ssemogerere sedition trial didn't start today. A few days ago, after I'd read what the papers were saying about this case, I decided that it would be better if the whole matter came before the High Court to be dealt with, so I sent instructions to the Registrar to bring the Chief Magistrate's court file before me to make an order. When he brought the file up he reported that defence counsel, Mulenga, had, in fact, just filed an application to remove the case to the High Court for trial. So I fixed it to come before me this morning (the original trial date) and gave my ruling this afternoon. Mulenga submitted that the law of sedition was complicated and required the expertise and experience of a High Court judge, and that the integrity of the Chief Justice should not be enquired into by any lesser judicial officer than a judge. In my ruling granting the application I said that it was appropriate that such a serious affair concerning imputations against the Chief Justice should be dealt with in this court.

Now it's up to the DPP to process the case for a High Court trial without delay. Meanwhile, I have directed that the bail stands as a High Court order and nobody is to interfere with it. I made a special point of this because it's clear that certain people want to keep these three chaps in custody if they can possibly arrange it. As the CJ is named as the complainant in this case, he cannot be involved in arranging the court proceedings, which I suppose might be slightly vexing for him.

Thursday 27 December

Not a very good Christmas this year. Since I don't usually bother to celebrate birthdays and Christmas I followed my normal procedure and paid my cook and *shamba* boy their wages for the month plus a Christmas bonus and sent them both off to their home villages to spend the period with their families. I've had plenty of experience of looking after myself so it was not likely to be a problem. Unfortunately we've had no piped water all month and I've managed to contract a streaming cold that has turned into influenza over Christmas. I feel like death warmed up and have had to resort to the, for me, unusual remedy of taking aspirins.

Monday 31 December

The Kirya case was the second treason trial in Uganda. The first was against the DP MP, Professor Yoweri Kyesimira, in which the evidence was heard early this year but the trial judge seems to be rather reluctant to write a judgment. It now appears that, following the ending of my Kirya trial, they are likely to free Kyesimira, but in return for that they apparently expect the professor to cross the floor and join the UPC. If he doesn't, as seems likely, he'll just stay in detention. I suspect no judgment will now be delivered in that case in any event.

1985

Wednesday 2 January

Last August Vice-President Muwanga visited North Korea and, as a result, they have sent somewhere around 700 military personnel to train the UNLA. Amin did the same for his army. Their expertise is in cruel and painful interrogation and unarmed killing methods. We really don't need this sort of thing, whatever Muwanga thinks. Now we have them here again teaching Ugandans how to be more efficient killers of their own people. They have been active up in the Luwero Triangle against the NRA, which has been getting the upper hand recently and has established its HQ in Ssingo county around the area of my old station at Mityana.

A short while back the NRA claimed to have killed about 140 UNLA troops and three North Koreans and to have taken seven North Koreans as prisoners in fire-fights in that area. Why on earth can't these people call off this stupid, senseless civil war and just talk together about sharing government and rebuilding this wonderful country instead of continuing with this meaningless killing and useless destruction?

Thursday 15 January

For years I've been dealing with the probate of wills and the administration of estates and it's become very noticeable that many more Ugandan men these days die of heart attacks caused by high blood pressure in the excessive stress and tension of modern life in Uganda; whereas before it used to be old age or, more commonly, the usual tropical diseases like malaria, sleeping sickness, smallpox and so on that carried them off. In one such matter this morning the death certificate said: 'Death due to high blood pleasure caused by hippo-tension'. It's an interesting variation.

Tuesday 5 February

Yesterday I came to Masaka to commence a long criminal sessions, with 12 murder and rape cases. In the course of the Tanzanian invasion in 1979 Masaka was almost destroyed. This was quite unnecessary but a part of Nyerere's plan to damage and destroy so as to punish Amin and Uganda. There was practically no fighting here as Amin's troops fled, so the TPDF simply blew up many of the buildings. Now, six years later, the buildings are still unrepaired. There are collapsed houses and shops everywhere; the modern hotel in town was so badly damaged that it is no longer safe to use, so I am staying in the guest house of the RDC, a foreign development company doing some rebuilding here. There's no water at the place and the fittings and furniture are very primitive. The court building was also badly damaged but there are parts of it that can be used, although I suspect that the structure is not all that stable. However, I have a court-room and the use of chambers, so I can manage. Amazingly enough for Masaka, I've actually had acceptable pleas of guilty to manslaughter in five cases, which has got us off to a good start.

Friday 8 February

I gave judgment yesterday in the trial of two men on four counts of aggravated robbery. Each was armed, one with a gun and the other with a *panga*, and they stood at the roadside near Namirembe swamp in Masaka district and robbed passers-by of money and watches. Most of the victims were on bicycles returning home from selling second-hand clothing at Kanamusabala market. One gunshot was fired at a man who was running away, but fortunately it missed. A chief and a group of people from the market came to the scene and the man with the gun, urged on by his companion, tried to fire his gun again at them, but it jammed. The robbers were then seized and the gun, an SMG with 25 rounds in the magazine, was produced as an exhibit. It was capable of being fired and so qualified as a deadly weapon. Their story was that they too were the victims of robbers and had been wrongly arrested by the chief and his people. But they were clearly identified by a number of witnesses in daylight and there was no doubt of their guilt. This is a capital offence and after I had convicted them both I had no choice but to sentence them to death. Wish I could have avoided it. I shall recommend that the President exercises the prerogative of mercy (commuting the sentence to imprisonment) in my 'Trial Judge's Report' if and when their appeal fails.

Tuesday 12 February

The second trial was for murder. A Second Lieutenant Ouma from the UNLA barracks at Masaka was charged with shooting and killing his friend Second Lieutenant Kalibo. At a place called Nabusanke they both arrested one Private Kassim, who they knew was wanted for stealing a lorry from a civilian. Instead of driving straight back to barracks with Kassim, they stopped at Lukaya Trading Centre for drinks and to visit Kalibo's girl-friend.

Kassim managed to escape there and Ouma blamed Kalibo, quarrelled with him indoors and fired three shots at him with his Chinese-made automatic pistol, hitting him in the head and heart and killing him. Ouma in court claimed that they were both very drunk when they quarrelled and Kalibo had fired at him first and then he fired back in self-defence. However, the evidence of other witnesses showed that only Ouma fired his gun, but he was very drunk at the time and had blamed Kalibo for the escape. I convicted him of manslaughter and sentenced him to six years to add to the two and a half years he had been in custody awaiting trial.

Thursday 14 February

I acquitted the accused men in two rape cases today. One case was so badly investigated by the police, with all the obvious evidential requirements omitted or ignored, and so poorly prosecuted by the state attorney, that I directed that a copy of my judgment be placed before the DPP and the IG Police – though I don't suppose it will do much good.

In the second case the 'victim' had clearly agreed to intercourse and then changed her mind later to avoid retribution from her husband. She was a dreadful witness in court, quite obviously lying, constantly contradicting herself and the evidence of other prosecution witnesses, and the case could not possibly succeed.

Thursday 28 February

This circuit ended today, the last day of the month. The last case involved another UNLA soldier, Lance Corporal Akicha, a regimental policeman 6 feet and 4 inches tall. It was alleged that he went to a house outside Masaka barracks and shot three people there, two of whom were a young woman and her baby. None of these people knew the accused and he didn't know them. There was no apparent motive for the killing and the case really depended upon identification of the accused, which is always tricky, especially in unlit huts at night.

Again the police made a mess of the investigation; no gun was produced as an exhibit; no sketch plan was made of the scene of the crime; no evidence was given of what duty the accused was supposed to be on at the time, nor whether he had been issued with a firearm and ammunition. There was no evidence to support or deny the accused's contention that all the troops were confined to barracks on that day and that he did not go outside, but remained on duty inside barracks; which should have been fairly easy to check. The prosecution merely relied on identification of the accused by two young boys and a girl, who picked out the accused from an identification parade which they should never have attended since they had already told the police that they knew the very tall accused well and had seen him many times before.

However, when I demanded to be shown the police record of the identification parade, which had not been put in as evidence as it should have been, it turned out that the two boys had not in fact picked out the accused at all. The remaining identification by the girl was so shaky and unconvincing, as was her testimony, that so much doubt was raised I felt bound to acquit him.

Friday 1 March

Back in Kampala, where I find that, according to *The Star* the Uganda Law Society has been publicly and strongly criticising the Judiciary for being irresponsible in its duties with long and unnecessary delays and slow trials. They named three judges, including myself, who they said were exceptions who started court promptly on time and dealt with cases properly and with despatch. They also complained about wasting the time of the court and advocates with cases withdrawn before completion – obviously referring to the recent Kirya treason trial – and the rearresting of people released by the courts on bail or acquittal. I don't suppose the CJ or anyone else will take much notice of that, though.

Wednesday 6 March

Ochienghs-Wellborn called into my chambers today for a chat. He's an advocate who normally practises in the Eastern Province, mostly around Tororo but, being a UPC supporter, he was recently appointed as Uganda's Ambassador to Moscow. He invited me to visit him at the embassy there; an invitation I'm extremely unlikely to take up. I just wonder how these chaps cope with such important jobs, with absolutely no experience in government or administration or diplomacy. I suppose they just rely on self-confidence and charm and a lot of bluff.

On the 17th it will be exactly 30 years since I first set foot in East Africa and, in spite of all the problems and difficulties, I wouldn't have wanted to spend the time in any other way.

Thursday 25 April

At last, after all this time, the new tiles which Works have managed to find from somewhere have been fixed to the roof of my house, replacing those which were forcibly removed, broken or cracked when the shell exploded over the roof in the 1979 Tanzanian invasion.

Friday 26 April

At a long and boring judges meeting today the matter came up of what to do about one of the judges, who was not present, who came back from many years of exile and is quite obviously going round the bend – even more noticeably so than the rest of us. He does not attend to his duties and wanders around the court building half-dressed and shouting at people and strays into other busy court-rooms and causes considerable embarrassment. His wife has to be fetched to collect him and take him home since he won't go with anyone else; and it's all rather disturbing.

Obviously he needs proper psychiatric treatment but he doesn't realise it and becomes violent when it is suggested to him. The other day I was warned by a colleague on the phone that he had announced that he was on his way 'to get' me. I waited in chambers and, when he threw the door open and came in, I greeted him in a friendly fashion and talked about an imaginary problem I told him I was having with the military which I said only he could advise me on because of his past experience as a legal officer in the army – until Amin got rid of him and he came into the Judiciary. After a brief chat he seemed calmer, and he got up and walked out. By then his wife had been fetched and she took him home. Apparently he had not been taking his sedation tablets regularly.

Monday 6 May

I was supposed to go on circuit to Jinja today but by the end of the afternoon they had not produced any cash to pay for it, so I didn't go.

The money allocated has unsurprisingly all been taken and misused elsewhere.

Thursday 9 May

I was asked to speak to a seminar for magistrates at the LDC this afternoon. It's really a refresher course for magistrates who have been many years in the field without attending one, so I met again some old Law School types whom I hadn't seen for a long time. I brought them up to date on various procedural matters and we discussed many of their problems, most of which unfortunately have existed for so long without any hope of change in the situation being in sight, and will no doubt stay that way.

Tuesday 11 June

The Ssemogerere sedition case involving the CJ has come before me again. In December I ordered that it should be prepared for trial in the High Court without delay. Three months later nothing had been done and the Chief Magistrate across the road dismissed the case for want of prosecution. The State then applied to this court to reinstate the case.

As I said in my ruling on this application, it had come up before the Chief Magistrate on eight occasions when, each time, a different junior state attorney appeared and simply applied for an adjournment as they said that they weren't ready to proceed. This clearly showed incompetence and a lack of interest in an important case which should have been handled throughout by an experienced senior state attorney making a real effort to achieve some results.

The CM in fact has no power to dismiss this case but he was obviously frustrated by the delaying tactics of the DPP's department. I have reinstated the case and ordered it to be committed to the High Court for trial by the end of June. If the DPP really doesn't want to go ahead with this case then why on earth did he ever bring it to court? Politics, I suppose. Someone else was probably pushing him. I wonder what the CJ thinks about it? Does he really want to appear in court as a witness and be cross-examined?

Wednesday 12 June

The BHC held a reception for the Queen's birthday at 5 p.m. today. Madame once again pretended she didn't know me and asked what I do here. I just said: 'Oh, nothing very important,' and moved on. The Police Band was there and, as always, put on an excellent performance, including a very well done British national anthem, which they probably haven't played for years. Most faces in the band were new but there were one or two I recognised from the past and we exchanged greetings.

Monday 17 June

I was supposed to lecture to the magistrates at the LDC this afternoon but there has been quite a lot of gun-fire and also a number of explosions around Kampala lately and nobody turned up. They were understandably all lying low, so I just checked in at the LDC office and drove home.

Saturday 22 June

Earlier this month I was invited to be the guest speaker at a lunch held yesterday by the Uganda Law Society at the Imperial Hotel. There were several matters that I took the opportunity to bring up. One of them was the reluctance of most advocates to take legal aid cases – because they are paid so very little that it is regarded by them as a completely non-profitable chore. I pointed out to them the importance of providing a defence advocate for poor accused persons in serious cases and that Uganda can't afford to pay high fees. I added that most of them had obtained their qualifications and professional careers from a scholarship paid for out of public funds and that they therefore owed it to their people to try and pay back some of it by way of giving such assistance without expecting to make any profit from it. I'm afraid this as usual fell largely on deaf ears. I'm told by those with TV sets that an extract from this talk was shown on UTV news.

One advocate complained afterwards that I did not offer any praise for what they were doing. So I asked: 'Praise for doing such as like what?'

Monday 24 June

Professor James Read called in to see me in chambers. He's from the London University School of Oriental and African Studies and I've known him since Law School days, when he was a lecturer in law at Dar-es-Salaam University in Tanzania, or Tanganyika as it then was. He's now an external law examiner for Makerere University and visits here each year on some sort of swan. I am an external examiner, too, but I'm not eligible for the free travel and hotel perks that he has, more's the pity. In fact, I don't even receive the often-promised examiner's fee. Probably because I haven't asked for it. Just as I refused a fee for the LDC lectures, as I regard it all as a part of my personal contribution to much-needed assistance. That was the general idea that I tried to put over to the members of the Law Society the other day, without mentioning my own part, of course.

Thursday 27 June

According to *The Star* the committal proceedings in the Ssemogerere sedition case are taking place in the nick of time, since I ordered that they be completed by the end of June. I wish they'd get on with things without the need for these constant nonsenses which somehow seem to find their way before me to be sorted out.

Thursday 4 July

Yesterday's and today's front page headlines in *The Star* concern the fact that, after Ssemogerere and the other two accused in the sedition case were committed for trial in the High Court by the magistrate, he quite rightly followed the order I had deliberately put there, not to interfere with the present bail conditions of the three accused imposed by me. The DPP for some reason desperately wants them in prison on remand. I don't know why, but I suspect it's due to political pressure from above, which is what I foresaw when I made the original order.

Normally, after committal proceedings, the magistrate can remand the accused in custody or release him or them on bail, but by interposing my order there, I have deliberately prevented their being remanded in custody. The DPP is apparently appealing against the magistrate having followed my order, which the lower court must do. Well, we shall see what we shall see.

Tuesday 9 July

Yesterday evening I had dinner with Peter Penfold, who is the Deputy British High Commissioner, at this moment acting as High Commissioner. There were various things to discuss and it was a very pleasant and enjoyable evening. I'd sent my driver home earlier, as neither he nor I wanted him to be out after dark these days, so I was given a lift home by two of the Royal Military Police SAS-trained Close Protection Unit. Apparently only the Kampala High Commission and the British Embassy at Bogotá, Colombia, are regarded as dangerous and hazardous enough to warrant such units. They told me that one night they were driving back to the High Commission here when someone opened fire on them from a compound as they passed. So they returned rapid and concentrated fire at that point which immediately shut them up.

This afternoon I lectured to the magistrates at the LDC on the important subject of the judicial conduct of magistrates. I think it went quite well, but at the moment I'm rather concerned with someone else's judicial conduct.

The people concerned with the sedition case have now seen my hand appearing and directing procedures in it several times, though not from my choice. The file has been laid before me each time and, like any other file, I then proceed to deal with it. I certainly haven't asked for the case. But someone, and I think I can guess who, has decided to try to end this and has worked out that the way to neutralise my efforts and prevent me from having any more to do with the case is by making me a witness in it.

So yesterday afternoon a senior CID officer came to my chambers saying that he had had orders from the IG to take my 'statement'. Since I know absolutely nothing about the affair outside of what I've been dealing with in court, it was a very brief statement and totally negative in value to either side. But now that they have it they are claiming that I am a potential witness, though they surely have no intention of calling me to testify since it would obviously give me an opportunity to say things that mightn't be helpful to the complainant CJ. Just so long as they don't try to mess around with the orders I've made so far.

Friday 19 July

When Amin was in power his Nubians, aided by Ugandans from western and eastern tribes, massacred many Acholi and Langi soldiers, who were thus fellow victims then. Now that Obote is President his Langi are on top and they and the Acholi have resumed their former intertribal hatred and are killing each other again. This, of course, is of considerable assistance to Museveni and the NRA westerners aided by the Baganda. They are carrying out a guerrilla warfare against an army that is also fighting itself, and all for no good reason.

Some time back Otai, the Minister of State for Defence, went to Bulgaria and purchased a large consignment of weapons destined for Langi units based around Lira. These were intercepted at Entebbe airport by Vice-President Muwanga's security officers and sent to an Acholi unit based at Mbuya barracks, just outside Kampala. So what is Muwanga up to?

Brigadier Opon Acak, a Lango and the Chief of Staff, sent Langi soldiers to Mbuya to collect the arms consignment, and there followed a fire-fight between Langi and Acholi soldiers. Muwanga tried to quell public alarm at the fighting by using gobbledegook and describing it as 'unco-ordinated troop manoeuvres'. The Army Commander, Major-General Tito Okello, has left Kampala and gone to Gulu, where many Acholi in the Army have joined him, including the powerful Lieutenant-Colonel Bazilio Okello, who Opon Acak has announced on the radio has been dismissed from the Army. In reply Tito Okello from Gulu has demanded Bazilio's reinstatement and that Opon Acak should be the one dismissed instead. Things are hotting up, it seems, and it doesn't look good for Obote now as all around him everything seems to be falling apart.

Monday 22 July

This wretched sedition case has been before me again. It was apparently fixed before another judge, but the CR told me that none of them wants anything to do with such a sensitive case involving the CJ and the DP party leader as it's too hot to handle. So it keeps being placed before me as they well know that I don't refuse to take cases.

The DPP filed an appeal against the committing magistrate's refusal to ignore my bail order and remand the three accused in custody, as required by a recent amendment to the procedure – which, incidentally, I knew nothing about as we in the High Court were not consulted about it by the CJ, or even given copies of the amendment afterwards. The usual shambles, in fact.

In court the DPP protested that I should not be hearing this appeal as I had made the original order that the magistrate had followed and that they were now appealing against. I said that it must surely be the magistrate's order they were appealing against, not mine, otherwise they'd have to go to the Court of Appeal. He then rather abruptly and rudely demanded a ruling on his application to remove the matter from me. I said that before considering that I must first discover whether there was in fact an appeal to be heard by anyone, and I wanted to hear what the defence counsel had to say about that. The DPP petulantly again demanded an instant ruling and I repeated what I had just said. He then snatched up his files and books and stamped out of court.

There was silence for a moment as everyone stared, shocked at this blatant discourtesy, which was in my view a clear contempt of court. I then asked the defence advocates for their submissions. None of them objected to my hearing the matter and I particularly wanted to put an opinion on record regarding this latest procedural amendment, which was probably the CJ's work.

I pointed out that due often to delays by the DPP in capital offences the High Court will very often have released an accused on bail before he eventually comes before a magistrate to be committed for trial. So, if the magistrate is now required by the amended statute to remand the accused in custody, he would have to overrule or ignore the bail order already made by the High Court, which he is not permitted to do. No subordinate court can ignore or change an order of the High Court. Because of not consulting the judges before hastily passing this legislation, this anomaly has arisen. It was obviously designed as part of the CJ's exercise to limit the bail powers of the High Court.

I said that the amendment was unconstitutional as it takes away bail rights granted by the Constitution and that this has been done for no good reason but is merely a malicious and mischievous interference with the discretion of the High Court.

On the present issue, I said there is no right of appeal against granting or refusing bail, as the DPP should well know. It is a matter of applying to a higher court to grant or cancel bail. The only statutory right of appeal by the prosecution is against acquittal and nothing else. The so-called appeal before the court is therefore incompetent and must be struck out. There is consequently no appeal to be heard and nothing to disqualify myself from hearing. I ordered that the three accused will remain on bail as previously ordered by me.

I also remarked that the DPP must accept decisions and rulings in court and not argue about them. He had shown considerable disrespect for the court by withdrawing without listening to my decision or explaining himself. Afterwards I let it be known that, as far as I'm concerned, he is in contempt of court and cannot appear before me again until he is ready to apologise in open court for his disrespectful conduct.

Sunday 28 July

On Friday the two Okellos made their move. They took Lira without a fight, then split their forces. One group went eastwards and then south to Soroti, Mbale and Jinja, while the other went westwards and south through Masindi, Hoima, Nakasongola and Bombo to Kampala. There was little or no resistance to these movements.

Yesterday mid-morning I had a phone call from the BHC representative with the message: 'Something's happening today. Keep your head down and don't go out.' Shortly after that all hell broke loose and there was gun-fire accompanied by explosions from all over Kampala, which continued all day long and all last night. It was a sleepless night. I think a lot of it was shooting in the air so as to keep the civilian population indoors. I don't believe there was any actual battle going on.

This morning I rang one or two people to see if they were all right. When I rang one of the judges, Seth Manyindo, his young nephew, Kenneth, answered the phone and told me that Seth had been out when the shooting started yesterday and had been mistaken for a UPC Minister and shot in the arm and leg. He's in Mulago hospital now. I must go there when this business is over and see how he is getting on.

Monday 29 July

A new government has been formed. There is a Military Council of nine men, with General Tito Okello as Head of State and Chairman of the Military Council. He's not calling himself President yet. The Deputy Chairman is Colonel Wilson Toko, from the West Nile, who was shunted out of the military by the previous government and was made chairman of Uganda Airlines. The DP leader, whose case I've been dealing with, Ssemogerere, is now Minister of Internal Affairs, and Mayanja-Nkangi, the Conservative Party leader is to be Minister of Local Government. The big question is who will be Prime Minister? I wonder if the CJ is still around and, if so, how long he will remain in this post. I imagine that the sedition case will now fizzle out.

Nick phoned from the UK to check that I'm all right and I told him what's been happening here. I rang Seth's home and Kenneth reported that Seth is recovering slowly in hospital and is not dangerously injured, which is a considerable relief.

Tuesday 30 July

I managed to get to court this morning in a borrowed small car. My official Mercedes was in for repairs and my driver, Laurence, went to collect it on Saturday morning when all the fun and games started. It wasn't ready and he naturally cleared off and took cover. He has since been to check up and has discovered that the military and civilian looters, who are out all over Kampala, have taken it. A few people turned up at the court but there was nothing doing except for an exchange of gossip and rumour.

It seems that the CJ fled eastwards, probably to Mbale, where he's been building a big house and some business premises. Everyone here is assuming he has gone for good and is speculating about who will replace him. There are not a lot of suitable candidates but several with ambitions that way. Obote has fled to Tanzania.

Thursday 1 August

Appalling news. Yesterday it was announced that the awful Muwanga has been appointed Prime Minister and today he was sworn in. I did not bother to attend the ceremony. What can they be thinking of to appoint him? He doesn't lead any faction and he's universally hated here. The Baganda certainly dislike and distrust him, although he is one of them. This is a very big mistake.

As usual after we've had a coup, someone from Amnesty International called in to see me. We had a chat and I put him on to a couple of matters that could do with his attention.

There's been a certain amount of canvassing among the judges for support by judges who have hopes of becoming Chief Justice or are supporting the name of someone whom they wish to see in the post. It may be that the new government has asked for suggestions. Although asked for my views, I have no influence in the matter as an expatriate and wish to keep out of it. Two judges actually came to my chambers and said they wanted me to be the CJ. I made it clear that my interest is in getting into the Court of Appeal, either to head it or as a member, I don't mind which. The post of CJ is too prominent and gets too much exposure for an expatriate these days and it also involves too much attendance on the President, which would not be to my liking at all.

Saturday 3 August

One of the judges, Mathew Opu, who has now recovered from his recent illness, called on me at home this morning. He said he is now almost sure that I shall be the next CJ. I think he'd been sent to sound me out about it. I said that it was an attractive idea but my real interest was only in the Court of Appeal these days so that I could continue working quietly in the background and out of the public eye, and would he please pass this on to his contacts.

I didn't say so, but my feeling is that, with Museveni and his NRA still out in the bush and growing stronger, this military government is unlikely to last long. Everything about it looks shaky and provisional to me. And with Muwanga heading the government there's bound to be a lot of dissension and oppression. I can't see it settling down easily.

Thursday 8 August

I'm still without transport but managed to get a lift to visit Seth in hospital this afternoon. He seems to be doing well and recovering slowly. He's lucky that someone came along and identified him as a judge and stopped the man from shooting him again and finishing him off. I took him a pile of magazines to occupy his time. Of all the judges, he's the one whom I'd most like to see as the new CJ. I've already mentioned this to Opu and others interested and just hope that it works out that way.

Friday 9 August

The Chief Justice has returned to Kampala. Perhaps he's expecting to take up the reins again now that things have quietened down in Kampala. But he's such a well-known Obote and UPC man that I can't see them agreeing to that – I certainly hope not. On the other hand they made the dreaded Muwanga PM, so I suppose it's possible. This is not a particularly happy thought.

There's been no postal service working since the balloon went up last month. But today a few letters appeared in the box, so it looks as if they're back in business again.

5

Chief Justice: August 1985–August 1986

Thursday 15 August

Because of the lack of transport, and the fact that the courts are not sitting yet, we go in to work for the mornings only at the moment. Just after lunch today my phone rang and the voice at the other end said he was Colonel Toko, the Vice-Chairman of the Military Council. He wanted to know if I could come round to the President's Office at 1630 hours to be sworn in as Chief Justice by General Tito Okello. I was not even asked if I would accept the post, so I said surely it would be better to have a Ugandan in such a prominent post? Toko replied that they were aware that the Judiciary was in a complete mess these days because of the activities of the previous CJ and that it had been agreed by the Military Council and those it had consulted that I was the right person to sort it out.

I then pointed out that I have always kept a very low profile and the idea of constantly being expected to appear at public functions with the Head of State was not to my liking. He replied that they already knew this about me and accepted it but would hope for my attendance at such functions as independence celebrations and those connected with the law. I said that was fair enough and, when he added that the post was substantive not acting, I agreed to be there at 4.30 p.m. But it's not too exciting as the holder of the post of Chief Justice has been changed every time there's a different government in Uganda, which means that my time is probably limited to however long this present government lasts, and my feeling is it will not be for very long. It's good to move to the top judicial post, of course, but not at all good to contemplate an approaching end to my service in Uganda.

I rang Mathew Opu at his home, as I was sure that he'd had a lot to do with this development, and he expressed his delight and couldn't resist saying: 'You see, I told you so!' Then I asked him for a lift to the President's office. They must now find a car for me, I can't rely

620

on lifts to get about. In fact, my predecessor still has the official car and it'll have to be obtained from him, as will the official residence on Nakasero hill.

At the swearing-in, for which I wore a suit, there was a UTV camera and a still photo cameraman from the Ministry of Information. I had a chat with Tito Okello, who seemed to be very pleased about my appointment, and with Colonel Toko, whom I had not met before. All the other judges were there with the Chief Registrar, and a couple of new ministers who were also sworn in. At home this evening, after the usual light meal, I spent the time reading and listening to music. I felt no inclination to celebrate.

Friday 16 August

Quite a day. Telegrams of congratulations came in from magistrates and advocates all over Uganda and phone calls from the UK and from the British High Commissioner and from other embassies. I even heard it announced on the BBC World News and Voice of America. I'm told it was also on German, French and Indian radio news. It seems that everyone was surprised that a Brit should be appointed to this high post in Uganda after what's been happening here for years. Richard Dowden of *The Times* called in and interviewed me, and two other journalists from British newspapers did short interviews over the phone from the UK. The local newspapers seem to be in favour of my appointment. As always, Africa is full of surprises.

Tuesday 20 August

The Germans got in first and I was invited to lunch yesterday with the West German Ambassador. He had some aid people with him and we discussed various projects where they could help. As usual I emphasised that cash should not be handed over, but only well-controlled projects offered.

This afternoon the newly appointed Minister of Justice/Attorney-General called on me. He is Sam Kutesa, a Munyankole advocate, and we discussed various matters concerning the courts and legislation that need urgent attention, like my predecessor's efforts at limiting bail and so on.

Wednesday 21 August

I called a special meeting today and invited the Minister of Internal Affairs, Ssemogerere, the new AG, the IG Police, the Commissioner of Prisons and the Head of CID. High on my agenda I emphasised the urgent need to release the masses of political detainees and all those persons already released by the courts and rearrested by the previous authorities. I added that there must be a stop to further rearresting of such persons, and I looked hard at the IG Police and Commissioner of Prisons, both of whom had for a long time knowingly co-operated in this with the last government. They both looked uncomfortable and, in fact, I decided to speak privately to their Minister about removing and replacing both of them as soon as possible. Ssemogerere, himself so recently having appeared in court before me as an accused in the sedition case and whom I had managed to keep out of the cells, agreed firmly about ending this rearresting practice.

When they were all leaving, after we had got through a useful discussion, I asked Ssemogerere if he could spare a moment. When we were alone I brought up this matter of replacements and he thoroughly agreed but said he didn't know whom to appoint. So I suggested that he should get Luke Ofungi back in the chair at Police HQ and he agreed to see to this. I don't know the prisons officers well enough so I couldn't suggest a replacement there.

Thursday 22 August

I visited Seth in hospital this afternoon and took him some more reading matter. He's definitely on the mend but will probably have to go to the UK sometime for a proper medical check-up. I shall certainly arrange that.

I'm having problems with my predecessor. He has not handed over the keys to the CJ's chambers and safe, nor has he returned the official car, although he has been requested several times to do so. I directed Zadok, the Chief Registrar, to go to the residence with at least two of the larger of our police orderlies and obtain the keys and car by whatever means necessary as he has no right to hang on to government property to which he's no longer entitled; though I can well understand how galling it must be for him to see me, of all people, in his chair. However, I have to have these things to do my job. The next item is the residence itself, and I've made it clear that he must move out without delay. It's not that I want to move; indeed I'd rather stay in my newly renovated house, but there's really no choice in the matter now. If the CJ's official residence is left vacant, some over-inflated army type will move in and the Judiciary will lose it.

The DPP, no doubt acting on orders from the AG, whom I had spoken to about this, today filed a *nolle prosequi* withdrawing the charges in the Ssemogerere sedition case, and for the last time the matter came before me and I ordered the dismissal of the case and discharged the three accused.

Saturday 24 August

People have been calling into my chambers all week with congratulations and good wishes. Some who have been lying low either in or out of the country for years, I was glad to see again alive and well. Breaking my usual practice of never giving interviews to journalists, a meeting with the editor, with a photographer present, was arranged at my home this morning for the Luganda magazine *Musizi*. I shall have to get a translation made when the issue comes out to find out what I'm supposed to have said. It gave me a chance to explain about how badly the Constitution and the law have been disregarded and degraded over the years and how this must now change. We hope.

Monday 26 August

At last this new government has seen sense, no doubt due to the many complaints and expressions of dismay in and out of government circles, and got rid of awful Muwanga. I've avoided meeting the man and know nothing good about him; he was definitely very bad news. He has been replaced as Prime Minister by Abraham Waligo, whom I don't know. Until now he has been Minister of Finance and was formerly Minister of Housing in Obote's recent government; but he doesn't seem to have been associated with any unpleasant hanky-panky in the past. I met him when I attended his swearing-in by General Tito Okello this morning.

Friday 30 August

As chairman, I called a meeting of the Judicial Service Commission (JSC) this morning as I wanted to discuss filling some of the vacant senior magistrate posts and to consider possibilities for promotion to the High Court. There is also a certain amount of dead wood to be got rid of; one of the main reasons why I was appointed, in fact. I've already met departmental heads and instructed them to sort out their sections where nepotism and politics have placed a number of unsuitable people. There are two or three judges who do very little useful work; one in particular, who is considerably senior to me in service, who occasionally hears cases but is very reluctant to write and deliver judgments, judging by the number of letters of complaint from advocates and plaintiffs on the files going back several years. He just doesn't like making decisions. However, I'm very glad to see that the government has acted quickly on my advice and brought in Luke Ofungi as Inspector General of Police once again.

Thursday 5 September – New Forest, England

My predecessor had made arrangements to attend the Commonwealth Magistrates Association conference in Nicosia, Cyprus, from 8 to 14 September. I have taken his place, and I flew to Gatwick yesterday and am spending a couple of days at home first before buzzing off to the Mediterranean.

Sunday 8 September – Cyprus

I flew to Cyprus yesterday and the conference was opened this morning by President Kyprianou of Cyprus at the Nicosia Hilton, where we are all staying. The Lord Chief Justice of England, Lord Lane, is also attending the conference, as are chief justices from a number of Commonwealth countries, including Australia and India and some African countries.

Wednesday 11 September – Cyprus

On Monday afternoon the various chief justices were driven to the presidential palace in Nicosia for a private reception and meeting with President Kyprianou. In the evening, after the conference programme for the day was over, all the delegates were taken to the presidential palace for a reception. There is tremendous security at the hotel and wherever we go because we're not far away from Beirut and the Palestinians and such who, it is felt, would find some useful hostages among us to kidnap and take back with them. Today was very hot; most of it we spent touring Cyprus and visiting Limassol, Paphos and the Episkopi Sovereign Base Area, where we were met and addressed by Major-General Sir Desmond Langley, the General Officer Commanding.

Saturday 14 September – London

The conference closed yesterday and I met Bob Whillock in the afternoon. He was in the Uganda Police with me and is now in charge of security at the British High Commission in Cyprus. At the closing dinner dance in the evening at the hotel there was a top table for the various CJs and VIP guests, but I found that we four African CJs had been parked at a table in the far corner of the room. The others were naturally not happy about this so I went to the Greek Cypriot appeal court judge who was responsible for organising the conference and pointed out that putting the Commonwealth CJs at the top table except for the African CJs was rather discourteous and appeared to be discriminatory. As Africans were naturally rather sensitive about such matters, couldn't he move one or two of them to that table? He looked rather arrogantly at me and said: 'Those are the arrangements we've made and they cannot be changed now.'

I replied: 'Well, I don't think that's a very good decision. We shall have our meal here and then walk out before the speeches start.' And that's what we did. But I doubt whether anyone else noticed.

Today we flew to London from Larnaca and I'm spending the night at the club, the Royal Commonwealth Society, after a spot of very rapid shopping. My secretary had asked me to bring her a dress and shoes and provided the sizes. I found a very helpful saleswoman in Marks and Sparks and handed the matter of choice of these items to her while I selected shirts of various sizes for myself and a few other people.

Tuesday 17 September

On Sunday the Uganda High Commission in London transported me to Gatwick, where I was taken to the VIP lounge until it was time to board. The flight to Entebbe was uneventful and my driver met me there with the CR, who told me that I could now move into the CJ's residence on Nakasero hill as my predecessor has at last moved out. So that's what I've been doing today. A large covered lorry came to collect my boxes and, after it was loaded, the driver tried to negotiate the right-angled corner from the back of my house on to the driveway to the gate. The huge vehicle couldn't manage it and the top part of its canvas covered frame struck the roof corner and neatly broke off most of the tiles that had replaced those damaged by gun-fire in 1979.

The CJ's residence is in a dreadful state and will need redecorating throughout. But first I called in the pest-control people. The large kitchen area of about five rooms, pantry, laundry and drying rooms is swarming with cockroaches and the house is also bat-infested; plus there's no water supply. Even when the supply is on elsewhere, none seems to reach Nakasero and the large water tank has previously been filled regularly by the Fire Brigade. However, so I'm told, the Chief Fire Officer is a friend and fellow tribesman of my predecessor and may not feel disposed to continue such assistance to his replacement. Furthermore, someone has removed the electrical pump to bring water from the tank to the house and a replacement has to be found first. This is a very large house – far too big for me – with two storeys plus basement rooms and garage in a compound cut into the hillside, which consists mostly of grass, trees and shrubs with a drive down to the main gates, where there lurk two police sentries day and night.

Saturday 21 September

Someone on the staff managed to find a replacement water pump, which was fitted today. The fire truck came, after all, and filled the water tank, so conditions are not quite so primitive at the moment. The pest-control people sprayed some very powerful stuff in the kitchen and laundry area and next day the floors of all rooms there were ankle-deep in dead cockroaches, which Vincent and his brother Godfrey have been shovelling up and removing. I've never seen so many of the creatures. The infestation was unbelievable. Some other noxious substance was introduced into the two partially blocked old chimneys and hundreds of bats soon took off and, I hope, will not return, since besides being unpleasant they carry rabies and make a mess. There are still a few lurking in the basement area that will have to be dealt with as they zoom through the rooms in the evening and I throw cushions at them. I was pleasantly surprised to find a TV set here in the house so, for the first time, I've been able to watch UTV news and programmes, most of which seem to be incredibly dull and uninteresting. Speeches of ministers and other leading political figures are shown in full and go on for hours.

Wednesday 25 September

There was a JSC meeting this morning to confirm various appointments, select a new chief magistrate and a judge and to arrange for some retirements. In the afternoon I went to the LDC to lecture and the Director was delighted and expressed considerable surprise that I should be willing to go on doing this now that I'm CJ. I said this appointment makes no difference to me and I want to continue occasional teaching as my personal contribution.

I sent a semi-official letter to Luke Ofungi the other day and he has kindly done as I asked and arranged the promotion to corporal of my long-serving police orderly, Wilson Outeke, who is today proudly sporting his stripes.

Monday 30 September

I gave judgment this morning in an undefended divorce petition between two Alur from West Nile who had married first according to their tribal custom and then later at All Saints Cathedral in Kampala. (There are three cathedrals here.) The only special interest in the case was that the co-respondent named was Professor Isaac Newton Ojok, who was a minister in Obote's Government and who had conducted a long-standing affair with the petitioner's wife. Ojok didn't appear in court as he is now out of the country.

Thursday 3 October

When checking the files here, I found that one of many matters neglected for a long time is the enrolment of newly qualified advocates, some of whom have been waiting for this for up to two years. I checked through the accumulated applications and found that out of 40 there were 33 properly qualified, so I had the CR summon them to court yesterday morning and enrolled them and called them to the Ugandan Bar. According to *The Star* I addressed them about standards of work, honesty and ethics, attendance at court and punctuality. I must have done so as it's in the paper.

Today I swore in a group of new magistrates, who had also been kept waiting for this for a long time, so that they could now commence their duties. The thoughtless delays by my predecessor in doing these simple but essential tasks meant that the lawyers and magistrates involved could not be employed at their proper jobs and so earning their salaries or fees.

From Police HQ I received a request to swear in a large number of their senior officers as JPs. This also should have been done long ago – yet another matter neglected for years – so I've arranged for them to come to my chambers in two batches.

Friday 4 October

The situation in Lira is very worrying. They have been out of contact for a couple of months. When the Okellos and the Acholi in the UNLA moved northwards in July, they expressed their feelings about Obote by ransacking his home town, Lira, and destroying or badly damaging most of the buildings in the town, including the court. All records and books were looted or destroyed. Hopefully the magistrates got away safely but we haven't heard from them. As the western areas and much of the north are now in the hands of Museveni's NRA, who have done more damage, we can't do anything about it at the moment. For the time being circuits are postponed and most communications are out.

What people here want above all is peace. If only Museveni and the Okellos would get together now that their common enemy Obote is out, and form some sort of coalition government to stabilise the country, we could start to get things sorted out. At the moment both sides are waiting and watching.

Wednesday 9 October

Today was Uganda's twenty-third anniversary of independence. There was a ceremony and a series of dreary speeches at the International Conference Centre attended by General Tito Okello and everyone else in government, including myself. I tried to look inconspicuous but, as I saw on the UTV news this evening, the cameraman seemed fascinated by my presence and kept pointing the thing at me. It was rather embarrassing.

Saturday 12 October

I've been fixing up for painters, carpenters and electricians to come and do something about the appalling state of this wretched house I now have to live in.

I had lunch today with the British High Commissioner, who has changed his attitude to me since my elevation to great heights. Madame actually managed for once the remarkable feat of remembering who I am. It probably won't last. Also there was the East African desk chief from the FCO/ODA visiting with regard to aid, and Ssemogerere and two other ministers. The colonel commanding the British Army Training Team was present and, having been most unsuccessful with trying to train the untrainable UNLA, as I had remarked before, he now seems to think he should continue with their successors, who are mostly the same people anyway and equally untrainable. What these people need is encouragement to disband their useless, murdering armies and give the country some badly needed peace and quiet. Fat chance of that, though.

Friday 25 October

Zadok, the CR, is off to the USA tomorrow for a month on some American-sponsored tour designed for African senior judicial officers, visiting courts and other places of interest. A pleasant and interesting break for him from this place, organised by the US Embassy here. I've called in a chief magistrate, Anthony Ochwo, ex-Law School of course, to act in his place. In fact, I'm hoping to arrange Zadok's appointment as a judge soon. His judicial work is better than his administration and he's senior enough.

Work on renovating the house has commenced at last and the painters are at work, while the electrician is scratching his head over the ancient wiring and wall plugs that all should have been replaced long ago.

Thursday 7 November

I delivered a long judgment this morning in a dispute between two tea estate companies quarrelling over the possession of the Kampala Tea Estate near Mukono, formerly owned by Asians thrown out in 1972. I took the opportunity of repeating my earlier views about the absolute illegality and the unconstitutionality (is that a word?) of Amin's seizure of non-Ugandan properties and referred to the later Court of Appeal judgment giving the contrary view to mine – that it was a legal nationalisation – as being totally unrealistic and deserving of no respect at all.

Monday 11 November – In the UK

I arrived in the UK this morning, having obtained Tito Okello's permission to spend a week here mainly for the purpose of attending my mother's ninetieth birthday celebrations, plus some urgently needed shopping and visits to the dentist and the bank manager.

Monday 18 November

I'm back in Entebbe today. The Uganda High Commission in London as usual was very helpful with arrangements and facilities during my short visit.

Saturday 30 November

Today is St Andrew's Day and I was invited as guest of honour to the Caledonian Society lunch. It used to be a dinner, but evening functions are still not on these days. At first I had declined because it involves making an after-dinner speech, or after-lunch in this case, something I've always managed to avoid. However, they twisted my arm and tortured me so I agreed to speak for only five minutes, and they could find someone else to fill in the rest of the time. So I recounted a few legal anecdotes and quickly sat down before they started to throw things, as I had no wish to be struck by a live haggis. Or even a dead one.

Actually, it went quite well and it's the first time I've tasted haggis. The bagpipes were deafening, of course, but unavoidable – like death, income tax and the OBE. Off-stage cries of: 'I don't wish to know that.'

1985

Sunday 1 December

While peace talks are going on in Nairobi between Museveni and General Tito Okello under the chairmanship of President Arap Moi, Lieutenant-General Bazilio Okello is busily fighting the NRA in the west and the north and seems to have no interest in peace at all. He is a big problem.

The popular local pop stars, Jimmy Katumba and the Ebonies, are giving a series of performances in aid of a school and using the theme 'Peace and Tranquillity'. I was invited by them to attend today's performance as guest of honour. At the interval Jimmy Katumba, whom I've met before, introduced me to the audience and, at his request, I said a few words about ending the fighting. According to *The Star* today I urged Ugandans to stop killing each other and to talk together to achieve peace in this lovely country. I added that if Ugandans put their heads together there is no reason why they shouldn't find a permanent peaceful solution to their disputes. After thanking me for attending, Katumba presented me with a set of his group's audio cassettes. It's actually very pleasant music.

Tuesday 17 December

Museveni and Tito Okello signed a peace treaty in Nairobi today and everyone is carefully rejoicing but, although we're sure that Okello wants it, nobody is quite so sure about Museveni. The feeling is that he wants all the cake and is not a sharer. Well, we all very much hope for the best and we have to wait and see. The one thing one can always expect in Africa is the unexpected. I also received a Christmas card from Tito Okello today.

Friday 20 December

A plaintiff called Rubale sued the government through the AG for damages for serious injuries sustained in a traffic accident caused by a government vehicle. There was a judgment by consent for 1.5 million shillings which has not been paid by Finance for over two years in spite of repeated requests. He now appeared before me asking for an order of *mandamus* directing the Treasury Officer of Accounts to pay the sum or take the consequences, which might include an arrest order. This is something the courts are very reluctant to do but, in the circumstances, I granted the application. I must speak to the AG about this one and get it sorted out.

Saturday 21 December

There was a large government function in the middle of Kampala this morning, attended by Tito Okello with all his government and large numbers of diplomats and invited guests. I was asked to attend and did so. There was tribal dancing, singing, speeches and so on, all in celebration of the peace treaty. Just about everybody wants it to succeed and end the many years of unnecessary fighting and quarrelling and bloodshed. If only...

Monday 23 December

A High Court Christmas party was held at my residence this afternoon. All the judges, magistrates, and court staff came, together with the Kampala advocates, Luke Ofungi and one or two other senior police officers whom I had invited. Also their Minister, Ssemogerere, and the AG. The Police Band attended and provided us with an excellent musical background.

Tuesday 24 December

I sent Laurence, my driver, to the market for some Christmas shopping in the Isuzu, which I've kept as a second official car for such jobs. However, as soon as he parked it at the market some armed soldiers came and took it and drove it away. He reported to the police station and we'll now see if they can recover it. This is usually a hopeless task, but the police know that their IG and I are close friends, so maybe they'll make an extra special effort this time.

There has been no airmail for over three weeks as the Uganda Airlines aircraft is grounded for repairs, so no letters or Christmas cards have been received from overseas. I have had a local one signed 'Balaki', which I suppose comes from Balaki Kirya, whom I had discharged at the end of the recent treason trial. Presumably he has since been released from unlawful detention with the others about whom I spoke to the new Minister of Internal Affairs.

At home this evening when I went into the kitchen and asked the *mpishi* what he was cooking, he said: 'Kitchen soup'. It's a good name for it but he actually meant chicken soup.

Monday 30 December

The last revision and updating of Uganda's law volumes was carried out in 1964. In the last 21 years many new laws have been passed and others amended, and the consolidation of these laws into revised volumes is long overdue. So I asked one of our judges, who has reached retirement age and is a former legal draughtsman, to start work on revising the laws. It's a very necessary job and it will give him something useful to do for some time to come.

1986

Thursday 2 January

Luke Ofungi phoned from Police HQ with new year greetings and the news that his chaps had recovered my Isuzu car and were bringing it to the court. He suggested that we change the registration number plate so that the soldiers concerned hopefully don't recognise it and try to seize it back. This was done today.

Tuesday 7 January

The American Ambassador, Mr Houdek, called on me today and we talked about aid needed by the Judiciary. I would like to put up a suitable building nearby for the Court of Appeal as we have no room in the High Court building for the two separate full-time courts. But, for some reason, they don't seem to be interested in really useful projects of long-term value like this one, which the British have also rejected. It's a great pity.

Sunday 19 January

My contact at the President's Office rang and confirmed what I had suspected and passed on to him. The Minister of Justice/AG has been very naughty and, instead of assisting me to sort out the Judiciary as required, he has been busy at the President's Office fouling up my proposed appointments of new judges and removal of dead wood. None of the new ones comes from his tribe and he has personal objections to two of them. I knew this before, of course, but not at first that he was actively sabotaging my efforts. I shall have to take steps.

Tuesday 21 January

There's been heavy gunfire around Kampala for the last two days and nights. No police sentries have turned up at the house, which is an indication of trouble brewing. It looks as though Museveni has unfortunately at last made up his mind and decided to have a go at taking over the government. This is very bad news and it won't be welcomed either here or anywhere else in East Africa, let alone outside. This country is never going to get on its feet again if we're to have these frequent violent coups like some South American banana republic, just because some ambitious populist guerrilla movement decides to take over. Why on earth couldn't they have tried to make the peace treaty work? It's not even been given a chance.

The power has gone off, of course, and the new water pump fixed in my residence has already broken down. I suspect they sold us a defective replacement – a frequent occurrence here.

Wednesday 22 January

I drove to court this morning but hardly any staff had come in and, when the gun-fire increased, even those few disappeared rapidly in the direction of their favourite bolt-holes and I suddenly found that I was the only one left in the building, with a very anxious Laurence urging me into the car.

Friday 24 January

The gun-fire is very heavy now and everyone is keeping indoors. It's heads down time and panic stations. There are bullets, missiles and mortar shells flying around and exploding all over Kampala. Through my binoculars I can see near Makerere University a multi-rocket launcher busily firing in this direction. This large house on the hillside makes a tempting target, I expect. So far only bullets have hit the walls. I hope it doesn't get worse.

Vincent and Godfrey are in the house with me – in the central corridor so that we have two thick walls on each side between us and the outside. It's rather strange that although the electricity has been off for five days, a small patch on one wall near the dining room and just above a switch is so hot it can't be touched – as if the wires are burning or red-hot somehow. Yet there's no smoke, no fire and no power. What does it all mean, I ask myself. I also asked my cook, Vincent, for his learned opinion and he replied: 'I don't know. I am not a scientific.' A great help.

Saturday 25 January

The battle continues and we are running out of food. With the power off for so long, all I had in the fridge has been consumed or gone bad now. It's still very unsafe to go outside. From an upper window I can see Museveni's men moving about in the area. They are recognisable because, being guerillas, they are not in any particular uniform, but in anything they've captured or looted in different places. Some are still in the partial police or prisons service uniform that they wore when they joined the NRA. Others wear parts of camouflage uniforms of various designs and colours taken from the UNLA, Tanzanians, Koreans and possibly purchased outside. They are also recognisable because most are from the western parts of Uganda and tend to be light brown in colour, in contrast to the black Nilotics in the UNLA.

Sunday 26 January

Well, it's clear that the NRA has won this one. Their armed groups seem to be all over Kampala. There are many very young boys among them carrying AK-47s as if they know how to use them.

This morning a group of them, some not yet teenagers, forced their way into my compound and demanded to know who I am and what I was doing for the last government. They had no idea of what is meant by the term 'Chief Justice' and then they demanded my official Mercedes standing in the carport. I said 'no', and several Kalashnikovs were swung in my direction, fingers on the triggers, one of them poked into my stomach. One trigger-happy Munyankole boy, thinking that I didn't understand, said to his companions: 'Let's shoot him. I haven't killed a *Mzungu* yet.'

Speaking slowly and steadily I said: Listen carefully. Your leader Museveni will want to be President now and it is my job as Chief Justice to swear in the new President. Nobody else can do it, by law. So I must have my official car to go there for that purpose otherwise he will be very angry with you for preventing me.'

'All right,' one of them said, 'then we'll take the other car. Give us the keys.' So I handed over the key of my recently recovered Isuzu and they all clambered into it and away they went, zigzagging down the drive. Quite clearly the youngster behind the wheel was not a competent driver and I suppose it will soon be smashed up. It didn't last long back here – first taken by UNLA looters, now by the NRA. I made a note of this as I intend to report it to Museveni when I meet him. As soon as they had gone Vincent and I let down two tyres of the Mercedes, threw dust and dirt over the wheels and put a cover over it so that it appeared to be out of working order, as no doubt we shall be getting other visitors.

Later a group of local Baganda, who know very well whose residence this is, tried to break into the back of the compound to loot, so I ordered them out. One young idiot had a piece of wood cut roughly in the shape of a rifle and he waved it at me and threatened to shoot me, claiming that it was real gun. I used a very insulting expression in Luganda which caused him almost to turn inside out with screaming fury. I then turned my back on him and walked towards the house.

By then two or three armed guerillas had joined the small crowd outside the fence and were staring in. This character screamed at them: 'Shoot him! Shoot him!' I kept walking away without turning round and hoped that none of them would oblige him. When I had entered the house I sighed with relief. This was no way to enjoy a Sunday afternoon.

Monday 27 January

Although there's been no power for over a week, we've all been listening to our battery radios for any official announcements. It's clear to me that Kampala is completely in NRA hands although Museveni and his staff are not in the city yet. My information is that they are up in Mengo at the *Lubiri*, where they have a temporary HQ now that the UNLA is no longer in residence.

As the former Head of State and the Prime Minister, who was Head of Government, have both fled, it leaves me, as Head of the Judiciary, as the senior government official in place and, I suppose, as a sort of acting Head of State. It's thus my job to see to it that there's some sort of legal government installed as soon as possible. It seems from the radio that Museveni is already starting to form a government to take over. This he should not do until he is formally appointed as the Head of State, otherwise nobody outside Uganda will recognise his government. Consequently I feel I have a responsibility to do something about it.

I rang up someone who I know has a close relative on Museveni's staff and asked him to make urgent contact and to inform Museveni that, if he wishes to set up a lawful and internationally recognised government, there are formalities to go through and I wish to meet him without delay to discuss the procedure for this. He agreed to make contact.

Tuesday 28 January

I thought it might be a courtesy to tell the British High Commissioner what I'm planning to do with Museveni, so I rang his residence, where he and his staff are holed up – just down the road, in fact. A very off-hand character answered the phone and told me that the High Commissioner was too busy to speak to me and I could therefore either leave a message or call back later. I replied: 'Of your two choices I've selected number three,' and put the phone down. The BHC could find out later what I'm up to.

At lunch-time a commandeered minibus arrived at my gates with several variously dressed armed types in it. The fellow who seemed to be in charge wore a red shirt and had a shifty, villainous-looking face. As he got out I said to him: 'I suppose you're in charge of Museveni's security people?'

He looked surprised and asked: 'How did you know that?'

I said: 'It must be the great intelligence shining from your eyes.' He seemed quite pleased with that and asked me to go with them to Museveni's HQ. I suggested that we should call round at the home of the Solicitor-General and collect him too as there would be a legal notice and proclamation to produce.

When we reached the SG's house I told them to remain in the vehicle as the occupants would be alarmed if armed men approached the place. I walked up to the door, knocked and called out my name. We talked and then assured his family of his safety and off we drove to Mengo hill. At the *Lubiri* the whole hill was covered with heavily armed guerrillas sitting around and generally idling about and cluttering up the place and making it look very untidy. They looked in surprise and curiosity at this *mzungu* in a jacket walking past them. I ignored them. Museveni, who was talking to some of his staff, looked up, saw me and came and greeted me in a friendly fashion. We went aside to sit under a mango tree – always the proper place for important discussions.

I explained the legal situation and the need for international recognition if he wanted to obtain aid and co-operation from other governments, and he asked what he should do. So I said: 'Whoever is to be your president should be sworn in properly and publicly on the steps of Parliament where everyone can see it and the press and TV people can record it.' I suggested that we should do it tomorrow at 10 a.m. and an announcement to that effect should be made on the radio and TV right away. I undertook to have the judges and legal staff informed and present and the SG said he would prepare the proclamation and legal notice and inform the other permanent secretaries and diplomats.

I looked at Museveni's scruffy, soiled bush uniform and said: 'Look, I have to wear wig and robes for this ceremony, so you should dress up too. Try to borrow a suit or at least a clean uniform, as photographers and TV people will be there and you must look authentic and reasonably respectable.' I added that if he and his staff appeared in uniform the people would assume that they had another military government, which might not make them too happy. He said he'd see what could be done and I took my leave and was given a lift into town in another vehicle. I wanted to contact the Chief Registrar and I knew where he had gone to ground during the recent fighting.

He appeared and I briefed him about tomorrow and what will be required, especially the presidential oath and signature book and to arrange with the Parliamentary Serjeant-at-Arms to open the parliament building and get chairs put outside above the steps and a table and Bible. The High Court has to be opened tomorrow as I need to go in to collect my robes. At the moment it's occupied by guerrillas, so heaven knows what state things are in there. Laurence turned up this afternoon and got busy pumping up the tyres and cleaning the car.

Wednesday 29 January

There were dead bodies and military detritus lying around in the courtyard area of the High Court and a number of guerrillas wandering around. I ignored the latter and went upstairs and unlocked my chambers and took out my red robes and full-bottomed wig. A young police inspector arrived and said he'd been sent by the IG to escort me.

When we drove to Parliament the streets were crowded with people. Not enough police had reported for duty to do any useful crowd control, so there was no way open for us to get through the mass of people to the steps of Parliament. I told Laurence to keep driving slowly forward and the inspector stuck his head out of the window and shouted to people to make way. The crowd was in a good mood and clearly excited by events. As we moved slowly forward they noticed me in my robes and guessed or knew what I was going to do. Some started to bang on the car roof with flat hands. In other circumstances it might have been menacing and both Laurence and the inspector looked rather apprehensive.

'Don't worry,' I said, 'they're friendly today and won't harm us. Just keep going forward.' I waved to them and some of them started shouting: 'CJ, CJ, CJ!' and laughing. Near the steps we stopped and I got out. The police had put together a small guard of honour and an officer approached me and asked me to inspect it. Normally I try to avoid this sort of thing, so I quickly walked round them and complimented him on their turnout and went straight up the steps and into the building. The table outside was covered with microphones and there were many foreign journalists and TV teams spread out on the wide steps and others still arriving. Judges, diplomats and other VIPs sat on the chairs at the top of the steps.

One of Museveni's staff met me and said that Museveni had been waiting for nearly an hour and he and his staff were very worried and afraid that I had decided against making them a legitimate government by avoiding the ceremony. I replied that 10 a.m. was the time we had agreed and there was still five minutes to go, so there was no need to panic. In a room by the entrance Museveni was waiting. He was wearing a clean green bush uniform and his entourage sat nervously, looking like patients at a dentist's clinic. The CR was in his barrister's wig and gown and held the presidential oath book and a Bible, well organised as usual. While we were waiting I mentioned to Museveni that his NRA men had taken my official car and he immediately replied, without any knowledge of the facts: 'Oh no, they were not NRA. My men would never do a thing like that. It's strictly forbidden.'

I walked with Museveni outside to the table and the others followed. People started to cheer, or maybe there were cheer-leaders out there. The CR took him through the oaths of office and he signed the book and became President. He then made a long off-the-cuff speech in English – it went on for over an hour – in which he reverted to his style as a one-time political scientist who had been a technical college lecturer. His speech/lecture covered unity, religious and tribal differences, calories, health in the bush, international relations and a great deal of Marxist-style talk about forming village committees and people's democracy and the need to politicise the population and the government service. This sounded to me like bad news. I can't visualise myself as having any part to play in such a communistic set-up.

Fortunately for us in this prolonged outdoor ceremony, the weather remained fine throughout. It was only later this afternoon that we had a heavy downfall of rain. I'm told that Museveni gets his name from the fact that his father was serving in the 7th Battalion KAR when he was born and so he was named Yoweri Mu-seven-i which means: Yoweri of the Seventh. So here he is: what he couldn't achieve by the ballot he has gained by the bullet.

Thursday 30 January

The guerrillas have been moved out of the High Court compound, with their equipment, at my request and most of the staff turned up this morning to tidy up the offices that had been occupied and fortunately not ransacked. Some ministers have been appointed but so far, no Minister of Justice/Attorney-General.

It seems we had a lucky escape yesterday. Having heard on the radio about the presidential installation ceremony, Lieutenant-General Bazilio Okello sent an Augusta Griffin AB 412 helicopter with side-mounted rockets to attack Parliament buildings at the swearing-in time and thus wipe out Museveni and his staff and, in the process, the diplomats, judges and foreign journalists and TV people. As I was standing next to Museveni in my scarlet robes, I would have made an perfect aiming point for the attacker. The pilot, a Ugandan captain in the UNLA, fortunately lost his way, panicked and had second thoughts about this mad order, then turned back and managed to find Nakasongola and land there, where he gave himself up to Museveni's troops and reported what had been his target for the aborted mission.

Thursday 6 February

Noel Guina, First Secretary at the British High Commission, called into my chambers this morning for a chat. I mentioned my thoughts about the likelihood of Museveni replacing me soon with his own appointee, as had happened previously with every change of government in Uganda. I just hope that I shall be consulted first, but I suppose it's not really very likely. My present contract expires in a few months and the question of renewal may be used as a pretext.

Afterwards, K dropped in. He's an old-time advocate from Ankole who has been a wealthy businessman in Kenya and the UK and maybe elsewhere for many years. He's certainly not lived in Uganda for a long time and hasn't been a guerrilla or given up his very comfortable life-style. But he now seems to have attached himself to Museveni and, as he comes from the right district and tribe, he may be hoping for a ministerial post or something like that; maybe even to replace me, though he has no judicial experience.

Our meeting did not go well. I happened to mention several unpleasant things that had happened to me and he immediately leapt to the defence of Museveni and his men and clearly implied that I was lying. He claimed that the NRA did not behave like that and I was obviously mistaken, and he added that it was definitely time I went on leave. I thought: So, he does want to get rid of me, and what does he know about what the NRA does or doesn't do – he hasn't been in the bush in his life. I don't take kindly to some buckshee lawyer walking into the Chief Justice's chambers and being arrogant and discourteous, and I made this quite clear to him. We did not part on good terms and I suppose a report will now go to Museveni that it's time I went.

There's still no electricity – I hope they get the power back on soon. Whatever mysterious gremlin was causing the tremendous heat above the wall switch in the dining room seems to have gone away; but I can't test whether it's the wiring that's been affected yet.

Friday 7 February

The new AG has been appointed – a western advocate, of course, Joseph Mulenga. He was Ssemogerere's defence counsel in the recent sedition case. He called on me this afternoon and we had a chat about judicial appointments which were interrupted by recent events and which I wish to continue with; particularly the appointment of new judges. I have a feeling, though, that there are going to be problems. We don't seem to have the same aims in mind.

Wednesday 12 February

I was told the unsurprising news this morning that there is already a move afoot to replace me. Well, I don't suppose Museveni has any particular reason for keeping me on. I'm due for leave in June and that will no doubt be the testing time when a decision will be made.

I went to the British High Commissioner's residence for lunch. Mrs Lynda Chalker, Minister of State at the FCO, is visiting to talk about aid requirements. I was granted half an hour with her without the BHC or his minions being present, so I was able to put over my views about aid without interruption or contradiction. Well-managed and supervised projects are the answer, not handing over bundles of cash to greedy politicians.

This evening I had cocktails at the US Ambassador's residence and met a group of American aid people and had a chat with them. The big problem is that outside governments say that they won't give aid without there being security in the country. In our present state of considerable insecurity we therefore don't qualify; but, if we don't get aid, we can't produce security. A Catch-22 situation.

Friday 21 February

The Prime Minister is an old man called Samson Kisseka, a Muganda, who was previously NRM external affairs co-ordinator. He's very much a long-winded political theorist but, as he has no ministry to run and there's an executive president, his powerless post is probably a suitable one. I received a message that he wanted to see the AG and myself this afternoon to be briefed about the Judicial Service Commission. It sounded nonsense to me. The JSC is nothing to do with the PM and I make a point of never calling on politicians if I can avoid it. However, I went along and was irritated to be left sitting in a corridor and kept waiting – no doubt to show how important he is – something I detest and never do myself. I had just decided to put up with the discourtesy no longer and I told the AG that I was going back to my chambers, when we were called in.

Kisseka didn't ask anything at all about the JSC; instead we sat silently listening to his long, boring diatribe about the politics of the NRM and an attempted justification for their actions. Since nothing could justify their civil war and the huge number of resultant deaths and misery simply to achieve a political victory and power, it was just a waste of time. This evening on the UTV news it was announced that the Chief Justice had paid a courtesy call on the Prime Minister, who had explained the aims and policies of the NRM. Since I didn't initiate the visit it was certainly not a courtesy call. Clearly it had just been set up as an excuse for the PM to get some news coverage in the media and to boost his ego. It was a discourtesy call.

Monday 24 February

The British High Commissioner has gone to London for consultations or something and his deputy, Peter Penfold, is acting as HE. He invited me to dinner yesterday evening at his residence. The main guest was an elderly person called Lady Alexandra Metcalfe, a daughter of the late Lord Curzon, who held high posts such as Foreign Secretary, Viceroy of India and others. She is doing something here with the Save the Children Fund.

Today at noon I went to the President's Office, where Museveni swore in my new judges, including our first woman judge and Zadok the Priest, the former Chief Registrar, now back from his visit to the States. Museveni has also appointed Wambuzi as President of the Court Appeal. I had no say in this – I was merely told that it was going to happen. I had wanted Seth Manyindo in the post but I was overruled, which is a pity as I know a great deal more about the personnel and our requirements than any of those who have intervened in this matter. However, I did succeed in moving Seth up to the Court of Appeal and having him appointed as Vice-President of that court.

Wambuzi has twice before been Chief Justice, the first time was when I was appointed to the High Court and the second briefly after the fall of Amin. I believe that this move bringing him back into the Judiciary is the first step towards reinstating him as CJ as soon as I can be disposed of – at the end of this present contract, for instance. I had various things that I wanted to talk to Museveni about rather urgently but, having caught an extremely inconvenient bad cold, I completely lost my voice. Not a peep. It was most frustrating, aggravating and embarrassing.

Monday 3 March

Something's got to be done about finding a place for the Court of Appeal to be located and to operate in now that the US and UK aid people won't assist us in this. The High Court building is overflowing with judges and has insufficient courts and chambers. As far as I can see, the only suitable place is the court building at Mengo originally built for the former Buganda courts. I drove out to have a look today. The road to Mengo is appalling. It's like driving on the moon's surface – craters and pot-holes all the way. There are repairs to be carried out to the court buildings there, but, otherwise, they are suitable for the appeal court; though further away than I had wanted. However, Wambuzi will no doubt be happy about that as I get the distinct feeling that he doesn't really want to be working near me.

Monday 10 March

The NRA took Gulu on Saturday and Lieutenant-General Bazilio Okello and his men have retreated northwards to Kitgum, which they are unlikely to hold for long. Lira is already in NRA hands, although they had to fight hard for it and more damage has been done to the town to add to the devastation caused there last August. In Teso and Karamoja the Karamojong are having a field day killing people and stealing cattle in large numbers. The rest of the country seems to be in NRA hands now, for the moment.

Balaki Kirya, whom I discharged at the end of his treason trial in December 1984, is now a Minister of State in the President's Office.

Thursday 13 March

Yesterday evening there was a reception at the senior police officers' mess and another this evening at the BHC's residence, both for the visiting ODA Overseas Police Adviser, John Kelland, who is here concerning the police training team. The team leader, Vivian Brook, and the IG, Luke Ofungi, were there, and we were able to discuss various matters with a view to getting the Force fully effective again.

Saturday 15 March

Museveni's coup and the existence here of a European Chief Justice seems to have caught the eye of the media in various parts of the world. I've been sent newspaper cuttings with the swearing-in photographs and articles from Hong Kong, Australia, Canada, South Africa, Kenya and various UK newspapers as well as *Time* magazine and *The Illustrated London News*. Apparently it was shown on TV news in many countries too. Fame at last.

Saturday 22 March

All the wheels were stolen from my official Mercedes last night and there were supposed to be two police constables on sentry duty here at the time. It seems that one of them cleared off early and went back to barracks for a sleep, while the other stayed but went into hiding in the servants' quarters when the gang of thieves entered the compound by making a gap in the security fence not far from the main gates.

Early this morning I placed that remaining constable under arrest, took away his gun and told him to remain sitting on the grass in front of the house. I rang up the IG and he sent the Senior Assistant Commissioner in charge of the Police in Buganda and several CID officers to deal with the matter. This evening I received a call to report that both constables had been dismissed from the Force and that, so far, the car wheels have not been located or recovered, nor the thieves traced.

Monday 24 March

It is Museveni's stated intention to politicise the whole of the civil service, including the Judiciary, in the same way that they indoctrinated their guerrilla cadres in the bush. They have set up training camps outside Kampala for this purpose and senior staff are being taken away to live in very primitive huts in the bush while they undergo this, in my view, totally unnecessary and improper left-wing indoctrination course when they are badly needed to sort out their own departments and get them organised and working again. They are drilled and given weapon-training and made to sing revolutionary songs and to chant responses to political rallying cries.

I tried to point out that such politicising is not appropriate for the Judiciary and staff, which should remain impartial and non-political, but I was quickly overruled and, as a mere expatriate, I don't see that I can interfere in these matters beyond expressing my views. They must be allowed to do things in their own way; and obviously will in any case. But I think it's sad that Uganda should now have a Marxist-style government in a continent where such governments have already failed so badly and have squandered their countries' resources and efforts on unrealistic political ventures, as was done in Tanzania and Zambia.

Another problem is the constant, very tedious, anti-British stand taken by Museveni and especially some of his guerrilla commissars, several of whom are also political scientists. These take every public opportunity on TV and in public speeches to denigrate the British and everything we did here before independence. Most of those spouting this stuff are not even old enough to remember that far back, so they're merely repeating what the left-wing political scientists taught them originally. Of course, it's all old hat now – the sort of rubbish the local half-baked politicians were trundling out 20 years ago, and have long since ceased to do. But these present chaps have been wandering around like Moses in the wilderness for so long that they are politically out of touch and they are still of the view that communism is the answer to their troubles.

But why do they call it political science? There's absolutely nothing scientific about any aspect of politics; if we must be polite, then politics is an art not a science, though I would prefer to put it in the faculty of jiggery-pokery, where it belongs. Exit right, muttering and mumbling.

Tuesday 1 April

Among other things, in the last month I've dealt with nine consent judgments. I've always encouraged parties in civil suits to try to come to an amicable agreement and so settle their dispute without the necessity and expense of a court trial. A good number of the claims filed and piled up in the civil registry awaiting trial are in this category, but frequently the parties won't talk to each other, or their advocates don't make a sufficient or even any attempt to bring them to a settlement. Thus, if from a perusal of the papers on the court file, it appears to me to be a possibility, I generally ask the advocates if they can settle out of court. Sometimes they say: 'We'll try' and go right to it; sometimes the advocates come alone into my chambers and say: 'Well, we advised them to settle but they won't consider it or agree to talk, or listen to us.'

Then I say: 'Well, they need their heads knocking together. Tell them that the judge says they must settle now or there'll be trouble and considerable delay in dealing with their dispute.' Then, if it's a simple, straightforward claim, I add: 'Tell them they've got an hour and then I expect an agreement to settle.' Quite often this approach works, especially because, although they may be suspicious of the motives of their advocates in advising a settlement, they know that the direction coming from the judge means that it's neutral and above board.

In other cases, such as the one before me this morning, the defendant indicates that he's willing to admit liability for causing the injury, loss or damage but they can't agree the amount of damages (compensation) to be paid. So the advocates inform the judge of this and ask him to assess the damages. Again, much time is saved since the facts are admitted and don't need to be proved, so it's just a matter for the judge to determine values and amounts or seriousness of injuries and then give judgment accordingly.

Thursday 3 April

I decided that it's time to get this show on the road, so I wrote to the President today to say that I wish to go on leave on 22 June and that I'm willing and available to return for another contract if he so wishes. But really I think that the consistently anti-British attitude of him and his supporters bodes ill for me. Also I'm dead against this proposed politicising of the Judiciary and the setting up of peoples courts in the villages. Why on earth do they want their disputes and crimes to be decided and judged by a bunch of ignorant peasants when they have in place a well-established and working magistrates courts system? The answer, I suppose, is nothing more than to satisfy a political theory.

Monday 7 April

I've put in a considerable effort organising and setting up the Court of Appeal in the Mengo court buildings, and all the judges went there this morning to attend the full dress official opening of the court. Ponderous speeches were delivered from Bench and Bar, though I declined the invitation to speak as I felt it should be all Wambuzi's show as President of that Court. Then we all dispersed back to our own courts, leaving them to it.

There was nothing interesting on UTV this evening, just the usual series of long, boring speeches by a succession of NRM political theorists politicising the population with their long-winded, very anti-British, left-wing outpourings. Fortunately the off switch works.

Wednesday 9 April

One of the chief magistrates, Gaudino Okello, a former Law School student of course, whom I put up for a well-earned judgeship, is an Acholi, and these days Acholis are regarded by the present administration as the enemy. However, my point was that such ideas are unacceptable in the Judiciary, which must represent and be represented by the whole country. And, of course, from the political point of view, I suggested that it would look good to aid-donors and others if the President is seen to be prepared to appoint a member of that tribe to a high judicial post. I was pleasantly surprised when Museveni agreed to this proposed appointment.

Okello should have been sworn in with the other new judges in February but there had been a problem contacting him as Gulu was then still not captured by the NRA, so we were out of touch. However, my message eventually got through and he travelled down to Kampala and reported to me on Tuesday last week. I then arranged with the President's Office for today's ceremony.

Afterwards I had a few private words with Museveni and brought up some worrying matters, such as the fact that, in spite of what he had earlier told me, several judges have now lost their official cars to members of this thieving NRA and the houses of two judges have been occupied by NRA men, and I wanted the cars and houses returned to us. He tried to tell me again that they were too saintly and politically committed to do such things, but I persisted and he then gave instructions to one of his ministers present to get the cars and houses recovered. I wonder if they will be.

The second matter that I brought up was the situation of all these youngsters, some still small children, wearing uniform and carrying guns around in the city and threatening people. I said that they should be taken out of uniform and sent to school. I know that most are Baganda orphans from the Luwero Triangle slaughters, so they have no families to return to, and it's a big problem. But they are no longer childlike and they've had no childhood. They are now small adults, solemn, surly and dangerous, with no smiles or laughter; just sad leftovers. Possible future killers and criminals, in fact.

There have been photographs of these gun-toting infants in local and international newspapers and magazines and descriptions of their military training, with interviews reporting their boasting of how many people they have shot and killed. We have all seen them and encountered them ourselves so it is ridiculous for Museveni to persist in saying, as he did then, that none of them has a gun or has been trained to fire a weapon, and that they are not permitted to carry guns. Perhaps he's trying to convince himself, but he certainly doesn't convince me – or anyone else, I suspect. I also mentioned my objections to his stated intention to politicise the courts and staff. I couldn't fail to notice that he definitely did not appreciate my bringing up any of these matters. Another black mark against my name, I suppose.

Friday 11 April

Well, hallelujah! The British High Commissioner actually called on me yesterday in my chambers for the first time. The other ambassadors and high commissioners called on me in August last year after my appointment, and several have dropped in again since then. At least Madame wasn't with him to ask me what work I do here.

This morning we had a judges meeting. Not one of those dreary, boring all-day affairs that my predecessor went in for. This was brief and I cut short the usual verbose outpourings. The main subject was salaries. Nobody is ever paid enough. I don't take part in such discussions as it would not come well from an expatriate and, in any case, I receive my topping-up allowance from ODA, which satisfies me. But I will certainly put forward and support their requests and suggestions as coming from them, whenever I can do so.

Later, one of the many Patels (the Indian equivalent of the Smiths) who had been expelled from Uganda by Amin in 1972, called in. He said he is now an extremely wealthy businessman in Leicester, which happens to be my birthplace, and we chatted about that city and his career since Amin gave him his big chance in life to make good. Yet another example of how sometimes good can come to people out of the evil done to them.

Wednesday 16 April

There were eight new advocates to enrol this morning, which brings us up to date with these applicants and gives them the opportunity to start earning money in their chosen careers.

There's an anonymous article from a 'Special Correspondent' in a recent issue of *The Star* deriding and sneering at those who complain about boy soldiers being armed and sent out to kill. The writer claims that this was done out of necessity after such children had witnessed their families being tortured and massacred, and nobody cared for or helped them until the kindly NRA came along and gave them guns and trained them. It strongly criticises people for saying that such young boys have killed and have no feelings for the wrongness of taking human life and that they will possibly turn into criminals. But the writer doesn't try to deny this likelihood, I notice. However, it struck me that the article covers just what I was recently saying to Museveni and I can't help wondering if this is a coincidence or perhaps someone who was present then decided, or was encouraged, to write this article. It would certainly be typical.

This afternoon two characters from Amnesty International dropped in and we discussed some areas of interest to them, and I passed on what I knew of the plight of a couple of people whom they might be able to assist.

Wednesday 23 April

I finished marking the law of evidence exam papers that I had set for my evidence class with the current magistrates course at the LDC, and sent the results to the Centre. Not too bad; several of them have done very well in this difficult subject.

This evening I went to a reception at the BHC residence and, when

I asked if it had anything to do with the fact that today is St George's Day, nobody there seemed to have noticed the significance of the date or was even aware of it. I suppose that proves something or other.

Thursday 1 May

I was supposed to fly to Gatwick yesterday by Uganda Airlines on my way to Banjul in the Gambia to attend a conference for Commonwealth African Chief Justices. However, when we were in the air heading northwards, the captain announced that we had to return to Entebbe for 'technical reasons'. So we all had to disembark and, when I was back in the VIP lounge, I was informed that they had received a report that there was a bomb planted on our aircraft. There were a couple of government ministers on board as well as myself, but none of us was an obvious target. It would hardly have been a disgruntled customer in some concluded court case before me; more likely just a haphazard act or even monumental incompetence by someone. Eventually, after a long search, no bomb was found and it appeared to be a hoax, so we were able to continue on our flight today. I'm staying tonight at an airport hotel at Gatwick and I'll fly on to Banjul tomorrow by British Caledonian.

Monday 5 May – In the Gambia

We had an idle weekend in the Kombo Beach Novotel, which is at Faraja on the Atlantic Ocean side, and on Saturday some of us took a taxi into Banjul, the capital, at the mouth of the River Gambia. The road crosses a large mangrove swamp and the Denton Bridge, which is a couple of hundred yards long over the Oyster Creek. We wandered around the small town but there wasn't much to see there. Later we attended a rather boring and dusty local wrestling contest. It's very hot and dry here, with a strong wind, but quite pleasant. The people seem very friendly and helpful and the tourist hotel is comfortable, and provided with a conference room just large enough to accommodate the 15 or so chief justices, or their representatives, attending from West, East and Central Africa and the Seychelles – with the Indian CJ as a special guest speaker. I was bombarded with questions from the judges about what's been happening in Uganda. Gambia is a tiny country and not able to find all the senior staff it needs. The Chief Justice here is a Nigerian and their Court of Appeal, now visiting, is made up of outside West African judges. An official car with a police orderly has been supplied to each one of us for our use while we're here. The conference was opened by the Gambian President, Sir Dawda Jawara, and we then had a group photograph taken with him and his Vice-

President and the Speaker. Afterwards I was asked to chair the first session.

Thursday 8 May

This morning, in a convoy of official cars, we were taken to State House, where we had coffee and a discussion with President Jawara. He's not very tall, quietly spoken and with a friendly demeanour. State House is a very old building, originally Government House of course, with beautiful grounds smothered in very colourful tropical flowering trees, shrubs and plants and myriads of brightly coloured birds. The afternoon conference session was about outside interference with the Judiciary and I was able to compare examples of this from the Amin and Obote regimes with some of their experiences. This evening we were taken back to State House for an enjoyable closing reception.

Friday 9 May – London

After the closing ceremony, at which each CJ was asked to speak briefly, we were driven to Yundum International Airport and flew back to Gatwick. The Uganda High Commission provided a car to take me to my club in town as I have some urgent shopping to do before I return to Uganda on Sunday.

Monday 12 May

In London on Saturday evening I went to see a film called *Out of Africa*, based on the writings of Karen Blixen. Apart from some mis-casting it was very good – made in Kenya, of course – but also sad; backed by the haunting adagio from Mozart's Clarinet Concerto. The significance of the film's title struck me as I realised that it might well describe my own situation fairly soon if things go the way they seem to be.

The helpful Uganda High Commission people took me to Gatwick yesterday evening and I arrived back at Entebbe this morning at 6 a.m. but found no car or driver waiting for me. It was much too early to try ringing anyone, so I waited for a couple of hours in the VIP lounge then rang the High Court and spoke to the telephone operator, who went to look for my car but couldn't see it. However, an aide of Museveni's was at the airport for some purpose and he said he thought it was very bad for the Chief Justice to be kept waiting like this and the President wouldn't like it; so he insisted on taking me to Kampala in the State House car he had with him. About 5 miles out of Kampala I spotted my car heading southwards at speed and asked our driver to signal to him to stop. I stuck my head out of the back window so that Laurence could see that it was me. After changing cars and thanking the State House chap I went straight home.

Thursday 15 May

When discussing aid projects at the British High Commission earlier, I had mentioned the fact that we are very short of transport in the Judiciary. A new post I have introduced is Inspector of Courts, and the chief magistrate now appointed to the post will travel around to all the lower courts inspecting, checking and reporting; then following up on action taken, whether judicial or administrative. Hopefully this will give the Chief Registrar and myself an up-to-date picture of the state of the courts throughout the country.

As for transport, yesterday morning Peter Penfold, once again acting as High Commissioner, came to the court with two brand-new Range Rovers as UK aid to the courts and handed them over to me in a small ceremony outside in the courtyard, at which a number of judges and staff were present. The Attorney-General was there and he, Peter and I each gave brief speeches, which were reported in today's newspapers and on the UTV news. As part of British aid myself, I felt it was rather odd and inappropriate for me to be on the receiving end of this aid on behalf of Uganda, but there it is – all just a part of the job.

In the afternoon a colonel in the British Army Legal Service called on me. He said he's in Uganda to assist in drafting new court martial procedures for the NRA and, apart from making a courtesy call, wanted some advice on a couple of local legal matters.

Friday 16 May

This is definitely a Black Letter Day for me. At last I've received the President's reply and decision concerning my job. He has not seen me to discuss it with me first, as I was hoping he would do, and as I had mentioned to the Minister of Justice some time back that I would like to do. Maybe there are reasons, but not necessarily good ones from my point of view.

His letter thanks me for mine, notes my willingness to continue under a new contract and points out that qualified Ugandans must be given the opportunity to serve their country (as if I need telling that). He says he has decided that a Ugandan should be appointed as CJ. Then the nasty bit: 'But recognising the fact that there are still areas of limited skilled personnel it is my intention to request the British Government to redirect to such areas this part of British technical aid which hitherto has been utilised to supplement your salary.' In other words they have a better use for the aid that I represent. I phoned Peter Penfold at the BHC and he came straight over to my chambers. When he had read it he borrowed the letter to take back and have a copy made to send to London as our copier, as usual, was out of action.

Monday 19 May

At the mid-morning coffee break I went along to our Common Room, where I had asked all the judges to assemble, and told them of my imminent departure. I refrained from saying to the two or three who I know have ambitions to take my place that this was their chance, but I could read it in their faces. I just told them the facts without any comment and left them to discuss it.

Tuesday 20 May

I asked the current President of the Uganda Law Society, Henry Kayondo, to call into my chambers this morning to inform him of the situation. He is an old friend since we were in the Police together, and he had later read for the Bar at the Law School.

I also rang Luke Ofungi at Police HQ and told him. After that I contacted a newly established firm called Export Packers and asked them to arrange to pack and fly my kit to the UK next month. I have a big job to do sorting out the boxes of papers and about 2,000 books and other possessions accumulated over 30-odd years in Uganda. As I've no idea where I shall be going next I must get rid of most of it.

The Kenyan newspaper *Sunday Nation* has already got on to the story and it has headlined: UGANDA TO REPLACE WHITE CHIEF JUSTICE. Most of the article is fairly accurate and somebody, referred to as a well-placed source, gave them an outline of my career. It also says: 'A letter from the President's Office explained that Uganda could do without the aid given to the country if Allen or any other Briton remained Chief Justice.' Apparently the local Luganda newspaper *Ngabo* also has this story. I wonder who's been talking to them. Still, it's not a secret, but they certainly got on to it quickly.

Tuesday 27 May

US Ambassador Houdek called to discuss the invitation that he recently passed on to me from the American Bar Association to attend their annual meeting in New York in August and to address the symposium on 'Judicial Systems in Crisis' and tell them something of the way it's been in Uganda. I shall spend a week in New York, my first visit, taking in all the sights as well as attending the ABA convention;

then a week in Washington visiting and calling on people in the Supreme Court, the State Department, Congress, various courts, the Pentagon, FBI HQ, the Police Academy and so on. It sounds interesting.

Wednesday 28 May

Several of the local newspapers, such as *Focus* and *The Sunday Review* and *The Equator,* have been speculating about who will be appointed to replace me. The names of K, the advocate who called on me in February, and the former CJ and now President of the Court of Appeal, Wambuzi, were mentioned; though the latter seems the most likely, in their opinion. I'm inclined to agree and I suspect it's been the object of the exercise from the start to remove me and put him in place, rather than having to look around for a likely replacement. The government newspaper, *Uganda Times,* because of its irregular appearance now known as the *Uganda Sometimes,* is silent.

Saturday 31 May

Various friends have been calling at the residence to pick up stuff they can use and find space for. Many of my books and bookcases and various household items, curtains, mats and so on have gone. Meanwhile I've been packing the remaining books and papers that I'm taking into strong cardboard boxes supplied by the packers and putting aside quantities of papers to be burned. The *shamba* boy has dug a large hole in which he buries the non-combustible items as there has been no rubbish collection in Kampala for very many years. Kitchen waste goes into the soil as humus.

I've already brought back the personal things from my chambers and sorted out some old police items and relevant books to give to the Assistant Inspector in charge of the court orderlies. He was very pleased, especially with the swagger cane with the old crowned badge on the silver knob; such things have been unobtainable for a very long time, so he can now swank with it among his colleagues.

Wednesday 4 June

The packers came to the house to deal with the household items and pictures that need proper wrapping and packing, and two more old friends called in to collect boxes of books.

On the 1st June there was an editorial in the new tabloid called *The Sunday Review* which used up five columns writing about me, including remarks such as: 'His hard work, impartiality in the

administration of justice ensured his meteoric rise to judgeship...'
and 'We hope that the practice of conferring a knighthood on Britons
who ascend to the highest judicial office of our country will be adhered
to.' Further on: 'The advocates we talked to said that Judge Allen
would be sorely missed. His strict discipline and impartiality, they
said, have endeared him to the Bar. Only one advocate expressed a
contrary opinion. He said: "Judge Allen is too much a policeman. He
barks at us." But perhaps this is not a contrary view after all as it is
proof of his strictness...' and so on.

It's now very clear that the Uganda Government is not going to give
me the customary official farewell party before I leave. Perhaps they
think it will be embarrassing on both sides because I'm not leaving
voluntarily and would no doubt say so in the obligatory speechifying
at such a function. Or, maybe, they just don't want to be bothered.

Wednesday 11 June

The British High Commissioner and his French wife have departed
for his eagerly awaited Strasbourg posting and Peter Penfold is now
acting High Commissioner. I was invited to the residence for the
Queen's birthday reception this afternoon, which gave me an opportunity to say farewell to various diplomats and others.

An announcement appeared in *The Star* this morning that the
Uganda Law Society is giving a farewell party for me tomorrow at the
Law Development Centre and all members of the Society are invited
to attend. When I saw their President recently, Henry told me that his
members were not happy about the failure of the government to recognise my long service and give me a proper official send-off. He added
that the ULS was determined not to let me go without a farewell party
from them at least. But I'll have to make a speech.

Friday 13 June

The Law Society farewell party was at 3 p.m. today and there was a
good turnout of lawyers, as well as judges and magistrates – some of
the latter former Law School students from up-country who happened
to be in Kampala. Henry Kayondo gave an excellent speech, ending
with a prediction that I shall receive a knighthood. There's not much
chance of that, however, since I know that nobody in the Uganda
Government has been moved to make such a recommendation and our
departed High Commissioner didn't do so either,* though some such
recognition might be helpful when I'm job-seeking. The Secretary of

*However, this was rectified by his temporary successor.

the ULS spoke, and managed to bring in the fact that he was a law student at Makerere in 1969 when he first met me, when I came from the LDC to talk to the undergraduates in the Makerere Law Society, and that I tore him off a tremendous strip for being late meeting me. The Baganda tend to have elephantine memories for slights and disagreements and seem to hold their grudges for ever. The Society presented me with a fine bas-relief carving on an *mvule* wood board, and then I was expected to say a few words. This I did with some difficulty and my usual brevity. I said:

> In my time in Uganda I've seen many people come and go and I've attended quite a number of parties given to departing expatriates in the past – but always before I was merely one of the guests. Somehow I never thought that the day would come when I would be the departing one … I can't hide my sadness at having to leave, nor do I want to hide it. It is not my choice that I am leaving Uganda and, indeed, I'm very sorry and upset about having to go and having to say goodbye to so many old friends … I take nothing with me from Uganda except a certain amount of experience, which I hope will be found useful somewhere.

I then referred to the tale that, when David Livingstone's body was carried to the coast by his African friends and sent to England for burial, his heart had already been buried in Africa. I remarked that 'I too shall be leaving at least a part of my heart in Africa.' I then thanked them for the party and the gift and wished them all well and left quickly.

Saturday 14 June

A lorry came to collect my boxes and take them to the airport and another came for my car, as I've decided to take my 'E' Type Jaguar back with me by air. I've had it for 20 years and I may as well go on using it. We removed the battery and, as I'd already drained the water, petrol and oil, I free-wheeled it down the slope from the main gates, picking up just enough speed to get it up on to the ramp and into the back of the lorry.

Humble Joe called in to say farewell and to express his disgust at my removal from office. He's a former Law School Bar student and now a long-standing and successful advocate in Masaka. I named him Humble Joe when he was a Finals student in London and used to end his letters 'Your humble student'.

Monday 16 June

I had previously contacted the Director of the LDC and arranged this afternoon to take my last class there. It was merely to go over the paper which I had set in the recent evidence exam and to say farewell to the students and wish them success. I'm really going to miss these teaching intervals most of all. Although it was an unofficial and unpaid voluntary effort, I regard it as my most useful, enjoyable and satisfying contribution. In a recent article in the Kenyan *Sunday Nation* some anonymous Ugandan advocate is quoted as saying: 'Justice Allen has been highly respected in legal circles here. He has been a keen teacher, always willing to sacrifice his time to give instruction at the Law Development Centre – something many of us find difficult to do.'

Wednesday 18 June

Yesterday evening Peter Penfold, the acting British High Commissioner, gave me a farewell dinner at his residence, inviting several old friends, including Luke Ofungi and Henry Kayondo. It was informal and very pleasant but rather sad. Today I had a farewell lunch with Edred Bowman, Managing Director of Barclays Bank, which has been my bank since I first came out here.

Thursday 19 June

Late this afternoon I went to the Senior Police Officers' mess (the former Kampala Club) for my farewell party given by the Police. There were a great many people there and I didn't get around to speaking to all of them. Luke Ofungi made an excellent speech and presented me with a large shield of *mvule* wood with the police badge carved on it. I said:

I'm very grateful to you all for this party and for this last chance to meet you before I depart on Sunday. Even though I left the Force as long ago as 1962, as you know, I've maintained contact ever since and I've tried to assist whenever I could because I have always had the well-being and good reputation of the Force at heart. I'm going to miss this very friendly relationship and co-operation very much indeed.

I hope and expect that the Force will soon regain most of its former high standards and quality. There is a very great deal to be done by you all before achieving this – but it's a very worthwhile target.

I believe you have a very good chance of eventually succeeding in this because the Force is fortunate enough to have as Inspector General a man of such high quality, ability and integrity as Luke Ofungi. If he is given your whole-hearted support and co-operation, and if you all make the maximum effort, then you will certainly succeed.

I know that I've met some of you only very occasionally, but even this will end now. It's not my choice that I'm leaving Uganda and I'm sorry to have to say goodbye to so many old friends. I hope that sometime in the future there will be an opportunity for us to meet again somehow; but at the moment I do not see how this could happen...

Thank you very much, my friends, for giving me this splendid farewell party and for the nice things that have been said about me today. You must know that I shall not forget you. I wish you all success and happiness and may God bless you and all members of the Uganda Police. Thank you.

With a heavy heart I somehow managed to get through this brief speech, but I was feeling very upset and I quickly took leave of them. As I left the mess the officers all lined up outside and I shook hands and said goodbye to each of them, then stumbled into my car feeling completely desolated and heart-broken. This is really happening, after all.

Friday 20 June

This whole morning was spent at State House. I had earlier indicated that although the Uganda Government has chosen to ignore my departure, I wished, out of courtesy, to take leave of the President. At first this was not agreed, probably by the Minister, but I pointed out to him that if the President refused to see his outgoing Chief Justice it would appear to the public as if I was being sacked in disgrace and, I added, what is the problem with just saying goodbye?

So I was told to appear at State House at 8 a.m. today. This was an absurd and most discourteous hour and I had to get up at dawn and drive over to Entebbe. At first a very dim-witted military sentry refused to let me enter State House grounds without giving me any reason. After hanging about outside for about 20 minutes, I had just decided to return to Kampala and forget the whole business, when Njuba, the Minister of Constitutional Affairs (whatever those are), arrived and told the fool to let me in.

When I reached State House nobody was even up. The house was empty. Eventually a sleepy servant appeared and said: 'Wait in that room.' No please and no greeting; perhaps it's all part of the Marxist equality nonsense. I quietly cursed the rude oaf who set up this wretched meeting.

After half an hour of just sitting there with nothing to do or even to read, and no offer of refreshments, Museveni came in and looked startled. He said: 'I didn't know you were here. Nobody told me.' Marvellous. Why was I not surprised?

I was feeling considerably irritated by now. There had been no need to drag me from Kampala at such an ungodly hour merely to be kept waiting first outside, then inside, for so long. I wanted to get away from this complete waste of my time, so I said: 'I just came to say goodbye as I'm leaving on Sunday, though I don't suppose anybody bothered to tell you.' Museveni said that we must wait for the UTV people so that there was a record of this that everyone could see. But why weren't the TV people there waiting for the President, instead of the other way round? The whole place struck me as being considerably disorganised.

There was nothing for us to discuss – I merely wanted to say farewell and get back to Kampala. We just sat there waiting for his miserable UTV unit and saying very little. I mentioned very briefly what I had been doing and planning in the course of sorting out the Judiciary; at which point Museveni said to Njuba: 'Isn't there some way we could continue to make use of Mr Allen's services in Uganda?' Njuba looked rather worried at such a suggestion and said he didn't think so.

I remarked: 'Well, it's too late now anyway. My arrangements have been made and all my property has gone to the UK and my flight is on Sunday.'

Museveni should have seen me privately long ago when I requested a meeting so that we could have discussed the possibility of my exchanging positions with the President of the Court of Appeal to enable me to continue working here out of the limelight. But those concerned had made sure I did not get the chance to see him until it was too late. However, that waste of useful aid gibe in the President's letter to me had clearly indicated the way things were going and, reluctant as I am to leave Uganda, I certainly have no wish to stay where I'm not wanted. The UTV team eventually turned up, having broken down on the way to Entebbe, so they said. What was supposed to be a picture of us saying a friendly farewell turned out to be the two of us sitting glumly staring ahead and not talking. There was nothing left to say and I certainly didn't feel friendly. I saw it on the UTV news this evening; it lasted for about five seconds on the screen. What a complete waste of time.

This afternoon at the court I was interviewed by a very polite local journalist from the government newspaper *New Vision*. I spoke of various laws in Uganda that needed reforming because of being out of date and no longer relevant to or adequate for present-day needs. I declined to talk about myself and when he asked what was my greatest achievement here, I merely said that if there was one it was for others to say so.

After that I was called to our Common Room, where the judges had assembled to bid me farewell. The AG was also there, and then in walked Professor James Read, once again visiting Makerere as an external law examiner. He said he'd been told at the university that I was departing this weekend.

Sunday 22 June

I spent yesterday packing my suitcases and handing over to Vincent and his brother a number of things that I couldn't cram into the cases. Vincent said he wanted to come to the airport with me.

This morning Laurence drove us to Entebbe airport and there was a longish wait in the VIP lounge. Most of the judges were there, the AG and some senior High Court staff, the Director of the LDC, also Henry Kayondo and various advocates. The biggest surprise was when we all went outside to walk across the tarmac to the waiting aircraft of Uganda Airlines. There was a tremendous shout from the large flat roof of the terminal building. It was crowded with former friends and students, many police, magistrates and court staff and others. They all started to shout in unison: 'Peter! Peter! Peter!'

There was a lump in my throat as I kept waving back at them while walking towards the aircraft. What a wonderful send-off. At the aircraft steps I said thanks and goodbye to everyone who had come to see me off, including Vincent and Laurence, and slowly and reluctantly I climbed the steps with an extraordinary strong feeling pulling me back. At the top I turned to those waiting below and to the crowd still waving from the terminal roof. I felt overwhelmed with sadness at having to leave this country when there was still so much work that I wanted to do with them and for them. I was leaving these wonderful, cheerful, friendly people who had made me so welcome and had enriched my life and let me live and work with them for so long.

I raised both my arms and gave them a final wave, and it really hit me then that I was leaving for ever and ending a considerable period in my life. Then I went inside the aircraft and was shown to my seat, where I sat numb and unhappy and feeling totally empty inside as we took off and I watched Entebbe airport disappear below us. I felt as if I really had left my heart behind in Africa, for so long my home.

POSTSCRIPT

Long, long ago Lord Lugard, that most understanding imperialist and proconsul in Africa, in his book *Dual Mandate* wrote these instructions to young administrators about to work in Africa:

> Your job is to learn how they govern themselves and assist that process. You'll be there for a very long time, you're there to give support to existing native structures, to enable them to evolve naturally – and there is no immediate necessity either to understand urban politics or transpose Westminster models of government.

The unfortunate result of a combination of excessive pressures and ignorance, plus the over-reaction to the then current rabid anti-colonialism in the UK, the USA and the UN, together with what some consider were rather over-hasty political efforts of Sir Andrew Cohen and his like-minded chums, may well have had a share in making possible the events in Uganda that have caused untold damage and misery that will no doubt take many years to rectify. Cohen introduced and encouraged useful changes and advances in local administration and adult education, but much later admitted that he had gone too far too fast with political development. Additionally, the personalities of the various Ugandan leaders had a great deal to do with subsequent events.

As for myself: a long time ago I read something that has stuck in my mind. I don't know who wrote it but it went something like this:

> A journey must come to its own end. We can choose our path, and with luck find another after it has ended. Without luck we become immobile, afraid to go back because we know what's there, unable to go forward because our way is blocked. The key is to seek out that next road and accept the transition it offers from the last.

GLOSSARY

(Ach = Acholi; Swa = Swahili; Lug = Luganda)

Acholi	–	Nilotic tribe and language and district in northern Uganda
ADC	–	Assistant District Commissioner; Aide-de-Camp
AG	–	Attorney-General
ALG	–	African Local Government
Anyanya	–	southern Sudanese rebel movement
askari	–	(Swa) and *acekere* (Ach) soldier, policeman
Ateso	–	Teso language in Eastern Uganda
Balokole	–	(Lug) born-again Christians
baraza	–	(Swa = verandah) official gathering, meeting of chiefs
BHC	–	British High Commission(er)
boma	–	(Swa) District HQ buildings; thorn enclosure for cattle, goats
BPTT	–	British Police Training Team – a British aid project
Buganda	–	southern Uganda Kingdom (Muganda – a person from Buganda; Baganda – the people; Luganda – the language)
Bwana Mkubwa	–	(Swa) big master; important person
CID	–	Criminal Investigation Department
CJ	–	Chief Justice
CM	–	Chief Magistrate
CP	–	Commissioner of Police
CPS	–	Central Police Station
CR	–	Chief Registrar (High Court)
DC	–	District Commissioner
debe	–	(Swa) 4-gallon petrol can used as water container or flattened as roofing or wall material
dhobi	–	(Hindi) laundry
DMO	–	District Medical Officer
DO	–	District Officer (includes DC, ADC, general service officer)

661

GLOSSARY

DP	–	Democratic Party (Uganda) made up of largely Catholic followers
DPP	–	Director of Public Prosecutions (in the AG's Chambers)
duka	–	(Swa) small general shop, usually Asian-owned
enguli	–	(Lug) also *waragi*(Swa) high-proof spirit distilled from green cooking bananas (*matoke*)
enzige	–	(Lug) edible large green grasshoppers
FCO	–	Foreign and Commonwealth Office (UK)
fundi	–	(Swa) expert, craftsman, skilled artisan
GSU	–	General Service Unit (secret police in Obote's first regime)
HE	–	His Excellency (Governor, President, Ambassador, High Commissioner)
HMG	–	Her Majesty's Government (UK)
HQ	–	Headquarters
IG	–	Inspector General of Police
Iteso	–	Teso people in eastern Uganda
Jambo!	–	(Swa) greetings!
JSC	–	Judicial Service Commission dealing with appointments and promotions in the Judiciary
Kabaka	–	Ruler of Buganda Kingdom, southern Uganda
KAR	–	King's African Rifles (East African Regiment in British Army)
Karamoja	–	District in NE Uganda (Karamojong = the people)
KCC	–	Kampala City Council
kiboko	–	(Swa) hippopotamus, rawhide whip made from hippo skin
Kitchen Swahili	–	simplified, non-grammatical Swahili usually used with domestic servants and in Asian *dukas* (known as 'ki-settler' in pre-independence Kenya)
ladit	–	(Ach) elder, important person (term of address)
Lango	–	Ugandan northern tribe and language (Lango – a person and Langi people of that tribe)
LegCo	–	Legislative Council (a colonial, mostly non-elected, parliament)
Lukiiko	–	(Lug) Buganda parliament, non-elected
manyatta	–	circular Karamojong village surrounded by fence of thorn bushes
matoke	–	(Lug) green cooking plantains (bananas)
mpishi	–	(Swa) cook

mweso	–	(Lug) or *bao* (Swa) a board game played with 32 or more holes in rows of four using pebbles, beans or seeds as counters
Mzungu	–	(Swa) and *Muno* (Ach) European, white man (includes Americans etc.). The plural is *Wazungu*.
NCO	–	non-commissioned officer
ngoma	–	(Swa) drum; tribal dance
NRA	–	National Resistance Army – military wing of Museveni's National Resistance Movement
Nubians	–	*nubis* (Swa) a southern Sudanese tribe
OC	–	Officer-in-Charge (of police station or unit)
ODA	–	Overseas Development Administration, overseas aid department in the British Foreign and Commonwealth Office
panga	–	(Swa) a large bush knife like a machete used for cutting meat, firewood, etc. .
PC	–	Provincial Commissioner, a colonial administrative head of a province; a police constable
pikipiki	–	(Swa) motor cycle or motor scooter
pombe	–	(Swa) native beer
posho	–	(Swa) daily food ration, often cooked porridge of maize flour
PS	–	Private Secretary
PSU	–	Public Safety Unit; a police anti-robbery unit used by Amin as a murder squad
PTS	–	Police Training School
PWD	–	Public Works Department
QM	–	Quartermaster (OC Police stores)
RC	–	Roman Catholic
RM	–	Resident Magistrate
safari	–	(Swa) an up-country touring, a journey
SB	–	Police Special Branch
SD	–	Police Station Diary, records all incidents and movements in/out
SF	–	Special Force, a police service unit dealing with border incidents, riots, etc.
SG	–	Solicitor-General
shamba	–	(Swa) garden, cultivated plot of land
simba	–	(Swa) lion
SRB	–	State Research Bureau (Amin's secret police)
Tanzania	–	Combined republics of Tanganyika and Zanzibar (1964)

tembo (also *ndovu*) – (Swa) elephant

TPDF	–	Tanzanian Peoples Defence Force
TUFMAC	–	The Uganda Fish Marketing Corporation
UHC	–	Uganda High Commission(er)
ULS	–	Uganda Law Society
uniport	–	A rondavel, a circular hut made of aluminium panels bolted together with a concrete base or earth floor.
UNLA	–	Uganda National Liberation Army (Obote's second regime army)
UPC	–	Uganda Peoples Congress (Obote's largely Protestant party)
UTV	–	Uganda Television
wakombozi	–	(Swa) liberators (lit. redeemers) name given to Tanzanians and returned Ugandan exiles who removed Idi Amin in 1979
waragi	–	(Swa) or *enguli* (Lug) high-proof spirit distilled from green cooking bananas (*matoke*)

INDEX

Kisitu, Douglas 441, 527, 533, 540, 547, 551, 554, 559
Kisseka, Dr Samson 640
Kisubi, St Mary's College 251
Kisumu 5, 59–60
Kitale 180
Kitante Government Hostel 5, 147
Kiwanuka, Benedicto 203, 207, 315–316, 318, 321, 339
Kololo Hill 162, 363, 550
Kyabazinga of Busoga 85, 231

Lake Victoria 5, 409, 456
Lango 103
Law courses for the administration 276, 288
Law courses for army officers 285, 288, 295, 297–298, 576
Law courses for police 578, 584
Law Development Centre 281, 287, 292, 301, 439, 473, 527, 529, 550, 553, 560, 581, 583, 614, 626, 647, 655
Law Reform Commission 290– 291
Law School 210–211, 214, 224, 245, 261
Legislative Council (LegCo) 16, 84–85, 101, 131, 163
Lennox-Boyd, Alan 115
Libyans 505–506
Lions Club 389
Lira 103, 551, 627
Looting 508–510
Lost Counties 245
Lototura 150
Lubiri 28, 98
Lubiri barracks 312
Luce, Richard 548
Luganda 63
Lugazi 34
Lugbara tribe 370
Lukiiko, Buganda 97, 200, 297
Lule, Godfey 412
Lule, Y.K. 253, 513–514, 517–520, 539
Lutembe Beach 485
Luwero Triangle 262, 578, 589, 606, 646
Luwum, Archbishop 442
Luzira Prison 63, 441

Macmillan, Harold 173
Macoun, Michael 145, 228
Magendo 399, 465
Magistrates Courts Act 265

Makarios, Archbishop 202
Makerere University College 25, 265, 296
Makerere University Law Faculty 540, 552
Makindye Barracks 372
Makindye, Governor's Lodge 11, 98
Malyamungu, Isaac 375, 409
Manyindo, Seth 562, 617–618, 622, 641
Masaka 469, 499, 607
Masindi 150, 373, 442, 591
Mau Mau 5, 80
Mayanja, Abubakar 163–165, 320
Mayanja, Joseph 654
Mayanja-Nkangi 245, 546, 617
Mbale 86, 150, 179, 185, 240, 388–389, 421, 453, 456–457, 478
Mbarara 208, 272, 307, 362–363, 370, 395–397, 442, 468, 492, 499
McNair-Wilson, Patrick 412
Mengo Court 641–642
Ministry of Internal Affairs 584
Mityana 109–112
Moroto 104–105, 161, 166, 168, 425–427, 462
Morrison, Herbert 107
Moses Ali, Brigadier 468, 549, 579
Mubende 119
Mulago Hospital 255, 432, 437, 487–490
Murchison Falls National Park 167, 265
Museveni, Yoweri as guerrilla 544, 548, 564, 578, 591, 614, 627, 630, 632–635
as politician 537, 539, 544
as minister 525, 528, 534
swearing-in 636–638
as President 639, 641, 643, 645–646
meetings with 525, 641, 657
Mutono, Addy 323, 352, 457
Muwanga, Paulo 534, 542–544, 567, 575, 584, 591, 599, 606, 614, 618, 623
Mweso 31, 112

Nabilatuk 162, 169–200, 530
Nakasero Hill 259
Namanve Forest 358
Namirembe Cathedral 11, 72
Nasur, Major 450–452
National Consultative Council (NCC) 517–518
National Resistance Army (NRA) 578, 591, 627, 634–635, 642, 646–647, 650
National Resistance Movement (NRM) 640, 645